Handbook of Global Economic Policy

PUBLIC ADMINISTRATION AND PUBLIC POLICY

A Comprehensive Publication Program

Executive Editor

JACK RABIN
Professor of Public Administration and Public Policy
School of Public Affairs
The Capital College
The Pennsylvania State University—Harrisburg
Middletown, Pennsylvania

1. *Public Administration as a Developing Discipline* (in two parts), Robert T. Golembiewski
2. *Comparative National Policies on Health Care*, Milton I. Roemer, M.D.
3. *Exclusionary Injustice: The Problem of Illegally Obtained Evidence*, Steven R. Schlesinger
4. *Personnel Management in Government: Politics and Process*, Jay M. Shafritz, Walter L. Balk, Albert C. Hyde, and David H. Rosenbloom
5. *Organization Development in Public Administration* (in two parts), edited by Robert T. Golembiewski and William B. Eddy
6. *Public Administration: A Comparative Perspective, Second Edition, Revised and Expanded*, Ferrel Heady
7. *Approaches to Planned Change* (in two parts), Robert T. Golembiewski
8. *Program Evaluation at HEW* (in three parts), edited by James G. Abert
9. *The States and the Metropolis*, Patricia S. Florestano and Vincent L. Marando
10. *Personnel Management in Government: Politics and Process, Second Edition, Revised and Expanded*, Jay M. Shafritz, Albert C. Hyde, and David H. Rosenbloom
11. *Changing Bureaucracies: Understanding the Organization Before Selecting the Approach*, William A. Medina
12. *Handbook on Public Budgeting and Financial Management*, edited by Jack Rabin and Thomas D. Lynch
13. *Encyclopedia of Policy Studies*, edited by Stuart S. Nagel
14. *Public Administration and Law: Bench v. Bureau in the United States*, David H. Rosenbloom
15. *Handbook on Public Personnel Administration and Labor Relations*, edited by Jack Rabin, Thomas Vocino, W. Bartley Hildreth, and Gerald J. Miller
16. *Public Budgeting and Finance: Behavioral, Theoretical, and Technical Perspectives, Third Edition*, edited by Robert T. Golembiewski and Jack Rabin
17. *Organizational Behavior and Public Management*, Debra W. Stewart and G. David Garson

18. *The Politics of Terrorism: Second Edition, Revised and Expanded,* edited by Michael Stohl
19. *Handbook of Organization Management*, edited by William B. Eddy
20. *Organization Theory and Management*, edited by Thomas D. Lynch
21. *Labor Relations in the Public Sector*, Richard C. Kearney
22. *Politics and Administration: Woodrow Wilson and American Public Administration*, edited by Jack Rabin and James S. Bowman
23. *Making and Managing Policy: Formulation, Analysis, Evaluation*, edited by G. Ronald Gilbert
24. *Public Administration: A Comparative Perspective, Third Edition, Revised*, Ferrel Heady
25. *Decision Making in the Public Sector*, edited by Lloyd G. Nigro
26. *Managing Administration*, edited by Jack Rabin, Samuel Humes, and Brian S. Morgan
27. *Public Personnel Update*, edited by Michael Cohen and Robert T. Golembiewski
28. *State and Local Government Administration*, edited by Jack Rabin and Don Dodd
29. *Public Administration: A Bibliographic Guide to the Literature*, Howard E. McCurdy
30. *Personnel Management in Government: Politics and Process, Third Edition, Revised and Expanded*, Jay M. Shafritz, Albert C. Hyde, and David H. Rosenbloom
31. *Handbook of Information Resource Management*, edited by Jack Rabin and Edward M. Jackowski
32. *Public Administration in Developed Democracies: A Comparative Study*, edited by Donald C. Rowat
33. *The Politics of Terrorism: Third Edition, Revised and Expanded*, edited by Michael Stohl
34. *Handbook on Human Services Administration*, edited by Jack Rabin and Marcia B. Steinhauer
35. *Handbook of Public Administration*, edited by Jack Rabin, W. Bartley Hildreth, and Gerald J. Miller
36. *Ethics for Bureaucrats: An Essay on Law and Values, Second Edition, Revised and Expanded*, John A. Rohr
37. *The Guide to the Foundations of Public Administration*, Daniel W. Martin
38. *Handbook of Strategic Management*, edited by Jack Rabin, Gerald J. Miller, and W. Bartley Hildreth
39. *Terrorism and Emergency Management: Policy and Administration,* William L. Waugh, Jr.
40. *Organizational Behavior and Public Management: Second Edition, Revised and Expanded*, Michael L. Vasu, Debra W. Stewart, and G. David Garson
41. *Handbook of Comparative and Development Public Administration*, edited by Ali Farazmand
42. *Public Administration: A Comparative Perspective, Fourth Edition*, Ferrel Heady
43. *Government Financial Management Theory*, Gerald J. Miller
44. *Personnel Management in Government: Politics and Process, Fourth Edition, Revised and Expanded*, Jay M. Shafritz, Norma M. Riccucci, David H. Rosenbloom, and Albert C. Hyde
45. *Public Productivity Handbook*, edited by Marc Holzer
46. *Handbook of Public Budgeting*, edited by Jack Rabin

47. *Labor Relations in the Public Sector: Second Edition, Revised and Expanded*, Richard C. Kearney
48. *Handbook of Organizational Consultation*, edited by Robert T. Golembiewski
49. *Handbook of Court Administration and Management*, edited by Steven W. Hays and Cole Blease Graham, Jr.
50. *Handbook of Comparative Public Budgeting and Financial Management*, edited by Thomas D. Lynch and Lawrence L. Martin
51. *Handbook of Organizational Behavior*, edited by Robert T. Golembiewski
52. *Handbook of Administrative Ethics,* edited by Terry L. Cooper
53. *Encyclopedia of Policy Studies: Second Edition, Revised and Expanded,* edited by Stuart S. Nagel
54. *Handbook of Regulation and Administrative Law,* edited by David H. Rosenbloom and Richard D. Schwartz
55. *Handbook of Bureaucracy,* edited by Ali Farazmand
56. *Handbook of Public Sector Labor Relations*, edited by Jack Rabin, Thomas Vocino, W. Bartley Hildreth, and Gerald J. Miller
57. *Practical Public Management*, Robert T. Golembiewski
58. *Handbook of Public Personnel Administration*, edited by Jack Rabin, Thomas Vocino, W. Bartley Hildreth, and Gerald J. Miller
59. *Public Administration: A Comparative Perspective, Fifth Edition*, Ferrel Heady
60. *Handbook of Debt Management*, edited by Gerald J. Miller
61. *Public Administration and Law: Second Edition*, David H. Rosenbloom and Rosemary O'Leary
62. *Handbook of Local Government Administration*, edited by John J. Gargan
63. *Handbook of Administrative Communication*, edited by James L. Garnett and Alexander Kouzmin
64. *Public Budgeting and Finance: Fourth Edition, Revised and Expanded*, edited by Robert T. Golembiewski and Jack Rabin
65. *Handbook of Public Administration: Second Edition*, edited by Jack Rabin, W. Bartley Hildreth, and Gerald J. Miller
66. *Handbook of Organization Theory and Management: The Philosophical Approach*, edited by Thomas D. Lynch and Todd J. Dicker
67. *Handbook of Public Finance*, edited by Fred Thompson and Mark T. Green
68. *Organizational Behavior and Public Management: Third Edition, Revised and Expanded*, Michael L. Vasu, Debra W. Stewart, and G. David Garson
69. *Handbook of Economic Development*, edited by Kuotsai Tom Liou
70. *Handbook of Health Administration and Policy*, edited by Anne Osborne Kilpatrick and James A. Johnson
71. *Handbook of Research Methods in Public Administration*, edited by Gerald J. Miller and Marcia L. Whicker
72. *Handbook on Taxation*, edited by W. Bartley Hildreth and James A. Richardson
73. *Handbook of Comparative Public Administration in the Asia-Pacific Basin*, edited by Hoi-kwok Wong and Hon S. Chan
74. *Handbook of Global Environmental Policy and Administration,* edited by Dennis L. Soden and Brent S. Steel
75. *Handbook of State Government Administration,* edited by John J. Gargan
76. *Handbook of Global Legal Policy,* edited by Stuart S. Nagel
77. *Handbook of Public Information Systems,* edited by G. David Garson
78. *Handbook of Global Economic Policy,* edited by Stuart S. Nagel

Additional Volumes in Preparation

Handbook of Organizational Consultation: Second Edition, Revised and Expanded, edited by Robert T. Golembiewski

Handbook of Global International Policy, edited by Stuart S. Nagel

Handbook of Global Technology Policy, edited by Stuart S. Nagel

Handbook of Global Political Policy, edited by Stuart S. Nagel

Handbook of Global Social Policy, edited by Stuart S. Nagel and Amy Robb

Handbook of Strategic Management: Second Edition, Revised and Expanded, edited by Jack Rabin, Gerald J. Miller, and W. Bartley Hildreth

Handbook of Organizational Behavior: Second Edition, Revised and Expanded, edited by Robert T. Golembiewski

Handbook of Administrative Ethics: Second Edition, Revised and Expanded, edited by Terry L. Cooper

Handbook of Public Quality Management, edited by Ronald J. Stupak and Peter M. Leitner

Handbook of Criminal Justice Administration, edited by Toni Dupont-Morales, Michael Hooper, and Judy H. Schmidt

Labor Relations in the Public Sector: Third Edition, edited by Richard C. Kearney

ANNALS OF PUBLIC ADMINISTRATION

1. *Public Administration: History and Theory in Contemporary Perspective*, edited by Joseph A. Uveges, Jr.
2. *Public Administration Education in Transition*, edited by Thomas Vocino and Richard Heimovics
3. *Centenary Issues of the Pendleton Act of 1883*, edited by David H. Rosenbloom with the assistance of Mark A. Emmert
4. *Intergovernmental Relations in the 1980s*, edited by Richard H. Leach
5. *Criminal Justice Administration: Linking Practice and Research*, edited by William A. Jones, Jr.

Handbook of Global Economic Policy

edited by

Stuart S. Nagel
University of Illinois
Urbana, Illinois

MARCEL DEKKER, INC. NEW YORK • BASEL

ISBN: 0-8247-0328-6

This book is printed on acid-free paper.

Headquarters
Marcel Dekker, Inc.
270 Madison Avenue, New York, NY 10016
tel: 212-696-9000; fax: 212-685-4540

Eastern Hemisphere Distribution
Marcel Dekker AG
Hutgasse 4, Postfach 812, CH-4001 Basel, Switzerland
tel: 41-61-261-8482; fax: 41-61-261-8896

World Wide Web
http://www.dekker.com

The publisher offers discounts on this book when ordered in bulk quantities. For more information, write to Special Sales/Professional Marketing at the headquarters address above.

Current printing (last digit):
10 9 8 7 6 5 4 3 2 1

PRINTED IN THE UNITED STATES OF AMERICA

Preface

This handbook on global economic policy is one in a set of six global policy handbooks. The other five deal with technology, social, political, international, and legal policy.

Public policy studies in the past have tended to emphasize domestic policy, rather than cross-national policy. This is especially true of American policy studies which tend to be especially nation-bound. This is also true to some extent of policy studies in France, Russia, China, Brazil, and elsewhere.

When American policy studies show an interest in other countries, those other countries tend to be exclusively Western European countries. This six-volume set, however, will include all the regions of the world, consisting of Africa, Asia, Europe, Latin and North America in alphabetical order with Western Europe being only one of the several regions.

Public policy studies also tend to place a lot of emphasis on methods of analysis and the policy process. They do not get much into substance, especially at the professional or scholarly level, as contrasted to undergraduate textbooks. This is so because scholars have traditionally considered substance to be not as philosophical or theoretical as methods or process.

In this six-volume set, however, each volume is devoted to a different substantive field, including economic, technology, social, political, international, and legal policy. The discussions will be more theoretical than most substantive discussions because they will emphasize comparisons across places, across times, and across different substantive fields. At the same time, the discussions will be practical in terms of applicability to real world problems.

Scholars and others who study comparative government unfortunately tend to overemphasize structures like federalism, separation of powers, legislatures, chief executives, and supreme courts to the neglect of public policy, which this series emphasizes. Comparative government people also tend to emphasize area studies which involve specializing in a single country or sub-region, as contrasted to this set of six volumes which cuts across many regions and many policy fields.

Thus the key objective of this set is to encourage more cross-national and cross-policy research and applications. The set not only advocates more of that kind of research, but practices what it advocates by providing almost 200 studies across six volumes which average about 30 studies per volume. This should be a landmark set in the disciplines of both policy studies and cross-national studies.

Stuart S. Nagel

Contents

Contributors

Jong Gook Back Professor, International Relations, Gyeongsang National University, Chinju, Korea

Noorjahan Bava Professor, Department of Political Science, University of Delhi, New Delhi, India

Morten Bøås Research Fellow, Centre for Development and the Environment, University of Oslo, Oslo, Norway

Yat Lun Chan Professor, University of Aberdeen, Old Aberdeen, Scotland

Rupa Chanda Assistant Professor, Department of Economics, Indian Institute of Management, Bangalore, India

Rekha Datta Assistant Professor, Department of Political Science, Monmouth University, West Long Beach, New Jersey

Zhong Zhu Ding Professor, Department of Political Science, New School University, New York, New York

Maiga Dzervite Deputy Director General, Latvian State Revenue Service, Riga, Latvia

Alex Kelvin Scheme Tutor International, Department of Management, University of Hertfordshire, Hertford, England

Henry E. Kilpatrick, Jr. Research Fellow, The Institute of Public Policy, George Mason University, Fairfax, Virginia

Thomas König Professor, University of Uonstanz, Uonstanz, Germany

Mark Owen Lombardi Associate Professor and Chair, Department of Government and World Affairs, University of Tampa, Tampa, Florida

Miriam K. Mills* New Jersey Institute of Technology, Newark, New Jersey

Maria Chan Morgan Professor, Department of Politics, Earlham College, Richmond, Indiana

Rosa Mulé Lecturer, Department of Politics and International Studies, University of Warwick, Coventry, United Kingdom

G. Mac Nie Associate Professor, Department of Business Administration and Economics, Fort Valley State University, Fort Valley, Georgia

Dora Orlansky Professor, Department of Political Science, University of Buenos Aires, Buenos Aires, Argentina

Laure Paquette Associate Professor, Department of Political Science, Lakehead University, Thunder Bay, Ontario, Canada

Sang-Chul Park Professor, Centre for East and Southeast Asian Studies, Göteborg University, Göteborg, Sweden

Louwrens Pretorius Professor, Department of Sociology, University of South Africa, Pretoria, South Africa

David A. Reingold Assistant Professor, School of Public and Environmental Affairs, Indiana University, Bloomington, Indiana

Lawrence Sáez Visiting Scholar, Center for South Asia Studies, University of California, Berkeley, California

---

*Deceased.

Sandip Singh Sahota Professor, Department of Government and World Affairs, University of Tampa, Tampa, Florida

Yoichiro Sato Lecturer, Department of Political Studies, University of Auckland, Auckland, New Zealand

Kenneth C. Shadlen Professor, Department of Political Science, Brown University, Providence, Rhode Island

Niels Christian Sidenius Associate Professor and Dean, Department of Political Science, University of Århus, Århus, Denmark

Gwynneth Singleton Senior Lecturer, School of Administrative Studies, University of Canberra, Canberra, Australia

J. Gunnar Trumbull Jean Monnet Fellow, Robert Schuman Center, European University Institute, Florence, Italy

Mark Turner Professor, School of Administrative Studies, University of Canberra, Canberra, Australia

Enbao Wang Assistant Professor, Department of Political Science, University of Hawaii at Hilo, Hilo, Hawaii

Feng Xiao Professor, University of Hertfordshire, Hertford, England

INTRODUCTION

Stuart S. Nagel
University of Illinois, Urbana, Illinois

Win-win or superoptimizing analysis of public policy problems tries to find feasible solutions that can enable conservatives, liberals, and other major viewpoints to all come out ahead of their best initial expectations simultaneously. The elements in the analysis include (1) conservative goals and alternatives, (2) liberal goals and alternatives, (3) relations between the major alternatives and goals, (4) the development of win-win solutions, and (5) feasibility hurdles to overcome.

The feasibility problems to be overcome include economic, administrative, political, psychological, legal, international, and technological hurdles, and the disruption of displaced firms and individuals.

As applied to economics, we are especially talking about the alleged tradeoffs among (1) unemployment and inflation, (2) economic growth and displaced workers, (3) increased government spending, reduced taxes, and a reduced deficit, and (4) the tradeoff between capitalism and socialism. We will also briefly refer to the economic policy problems of land, labor, and capital, but with less detail in view of space limitations.[1]

I. UNEMPLOYMENT AND INFLATION

A. Conservative Alternatives

Doing nothing is not likely to worsen unemployment or inflation, but it is also not likely to help. Decreasing the money supply and increasing interest rates may decrease inflation but increase unemployment. The same is true of decreasing government spending and increasing taxes. The ''Reaganomics'' approach involves decreasing taxes to stimulate employment, and decreasing domestic spending to reduce inflation. The Democratic counterpart as of 1980 was to increase employment through government jobs and decrease inflation through price control. (See Table 1.)

Raising interest rates to decrease inflation may have the effect of decreasing prices by reducing spending from borrowed money. Those benefits may be more than offset by the undesirable effects on reducing the ability of business to borrow for expansion, inventory, and other purposes. The reduction in spending may also have an adverse effect on employment.

Raising taxes and decreasing spending to fight inflation may not be politically feasible. It would also reduce the ability of the government to give tax breaks and well-placed subsidies to increase productivity.

B. Liberal Alternatives

Increasing the money supply and decreasing interests may stimulate employment but increase inflation. The same is also true of increasing government spending and reducing taxes. Lowering interest rates to decrease unemployment may have little impact because businesses are reluctant to borrow when they are reducing their operations and sales are down. Likewise, consumers are reluctant to borrow when they are already heavily in debt and fearful of a reduction in employment or hours.

Lowering taxes and increasing spending to fight unemployment may not be politically feasible when the national debt and deficit are already too high.

Table 1 Analysis of Inflation and Unemployment

	Criteria	
Alternatives	Conservative: Lower inflation	Liberal: Lower unemployment
Conservative:	+	–
Monetary policy (change interest rates)	Rates up (bad impact on profits and wages)	Rates down (no impact on profits and wages)
Liberal:	–	+
Fiscal policy (change taxing & spending)	Surplus (not politically feasible)	Deficit (not politically feasible)
Neutral:		
Little of both	0	0
SOS or win-win:		
Economic growth policy	++	++
1. Increase technology		
2. Increase skills		

C. A Win-Win Alternative

The adoption of new technologies and raising the skills of workers help to reduce inflation by (1) increasing the productivity of labor to offset increased wages, (2) increasing the quality of goods to offset increased prices, and (3) increasing the GNP and domestic income to further offset increased prices.

Increasing the adoption of new technologies and raising the skills of workers help to reduce unemployment by (1) making the workers more employable, (2) increasing the GNP and domestic spending to stimulate the creation of more jobs, and (3) increasing the productivity and wage rates, thereby offsetting a possible reduction in hours.

The conservative alternative of having interest rates up in time of inflation and down in time of unemployment does not make sense if inflation and unemployment are problems simultaneously. That would be so if both were over 3%. Likewise, the liberal alternative of having a budget surplus in time of inflation and a budget deficit in time of unemployment does not make sense when both inflation and unemployment are over approximately 3%. One can, however, stimulate new technologies and upgrade skills when inflation and unemployment are both occurring simultaneously.

II. ECONOMIC GROWTH AND DISPLACED WORKERS

A. Economic Growth

1. Definition and Importance

''Economic growth'' refers to the annual rate of increase in the gross national product or the gross domestic product. The GNP refers to all income generated in the United States even if some of it goes to foreigners. The GDP refers to all income generated anywhere in the world that goes to Americans.

Economic growth is highly important because it provides the increased income that generates increased spending, taxes, jobs, money for government programs, and appropriations for dealing with schools, crimes, health, transportation, communications, food, housing, defense, new technologies, upgrading skills, etc. (See Table 2.)

2. Conservative and Liberal Approaches

The conservative approach tends to emphasize taxing and spending in a way that is helpful to investment and business. The increased investment stimulates economic growth. Conservatives advocate increased investment through lowering taxes on the upper income brackets and lowering the capital gains tax. They

Table 2 Economic Growth

	Goals	
Alternatives	Conservative: Investment	Liberal: Consumption
Conservative:		
Trickle down	+	−
Liberal:		
Percolate up	−	+
Neutral:		
Both	0	0
SOS or win-win:		
Package	++	++

also advocate spending for highways, airports, railroads, and other expenditures that will facilitate business profits.

The liberal approach tends to emphasize taxing and spending that is helpful to consumption and workers. The increased consumption stimulates economic growth. Liberals advocate increased consumption through lowering taxes on the lower income brackets and raising exemptions for dependents and the standard deduction. They also advocate government spending for food stamps, housing vouchers, welfare, teacher salaries, health care, and other government expenditures that result in high consumption.

3. A Win-Win Package

An SOS package can promote economic growth more directly rather than indirectly through private investment and consumption although the SOS package could also possibly increase investment and consumption. Such a package might include the government's providing:

1. Long-term, large-scale risk capital
2. Stimulus to competition by readily granting entry permits into all industries and entry of foreign goods into the United States
3. Stimulus to business and labor to adopt new technologies and upgrade worker skills
4. Funds for relocating workers displaced by tariff reduction, immigration, new technologies, or conversion from defense production
5. Reductions in foreign tariffs to open new markets
6. Immigration policy that brings in innovative, ambitious people with needed skills

7. Free speech to encourage creativity, including suggestions to improve productivity
8. Grants, patents, and purchasing to stimulate inventions but requiring licensing to stimulate diffusion and competition
9. An educational system that is oriented toward preparation for productive jobs and careers
10. Conservation of natural resources and a productive, healthful environment

Other important economic indicators besides economic growth include unemployment, inflation, and measures of income equality. Big economic growth is offset if those other indicators worsen or do not improve.[2]

B. Displaced Workers and Firms

Displacement of labor is the result of (1) productivity downsizing, (2) free trade, (3) immigration, (4) civilian conversion, or (5) jobs for public aid recipients, the disabled, the elderly, minorities, and women.

The issue here is how to find jobs for displaced workers. The conservative emphasis is to leave it up to the recipient to find a job on his own and not make it a responsibility of other people. The liberal emphasis is on the welfare agency or another government agency doing most of the job finding work. The neutral position might involve delegating the activity to a nonprofit organization. (See Table 3.)

A key conservative goal is to save tax money. That means encouraging job finding to reduce welfare payments, but not incurring high fees for job finding. A key liberal goal is to find jobs for displaced workers or welfare recipients not just to save welfare payments but also because jobs can increase the income, quality of life, and dignity of welfare recipients. Doing so also has effects that relate to multipliers, compounding, role models, and reducing illegal activities.

An SOS alternative is to contract out to a private profit-making firm at a commission of $X per welfare recipient who receives long-term employment. Half of the commission is paid after four months on the job and the other half after eight months. The firm is responsible for providing training, day care, employment leads, advice, and dispute resolution, all of which the government agency might otherwise provide.

This is a good example of contracting out. The profit motive stimulates more success in finding jobs than the rate of success by a government agency or a nonprofit organization. The firm also has more capability than the recipient. Tax money is saved in the long run as a result of replacing welfare with work. It may also be saved in the short run by costing less money per long-term job

Table 3 Equity Versus Efficiency in Displacement of Labor[a]

Alternatives	Goals: Conservative: Efficiency (merit or survival of the fittest)	Goals: Liberal: Equity (i.e., fairness to those unemployed to no fault)
Conservative:		
Marketplace (leaves to the labor marketplace)	+	−
Liberal:		
Welfare handouts with few conditions	−	+
Neutral:		
Welfare with conditions:		
1. No able-bodied eligibles, especially males	0	0
2. Bare minimum benefits		
3. Residence requirements		
4. Provide no due process		
SOS or win-win, i.e., job facilitators		
1. Training		
2. Wage subsidy		
3. Employment agency commissions	++	++
4. Rising GNP		
5. Relocation		
6. Welfare conditional on training and job cooperation		

[a] Displacement of labor means displaced because of (1) productivity downsizing, (2) free trade, (3) immigration, (4) jobs for public aid recipients, disabled or aged, (5) minorities and women.

found than the cost with a government agency or nonprofit organization. Related activities can also help displaced businesspeople find new jobs or new businesses.

III. SPENDING, TAXING, AND THE DEFICIT

A. SOS Spending

1. Arriving at a Win-Win Budget

Each allocation is arrived at by (1) multiplying the percentages in the goal columns by the neutral, conservative, or liberal weights; (2) summing across the products; (3) dividing the sum by the total of the appropriate weights to obtain a weighted average allocation percentage; and then (4) multiplying the total budget of \$200 by that allocation percentage. (See Table 4.)

The superoptimum budget is \$243 since that is the minimum amount that will allow for a bigger allocation than the best expectations of both the conservatives (\$112 + \$1 to the police) and the liberals (\$129 + \$1 to the courts).

2. Obtaining a Bigger Budget or Using the Present Budget More Efficiently

The next step would be to analyze various ways of increasing the budget from \$200 to \$243, and then taking the best combination of those in light of various criteria. There is an alternative approach to increasing the budget to an SOS amount that satisfies the best initial expectations of both liberals and conservatives. The alternative involves satisfying conservatives by enabling the police and the courts to be more efficient in crime reduction so that they will not need so much money.

The police can be more efficient by being more visible—for instance, by covering highway policing with their red lights continuously flashing. The courts can be more efficient in crime reduction by using better screening and reporting with regard to those who have been released on bail prior to trial.

The alternative also involves satisfying liberals by enabling the police and the courts to be more efficient in using fair procedures. The police can be more efficient and effective by giving a summons to appear in many arrest cases rather than booking and jailing the suspect. The courts can be more efficient and effective regarding fair procedure by allowing jurors to view each day's trial on videotape. This helps clarify matters that might otherwise be forgotten. Jurors can also be allowed to take notes, ask questions of judges and the lawyers, and receive some training before becoming jurors.

B. SOS Taxing

1. Conservative and Liberal Alternatives

The conservative position on tax sources tends to emphasize consumption taxes, which are roughly equal across the general public. The liberal position tends to emphasize income taxes, which bear more heavily on those with greater ability to pay. Conservatives tend to emphasize taxes on consumption such as the sales tax or the value-added tax. Liberals tend to emphasize taxes on income, especially progressive income taxes, where the rates are higher on higher incomes. The neutral position is to have both sales taxes and income taxes, but with the sales tax rates lower than conservatives advocate and the income tax rates lower than liberals advocate. (See Table 5.)

Table 4 SOS Spending

	Goals		Allocations			
Budget categories	Conservative: Crime reduction	Liberal: Fair procedure	Neutral: Wts. = 2 & 2	Conservative: Wts. = 3 & 1	Liberal: Wts. = 1 & 3	SOS
Conservative:				(X)		X+1
Money for police	2	1	$92[a]	$112	$71	$113
	(67%)	(25%)	(46%)	(55%)[b]	(35%)[c]	(46%)
Liberal:					(Y)	Y+1
Money for courts	1	3	$108	$88	$129	130
	(33%)	(75%)	(54%)	(44%)	(65%)	(54%)
Totals	3	2	$200	$200	$200	$243
	(100%)	(100%)	(100%)	(100%)	(100%)	(100%)

Abbreviations: Wts. = Weights for multiplying the allocation percentages for each of the two goals. X = Conservative allocation to exceed. Y = Liberal allocation to exceed.

[a] Dollars are in millions.

[b] The conservative 55% = [(3 times 67%) plus (1 times 25%)]/4.

[c] The liberal 35% = [(1 times 67%) plus (3 times 25%)]/4.

Table 5 Tax Sources

Alternatives	Goals: Conservative: Stimulating investment	Goals: Liberal: Ability to pay
Conservative:		
Sales tax	+	−
Liberal:		
Income tax	−	+
Neutral:		
Other or both	0	0
SOS or win-win:		
Decrease tax rates, but increases taxes with lots of well-placed subsidies	++	++

2. Conservative and Liberal Goals

A key conservative goal is to stimulate investment. A key liberal goal is to stimulate consumption and to take into consideration the equity goal of ability to pay.

Both conservatives and liberals recognize the need for some tax money to support the government activities they like. The superoptimum solution, therefore, is not to abolish all taxes. That would be undesirable to both conservatives and liberals if it means abolishing the government activities they endorse. Likewise, the neutral position may result in a decrease in the government activities endorsed by conservatives and those endorsed by liberals.

3. Relations Between Alternatives and Goals

Sales taxes score low on consumption and ability to pay, whereas income taxes score higher. On the matter of stimulating investment, one can argue that relying on sales taxes rather than income taxes frees up more income for investment purposes. Therefore, the scores in the column on stimulating investment should probably be 2, 3, and 4, rather than all 4's. The justification for having a 4 on income tax is that such a tax lends itself well to giving tax credits to stimulate investment.

Regardless of how the different taxes are scored on the two goals, there does tend to be a tradeoff. Reliance on income taxes generally does better on ability to pay than on stimulating investment. That, however, depends on the extent to which the income tax provides for meaningful credits. Likewise, reliance on sales taxes generally does worse on ability to pay than on facilitating investment.

4. The Win-Win Alternative

The SOS alternative involves substantially decreasing both kinds of tax rates while at the same time increasing the total tax revenue by increasing the GNP tax base. That can be partly done by well-placed tax breaks and subsidies to encourage greater national productivity.

An SOS alternative would do well on both goals. That kind of alternative might involve a combination of the two taxes, but accompanied by well-placed subsidies and tax credits to stimulate increased productivity. The tax credits could also include an earned-income payment for those who are regularly working but not earning very much and thus without much ability to pay high taxes.

C. The Deficit

1. Dealing with the Deficit

A statement of the conservative goals might be: (1) have a strong national defense and (2) stimulate investment through low taxes on the relatively rich. A fuller statement of the liberal goals might be: (1) have strong domestic policies in such areas as education and housing and (2) stimulate consumption through low taxes on the relatively poor. (See Table 6.)

Table 6 The Deficit of Spending over Taxes

	Goals	
Alternatives	Conservative: Defense and investment	Liberal: Domestic and consumption
Conservative:		
1. Decrease domestic spending	+	−
2. Increase taxes on poor		
Liberal:		
1. Decrease defense spending	−	+
2. Increase taxes on rich		
Neutral:		
1. Decrease both spend	0	0
2. Increase taxes on both		
SOS or win-win:		
1. Increase spending	++	++
2. Decrease taxes		

The SOS involves a reduction of taxes in the form of tax breaks designed to stimulate greater productivity. Likewise, the SOS involves an increase in spending in the form of well-placed subsidies designed to stimulate greater productivity. The increased productivity means an increased gross national product, which means an increased base on which to apply the national tax rate. Thus the tax rate can drop and still bring in increased tax revenue, making more money available for government spending on defense, domestic policies, deficit reduction, and more well-placed subsidies.

2. A Balanced Budget Amendment

A related issue here is whether there should be an amendment to the Constitution that requires the federal budget to be balanced each year, with federal spending not to exceed federal tax revenue.

Conservatives endorse the amendment to keep down federal spending that is considered too liberal, especially if an exception is made for defense spending. They would also like a requirement of 60% congressional approval for tax increases.

Liberals oppose the amendment because they want to allow for federal spending to fight unemployment and to promote economic growth. If those considerations are covered, they would endorse a prohibition on deficit spending since deficits lead to government borrowing which boosts interest rates. Such increases interfere with consumer purchasing and business expansion.

The neutral position is to have a balanced budget amendment, but with exceptions. The conservatives, especially, want an exception for a declared war or a joint resolution relating to military action. Liberals want exceptions for (1) high unemployment and (2) when 60% of Congress votes for an increase in the national debt.

An SOS alternative would be to promote economic growth through training, new technologies, competition, exports, government capital, and other means. Growth in the GNP allows for a reduction in income tax rates, with an increase in tax revenue. It also allows for a reduction in spending for welfare, with increased spending for economic growth activities. Such growth can mean increases in both profits and wages.

What may be needed is an economic growth amendment that requires or recommends that the federal government promote at least 3% economic growth per year. The amendment can mandate the establishment of a quasi-public Consortium for Economic Growth. Its governing board could consist of three representatives from the National Association of Manufacturers and the U.S. Chamber of Commerce, three representatives from the AFL-CIO, and three representatives from the Senate, the House, and the Presidency. It could have a substantial appropriation for encouraging economic growth activities.[3]

IV. ORGANIZING THE ECONOMY

A. Alternative Ways of Relating the Government to the Economy

Socialism refers to government ownership and public policy designed to facilitate equality of income and wealth. *Capitalism* refers to private ownership with no public policy designed to facilitate equality of income, wealth, and opportunity. One could conceivably talk in terms of four policies: (1) private ownership and no equality; (2) private ownership and equality; (3) government ownership and no equality; and (4) government ownership and equality. The two elements of capitalism (private ownership and inequality) tend to go together, and likewise the two elements of socialism (public ownership and equality).

One can have democratic or dictatorial capitalism and democratic or dictatorial socialism, depending on whether there are universal voting rights, and minority political rights. One can have responsive or nonresponsive capitalism and responsive or nonresponsive socialism. Responsiveness in this context means being responsive to consumers and workers. Socialism is traditionally thought of as being more responsive to consumers and workers.

B. Government Versus Private Ownership and Operation

The SOS alternative of contracting out to private operation can apply even to public schools, post offices, and municipal transportation. In former socialistic countries, it could also apply to contracting out government-owned factories and land. (See Table 7.)

Table 7 Ownership and Operation

	Goals	
Alternatives	Conservative: High productivity	Liberal: Equity
Conservative:		
1. Government ownership and operation (socialism)	+	−
Liberal:		
1. Private ownership and operation (capitalism)	−	+
Neutral:		
1. Some government and some private	0	0
SOS or win-win:		
1. 100% government owned and 100% private operation	++	++
2. 100% private with government incentives; both SOSs.		

The contracting out does not have to be to only one private entrepreneur. The two most qualified lowest bidders can both receive contracts for different geographical areas, sectors of the industry, or other aspects of the contract in order to encourage competition.

Productivity and the liberal goals can be further increased through appropriate government incentives by way of well-placed tax credits and subsidies. That goes beyond what can be achieved by way of government ownership or control combined with contracting out to private operation.

Workplace quality, environmental protection, and consumer protection are not necessarily promoted by government ownership. The socialist steel mills in Poland were a good example of poor workplace quality under socialism. The socialistic TVA in the United States was a good example of poor environmental protection under socialism. Government-owned power companies having monopoly control are good examples of the lack of consumer protection under socialism.

All those goals can be better achieved by requiring them as part of the contract in contracting out. That is likely to produce greater compliance than traditional government regulation. The threat of not having the contract renewed but instead having it go to a competing company can generate greater compliance. That is better than relying on the supposed altruism of managers of government factories who are not rewarded or punished for complying with goals. The government can provide further incentives by way of well-placed subsidies and tax credits to supplement the liberal contract provisions.

C. Competition as a Key Factor

The conservative alternative of an unregulated marketplace may lead to only one or a few firms dominating most industries. That arrangement may be profitable in the short run, although contrary to low prices. The liberal alternative of government ownership or tight regulation tends to mean a government monopoly or stifled private enterprise. That means reduced business profits, although it might mean artificially low prices to satisfy consumers as voters. The mixed economy scores in the middle on both business profits and low prices. (See Table 8.)

The SOS alternative may draw on the stimulus to innovation and efficiency of private profit making. The SOS alternative may encourage competition through well-placed seed money and other competition facilitators. Doing so results in lower prices through a competitive marketplace, rather than through a monopolistic one or through artificial price constraints.

The marketplace is associated with capitalism. It may not be associated with competition if the marketplace leads to monopolies or firms working together to decrease competition. Regulation and government ownership are associated with socialism. It is even more likely to lead to monopoly, but monopoly in the hands of the state rather than private enterprise. The marketplace may lead

Table 8 Competition

Alternatives	Goals: Conservative: Business profits	Goals: Liberal: Low prices
Conservative:		
Marketplace (monopoly)	+	−
Liberal:		
Government ownership or tight regulation (monopoly)	−	+
Neutral:		
Some of both (mixed economy)	0	0
SOS or win-win:		
Stimulate competition through well-placed subsidies	++	++

to better business profits than regulation does. Regulation may lead to better consumer prices than the marketplace does.

An SOS alternative is competition, which is likely to lead to even better total business profits than the marketplace, although not necessarily better profits for each firm. Competition is likely to lead to better consumer prices and quality of products than regulation. Competition can be stimulated through laws that require (1) licensing of patents and facilities, (2) lowering of tariffs to increase international competition, (3) seed money to get new businesses established or expanded to make an industry more competitive, and (4) leasing of networks of electricity, telephone, and cable TV.

D. Equality in Socialism and Capitalism

Capitalism differs from socialism mainly in terms of government versus private ownership and operation of the major means of production and distribution. Capitalism also differs from socialism with regard to the extent to which inequality of income and wealth is allowed.

Under pure capitalism, there are no limits to the degree of permissible inequality in income and wealth. Under socialism, there are progressive income taxes and inheritance taxes designed to promote a substantial amount of equality in income and wealth.

Capitalism justifies economic inequality as a stimulus to increased productivity. The theory is that people will work harder and be more innovative in order to receive the rewards of greater income and wealth. Socialism justifies having greater income equality as the fair or equitable thing to do, especially in the context of providing a minimum floor regarding food, shelter, and clothing to the poor.

An SOS alternative that does well with both the conservative and liberal goals involves allowing considerable inequality in income and wealth but providing a minimum floor. That can be done through a negative income tax whereby people who are below that minimum level receive a payment from the Internal Revenue Service instead of paying to the IRS. (See Table 9.)

A better approach is to emphasize earned income credit whereby the people below a minimum level who work are rewarded by receiving an IRS payment. Those who do not work receive public aid and assistance in finding a job. The SOS may also provide tax breaks and subsidies for upgrading individual skills in order to increase productivity.

E. Political-Economic Competition and Prosperity

Table 10 includes only industrial nations; a separate table could be compiled for developing nations. Among industrialized nations, those that provide for competition in politics and economics have more prosperity than those that do not provide for competition in both activities. Industrialized nations that provide for competition in only one of the two activities are likely to have middling prosperity, although competition in politics may be more important to prosperity than competition in economics.

Table 10 is designed mainly to relate political and economic competition as key causes in prosperity. One could also interpret Table 10 as showing that

Table 9 Equity

Alternatives	Goals: Conservative: Productivity	Goals: Liberal: Equity (minimum floor)
Conservative:		
1. Income inequality (capitalism)	+	−
Liberal:		
1. Income equality (socialism)	−	+
Neutral:		
1. In between	0	0
SOS or win-win:		
1. Negative income tax or earned income credit	++	++
2. Tax breaks for upgrading skills		

Table 10 Political and Economic Competition as Key Causes of Prosperity

	Competition (causal variable)	
	NO (in politics and economics)	YES (in politics and economics)
YES		West Germany (capitalism)
Prosperity or high standard of living (effect variable)		Sweden (socialism)
NO	East Germany (socialism) Spain Pre-1980 (capitalism)	

countries that have economic competition are more likely to have political competition, and vice versa. In addition, one could interpret Table 10 as indicating that industrialized nations are more likely to have a higher standard of living than nonindustrialized nations regardless of political and economic competition. Another conclusion, which Table 6 generates, is that whether a country has capitalistic private ownership or socialistic government ownership is virtually irrelevant to prosperity in comparison to political-economic competition and industrialization.[4]

V. OTHER ECONOMIC ISSUES

The economic issues we have discussed all deal with the economy as a whole. They are macroeconomic issues, as contrasted to issues that deal with the individual firm or with land, labor, and capital as the major factors of production. Sometimes government policy is added as a fourth factor. We consider government policy to be present in discussing how to promote effectiveness, efficiency, and equity in using the other three factors and other societal resources.

A. Land

A key tradeoff issue dealing with land or natural resources in the United States is the alleged conflict between high farm production and high farm income. The

United States may be the only country in the world in which farmers have been encouraged to produce less in order to create artificially high prices. In other countries, farmers are encouraged to grow more in order to feed the population and have crops for export. A win-win solution recently adopted under the title ''Freedom to Farm'' allows farmers to produce all they want in anticipation that the world market will be able to absorb their extra production.

Unfortunately, when subsidies were abolished for setting aside land, the Asian and Russian markets became less able to buy. The problem is not the lack of demand, or that American farm products are high priced. There is plenty of demand, and American farmers are highly efficient. The problem seems to be that when China or Russia wants to buy wheat, they are likely to buy it from Australia, Argentina, or Canada because they can afford Australian, Argentine, and Canadian dollars better than they can afford U.S. dollars. The U.S. dollar is high priced compared, for example, to the Canadian dollar.

The American government drives up the price of the dollar whenever it seeks to sell U.S. Treasury bonds in order to borrow from new lenders to pay off old lenders. We could reduce the national debt (as we have reduced the annual deficit) through economic growth which provides (1) increased government revenue and (2) decreased welfare spending. The price of the dollar would go down. As a result, farmers could sell more goods overseas, and so could all American producers. That would be a super win-win for America and the consumers of American products.[5]

B. Labor

A good example of win-win labor policy relates to the minimum wage. Whenever there is a suggestion of raising the minimum wage, management talks about having to lay off workers whose families will then starve. Labor talks about families already starving because the minimum wage is not a living wage. The usual result, however, is a compromise in which both sides are allowing for some alleged starvation. A win-win solution is needed whereby, for example, management could pay less than $4 an hour and labor could receive more than $5 per hour. Such a procedure involves minimum-wage vouchers, which are worth $1. The $1 vouchers are given to employers to enable them to pay their workers $4 an hour plus a $1 voucher that can be cashed at the bank.

To receive this $1 subsidy, the employer must agree to provide on-the-job training to bring the worker's skills up to the $5-an-hour level within six months. Likewise, to receive this $1 subsidy, the worker must agree to participate in the on-the-job training and to pass the final exam. This is a win-win situation for management and workers alike. It is also a win-win situation for society because it saves tax money that might otherwise go to unemployment compensation, public aid, food stamps, public housing, anticrime expenses, Medicaid, and other services for the unemployed. Society also benefits because these newly employed people pay taxes which support productivity-increasing public policy. The workers are also better role models for their children and grandchildren.

Workers who already work for the firm would also be eligible to take on-the-job training to be in the voucher program to increase their wages above the minimum wage. The voucher program is especially beneficial to the economy, however, if it enables people to work at the minimum wage or above when they otherwise would not be employed at all. This kind of wage voucher could also apply to elderly workers, disabled workers, and others to temporarily fill the gap between what employers are willing to pay and what might be considered a living wage.[6]

C. Capital

As an example that deals with capital in our set of land, labor, and capital examples, we can deal with the stock market. It is a big source of capital under U.S. capitalism, although Japan relies more heavily on bank savings and the tax-supported MITI. A conflict of interest in stock brokerage is between small investors and the middlemen brokers who facilitate obtaining capital for big firms. The problem is that those who sell stocks and bonds would like to get as big a cut of their sales as possible. Those who buy stocks and bonds would like to pay as small a commission as possible.

Commissions could be increased to make both sellers and buyers happy by changing the present payment system. The current system pays sellers a percentage of what they get the investor to buy. This inherently encourages brokers to encourage investors to buy more than they possibly should, and to buy more of certain shares that pay high commissions. A win-win alternative would be to pay on the basis of good performance. That way a broker would get a substantial percentage of the dividends within the first five years, or whatever percentage and time period are negotiated. The broker could also get a substantial percentage of the increase in the value of stock upon resale. Such an arrangement could enable good brokers to make a lot more money, which would also benefit the stock buyers. A minimum fee could be provided on the basis of hours worked.

There is a need for more performance pay in all fields of the private and public sectors to enable both sellers and consumers to come out ahead of their best initial expectations. Total profits of stock sellers could also be increased if banks were allowed to sell stock. The competition could allow qualified banks to make a legitimate profit, which they are currently denied. The stock buyers would also benefit from the competition. Indeed, stimulated competition and the structured or channeled profit motive may be the two most important concepts in win-win economic policy.[7]

This *Handbook on Economic Policy* contains chapters dealing with the above and other economic issues. The chapters are organized in terms of economic policy in Africa, Asia, Europe, and Latin America/North America.

ENDNOTES

1. For further details on win-win analysis, see S. Nagel, *Super-Optimum Solutions and Win-Win Policy: Basic Concepts and Principles* (Quorum, 1997); S. Nagel, *Public Policy Evaluation: Making Super-Optimum Decision* (Ashgate, 1998); and S. Nagel, *Policy Within and Across Developing Countries* (Ashgate, 1998).
2. For further details on inflation and unemployment, see Charles Schultze, *Memos to the President: A Guide Through Macroeconomics for the Busy Policymaker* (Brookings, 1992); and Melvin Dubnick and Alan Gitelson (eds.), *Public Policy and Economic Institutions* (JAI Press, 1991).
3. On taxing, spending, and the deficit, see Robert Reischauer (ed.), *Setting National Priorities: Budget Choices for the Next Century* (Brookings, 1997); and Warren Samuels and Larry Wade (eds.), *Taxing and Spending Policy* (Lexington, 1980).
4. On organizing the economy, see Randy Ross, *Government and the Private Sector: Who Should Do What?* (Rand, 1988); and Dennis Thompson (ed.), *The Private Exercise of Public Functions* (Associated Faculty Press, 1985).
5. On land and agriculture, see Emery Castle (ed.), *The Changing American Countryside: Rural People and Places* (Kansas, 1995); and Don Hadwiger and William Browne (eds.), *The New Politics of Food* (Lexington, 1978).
6. On labor and management, see Thomas Moore, *The Disposable Work Force: Worker Displacement and Employment Instability in America* (Aldine De Gruyter, 1996); and Lawrence Flood (ed.), Unions and public policy, in *The New Economy, Law, and Democratic Politics* (Greenwood, 1995).
7. On business and consumers, see Rogene Buchholz, *Business Environment and Public Policy: Implications for Management and Strategy Formulation* (Prentice-Hall, 1986); and Richard Judd, William Greenwood, and Fred Becker (eds.), *Small Business in a Regulated Economy: Issues and Policy Implications* (Quorum, 1988).

Handbook of Global Economic Policy

1

Environmental Policy in the African Development Bank and the Asian Development Bank

Morten Bøås
University of Oslo, Oslo, Norway

I. INTRODUCTION—MULTILATERAL DEVELOPMENT BANKS AND THE ENVIRONMENT

In the Multilateral Development Banks (MDBs), environmental considerations are a relatively new theme,[1] and both the African Development Bank (AfDB) and the Asian Development Bank (ADB) have been described as late-comers within this issue-area. Stein and Johnson (1979) described the situation in the ADB as one where the institution lacked any formal commitment to environmental protection or to specific procedures for considering environmental impacts in loan preparation and negotiation, and as late as 1988, Mikesell and Williams (1992) found that the Environmental Unit of the ADB had little more than an advisory role. Its staff had not veto power on the approval of projects. In the AfDB, the situation was quite similar. In 1991, while officially advocating environmental policies similar to those of the World Bank, it had not taken any steps to embody these policies in its operations and its Environmental Unit was without any permanent staff.

Even though most observers agree that the environmental record of the AfDB and the ADB has improved during past years, this issue-area is still one of the most controversial and contested in the Banks. And it does not look like the political controversies related to environmental policy will diminish in the near future. On the contrary, they seem more likely to increase, because the Banks are now in the process of entering into the unknown field of post-industrial environmental policy inhabited by cross-cutting issues like environment, indigenous people, involuntary resettlement and social forestry just to mention a few.[2] The main aim of this article is therefore to investigate into what kind of factors that have limited and what kind of factors that have prompted the development of an environmental policy in the AfDB and the ADB. The rationale for undertaking such an exercise is that improved knowledge of these factors may make it easier for these two important development institutions to overcome the challenges they are faced with today. It is also assumed that an interpretative comparative approach will help us to highlight constraints to the development of environmental policy in such institutions, but also throw light on factors that can promote such policies.

In order to accomplish this task two single case studies of the AfDB and the ADB are presented before we, on the basis of these case studies, draw our conclusions. However, before we can proceed with this task we need a theoretical toolbox that can guide us in our search for factors that have limited and prompted the development of environmental policy in the AfDB and the ADB. The major assumption that guides the composition of the theoretical toolbox is that MDBs are political institutions. Subsequently, we will look at these processes in the Banks in light of a theoretical framework that highlights both competitive bargaining and the development of generalized principles of conduct for behavior. The theoretical toolbox is therefore constituted by Young's (1989, 1991, 1992) games of institutional bargaining and Ruggie's (1993) brand of multilateralism. Drawing on this theoretical reserve, we will start with the Bank on the African continent before we turn our attention to its Asian counterpart.[3]

II. MULTILATERAL DEVELOPMENT BANKS AS POLITICAL INSTITUTIONS

The main assumption for the analysis is that MDBs are political institutions because their loans affect both domestic priorities and the distribution of wealth and power.[4] They are therefore interpreted as arenas that promote international order and cooperation, but also as battlefields between various actors in world politics. However, the MDBs have since their founding advocated the doctrine of political neutrality. They have embraced the functionalist logic that technical economic questions could be separated from politics.[5]

Contrary to this view, a growing body of literature on MDBs gives attention to political conflict and how countries seek to use the MDBs as an arena to facilitate their own political and economic interests. Sanford (1982) argued that the United States strongly influences MDBs and their policies. According to Yasutomo (1983, 1995), Japan seeks to use ADB as a foreign policy tool, and Japanese ODA and MDB policies are not isolated cases but rather crucial components in a new activism in Japan's overall foreign policy. On the contrary, Krasner (1981) argued that the large donors do not enjoy voting influence commensurate with the size of their contributions. With respect to the AfDB, Mingst (1990) argued that even though the hegemons who had played such a key role in the other MDBs had been prevented from exercising inordinate influence in the Bank, the level of political conflict penetrated deeply into the institution. In short, MDBs are not technical institutions like functionalists or the institutions themselves have argued.[6] Instead, they are political institutions which in an interdependent world cannot be separated from the harsh world of politics nor from the process of change within it.[7]

A. The AfDB and the ADB as Negotiated International Regimes

The AfDB and the ADB are intergovernmental organisations, and thus negotiated international regimes.[8] They are instruments of foreign policy that provide arenas for exchange of viewpoints and legitimation of norms, principles and values. However, they are used not only to encourage coalition-building and linking of issue-areas, but also to perpetuate conflict and block cooperation. As such, a negotiated international regime is the outcome of conscious efforts to agree on the regime's major provisions, and they embody the explicit consent of the individual participants and the formal expressions of the results (Young 1982).

In the AfDB, the participants are the recipient countries, all African, which hammered out the major provisions expressed in the *Agreement Establishing the African Development Bank*, and the donor countries, all nonregional, which joined after 1982. The formal expression is the institution itself. In this respect, the AfDB is a unique case among the MDBs. It is a lending institution controlled and even originally funded by its recipient member countries.[9] In the ADB, the situation is different. The participants are the recipient countries, all Asian, and the donor countries, mostly nonregional but also from within the region, who together agreed on the major provisions expressed in the *Agreement Establishing the Asian Development Bank*. As in the case of the AfDB, the formal expression is the institution itself.[10] Thus, the agreements can be interpreted as an expression of a multilateral architectural principle. The question, however, is whether the regimes in fact embody the explicit consent of the individual participants.

B. Institutional Bargaining

The objective of institutional bargaining is to analyze efforts from autonomous actors to reach agreement among themselves (Young 1989). In institutional bargaining games, the number of autonomous actors is to a certain extent fixed.[11] It is seldom possible to collapse the participants into two blocks, and those engaged in this type of bargaining normally operate under an unanimity rule instead of a majority rule. When the membership of the relevant group is set negotiations are assumed to revolve around efforts to come up with an arrangement that all participants may accept, because regime formation in international politics is supposed to involve a large element of integrative (productive) bargaining in contrast to distributive (positional) bargaining. Moreover, it proceeds under a veil of uncertainty because institutional arrangements, unlike specific or self-contained choices, typically apply across a wide range of contexts and over a more or less extended period of time. Thus, ''as both the generality and the performance of rules are increased, the individual who faces choice alternatives becomes more uncertain about the effects of alternatives on his own position'' (Brennan and Buchanan 1985:29).

According to Young (1989), this observation is applicable to the behaviour of collective entities as well. Actors involved in institutional bargaining usually focus on some main problems, and seek to find solutions that each participant can accept as fair in the sense that the outcome generated under the arrangement will be broadly acceptable, regardless of where the participants might be located in the outcome.[12]

States as complex collective entities encompass numerous groups whose interests often differ with respect to any given issue-area. This implies that institutional bargaining involves extensive intraparty bargaining which occurs simultaneously with relevant interparty bargaining. The potential for the development of transnational alliances among interest groups supporting the formation of specific outcomes of the bargaining process is therefore present.[13]

> At a time when some participants are anxious to conclude the bargaining process, others may be paralysed by internal disagreements over the terms of the proposed contract. Similarly, domestic elections or civil strife may divert the attention of some participants from institutional bargaining just as the political context within others makes it easy for them to exercise the political will required to bring the bargaining process to a close (Young 1991:285).

Thus, whereas traditional utilitarian negotiation models emphasize interaction within the issue-area in question, institutional bargaining features an array of linkages to other events occurring in the international political economy. These linkages are a double-edged sword. Participants may deliberately complicate the negotiations by linking together several issues in such a way that an agreement necessitates too complex bargaining to be achieved. On the other hand, the linking of disparate issues together may pave the way for mutually acceptable arrangements by creating opportunities for the international equivalent of log-rolling and formulation of package deals. The question is, then, how Young's model of institutional bargaining is compared to the concept of multilateralism. Are they contradictory or complementary?

C. Institutional Bargaining and Multilateralism

Whereas institutions as persistent and connected sets of rules, formal and informal, that prescribe behavioural roles, constrain activity and shape expectations (Keohane 1990), can take the form of bilateralism, imperialism, and multilateralism, Ruggie's (1993) understanding of multilateralism is as an adjective that modifies the noun *institution*.[14] We must therefore draw a distinction between multilateral institutions (formal organisations) and the institution of multilateralism (an architectural form/a deep organising principle of international life) (Caporaso 1993). Thus, the generic question is how the practice of ''multilateralism'' can modify an institution?

The answer to this question lies in its proposed ability to coordinate relations among three or more states on the basis of generalised principles of conduct—principles which specify a certain behaviour to a certain issue-area without regard to any particularistic interests of the concerned parties.[15] Adherence to a particular norm makes the system in question an indivisible whole that spreads costs and benefits among the concerned parties. The presence of generalised principles of conduct and indivisibility establish a diffuse reciprocity among the partners in which they adjust their utilitarian lenses for the long view and vice versa. These properties are not three detachable indicators of multilateralism, but rather a coherent ensemble which is, in itself, indivisible. This indivisibility is a social construct and not a technical condition. Accordingly, for multilateralism to be present in this particular form, the concerned members must have the ability to construct it because it only exists if the members act in a certain way to make it so. Subsequently, the argument is that an arrangement based on generalised principles of conduct, indivisibility and diffuse reciprocity is more flexible than one based on particularistic interests and situational strategies.

The AfDB and the ADB are without doubt multilateral institutions, the question is whether they also embody elements of the institution of multilateralism. With respect to environmental policy in the Banks this means that the costs and benefits of the Banks' environmental policy is spread in a legitimate manner between the concerned parties (indivisibility). Universal modes of interaction on environmental policies are established, rather than differentiating relations case-by-case on the basis of individual preferences, situational strategies, or pregiven particularistic grounds (generalized principles of conduct). Whereas diffuse reciprocity within this issue-area in the AfDB and the ADB would entail that each actor involved in the process of developing these policies expect to reap a fair share of benefits in the long run and not every time on all issues.

The formation of Ruggie's (1993) generalized principles of conduct may be the outcome of a process of institutional bargaining. However, Young's vision of institutional bargaining is crowded with barriers to overcome and puzzles to solve. Whereas institutional bargaining may lead to the formation of generalized principles of conduct it is much harder to imagine that if institutional bargaining is present that the principles of conduct will be durable and adaptive. Rather, it seems more likely that under institutional bargaining the outcome of political processes is a Pandora's box constantly reopened by different actors for different political reasons. However, according to Young (1991, 1992), the probability for cooperative settlements of institutional bargaining games are enhanced by exogenous shocks and/or effective leadership. Exogenous shocks is a contextual variable, and not an inseparable part of the bargaining process per se.

> Even in negotiations that allow considerable scope for integrative bargaining under a veil of uncertainty, institutional bargaining exhibits a natural tendency to bog down into a kind of sparring match in which participants jockey for positional advantages and lose track of their common interest in solving the relevant collective-action problem (Young 1989:371).

Thus, it is supposed to enhance the probability of success by breaking logjams and propelling the actors towards agreement by changing their perception of the situation they are faced with. Leadership in the form of a structural leader, an entrepreneurial leader and an intellectual leader can perform the equivalent function.[16] The exogenous shocks we will be concerned with here are severe environmental degradation and natural disasters. Concerning leadership emphasis will be placed on the role of Japan and the United States in the Banks.

III. THE AFDB AND THE ENVIRONMENT—A SLOW START, AND A SLUGGISH LEARNER?

A. Origins

The AfDB was established in 1964 by the African countries themselves, and membership was confined to Africa.[17] In the early years, when the lending capacity depended solely on the capital subscriptions of its African members, the Bank had few resources for loans.[18] It was expected to be able to borrow in the international capital markets on the basis of capital subjected to call. However, the international credit standing of the member countries was not good enough to provide a credible guarantee on amounts borrowed (Krasner 1981). The AfDB was finally opened to non-regional countries in 1982 as a consequence of inadequate financial funding.[19]

B. The Official Picture

Since 1970, the AfDB has taken part in most major international initiatives on the environment. Prior to the 1972 United Nations Conference on the Human Environment in Stockholm, the Bank participated in international forums on the environment. According to the Bank, since then it has shown a commitment to assist regional member countries in their efforts to reverse the environmental damage which the continent is experiencing (AfDB 1990). In 1981, along with most other international development institutions, the Bank signed the Declaration of Environmental Policies and Procedures related to Economic Development for ensuring environmental soundness and viability of their operations.[20] In 1988, the AfDB, in collaboration with the United Nations Economic Commission on Africa (UNECA), published an Economic Recovery Report which highlighted the direct relationship between the economy and the environment. In this report, the dependency of Africa's development upon its natural resource base was underscored, and the need for urgent actions to arrest the process of ecological decline on the continent was stressed. Furthermore, the AfDB took part in the preparatory process of the UNCED as well.

Environmental issues have thus formally been an official part of the AfDB agenda since 1971. According to the institution itself, it has closely followed the work of the African Ministerial Conference on the Environment, the recommendations of the Lagos Plan of Action 1980–2000 and the report of the World Commission on Environment and Development.

Thus, if we look simply at the Bank's participation in international forums concerned with the environment, the Bank may be interpreted as a relatively fast starter. However, as we will see when we turn to the matter of developing and implementing an operational environmental policy for the AfDB, it is highly questionable whether the Bank acted fast, or is in fact a slow starter and a sluggish learner in this issue-area.

C. Organization and Staffing

On the contrary, the IIED (1979) described the situation of an institution without any formal procedures for evaluating environmental issues, and with a limited understanding among staff for the broader environmental consequences of loans to development projects. Until 1983, the situation was more or less similar to the one described by the IIED.[21] The first significant organizational change was an internal environmental guidance paper. It dealt with the treatment of environmental questions in planning and evaluation of projects. Furthermore, in 1983 the AfDB announced that it would incorporate environmental guidelines from the World Bank. The responsibility for organisational co-ordination of environmental issues and questions was placed on the Central Projects Department.[22] In 1985, the first environmental specialist in the AfDB was appointed to this department, followed by the creation of the Social and Environment Policy Division within the same department in 1987. By 1988, the Division had three full-time environmental specialists. In early 1994 the number had increased to a core team of 14 professional staff members dealing with the environment and related fields such as population, poverty, health, and economics. Ten members of this core staff dealt with environment policy formulation and oversight, while four were assigned to operations.

D. Environmental Policy

However, it was not until 1989 that the AfDB started the process of developing an environmental policy for the whole spectre of loans and credits in which it was involved, and until June 1990 that the suggested policy was approved by the Board of Directors. The overall objective of AfDB's environmental policy is to ensure that environmental viability is present in all investment projects in the Bank's lending programmes. The adoption of the policy paper was without doubt a major turning point with respect to the incorporation of environmental concerns in the Bank's operations.[23]

However, only one month after the environmental policy was approved by the Board of Directors, George Folsom, Deputy Assistant Secretary in the U.S. Treasury Department, in a letter dated August 23, 1990, urged the Bank to increase the number of environmental specialists to at least 10, and to integrate environmental considerations into all of its lending activities.[24] In addition, Folsom advised the AfDB to implement procedures to ensure that Environmental Impact Assessments be completed for all projects that significantly affect the environment. Furthermore, as late as 1991, the AfDB had still not taken any steps to embody the environmental guidelines from the World Bank into its operations, as it officially stated it would do in 1983. In sum, the AfDB was quite fast to show up in international forums on the environment, but it is also clear that the Bank was a sluggish learner regarding formulation and implementation of its own environmental policy.

On the other hand, even though the creation of environmental awareness in the AfDB was a sluggish process these issues have increased in importance in the Bank. If we look back in history, the decisive period for formulation of an environmental policy was the period between 1983 and 1989. The reason why environmental issues suddenly received increased attention and were taken more seriously in the AfDB is due to several factors. However, it is likely that exogenous shocks in the form of the dramatic events in Africa, with long periods of drought and widespread famine in the early 1980s, demonstrated convincingly the close connection between environmental factors and the economic difficulties in Africa to the Bank and its members.

How have these events influenced the process of formulating an environmental policy for the AfDB? The causes offered by the AfDB itself to explain why an issue-area which was virtually nonexistent in the Bank prior to 1983 suddenly received increased attention are in accordance with a picture where exogenous shocks play an important role in breaking logjams and propelling actors toward agreement and institutional change. According to the AfDB (1994a), its mandate became more challenging during the last decade, when many of its regional members faced unprecedented economic crisis triggered by foreign debt and deterioration of their terms of trade. This economic crisis was compounded in some regional member countries by drought, civil strife, environmental degradation, weak institutional capacity and decaying infrastructure. According to the AfDB, it was within this context that it began to rethink and reorient its country programming and lending operations, in order to conserve the natural resource base and social fabric of African societies on which development depends. It was in response to increased concern over the state of the environment from both recipient and donor countries that the AfDB initiated a program of activities that addressed environmental issues in Africa.[25]

How did this process of policy formulation occur within the AfDB? Did this process entail the evolution of Ruggie's brand of multilateralism?

E. Decision Making and Organisational Procedures

The answers to these questions are conditioned by the interaction between the involved participants, and the AfDB's rules for decision making and organisational procedures.

Formally, the AfDB has a multipolar structure with power shared between regional and nonregional members. The regional members hold the majority of the votes in the Bank and in the Fund[26] voting power is shared between donor and recipient countries.[27] Nevertheless, the experience during the "independent" years suggests that the AfDB is strongly dependent on the contributions from the non-regional members. Their main influence is in the Fund, where the votes of these countries are allocated in proportion to their share of financial contributions. All operational decisions of the Fund require 75% approval, and authorisations of general increase in subscriptions require 85% approval. A member state is not obliged to contribute if it votes against an increase. This implies that the Fund is operating with a mutual veto arrangement in which either the recipient or the donor countries can block action, but it is obviously more influential when some of the large contributors, for instance, the United States, vote against an increase in capital subscriptions.

The AfDB's main governing body is the Board of Governors, which normally meets once a year. Each member state appoints a governor, who is entitled to cast the number of votes he represents, with issues decided by majority, but in practice consensus is the norm at the Board of Governors' meetings. At the Board of Directors political controversy is more apparent. The executive directors responsibility is to supervise the general operations of the Bank. There are 18 executive directors—12 from the regional members and six from the nonregionals. These directors and their alternates represent constituencies of countries, or in one case, one state, namely the U.S. With respect to the regional constituencies, these are generally based on a combination of geographic proximity and linguistic community, while the nonregional constituencies represent a haphazard conglomeration of states put together for a variety of reasons. The voting ratio, two-thirds for the regional and one-third for the nonregionals, is critical for the functioning of the executive directors. But in the actual meetings votes are seldom taken. Usually voting on projects is by resolution, with countries expressing their disapproval by abstention.

In general, the most influential of the regionals are the four largest contributors—Algeria, Ivory Coast, Egypt, and Nigeria—who together control approximately 24% of the votes.[28] Canada, Japan, and the United States are in general the most influential of the nonregionals. The constituency of Australia, Saudi Arabia, Brazil, and Japan is dominated by Japan. Japan as a large donor[29] always occupies the executive director position, while the alternate position rotates among the other members. The Japanese director receives considerable input and guidance from his home office, but he consults less frequently with the other members of the group. The group composed of Canada, Spain, China, Korea, and Kuwait follows much of the same procedure, with Canada as the main leader.[30] For the other nonregional groups, the executive directorship is rotated every three years, and when one country holds the directorship, the other countries play a more passive role. Most often the director in place makes decisions in consultation with his home office.[31]

If extensive consultation by executive directors representing several nonregionals is rare, consultation by regional executive directors is even less institutionalized. Several executive directors represent many small states, and most often only pro forma ad hoc coordination occurs. In most African capitals, it appears that it is left to the executive director of each constituency to formulate positions on concrete issues on his own. It seems most African states only care about getting their own projects passed and to receive their loans (Jerlström 1990).

One executive director in the AfDB constitutes a unique case, namely the U.S. representative. He does not represent a constituency, only the United States, and his level of consultation with his home office is higher than any of the other executive directors (Mingst 1990). All loans proposed by the AfDB are sent to Washington, DC, to the Working Group on Multilateral Assistance (WGMA). The group is headed by Treasury Department officials, with members from the Departments of State and Commerce, and the U.S. Agency for International Development (USAID). WGMA's task is to assess loans proposed in the MDBs on the basis of whether they are in accordance with general American foreign policy, as well as whether the projects are properly conceived.[32] The American executive director is therefore more circumscribed by his country's domestic politics than most of the other executive directors. His hands are tied by American domestic politics. The strategy of ''tying hands''—to reshape domestic constraints to promote favoured policies—is not uncommon in the literature, but evidence suggests that it is less effective than traditional wisdom assume (Evans 1993).[33] Subsequently, the U.S. executive director has less to bargain with. The result has often been that without formal veto power and in many cases little bargaining capacity and real political commitment, the United States has opposed loans without affecting either the specific project or the policies of the institution (Mingst 1990; Mule and English 1996).

Before we turn our attention to how these different players interact in policy formulation, it is necessary to introduce one remaining key player, namely the president. The president is the Bank's legal representative. He is responsible for the daily business carried out under the management of the executive directors, for the Bank's organization, staff matters, and the implementation of all policy decisions. In addition to his formal powers, he has great informal power over the agenda and the speed of organisational change. Unlike some of the other MDBs which have either constitutionally mandated stipulations or strong precedents that the president come from a certain country,[34] the principle in the AfDB is only that he should be an African.

Even this general description of the key players and their interaction entails that we must question the validity of the argument that ''multilateralism'' is modifying an institution. On the contrary, the situation looks more like one of Young's games of institutional bargaining under exogenous shocks, but without the supervision of clear leadership.

F. Resolution by Consensus

The records of the AfDB show that no African country has ever voted against or officially opposed any loan. The norm for bargaining and coalition building among the regionals is therefore consensus. The shadow of the future[35]–the high probability that loans approved today may facilitate a state's own loan approval in the future and vice versa—is the cornerstone for consensus among the regionals. On the contrary, the nonregionals face quite different pressures and cleavages among themselves, which tend to render in vain attempts to build coalitions similar to those of the regionals. The former colonial powers often base their actions on relations which lie well outside the boardroom. For instance, even if the United States and France can agree that a certain project is objectionable on the basis of flawed environmental consequences, there still may be good reasons for France to support it. Japan's support of AfDB is characterised by substantial financial contributions and low levels of conditions and demands. The result is that the nonregionals seldom have managed to combine their forces to achieve common goals. Instead, most of them prefer to engage in direct bilateral bargaining to secure contracts, improve loan quality or advance other policy priorities.

In fact, the United States is often, as a one-nation voting block, the only actor with an ability to speak with a single substantial voice at the bargaining table. However, in AfDB, the United States is just another ordinary player, but a powerful one. Coordination of nonregional policy becomes therefore difficult because, whereas the United States takes inflexible positions on loans mandated from Washington, several other nonregionals voice similar concerns less stridently through abstention or by presenting a memo. For instance, the United States opposed 15 loans due to harmful environmental effects between 1982 and 1989. The problem is that the United States does this in isolation, and the net result is most often that American opposition in this form entails a closing of the conversation and shrugging of African shoulders rather than the reshaping of a loan agreement on the basis of institutional bargaining. There is little evidence that the United States through unilateral action has ever successfully modified the terms of a particular loan, or that the concerns expressed by the Americans unilaterally have led to a clear change in policy (Mingst 1990; Mule and English 1996).[36] Hence, the experience suggests that distributive bargaining is quite common in the AfDB, and it looks as though the so-called veil of uncertainty effect, if present at all in the Bank, is significantly diminished by the "shadow of the future."

G. Example of a Formative Policy Discussion

Let us now turn to a particular project which had substantial influence on the formation of an environmental policy for the AfDB, in order to understand how these actors and the constraints placed on them by different factors (structural and agency based) have interacted in the bargaining process.

In 1986, Botswana submitted a loan request to finance the construction and initiation phase of an *abattoir* to process and export meat products. In addition to a slaughterhouse and boning facility, the project called for the construction of fencing to enclose the cattle prepared for slaughter.[37] During the planning process, environmental NGOs based in the United States started raising objections to the project, based on a widely circulated film describing the deaths of indigenous and migrating species due to cattle fencing in Botswana sponsored by the World Bank.[38] The area in question, Francistown, lies in a region with several national wildlife preservations, and the NGOs were worried that the AfDB would repeat the mistakes of the World Bank. The claim from American environmental NGOs, and in particular from the National Resources Defense Council, which headed the campaign, was that the project would lead to an unsustainable enlargement of the stock of cattle in Botswana, which in turn would lead to overgrazing and desertification (Shaw 1991). These objections were brought directly to the Bank, and they were supported by the Treasury Department, which received significant pressure on the issue from environmental lobbyists in Washington. The immediate outcome was that the U.S. executive director at that time, Donald Sherk, was instructed to demand environmentally responsible action from the Bank.

When the opposition from the American NGOs and Washington reached AfDB, the Environmental Unit in the Bank tried to take advantage of the situation. The unit made it clear to top management that it was not comfortable with the project and its environmental implications. In fact, the environmental coordinator demanded for the first time to make a field study of the project before it could be approved by her office,[39] and she was granted five days of fieldwork in Francistown. Her conclusion was that the project, with some modification—the planned fences moved to double the effective wildlife management area, greater access permitted to water and fodder sources, and confirmation of the government of Botswana's plans for setting aside larger tracts of land in the south for wildlife preservation—in fact would not lead to further desertification, but rather prevent it (AfDB 1987). Since the U.S. director had urged such action, he anticipated being able to support the loan.[40]

However, the Working Group on Multilateral Assistance concluded that the environmental improvements to the project were purely cosmetic and therefore instructed him to vote against the loan. Only upon personal appeal to the Treasury Undersecretary for International Affairs was the executive director able to modify his instruction. The final result was that the United States abstained. It therefore missed the opportunity to advance its stated interests in environmental policies by supporting with a formal approval the modifications it had required itself. The American position and handling of this project was not understood by the regionals. The regional members from Southern Africa were especially upset by this behaviour. The United States was interpreted as an actor without the ability nor the willingness to make compromises. The Africans made their part of a productive institutional bargaining by revising the project, while the United States just abstained from voting.

The basic point is that bargaining can only facilitate cooperation if it includes policy co-ordination among the concerned parties. In this case, the Bank, and in particular the regional members from Southern Africa felt that they made the necessary adjustment for a more cooperative atmosphere to emerge, but their counterpart the United States abstained from similar adjustment. Ruggie's brand of multilateralism is a social construct. It must be constructed by the concerned parties through processes of policy coordination in which all parties conduct necessary adjustment. In this case, the United States was prevented from fullfilling its part of the process by domestic constraints.

H. Recent Developments

At the Bank's 30th Annual Meeting in Nairobi in 1994, a report from a task force on project quality was submitted to the Bank's Board and its Governors.[41]

On the background of the recommendations of this report it was decided to reorganise the Bank.[42] Environmental policies were not a major part of this process, but what happened with the Bank's environmental policy gives us a good indication that this is still a controversial issue-area in which generalized principles of conduct are still not well developed.

Just after the conclusions of the Knox report reached Abidjan in April 1994, the discussions on what to do with the Bank's Social and Environment Policy Division started. Several suggestions were put forward. The division itself argued strongly that it should be turned into a department directly under one of the vice-presidents. Their view was supported by the NGO community in Washington and most of the nonregional members. In a Board meeting on November 21, 1994, it was decided that the Bank should have country programming departments with one sustainable development unit added on to the structure of the operational sector. Thus, it looked like the Environment and the Social Policy Division had won the day. However, in the following Board meeting in January 1995 when the new organisational structure was presented, the sustainable development unit promised in the November draft had disappeared from the organisational chart. Nevertheless, the new organizational structure was approved by the Board with the consequence that the Social and Environment Policy Division vanished. It may have been left out by mistake or it may have been on purpose. More serious is the question how it was possible for the Board not to notice that a whole unit was missing from the draft they approved in the November meeting. Nobody seems to know why and nobody was willing to accept responsibility for it. In short, this does not add up to a picture of emerging generalised principles of conduct within the issue-area of environmental policies. It rather looks like a case in which rules are bent in accordance with the issue at stake and the actors' agenda, and where nobody is willing to assume leadership of any kind.

The question is, then, what the bargaining games around the Francistown case and the last illustration from the AfDB tell us. Institutional bargaining may entail the emergence of Ruggie's brand of multilateralism, but not necessarily if the participants are easily divided into blocks, and they involve themselves in both productive and distributive bargaining in accordance with the issues at stake and their domestic agendas as the members of the AfDB does. Exogenous shocks and effective leadership may enhance the probability of success by breaking logjams and moving the participants toward agreement. Exogenous shocks constitute a contextual variable in the development of environmental policies in the AfDB, but effective leadership has not been present. The Francistown project demonstrated that by denying the U.S. representative to the Bank the opportunity to act with some degree of autonomy in games of institutional bargaining, the opportunity to assume leadership and promote actions in accordance with stated U.S. interests is easily lost. The evidence at hand therefore lead me to conclude that "multilateralism" as practice has not modified the AfDB to the extent that we can talk about environmental policies in the Bank as a subfield with generalized principles of conduct, indivisibility, and diffuse reciprocity.

IV. THE ADB—THE FAST LEARNER?

A. Origins

The idea of an Asian Development Bank was advocated by the UN Commission for Asia and the Far East, and Japan expressed strong interest in assisting to establish an Asian Bank.[43] In 1963 a Ministerial Conference for Asian Economic Co-operation endorsed the idea of an Asian Bank, and in 1964 the charter was completed, modelled after the World Bank. The U.S. government was sceptical about the need for a new regional institution, but geopolitical factors worked in its favor. In 1965, President Johnson called for a peace effort in Indochina, which he hoped to encourage by an economic development program supported by U.S. aid. The outcome of the process was that the ADB was inaugurated in November 1966 in Manila, with American blessings and a Japanese president. Since the modest start in 1966, the ADB's history has been characterized by steady expansion and evolution over the past three decades. Initially capitalised at $1 billion, the ADB's authorized capital stood at $51.9 billion by the end of 1996.

B. Decision Making and Organization

Like the AfDB, the ADB formally has a multipolar structure, with power shared among the present 56 recipient and donor country members of the Bank.[44] While four members graduated from recipient countries to donors—a reflection of the fact that the Asia Pacific region is the region with the most rapid economic growth in the world—two new important recipient countries appeared on the scene in the last half of the 1980s.[45] India, a founding member, converted to borrowing status, and China entered as a recipient country in 1986. This blend of regional members in the form of both donors and recipient countries makes the Bank unique among the regional development Banks, and it creates a potential for less clear-cut cleavages than the one between regionals (recipient) and nonregionals (donor) that we found in the AfDB.[46]

With respect to policies and decision making, the Board of Governors, which consists of 56 members representing 40 regional members and 16 nonregionals, is the highest policy-making body in the Bank. Under article 28 of the *Agreement Establishing the Asian Development Bank*, the Board of Governors is vested with all the powers of the institution. However, most of these powers are delegated to the Board of Directors, because the governors normally meet once a year for the annual meeting. Under the article mentioned above, the governors elect a 12 member Board of Directors at the annual meeting, eight elected by the regionals and four by the nonregionals. The president of the Bank is the chairman of this board. It performs its duties on a full-time basis at the headquarters in Manila, and the directors exercise their authority and functions through their quarterly and annual supervision of the Bank's financial statements, their annual approval of the administrative budget and their continuous review and approval of policy documents and all loans, equity, and technical assistance operations.

With respect to voting power, the regionals hold 64.34% and the nonregionals 35.66% of the votes. The ones with the largest voting power are Japan, United States, China, India, and Australia,[47] but the main players are without doubt Japan and the United States.

The factor of exogenous shocks is not present in the ADB in the similar form that they were in the AfDB in the formative period. However, the close relationship between Japan and the ADB may indicate that the question of leadership may play an improtant role in the formation of Bank policy.

C. Leadership: Japan and the United States

Since 1966, the president of the ADB has always been from Japan. At present he is joined by American, French, and South Korean vice presidents. More important, Japan has remained a steadfast supporter of the ADB. Tokyo's relationship with the Bank is the most intimate of all its ties with international organisations (Yasutomo 1993). It took an active role in the shaping of the ADB's organization and practices in the early years, but during the 1970s and into the early 1980s, Japan's policy approach was mostly low profile and narrowly focused. It lacked a concrete policy agenda. However, in the 1980s,[48] the Japanese came to realize that economic assistance was a foreign policy tool of particular attraction, and this new activism was in particular directed towards the MDBs.[49] Japan's ADB policy has reflected this new activism in multilateral aid policy since the mid-1980s. Japan's involvement is no longer low profile and passive. It has begun to define more clearly the Bank's purpose as a strategic foreign policy tool, having amended its past policy of passivity and anonymity in an effort to gain a preeminent position in the Bank, even differing openly at times with the other major power in the ADB, the United States.

Since the institutions's establishment Japan has expressed a strong will to be its main financial supporter,[50] but it left the use of the funds primarily to the Bank. Therefore, when the quotas for loan commitments established under President Fujioka (1981–89) triggered severe opposition from the United States,[51] the Americans accused both the Bank of cooking projects, Fujioka of a ''lend or perish'' policy, and Japan of focusing only on amounts of aid and not on aid quality. There may be some truth to these allegations, at least in the sense that

Japan during its history as a donor has tried hard to avoid interference in the domestic affairs of recipient countries. ''Aid is a cooperative joint work between two countries. Starting from this philosophy, we as a donor should be careful not to force certain economic policies on the recipients'' (Ministry of Foreign Affairs, Japan 1989:29).

The fact that MDBs, even though they are without doubt political institutions, officially advocate the doctrine of political neutrality may explain why Japan has taken such a keen interest in them. The ADB norm of noninterference and nonpoliticization accords well with Japanese principles.

Japan–United States cooperation has constituted the major pillar of Japan's policy toward the ADB since the inaugural period. However, during the Fujioka tenure (1981–89) this relationship was put under significant strain. The U.S. executive director, Joe Rogers,[52] was very critical of Fujioka's lending targets and his lack of willingness to engage in policy dialogue and conditionality. Thus, Japan was caught between its policy of supporting the president and working closely with the United States. The Japanese government found the American emphasis on conditionality too inflexible. It agreed with Fujioka's view that development policies must be tailor made. The underlying Japanese position was that conditionality and policy dialogue should be based on recognition of the distinctiveness of Asia. Whereas Japan wanted the ADB to follow a nonconfrontational consensus style of engaging in two-way dialogue, the United States expressed strong preferences for an across-the-board application of principles. The answer from Japan to the mid-1980 conflict with the U.S. was to attempt to balance between mitigating problems with the United States on the one hand, and on the other hand seeking greater predominance in the Bank. Japan has increased its share of votes and subsequently abandoned its traditional policy of parity with the United States. It sent a new breed of executive directors who have actively countered the U.S. director on specific policy issues ranging from support for environmental policies and poverty alleviation to program-based lending and concerns on gender questions in development, and subsequently forged a stronger relationship with recipient countries.[53]

By looking at the broad picture of interaction on policy formation between the two main players in the ADB, we are led to question to what extent multilateralism as generalized principles of conduct, indivisibility, and diffuse reciprocity is present in the Bank. On the contrary, it looks more like the process of policy formation in the ADB is the outcome of institutional bargaining, conducted under a double leadership which sometimes is competing and sometimes cooperating, entailing both cooperation and discord within the process of policy formation. Nevertheless, the evidence suggests that the ADB has been quite successful, after a slow start, in formulating an environmental policy that the various participants can agree upon.

D. Environmental Issues and Orientation

According to the ADB, it soon recognized that environmental issues should be incorporated into its operations. However, the first expression of environmental awareness in the Bank came in 1978 through a paper entitled *Environment Protection and Development Financing by the Asian Development Bank*. This paper summarized the nature of the environmental problems of the region, discussed national and international efforts to remedy them, and concluded that the Bank should systematize its approach to environmental issues and incorporate environmental concerns into each stage of the project cycle. In 1980, the Board started to discuss more specific recommendations on how a systematic approach to environmental issues could be incorporated into Bank operations. The next significant step toward a more fully developed environmental policy came according to the ADB in 1986, when the board endorsed a working paper entitled *Review of the Bank's Environmental Policies and Procedures*, which identified the scope of the Bank's future environmental activities and provided a framework of action.[54]

To some extent, there is support for the ADB view that, since 1986, environmental activities have been formally institutionalized. The creation in 1987 of an environmental unit did provide a focus within the Bank for review of environmental aspects of projects and for promotion of awareness and institution building with respect to environmental issues. Furthermore, the upgrading of the unit in 1990 to the Office of the Environment suggests a deeper environmental awareness in the Bank. The official aim of the office is to ensure that environmental protection measures are incorporated into relevant Bank operations from the outset. In pursuit of this goal, the office is mandated to support the operational departments to prepare country operational strategies and operational program papers, to assist in the identification of projects and programs, to assess their environmental impacts, and to participate in the project cycle to ensure compliance with the measures necessary to mitigate adverse impacts on the environment.

The official ADB picture is supported by the significant increase in environmental lending in the last part of the period from 1970 to 1993 (see Figure 1).[55]

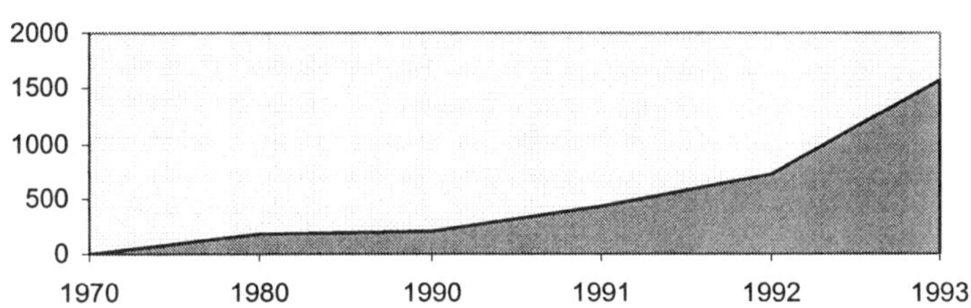

Figure 1 Annual pattern of environmental lending for 1970–1993.[56]

From a very modest level in the 1970s and 1980s, environmental lending escalated between 1992 and 1993 to the extent that as a percentage of total lending in 1993, it exceeded 25%.

As opposed to the official ADB, several NGOs have argued that this categorisation is highly questionable and more lip service than actual awareness. Furthermore, observers have also argued that it took quite an amount of time before the Bank recognized the importance of the environment in its projects. ADB was described in 1979 as without any formal commitment to environmental protection or to specific procedures for considering environmental impacts in loan preparation and negotiation (Stein and Johnson 1979). In 1981, the first two environmental specialists were appointed, but it took several years before a system of review of Bank projects and application of environmental guidelines were put into operation (Mikesell and Williams 1992). Between 1981 and 1987 more than 500 projects were the subject of environmental reports, but the problem was that such a small staff could not supervise and make suggestions on such a large number of projects. However, in 1987 the working conditions of the environmental staff were improved when the Environmental Unit was established, but prior to 1989 the Environmental Unit had little more than an advisory role. Its staff had no veto power over proposed projects and the incorporation of environmental practices into loan covenants. The influence of the environmental staff was limited once a project reached the appraisal stage, due to the lack of a formal environmental clearance process (Runnals 1986). However, it is admitted even by observers who are critical to the environmental practice of the ADB that the promotion of the Environmental Unit to office status enlarged its scope of action and internal bargaining power. The office plays a more direct and independent role in the project review and appraisal process than the previous environmental unit.

The question is how the process of policy formulation went on within the ADB. What was the level of adaption, and did the process lead to cooperation and the development of generalized principles of conduct, indivisibiltiy, and diffuse reciprocity?

With respect to the ability to adapt to new circumstances, the experience suggests that the bargaining games of multilateral institutions are time-consuming. It looks as if institutional bargaining in order to produce something other than stalemate is dependent on a considerable amount of time. However, it is still possible that during this slow and tiresome process some generalized principles of conduct were developed.

We will therefore return to those years when the ADB was characterized by observers without any formal commitment to environmental issues. To be more precise, we will turn our attention to one of the first discussions by the Board with respect to the development of an environmental policy for the ADB.

E. Example of a Formative Policy Discussion

In 1980, a working paper entitled *Environmental Considerations in Bank Operations* was presented to the Board of Directors. It outlined a general strategy by which Bank operations could systematically take account of environmental issues.[57] It recommended that as far as possible, systematic attention should be given to environmental aspects in all phases of the project cycle, from project identification to post evaluation. It argued that Bank lending should continue to be in traditional areas, but projects should be modified by the inclusion of environmental components or of regulatory safeguards to ensure that environmental damage is avoided as much as possible. Moreover, it recommended that the Bank make a modest beginning by recruiting an environmental specialist to assist in systematizing and monitoring considerations of environmental aspects of Bank loans and technical assistance projects. How did the different executive directors of the Board react to these suggestions?

The response from the Board as a collective decision-making body was to endorse the general approach of the paper.[58] It agreed that in due course, more specific recommendations for guidelines on environmental considerations should be submitted for consideration by the Board, i.e., entailing that the Bank should proceed slowly and make a modest start. With respect to individual executive directors, several from regional recipient countries expressed substantial skepticism toward Bank involvement in environmental issues. They stressed the need for a balanced approach to prevent environmental experts from achieving the power to veto proposals from other departments. Regional executive directors expressed outspoken fear of environmental issues becoming a new religion that could create a diversion in terms of greater costs and difficulties in the path to development and progress. In other words, no diffuse reciprocity was assumed within this issue-area. As one regional executive director expressed it, ''The critical issue for developing member countries, particularly after the energy crisis, is survival, and poor people in these countries do not object to pollution if it means more jobs.''

The message from the regional recipient countries was therefore clear. Project processing should not be stopped just because of the fear of environmental damage in itself. With respect to the Japanese director, his response was on one hand to welcome the paper and support the conclusions and recommendation, while on the other hand he stressed the need for caution and a balanced approach to environmental issues. The net result was the compromise outlined above, a cautious approach built on modesty and balance, but it was agreed that an environmental specialist should be employed.

These discussions initially created a clear-cut donor-recipient country divide, with one exception—Japan. The NIC regional members were not interested in a dimension which they perceived as a possible barrier against their industrial development, whereas the poorest regional members perceived environmental protection as a luxury they could not afford. Even though the approach chosen by the Board may seem very defensive and too cautious, it may with hindsight be a sensible solution. The decision to approach this question slowly and in a balanced way may have contributed to both putting the environmental question firmly on the agenda while simultaneously calming the expressed fear from the regional recipient countries.

F. Summing Up the ADB Experience with Environmental Policy

Contrary to the official ADB view of an institution with a rapid and growing environmental awareness since the late 1970s, the evidence thus suggests that the Bank's environmental awareness has been growing slowly, but at a steady pace. This interpretation is supported by Figure 1, which suggests that the importance of environmental questions has increased over the latest year and that both Japan and the ADB's attitudes toward policy dialogue with respect to environmental issues have changed. In a document on Japanese ODA from 1993, Japan suddenly finds it extremely important to have a policy dialogue with developing countries for the purpose of conserving the environment and in terms of deepening mutual understanding on the importance of taking the environment into consideration. Furthermore, the text says that Japan believes in using every available opportunity to have detailed dialogue with developing countries (Ministry of Foreign Affairs 1993). The following statement made by ADB President Mitsuo Sato on the opening of the *First Regional Conference on Biodiversity Conservation* may be interpreted in a similar way[59]: "The fight for biodiversity is being threatened by rapid economic and population growth and exacerbated by inadequate and unfocused legislation, weak national institutions, a lack of political will and a shortage of financial resources" (ADB Review July/August 1994).

It may therefore be argued that the slow and gradual approach adopted by the Board has been quite successful in achieving some sort of cooperation on these issues. Whether this has led to the development of multilateralism as generalized principles of conduct, indivisibility, and diffuse reciprocity is less clear, because as recently as the 1994 Annual Meeting of the Board of Governors in Nice, one witnessed a clear cleavage between nonregional donor countries and some regional members on the issue of a greater ADB focus on social problems and improvement of the Asian environment. Similarly, the U.S. insistence that capital increase should be linked to changes in ADB lending to such issues led to accusations of political interference from regional members. For instance, Zhou Zhengqing, the senior Chinese official attending the 1994 Annual Meeting, stated that China did not agree with a linkage between capital and policy. According to China, these were completely separate issues.[60] It is therefore reason to question the presence of Ruggie's brand of multilateralism. Evidence suggest that some sort of generalised principles of conduct has been developed within the field of environmental policies in the ADB. However, as the experience of the 1994 Annual Meeting shows, the development of such principles does not mean that discord and tension are out of the picture. Rather, when actors reach agreement on one part of an issue-area, another field of conflict emerges in which particularistic interests are highly important.

V. CONCLUSION

The evidence suggests that the process of environmental policy formation has been less ridden with conflicts in the ADB than in AfDB but it does not seem like any of the two multilateral institutions in question have developed the sort of generalized principles of conduct that are the hallmark of the institution of multilateralism (Caporaso 1993; Ruggie 1993). As we have seen, the question of what constitutes a legitimate level of political interference in recipient countries policies is still unsolved in both institutions. However, it looks like the deliberate, cautious approach adopted by the Board in the ADB has been more successful than the political controversies of the AfDB.

The difference with respect to leadership in the two institutions may be one important explanation. In the AfDB, the contextual framework for environmental policy formulation was exogenous shocks and missing leadership, while the ADB contextual framework was the lack of such specific external shocks and a double leadership. The different role played by Japan in the Banks may have had a significant impact on their differences. In the ADB, the Japanese position on conditionality acted as a constraint on the more aggressive position of the United States and hence contributed, through demands for moderation and caution, to prevent recipient countries from entering the trenches in this issues-area. In the AfDB, the low-profile position of Japan in the formative years excluded the possibility of a viable double leadership and left the U.S. executive directors more or less alone in the arena with positions that most often led to a closing of the debate and the shrugging of African shoulders.

In sum, it seems like multilateralism in Ruggie's understanding is too demanding to have a significant relevance in true multilateral contexts in which different cultures, perceptions, ideologies, and political systems are to interact to achieve some sort of cooperation. However, the argument is not that some sort of consensus or generalized principles of conduct are not possible to cultivate. Young's model of institutional bargaining is not by necessity contradictory to Ruggie's brand of multilateralism. The evidence from both institutions suggests that this is not the case, but the experience from the AfDB and the ADB also clearly suggests that even if some sort of principles for conduct evolve, this does not mean that the game of institutional bargaining is closed. On the contrary, the more successful case, the ADB, shows that bargaining within multilateral institutions is a Pandora's box which is constantly reopened by different actors for different political reasons. The point, as Ruggie correctly argues, is that these institutions are what the actors make them. They are social constructs, depending on their members' perception of the issues at stake for their behavior within any issue-area. Nevertheless, the evidence also underscores the importance of leadership, and in particular the presence of a regional leader that can act as a buffer and bridgehead between nonregional donor countries and regional recipient countries. Japan played this role in the ADB, no actor seems to have been able or willing to take on such a role in the AfDB.

ENDNOTES

1. Of the MDBs, the World Bank has historically been the leader with respect to environmental questions. In 1970 under the presidency of Robert McNamara, it became the first MBD to appoint an environmental adviser, and McNamara's successor have continued to upgrade the World Bank's involvement in environmental issues, to the extent that in 1987 the environment office was upgraded to the status of department under the vice president for Sector Policy and Research.
2. This observation is drawn from fieldwork in Abidjan Côte d'Ivoire, September 1995 and September 1996, in Manila, Philippines, January and November 1996 and from participation in the 29th and 30th Annual Meetings of the ADB, held in Manila, May 1996, and Fukuoka, Japan, May 1997.
3. The minor comparisons presented are not built on a formal scheme of comparative methodology, because the ambition is not to present a comprehensive picture but to indicate areas for further research.
4. See Baldwin's (1965) study of the World Bank. According to Mingst (1990) it was due to Baldwin's observation that scholars began to systematically dispel the myth of political neutrality.
5. For instance, in the *Agreement Establishing the African Development Bank* and the *Agreement Establishing the Asian Development Bank*, the following principle of political neutrality is stated: "The Bank, its Presidents, vice-presidents, officers and staff shall not interfere in the political affairs of any members, nor shall they be influenced in their decisions by the political character of the member concerned. Only economic considerations shall be relevant to their decisions" (AfDB 1964: Art. 38; ADB 1966:Art. 36).
6. For functionalist approaches to IGOs, the classical piece is Mitrany (1943). For a more contemporary work see Selim (1983).
7. Or in Kratochwil's (1993:467) words: "Thus the characterisation of certain agencies as merely 'functional' is misleading.".
8. An international regime is commonly defined as a set of implicit and explicit principles, norms, rules and decision-making procedures around which actors' expecta-

tions converge in a given issue-area (Krasner 1982). Even though the concept of international regime is widely acknowledged among students of international relations, it is not universally accepted. For an excellent critical review see Strange (1982).

9. The AfDB was established by African countries in 1964. In 1982, the first non-regional members joined the institution. In the Bank, the regionals have 64.172% of the votes and the non-regionals have 35.828%. In the Fund, the regionals have 50.00% and the non-regionals have 50.00%.
10. The ADB was established by both Asian and non-Asian countries in 1966.
11. While there may be disagreement, and even hard bargaining with respect to the identity of the parties that are or should be included in a specific case, efforts to devise international regimes generally involve a number of autonomous participants. See Young (1989:360–361).
12. For a more detailed discussion of such processes, see Brennan and Buchanan (1985).
13. In this respect, the model of institutional bargaining has some significant similarities with the two-levels game approach of Evans et al. (1993).
14. See also Wæver (1997).
15. Ruggie (1993) mentions MFN treatment as an example of such generalised principles. Adherence to the MFN norm makes the system of world trade an indivisible whole, not some inherent attribute of trade itself.
16. Whereas the structural leader relies on its ability to translate material resources into bargaining power, the entrepreneurial leader relies on its negotiating skills and the intellectual leader on its ability to shape the intellectual capital available to those involved in the bargaining process. We are in this paper mainly concerned about the possibility of structural leadership of Japan and the United States.
17. With one exception. South Africa was not eligible for membership until apartheid was terminated. South Africa joined in August 1995 with 1% of the Bank's share capital and the option to increase this holding at a later stage.
18. The initial capitalisation of the AfDB was $300 million, of which 50% was paid-in convertible currency, the rest callable. The present capitalisation is $22.25 billion of which $2.56 billion is paid-in capital.
19. The decision to admit nonregional countries to join the AfDB was highly controversial and it led to the fall of Kwame Donkoh Fordwar, the president who initiated the process. See Fordwar (1981) and Mingst (1990).
20. It was this declaration that established the Committee of International Development Institutions on the Environment (CIDIE).
21. See Wettestad 1987. This observation was confirmed in interviews with informants who worked in the AfDB during this period.
22. Prior to the current reorganisation of the AfDB this department was responsible for issue-areas such as infrastructure development polices, procurement policy, agrarian development polices, social and environmental policies and the issue-area of women in development. In other words, it was a policy department, not an implementing agency.
23. The following six principles constitute the core of the AfDB's policy on the environment: (1) Promotion of strategies and practices that foster sustainability of develop-

ment, by emphasising rational utilisation of natural resources for the long-term needs of regional member countries. (2) Support of regional member countries' efforts in making environment an integral part of their national strategic framework for sustainable development. (3) Empowerment of the poor and other vulnerable groups, such as women and youth, to enable them to participate in the management of natural resources. (4) Strengthening institutions and human resource capabilities in the regional member countries to enable them to undertake environmentally sound management and development activities. (5) Adoption of an integrated approach to natural resource management, given the holistic nature of environmental issues in Africa. (6) Harmonization of environmental policies, procedures, and practices among the various international institutions and donor agencies, for the ultimate benefit of regional member countries.

24. Letter from George Folsom to Babacar N'Diaye, August 28, 1990. Quoted in Mikesell and Williams (1992:25).
25. According to informants who worked in the AfDB during this period, the drought in Africa from 1983–85 did increase the staff's preoccupation with environmental issues. In addition, the international trend in general, and in particular the Brundtland Commission and its report ''Our Common Future'' is mentioned as important.
26. The African Development Fund is the soft window of the Bank with repayment periods of 50 years and a service charge of 0.75% per annum.
27. In the Bank, the regional countries hold 64.172% of the votes and the nonregionals 35.828% of the votes.
28. In 1995, Algeria held 4.007%, Côte d'Ivoire 4.101%, Egypt 5.861%, and Nigeria 10.143% of the votes.
29. In 1995, Japan held 4.701% of the votes. Recently, the Japanese have signaled that they are eager to cash in greater political influence on their financial contributions.
30. In 1995, Canada held 3.227% of the votes. Canada has played an important role in the AfDB, for instance, it played an instrumental role in the establishment of the Fund and convinced France to participate in the undertaking.
31. Some of the nonregionals only take an active interest in the AfDB when procurement contracts are on the agenda. See Mingst (1990). This information has been confirmed by informants who have worked in the AfDB.
32. For instance, U.S. law requires that copies of Environmental Impact Assessments (EIAs) are available to board members at least 120 days in advance of loan consideration, and that copies of EIAs or a comprehensive summary are made available to the public. U.S. directors cannot support loans unless these procedures are followed.
33. ''The strategy of ''tying hands''—deliberately shrinking the win-set in pursuit of an agreement closer to the COG's preferred outcome—is infrequently attempted and usually not effective. The tying-hands strategy, suggested by Thomas Schellings's work, is logically plausible but lacks efficacy in practice'' (Evans 1993:399). See also Schelling (1960).
34. For example, in the World Bank an American and in the ADB a Japanese.
35. With respect to the concept ''the shadow of the future,'' see Oye (1986:12–14).
36. This information has been confirmed by informants in the AfDB. An interesting question is why the U.S. is pursuing this kind of a strategy. One reason may be a lack of knowledge in Washington with respect to the specific nature of the AfDB,

another is that NGOs are paid off with an aggressive environmental policy in cases where no American interests are at stake.

37. The information concerning this case was obtained through interviews with former AfDB staff, and from Shaw (1991) and internal memorandums from the Bank.
38. The film in question was made by a South African, and it was latter rumoured in Botswana that the film was sponsored by the South African meat industry.
39. The environmental coordinator during this period was Ingrid Bertilsson. As in the case of the Norwegian environmental specialists in the early stages, she was formally employed by the AfDB, but her salary was paid by the Swedish Ministry of Foreign Affairs.
40. At least this is how his position was understood by Southern African constituencies and the staff of the environmental unit.
41. This report was quickly known as the Knox-report after the chairman of the task force, David Knox, a former vice president of the World Bank. The report described the Bank as a top-heavy bureaucracy, weakened by the impoverishment of the continent it was meant to help, and full of political intrigue and suspicion. The argument was that if the Bank was not significantly reformed it might end up by destroying itself. See AfDB (1994b).
42. For a more general review of the reorganisation process in the AfDB see Bøås (1997).
43. For an excellent review of the relationship between Japan and the ADB see Yasutomo (1983).
44. Contrary to the AfDB, it is not as easy in the ADB to divide the members into regionals and nonregionals, because among the regionals we find donor countries such as Australia, Hong Kong, Japan, New Zealand, Singapore, South Korea, and Taiwan. All nonregionals are donor countries.
45. The ones that graduated were Hong Kong, Singapore, South Korea, and Taiwan.
46. According to Young (1989), blurred cleavages facilitate the prospects for success in institutional bargaining.
47. Japan holds 15.601%, the United States 7.979%, China 6.651%, India 6.541%, and Australia 6.009% of the votes.
48. From 1981 to 1985 Japan's foreign aid budget expanded faster than any other item. In this period the average increase was 10% per annum. See Yasutomo (1986).
49. Japan is the largest contributor to the ADB. It joined the African Development Fund in 1973 and became a full member of the AfDB in 1983 and it has been active in the Inter-American Development Bank since it gained membership in 1976. Since 1984, Japan and the United States have been the largest suppliers of funds to the World Bank. For a study of the new multilateral activism in Japan's foreign policy see Yasutomo (1995).
50. At establishment, Japan and the United States contributed $200 million each, the first time any country matched an American contribution to an international organization. From the beginning Japan sought to maintain funding parity with the United States. Since the early 1970s, Japan has pledged to provide at least one-third of the ADF. In addition, it created a Japan special Fund within the Bank in 1988 and in 1990 offered to set aside $4 million out of a planned $59 million allocation to the Japan Special Fund for a new environmental preservation fund.

51. Under Fujioka's leadership, a quota for loan commitments of 15% and then 21% a year was instituted. This issue became especially acute in the mid-1980s, when the ADB was awash with liquidity because of a drop in loan requests from recipient countries.
52. The American executive director in the ADB is in the same positions as the U.S. executive director in the AfDB. All loans proposed by the ADB are sent to Washington to be evaluated by the Working Group on Multilateral Assistance.
53. Japan has envisioned its role as co-ordinator and balancer because of its status as both an Asian country and a donor, and its preferences are pivotal, for its vote may tilt the balance toward either the recipient or the donor countries.
54. In particular, the paper recommended that the ADB should concentrate on (1) reviewing the Bank's projects to ensure that all potentially significant environmental impacts are identified, and that appropriate measures are taken to avoid adverse impacts; (2) promoting environmental awareness among Bank staff; (3) acting as a regional resource center; (4) supporting projects with direct environmental benefits as well as initiating and processing environmentally oriented projects per se, and (5) strengthening the institutions dealing with the planning and management of environmental and natural resources, together with the line agencies concerned with the monitoring and enforcement of environmental laws and regulations.
55. Unfortunately, no comparable figures exist for the AfDB.
56. Source: ADB (1994). Environmental lending includes environmental-oriented projects such as forestry, and use planning, urban environmental improvement, and environment projects per se such as biodiversity conservation, institution building, and pollution control and projects with environmental components—i.e., those which include a component to mitigate the environmental impact.
57. In this paper, the need for such a strategy is legitimized by pointing at the Stockholm principles and the guidelines already prepared by the World Bank and USAID.
58. The following information was obtained from Bank documents and interviews with former members of the ADB staff.
59. The conference, which was cosponsored by the ADB and the IUCN, was the first concerted action for the region since the signing of the Convention on Biological Diversity by over 150 governments at the Rio Summit. According to Tahir Qadri, an ADB forestry specialist, the conference was a success in the sense that it brought home the message that the Bank would support efforts in gearing members policies to biodiversity conservation.
60. See the *Financial Times* 5/5/94.

REFERENCES

Agreement Establishing the Asian Development Bank. Manila: ADB, 1966.

Environmental Protection and Development Financing by the Asian Development Bank. Manila: ADB, 1978.

Environmental Considerations in Bank Operations. Manila: ADB, 1980.

Review of the Bank's Environmental Policies and Procedures. Manila: ADB, 1986.

Annual Report. Manila: ADB, 1993.

Summary of Proceedings. Twenty-Sixth Annual Meeting of the Board of Governors. Manila: ADB, 1993.

ADB Review July/August 1994. Manila: ADB, 1994.

The Environment Program of the Asian Development Bank. Past, Present and Future. Manila: ADB, 1994.

1995 Annual Report. Manila: ADB, 1996.

Agreement Establishing the African Development Bank. New York: United Nations, 1964.

Memorandum: Botswana—Loan Proposal for the Financing of the Francistown Abattoir Project. Abidjan: AfDB, 1987.

African Development Bank Environmental Policy Paper—Draft. Washington, DC: Development Alternatives Inc., 1988.

Environmental Policy. Washington DC: Development Alternatives Inc., 1989.

Agricultural Sector Policy. Abidjan: AfDB, 1990.

Environmental Policy Paper. Abidjan: AfDB, 1990.

Environmental Asseement Guidelines. Abidjan: AfDB, 1992.

1992 Annual Report. Abidjan: AfDB, 1993.

The African Development Bank and the Environment. Abidjan: AfDB, 1994a.

Report of the Task Force on Project Quality. Abidjan: AfDB, 1994b.

1995 Annual Report. Abidjan: AfDB, 1996.

AfDB/UNECA. (1988). *Economic Recovery Report*. Abidjan: AfDB.

Baldwin, D.A. (1965). The international bank in political perspective. *World Politics*, *18*, 68–81.

Bøås, M. (1997). Between international politics, intraorganisational rivalry and individual strategic behaviour: reforming the African Development Bank. Like flogging a dead horse? In The Norwegian Research Council *The Research Programme on Multilateral Development Assistance—Leangkollen Papers I*. Oslo: NFR. (23–47).

Brennan, Geoffrey and James Buchanan. 1985. *The Reason of Rules: Constitutional Political Economy*. Cambridge: Cambridge University Press.

Caporaso, James A. 1993. ''International Relations Theory and Multilateralism: The Search for Foundations.'' In John Gerard Ruggie [ed.] *Multilateralism Matters. The Theory and Praxis of an Institutional Form*, 51–90. New York: Columbia University Press.

Evans, P.B. (1993). Building an integrative approach to international and domestic politics: reflections and projections. In P.B. Evans, H.K. Jacobson, and R.D. Putnam (eds.), *Double-Edged Diplomacy. International Bargaining and Domestic Politics*, 397–430. Berkeley: University of California Press.

Evans, P.B., and Jacobson, H.K. and Putnam, R.D. (eds.). (1993). *Double-Edged Diplomacy. International Bargaining and Domestic Politics*. Berkeley: University of California Press.

Financial Times. 05.05.94.

Fordwar, K.D. (1981). *The African Development Bank: Problems of International Cooperation*. New York: Pergamon Press.

Gardiner, R.K.A, and Picket, J. (1984). *The African Development Bank. An Experiment in Economic Co-operation and Development*. Abidjan: AfDB.

Jackson, R.H., and Rosberg, C.G. (1982). *Personal Rule in Black Africa. Prince, Autocrat, Prophet and Tyrant*. Berkeley: University of California Press.

Jerlström, B. (1990). *Banking on Africa. An Evaluation of the African Development Bank*. Stockholm: Ministry of Foreign Affairs.

Keohane, R.O. (1990). Multilateralism: an agenda for research. *International Journal 45*, 731–764.

Krasner, S.D. (1981). Power structures and regional development banks. *International Organization 35*(2), 303–328.

Krasner, S.D. (ed.). (1982). *International Regimes*. Ithaca, NY: Cornell University Press.

Kratochwil, F. (1993). Norms versus numbers: multilateralism and the rationalist and reflexivist approaches to institutions—a unilateral plea for communicative rationality. In Ruggie, J.G. (ed.), *Multilateralism Matters. The Theory and Praxis of and Institutional Form*, 443–474. New York: Columbia University Press.

Mikesell, R.F., and Williams, L.F. (1992). *International Banks and the Environment. From Growth to Sustainability: An Unfinished Agenda*. San Francisco: Sierra Club Books.

Mingst, K.A. (1990). *Politics and the African Development Bank*. Lexington: University Press of Kentucky.

Ministry of Foreign Affairs. (1989). *Japan's ODA 1988*. Tokyo: Association for Promotion of International Cooperation.

Basic Facts on Japan's ODA. (1993). Tokyo: Ministry of Foreign Affairs.

Mistry, P.S. (1995). *Multilateral Development Banks. An Assessment of their Financial Structures, Policies and Practices*. The Hague: FONDAD.

Mitrany, D. (1943). *A Working Peace System*. London: Royal Institute of International Affairs.

Orr, R.M. Jr. (1990). *Japan's Foreign Aid Power*. New York: Columbia University Press.

Oye, K. (1986). Explaining cooperation under anarchy: hypotheses and strategies. In K. Oye (ed.), *Cooperation Under Anarchy*, 1–24. Princeton: Princeton University Press.

Ruggie, J.G. (ed.). (1993). *Multilateralism Matters. The Theory and Praxix of an Institutional Form*. New York: Columbia University Press.

Ruggie, J.G. (1993). Multilateralism: the anatomy of an institution. In J.G. Ruggie (ed.), *Multilateralism Matters. The Theory and Praxis of an Institutional Form*, 3–47. New York: Columbia University Press.

Runnals, D. (1986). Factors influencing environmental policies in international development agencies. In ADB (ed.), *Environmental Planning and Management*, 191–235. Manila: ADB.

Sanford, J.E. (1982). *U.S. Foreign Policy and Multilateral Development Banks*. Boulder, CO: Westview.

Schelling, T.C. (1960). *The Strategy of Conflict*. Cambridge, MA: Harvard University Press.

Selim, H.M. (1983). *Development Assistance Policies and the Performance of Aid Agencies: Studies in the Performance of DAC, OPEC, Regional Development Banks and the World Bank Group*. New York: St. Martin's Press.

Shaw, C.L. (1991). *Par inter paribus*: The nature of power in cooperation lessons [for the United States] from the African Development Bank. *African Affairs 90*, 537–558.

Stein, R., and Johnson, B. (1979). *Banking on the Biosphere? Environmental Practice and Procedures of Nine Multilateral Development Agencies*. Lexington, MA: IIED.

Strange, S. (1982). *Cave! Hic dragones*: A critique of regime analysis. *International Organization 36*(2), 337–354.

Wæver, O. (1997). John G. Ruggie: transformation and institutionalisation. In I.B. Neumann and O. Wæver (eds.), *The Future of International Relations: Masters in the Making, 170–204*. London: Routledge.

Wettestad, J. (1987). *Multilateral Bistandsorganisasjoner og Miljøvernet*. Oslo: FNI.

Wilson, D. (1987). *A Bank for Half the World. The Story of the Asian Development Bank 1966-1986*. Manila: ADB.

Yasutomo, D.T. (1983). *Japan and the Asian Development Bank*. New York: Praeger Special Studies.

The Manner of Giving. Strategic Aid and Japanese Foreign Policy. (1986). Lexington, MA: Lexington Books.

Japan and the Asian Development Bank: multilateral aid policy in transition (1993). In B.M. Koppel and R.M. Orr Jr. (eds.), *Japan's Foreign Aid. Power and Policy in a New Era*, 305–340. Boulder, CO. Westview Press.

The New Multilateralism in Japan's Foreign Policy. (1995). New York: St. Martin's Press.

Young, O. (1982). *Resource Regimes: Natural Resources and Social Institutions*. Berkeley: University of California Press.

The politics of international regime formation: managing natural resources and the environment. (1989). *International Organization 43*(3), 349–375.

Formation. On the development of institutions in international society. (1991). *International Organization 45*(3), 281–308.

2

Reforming Transport with Dominant State-Owned Enterprises

Democratic Republic of Congo (Formerly Zaire)

Alex Kelvin
University of Hertfordshire, Hertford, England

I. BACKGROUND

The purpose of this chapter is to help you with a reform project in the sectors with quasi-monopolistic public provision. You can be in Slovenia, Brazil, Nigeria, France, or the People's Republic of China. Shortcomings of two versions of reform in Onatra (National Transportation Authority) are assessed. A third, more thoroughgoing blueprint of *strategic partnerships* is formulated. Its advantages in human motivation, organizational arrangements, and efficient satisfaction of customer needs are illustrated.

After independence of 1960, the state-owned enterprises (SOEs) enjoyed monopolies over seaports, river ports, railways, and transport of mineral exports. But instead of a uniform policy of administrative tariffs for multiple products, a more realistic market segmentation was needed. Preferential use of the national network for exporting minerals from the southeastern province of Katanga via the port of Matadi was the cornerstone of transport policy. However local agriculture and manufacturing suffered from transportation shortages (Kelvin 1997c).

The public monopoly argument that minerals could not be shipped by private operators did not stand scrutiny. With containerization, the public corporations experienced numerous difficulties to balance traffic, plan maintenance, and manage empty boxes. The range of services could not accommodate the changing scope of demand. Since 1960, the managers in public corporations have resisted competition and privatization, using their influence on political and legislative decision making. Delegation of responsibilities and decentralization proved inconclusive.

Onatra pursued the following official objectives: at the corporate level—efficiency, financial viability, quality of service; at the sectoral level—modal integration, regional integration, and transport of more minerals via the national territory, at the national level—export competitiveness, economic integration, and growth. Survival was added by the author as an unofficial corporate objective, and it proved highly significant in explaining the gaps between the public provision and the beneficiaries' needs.

In 1991 the public corporation defaulted on repaying debts. Recommendations emerged in favor of reallocating provision from the public to the private operators. It was proposed that the private operators take over all transport services which they could provide covering costs. For the remaining balance, public support could be envisaged. In 1985, the Organization of African Unity adopted Africa's Priority Program for Economic Reforms, stressing the need for a larger economic role for the private sector. About the same time, reports by the Economic Commission for Africa and the African Development Bank pointed out that mistaken policies depressed agriculture and industries and lessened incentives for the private sector. In 1986 the living standard of the population was 27% of its level in 1965 (IMF). All attempts of the IMF, the World Bank, and other lenders to stabilize the economic situation failed. In the wake of crumbling of the Second Republic in 1990, the country defaulted on servicing debts.

The country possesses exceptional assets. The cost of copper production was the lowest among the major copper-exporting countries, followed by Zambia, Chile, United States, Peru, and Canada (Pindyck et al. 1992). The rent from copper sales on the international market was highest. It possesses as well the largest reserves of industrial diamonds in the world. Soil and climate are extremely favorable for agriculture. Over 50% of African tropical forests grow in the country. The National Development Plan 1986-90 listed the reasons for the crisis such as generalized public managerial failure; inability to maintain capacity; wrong choice of investment projects; extreme bias toward external finance; lack of budget discipline; failure to create a favorable business environment; inability to initiate vital institutional reforms.

You can list the main assets for national growth in your country and make a brief outline of how well they have been used. A summary of how your public corporation has been satisfying demand is useful.

II. METHOD AND STUDY DESIGN

Field research is based on personal working experience of the author as responsible for corporate economic studies at the National Transportation Authority and interviewing 10 managers from SOEs, four managers from relevant ministries (Transport, Finance, Economy, and Planning), three representatives of consumer associations, 12 managers from private companies, and three representatives from regional/local authorities. The theoretical method draws on cultural realms, transaction costs, and strategic partnerships.

Question 1. What cultural characteristics can be used to improve efficiency?

A. Cultural Realms

Cultural realms explain interactions among individual motivation, social behavior, and organizational efficiency (Hyden 1983). Behavior is conditioned by them but it is too complex to be directly explained by any single motive. The *primordial* realm is associated with the traditional African clan. It determines values and the norms of social behavior. Individual behavior is explained by the *private* realm, which is based on self-interest. It defines the limits of individual responsibility and conditions motivation and effort. The important point is that the private and the primordial realms are based on similar values (Kelvin 1997d).

The *public* realm expresses the idea of an economy with a strong public sector. Prior to colonization, sub-Saharan Africa knew no states in the Western or Oriental sense (Young 1984). Modern economic concepts such as large-scale enterprise, planning, manufacturing, marketing, finance, and fund raising, accounting, and depreciation are still not integrated with the *economy of affection*. Several top local economists reiterated the difficulty of long-term thinking because people were bogged down in daily concerns. With an average four-child family in the Kinshasa area, in 1988 monthly salaries of the graduates in SOEs were sufficient to buy food up to 20 days. Public assets and budgets were the natural source of gain. The public debt was not perceived as future tax liability.

Fallers (1965) emphasized how hard it was to isolate SOEs from lineage influences. The employees continue to be guided by the *primordial* realm. In trying to develop formal authority, public organizations clash with clans. Interpersonal conflicts and organizational instability result. Since cultural behavior patterns are complex, no consideration is given to them in feasibility studies or reengineering proposals. When cultural values and anthropological customs are assumed away, large public corporations are similar to surrealistic theaters, where employees act out informal scripts. This gap among formal objectives, organizational structure, and expected conduct at the SOEs, on the one hand, and the actual motives and behavior, on the other, seems to be fundamental.

After independence the preference in resource allocation was given to bureaucracy. Political bans and restrictions multiplied, and the state bureaucracy expanded. Hyden (1983) cited Zaire as an extreme example, where officials gained advantages through organized disarray (p. 63). Meantime, the objectives of competitive exports, regional and economic integration, and growth remained frustrated.

To conclude this section: competitive market structures appear to be in tune with the primordial cultural realm which is associated with multiethnic population. The primordial realm points to the pluralistic civic and economic organization of the society. At the same time, monopolistic structures are part and parcel of the public realm. The theory of transaction costs provides a framework for studying market structure, motivation, effort, and performance.

Question 2. How can the firm size and the market structure be determined?

B. Transaction Costs

This theory treats markets and organizations as alternatives for allocation of resources, production, and distribution of incomes. Coase (1988) fashioned economic activities in two alternative ways: either as series of market transactions or as coordinated activities within the organization, whichever allows savings in transaction costs. The upper limit for the size of efficient operations is reached when the costs of organizing an extra transaction within the organization becomes equal to the costs of the same transaction in the market. In larger organizations transactions multiply, and it becomes increasingly difficult to maintain efficient production. Coase named this phenomenon decreasing returns to the entrepreneur's function (p. 394), or diminishing returns to management (p. 395).

Williamson (1975, 1986) based his transaction costs approach on Coase's theory of the firm. The basic concepts are bounded rationality, uncertainty associated with complexity, opportunism, and information impactedness. Bounded rationality limits the amount of information that individuals can assimilate and use. Uncertainty results from complexity of choices. Opportunism implies that people take decisions and act from their individual standpoint. Information impactedness specifies the limits in assimilating knowledge and transmitting information. Therefore costs are involved in selecting and training staff, as well as in establishing networks of communication. Transaction costs include the costs of information, negotiation, decision making, contracting, and enforcement.

On the supply side, it is assumed that, given technology and resource endowments, institutions are minimizing transaction costs. On the demand side, economic actors are guided by their preferences and presumably select the alternative minimizing transaction costs (Datta and Nugent 1989). The transaction efforts are related to the diversity of customer base, productive and regulatory arrangements, and market structure. This method covers the whole spectrum from perfectly competitive private markets to tightly controlled public monopolies. The advantage is that the method is politically neutral and can be used by decision makers with different value judgments in various political systems. Moreover, the framework allows the integration of both internal and external factors. Cultural factors, for example, can considerably influence motivation, efforts, and conduct of the employees, affecting the outcomes of corporate activities.

In the public theory of resource allocation, the assumptions are made that transaction costs are zero, resources are fully employed, the same quality and quantity of information can be generated by the quasi-monopolistic public sector as by the perfectly competitive market, and administrative prices are equal to the long-term marginal costs. However, the discretionary behavior of managers and employees in the SOEs considerably enhances information impactedness and transaction costs. The assumption that the decision makers in the SOEs act in the interests of beneficiaries was rejected by empirical testing (Kelvin 1994, 1995b). Therefore, the intangible factors do explain the behavior of bureaucrats and are central to the theory of public sector failure (Aharoni 1982). Attenuation of property rights in the SOEs discourages advantageous specialization, and collected rents can favor narrow interest groups. Across-the-board wage increases are easier to administer than the remuneration systems based on individual merit, but arising apathy saps motivation and deflates productivity.

Question 3. How close is the level of public provision to demand?

The main argument in favor of public provision is that it takes account of externalities. However, the crucial question is how closely the public provision comes to the socially desirable level of output. An impact model of socially low tariffs in river transportation (Kelvin 1997) showed that the expected increase in demand for river transportation did not occur because Onatra rationed capacity provision. Although tariffs remained low, the users were overcharged unofficially if they wanted goods to be shipped. Corporate claims for budgets multiplied. The overhead costs were five times higher per unit of traffic in the public than in the private sector. Therefore the service provision was much lower than the socially desirable or the efficient throughputs.

The reader is invited to assess two types of throughput for your public company: competitive and socially desirable. Compare both to the level of demand and supply. What blend in the public/private provision would accommodate the demand better? This leads to the concept of strategic partnerships.

Question 4. What are the benefits of strategic partnerships compared to exclusively public or private provision?

C. Strategic Partnerships

Woodward (1980), Jackson (1982), and Arndt (1983) treated organizations as open social systems, dynamic, adapting, and internally differentiated. Businesses are strategic partnerships among providers of service, their suppliers, lending institutions, customers, and public authorities (Webster 1992). The core holding firm is defined by its knowledge base and its markets. The subsidiary companies develop customer-oriented information technology, segment and differentiate the markets, and position services in relation to competition. Badaracco (1991) emphasized the focus on long-term partnerships.

The detailed blueprint for privatization was formulated (Kelvin 1995a). Objectives of privatization, scenarios, and techniques were outlined. The best candidates to take over the ailing SOEs were identified. Impacts of hypothetical privatization were simulated on the port component of the Corporate Capital Investment Program 1989–1993. For the *selected* port projects, up to 90% of funding at the main seaport of Matadi and up to 75% at the main river port of Kinshasa could have been provided by the private sector. Moreover, several *shelved* expansion-type projects could have become feasible with private commitment. The following recommendations were suggested: end the public monopolies on seaports, river ports, railways, and transportation of mineral exports; shift the ownership toward a more natural balance of 80% private and 20% public; encourage strategic partnerships of leaner public organizations with private carriers, freight forwarders, producers, traders, and consumers; phase out cross-subsidizing of inefficient public river transportation.

D. Methodological Summary

Cultural characteristics set the stage for understanding human motivation and efficient organizations. Transaction costs determine the contestable and sustainable market structure and the size and number of suppliers. Strategic partnerships shift the focus from rivalry to the spirit of association, showing how to pool resources to provide value for all economic actors. Two conditions appear important (Casella and Frey 1992). Firstly, the probability that one group could dominate and bias the rules in its favor to the detriment of important economic groups should be greatly reduced. Secondly, the economic actors should be able to fulfill their preferences by having a choice of alternatives. The theory of clubs emphasizes that both public and private services are sustainable as long as the interested public is prepared to pay for them.

III. THREE VERSIONS OF CORPORATE REFORM

Customers perceived Onatra as too vast and remote from their preoccupations. Where contestability was allowed, the traffic was lost to the private competition. Reform had to save the recoverable units and divest from the money-losing activities. Tariff reform has to improve revenues by automatically adjusting tariffs for changes in costs. Three versions of reform are outlined: divisionalization, holding company, and partnership.

Question 5. Have the considered versions of reform succeeded?

A. Divisionalized Version of New Corporate Organization

Divisionalization provides parallel decentralization in the vertical dimension (Mintzberg 1989). This version of reform was formulated by the consultant. Each business unit or division had to make decisions that affected its own services or geographical areas. The business units were to receive objectives and performance standards. As long as they met them, they would preserve their autonomy. Financial controls were retained at the headquarters. This was similar to the model applied by Alfred Sloan to General Motors in the 1920s. But too much power was left in the hands of a few managers whose decisions affected millions of beneficiaries. This type of reform seemed too cosmetic: it would not end public quasi-monopoly.

B. Holding Version of Corporate Organization

This second version was also formulated by the consultant and it was favored by the lending institutions. A slim holding company could have partial ownership in subsidiary companies. But information gathering, operational decision making, and execution would be transferred to the subsidiaries. The central corporate services employed approximately 4200 of the total workforce of 18,800, that is, 22%, but their overhead costs accounted for 56% of the total. Divisions would have the choice of services either from the company or from alternative suppliers in the market. In other words, the departments had to become operationally independent companies.

In 1962 the mission of the EEC pressed with the decentralization of the Matadi-Kinshasa railway, river transport, privatization of operations on the river tributaries, and divestment from food farming, timber harvesting and dockyards. Also in 1962, the World Bank mission insisted that the corporation operate on the basis of technical and commercial considerations and get rid of politicians nominated to its Board of Directors. In 1963, the Belgian cooperation mission urged to scale down the public monopolies in transport. In 1969, the World Bank mission pressed for a new holding structure for Onatra. None of the recommendations were followed. Attempts to make public monopolies more competitive by introducing several smaller SOEs failed to improve efficiency because of the entrenched bureaucratic culture.

Pirie (1988) emphasizes that to subject state monopolies to competition misses the point. "The purpose is to make state operations *private*. Only when they become free from the state intervention, most of the decisions will become economic'' (p. 53).

The corporate president taking over in 1985 delegated much responsibility. However, this led to abuses and diversion of public funds. Experience of several corporate presidents showed that it took at least three years for them to develop a reasonable grasp of the activities. Over the period of 1985-1993 four corporate presidents were replaced. But the corporate performance continued to deteriorate.

Make notes on limitations of the previous reforms and on the challenges facing your organization or sector now. If such studies have not been done, list the main issues for the reform to address.

Question 6. How can one discover the effective organizational structure?

C. Strategic Partnerships

Since both reform proposals above had important limitations, the third, more unmitigated blueprint was devised by the author. It comprised the following measures: (1) end Onatra's monopoly on terminal operations in the seaports and the river ports; (2) open the seaports and the river ports for private operators; (3) end the monopoly over mineral export traffic; (4) contract out railway operations to private or mixed companies; (5) privatize all three public dockyards; (6) increase contestability in all modes of transport so that a natural blend in public/private provision could emerge; and (7) privatize the auxiliary services.

Strategic partnerships involve close cooperation between parties with specified joint rights and responsibilities. In a joint venture for the Kinshasa container terminal, outside the port, Onatra had a 35% share and contributed the site for the terminal which handled all imported containers for the Kinshasa area and containerized exports originating from the capital. Two largest freight forwarders and the leading private transportation company were the other shareholders. This successful joint venture with private management can be a prototype for other mixed companies.

The increasing shipping of mineral exports from Katanga via the national port of Matadi was severely restricting capacity for transporting agricultural exports and consumer goods. In the early 1980s construction of container terminals in the ports of Matadi and Kinshasa opened the national network for containerized traffic. Containerization limit was estimated at 45% to 50% for imports and 60% to 65% for exports by the consultant. Onatra had to start a new joint venture or to contract container traffic out. Private carriers and freight forwarders appeared to be better positioned for transporting minerals. Balanced growth requires adequate entrepreneurial and managerial abilities.

Suykens (1988) presented the advantages of a well balanced blend of official and private interests and responsibilities in the port of Antwerp, where public investment in industrial sites brought about 10 times higher private investment.

Therefore operational and maintenance management, supplies, marketing, financial control, capital budgeting, recruitment, pay, and pensions should become the responsibility of private or joint companies. In 1989 support was provided for the legal and technical mechanisms for a debt/equity swap in the country. Government corporations could be converted into limited liability companies with new management, financial structures, accounting practices, and personnel policies.

In implementing reforms it is important to consider those involved. In the late 1980s, personal interviews with typical workers and employees in Kinshasa revealed that approximately one-fifth or at best one-quarter of their family expenses were covered from wages. Housing provided by Onatra, health care and pension schemes were considered sufficient benefits for the public employees. Obedience was reinforced, and promotion was based on seniority. Onatra selected and promoted *field-dependent* members (Witkin et al. 1977) who expected too much guidance and supervision and were neither encouraged nor trained to think about alternatives. In terms of Belbin's (1992) business team roles, the public corporation was disproportionately staffed *with company workers* and *team workers* whose main characteristic was compliance. At the same time *shapers* (the most efficient project leaders), *resource investigators*, and original thinkers were in short supply. At the main seaport of Matadi only seven of 2230 employees were university graduates. Kanku (1986), Director of the Container Terminal at Matadi, emphasized that it was myopic to make important capital investments in infrastructure (container, log, and other specialized terminals) without upgrading the quality of management and workforce.

In the privatization scenario employees and managers would be tested prior to signing new contracts. Salaries and wages in private compaines were four to five times higher than in the public corporations. But relatively generous compensation packages were envisaged by the lending institutions for those who would either choose not to continue working or were not selected to do so.

List a range of services which your reformed SOE could efficiently provide. Who are the best potential partners for joint ventures? Sketch a new organizational chart for divisions and units.

IV. OPTIMAL COMBINATION OF PRIVATE AND PUBLIC PROVISION.

Question 7. How can one determine the advantageous blend in public and private provision?

It emerged from the questionnaires that the overstretched SOEs had no advantage in running too many activities, whereas private companies were vigorous, eager to invest, and eager to provide efficient service. Up to 500% improvement in productivity and quality of service was expected by those interviewed from the change in ownership. This is in line with the wage differential up to five times higher in the private sector. Market liberalization was perceived as a useful supporting dimension. The deregulation experience in river transport since 1978 showed the potential of competitive private provision and the avenue for reform in other modes of transportation. There were no doubts among those interviewed that the private operators could better satisfy demand than the public monopoly.

Economies of scope appeared influential. They originate from indivisible transport infrastructure, which can provide multiple service simultaneously (Baumol et al. 1986). Smaller river transport and trucking companies increased fluidity and contestability of markets. Liberalized road and river transportation showed that firm size was not a determinant factor of efficient service (Kelvin 1996). Three seaports—Matadi, Boma, and Banana—would be managed by separate and autonomous port authorities. No private operator should become the owner or franchisee of terminals on long-term basis at more than one seaport at a time. This is to guarantee choice for the users at least between the ports of Matadi and Boma. It is healthy to promote competition not only between the port ranges but between national ports, as well as between terminals in the same ports (Verhoeff 1981).

V. REGULATION CONUNDRUM

Question 8. How can regulation help improve service provision?

Kelvin (1995a) showed a wide chasm between the SOEs and the beneficiaries. The users and beneficiaries wanted growth and regional and economic integration. The monopolistic throughput in the main seaport of Matadi was about six times smaller than competitive throughput could have been. This shows potential long-term gains from privatization and deregulation.

Financial dependence of SOEs on heavy shipping of mineral exports over the national network was seen as a liability because of capacity rationing for agricultural commodities and consumer goods. As a consequence national growth was thwarted. Since monopolistic seaport charges of \$21/ton in the seaport of Matadi appeared to handicap nonmining exports, it seemed advisable to cut seaport charges closer to the average costs of \$3/ton.

Corporate Boards of Directors at the SOEs failed in designing development plans and strategies. Their members, Corporate Presidents and Deputy-General Managers were nominated by the President of the Second Republic. There was no mechanism to monitor their performance; their fixed remuneration was in no way related to performance. Often important issues of SOEs were decided at the high political level without consulting the Boards of Directors. In contrast, the

Boards of Directors in mixed companies appeared much more effective. The only objectives for joint companies were cash generation and return on dividends.

VI. CONCLUSION

The purpose was to furnish guidelines for public servants, researchers, consultants, lenders, and students to reform quasi-monopolistic sectors with inefficient public corporations. Equipped with such methodology, the reader can work out a reform project to bridge the gap between inadequate supply and unsatisfied demand. Limitations of the first two variants of reform were examined. The third solution of strategic partnerships was proposed.

Previous studies (Kelvin 1994, 1995b, 1996, 1997) made economic case for the reallocation of property and production rights to those suppliers who were able to provide better service. Deregulation of the river traffic since 1978 showed that Onatra was unable to compete in a contestable environment and its survival depended on the monopolistic privileges.

The private and public balance changes over time. In the 1930s the private operators could not earn a return. The government had to step in to continue investment programs and operations. Today the situation is very different. The prevailing mentality seems to favor a contestable service provision. The sustainable balance in public/private provision will be achieved by reallocating property and production rights to private operators who are better suited for efficient provision. Strategic partnerships and the theory of clubs seem to provide vehicles for testing and ascertaining the best private-public blend in each market.

You can sketch a reform proposal for your SOE or for the whole sector, and outline its advantages.

REFERENCES

Aharoni Y. (1982). State-owned enterprises: an agent without a principal. In L. Jones (ed.), *Public Enterprise in Less Developed Countries*. Cambridge: Cambridge University Press.

Aharoni, Y. (1986). *The Evolution and Management of State-Owned Enterprises*. Cambridge, MA: Ballinger Publishing Company.

Arndt, J. (1983), The political economy paradigm: foundation for the theory building and marketing. *Journal of Marketing 42*(3), 44–54.

Badaracco, J. (1991). *The Knowledge Link: How Firms Compete through Strategic Alliances*. Boston: Harvard Business School Press.

Bailey, F. et al. (1982). Market structure and multiproduct industries. *Journal of Economic Literature 20*(September), 1024–1048.

Baumol, W. et al. (1982). *Contestable Markets and Theory of Industrial Structure*. New York: Harcourt Brace Jovanovich.

Baumol, W. et al. (1986). Contestability: developments since the book. In D. Morris et al. (eds.), *Strategic Behavior and Industrial Competition*. Oxford: Clarendon Press.

Bazerman, M. (1986). *Judgment and Managerial Decision Making*. New York: John Wiley.

Belbin, R. (1991). *Management of Teams*. Oxford: Butterworth-Heinemann.

Berne, E. (1963). *The Structure and Dynamics of Organizations and Groups*. Philadelphia: J.B. Lippincott.

Blumenthal, E. (1982). *Zaire*: *Report of her International Financial Credibility*, April 7.

Callaghy, T. (1990). Lost between state and market: the politics of economic adjustment in Ghana, Zambia and Nigeria. In J. Nelson (ed.), *Economic Crisis and Policy Change*: *The Politics of Adjustment in the Third World*. Princeton: Princeton University Press.

Casella, A. et al. (1992). Federalism and clubs: towards an economic theory of overlapping political jurisdiction. *European Economic Review 36*, 639–646.

Coase, R. (1988). *The Firm*, *the Market and the Law*. Chicago: University of Chicago Press.

Datta, S. et al. (1989). Transaction cost economics and contractual choice: theory and evidence. In M. Nabli and J. Nugent (eds.), *The New Institutional Economics and Development*. Amsterdam: North-Holland.

Fallers, L. (1965). *Bantu Bureaucracy*. Chicago: University of Chicago Press.

Gould, D. (1980). *Bureaucratic Corruption and Underdevelopment in the Third World*: *The Case of Zaire*. Elmsford, NJ: Pergamon Press.

Hofstede, G. (1980). *Culture's Consequences*. *International Differences in Work-Related Values*. London: Sage Publications.

Huybrechts, A. (1970). *Transports et Structures de Développement au Congo*. Paris: Mouton.

Hyden, G. (1983). *No Short Cut to Progress*. *African Development Management in Progress*. London: Heinemann Educational Books.

IMF. (1965–87). *International Financial Statistics* 1965–87. International Monetary Fund.

Jackson, P. (1982). *The Political Economy of Bureaucracy*. Hemel Hempstead: Philip Allan.

Kanku, T. (1986). *Comment Combattre les Causes de la Fluctuation du Rendement au Port de Matadi*. Tokyo: Third Prize of the International Association of Ports and Harbours.

Kelvin, A. (1993a), Estimate of timber production, capacity utilization and export potential in Zaire. *Commonwealth Forestry Review 72*(3), 175–180.

Kelvin, A. (1993b). *Effectiveness of Decision Making in Capital Investment*: *Case Study of the National Transportation Authority in Zaire*. *Ph.D. Thesis*, Department of Maritime Studies and International Transport, University of Wales.

Kelvin, A. (1994). Sequential ordinal method of capital investment project selection. *Project Appraisal 9*(3), 183–194.

Kelvin, A. (1995a). *Effectiveness of Decision Making in Capital Investment and a Blue-*

print for Reform: *Case Study of the National Transportation Authority in Zaire*. Research Project, Brussels: Belgian Academy of Sciences for Overseas.

Kelvin, A. (1995b). Planning framework of analytical approaches applied to Zairian transportation. *Maritime Policy and Management 22*(2), 135–153.

Kelvin, A. (1996). From state monopoly toward contestable and sustainable market structures. *Dutch Journal of Transport Science 2*, 145–168.

Kelvin, A. (1997a). Impact model of socially low tariffs in Zairian river transport. *Annals of Public and Cooperative Economics 68*(1), 107–128.

Kelvin, A. (1997b). *Upgrading Private Contribution to Partnerships in View of Failure in the Public Provision*. Conference Paper. 24th *Annual (1997) Conference Proceedings, The Organization of International Business*. Leeds: Center of International Business, University of Leeds, April 4–5, 1997.

Kelvin, A. (1997c). Developmental suitability of government intervention in mineral traffic allocation in Zaire. Conference paper. 24th *Annual (1997) Conference—The Organization of International Business*. of the UK Chapter of the *Academy of International Business*. Leeds: Leeds University Business School, April 4–5, 1997.

Kelvin, A. (1997d). Closing the gaps between decisions, implementation and performance. Flemish Journal of Economics and Management *XLII*(4) 409–424.

Kronsten, G. (1986). *Zaire to the 1990s*: *Will Retrenchment Work*? Economic Intelligence Unit, Special Report No. 227. London: Economist Publications.

Leslie, W. (1993). *Zaire*: *Continuity and Political Change in an Oppressive State*. Boulder, CO: Westview Press.

Lynn, J. and Jay, A. (1981). *Yes Minister*. London: BBC Books.

McKean, R. (1970). Products liability: implications of some changing property rights. *Quarterly Journal of Economics 84*, 611–626.

Malkin, J. et al. (1987). *Studies on Improving Institutional and Legal Framework of Public Enterprises in Zaire*. Kinshasa. Unpublished Consultant's Report.

Myrdal, G. (1957). *Economic Theory and Underdeveloped Regions*. London: Gerald Duckworth.

Nabli, M. et al. (eds.) (1989). *The New Institutional Economics and Development*. Amsterdam: North-Holland.

Onatra. (1989). *Contrat-Programme 1989–1992*.

Paelinck, H. (1993). *Study of Transport Systems in Zaire*. Brussels: General Administration for Cooperation and Development.

Pindyck, R. et al. (1992). *Microeconomics*. New York: Macmillan.

Reich, R. (1987). Entrepreneurship reconsidered: the team is a hero. *Harvard Business Review 3* (May–June), 77–83.

Sangmpam, S. (1994). *Pseudocapitalism and the Overpoliticized State: Reconciling Politics and Anthropology in Zaire*. Brookfield, VT: Ashgate Publishing Company.

Suykens, F. (1988). The port of Antwerp and the 1992 horizon. *Hinterland 138*(2), 5–16.

Verhoeff, J. (1981). Seaport competition: some fundamental and political aspects. *Maritime Policy and Management 8*(1), 49–60.

Webster, F. (1992). The changing role of marketing in the corporation. *Journal of Marketing 52*(4), 1–17.

Williamson, O. (1975). *Markets and Hierarchies: Analysis and Antitrust Implications*. New York: Free Press.

Williamson, O. (1986). *Economic Organization, Markets and Policy Control*. Brighton, U.K.: Wheatsheaf Books Ltd.

Witkin, H. et al. (1977). Field-dependent and field-independent cognitive styles and their educational implications. *Review of Educational Research 47*(1), 1–64.

Wolf, C. (1988). *Markets of Governments*. Cambridge, MA: MIT Press.

Woodward, J. (1980). *Industrial Organization. Theory and Practice*. London: Oxford University Press.

Young, C. (1984). Zaire: is there a state? *Canadian Journal of African Studies 18*(1), 80–82.

3

From Conflict to Order? Corporatism in South Africa

Louwrens Pretorius
University of South Africa, Pretoria, South Africa

I. INTRODUCTION

In this paper the viability of corporatism as a mode for alleviating deep conflicts of interest between labor and business in South Africa is explored. This is done by contrasting scholarly analyses of the functions of corporatism with South African trade unionists' views on the purposes of corporatism. Although I cite a number of scholars, the exposition is constructed mainly around ideas culled from Claus Offe's (1985) article "The attribution of public status to interest groups."

Besides the introduction, this paper consists of five sections. In the first section I provide an outline of corporatism in South Africa. Because corporatism was declared dead by one of it's foremost theorists (Schmitter 1989), the first section also offers reasons for continued attention to the phenomenon. In the second section I look at the question, What is corporatism for? There scholarly specifications of functions are contrasted with South African actors' responses to the question. Much of the literature seems to suggest that rationales for liberal, democratic, and social corporatism are mainly pragmatic. Such pragmatic rationales for corporatism often turn on the proposition that corporatism serves to alleviate problems of economic governance which arise within pluralist systems. The third section of the paper suggests, in contrast, that elements within the major South African trade union federation, the Congress of South African Trade Unions (Cosatu), have substantive ideological goals in mind. The fourth section continues the exposition in part three, but moves on to suggest that labor in South Africa may be interested in using corporatism to subject business, rather than to simply smooth out difficulties of governance. Section five contains speculation on the question whether corporatism in South Africa could assist a transition from conflictual to consensual relations between business and labor.

With regard to the following discussion, two qualifications are in order. The first arises from the consideration that the internal unity of, and the external divisions among, the state, business, and labor which is presumed in the relevant discussions, can often be shown to be nonexistent. Even where the language used in this paper ignores the internal diversity of the major ''social partners'' (as state, business, and labor are optimistically called in South Africa), the existence of ideological and organizational diversity within their ranks is not denied. Actors and commentators are identified as clearly as possible in order to avoid the error of representing, for example, an individual union intellectual's views or the opinions expressed in a discussion document, as the official position of a complex organization such as Cosatu.

Secondly, this paper contains much more about the unions than about the other parties to corporatism. One reason is that the current phase of South African corporatism is largely a creation of labor interests. Another follows from the argument that business and labor have different ''logics of collective action'' (Offe, 1985a). This implies that trade unions need corporatism more than business organizations do, and that their stances towards corporatism is thus of special significance for its outcomes.

II. CORPORATISM IN SOUTH AFRICA

The still fragile South African democracy was achieved through a negotiated elite pact. The main parties to the pact were the previously ruling National Party (NP) and the now ruling African National Congress (ANC). Much of the political activity of the interregnum between 1990, when the then NP government formally opened the way for negotiations, and 1994, when the first democratic elections took place and the Government of National Unity was installed, was marked by an extensive *forum movement* (see Shubane and Shaw 1993). The forums were created by antiapartheid civil society formations with the purpose of shaping policy directions across a wide range of social and economic issues. In the end, the forums were unsuccessful as formulators of policy, but they were seedbeds for an ongoing experiment with corporatism.

At present the most important descendant of the forum movement is the National Economic Development and Labour Council (Nedlac), which was established by parliamentary act in late 1994 (Act 35 of 1994). The intended scope of Nedlac's policy activities is indicated by the existence of four ''negotiating chambers'' dealing with, respectively, public finance and monetary policy, trade and industry, labor market, and socioeconomic development issues. The roughly 60 members of Nedlac's Executive Council represent the state and organizations of labor, business, and ''the community,'' respectively. The inclusion of community-based interest organizations is, however, limited to the Development Chamber. In the other chambers, representation is strictly corporatist in the sense that only labor, business, and government are present. One other exception is that officials of the South African Reserve Bank are included in the chamber for public finance and monetary policy.

Formally, Nedlac is ''a negotiating, not an advisory body, whose brief is to produce agreements, not recommendations'' (Naidoo 1995). An ambitious interpretation of Nedlac's formal terms of reference would open even more possibilities. It must ''seek to reach consensus and conclude agreements on matters pertaining to social and economic policy'' and ''consider all significant changes to social and economic policy before it is implemented or introduced in Parliament'' (Act 35 of 1994, section 5 (1)). This wording contains the potential for placing a very wide range of policy issues within the competence of Nedlac.

Nedlac is an attempt to institutionalize corporatist ideas and trends which, depending on the definitions accepted, could be traced as far back as the 1930s (Pretorius 1994, 1996). However, in its deracialized mode and in the sense of formalized corporatist interest *intermediation*, rather than as a set of tripartite advisory bodies, the trend is less than a decade old. The enactment of the 1995 Labour Relations Act (LRA) set in place a legislative framework which has the potential to institutionalize corporatism down to the workplace. This potential, supported by Nedlac's own attempts to expand the arena of negotiated involvement in socioeconomic programs to various levels of society, has prompted some commentators to declare South Africa to be in a relatively advanced stage of corporatization (Baskin 1996; Webster and Adler 1997).

However, the future of corporatism is not assured. Since the establishment of Nedlac, the representatives of state, business, and labor have failed to reach agreement on some central issues. The failures stem largely from deep ideological divisions between the social partners. The current focus of ideological conflicts is the government's programme for Growth, Employment and Redistribution, commonly known as Gear (see Section IV). In policy terms, the differences were, during 1997 and 1998, reflected in failure to achieve agreement on government legislative proposals which were intended to govern basic conditions of employment and the demographic profiles of worker and management corps. The attendant controversies clearly revealed organized business's preference for a flexible labor market, as against the unions' insistence on a strictly controlled market. In line with liberal and capitalist orthodoxies, business also expressed concern about the large degrees of decision-making autonomy which the relevant legislation conferred on the Minister of Labour. The government, in it's turn, advocated ''controlled flexibility.'' Although it supported the unions in principle and in much of the detail of their positions, government tended to encourage pragmatic concessions from both sides. In the case of the 1997 Basic Conditions of Employment Bill (BCEB), for example, this was done mainly with a view to containing labor costs for both business and the state, while at the same time limiting undue exploitation of workers. When, after some 18 months of intense acrimony, the social partners failed to reach agreement on the BCEB, the government took its own version of the bill to Parliament. There it was approved after discussion in legislative committees which were dominated by the ANC and chaired by former Cosatu unionists. In the case of the 1998 employment equity legislation, business in effect acceded to labor and government demands.

In their campaigns around the labor legislation, as previously in those around the labor rights clauses in the Constitution, the unions' major weapons were, arguably, not corporatist or tripartite negotiation but collective action and direct lobbying. Business leaders are wont to criticize the unions' use of such instruments as being inimical to bi- and tripartite negotiations. But business organizations themselves favor conventional lobbying techniques. In fact, the government, unions, and business all have on important occasions bypassed Nedlac when dealing with issues which ostensibly fall within its brief. Moreover, it can be argued that effective political influence by business is more often than not exercised trough nonpublic lobbying by alliances of corporations or groupings of individual business leaders, rather than by organized business interest groups.

Predictions of South African corporatism's demise were strengthened by the government's and the main interest groups' ambivalent and muted responses to the report of the President's Labour Market Commission (LMC) (LMC 1996). The LMC argued that "the practice of voice regulation at the national level must be enhanced by means of a nationally negotiated Accord for Employment and Growth, involving all the social partners." In pursuit of this objective, the Commission recommended a "Presidential Jobs Summit" (LMC 1996:191, 192). After much prevarication by all concerned, the summit materialized in late 1998. It produced a number of resolutions and plans for the creation of jobs, but the participants agreed to avoid the central labor market issues and, more generally, Gear itself.

The failure of corporatist processes to resolve core disagreements about national economic strategies and basic labor policies indicates the fragility, but not necessarily the demise, of South African corporatism. The present phase of corporatism is relatively young, and Nedlac was instituted with the hard task of dealing with deeply entrenched social and political antagonisms. It is unrealistic to expect immediate or continuous success in the negotiation of such divisions. Moreover, all the major interest organizations have repeatedly reaffirmed their support for Nedlac.

Whatever the future of corporatism in its present form might be, the question whether or not South African corporatism is declining or ascendant is not the only important issue for inquiry. It is equally important to ask what the concepts and the accompanying propositions tell us about the likelihood of successful negotiation politics.

If theorizations of corporatism (and of similar configurations such as consociationalism) in Europe are taken as benchmarks, there could be little doubt that, in South Africa, the relevant structural conditions are not conducive to negotiated agreements between "class enemies." However, the depth and intractability of social divisions which some observers have noted as obstacles to corporatism in South Africa have been identified by others as the main reasons for instituting it. Also, it was for long predicted that apartheid could not be ended by negotiation. It was ended by negotiation. So perhaps corporatism or, more generally, the creation of political order through negotiation is possible.

III. WHAT IS CORPORATISM FOR?

Philippe Schmitter (1989:61) has commented that corporatism is "but one of several possible patterns of interest politics in capitalist societies [and this] in turn should alert analysts to the fact that it is not a necessity, but a choice." In South Africa Nedlac was consciously contrived as a corporatist body. Its architects copied much of the form directly from the democratic, liberal, and social corporatisms of the scholarly literature (Nedlac 1995:2). However, while the form replicates the European model, the purposes which South African corporatism are intended to serve, seem to differ in important respects from the model.

Formally, Nedlac is charged with meeting "three defining challenges"—the achievement of sustainable economic growth, social equity (in particular with regard to the distribution of wealth), and increased participation in economic decision making (Nedlac 1995a:4.1–4.3). It is instructive to compare this statement with scholarly views on the purposes of corporatism as it has been practiced in European democracies. According to Markus Crepaz (1992:143), the primary goals are "desired macroeconomic outcomes" (economic growth, low inflation) and "social harmony." Though the empirical relationships between the two sets are likely to be reciprocal, it seems that macroeconomic outcomes are posited to be instrumental in achieving social harmony, which is itself defined as an absence of industrial strife. Crepaz (1992:144) also proposes that "social partnership is not a means to redistribute dramatically social wealth nor to revolutionize society." This is an important consideration when South African corporatism is assessed.

If I understand him correctly, Claus Offe placed the emphasis somewhat differently. In this view corporatism achieves its purposes through the way in which it operates rather than through its products or outcomes. Corporatism is then seen not so much as an attempt "to satisfy demands but to channel them so as to make them satisfiable'' (Offe 1985:225). It is, according to Offe, a form of policy management which leans towards *structural policies*, as distinguished from *conjunctural policies*. Structural policies are designed for the ''shaping of political input and economic supply,'' whereas conjunctural policies are aimed at maximizing the responses to ''as many of the specific demand inputs as possible.'' Conjunctural policies are associated with liberal-pluralist politics. The role of the state here is, if not neutral, that of intervention. Structural policies are associated with conditions of relatively deep social, economic, and political division. Here the search is not for satisfying as many demands as possible, but for structuring demands in order to achieve social harmony (Offe 1985:223–226). The role of the state becomes that of matchmaker for a ménage à trois in which it is itself a partner.

According to Offe (1985:224–226), the type of political rationality which is associated with structural politics follows the imperative of keeping output constant, that is, at levels that are considered reasonable or affordable, while channelling demand inputs in a way that appears compatible with available resources.

I am not sure how strictly one should read this proposition. It seems that it would not make much empirical sense to think of it as an accurate representation of particular realities. A regime that emphasizes structural policies is unlikely to persist if the management of demands does not, within some reasonable period of time and to some materially adequate extent, meet some of the demands of ''strategic actors'' (Magagna 1988:421) and if the outputs do not respect the underlying interests. Furthermore, if the notion that output must be kept constant is to be taken literally, Offe was here swimming against a stream of analyses which indicated economic growth as a major objective of corporatism. So it must be a matter of analytic approach—or, as Offe (1985:226) says, ''conceptual distinction''—rather than empirical assertion, to claim predominant regime and institutional tendencies in one direction or another.

Proponents of corporatism for South Africa hold that the structure of SA society renders politics of the liberal-pluralist type very hard to achieve. It is depicted as a social structure marked by a large measure of coincidence between deep class and race divisions and an economic structure which is characterized by extreme inequalities of opportunity and reward. Major political and economic formations tend to mobilize around the divisions, and so reinforce them. The structure and performance of the South African economy are, furthermore, such that responses to the conflicting demands of class and race-based interest groups cannot be maximized. If the economy performed better, the divisions would presumably be easier to bridge. The problem for democracy is both to survive these unfavorable conditions and to reshape them (see, for example, Nedlac 1995:1, 3). Hence the designers of the pact which cleared the way for both the interim and the 1996 constitutions leaned in the direction of consensual political mechanisms.

Nedlac embodies an attempt to replicate in the socioeconomic field the achievements of negotiation in the political field. The experience of successful negotiation is reinforced through an interpretation of the history of Nedlac's immediate predecessors, the National Manpower Commission (NMC) and the National Economic Forum (NEF) (see, for example, LMC 1996:189). At least in terms of the publicly announced intentions, Nedlac was thus designed as a place and a process where conflicting class and other group interests can be accommodated, if not reconciled. In this sense, Nedlac is intended for demand management. But the ruling party's, and its allies', conceptions of the goals of corporatism go beyond a mere accommodation of interests. From the ANC's point of view, corporatism has the purpose of effecting quite thoroughgoing social and economic transformation:

> The democratic state must . . . seek to forge a democratic and equitable partnership as well as a working relationship between labour and capital in the interest of social stability, economic progress, reconstruction and development (ANC 1996:7).

In South Africa, terms such as *reconstruction* and *development* frequently indicate the goals of radically reducing inequalities and redressing inequities which are seen as the results of apartheid and the associated ''racial capitalism.'' As expressed in a document prepared for the party's 1997 Congress, the ANC's ''programme of social transformation'' specifies the

> strategic objective of the National Democratic Revolution . . . [as] the creation of a united, non-racial, non-sexist and democratic society. This in essence means the liberation of Africans in particular and black people in general from political and economic bondage. It means uplifting the quality of life of all South Africans, especially the poor (ANC 1997:5).

Traditional ANC policy incorporated measures such as the nationalization, or some other form of socialization, of banks, mines and industrial monopolies. Current ANC policy accepts (some would say in deference to global economic forces) neoliberal claims regarding the indispensability of private capital and the close integration of national economies into global capitalism. This is reflected in the claim that a ''dialectical relationship with private capital as a social partner for development and social progress'' is of particular importance, given the centrality of ''capital . . . to the creation of the material conditions which make it possible continuously to improve the conditions of life of the people,'' as well as the mobility of capital that comes with globalization (ANC 1996:10). However, such purposes, like those formulated for Nedlac, cannot be served by policies that ''keep output constant.'' They require firm efforts to achieve and sustain substantial rates of economic growth. The main social partners share this view. But that is as far as agreement goes.

IV. CORPORATISM: PRAGMATIC OR IDEOLOGICAL?

Justifications for *liberal* corporatism are usually (and can be only?) pragmatic (Anderson 1990; Cawson 1983; Magagna 1988; Offe 1985). Pragmatic arguments for corporatism have also been advanced by some of its South African proponents (notably Baskin 1993; also Adam et al. 1997). However, the arguments tend to refer to the necessity to overcome deep social divisions through negotiation rather than to matters such as inflation, recession, and the like. Moreover, the recent acrimony between the main participants suggests the continued influence of ideologically informed positions in the ranks of labor and business and within those of the ruling ANC and its allies, the South African Communist Party (SACP) and Cosatu.

Arguments offered by union-linked intellectuals usually project some form of socialist order. Geoff Schreiner (1991:135), for example, insisted that Cosatu's involvement in the restructuring of one of Nedlac's predecessors, the NMC, should "culminate in socialism" and that "any agreement with any party should be measured in terms of its value in taking the working class towards this objective." Writing in their personal capacities, Schreiner and his colleague Adrienne Bird (1992:33) proposed "a multi-partite model" instead of the "corporatist model," which they saw as disadvantageous for socialism, because

> moving towards socialist democracy requires an ongoing process of empowering institutions and organizations, outside of the state, to participate in the decision making process and thereby to exercise meaningful control over that state between elections.

This is in clear contrast to arguments which posit pragmatic responses to deficiencies of governance in pluralist democracies as motives for corporatism (see Section V). Schreiner and Bird (1992:26–27) supported a modified corporatism—not for functional or pragmatic reasons but as an instrument for fundamental political and socioeconomic restructuring.

Support for corporatism has never been unanimous in the union movement. To the left of the movement, Karl von Holdt (1993:48) has argued that corporatism is inimical to democracy and socialism, that it alienates the mass membership from the union leadership, that it is elitist, that it "co-opts labour into accepting the economic perspectives of capital," that it "stabilises capitalist society and ensures that the labour movement cannot struggle for socialism," and so on. The SACP, which wields considerable intellectual influence within the labor movement, has been quoted as "stating categorically that 'social democratic pacts between organised labour and capital are destined to fall far short of providing basic remedies. Such pacts . . . leave the capitalist class in the economic and political driving seat' " (Eidelberg 1997:10).

In fact, Cosatu has never committed itself to corporatism (or multipartism) over other instruments for achieving its purposes. This has been emphasized by speakers with regard to every major Cosatu campaign of the past decade. In particular, the tactics of "mass action" are viewed and used as instruments to strengthen the federation's negotiation positions, rather than as actions which could be replaced by negotiation. In Schreiner's (1991:37) words,

> Cosatu should never allow itself to accept limitations on the right to mass action *as a precondition* for participating in the institution [NMC]. This is quite different from the case where, *as part of* a social contract negotiated *through* the institution, the trade union movement could conceivably agree to restrict strikes (on certain issues, for a certain period of time) provided the trade-offs were sufficiently attractive.

The major business organizations have supported Nedlac and its predecessors both formally and actively. But their support has always been ambivalent. Moreover, their support does not imply support from the wider business sector. From the right of the spectrum, influential shapers of business opinions such as *Finance Week* and the *Financial Mail* have been consistent opponents of corporatism, even while the peak business associations have cautiously endorsed tripartite forums. One of the *Financial Mail*'s concerns is the possibility that corporatist processes in general, and social accords in particular, would undermine the freedom of business to pursue profit. It has repeatedly expressed opinions to the effect that "wage and price decisions have no place in a collective forum. They should be taken on commercial criteria gleaned from competitive experience" (*Financial Mail* 1996). Similar views are regularly publicized by *Finance Week*, whose editors see Nedlac as an instrument of Cosatu. Such expressions of free-market ideology are linked to a concern about the fate of democracy in the presence of corporatism and "Cosatu's political strikes."

To the extent that business organizations do support institutionalized corporatism, some are wont to express the view that it should be preceded by "a common economic vision between business and labour" (*Mail & Guardian* 1996; SALB 1996:27–28). How the visionary chicken and the institutional egg could be so sequenced is not clear. Nevertheless, the view that Nedlac is an important instrument in building "an economic dimension of reconciliation and nation building" in South Africa and in "helping to build confidence and trust amongst leading players in the economy" has been a recurrent message from the executive director of the South African Chamber of Business (Sacob), Raymond Parsons (1997). However, Sacob economic policy director Ben van Rensburg's response to the question whether macroeconomic policy should be discussed in Nedlac, is also revealing:

> It is the ruling party's responsibility to lay down macro-economic policy. That cannot be negotiated. It can be negotiated between the parties who form

> part of the ruling party. It's the job of the ANC and its constituents to sort out any differences, that's not for Nedlac (SALB 1996;27–28).

It may or may not be significant that he commented after the government announced its macroeconomic strategy for *Growth, Employment and Redistribution* (Gear; see below). Gear was favorably received by business but roundly condemned by labor. Labor reiterated its support for the *Reconstruction and Development Plan* (RDP).

Hard ideological divisions are not conducive to successful concertation. A number of theorists have suggested that there seems to be affinity between a broadly ''Keynesian consensus'' and effective corporatist interest intermediation (for example, Lehmbruch 1979:170–172). In South Africa ''left-Keynesian thinking'' is expressed in Cosatu's economic plan, *Social Equity and Job Creation* (Webster and Adler 1997:15). In contrast, business, speaking through the South Africa Foundation's document *Growth for All*, supports mainstream neoliberal policies. In its turn, the governing ANC has repeatedly affirmed commitment to its own plan for Gear. This plan is distinctly neoliberal (see Natrass 1996; Le Roux 1997). However, the government claims that Gear is an instrument for the implementation of the RDP (Mbeki 1996); that it ''seeks to be a macroeconomic framework for and not against the RDP'' (ANC 1997a:4). This means, in effect, that the ANC presents Gear as sharing the redistributive objectives of the RDP.[1]

The basic differences between the major interest groups are as follows: Business supports capitalism. The ANC has largely dropped the label *socialism* from its lexicon, but pursues broadly redistributive goals which it claims to be achievable within the framework of a ''mixed economy'' (see ANC 1997). The ANC's labor ally, Cosatu, remains explicitly socialist (Cosatu 1997). Business seeks economic growth through a free market, while labor seeks economic growth through socialist redistribution. Business and, to some extent, government see economic growth as a precondition for the reduction of social inequalities. Labor believes that the causal nexus lies in the opposite way.

Consistent with the doctrinal substance of socialist socioeconomic transformation, union speakers have offered, as was indicated above, the procedural ideal of participatory democracy in justification for corporatism. In the words of Nedlac's executive director, himself formerly a leading figure in the union movement,

> Participatory democracy in SA suggests a policy-making process which engages those affected by such policies more frequently than an election every five years. The Nedlac process deepens democracy by bringing the partners, on a continuing basis, into the policy-making process (Naidoo 1996).

This, like the views of the LMC (1996:198), echoes a position advocated by (amongst others) sociologist Eddie Webster, who has for long been closely involved in the union movement. Webster and his colleague Glen Adler have also suggested—in apparent contradiction of many scholarly assertions that corporatism decreases the autonomy of trade unions—that corporatism, in conjunction with modes of collective action, is a vehicle for enhancing union autonomy (Webster and Adler, 1997:3). The question that must follow is, What should the accompanying balance of power between the "social partners" be?

V. CORPORATISM: RESOLVING PROBLEMS OR IMPOSING UNION HEGEMONY?

According to Offe's analysis, corporatism in advanced capitalist societies came about in response to problems which could not be contained by party-based parliamentary governments. The problems derive from the power exerted by large organized interests within the *laissez-faire* environment of liberal pluralism, i.e.,

- Organized interests undermine parliamentary government
- Organized interests cause fiscal problems by overbidding
- Organized interests' freedom to pursue their own agendas undermine long term planning processes
- Conflicts between powerful groups are often settled at the expense of weaker or less organized groups (Offe 1985:227–228; see also Lehmbruch 1979:156).

Insistence on purely party-based parliamentary government would require measures to bar interest organizations from "politics." Offe (1985:230) points out that such a remedy is inappropriate in complex economies because of the power which interest organizations wield over their constituents and the value of the information which they control. Hence, Offe (1985:231–232) claims the "political problematic" shifts from debates about the desirability of specific policy goals (like containing inflation) to ways of structuring power between interest organizations.

Offe (1985:242–247) further explored the need for corporatism by considering the performance of party functions and problems of bureaucratic policy making and implementation. With regard to the former, he argued that it is problems concerning party government rather than the domain specific characteristics of macroeconomic policy which underlie corporatist arrangements. As Offe saw it, political parties in the GFR were not particularly efficient in performing functions such as interest aggregation and policy formulation. One of the notable attributes of these parties was that there were more divisions within them than between them. This, Offe argued, was a consequence of the broadening of electoral bases and the dilution of ideological positions. It was "this condition of often unresolvable intra-party conflict, plus the concomitant instability of governing party coalitions" which gave rise to corporatism (Offe 1985:243, 244).

In contrast, Lehmbruch (1979:151, 154, 155) interpreted corporatism in terms of ''increasing *structural differentiation and functional specialization* of the political system brought about by certain requirements of consensus-building specific to economic policy making.'' When parties are incapable of providing appropriate policies, the function of consensus building may shift to the ''subsystem of interest associations.'' Interestingly, and perhaps contradictorily, the incapable parties nevertheless remain important for the successful pursuit of concertation because, Lehmbruch (1979:167, 169) hypothesized, ''consensus-building in liberal corporatism is . . . largely contingent on the degree to which the labor union movement is integrated into the process of policy-formation.'' This, in turn, seems to depend on unions gaining power ''by the channel of the party system.''

Despite some ambiguity about the importance of political parties in corporatism, Both Offe's and Lehmbruch's propositions direct attention to the association between party-union coherence and the prospects for corporatism. I want to look at the South African case at two ''levels'': first, and briefly, with regard to problems of governance, and then with regard to relations between the ANC and the unions.

In South Africa, corporatism and debates around it do focus strongly on structuring relations between social partners and, by implication, within the wider society. But if South African corporatism is a response to problems of governance, then all the problems did not arise from the dynamics of a liberal pluralist society, nor from those of the very young postapartheid political and party systems. Rather, pragmatists tend to justify corporatism in terms of the prediction that governance would be extremely difficult given the legacies of apartheid and the structural conditions mentioned before (section I of this paper). They also justify it with reference to the vulnerability of the economy and the state to centrifugal interests and ideologies and to the ''demands'' of a globalized economy (for example Adam et al. 1997:140–159).

However, I would argue that elements within the unions see the purpose of corporatism differently. For them corporatism is about gaining decisive control over policy agendas and policy formulations. This position was already visible in their insistence, during the interregnum of 1990 to 1994, that the decisions following from corporatist processes should be binding rather than merely advisory (Webster and Keet 1992:15). Furthermore, influential elements within the unions are not concerned about problems of governance as such, but about enforcing a particular programmatic direction in order to achieve, ultimately, a socialist transformation of society. In other words, and in contrast to a suggestion by Schmitter (1985:40) about the emergence of corporatism in advanced capitalist societies, corporatism in South Africa may well be connected to ''the elevated goal of attaining hegemony and imposing a distinctive 'class project' upon the whole of society.''

Business, on the other hand, seems to vacillate between the objectives of advice and control, depending on perceptions of how well government's policy declarations fit its own. During the interregnum, as during apartheid, the nationalist government was concerned about its sovereignty and preferred purely advisory processes. The ANC government from time to time threatens to govern alone, and did in fact do so when it took the BCEB to Parliament. However, it is hamstrung by divisions in its own ranks and that of the *Tripartite Alliance*.

As noted before, corporatism was formally conceived as a vehicle for resolving conflict between capital and labor. But the fate of corporatism is likely to depend quite significantly on the ability of the ruling party to accommodate its own internal divisions and those between the parties to the Tripartite Alliance.

The ANC is itself a complex of formations. It rules as a member of the Tripartite Alliance comprising itself, the SACP, and the major trade union federation, Cosatu. Furthermore, the ANC's membership and support overlaps with that of its two allies. This overlap is especially significant at the level of the higher party organs and the national, provincial, and local levels of government. For example, after the 1994 general elections the SACP claimed that four cabinet ministers and one deputy minister owe allegiance to it, and that it also had two of seven provincial premiers and between 50 and 80 MPs as members. Between 1994 and 1998 some 20 Cosatu officials were members of parliament, and many more sit in provincial and local legislatures (of which a significant number are likely to be the same individuals claimed by the SACP).

Differences of interest base and ideology *between* the constituent organizations of the Alliance are, given the interlocking membership and directorates, presumably repeated *within* the ANC as well as within the other two components of the Alliance. Moreover, Cosatu includes unions which prize their autonomy, which are not equal in influence within the federation, and which possess their own, often divergent traditions of relating to (or diverging from) the ANC and which have their own ideological proclivities.

The Alliance and its unity of purpose has been partially dependent on the existence of common enemies: the nationalist government and apartheid. The extent to which opposition to capitalism and capital was uniform among members of the Alliance is less easy to say. The general tendency was to equate capitalism and apartheid with each other and to lean in a socialist, or at least a "mixed economy, state-welfarist," direction. With the ANC in power, the issues have become more involved and this is showing its effects in intensifying disputes about economic strategy.

The dissatisfaction of influential factions within Cosatu with the government has found strong expression in a November 1996 discussion paper presented to the Cosatu executive. The document alleges the absence of a "systematic Alliance approach to the development of policy" and the existence of a generally reactive approach to policy on Cosatu's side (Cosatu, 1996:2, 3). In fact, members of the Cosatu leadership have often threatened to make the federations' support for the ANC's 1999 election campaign conditional on such agreements (Cosatu 1997:Chapter 3).

In the 1996 Cosatu discussion paper it was claimed that the lack of joint planning within the Alliance resulted in ''conflicting perspectives emerging between the democratic forces'' in various state institutions and in Nedlac. The document then proposed, not a social pact between the social partners as per corporatism, but an intra-Alliance

> Accord or National Agreement on strategic issues, as well as a programme to implement these at different levels of government. This would clearly bind the Alliance forces to actively pursue this agenda in all areas. It would guide, for example, Cosatu and the Government as to how to approach the various issues in Nedlac, rather than the two parties going there with separate and often competing agendas. It would remove the impression that the government is acting as a neutral referee sitting above the other players in society. Rather the mass bias of government and its commitment to the implementation of a particular programme, would be the lodestar which would clearly reflect the mandate of the majority party. The Alliance would therefore openly mobilise the people for the implementation and defence of agreed programmes at the level of Parliament, Nedlac and other areas of governance (Cosatu 1996:13).

The clear intent of the authors is to ensure the elveation of an intra-Alliance agreement above any possible agreement between state, capital and labor, and to subject forums such as Nedlac to the purpose for which ''they were historically conceived—as fora for transformation'' (Cosatu 1996:21). Capital must itself be subjected to the Tripartite Alliance and its pruposes:

> While there is a common perception that accords have to be between unions, government and business, there is no law which says that Accords have to be negotiated with capital. Obviously an Alliance agreement will for its implementation need certain elements to be negotiated with capital . . . but this is different from deciding that you want the agreement itself to be tripartite in character (Cosatu 1996:15).

The discussion document did foresee a need for agreement with business on what it calls ''state regulated activity'' such as incomes and wages policy, investment policy and supply side measures (Cosatu 1996:18–19). However, those are mostly areas in which South African business has—consistent with a quite purist free market ideology—traditionally opposed government intervention. Moreover, the authors of the document makes the intention to subordinate business to labor quite clear by presenting the union vision of labor-business agreements as

> an opportunity for business to make reparations for the devastation they have created in this country over the apartheid years; to create social stability;

> to allow people to benefit from economic participation; and to themselves ultimately share in the huge economic expansion which they have been too short sighted to invest in (Cosatu 1996:21).

In the South African case a union way of looking at corporatism is thus to see it as a vehicle for radical transformation strategies. Pushed to its logical conclusion, the view is, however, one which rejects corporatism. It projects state intervention to force socialist transformation under union leadership. Neither Offe's nor Lehmbruch's propositions have much bearing, then, on the way in which the Cosatu discussion document perceives the relationship between the unions, the governing party and business. If corporatism is engineered consistently with the discussion document, the task of Nedlac will be limited to mediating concessions to business as a political subject, rather than that of brokering agreements with business as a social partner.

The fact that government has tended to ignore business demands on core aspects of labor legislation could indicate that reality approximates the union ideal of subjecting business. And Cosatu is, after all, a member of the governing Alliance—even if the Alliance does not operate to it's satisfaction. On the other hand, Cosatu did not achieve all it wanted from, for example, the BCEB. Moreover, ANC leaders have claimed—despite subsequent denials by Cosatu leaders—that the ANC's December 1997 congress endorsed Gear. This came shortly after President Mandela apologized to the 1997 Cosatu conference for the government's unilateral adoption of Gear, but also made it clear that, in "situations, where no agreement [between the partners of an alliance] is possible . . . the ANC government's view will hold sway" (*Sunday Independent* 1997; Mail & Guardian January 1998). ANC President Thabo Mbeki's mid-1998 addresses to Cosatu and SACP structures clearly implied the ANC's impatience with criticism from its partners, as well as the warning that the ANC is the senior partner. But—as Mbeki's statements also implied—the partners are interdependent (Mbeki 1998, 1998a). Awareness of this interdependency is likely to suppress intra-alliance conflicts until after the general elections scheduled for 1999.

An October 1998 meeting between ANC, Cosatu and SACP leaders announced that budget deficit targets set by Gear would be eased. However this, and the Jobs Summit, left Gear's neoliberal thrust largely intact. But Gear remains in place alongside government policies which protect an inflexible labor market. The seeming anomaly may reflect a fragile balance of power and preferences between the relevant interest groups. But it may also reflect the ANC government's compromise between global economic interests and national union demands.

In short, it is not clear whether or not current policy processes and directions indicate the ascendancy, or otherwise, of Cosatu's hegemonic ideals. Nor do they unambiguously indicate the balance of interests within a putative corporatist system. What is clear is that there are strong ideological disagreements between the unions and organized business and within the governing Tripartite Alliance. It is also clear that influential elements within the major union federation see corporatism as an instrument for working class hegemony.

VI. FROM CONFLICT TO ORDER OR FROM ORDER TO CONFLICT?

Can corporatism contribute to political order in a deeply divided society? Offe's views are useful once again. He asked, "In what direction and within what limits will corporatist changes in political structure affect the intensity of social and political conflict?" (Offe 1985:253).

In answer, Offe suggested three scenarios—stable corporatism, noninstitutional political conflict, and balancing the class bias of corporatism (Offe 1985: 253–258). All three scenarios contain propositions which are relevant to answering the question in the South African context. For present purposes, attention to the first scenario will suffice. "Stable corporatism is a condition in which corporatist political structures succeed in providing an interest-group consensus unchallenged by radical or 'immoderate' demands or tactics of conflict" (Offe 1985: 253).

In other words, stability depends on the legitimacy afforded the corporatist system, and legitimacy becomes a critical variable "when significant material advantages are at issue" (Offe 1985:253–254). The achievement of stable *liberal, democratic, or social* corporatism becomes a very hard project when there are serious differences amongst the social partners—and within society generally—about the interests to be represented, the issues to be intermediated, the political means to be used and, ultimately, the goals to be achieved. A fundamental dilemma is that

> corporatism, in order to be stable, must not only continually generate consensus; it must first of all presuppose consensus, that is, a solid and undisputed acceptance of a certain mode of interest representation and accommodation (Offe 1985:254).

A somewhat similar point has been made by Nedlac's executive director (Naidoo 1997). However, as Sacob spokespersons have argued, in South Africa it is also a pre-existing consensus about substance, and not only one about process, that is lacking. This takes us back to where we started. The pragmatic supporters of corporatism advocate it as a means of generating consensus. But it seems clear that the content of the desired consensus, as well as the associated processes, will be heavily disputed for some time to come. If that is the case, we may not yet be crossing the threshold from conflict to order.

The power of local interest organizations and the force of ideology must not be overestimated. The caution applies particularly in the case of a relatively weak economy which is highly dependent on inflows of foreign investment and which is thus sensitive to global economic and political forces. South Africa has been analyzed in overly ideological terms before, but the pragmatists were much closer to the mark. It could be that Cosatu's militant and ideological face indicates a decline in its power. It could be that the manifest ideological disagreements will be undermined surreptitiously but certainly by the many negotiated agreements which are being reached on specific issues at many levels of society, and in Nedlac itself. But there is also the possibility that pragmatism could wither away if the material conditions for its sustenance cannot be created. Then ideology rules the political process and the prospects for order recede.

ENDNOTE

1. In 1994, the ANC presented the RDP as the basis of its electoral campaign. The RDP originated in the union movement, but went through some revision (from relatively socialist to a position reaching towards neoliberalism before it was released for ''electoral approval'' (see Webster and Adler 1997). In essence, it proposed economic growth, social development, and the redistribution of wealth and opportunities, with the state playing a guiding role in the economy. Analysts disagree whether or not the RDP has any Keynesian elements. See Adelzadeh (1996) and Le Roux (1997).

REFERENCES

Adam, H., Van Zyl Slabbert, F., and Moodley, K. (1997). *Comrades in Business. Post Liberation Politics in South Africa* Cape Town: Tafelberg.

Adelzadeh, A. (1996). Growth and development: labour and business perspectives on development. in J. Baskin (ed.), *Against the Current. Labour and Economic Policy in South Africa* Johannesburg: Ravan Press.

ANC. African National Congress. (1996). The state and social transformation. Discussion document. Internet, http://www.anc.org.za.

ANC. African National Congress. (1997). All power to the people! draft strategy and tactics of the African National Congress. Internet, http://www.anc.org.za

ANC. African National Congress. (1997a). The core values of the RDP—a discussion document. Internet, http://www.anc.org.za.

Anderson, C.W. (1990). *Pragmatic Liberalism*. Chicago: University of Chicago Press.

Baskin, J. (1993). *Corporatism: Some Obstacles Facing the South African Labour Movement*. Johannesburg: Centre for Policy Studies, Social Contract Series, Research Report No. 30.

Baskin, J. (1996). The social partnership challenge. In J. Baskin (ed.), *Against the Current. Labour and Economic Policy in South Africa*. Johannesburg: Ravan Press.

Cawson, A. (1983). Functional representation and democratic politics: towards a corporatist democracy? In G. Duncan (ed.), *Democratic Theory and Practice*. Cambridge: Cambridge University Press.

Cosatu (1996). A draft programme for the Alliance. Discussion paper presented to the Exco. Internet, http://www.anc.org.za

Cosatu (1997). *The Report of the September Commission on the Future of the Unions*. Internet, http://www.anc.org.za.

Crepaz, M.L.M. (1992). Corporatism in decline? *Comparative Political Studies 25*:2.

Eidelberg, P.G. (1997). The Tripartite Alliance on the Eve of a New Millennium: The Congress of South African Trade Unions, African National Congress, and the South African Communist Party. Paper presented to the Institute for Advanced Social Research, University of the Witwatersrand, March 1997.

Financial Mail 6 July 1996.

Lehmbruch, G. (1979). Liberal corporatism and party government. In P.C. Schmitter and G. Lehmbruch (eds.), *Trends Toward Corporatist Intermediation*. Beverly Hills: Sage Publications.

Le Roux, P. (1997). The growth, employment and redistribution strategy (GEAR): a critical discussion. *Africanus 27*:2.

LMC. Labour Market Commission. (1996). *Restructuring the South African Labour Market. Report of the Commission to Investigate the Development of a Comprehensive Labour Market Policy*. Pretoria: Government Printer/Department of Labour.

Magagna, V.V. (1988). Representing efficiency: corporatism and democratic theory. *Review of Politics* 50.

Mail & Guardian, 2 to 9 June 1996.

Mail & Guardian, 16 to 22 January 1998.

Mbeki, T. (1996). Statement of Deputy President Thabo Mbeki at the National Assembly, Cape Town, 14 June 1996. Internet, http://www.anc.org.za.

Mbeki, T. (1998). Statement of the President of the African National Congress, Thabo Mbeki, at the meeting of the Central Committee of Cosatu, Johannesburg, June 22, 1988. Internet, http://www.anc.org.za

Mbeki, T. (1998a). Statement of the President of the African National Congress, Thabo Mbeki, at the 10th Congress of the SACP, Johannesburg, 2 July 1988. Internet, http://www.anc.org.za.

Naidoo, J. (1995). Interview with Louise Stack. *TransAct 2*:7.

Naidoo, J. (1996). How Nedlac tackles the tasks it faces will determine the future. *Business Day* 29 January.

Naidoo, J. (1997). Don't fracture the negotiating forum. *Sunday Times* 21 September.

Nattrass, N. (1996). Gambling on Investment: Competing Economic Strategies in South Africa. Paper presented to the Conference on Democracy in One Party Dominant Systems, Cape Town and Arniston, 6–9 November.

Nedlac. (1995). Discussion on a Framework for Social Partnership and Agreement-Making in Nedlac. Internet, http://www.nedlac.org.za

Nedlac. (1995a). Founding declaration. Internet, http://www.nedlac.org.za.

Offe, C. (1985). The attribution of public status to interest groups. In J. Keane (ed.), *Disorganized Capitalism*. Cambridge: Polity Press.

Offe, C. (1985a). Two logics of collective action. In J. Keane (ed.), *Disorganized Capitalism*. Cambridge: Polity Press.

Parsons, R. (1997). Don't write Nedlac's obituary just yet. *Sunday Independent Business* 7 October.

Pretoria News 4 September 1997.

Pretorius, L. (1994). The head of government and organized business. In R. Schrire (ed.), *Leadership in the Apartheid State. From Malan to De Klerk*. Cape Town: Oxford University Press.

Pretorius, L. (1996). Relations between state, capital and labour in South Africa: towards corporatism? *Journal of Theoretical Politics 8*(2).

SALB. (1996). Interview with Ben van Rensburg. Nedlac courting consensus. *South African Labour Bulletin 20*(6).

Schmitter, P.C. (1985). Neo-corporatism and the state. In W. Grant (ed.), *The Political Economy of Corporatism*. London: Macmillan.

Schmitter, P.C. (1989). Corporatism is dead! Long live corporatism. *Government and Opposition 24*(1).

Schreiner, G. (1991). Fossils from the past: resurrecting and restructuring the National Manpower Commission. *South African Labour Bulletin 16*(1).

Schreiner, G. and Bird, A. (1992). COSATU at the crossroads: toward tripartite corporatism or democratic socialism? *South African Labour Bulletin 16*(6).

Shubane, K. and Shaw, M. (1993). *Tomorrow's Foundations? Forums as the Second Level of a Negotiated Transition in South Africa*. Johannesburg: Centre for Policy Studies, Social Contract Series, Research Report No. 33.

Sunday Independent 21 September 1997.

Von Holdt, K. (1993). The dangers of corporatism. *South African Labour Bulletin 17*(1).

Webster, E. and Keet, D. (1992). National economic forum. Parallel to Codesa? Interview with Sam Shilowa. *South African Labour Bulletin 16*(3).

Webster, E. and Adler, G. (1997). Exodus without a map? The labour movement in a liberalising South Africa. Unpublished draft paper.

4

International Financial Institutions and the Politics of Structural Adjustment

The African Experience

Mark Owen Lombardi and Sandip Singh Sahota
University of Tampa, Tampa, Florida

I. INTRODUCTION

> The experience of several developing countries with the IMF supported adjustment programs seem to indicate that the strategy supported by the IMF is conducive to improved economic performance.
>
> IMF Occasional Paper 118[1]

> But when these general principles get translated into specific programs for action, there seems to be a wide gulf between the fund's and the African's diagnosis of the true cause of the malaise, the prescriptions of remedies, the perceptions of how the remedies will work in practice, and the periods within which a more healthy and normal condition will return.
>
> C. M. Nyirabu, Governor, Bank of Tanzania[2]

As Africa wallows in its second decade of adjustment, the effectiveness of Structural Adjustment Programs (SAPs), commonly advocated by International Financial Institutions (IFIs) is still being challenged. For two decades, numerous African governments have resorted to agreements with the International Monetary Fund (IMF) and the World Bank that have left them reeling from the shock therapy of adjustment policies.[3] Today most African states are mired in a cycle of debt, unemployment, capital drain, declining exports, and limited investment as SAPs have thus far failed to adequately respond to Africa's needs. The result is a grave social, political, and economic crisis as fragile states struggle to halt declining standards of living and the social and political decay that often accompany economic collapse.

In addition to the economic burden imposed by SAPs, IFIs (and their Western governmental sponsors) linked political liberalization to debt relief and foreign investment resulting in significant political transformations further destabilizing the African political economy. Many African regimes are now grappling with the demands of IMF/World Bank conditionalities that bring short-term economic upheaval (e.g., rising unemployment, spiraling inflation, reduced state subsidies, and decreased currency value) and subsequent political instability while simultaneously heeding calls for political liberalization along Western democratic lines. In several respects Africa now lies prostrate on the operating table of Western medicine where the "cure" seems as bad as if not worse than the "disease."

Governments and people across Africa are trying to comprehend how this Structural Adjustment Regime (SAR) will address their daunting economic problems when its effectiveness in halting Africa's economic decline has thus far been suspect. They are also struggling with political and social reforms amidst an economically unstable environment adding to the sense of disorder and decline that already pervades the African political landscape. How will the two-pronged attack on the economy and the political structure be successful when the intellectual linkage of political liberalization and economic development so prevalent in Western discourse remains questionable? How can Africa withstand the "remedy" of SAPs when the very fabric of some societies is splitting apart under the imperious weight of economic collapse? Can Africa find any path out of the SAR in an era of political marginalization by the North and victorious arrogance in the Western capitalist world? Are there avenues of reform and change that can halt the decline and at least give Africans a fighting chance at sustainable development? What are the ways that NGOs, local states, and IFIs can refashion strategies that will meet both economic and political realities in various African societies? It is these and other questions that we attempt to analyze in this paper.

This paper briefly traces the development of the SAR and its central precepts. We then outline the general economic performance of the SAR in the 1980s and '90s. From this performance, we analyze the politics of adjustment policy focusing on the intellectual linkage of political liberalization and economic reforms and its fundamental problems in conceptualizing the relationship between NGOs, the State, and the people. Finally, we evaluate the theoretical basis of neo-liberalism and explicate how the theoretical assumptions underlying the SAR are flawed. Our central thesis is that the SAR is flawed at the theoretical level due to its spurious assumptions regarding the linkage of economic and political liberalization along with its orthodox and somewhat antiquated notion of inter-actor relationships within the international political economy.

II. STRUCTURAL ADJUSTMENT DILEMMA

The current adjustment dilemma has its roots in the continental and international policies and prescriptions of the 1970s.[4] With the oil shocks of 1973 and 1979, many African states were faced with severe balance of payment deficits that underscored several problems festering in the political economy of the continent. First among these was a consistently poor performance in export earnings due to commodity pricing and declining market share.[5] Second, the colonial/neocolonial African cash crop economy (coffee, cocoa, etc.) suffered greatly under the weight of technological diversification, Transnational Corporate (TNC) control of the market, and price instability thus limiting or destabilizing export earnings even for some of Africa's better and more stable economies (e.g., Ivory Coast, Ghana, and Zambia).[6] Third, import substitution policies suffered under the burden of reduced revenues and thus failed to produce any positive impact.[7] Finally, Africa's problems with increasingly exploitive state governments became more pronounced as leaders and regimes developed more intrusive methods of maintaining power in periods of scarce resources.[8] Corruption and dubious state-managed projects usurped excess capital which fed a financial crisis as export earnings dropped and investment declined. All of these factors coalesced in the third decade (1970s) of African independence forcing many states to either undergo fundamental reform or opt for the international quick fix of access to liquidity, i.e., borrowing.

Most regimes chose to borrow their way out of this dilemma and indebtedness significantly increased in the late 1970s and '80s.[9] African governments borrowed extensively in order to maintain public expenditures and social programs as well as pay for the increased energy costs of the second oil shock of 1979.[10] Regimes hoped to repay the debt from the income generated by commodity exports, but drops in commodity prices coupled with suspect investment policies provided little of the projected return.[11] In a relationship not unlike that of a loan shark and his prey, Africa was caught in a spiraling debt cycle forced to borrow more and more to finance internal budget and balance of payments deficits as well as social programs and infrastructure projects begun in better times.

At this juncture the IFIs changed the nature of African borrowing and investment by linking short-term lending pakages to correct balance of payment deficits with structural reforms in the economies of target states.[12] These conditionality programs introduced by the IMF and later adopted by the World Bank and private banking institutions became the operating framework for the current SAR.

The concept of conditionality "refers to agreements between donors and recipients that exchange financial transfers (either grants or loans) by the donors for policy changes by the recipients."[13] Central to this set of policies is the goal of creating an impetus for investment flows from largely private sources, based in the North. It dictates that loans are made with explicit policies that members must follow if they are to receive assistance now and in the future.[14] In addition, a set of implied conditions exists regarding a state's future access to markets and investment capital from the West. These conditions were attached in an effort to provide confidence to lender nations (First World) that measures were being taken to stabilize the balance of payment equilibrium in the short run and restructure the economy to preempt further economic breakdowns. Minimally, the application of conditionalities was designed to secure the creditor nations that make up the IMF that the environment within target African economies would facilitate the return of the borrowed capital. Through both Paris and London Club meetings, private banks followed IMF program recommendations and this closed any loopholes for African regimes and their access to capital.

During this initial period of conditionality, many African states turned to the World Bank for access to linkage-free capital, only to experience IMF style conditionality as well. The World Bank adjusted its policies after many internal reports had concluded that "poor outcomes of Bank projects, particularly in the agriculture sector, has been due to inappropriate overall economic policies that thwarted even the best designed projects."[15] Following the lead established by the IMF, the Bank proceeded to develop mechanisms that increased Bank authority and policy influence in target states under the assumption that greater Bank control meant greater chances for success.[16]

Due to this shift in emphasis, the 1980s saw the evolution of what Pollin calls a "Creditor Cartel." The IMF, World Bank, and private banking institutions all acted to insure that borrowing states were following IMF prescriptions. The IMF became the stepping stone or gatekeeper for additional funding from other sources. "The fund's power does not depend on its net lending. . . . It arises because a highly conditional agreement with the fund is a pre-condition for a Bank SAP, a Paris club debt re-scheduling and enhanced bilateral assistance."[17] A positive rating from the IMF can open the door to much needed foreign exchange and investment in the local economy. Whereas a negative or noncompliant rating could be detrimental to the economic future of any developing nation that was dependent on that foreign capital. Thus, the IMF became the de facto arbiter of foreign investment and external development assistance in African states who entered the SAR. As a lender of last resort and now as a lender of choice, the IMF had the ability to pick and choose who to help and at what expense to the sovereign nation.

This new strategy of increased IFI influence and expanded authority over the design and impact of economic programs was adopted for a variety of political, economic, and ideological reasons. First, foreign investors (private banks and companies) were reluctant to lend capital due to the economic failures (perceived and real) in the 1970s. Second, the IMF and other lending agencies increasingly felt that short-term loans at relatively high interest rates would not provide the long-term basis for economic stability, so they demanded more structural remedies to accompany monetary assistance. Third, Afro-Marxism was showing signs of strain in the 1980s and politicians in the First World saw a good opportunity to promote capitalist development, undermining Socialist-Marxist doctrine and the regimes that espoused it (Angola, Ethiopia, Mozambique, Congo, Benin, and Tanzania). Fourth, the 1980s saw a resurgence of orthodox neoliberalism emerge in several key states (United States, United Kingdom, Germany) ushering in a more economically conservative climate that was reflexively imposed on most IFIs. Finally, resources from alternative sources (i.e., Second World) were drying up and thus the West became the only secure bankroll for short-term African development and hence political survival. Consequently, the international community surmised that Africa's economic problems were structural (i.e., statist-ideological) and that political opportunities were ripe for capitalist reform.

The influence of the IFIs on many African regimes was unquestionable. Several African states were increasingly dependent on the IFIs for support and financial backing (Ivory Coast, Mauritania, Congo, and Mozambique). IFIs enjoyed access to local leaders, conducted policy dialogues, and provided the assistance needed to establish the initial foundation for change. Realistically, countries had no choice but to accept the new nature of funding with its underlying conditions. In the face of such intense criticism, the IMF argued, that "the decision to approach the fund for help is a sovereign decision of the member and cannot be taken for granted."[18] But how sovereign is such a decision when the fund is the only source of financial backing and plays the decisive role in an increasingly collusive credit/corporate system serving as the gatekeeper to capital, TNC investment, and ultimately expanded trade?

As the SAR took hold and the ideological vigor of Afro-Marxism and its second world supporters faded, neoliberalism reigned supreme. IFIs and their Western governmental sponsors saw themselves as both victors and vindicated in the great ideological tug-of-war with communism. Consequently, advocacy of free markets, decreasing statism, increased privatization, and democratization became basic lessons of the collapse of Communism. Almost by fiat, political and economic leaders embraced the rather simplistic notion that not only was Communism defeated but capitalism was vindicated and in fact "proven" to be right and universally applicable. Therefore, economic and later political conditionalities became de facto "right and necessary" and part of the West's unchallenged answer to development.

III. STRUCTURAL ADJUSTMENT LEGACY

Despite the IFI's strong-arm tactics and the infusion of much needed foreign exchange into the political economy of Africa, the 29 states that adopted SAPs have had a largely negative experience with adjustment.[19] During the initial stages of adjustment in the late 1970s, the annual mean rate of growth in per capita income in Africa was 0.8%; from 1980 to 1989 this dropped to −2.2%.[20] Africa's total debt, which was $55 billion in 1980, almost tripled to $160 billion in 1992 with an average debt service ratio of 25%.[21] By 1990, Africa's external debt as a percentage of GDP averaged between 60% to 80% with Mozambique, Tanzania, Ivory Coast, Mauritania, and Zambia saddled with at least 250%.[22] In the 1980s the average commodity prices for manufactured goods was the lowest this century with 25% of Africa's purchasing power lost.

Africa's dismal performance continued into the 1990s, and "though it had been hoped that Africa's economic performance would show improvements beginning in the early 1990s, economic growth in the 1992–1993 biennium remained lackluster."[23] By 1994, there was still no visible sign of economic recovery or significant improvement in the standards of living which fell through the 1980s.[24] This decline continued on all fronts into 1995 as Africa was gripped by a steadily declining share of world economic production coupled with population growth rates twice the global average.[25] In the 1990s the debt service ratio for African states rose to 40%.[26] Foreign investment lagged behind IFI projected levels, and both the agricultural and manufacturing sectors have contracted throughout the decade (1990–1996).

There is no evidence that the performance of low-income countries in terms of balance of payments, growth, inflation, savings, and investment was any better for countries with Fund programs than those without.[27] In a study of adjustment experience in 1980–1981, the Fund admitted that only a minority of countries in Africa had met their targets. Only five countries out of 23 reached their growth targets, 13 out of 28 reached their inflation targets and 11 out of 28 reached their trade targets.[28] Further, in 1980 and 1982 there was a significant increase in the number of SAPs in Africa that were breaking down in their first year, from 36% to 58%.[29]

In two recent studies done by Sayre Schatz, data show that this trend has continued through the 1990s. Both analyses argue that those with and without fund programs have no appreciable differences in economic performance. And these studies further show that promised economic growth did not materialize for those who embraced SAPs. Schatz argues that "it is appropriate to say that no relationship was shown between fiscal reform and economic growth."[30]

In the halls of corporate and state power, it was widely believed that the solution to Africa's crises rested in the market. Therefore SAPs in Africa have "generally involved a set of policy reforms to maximize reliance upon markets in domestic and external trade and capital flows, minimize the governments interventionist role; by reducing public ownership, subsidies and regulation, and improve the state's efficiency in allocating and using resources."[31] Such a neoliberal approach was intended to open markets to free competition and strengthen the African economic structure bringing with it much needed private capital investment, growth, and inevitably development across the board. But the SAPs only served a self-fulfilling purpose. Donors and the IFIs concerned about their investments and past development failures hoped that through effective conditionality, structural changes would take place and subsequently African economies would provide a return on their costly investments. Yet, First World investment did not materialize.

Commercial investment declined as the need for strategic minerals and other like products in Africa dissipated with the end of the cold war coupled with the development of alternative sources elsewhere. In addition, the opening of the Asian and Eastern European markets in the wake of Communism's collapse, decreased Africa's bargaining power further. In 1992, investment in the continent totaled $500 million, or less than 2% of total investment in the Third World.[32] In fact, investment in Africa declined over the past two decades for reasons mentioned above as well as TNC concerns regarding political stability and economic commitment to capitalism and adjustment reforms. Essentially, the promised return on Africa's "investment" in the SAR has not materialized further undermining the adjustment process.

While primary criticism of the SAR came from African leaders and scholars, the United Nations Economic Commission for Africa (UNECA) grappled with the problem trying to explain the downward trend. UNECA examined all of the facets of Africa's economic position and concluded that the common Western rationale for poor performance including political instability, ethnic conflicts, hostile economic investment climate, and climatic catastrophe in agriculture (in other words, *indigenous events and trends*) simply did not explain the economic performance of the continent.[33] The UNECA along with several other African and non-African critics place a great deal of the blame on the SAR. The UNECA report of April 1994 states, "Despite several years of implementing SAPs, most African countries are yet to outgrow the narrow confines of inherited colonial economic structures or to diversify their economies beyond the groundnuts, coffee, cocoa-based system of monoculture."[34] Economic indicators show that even the most basic goal of the adjustment programs to set up a free market that produces incentives for the accumulation of capital and the best allocation of resources has yet to be achieved.[35]

In addition, the political and social ramifications were not lost on the UNECA study as concerns were raised regarding the impact of poor growth and economic contraction on African political systems and culture. As the March 1995 UNECA report states,

> The fact is that most of the African countries have yet to take even the first faltering steps in the transition towards a modern industrial and technological society. They have remained essentially the fragmented mini-states they were when they achieved political independence, increasingly incapacitated and unable to sustain even a modicum of modern institutions and consistent gov-

> ernment policies, not to talk of the lack of an overall enabling environment for development.[36]

Africa's economic decline and experience with the SAPs is well documented. Much of the past political and scholarly debate centered around two fundamentally different conceptions of responsibility underlining the philosophical and political differences between Africa and the West. The neoliberal, Western argument is that local regimes failed to adequately embrace the SAR. IFIs and the G10 contend that Africa's poor results reflect the indigenous problems and mistakes made by African regimes. They contend that local factors must account for the failure as IFIs continue to insist that only the consistent, long-term application of SAPs will work. As part of this argument, a few so-called success stories are offered up, especially Ghana, to vindicate this argument. In addition, when marginal signs of economic growth are identified, they are offered as proof of the righteousness of SAPs and the need for continued application.

Technically, IFIs are partially correct in their criticism of African implementation. With empty coffers and limited financial support to back the drastic changes sanctioned by the IFIs and donors, many African regimes have failed to fully implement conditionality programs.[37] Also, several African regimes mired in corruption-ridden systems (Nigeria) or outright kleptocracies (Zaire) have served to work against the goals of the SAR through their own mismanagement. However, blaming Africa for a failure to "try hard enough" misses the larger issue, which is that the very limitations that inhibit regimes from fully adopting SAPs are complex and interconnected and not merely a product of one artificially demarcated area (domestic) over another (international).

The second viewpoint which comes from Africanists and many African regimes argues that SAPs failed in terms of program conceptualization and the values and assumptions inherent in the neoliberal model of development. Many contend that the root of the problem lies in the inherent Western centric concepts of "development," "market," and "progress" so embedded in the logic of capitalism. These critics maintain that it is nearly accepted as scientific fact and an article of faith that capitalism, modernization, and development are synonymous and that such policies that promote the market are inherently positive even if success is not readily apparent.[38] They contend that Western models of industrial development are predicated on uniquely Western political and social experiences that took place in a fundamentally different international system. In addition, this view contends that a mythology of laissez-faire state involvement that has gained credence in the West is largely untrue. They point to the nurturing and outright partnership between 19th and 20th century state governments and private industry designed to promote and encourage indigenous economic growth.

These two orthodox views have been challenged in recent years both within the IFI and African political community and among scholars themselves. More moderate and balanced views have emerged within the World Bank and among

African leaders as blame and ideology has given way to pragmatism and problem solving. Recent World Bank reports have shown a more moderate wing of the IFI community willing to accept the shared responsibility of failure while Africanists have shunned some of the more leftist rhetoric of years past for a more pragmatic problem-solving approach.[39]

This has opened up the dialogue to include heretofore underrepresented perspectives including the potential of NGO-state partnerships based on local projects aimed at sustainable development. While the exact nature of NGO-state relations is ambiguous and potentially combative (IFI-state relations) the argument rests on the assumption that by developing locally defined goals and exploring ways that NGOs and states can work together to satisfy them, true developmental progress can be made.[40] This argument is particularly persuasive when examined at the grassroots level, where community development and empowerment are fostered by NGO work in selected states. This builds on the more pragmatic voices emerging in both the IFI and African communities.

IV. POLITICS OF ADJUSTMENT

With the collapse of the Soviet Union and the democratic reforms in Eastern Europe and Latin America, IFIs and their Western donors placed increasing emphasis on political liberalization. While political reform has always been a rhetorical demand of Western states, it was usually sacrificed on the altar of bipolarity and cold war power politics. Some African leaders were particularly adept at playing to the fears of Western states in order to maintain a degree of political integrity from Western interference.[41] This situation is no more. Africa has faded as a cold war battleground to combine with its decreasing importance in the international division of labor.[42] Thus Africa is faced with the unenviable position of reversing an endless spiral of underdevelopment and economic decline in an era of increasing marginalization and intensifying pressures for political liberalization.

The end of the 1980s saw a new push directed at reforming the political arena to better accommodate development. Part of this grew out of the conservative, neoliberal resurgence in the West as the virtues of ''democratic capitalism'' were increasingly voiced in Washington, London, and elsewhere. The central precept was and is that capitalism and political liberalization are mutually reinforcing processes and indeed linked together such that changes in one must naturally coincide with reform in the other.[43]

This approach among the IFIs and Western donor states evolved into an assumed precondition for capital and investment. For IFIs the process was clear: ''economic liberalization creates sustained growth, growth produces winners as well as losers, winners will organize to defend their newfound welfare and create sociopolitical coalitions to support continued economic reform.''[44] Good governance or political conditionality as it's referred to, was highlighted by the World Bank in its report *Sub-Saharan Africa: from Crisis to Sustainable Growth*, in which it stressed the importance of good governance as a key lesson of the adjustment process.[45] It is our assessment, and the conclusion of many scholars who criticize the SAR, that this supposed lesson of the adjustment era fundamentally undermines the entire developmental process and the credibility of the IFIs. Essentially, the inherent conflict of interest that political reform and economic restructuring pose for a developing nation-state, can cause the balancing of both measures for a preference for the status quo that benefits primarily IFIs and TNCs. In addition, there is no guarantee that political liberalization leads to new actors predisposed toward either democratic development or sustained economic growth.

The neoliberals downplay or omit large dimensions of political economy that go to the heart of development in Africa and indeed throughout the Third World.[46] This inevitably leads IFIs to base their policies and approaches on their own flawed and alien sociopolitical assumptions. The ramifications of not factoring in the political process or the role of the state in the developmental approach can be disastrous. There is a need for a clearly defined role for the state within the economic sphere. In a young economic market with little free-flowing capital, the state can be instrumental in effectively operating and assisting the market in its growth and management. But IFIs, following neoliberal thinking, ensure that the state is distanced from the economic markets and limited in its powers of control or persuasion. Such policies ignore the need for embryonic African states to take responsibility in the developmental capitalist process. The lessons of development from the NICs, Japan, and even to some extent the Western world, clearly indicate the need for a strong apparatus that can lay the necessary foundation for the growth and the continued perseverance of capitalism. As Barnet and Cavanagh point out, ''So far only those developing countries with governments *strong enough* to set their own priorities have succeeded in becoming industrial nations.''[47]

This continued denial of a state role within the African economy is based on the neoliberal bias against the state that has gained such credence in the wave of recession, failed domestic social policies, and flourishing corporate power since the 1970s. Neoliberals increasingly downplay the potential for supportive partnership arrangements between state and market.[48] The examples of successful state roles in the economy are voluminous (China, Japan, South Korea, Taiwan, parts of Europe, and North America). But why is it that in Africa the state is limited in the role it is allowed to play? IFIs indicate that the political instability of African regimes and their institutions requires a de-linking of the two structures. But what is to suggest that a young market can survive in a highly competitive international arena without any guidance and assistance by the government? As Callaghy points out:

> Ultimately, it is not just a question of finding the "precarious balance" between state and market or state and society, but rather searching for the precarious trialectic between state, market and the international arena. Such a precarious trialectic can be very difficult to achieve, however, as domestic politics and the international arena have a habit of presenting new and unexpected challenges for African rulers.[49]

Arguably, the establishment of market principles in Africa would need all the support of the government to provide political stability and legitimacy as well as a partial shield for the domestic market from the domination of the international sector. However, the reflex-like neoliberal fear of the state underlies a fundamentally paternalistic Western assumption that African governments do not have the administrative capacity, leadership sophistication, or self-discipline to solve complex economic and political problems.[50] Consequently, IFIs see political liberalization as a necessary "growth step" in order for SAPs to succeed. Yet, as Manor eloquently points out, "It makes one wonder whether the tendency of some neoliberals to exclude things political from their analyses is not intended to distract attention from the inconveniently draconian implication of their prescriptions."[51]

The neoliberal approach further argues that it is precisely previous state intervention that accounts for Africa's deep economic crisis. For example, conservative/orthodox elements in the World Bank are adamant in their "view that the chief cause of Africa's problems lies in the market distortions that have been generated by internal political forces using state policies to serve their own short term interests."[52] But such classic neoliberal thinking is criticized by Robert H. Bates, who concedes "some validity in the neo-liberal view that political activity imposes economic costs upon society, but this idea so dominates the analysis that it obscures deeper political questions."[53] What is the role of the state? Can neoliberalism provide the answers to the political questions that it ignores? What is the proper role of the state vis-à-vis both international and domestic NGOs? The focus on the economic sphere is a fundamental part of IFI development analysis, yet the underlying political equation is nonchalantly ignored. As Bates remarks, neoliberals display, in their theories, "their disinclination to engage in serious analysis of things beyond their narrow economic concerns."[54] Charles Harvey further "calls attention to the compelling array of political difficulties which assail attempts by African states to implement structural adjustment programs and which the neo-liberals tend to ignore."[55] This continued disregard of the political implications of their economic policies only clarifies the fundamental problem with neoliberalism, which is that policy prescriptions are often highly specific and artificially compartmentalized thus ignoring the realities of political economy in an international context.

Not only has the conditionality attached to the aid and financing increased but the introduction of the concept of good governance and political reforms has only further exposed the shortcomings of the neoliberal approach. The SAR has served to increase political tension and decay thus creating a very real and stark contradiction. Miles Kahler, writing about Cameroon, labeled this contradiction as the ''orthodox paradox'': ''the expectation that governments will implement reform programs that undermine the foundations of their political support and that a capable state is necessary to implement a neo-classical strategy of economic adjustment.''[56] The application of SAPs has proven to be politically problematic and their impact seems *to increase* (and not decrease) the need for a stronger state at the helm of government and the economy.

The example of Ghana is illustrative here. Ghana is consistently offered as the IFI/World Bank success story and proof of the viability of SAPs.[57] Ironically, Ghana has managed to see some strong economic growth of late and developmental achievements under the lengthy and quasi-authoritarian tutelage of Jerry Rawlings. This is the same Jerry Rawlings who was branded a leftist by the West, undermined by the Western intelligence agencies, and castigated for his strong statist bias during his first tenure as ruler of Ghana. Arguably, Ghana's success can be attributed as much to his authoritarianism in the midst of significant political and economic reform as to the strength of adjustment policies. The contradiction of using Ghana as the prime example with the neoliberal arguments regarding political and economic liberalization is stark.

The tension between committed reformers and those resistant to the reform process has been extreme. The apparent belief that governments will implement reform programs that will jeopardize their political existence seems to be an acceptable cost for the IFIs even though logic dictates that this reality will only serve to decrease the chances for success.[58] Most politicians understand the need for economic development, albeit defined in different terms, yet the immediacy of political realities (i.e., coalition building, ethnic balancing, bureaucratic inertia, and the like) often pushes developmental decisions to the background (witness Nigeria and Zambia). It is not the intention or the desire of African regimes to become increasingly dependent on the IFIs and Western donors, but political conditionality has only increased their dependence on external actors asking for widespread reform in exchange for limited concessions.

Can political and economic liberalization coexist? Can Africa pioneer successful changes in its economies and political systems? One area that has drawn IFI attention and perhaps has the seeds of answers to these questions has been the agricultural sector. IFIs have promoted economic reforms that would benefit the agricultural industry hoping that success would prompt the creation of an agricultural elite sparking political constituencies that would champion their own interests. The World Bank's focus on agriculture was evident in the Berg Report in which it stressed that ''agricultural output is the single most important determinant of overall economic growth'' and attributed it as ''the principal factor underlying the poor economic performance of the countries of the region.''[59] Consequently, IFI policies hoped to foster the creation of an agricultural elite that would take the political challenge, protect their interests, and subsequently, under the capitalist credo, reap political as well as economic benefits.

However, once again, a lack of understanding of agricultural interests and their various political, social, and ethnic cleavages left the political empowerment of agricultural constituencies unrealized.[60] African farmers have been unable to form any significant interest groups or effectively challenge the political structure.[61] Within the majority of Africa the political impact of agrarian societies is limited due to the "very high transaction costs (e.g., to peasants in the rural areas) that prevent certain constituencies from mobilizing to support a government that has embarked on significant reforms to help agriculture."[62] Robert H. Bates divides the blame for the political weakness of the agrarian producers between the African state and its urban bias and the "atomistic" and isolated nature of rural producers.[63]

Overall, the success of these agricultural policies, aimed at increasing the output of the economies and catering toward what the World Bank feels is the comparative advantage of the African economies in the commodity markets, has failed. The IFIs placed incredible importance on the need for higher prices for agricultural products which in turn would stimulate long-term agricultural growth. But Africa's collective experience brought about "universal agreement that non-price factors such as inadequate infrastructure, lack of availability of key inputs such as irrigation or fertilizers, and unproductive research and extension services are significant constraints on supply."[64] The increased incomes of the farmers, a direct result of the increase in production prices, had a limited impact since consumer product development and availability did not keep pace.[65] In addition, Western agricultural products heavily subsidized by their governments are routinely dumped on the world market undercutting local producers, artificially lowering the market value and flooding local African markets with cheaper alternatives.

Overall, the IFIs focus on increasing commodity prices worldwide has not achieved the desired results.[66] African governments find it increasingly difficult to offer higher prices to stimulate production growth. Critics of the World Bank's policies had "warned against the fallacy of composition in the [Bank's] prescriptions: the argument that what is good for one country acting individually is not necessary beneficial if a number of countries simultaneously pursue the same policy."[67] Masterminded by the World Bank, output across the world has risen while the consumption is unable to keep pace. This basic misconception challenges the sociopolitical culture of the World Bank, the neoliberal approach that advocates standardized policies for all nations and highlights the needs for a new approach that realizes the impact such fundamentally flawed policies can have on Africa's political economy.

V. THE SAR AND THE FAILURE OF NEOLIBERALISM

Fundamentally, African governments in the SAR are now required to balance competing international and domestic forces like no other states on Earth. They are required ''to live up both to people's expectations, raised by old and new populist policies, and to IMF conditionalities—at the same time!''[68] Political reforms are being used as criteria for the continued aid or assistance from the IFIs and the donor community. The blanket application of this policy disregards the dilemma ''that sound economic policy is inconsistent with consolidating the political legitimacy, particularly of countries in the process of transforming disintegrating dictatorships into some kind of pluralist democracies.''[69] The crisis in development is a clear indication of a political crises of the sovereign nation-state. Neo-liberal theory advocates a limited role for the state yet, the application of its policies that have grave economic and political ramifications presupposes a strong state that can face the resolve of its people. The introduction of political reforms that question the legitimacy of the very government that is responsible for the economic reforms is a clear formula for political instability. Concomitantly, IFI policies incite the nationalistic feelings of the indigenous people by introducing reforms that are ethno-centric, foreign and have an immediate negative impact on their economic prosperity while questioning the credibility and legitimacy of the government in power that attempts to enforce their reform packages. Are the IFIs not undermining their own success?

Let's disregard the nature of the political regimes in Africa and their relative desire for political liberalization. The underlying assumption of IFI policy is that intrusive, exploitative authoritarianism in Africa caused its economic decline and only economic restructuring and political liberalization will alleviate it. This extension of neoliberal economic logic is further based on the presupposition that the African state is homogenous and autonomous from other internal and external actors as well as formally in control of the mechanisms of power, i.e., it is a sovereign state in the Western-centric model. As Herbst points out, these theories

> cannot make a substantive contribution to the demarcation of the African state because these theories are . . . incapable of taking account of African realities. Only an eclectic mix of guidelines which are grounded in the realities of how the economy and the state actually work . . . will usefully suggest what the state should do for whom.[70]

Therefore, IFIs need to reexamine the nature and role of the state in the African political and social context and in the international environment. This involves a fundamental reworking of development theory along with theories of state sovereignty already providing fruitful results.[71] Before a constructive approach can be deployed in Africa, the role of the state needs to be redefined within this political and economic climate. Also, NGO-state-market relationships need explication based on the assumption that economic development is part of a planned partnership between these groups and forces and not a competitive, artificial division between them. As Bienfeld points out in his analysis of the African crisis with adjustment, IFI ''policy prescriptions do not inspire confidence. Not only are the policies that are now proposed as solutions for Africa essentially the same policies that have led to the present debacle, but they also contain internal contradictions which undermine their plausibility and reveal fatal flaws in the underlying analysis.''[72]

The continued failure of SAPs stresses the need to reform those policies and shift our focus and assumptions to actors that may be crucial in the developmental process. For example, the role of tribes in Africa has been downplayed and ignored in the Western developmental model. For centuries tribes have been an integral part of African society and culture. They have enjoyed power, prestige, and the respect of their followers and the recognition of their counterparts. ''In the absence of strong nation-states and national political structures, the tribe may be an effective intermediary association providing services and brokering relations between the individual, family or clan and the national government.''[73] In the SAR, the role of the indigenous people is relegated to spectators or, more accurately, individualized consumers. The inclusion and extended empowerment of these groups may add credibility to the developmental process and help to develop more indigenous, grassroots solutions to local economic issues. In the face of constant criticism and rejection, IFIs need to abandon their ethnocentric policy domination and consider the implication their sociopolitical culture has on the developmental process.[74] Vrajenda Raj Mehta unequivocally rejects the conceptualization of a single and universal pattern of development. He suggests an ''indigenous process of change attuned to the needs of individual societies: A welcome process of social change in all societies is a process towards increasing self-awareness in terms of certain normatively-defined goals in each case, and that the direction of the process and the definition of ends is largely defined by the society's own distinct history and the way of life.''[75]

Wiarda goes on to argue:

> Hence, we need to see local indigenous institutions not necessarily as dysfunctional or doomed to history's ash cans but frequently as viable and necessary in the society we are studying, as filters and winnowers of the modernization process, as agencies of transition between traditional and modern, and as a means for reconciling and blending the global with the indigenous, the nationalist with the international.[76]

Therefore IFIs need to *Africanize* their agenda and minimize their own sociopolitical culture that is breaking down IFI policy prescriptions and severely affecting the future development of Africa.

In an attempt to provide more complex and indigenous plans for economic reform and increase the true dialogue between IFIs and African regimes, the United Nations Economic Commission for Africa (UNECA) has created an alternative framework to SAPs.[77] Their document, *African Alternative Framework to SAPs* (AAF-SAP), was created in an effort to counter the IFIs prescriptions.[78]

The functionalist attitude of the ECA which gathers its policy advisors from all over Africa is criticized as vague and too conservative in some respects, yet it still attempts to bridge the gap between orthodox viewpoints on both sides and therefore fits within a more pragmatic school of thought.

The ECA contends that the "center of the alternative framework is the human dimension," something the World Bank has ignored till recently.[79] The three major characteristics of the framework directly counter the approaches advocated by the neoliberal school of thought. First, the framework is not universally applicable. Rather the ECA's framework relies on the individual characteristics of the respective countries and their peculiarities. The goal is to design country-specific programs selecting appropriate policy instruments. Second, "as a human-centered framework, [the framework] implies full democratization of all aspects of economic and social activities and in all stages from decision-making to implementation."[80] Finally, in line with the past emphasis on economic unity and integration, the framework advocates intercountry cooperation and coordination of developmental policies and adjustment programs aimed at transforming the economies.[81]

Unfortunately, the differences between the ECA and the IFIs continue. Can there be a compromise in their policies? Will the IFIs consider the ECA a partner in the process toward the development of Africa or will the ECA continue to search for credibility and legitimacy within international financial circles? As the failure of SAPs becomes clear in Africa, the role of the ECA as an agency representing the interests of Africans from a neutral standing becomes increasingly important. The IFIs need to establish a working relationship between all parties; the states, the ECA and other NGOs, and the people that will bear the brunt of their changes. A better-coordinated approach with increased input will help in the creation of realistic policy prescriptions that could be more effective and create the foundation for growth and sustained development. They "must find a proper balance between global, holistic and interdisciplinary approaches on the one hand, and studies on economic sectors, individual countries and particular issues on the other hand."[82]

VI. CONCLUSION

"There can be no instantaneity, no quick fix. Our friends from the West often forget that true democracy became a reality in most of their countries only recently. A holier-than-thou attitude with harsh conditionalities will only abort the process."[83] SAPs have failed for a variety of reasons. Despite debates about specific policies and unique examples and conditions, it can be argued that the SAR was doomed from the very outset due to its sociopolitical culture, flawed neoliberal approach, and the undermining effects of linking political and economic liberalism. Amidst this reality, external support from donors and the IFIs has been limited and well below the required amount to sustain SAPs. Further, the international climate is not very forgiving. In an age where the neoliberal approach is basking in its hegemony, as evidenced by the lack of a contradictory approach, Africa is hostage to its worst excesses while facing increasing marginalization.

By critiquing the double barrel approach of political and economic liberalization, it is not our intention to discount the values of democracy, good governance, or political responsibility. Africa and its people can benefit from the implementation of such values within their own distinct sociocultural framework. Our argument is that by linking economic reforms with political liberalization, IFIs are undermining the very goals they purport to embrace. Democracy is not for the faint of heart and if competing pressures are not properly balanced, polarization and conflict will surely result. African countries need to decide their own priorities and fashion strategies that are mutually reinforcing of both political and economic development goals. This may involve concurrent reform strategies or perhaps more the promotion of one over the other. That decision is certainly best left to local decision makers.

Through a balanced analysis of the effects of conditionality, one must accept that a change in policy assumptions and prescriptions is in order. The need for economic development is still necessary. But the persistent linking of both political and economic reforms has to be questioned. ''Any justification of democratic regimes that relies on their development capabilities is at best weak . . . assertions by external factors to the effect that economic liberalization requires political liberalization ring more than a little hollow.''[84] External actors need to understand the constraints on Africa better and realize the impact of these hollow restrictions. They also need to examine and ultimately embrace the unique partnerships that must evolve among NGOs, state governments, and IFI/TNC entities based on mutual responsibility and pragmatism. If a new understanding on the part of IFIs is not achieved and a new dialogue is not developed, then marginalization, political decay, and social upheaval will prevail. The responsibility for that phase in Africa's development will most surely be a shared one.

ENDNOTES

1. IMF. Sub-Saharan Africa-Growth, Savings and Investment, 1986–1993. M.T. Hadjimichael, D. Ghura, M. Muhleisen, R. Nord, and E.M. Ucer. Washington: IMF Occasional Paper 118, January 1995:1.
2. Nyirabu, C.M. (1986). A view from Africa: 2. In G.K. Helleiner (ed.), *Africa and the IMF*. Washington: IMF, 1986:32.
3. For an overview see Ravenhill, J. (1993). A second decade of adjustment: greater complexity, greater uncertainty. In T.M. Callaghy and J. Ravenhill (eds.), *Hemmed*

In: Responses to Africa's Economic Decline. New York: Columbia University Press. Commins, S.K. (ed.). (1988). *Africa's Development Challenges and the World Bank*. Boulder, CO: Rienner. Ghai, D. (ed.). (1991). *The IMF and the South—The Social Impact of Adjustment*. London: UN Research Institute for Social Development. Onimode, B. (ed.). (1989). *The IMF, The World Bank and The African Debt: The Social and Political Perspectives*. London: Institute for African Alternatives/Zed Books. Clapham, C. (1996). *Africa and the International System: The Politics of State Survival*. New York: Cambridge University Press.

4. Many would argue that its roots are colonial in nature and much literature exists to support that thesis. For the purposes of this paper we will concern ourselves only with the postindependence period beginning with the decade of the seventies.
5. Chazan, N., Mortimer, R., Ravenhill, J. and Rothchild, D. (1992). *Politics and Society in Contemporary Africa*, 250–267. Boulder, CO: Lynne Rienner Publishers.
6. *Ibid*., pp. 258–267.
7. UNIDO. (1985). *Africa in Figures*. New York: UNIDO/LS517. Riddell, R. (ed.). (1990). *Manufacturing in Africa*, 250–258. London: James Currey. Chazan, pp. 250–258.
8. Gordon, D.F. (1993). Debt, conditionality, and reform. In T.M. Callaghy and J. Ravenhill (eds.), *Hemmed In*: *Responses to Africa's Economic Decline*, 97. New York: Columbia University Press.
9. McCarthy, S. (1994). *Africa*: *The Challenge of Transformation*, 139. London: I.B. Tauris & Co. Sachs, J. (ed.). (1989). *Developing Country Debt and Economic Performance*. Chicago: University of Chicago Press. Humphreys, C. and Underwood, J. (1989). The external debt difficulties of low-income Africa. In I. Husain and I. Diwan (eds.), *Dealing with the Debt Crisis*. Washington: World Bank.
10. Gordon, p. 95.
11. *Ibid*., pp. 95–96.
12. World Bank. (1981). *Accelerated Development in Sub-Saharan Africa*: *An Agenda for Action*. Washington: World Bank.
13. Gordon, p. 105.
14. IMF. The IMF—Its evolution, organisations and activities. A.W. Hooke. Washington: IMF Pamphlet Series No. 37, 2nd ed., p. 12.
15. World Bank. (1981). *Accelerated Development in Sub-Saharan Africa*: *An Agenda for Action*. Washington: World Bank. *Adjustment in Africa*: *Reform*, *Results and the Road Ahead*. Washington: World Bank. *Adjustment Lending—An Evaluation of Ten Years of Experience*. Washington: World Bank.
16. *Ibid*.
17. Green, R.H. (1993). The IMF and the World Bank in Africa. In T.M. Callaghy, and J. Ravenhill (eds.), *Hemmed In*: *Responses to Africa's Economic Decline*, 58. New York: Columbia University Press.
18. Erb, R.D. (1986). A view from the Fund. In G.K. Helleiner (ed.), *Africa and the IMF*, 23. Washington: IMF.
19. See Schatz, S.P. (1996). The World Bank's fundamental misconception in Africa. *Journal of Modern African Studies 34*(1):239–247, Schatz, S.P. (1994). Structural adjustment in Africa: a failing grade so far. *Journal of Modern African Studies 32*(4): 679–697. Clapham, 1996, pp. 163–186. Evans, P. (1992). The state as problem and

solution: predation, embedded autonomy, and structural change. In S. Haggard and R.R. Kaufman (eds.), *The Politics of Economic Adjustment*. Princeton: Princeton University Press.

20. Data for 1970s from *Accelerated Development in Sub-Saharan Africa*. (1991). Washington: World Bank. Data for 1980–1989 from *World Development Report 1990*. New York: Oxford University Press. Projected figures from *World Development Report 1992*, 32. New York: Oxford University Press.
21. Data from the International Monetary Fund. (1991). *World Economic Outlook May 1991*, 16. Washington: IMF.
22. McCarthy, p. 139.
23. UNECA. (1994). Biennial Report of the Executive Secretary 1992–1993. E/ECA/CM.20/4, April, p. viii.
24. UNECA. (1994). Economic Report on Africa 1994. E/ECA/CM.20/2, April, p. 3.
25. UNECA. (1995). Report on the economic and social situation in Africa, 1995. E/ECA/CM.21/3, March, p. 2.
26. McCarthy, pp. 137–140.
27. Loxley, J. (1984a). *The IMF and the Poorest Countries*. Ottawa: North-South Institute.
28. Zulu, J.B. and Nsouli, S.M. (1984). Adjustment programs in Africa. *Finance and Development 21*(1):5–9.
29. Loxley, J. (1986). Alternatives approaches to stabilization in Africa. In G.K. Helleiner (ed.), *Africa and the IMF*, 117–147. Washington: IMF.
30. Schatz, p. 684.
31. Sandbrook, R. (1991). Economic crises, structural adjustment and the state in sub-Saharan Africa. In D. Ghai (ed.), *The IMF and the South—The Social Impact of Adjustment*, 95. London: UN Research Institute for Social Development.
32. World Bank. *World Bank Development Report*, 1994, pp. 202–203.
33. "The economic regression has lasted far too long in the African region without real recovery or accelerated upturn for it to be explained only in terms of political instability, ethnic conflicts, the unfavorable international economic environment or fluctuations in weather-constrained agricultural output. See UNECA. (1995). Report on the economic and social situation in Africa, 1995, E/ECA/CM.21/3, March, p. 3.
34. UNECA. (1994). Economic Report on Africa 1994. E/ECA/CM.20/2, April, p. 2.
35. World Bank. (1994). *Adjustment in Africa: Reforms, Results and the Road Ahead*, 2. Washington: World Bank.
36. UNECA. (1995). Report on the Economic and Social Situation in Africa, 1995. E/ECA/CM.21/3, March, p. 4.
37. Ravenhill, J. (1993). A second decade of adjustment: greater complexity, greater uncertainty. In T.M. Callaghy and J. Ravenhill (eds.), *Hemmed In: Responses to Africa's Economic Decline*, 19. New York: Columbia University Press. Dorraj, M. (1995). *The Changing Political Economy of the Third World*, 85–114. Boulder, CO: Lynne Rienner Publishers.
38. Callaghy, T.M. (1993). Political passions and economic interests: economic reform and political structure in Africa. In T.M. Callaghy and J. Ravenhill (eds.), *Hemmed In: Responses to Africa's Decline*, 464–471. New York: Columbia University Press.

39. World Bank. (1989). *Sub-Saharan Africa: From Crisis to Sustainable Growth.* Washington: World Bank.
40. For discussions of this see Fowler, A. (1991). The role of NGOs in changing state-society relations: perspectives from Eastern and Southern Africa. *Development Policy Review 9*(1), 53–84. Gibbon, P. (1992). The World Bank and African poverty 1973–1991. *Journal of Modern African Studies 30*(2), 216–220.
41. Some of the masters of this game included Mobutu of Zaire, Numeri of the Sudan, Hassan of Morocco, and of course the Afrikaner regime of South Africa.
42. Callaghy, T.M. (1994). Africa: falling off the map? *Current History* p. 31.
43. For a discussion of this perspective and those that have espoused it see Kohli, A. (1986). Democracy, and Development. In J.P. Lewis and V. Kallab (eds.), *Development Strategies Reconsidered*. New Brunswick, NJ: Transaction Books. Rueschemeyer, D., Stephens, E.H., and Stephens, J.D. (1992). *Capitalist Development and Democracy*. Chicago: University of Chicago Press.
44. Callaghy, 1994, p. 34.
45. World Bank. (1989). *Sub-Saharan Africa from Crisis to Sustainable Growth: Long Term Perspective Study*. Washington: World Bank.
46. Manor, J. (1991). Politics and neo-liberals. In C. Colclough and J. Manor (eds.), *State and Markets—Neo-Liberalism and the Development Policy Debate*, 308. Oxford: Clarendon.
47. Barnet, R.J. and Cavanagh, J. (1994). *Global Dreams, Imperial Corporations and the New World Order*, 354–355. New York: Simon & Schuster.
48. *Ibid.*, p. 312.
49. Callaghy, T.M. (1993). Political passions and economic interests: economic reform and political structure in Africa. In Callaghy and Ravenhill (eds.), *Hemmed In: Responses to Africa's Economic Decline*, 477. New York: Columbia University Press.
50. *Ibid.*, p. 313.
51. *Ibid.*, p. 314.
52. Bienfeld, M. (1988). Dependency theory and the political economy of Africa's crisis. *Review of African Political Economy 43*, 69.
53. Bates, R.H. (1988). *Macro-Political Economy in the Field of Development*. Working paper 40, Duke University Program in International Political Economy, Durham, NC.
54. *Ibid.*, p. 23.
55. Manor J. (1991). Politics and neo-liberals. In C. Colclough and J. Manor (eds.), *State and Markets—Neo-Liberalism and the Development Policy Debate*, 318. Oxford: Clarendon.
56. Kahler, M. (1990). Orthodoxy and its alternatives: explaining approaches to stabilization and adjustment. In J.M. Nelson (ed.), *Economic Crises and Policy Choice*, 33–61. Princeton: Princeton University Press.
57. For discussions of Ghana as success story, see Chand, S.K. and van Til, R. (1988). Ghana: toward successful stabilisation and recovery. *Finance and Development 25*(1), 32–35. Hodges, T. (1988). Ghana's strategy for adjustment with growth. *Africa Recovery 2*(3). Rothchild, D. (ed.). (1991). *Ghana: The Political Economy of Recovery*. Baltimore: Johns Hopkins University Press.
58. Callaghy, T. (1993). Political passions and economic interests: economic reform and

political structure in Africa. In T.M. Callaghy and J. Ravenhill (eds.), *Hemmed In: Responses to Africa's Economic Decline*, 478. New York: Columbia University Press.

59. World Bank. (1981). *Accelerated Development in Sub-Saharan Africa—An Agenda for Action*, 45. Washington: World Bank.
60. For examples of this analysis see Hirschman, A.O. (1970). *Exit, Voice and Loyalty*. Cambridge, MA: Harvard University Press. Bates, R.H. (1981). *Markets and States in Tropical Africa*. Berkeley: University of California Press.
61. Their success in Kenya and Zimbabwe can be attributed to the strong settler community that has remained in the countries following independence and the predominantly bourgeoisie involvement that exercises direct influence within the state bureaucracy.
62. Herbst, J. (1993). The politics of sustained agricultural reform in Africa. In T.M. Callaghy and J. Ravenhill (eds.), *Hemmed In: Responses to Africa's Economic Decline*, 333. New York: Columbia University Press.
63. Bates, 1981, pp. 106–119.
64. Cord J. (1993). Reviving Cocao: policies and perspectives on structural adjustment in Ghana's key agricultural sector. In Rothchild, D. (ed.), *Ghana: The Political Economy of Recovery*, 223.
65. Ravenhill, 1993, p. 31.
66. Overseas Development Institute. Commodity Prices: Investing in Decline? Briefing paper, March 1988, p. 1.
67. Ravenhill, 1993, p. 32.
68. Hettne, B. (1990). Crises in development theory and in the world. In *Development Theory and the Three Worlds*, 72. London: Longman Scientific & Technical.
69. *Ibid*., p. 28.
70. Jeffrey Herbst, J. (1990). The economic frontiers of the state in Africa. Manuscript, p. 26.
71. Bjorn, 1990, p. 28. Denham, M.E. and Lombardi M.O. (eds.). (1996). *Perspectives on Third World Sovereignty*. London: Macmillan Press.
72. Bienfeld, M. (1988). Dependency theory and the political economy of Africa's crisis. *Review of African Political Economy 43*, 76.
73. Wiarda, H. Toward a non ethnocentric theory of development: alternative conceptions from the Third World. In *The Political Economy of Development and Underdevelopment*, 70.
74. Pradervand, P. (1990). *Listening to Africa: Developing Africa from the Grassroots*. New York: Praeger. Weaver, J.H., Rock, M.T., and Kusterer, K. (1997). *Achieving Broad-Based Sustainable Development*. West Hartford: Kumarian Press.
75. Mehta, V. (1978). *Beyond Marxism: Towards an Alternative Perspective*, 104. New Delhi: Manohar Publications.
76. Wiarda, p. 76.
77. Green, 1993, p. 68.
78. *Ibid*., p. 69.
79. UNECA. (1995). African alternative framework to structural adjustment programmes for socio-economic recovery and transformation (AAF-SAP). E/ECA/CM.15/6/Rev.3, June 1995, p. iii.

80. *Ibid.*
81. *Ibid.*
82. Bjorn, 1990, p. 34.
83. *Ibid.*, p. 32.
84. Callaghy, 1993, p. 509.

REFERENCES

Abubakar, A. (1989). *Africa and the Challenges of Development*. New York: Praeger.

Adedeji, A., Teriba, O., and Bugemebe, P. (1991) *The Challenges of African Economic Recovery and Development*. London: Cass. Chapters:

Benachenhou, A. Structural trends in African economies.

Philips, A.O. Structural change and transformation of African economies.

H.M. Onitiri. Measures and mechanism for a new momentum for African economic recovery and development.

Nana-Sinkam, S.C. General framework for an analysis of economic adjustment programs in Africa with reference to the rural sector.

Adedeji, A., and T.M. Shaw, Shaw (eds.), In *Economic Crises in Africa-: African Perspectives on Development Problems and Potentials*. Boulder: Lynne Rienner Publishers.

Adedeji, A. (1992). Sustaining democracy. *Africa Report* January-February.

Adedeji, A. (1993). Former Executive Secretary, United Nations Economic Commision for Africa.

Interview with Margaret A. Novicki. *Africa Report* November-December.

Adedeji, A. (1989). *Towards a Dynamic African Economy: Selected Speeches and Lectures 1975–1986*. London: Cass.

Acheson, C. and Prachowny, D. (eds.). (1972). *Bretton Woods Revisited*. Toronto: UP.

Aina, T.A. (1994). Things need not fall apart. *International Development Research Centre Reports Magazine 21*(4).

Anunobi, F.O. (1994). *International Dimensions of African Political Economy*. Boston: UP.

Apter, D.E. and Rosberg, C.G. (1994). Changing African perspectives. In D.E. Apter and C.G. Rosberg (eds.), *Political Development and the New Realism in Sub-Saharan Africa*. Charlottesville: University Press of Virginia.

Asante, S.K.B. (1991). *African Development: Adebayo Adedeji's Alternative Strategies*. Kent: Hans Zell.

Barnet R.J. and Cavanagh, J. (1994). *Global Dreams Imperial Corporations and the New World Order*. New York: Simon and Schuester.

Balogun, M.J. and Mutahaba, G. (eds.). (1989). *Economic Restructuring and African Public Administration: Issues, Actions and Future Choices*. Hartford, Connecticut: African Association for Public Administration and Management.

———. (1992). *Enhancing Policy Management Capacity in Africa*. Hartford, Connecticut: African Association for Public Administration and Management.

Berman, B.J. and Leys, C. (eds.). (1994). *African Capitalist in African Development*. Boulder: Lynne Rienner.

Bush, R. and Szeftel, M. (1994). Commentary: state, markets and Africa's crisis. *Review of African Political Economy, 60.*

Callaghy, T. (1994). *Africa: Falling off the Map? Current History*, January.

Callaghy, T.M. and Ravenhill, J. (eds.). (1993). *Hemmed In: Responses to Africa's Economic Decline*. New York: Columbia University Press. Chapters:

Callaghy, T. Political passions and economic interests: economic reform and political structure in Africa.

Callaghy, T.M. and Ravenhill, J. How hemmed in? Lessons and prospects of Africa's responses to decline.

Callaghy, T.M. and Ravenhill, J. Vision, politics, and structure: Afro-optimism, Afro-pessimism or realism?

Chazan, N., Mortimer, R., Ravenhill, J., and Rothchild, D. (1992). *Politics and Sopciety in Contemporary Africa*. Boulder: Lynne Rienner Publishers.

Clapham, C. (1996). *Africa and the International System*. Cambridge: Cambridge University Press.

Denham, M.E. and Lombardi, M.O. (eds.). (1996). *Perspectives on Third World Sovereignty*. London: Macmillan.

Dorraj, M. (1995). *The Changing Political Economy of the Third World*. Boulder: Lynne Rienner.

Fowler, A. (1991). The role of NGOs in changing state-society relations: perspectives from eastern and southern Africa. *Development Policy Review 9*(1).

Gibbon, P. (1992). The World Bank and African poverty, 1973–1991. *Journal of Modern African Studies 30*(2). Articles:

Gordon, D.F. Debt, conditionality and reform: the international relations of economic restructuring in sub-Saharan Africa.

Green, R.H. The IMF and the World Bank in Africa: how much learning?

Herbst, J. The politics of sustained agricultural reform in Africa.

Ravenhill, J. A second decade of adjustment: greater complexity, greater uncertainty.

Commins, S.K. (ed.). (1988). *Africa's Development Challenges and the World Bank*. Boulder: Rienner.

da Costa, P. (1992). The capitalist credo. *Africa Report*, January-February.

Ghai, D. (ed.). (1991). *The IMF and the South—The Social Impact of Adjustment*. London: UN Research Institute for Social Development.

Glickman, H. (ed.). (1988). *The Crisis and Challenges of African Development*. New York: Greenwood.

Gondwe, D. (1992). *Political Economy, Ideology, and the Impact of Economics on the Third World*. New York: Praeger.

Hadjimichael, M.T., Ghura, D., Muhleisen, M., Nord, R., and Ucer, E.M. (1995). Sub-Saharan Africa—growth, savings and investment, 1986–1993. Washington: IMF Occasional Paper 118, January.

Helleiner, G.K. (ed.). (1986). *Africa and the IMF*. Washington: IMF. Chapters:

Erb, R.D. A view from the Fund.

Saitoti, G. A view from Africa: 1.

Nyirabu, C.M. A view from Africa: 2.
Ndegwa, P. The economic crisis in Africa.
Sansui, J.O. African economic disequilibria and the international monetary system.
Ouattara, A.D. Design and implementation and adequacy of fund programs in Africa.
Mawakani, S. Fund conditionality and socioeconomic situation in Africa.
Loxley, J. Alternatives to stabilization in Africa.
de Azcarate, L. The World Bank in adjustment and economic growth in Africa.

Hellinger, D. and Hammond, R. (1994). Debunking the myth. *Africa Report*, November-December.

Herskovits, R. and Harwitz, D. (eds.). (1964). *Economic Transition in Africa*. Evanston: Northwestern UP.

Hettne, B. (1990). Crises in development theory and in the world. In *Development Theory and the Three Worlds*. London: Longman Scientific & Technical.

Hill, H. (1992). The cycle of dependency. *Africa Report*, January-February.

Hooke, A.W. (1992). The IMF—Its evolution, organisations and activities. Washington: IMF Pamphlet Series No. 37, 2nd ed.

IMF Research Department. (1987). Theoretical aspects of the design of fund-supported adjustment programs. Washington: IMF Occasional Paper 55, September.

Islam, S. (1994). Try harder. *Far Eastern Review*, May 5.

Kennedy, P. (1994). Political barriers to African capitalism. *Journal of Modern African Studies 32*(2).

Khan, M.S. and Knight, M.D. (1985). Fund supported adjustment programs and economic growth. Washington: IMF Occasional Paper 41, November.

Killick, T. (ed.). (1984). *The IMF and Stabilization*. London: Heinemann, 1984.

Klein, M.W. (1994). A return to Bretton Woods? *Journal of Commerce*, August 25.

Lewis, P. (1994). The politics of economics. *Africa Report*, May-June.

Leys, C. (1994). Confronting the African tragedy. *New Left Review 204* (March/April).

Loxley, J. and Seddon, D. (1994). Stranglehold on Africa. *Review on African Political Economy 62* (December).

McCarthy, S. (1994). *Africa: The Challenge of Transformation*. London: I.B. Tauris & Co.

Mukerji, S. and Bernard, A. (1993). The significance of co-operation. *International Development Research Centre Reports Magazine 21*(2).

Ndiaye, B. (1992). President, African Development Bank. Interview with Margaret A. Novicki. *Africa Report*, January-February.

Nyang'oro, J.E. and Shaw, T.M. (eds). (1992). *Beyond Structural Adjustment in Africa*. New York: Praeger.

OAU. (1991). Treaty Establishing the African Economic Community, Abuja, June. *Lagos Plan of Action for the Economic Development of Africa 1980–2000*. 1981, Geneva.

Payer, C. (1974). *The Debt Trap: The IMF and the Third World*. Harmondsworth: Penguin.

Pradervand, P. (1990). *Listening to Africa: Developing Africa from the Grassroots*. New York: Praeger.

Pronk, J. (Minister of Development and Co-operation, Netherlands). (1992). Interview with Anne Shepherd. *Africa Report*, July-August.

Ravenhill, J. (ed.). (1986). *Africa in Economic Crisis*. London: Macmillan.

Riddell, B.J. (1992). Things fall apart—structural adjustment programs in sub-Saharan Africa. *Journal of Modern African Studies*, *30*.

Rueschemeyer, D., Stephens, E.H., and Stephens, J.D. (1992). *Capitalist Development and Democracy*. Chicago: University of Chicago Press.

Sachs, J. (1994). The ''M'' stands for mediocrity: a Report card for the IMF. *International Economy*, July/August.

Sanford, J.E. (1991). World Bank: answers to 26 frequent question. *Congressional Research Service Report for Congress*, November, 91-847F.

Schatz, S.P. (1994). Structural adjustment in Africa: a failing grade so far. *Journal of Modern African Studies*, *32*(4).

———. (1996). The World Bank's fundamental misconception in Africa. *Journal of Modern African Studies*, *34*(3).

Shaw, T.M. (1996). Conditionalities without end: hegemony, neoliberalism and the demise of sovereignty in the South. In Denham and Lombardi (eds.), *Perspectives on Third World Sovereignty: The Post-Modern Paradox*. London: Macmillan.

Shepherd, A. (1992). The lost decade. *Africa Report*, January-February.

Sylvia Ostry Foundation. (1995). *The Challenges Facing the IMF*. Toronto: PAC (Channel 21), Parliament Channel, 3–4 pm, August 21.

UN. (1995). The social dimensions of adjustment: a general assessment. Department for Policy Coordination and Sustainable Development, April.

———. (1995). Integrating environment and development in decision making. Department for Policy Coordination and Sustainable Development, April.

———. (1995). General discussion on progress in the implementation of Agenda 21, focusing on cross-sectoral issues and the critical elements of sustainability. Commission on Sustainable Development, April.

———. (1995). Agenda 21: an overview. Commission on Sustainable Development, April.

Boutros-Ghali, B. (1993). *Report on the Work of the Organisations from the 47th to the 48th Session of the General Assembly*. New York: United Nations.

UNDP. (1994). A forward strategy for UNDP's sustainable development networking programme. Kate Wild, July.

UNECA. (1994). UNECA activities in the field of emergency, humanitarian, rehabilitation,

———. (1994). Reconstruction and development in Africa: progress report. E/ECA/CM.20/23, March.

———. (1995). Issues before the twenty-first meeting of the Conference on Ministers. E/ECA/CM.21/2, April.

———. (1995). Resolutions and decisions in the economic and social sectors that are of interest to Africa adopted by the Economic and Social Council at its substantive session of 1994 and by the General Assembly at its forty-ninth session. E/ECA/CM.21/CRP.2, February.

———. (1995). Programme of work and priorities for the biennium 1996-1997. E/ECA/CM.21/12, March.

———. (1995). Progress report on programme evaluation in ECA. E/ECA/CM.21/13, March.

———. (1995). Human development in Africa, 1995 report. E/ECA/CM.21/8, March.

———. (1995). Global mid-term review of the implementation of the Paris Declaration and Programme of Action for the least developed countries for the 1990's. E/ECA/CM.21/15, April.

———. (1995). Report on the economic and social situation in Africa, 1995. E/ECA/CM.21/3, March.

———. (1995). Draft report of the twenty-first meeting of the Conference of Ministers. E/ECA/CM.21/L, May.

———. (1994). Rationalization and harmonization of ECA-sponsored institutions (Phase II). E/ECA/CM.20/21, April.

———. (1994). Strengthening ECA operational capacity extra-budgetary resources: current status and prospects. E/ECA/CM.20/28, April.

———. (1994). Proposals for updating the 1994–1995 programme of work and priorities in the light of General Assembly appropriations. E/ECA/CM.20/26, March.

———. (1994). Programme evaluation in the United Nations Economic Commission for Africa. E/ECA/CM.20/27/Add 1 and Add 2, April.

———. (1994). Programme evaluation in the United Nations Economic Commission for Africa. E/ECA/CM.20/27, April.

———. (1994). Science and technology for the development of Africa. E/ECA/CM.20/29, March.

———. (1994). Preparations for the International Conference on Population and Development: progress report. E/ECA/CM.20/19, February.

———. (1994). Anticipated impact of the Uruguay Round Agreements on African economies: a preliminary analysis. E/ECA/CM.20/31, April.

———. (1994). Implementation of the Addis Ababa Plan of Action for Statistical Development in Africa in the 1990's: progress report. E/ECA/CM.20/22, February.

———. (1994). Preparatory activities of the World Summit for Social Development: progress report. E/ECA/CM.20/17, March.

Public Administration and Management Innovations for Increased Popular Participation in the Design and Implementation of National Development Programs. (1994). Public Administration, Human Resources and Social Development Division. Addis Ababa: UNECA Development Management Series No. 3.

———. (1994). Preliminary assessment of the performance of the African economy in 1994 and prospects for 1995: end of year statement. Layashi Yaker, Executive Secretary ECA, December.

———. (1995). African alternative framework to structural adjustment programmes for socio-economic recovery and transformation (AAF-SAP). E/ECA/CM.15/6/Rev.3, June.

———. (1991). AAF-SAP: selected policy instruments. Addis Ababa, June.

———. (1994). Report on the implementation of the United Nations new agenda for the development of Africa in the 1990's (UN-NADAF). E/ECA/CM.20/3, March.

———. (1994). Implementation of the African strategies for the implementation of Agenda 21 and the African common position: progress report. E/ECA/CM.20/16, March.

———. (1994). Policy convergence for regional economic cooperation and integration: implementation of the treaty establishing the African Economic Community. E/ECA/CM.20/15, April.

———. (1994). Critical capacities in support of good governance, political stability, peace and security in Africa. E/ECA/CM.20/7, March.

———. (1991). Economic crisis in Africa: final review and appraisal of the implementation of the United Nations Programme of Action for African Economic Recovery and Development 1986–1990 (UNPAAERD). Report of the UN Secretary General for the General Assembly, September.

———. (1994). Capacity building for food production, food security and self-sufficiency in Africa. E/ECA/CM.20/13, March.

———. (1994). A framework agenda for building and utilizing critical capacities in Africa: preliminary report. E/ECA/CM.20/6, March.

———. (1994). Critical capacities for effective socio-economic policy analysis and management. E/ECA/CM.20/8, March.

———. (1994). Building and utilizing physical infrastructural capacities in Africa. E/ECA/CM.20/12, March.

———. (1994). Economic report on Africa 1994. E/ECA/CM.20/2, April.

———. (1993). Survey of economic and social conditions in African least developed countries 1992–1993. E/ECA/LDCs/93/005, Addis Ababa.

———. (1991). Economic report on Africa 1991. E/ECA/CM.17/2, April.

———. (1991). Critical capacities for the mobilization and efficient allocation of domestic and external financial resources. E/ECA/CM.20/11, March.

———. (1994). Developing entrepreneurial capacities for public and private sector enterprise. E/ECA/CM.20/10, March.

———. (1994). Biennial report of the Executive Secretary 1992–1993. E/ECA/CM.20/4, April.

———. (1994). Building, strengthening and effectively utilizing human capacities for sustained development in Africa. E/ECA/CM.20/9, March.

———. (1995). Implementation of the Abuja Treaty establishing the African Economic Community: progress made and prospects. E/ECA/CM.21/4, March.

———. (1995). Progress report on a framework agenda for building and utilizing critical capacities in Africa. E/ECA/CM.21/5, March.

———. (1995). Reviving private investments in Africa: policies, strategies and programmes. E/ECA/CM.21/5, March.

Verbit, G. (1975). *International Monetary Reform and the Developing Countries*. New York: Columbia UP.

Weaver, J.H., Rock, M.T., and Kusterer, K. (1997). *Achieving Broad-Based Sustainable Development*. West Hartford: Kumarian Press.

Wilber, C.K. and Jameson, K.P. (eds.). (1992). *The Political Economy of Development and Underdevelopment*. Toronto: McGraw Hill. Chapters:

Freire, P. Pedagogy of the oppressed.

Sen, A. Development: which way now?

Wiarada, H.J. Toward a nonethnocentric theory of development: alternative conceptions from the Third World.

World Bank. (1981). *Accelerated Development in Sub-Saharan Africa—An Agenda for Action*. Washington: World Bank.

———. (1988). *Adjustment Lending—An Evaluation of Ten Years of Experience*. Washington: World Bank.

———. (1994). *Adjustment in Africa—Reforms, Results, and the Road Ahead*. Washington: World Bank.

———. (1989). Growth and structural change in East Africa: domestic policies, agricultural performance and World Bank assistance, 1963–1986, Parts I and II. In U. Lele and L.R. Meyers (eds.), *Managing Agricultural Development in Africa*. Washington: World Bank.

Zulu, J.B. and Nsouli, S.M. (1985). Adjustment programs in Africa: the recent experience. Washington: IMF Occasional Paper 34, April.

5

Mechanisms for Labor Harmony

Dispute Resolution in the Industrial Courts of Kenya and Zambia

Miriam K. Mills
New Jersey Institute of Technology, Newark, New Jersey

I. OVERVIEW AND INTRODUCTION

This paper derives from a visit to Nairobi, Kenya, and Lusaka, Zambia, which included unions, the industrial courts, the judges of the courts, and material provided to me by the parties.

A. Kenya

In Kenya, the trade unions, as opposed to the craft unions, are organized on an industrial basis. There are at present 55 (15 employers' and 40 employees') registered trade unions in the country. All the employees' trade unions, with the exception of the Kenya National Union of Teachers and the Kenya Civil Servants, are affiliated to the Central Organisation of Trade Unions (Kenya)—COTU(K). Employers have also formed their own groups in the various industries and the majority of them are affiliated with or are members of the Federation of Kenya Employers (FKE).

Slightly more than half of the population is under the age of 16. Only 1 million persons out of 14 million are wage earners in Kenya. The 1979–83 Government Development Plan envisaged that the private sector would create about 50,000 new jobs every year. It is a major goal of the Kenya government to maintain the long-term growth and development of the nation. A serious impediment to productivity is, however, the high birth rate of the nation which tends to undercut any increases in national growth. Yet labor peace is considered a vital force at least in maintaining national growth. As Judge Saeed Cockar wrote:

> About four hundred thousand young boys and girls take the formal CPE exam and how many of them are going to go to secondary schools? I think no more than about 40 to 60 thousand, not more than that. The others will have to fend for themselves and in a couple of years they will be adults and they will be looking for jobs and they will swell the labor market. So we have to take all these harsh realities into account when we are talking in terms of industrial relations (Cockar 1985).

The Industrial Court in Kenya is the final arbiter of all disputes, those dealing with both contract formulation and interpretation.

B. Zambia

The situation in Zambia differs in certain respects. The Zambian economy is characterized by a comparatively high level of economic advancement. Net annual income per head was US $300 a year—a high figure compared to the majority of developing countries. The proportion of people employed for wages and salaries (over a quarter of the total population if their families are included) is also high compared to most African countries. Net investment (including changes in stocks) was about a quarter of the gross national income—a high rate by international standards—and Zambia also has one of the highest rates of educational expenditure per head in Africa. The main reason for this was the incomes generated by the copper industry; in 1967, sales of copper counted for 45% of the total national income and 90% of the country's export earnings (Olsson 1980).

However, this copper-based prosperity is likely to be short-lived. The price of copper has been depressed and in the developed nations synthetics and other alternatives tend to preempt the need for the natural mineral. Embassy officials report that the cost of extraction exceeds the price received but the extractions continue so as to bring in foreign currency.

Zambia had since 1969 become a relatively poor country due largely to external circumstances including the world recession, falling copper prices, and world inflation. However, a very wide gap has developed between the standard of living of the urban Zambian employees (in the mining sector as well as in public administration) on the one hand and the Zambian villagers on the other. It is estimated that the approximate annual earnings had risen by 3% in real terms for the peasant farmer. In the halycon copper days, mine workers saw 35% increases.

Some ILO observers have reported there is little incentive for personal performance since the wages or salaries are paid on a fixed monthly basis (ILO 1969:8).

II. GOING TO COURT

Sybill Bedford (1961) spoke about the symbolic impact of physical structure of perceptions of justice. The Industrial Court in both Kenya and Zambia are imposing and somewhat intimidating entities. As such they represent the final hope of the parties for an equitable resolution of their differences. There is no appeal to the decisions of the Judge of the Court in either country.

The cases are heard in a traditional courtroom. In Kenya, the court established in 1964 is located in the Social Security Building, a center of public administration. The Industrial Court in Zambia is a free-standing modern, dignified building. The judges are addressed as My Lord or My Lady, as the case may be, and the proceedings go forward carefully and deliberately at an almost stately pace. The courts exemplify the goals of the respective governments.

> Rather than have a test of strength between the employers and the workers bringing about a direct confrontation between them with undesirable consequences to both sides, they should take their problems to a forum in which they all have confidence and which is expected to be objective in its deliberations and to hand out impartial awards. After all, the parties desire a fair settlement and rather than getting it through direct action, it is preferable to obtain it through arbitration. The parties to industrial disputes in Kenya somehow appreciate this and there is a threat of strike on the part of the workers only when an employer in a non-essential service is trying to delay or avoid submitting the disputes to the jurisdiction of the Industrial Court (Cockar 1981:8).

In the absence of an official wages and incomes policy, it is up to the Industrial Court to ensure that the national interest be given maximum consideration. It was this national interest that persuaded the government to create a system for the parties to resolve their differences through the medium of reason. As the Industrial Court is the final arbiter of all trade disputes in the country, it is taken very seriously by the parties.

A. The Judge of the Kenya Industrial Court

Judge Saeed Cockar represents the most significant force in maintaining industrial harmony in Kenya. As the court of last appeal, his own nature and personality have molded the system. In discussions with unions and embassy officials prior to the meeting with Judge Cockar, I was struck by the high esteem in which he was held by all who knew him.

Judge Cockar stressed the desirability of disputes being resolved at the work site. However, such is the respect with which the court is viewed, that many individuals will be willing to wait great lengths of time in order to have him resolve their disputes.

The Kenya Court has served as a prototype for the African continent. In fact, the Industrial Court of Zambia was modeled on the Kenya experience. Judge Cockar indicated that his own experience derived from studies of the British, Australian, and Indian application. He informed me that the oldest Industrial Court had been established in Australia in 1986.

That court, similar to the Kenya Court, dealt with both rights and interests arbitration. Judge Cockar indicated that one of his major responsibilities is dealing with total economic packages. Engaging economists to do reports and analyses assists the judge in making his decisions which are final and binding on the parties and from which there is no appeal.

When queried as to his view of the American approach of having individual arbitrators make final and binding decisions, he seemed to suggest that the method used in Kenya was more congenial to the parties. He said he would rather see cases heard in settings run by the most rigorous legal standards. Although some discussion of expedited tribunals had been discussed earlier, this had been rejected.

Judge Cockar, working with two assistant judges, has the power to examine the case and to occasionally advise the parties to reach an amicable agreement. Since he hears cases for the entire country, this can mean a very significant delay. Based on my observations and discussions with the unions, the disputants seem to feel that the wait is warranted.

> In the early days, when the Industrial Court was first established the parties tended to reduce conciliation to a mere formality, but the Court soon put an end to that mockery of the whole process by castigating the parties for their perfunctory attitude to this important pre-Industrial Court procedure. Many a time the Court has come across issues which could and should have been settled at an earlier stage without having to waste its valuable time (Cockar 1981:29).

Yet despite his admonitions, the parties still prefer to use the Industrial Court regardless of delays.

When there is dispute on a labor contract, his rulings hold in economic issues. He insists that the parties disclose their latest positions. Because of this ultimate power, the result is that many times the parties will rush to the courts and avoid resolving their own issues. Sometimes their demands will be exorbitant.

He reported with pride on his activities in the coffee industry. The major industries of Kenya are coffee, tea, and tourism. He said that after 22 years the coffee workers made only $420 annually. At the same time the employers had difficulty in filling their vacancies. The employees were so disturbed at the intransigence of management that they went to the State House and the President. The coffee industry managers complained about the fact that the beans were drying on the vines. Through the judge's intervention they were able to increase the prices for the workers, but also were able to increase the revenues for management. The next agreement went very peacefully. Judge Cockar said he gave priority to those cases which had the greatest economic impact for the largest number of people. The road to Industrial Court is not an easy one, however.

> The importance of pre–Industrial Court procedures cannot be over-emphasized because they play, or should play, a vital role in the settlement of disputes between trade unions and employers. The parties are not allowed to cut out these procedures and the Industrial Court cannot accept a dispute unless it is accompanied by a certificate signed by the Labour Commissioner under 9(9)(e)(f) stating that the Minister has accepted the report of the trade dispute and that all available machinery (including statutory machinery) for the voluntary settlement of disputes prior to reference to the Court has been exhausted (Cockar 1981:33).

Judge Cockar recognized very clearly the enormous responsibilites faced by his court. It is necessary for him to make awards that permit the expansion of an enterprise so that new positions are created. He is also concerned that the decisions do not result in a redundancy situation wherein employees are laid off.

As a whole, the private sector is more concerned with generating profits rather than creating jobs. It is therefore the special responsibility of the Industrial Court to play a significant role in the application of social justice. Because of the close link between governmental aspirations for increased employment and productivity, it becomes incumbent on the court to make decisions within the larger framework of national economic growth. The court works with the realization that its decisions are inextricably intertwined with the very lifeblood of the country.

In considering necessary characteristics of future judges of the Industrial Court, Judge Cockar feels that not only should that individual be legally trained, but he should also be an economist and sociologist: "He should be able to understand and literally feel the pulse of the underprivileged and should be imbued with the spirit of uplifting the lot of mankind, particularly of the poor" (Cockar 1981:147). The weighty responsibility of dealing with cases which in totality affect the economy of the country calls for major caution and circumspection.

It would almost appear that individual decisions affecting small groups of employees or subsets of larger industries is a luxury for a developing nation. All the spokes of the wheel must converge on the fulcrum of national growth and productivity.

B. Attending the Court Hearing

In attending the court hearing, there was definitely a very strong formal air. Judge Cockar was addressed as "My Lord" throughout. All stand upon his arrival. He sits at an elevated podium with two associates. The case that was heard dealt with the manager of a diesel generator firm that engaged 50 employees. There were four grievants, all discharged for a variety of reasons. One of them was discharged for substandard work. It turned out that he was basically a laborer who, because of his knowledge of written and spoken English, was assigned to higher-level tasks without title change or salary change. The judge raised some very reasonable comments such as that it was really unfair to have a person working out of title and salary range and nonetheless be penalized for not doing his task. The judge seemed relatively intrusive. He raised the same kinds of objections that a U.S. arbitrator would have brought in terms of the proximate cause of discharge. Because management did not have a strong enough case, they tended to dredge up issues from the past. They spoke of the fact that this more qualified laborer was asked to place an order for a special cutter in order to expedite the task. The employee received his warning for not processing the order quickly. When confronted with the warning according to management, he ''impertinently'' crumpled it up, threw it away, and asked, ''What is this?'' On the basis of that fairly innocent behavior, he received another warning notice for insubordination.

Another worker was being let go for having falsified safari allowance receipts. (''Safari'' in Swahili means travel, but it has a far more exotic ring.) Evidently, on the previous day, testimony had been offered about his having had two receipts for the same day. A related problem was that a management official had been at that same lodge the following week and was charged only 30 kwashas for the same accommodations for which the worker claimed 50 kwashas. This led management to infer that the worker had, in collusion with management, arranged to pocket the difference. The contract was silent, however, on the issue of dollar limit for accommodations. Management argued that they were not quarreling about the amount of money but rather the apparent falsification of records. The worker staunchly maintained that he only had one receipt. There was also some question as to whether the two instances were identical as there was only a double room available for which the worker had to pay more. More important, there was no proof of collusion. (This is similar to the famous U.S. case of Anchor Hines where workers were suspended for falsification of motel receipts and the union declined to represent them. It later turned out that the motel clerk was the guilty party and had pocketed the difference. The clerk had charged the workers one figure but only claimed a lesser amount on his records, which permitted him to pocket the difference. The key element in that case was that the union had failed to adequately represent its members.)

The award of the court would not be announced until some weeks later. Judging by the gentle irony of some of his questions, one could expect that the grievances would be upheld. Under no circumstances, no matter how apparent the final decision might be, would a summary award be given. Because of the importance of trade disputes as they relate to national economic impact, the court must deliberate carefully. The court is concerned not only with rendering justice in the case at hand, but also in making those decisions which are conducive to overall industrial harmony. While Judge Cockar appeared very sympathetic and raised questions of basic equity, both sides were afforded ample opportunity to present their case at their own pace.

The final awards (Table 1) that are prepared similar to the American system give justification for the findings. When the Industrial Court began to explain reasoning in its written awards, the Federation of Kenya Employers initially objected. However, their position was overruled by the court and the government. While all the submissions of the parties are not specifically addressed, the court does provide the major persuasive factors which have led it to its conclusion.

C. The Judge of the Zambia Industrial Court

Judge Lombe Chibesakunda has served for six years on the Industrial Court of Zambia which was formed on the basis of the 1971 Industrial Relations Act. Similar to the reputation enjoyed by Judge Cockar of Kenya, Judge Chibesakunda was highly regarded by everyone with whom I spoke. Colleagues from the law association, the embassy, and labor unions were uniform in praise of her intelligence, capability, and clearly articulated awards. She was one of the first women ambassadors from Zambia. Her legal training was in Britain and she is not only gracious but extremely knowledgeable about labor dispute mechanisms throughout the world. While there are many similarities with the Kenya Industrial Court on which the Zambia Court is based, there are differences in the labor picture.

Worker councils are an integral part of the labor situation and they play a significant role in many aspects of the work situation above and beyound griev-

Table 1 Categories of Awards Announced for 1984

Category	Number of awards
Issues concerning terms of service—wages, working hours, etc.	16
Issues concerning termination/dismissals	30
Issues concerning redundancy	3
Issues concerning union recognition/demarcation	6
Other—interpretation of court awards, etc.	12
TOTAL	67

Source: Division of Manpower Planning, 1985.

ances. At the time of my visit Judge Chibesakunda was no longer with the Industrial Court, having been promoted to the High Court.

I asked her about her feelings on leaving the Industrial Court in which she had been so instrumental and where she enjoyed such a formidable reputation. She said that at the High Court there are far more sophisticated problems dealing with a much wider range of law and contract. The legislation that guides her decisions (a copy of which she gave me) is of a much narrower nature and provides less opportunity for over-arching analysis.

As in Kenya, this court has exclusive and binding powers. Since it is a duly constituted court, precedent does apply. The majority of cases deal with individual issues.

All of the procedures under which Judge Chibesakunda acted, and under which her successor continues are derived from Chapter 517 of the Laws of Zambia. This is described as:

> An Act to provide for the registration of trade unions, the Zambia Congress of Trade Unions, the Employers' Associations and the Zambia Federation of Employers; to provide for the establishment of Works Councils, collective agreements, the settlement of collective disputes and the establishment of an Industrial Relations Court; to repeal certain enactments relating to trade unions and trade disputes and industrial conciliation; and to provide for matters incidental to or connected with the foregoing.

D. Attending the Court Hearing

The Zambia Industrial Courthouse is a three-story new and modern building near the interior of the city. One is given admission through a guard posted outside. In the anteroom there is a flurry of activity as interested parties plan their presentations. Upon entering the hearing room, here again as in Kenya, there are three judges sitting at an elevated table. The disputing parties, similar to an American courtroom, are placed to the right and left of the platform. There is a brief discussion outlining the case by the management side and then the attention focuses on the grievant. In the case that I observed the grievant was a 31-year-old bookkeeper who had lost his job two and a half year prior. He evidently had been unable or unwilling to engage an attorney and consequently defended himself. Although he was a member of a union, no union representative was present. He was interrogated in a kindly manner by the judge and cautioned to speak only of what he had said or heard. He addressed the judge as "My Lord" and had to be drawn out on each point. Because the process went so slowly with the repeated encouragement of the judge who queried, "And what next?," I was only able to hear the grievant's position. There was relatively little interruption by the management attorney. The issue centered on the bookkeeper's having made repeated mistakes. There had been no preliminary warning or penalty and although he conceded he had been called to task verbally, he apparently had not recognized the consequence of his errors. (I must say that if the deliberate and plodding manner in which he responded was indicative of his normal work tempo, he was fortunate to have been employed six years.) This may be a disservice, however, because he may have felt very anxious and pressured in the course of this judicial hearing.

III. ISSUES IN DISPUTE RESOLUTION

In both countries the parties are encouraged to attempt to settle the dispute at the lowest possible level through the mechanism established by their contract. It is only in the absence of success that they are officially required to turn the problem over to the government which will then attempt to effect a settlement. Only in those areas where the parties have been unsuccessful does the Industrial Court serve as the final arbiter. The labor legislation in Kenya, for example, obliges the court to ignore any trade dispute unless the court has received a signed certificate from the labor commissioner stating that the minister has accepted the report of the trade dispute and that all existing mechanisms for dispute resolution have been explored and exhausted. Only then can the issue come to court.

The Trade Disputes Act of 1965 was amended in 1971. The major change was that the definition of "trade dispute" was expanded to cover disputes relating to the dismissal or suspension of employees and the allocation of work as well as recognition agreements. This extension to the grievances of individual employees was a significant one. Prior to this change it would only be large groups of employees or major issues of contract interpretation that would come to the courts.

As in the United States there is a certain degree of rigidity and intransigence by the parties in the framing of the issues:

> The parties are rigid on the technicalities of the dispute and they labour under the supposition that if they give in to the other party's version of the issue in dispute, then they will be at a disadvantage during the hearing. They want to maintain their legal and technical positions. In these circumstances, the court has encouraged the parties to put their respective versions on the issue in dispute in Form 'A' so that the court would have clearly before it what their respective position on the dispute is. In both examples cited above, the court accepted the Notification of Dispute Form 'A' with both parties' respective versions included and proceeded to hear the dispute and make an award (Cockar 1981:40).

The judge in this case has taken on the highly diplomatic and effective method used by arbitrators in the United States. Rather than becoming stymied on the question of stipulation, he proceeds directly to the issue at hand.

One of the more complex issues facing the court is that of resolving wage issues. As Justice Higgins in the Australian Commonwealth Court noted:

> The living wage represents the normal needs of the average employee regarded as a human being living in a civilized community. . . . Treating marriage as the usual fate of adult men, a wage which does not allow of matrimonial condition and the maintenance of about five persons in a home would not be treated as a living wage (Cockar 1981:70).

According to the economists and union officials with whom I spoke, the principal economic criteria that are used include (1) the basic needs of the workers or the family budget (the basket of goods); (2) movements in the cost of living; (3) wage comparisons, i.e., wages paid in other industries and places; and (4) money, i.e., the financial position of the employer, the ability or inability to pay.

Arbitrators in the United States claim to be less concerned with the ability to pay. Some will say that it is their intention to resolve the conflict rather than to explicitly deal with ability to pay.

Within the developing countries there are problems of income inequality between the urban and rural areas. The government's position is that pay increases, especially in the public sector, can only be given in accordance with the company's ability to propose cost-saving economics. This is frequently easier said than done. One of the intermediary groups in Kenya that plays an important role in wage deliberations is the Wage Advisory Board and Wage Council. These bodies are involved with the regulation of remuneration and conditions of employment. The Wage Council prescribes a basic minimum consolidated wage for the various job classifications in the industry they are intending to cover. Housing allowance, hours of work, overtime, holidays with pay, annual leave, sick leave, meals and accommodations allowances, redundancy, acting allowance (pay change for temporary assignment), termination of employment, casual labor, and working system are some of the other areas where minimum standards are prescribed.

The leader of the Domestic Worker's Union made an appealing case for the plight of some of the workers he represented. He indicated that at the major hotels the workers cannot use the facilities even on their off hours. In forthcoming negotiations he was going to attempt to get the hotels to support some nearby small native restaurants to which employees could go during their breaks or their days off. He further said that many of the Kenya workers have never been to the game reserves because they are so expensive. This seemed to him a particularly bitter deprivation for those in a country renowned for its wildlife. Consistent with this observation was his plan to establish a budget level resort for the workers which would permit them to enjoy the beasts of the wild. He said he had seen similar such projects in Czechoslovakia.

The union representative of the local government workers noted that the

Minister of Labor sits in on the negotiations of local government workers to determine that there are sufficient funds to meet the salary demands. In instances where the employer refuses to implement what has been promised, the Industrial Court will hear the justification. Sometimes the financial standing of the parties may have altered substantially from the time the contract was initially made. The position of the government is to see that the agreement is implemented as soon as it is signed so that there may be productivity resulting from salary incentives.

Sometimes the Industrial Court makes awards that are unsatisfying to the parties. Because the Industrial Court has the ultimate and final authority, it is obliged to consider the overall economy rather than that of a particular industry. In developing countries it is sometimes difficult to have increases if the population vastly outstrips the performance of the economy.

> When a worker is dismissed without any fault on his part then the poor worker and his children and wife have been condemned to death, slow death, starvation death. If a worker is doing his job nicely, not very good, but nicely, reasonably well and he is alright, he is not dishonest, he has not committed any gross misconduct then through the Industrial Court we have granted them security of employment (Cockar 1985).

This view seems at variance with the activities in the United States. Perhaps because there are more vocational alternatives, discharge is not seen as being quite as perilous.

As to layoffs, the union leadership is to be advised in advance of future redundancies and discharges. In the case of Kenya Petroleum Oil Workers and Kenya Shell, the company maintained that layoff was not subject to negotiation because of its right to organize business as it saw fit. While the court found strong basis for the argument, it ruled that giving the union notice of the proposed layoff was not equivalent to compelling the employer to surrender management rights.

In instances where discharge does occur, the Industrial Court is most likely to reinstate an employee or award heavy compensation for wrongful dismissal if the employer has denied the employee an appropriate opportunity to defend himself. In cases of reinstatement all files relating to termination are removed from the employee's dossier. Sometimes in reinstatement, if no alternative position is found, the award may be as much as 12 months' salary. The more common remedy is three months' salary in lieu of notice after it has been proved that the employee was discharged for just cause and was given due process.

When layoffs occur an investigation takes place to determine the contributing factors. Employees are interviewed and company records are examined. The investigator's report is provided to the union and the employer, and both sides can challenge the analysis on the basis of error or bias.

In summary, barring serious misconduct which could result in a worker's summary dismissal, management is obliged to give the employee a chance to improve by issuing a warning letter. The procedure has developed over the years that requires two or three warning letters before the employer can take steps to terminate his services.

IV. ROLE OF THE GOVERNMENT

In both Kenya and Zambia there is an understanding that it is in the national interest for employers and workers to cooperate in the undertaking and that progress can be made only upon the foundation of fair terms and conditions of employment. (In the United States it is the public sector that tends to be influenced by national goals and pressures.) In these Third World countries there is a much broader and even-handed approach by the government to both private- and public-sector employees.

Both Kenya and Zambia, similar to other developing countries, are frequently buffeted by external events which are beyond the expectation or control of the parties. This can include revolution, monetary depression, synthetic substitutes, and unfavorable climate. The governments have frequently attempted to alleviate these events by exercising persuasion to the unions. Perhaps because the union receives due deference from the government, it is generally cooperative in moderating its salary demands at difficult times. Employees are willing to accept less with the understanding that more of their fellow workers could be retained and that their general lot in life would be improved:

> All the developing nations of the Third World find that one of the challenges is to create wealth, to create national prosperity by educating your people, by creating jobs for them, by placing them in gainful employment where they will feel that they are serving a very essential purpose and it will lead to self-fulfillment. How do you achieve national wealth, how do you increase it? You increase it by expanding your industrial sector, your agricultural sector, and by expanding your service sector (Cockar 1985).

Shortly after independence, in 1962, the government, employers, and worker organizations realized that strikes and lockouts should only be resorted to when all other efforts have failed. The underlying message of all communication between the government and the parties was that the two were obliged in the national interest to maintain harmonious relations. To this end, on May 19, 1964, the Industrial Court was first established in Kenya. In 1973 guidelines began to be enunciated which aimed at increasing employment. In 1979 there were further changes with the express intention of creating more employment through the reduction of working hours. Some of the union officials with whom I spoke indicated that operationally this was a bit of a sham. The employers would pay the individuals for the reduced hours but still require them to show up and perform for the regular length of time.

In December 1983 the President of Kenya decreed that employers in both the public and private sectors increase the number of their employees by 10%. This agreement was enacted among the government, the unions, and the employers. The implicit understanding was that in return for the generation of new jobs that the union would tone down its wage demands. In another example of government involvement with employment policy, in May 1986 the President instituted the five-day work week for civil servants. This was not extended to the private sector, however. The intention was to improve manpower utilization and increase productivity. Although unexpressed, another expectation was that people would perform better rested. Here too, the implementation has differed from the original plan. Officials in the civil service have tended to increase the daily working hours to make up for the sixth day that was given up.

In Zambia, the South African Team for Employment Promotion (SATEP) has a joint responsibility for technical, advisory, and consultancy services to five countries in the subregion including Zambia, Zimbabwe, Botswana, Lesotho, and Swaziland. The main objective here is to assist the governments to formulate and implement employment strategies to increase employment and minimize the traditional dependence on South Africa.

The demands on the unions of both Kenya and Zambia are considerable in terms of maintaining labor harmony. Consequently, the Ministry of Labor officials must be strongly involved in the maintenance of industrial peace so that greater national productivity and employment can occur. As Judge Cockar wrote:

> The trade unions should appreciate and accept a statement by an employer made in good faith that a certain percentage of the profits is going towards the creation of more job opportunities in the country. After all, a lot of people in the labour force in the future will no doubt be from the families of these very workers. And nobody can seriously quarrel with the fact that the future prosperity of the country is the responsibility of all Kenyans (Cockar 1981: 144).

In an earlier case Judge Cockar had emphasized the importance not only of maintaining the employment of existing workers, but also of concentrating on creating more new jobs which were so vital to the economic growth of the country (Cockar 1981:128). Because of this high emphasis on employment, the courts tend to be relatively forgiving of individual employees who are disciplined. Wherever possible, the employee is retained.

No matter how generous and supportive the courts are of employment stability in their respective countries, there continue to be problems on the part of employers based on a number of difficult-to-reconcile conditions. Among the constraints on employment and labor unions are the following factors (Cockar 1985):

1. The conflict between increasing the number of employed and raising the wages of those already in employment.

2. The limits imposed by world markets, price levels, and export quotas on the capacity of our basic industries to pay.

3. The limits set by local purchasing power and by our tax revenues on the capacity of both home market producers and the public services to better the conditions of their employees.

4. The shortage of investment capital—both local and external—to promote the big economic expansion that Kenya so desperately needs in order to overcome its problems of poverty and population increases.

5. The subtle problem of redistributing the national wealth so as to benefit the mass of the people, while at the same time permitting profit margins which are sufficiently attractive to investors.

6. To lay a foundation for future prosperity by making the present generation of Kenyans accept the harsh facts of life—that hard work and sacrifice (by frugal living, savings, and investment) are the only way to provide a better life for our children.

V. CONCLUDING COMMENTS

In the United States, there will sometimes be deliberate ambiguity left within a labor contract just to reach settlement. It is assumed that these ambiguities will be resolved within arbitration. This state of events is foreclosed within Kenya and Zambia. In both instances the agreement before being approved must be submitted to the Industrial Court for examination and final approval. Many problems are thus averted because of this ultimate review. Questions of the power of external law are also dealt with through this review.

In the United States there is a stronger onus on the unions to practice the duty of fair representation. This leads shop stewards to sometimes pursue even the most trivial case to arbitration which is contrary to practice in Kenya and Zambia. Many can represent themselves. The union can decide whether or not to go to court, but the individual is not foreclosed from proceeding individually. Hearings on individual grievances can take months or even years but the people seem accepting of this delay.

American observers may well question the approach of having a single body deliberate the merits and provide final and binding decisions for the country. The U.S. model of individual arbitrators rendering decisions based on the issues at hand within the particular organization is an alien one to Kenya and Zambia. Yet even in the United States there are opponents to dispute resolution that takes place outside of the courts, even if it does initially seem more expeditious.

> It is sometimes claimed that there are those who subscribe to the ADR movement because they view efficient and inexpensive dispute resolution as an

> important societal goal without regard for the substantive results reached (Edwards 1985:669).
>
> This is not to say that private settlements can never produce results that are consistent with the public interest; rather, it is to say that private settlements are troubling when we have no assurance that the legislative- or agency-mandated standards have been followed, and when we have no satisfactory explanation as to why there may have been a variance from the rule of law. . . . Inexpensive, expeditious, and informal adjudication is not always synonymous with fair and just adjudication. The decision-makers may not understand that values at stake and parties to disputes do not always possess equal power and resources (Edwards 1985:678).

This view seems reasonable especially for a developing country where the national good must sometimes preempt individual benefits.

Some might suggest that mediation between the parties might be a valuable mechanism. Yet here too, for these countries at this time, there might well be serious hindrances.

> The principal thrust of recent criticism of ADR has been aimed primarily at mediation, perhaps because that process blends third party facilitation with disputant control of outcome, and hence is inherently imprecise and manipulable. In theory, mediation is a voluntary process whereby two or more disputants arrive at a mutually acceptable solution with the help of a neutral third party.
>
> In a recent piece. Professor Owen Fiss of Yale Law School launched a ringing attack on one of the fundamental premises of the alternatives movement—that settlement as a general rule is a social good. Fiss contends that settlement necessarily involves a compromise of legal entitlements, which is of particular concern when there is a sharp power disparity between the parties (Goldberg et al. 1986:292–293).

It is also argued that by focusing resolution of individual disputes, aggregate solutions are minimized.

It has also been observed that:

> This segregation of alternatives from the judicial process also has other adverse consequences, such as the common absence of public funding, which sometimes requires disputants to pay for alternative dispute resolution services even as the judicial ones are provided free. More subtle discouragement derives from the distrust that often accompanies processes that are new and unfamiliar and that appear to be unaccompanied by the legal protections that disputants have been taught over the years to value so highly. A related deterrent may be the absence of mechanisms for ensuring high standards in the provision of alternatives (Goldberg et al. 1985:291).

The method of dispute resolution in both Kenya and Zambia is quite centralized. Although both of the industrial judges emphasize the importance of settlement at the workplace level, there still tends to be a great reliance on bringing the hearing to the highest level possible. Despite the attendant delay because of the crowded court calendars, the system appears well accepted by the individual grievants, the union, and the managers. It is perhaps the very formality and sense of ceremony that makes this approach more desirable. The outstanding reputation of both judges may make it difficult to separate the system from its individual leaders. The first incumbent in a position has a unique ability to mold the organization. The countries will be well served if the successors to these individuals will earn the same high degree of eminence and national regard.

The reliance on alternative dispute resolution becomes more relevant when the existing dispute resolution systems are easily and efficiently used. Given the small number of employees working for wages, the absence of full literacy, and the varying tribal allegiances at this time, the Industrial Court may well be the most responsive solution.

Before one can consider any other alternatives, such as ad hoc arbitrators or mediators, it will be necessary for the population to gain greater experience and ease in dispute resolution at the plant level.

As indicated earlier, both Kenya and Zambia are very much obliged to consider national goals and purposes which is indeed reasonable when the courts are called upon to deal with issues that may have greater implications for different sectors of the economy. The motion of expedited hearings or individual arbitrators might be more feasible in those instances where individuals press grievances against companies. But here too, union officials may need to upgrade their persuasive skills so as to minimize going to court.

Systems develop organically from their own national experience. The influence of England on India places great stress on formalism. Despite the independence of the Commonwealth, both nations have been exposed to a highly ceremonial tradition. In future years there may well emerge new and even more responsive forms of dispute resolution. For now, the system works well largely because of the trust that all parties feel in the Industrial Courts.

REFERENCES

Bedford, S. (1961). *The Faces of Justice*. New York: Simon & Schuster. Central Organization of Trade Unions (COTU). (Undated). Kenya Constitution and Rules.

Cockar, S.R. (1981). *The Kenya Industrial Court: Origin, Development and Practice*. Kenya: Longman.

———. (1985). Speech before convocation of the Union of Hospitals, Hotels and Domestic Workers.

Edwards, H.T. (1986). Alternative dispute resolution: panacea or anathema. *Harvard Law Review*, *99*, 668–684.
Goldberg, S.B., et al. (1986). ADR problems and prospects: looking to the future. *Judicature*, *69*(5), 291–299.
Industrial Relations. (Undated). Chapter 517 of the Laws of Zambia. Lusaka, Zambia.
Olsson, U.K. (1980). Prices, wages, and incomes in Zambia: policies and their implementation: Southern African team for employment promotion. Discussion paper.
Report of Industrial Award Categories in Kenya. (1985). Division of Manpower Training 4-15-85.

6

Industrial Policy and Regional Development

A Diachronic Comparison of Japanese and South Korean Economic Strategies

Sang-Chul Park
Göteborg University, Göteborg, Sweden

I. INTRODUCTION

Since World War II Japan has been regarded as a country of economic miracle. Following World War II, the Japanese government tried to overcome its technical backwardness to Western countries while at the same time practicing a high productivity and growth-oriented economic policy. It led to a rapid economic growth during the 1960s. With the collapse of the Bretton Woods system and the two oil crises in the 1970s, Japan faced severe economic problems. Although the external economic environments restrained its economic growth, it handled it wisely. Its reaction was based on industrial rationalization, rationalization of firms, improvement of industrial structure, and industrial restructuring (Komiya 1984). Through these various policies the Japanese industrial structure shifted from capital-energy-intensive sectors such as heavy and chemical industries to knowledge-intensive sectors such as the electronics industry.

On the basis of these policies Japan succeeded in recovering from its economic recession faster than any other industrialized country and at the same time gained an advantage by expanding its world market shares. Additionally, the Ministry of International Trade and Industry (MITI) created a new phrase, "industrial policy," which has been internationally recognized as a perception of industrial development strategy.

South Korea, as a latecomer, has followed the Japanese economic development. It has imported know-how and capital goods from Japan and has become a competitor in certain industrial sectors such as semiconductors, steel, automobiles, etc., on the world market.

A theory of economic development by Kaname Akamatsu as the "flying geese" paradigm explains the development of industry from the introduction of its products to an economy through imports through the establishment of local production facilities to the emergence and growth of exports. Akamatsu's model is a catching-up cycle model based on a latecomer's point of view. It presupposes dynamic changes in economic relations among advanced and developing countries. The "lead goose" (advanced nation) eventually tires out and falls back. Its position is taken over by a more vigorous one (developing nation). His analysis focuses on the structural catching-up mechanism of latecomer countries rather than the decline of a lead country. His basic idea is that a developing country industrializes and goes through industrial upgrading by capitalizing on the learning opportunities made available through its external relations with more advanced countries (Akamatsu 1961). In this case, the role of government as a major planner of strategic industrial policy is very important (Korhonen 1994).

This paper focuses on the development of Japanese and South Korean economy, the role of government as planner, and regional development based on high technology.

II. ECONOMIC RECONSTRUCTION AND RAPID GROWTH

After the end of World War II Japan was confronted with all the same postwar problems that emerged in many European countries, such as unemployment, destroyed production facilities, lack of energy and food supply, and high inflation. In Japan there were about 13 million unemployed, mainly demobilized soldiers and workers from the former weapons industry (Klenner 1989). The challenge was to shift the war economy to a free-market system in order to rebuild the country and to create advantageous conditions for growth. To cope with this challenge, Japan attempted to encourage experienced economic leaders to participate in business and public institutions, and guided its disciplined workers to take part in the free-market economy.

In the beginning of the American occupation in Japan, the supreme commander, General Douglas MacArthur, took steps to destroy the political economy of the prewar time. He tried to break up the Zaibatsu, to eliminate the landlords as a class, and to create antimonopoly laws. Furthermore, labor unions and left-wing parties as counterpowers were allowed to build by the American occupation authority so that Japan could become a democratic country (Cumings 1989).

These left-wing-orientated organizations were suppressed by the government after the Korean War (1950–1953).

The Korean conflict helped Japan to realize its economic plans. Just before the war, the general directions of the economic policy were decided. In 1949 MITI was formed to create an industrial structure for the heavy and chemical industries that was similar to the one in the Western industrialized countries (Pauer 1985). For the realization of such a goal, Japan emphasized two different directions in its economy: First, it should invest huge amounts of capital in those industrial sectors. Second, it should import the most modern technology, mainly from the United States.

In spite of attempts at industrial rearranging, Japan had continually huge trade deficits, a weak capital market, and a low living standard until shortly before the beginning of the Korean War, in 1950. The war gave the economy a chance to vitalize a labor market for industries before the government took steps toward disarmament (Uchiyama 1986). Increasing export quantities and supplies of military equipment to Korea created a strong stimulus for the economy, and with it industries experienced a drastic upswing.

By 1950, manufacturing and mining had already reached a production level equal to that of the prewar period. During the Korean War the domestic production began to overcome the economic recession, and the Japanese living standard in the middle of the 1950s was higher than in the prewar period. The annual average growth rate of the GNP in 1946–1955 was around 8.9%. The number of employees increased from 33.3 million to 39.3 million between 1947 and 1955. Even more importantly, there was a shift in the structure of employment. During this time, many farmers left their land and moved into cities, where a large industrial reservoir emerged on the labor market. The government attempted to educate the labor force to improve its skill.

The economy profited not only by the rise of export and domestic production through the Korean War but also by the advantageous currency system during the Bretton Woods system. The fixed rate of exchange between the U.S. dollar and the yen in 1949 was $1 to 360 yen. This rate of exchange facilitated export growth during a sensitive period. Additionally, a new political independence from the victor powers was achieved through the peace treaty in San Francisco (1952).

Because there was a shortage of raw materials, the economic change was based on a search for export orientated economic mechanisms. These mechanisms made a rapid upswing of exports possible. Furthermore, economic growth was achieved through high investment and the introduction of modern technologies. Modern technology contributed greatly to the economic growth. It is no exaggeration to say that more than half of Japan's economic growth was based on technical progress. The most powerful economic growth aid was private investment in new industrial facilities. The portion of private investment in the industrial facilities ran up to about 8% of the GNP in the first half of the 1950s. This portion amounted to approximately 18% of the GNP in the second half of the 1950s. Productivity that resulted from private investment for industrial facilities was extraordinarily high in the economy. State investment was also high. It totaled more than half of the total state expenditures in the middle of the 1960s. During the systematic increase of technological production and the improvement of efficiency in productivity, the government played an important role. Traditionally, the policy of research and development in Japan is a part of the economic policy and the national self participation more than in any other countries (Kubler 1986). As a result of such a high investment in the industrial facilities, the GNP had reached the second largest in the Western world in 1968, and the presence of Japanese companies was significant in the world market.

III. TECHNOCORPORATISM

With the dissolution of Zaibatsu and the passing of antimonopoly laws, medium and small-size enterprises had the chance to participate in the reconstruction of the economy. Akio Morita, president of Sony company, established the Tokyo Telecommunications Engineering Corporation in October 1945 (Tatsuno 1986).

In 1949 the companies (NEC, Toshiba, Fujitsu, Sony, etc.), scholars (Professor Hiroshi Watanabe; Akio Kobayashi at the University of Tohoku; Jiro Yamasaki at the University of Tokyo, etc.), and MITI focused on developing the transistor, which was used in electronic implements instead of the vacuum tube. At that time, almost every participant except Professor Watanabe was very skeptical about the transistor project. Despite such skepticism, Watanabe and his coworker Kikuchi had finally succeeded in producing a transistor in their laboratory in the beginning of the 1950s.

MITI supported the transistor project very strongly. It wanted to reduce the technological dependence on the United States and increase economic growth through exports of new transistor products. Related to the strategy of MITI, foreign investment laws and the foreign trade control law were passed by Parliament. With these new laws, the possibility of foreign investment into Japan was increased.

In the beginning of the 1950s, the electronic industry had a boom because its market was enlarged by the Korean War and a growing domestic consumer market. A private radio broadcasting company was opened in 1951 and two years later TV broadcasting was established. To protect the domestic market of the electronic industry, MITI prohibited foreign investments in this area and transistor imports from the United States. Instead of transistor imports, MITI recommended companies to procure the new transistor technology from the United States. For the direct technology transfer, the electronic companies should pay royalties. Toshiba and Hitachi paid their royalties to the American electronic companies RCA and Western Electric. With these royalties, Fujitsu, Hitachi, Matsushita, NEC, and Toshiba produced their own transistors in 1955.

The industrial policy of MITI was composed of four different fields. First, it selected industrial sectors, which would be developed during the planning period. During this period, certain promotional measures, such as tax benefits, credits with low interest rate, and tariff barriers against foreign competition were taken. Secondly, modernization and rationalization through the consolidation of companies in the selected industrial sectors was supported. Thirdly, it targeted its support of the iron and steel industry, the cement industry, and the electronics industry. Fourth, it encouraged the companies to avoid an excessive production capacity and a rise of extreme competition between companies. The last part of MITI's industrial policy was called the Sunset Industry. The mining industry belonged to this area, which needed state subsidies for the energy production (Klenner 1989).

After the 1950s, heavy industry, the chemical industry, and the electronic industry in Japan achieved high growth rates, which were attributed to high investments and industrial political measures of MITI in these areas. Completely modern technologies were introduced in those industries. For this reason, shipbuilding, petrochemistry, the automobile industry, and the electronics industry reached extraordinary high growth rates until the end of the 1960s. MITI ordered the electronic industry to make up for the country's inability to produce transistors with the then most modernized electronic product—''IC-Chips'' (Integrated Circuit)—in the middle of the 1960s, so that Mitsubishi, NEC, Toshiba, Fujitsu, and Sharp produced these chips in the late 1960s.

To support the domestic computer industry and to reduce the share of American computer products on the domestic market, MITI commissioned the Electronic Industry Deliberation Council (EIDC) to recommend appropriate computer strategies. Additionally, it established a computer institution for data and analyses. Furthermore, MITI organized the Japan Information Center (JIC), in which the six biggest electronic companies could exchange information to develop computer technologies together. With the guidance of MITI's electronics and technical laboratories, the Super High-Performance Electronic Computer Development Project (1966–1971) was created.

For the realization of this project, MITI provided legal support related to new computer technologies. The Diet passed ''Kidenho,'' a law for electronics and machines in 1971, which contained equitable interest rates from state banks with a fund of about U.S. $4 million. This support contributed to the development of microelectronic and industry robots from 1971 to 1978 (Tatsuno 1986).

IV. ECONOMIC CRISES, INTERNATIONAL TRADE FRICTION, AND DOMESTIC MARKET OPENING

The prospects for further economic growth seemed to be very positive at the beginning of the 1970s. Despite positive expectations in Japan, the world economic situation restrained the continuous growth figures. The Nixon government was forced to initiate a reform of the world currency system in 1971 because of the growing trade deficits and high inflation rates in the United States. That fixed exchange rate system had provided a stable environment for reconstruction and helped Japan avoid the reliance on competitive devaluation seen in the 1930s. The new floating exchange rate system changed the previous favorable rate from 360 yen U.S. $1 to 308 yen U.S. $1. Japan experienced an economic recession with the revaluation. Companies were afraid of high export prices of their products, which reduced their competitiveness on the world market. Further, economic difficulties awaited in the fall of 1973. A drastic price increase in crude oil affected the whole country strongly, because three-quarters of its primary energy requirement was covered by imported crude oil. The higher oil price led to price increases for export products and in the service sectors.

As the result of the high crude oil price, the index of wholesale prices rose about 7.7% in 1973 and 17.7% in 1974 (International Monetary Fund 1990). In particular, heavy industry had extreme economic difficulties because this sector had huge energy requirements. Therefore, these industries tried to conduct measures of rationalization of their energy consumption in order to reduce costs.

To reduce inflation the government attempted to limit cash flow. In spite of this endeavor, an economic crisis followed. It resulted in trade deficits with foreign trade partners. This crisis was resolved at the end of 1975. Thanks to the industrial adjustment that took into account the new economic conditions, domestic products in the field of machines, motor vehicles, and electronics tools regained their competitiveness on the world markets. During the second oil crisis, in 1979–1980, the government and industries reacted in time. Therefore, Japan could conduct adequate adjustments and avoid the price increases that occurred during the first one.

During the periods of high economic growth in the 1960s and in the second half of the 1970s, Japan experienced serious environmental problems and conflicts between employer and employee. Heavy and chemical industry created environmental damage, like ''Itai Itai'' and ''Minamata,'' which resulted from polluted water from heavy industry (An 1991). The construction of Shinkansen tracks and a new international airport in Narita also gave rise to huge debates.

Supply of labor force was another problem. Because of the reduction of labor forces in cities, companies could no longer employ the required number of workers. At this time, the labor unions demanded higher wages. To avoid conflicts, companies attempted to open up new markets abroad. These efforts were criticized by the United States and Western European countries because of strong export activities and the low-valued yen.

In spite of the critics, the United States and Western European countries could only request Japan cooperate by restricting exports because of the geopolitical situation in the era of the cold war. To reduce the trade friction, Voluntary Export Restraint Agreements (VERAs) were negotiated either by government officials or by industries. They covered a large part of the total of Japanese exports to the United States and Europe. These exports were radios, tape recorders, television tubes, steel, cars, and so on, and were restrained voluntarily (Wilkinson 1991).

Due to a rapidly growing trade surplus with the United States and Europe, by the end of the 1970s and the beginning of the 1980s the trade frictions between Japan and the West became a focus of concern again. This time the sensitive sectors were not only ships, televisions, bearings, and cars, but also machine tools and computers. To reduce the trade surplus, both the United States and Europe limited Japanese exports in specific sectors, including numerically controlled machine tools, color televisions, VCRs, and automobiles. In addition, different forms of restriction were used, including VERAs, quotas, and antidumping investigations. On the Japanese side, a Special Committee for International Economic Measures was set up in the ruling Liberal Democratic Party (LDP). The new committee got rid of unnecessary ministerial rivalries and announced two sets of measures to ease access to the domestic market, which included advance tariff cuts and the removal of 67 of a combined U.S. and E.C. list of 99 nontariff barriers. Additionally, the committee established a new Office of Trade Ombudsman (OTO) to solve specific complaints from foreign businessmen.

Despite efforts of both sides, the trade surplus with the United States and Western Europe grew continuously, and Japan became the world's largest net creditor nation in 1985. In contrast, the United States stopped being a creditor to the world and became its largest debtor in the same year (Katsuzo and Conquest 1992). Finally, the G-5 countries (United States, Japan, Germany, France, and the United Kingdom) agreed to meet at the Plaza Hotel in New York in September 1985 and announced a joint effort to limit the global imbalance by cutting the value of the U.S. dollar, which lost 29% of the exchange value against the yen within a year. In the same year the yen rose by 22% against European currencies. By August 1986 the value had soared from 240 yen to the dollar to 160 yen, and by January 1988 it had reached 120 yen (Steven 1991).

Under these domestic and international economic conditions, the government and companies fundamentally changed their economic policy in the 1980s.

The new economic policy was based on three decisive areas: the new industrial revolution in the technology of manufactures; the concentration of the service sectors; and the expansion of activities for research and development. Japan resolved to take over the leading position in the process of the new industrial revolution. That means that Japan leads control systems in the process of productions through the new microelectronics and laser technology. The electronic control systems could reduce a large number of employees on the assembly lines and increase the flexibility in the process of the productions (Vogel 1989).

The pressure of the United States and Europe caused Japan to accelerate foreign direct investment (FDI) in its manufactures and financial institutions. It also tried to stimulate domestic demand with boosted imports. These economic activities had two different effects: first, businessmen were sent overseas to carry out production from foreign bases; second, foreign business came to Japan to profit from the high yen (Sadako 1992).

To reconstruct the economy to the new world economic situation, the government provided a macro-economic framework in 1986:

> First, slower growth itself forced companies and industries to undergo structural adjustment. Second, the rapid appreciation of the yen and improved terms of trade on at least three occasions (in 1972 before the first oil crisis, in 1978 and after 1985) severely hit export-oriented and import-competing industries and drastically undermined their competitive edge. Third, trade imbalance, trade conflicts, and the resulting series of market liberalization measures encouraged imports and increased competition within the domestic market. Fourth, the stimulation of domestic demand encouraged more firms to produce for the domestic market and to search for new products (Ippei 1992).

Under such a macro-economic framework, the government accepted advice from the Maekawa Committee in 1986, which introduced structural changes in the economy with the liberalization and internationalization of financial and capital markets, reducing Japan's dependence on export-led growth through domestic-led growth. The changes also promoted international cooperation and the contribution to the world economy. The most significant fact about the acceptance of the Maekawa Report was that it signalled the priority that the government wanted to place on international harmony. The goal of the government was the reduction of both economic tensions and imbalances in trade and payments with its major trade partners.

Maekawa himself described this new tendency of structural change in the economy as a historical transformation of the traditional policies on economic management and the nation's lifestyle. The five-year plan for 1988 to 1992 was carried out within a global economic context. The plan promoted the domestic-led growth and aimed to change three different areas:

> First, improvement of individual lifestyles by making more land available for private housing, reducing work hours and lowering consumer prices by simplifying the distribution system, and dismantling the protection for agriculture, second, development of regional economic centers, and third, rectification of external imbalances and increase of contributions to development aid and to the cost of the Western alliances (Wilkinson 1991:198).

In 1996, the GDP ran up to 500,356 billion yen and the per capita reached 3,978,657 yen (International Monetary Fund 1997). In spite of this prosperity the economy had a serious problem with regard to the insecure energy supply of the world. Japan is totally dependent on the supply of foreign energy, which makes up about 89% of total energy consumption. In addition, constantly growing wages, an increasingly aging population, and high individual claims tend to change the traditional view of the Japanese. On the international level it will not be possible anymore to concentrate only on its economic expansion without taking appropriate responsibilities for the securing of world trade, maintaining world peace, and aid to developing countries (Nojiri 1986).

Japanese direct investments in foreign countries follow roughly two different patterns, which can be distinguished by the geographical relocation and strategic capital investments for the internationalization of Japanese industries. The first is that Japan invests its capital in Asia, which has been a traditional target due to the problem of escalating costs from the high yen and to the establishment of production base for labor-intensive manufactures. The second pattern of foreign direct investment consists of high-technology projects, new joint ventures, and technical tie-ups in other industrialized countries. Traditionally, Japanese manufacturing companies invested in the United States and Europe mainly to service their export products in these markets. With the growing regional protectionism within the North American Free Trade Agreement (NAFTA) and the European Communities (EC), Japan must either make these high-tech products locally or cooperate with local partners.

V. TECHNOLOGICAL INNOVATION AND DECENTRALIZATION OF THE INDUSTRIAL DEVELOPMENT

In 1979, MITI decided to carry out a future-orientated project in the 1980s in order to minimize the effects of the second oil crisis and to reduce the trade surplus. The minister of international trade and industry, Keichi Konaga, explained his presentation about the project: ‘‘Technical innovation is a driving force for economic development. To build a creative knowledge-intensive industrial structure in the next decades depends on our capacity, that leads to development of basic technologies’’ (MITI 1980).

In 1980, MITI prepared a 10-year national project for R & D in the fields of supercomputers, robots, new materials, biotechnology, and mechatronics. To carry out this project it would have been more beneficial for MITI to have decreased trade protectionism, which prevented Japan's future-orientated industries from competing in domestic and international markets. In addition, trade protectionism hindered information exchange about high technologies and improvement of R & D projects with the participation of foreign companies.

Instead, the government launched industry plans in the beginning of the 1980s, which consisted of six different strategies:

Strategy 1: Joint R & D projects
Strategy 2: Strategic alliances with foreign companies
Strategy 3: The technopolis plan
Strategy 4: Telecommunication network
Strategy 5: Venture capital and venture business
Strategy 6: Promotion of selected imports

Among these strategies, the technopolis plan plays a very important role because it aims to decentralize industrial development and encourage cooperation among industry, scholars, and technopolises. The strategy of the technopolis should promote the development of high technology, which could contribute to Japanese society in the future (Tatsuno 1986). To succeed in this strategy, three steps should be followed. MITI defined these: ''First, new applications and combinations of existing technologies; second, emerging of new technologies as a result of new applications and methods from scholars and technologies and third, preparing for epoch-making technical innovations after 1990'' (MITI 1989).

The development of high technology in Japan has been part of economic policy. The central government, especially MITI, has played a very important role by advising industry and leading to the creation of industrial policies.

MITI is deeply involved in the technopolis plan although its role is limited to serve as a catalyst and moderator. Since national research policies are heavily centralized, the prefectures cannot enjoy independent research activities. MITI sets a target in the four major R & D areas of microelectronics, biotechnologies, new energies, and new materials toward which all of technopolises prioritized their R & D activities. They also focus on development of existing technologies in their regions.

VI. SUCCESSFUL MODEL OF TECHNOCORPORATISM IN JAPAN

Generally speaking, Japanese economic and technological policy seems to be successful. There are several different reasons for its success. The reasons are clearly distinct from the experience of Western industrialized countries.

First, the Japanese government strengthened its influence on economic and technological policy with the establishment of MITI. MITI could arrange an industrial policy which was aimed at a growth-orientated economic policy and, simultaneously, at a market-oriented technology policy. To carry out this policy successfully, MITI dealt with financial support for chosen economic sectors and with control of R & D for manufactures.

Second, compared to Western industrialized countries there was stronger competition and only limited cooperation between Japanese companies because the domestic market is relatively small in comparison with North America and the E.C. The Japanese companies improved their competitiveness through high productivities on the domestic market. The companies competed intensively to remain competitive not only on the domestic market, but also internationally. At the same time they avoided unnecessary competition with one another on the world market, which would have allowed other industrialized countries to take advantage of this comparative competitiveness and damage Japanese national interests. The cooperative relationship between Japanese companies on the world market was recommended by the MITI. On the domestic market, a limited cooperation was carried out, mainly in research areas.

Third, universities in technopolis areas contributed to improvements in industrial technologies through cooperations with companies. A major part of R & D activity at the universities was the researching for possibilities in manufacturing and their development. For that, a few Japanese national technical universities invited private companies and government institutes to launch joint research programs.

Fourth, the cultural background in Confucianism and Buddhism played an important role. Confucianism contains a strong loyalty to the state and a high respect for elders. These principles are applied in the lifelong employment system and the seniority system. In Buddhism, an achievement of "No-I" is regarded as an important goal. The group-oriented mentality is based on this Buddhist influence. It results in the group mentality that families and companies are more important than the individual. In addition, Buddhism teaches that nothing is permanent or absolute. It gives the people reason to continually improve in their field of work. Continuous progress is a way of life in Japan. As a result, workers always attempt to improve the quality of products, reduce production costs, and improve customer services (Kang 1989).

The given reasons were important factors for Japanese technocorporatism until the end of the 1970s. The close and cooperative relationships among the government, industries, and universities was called "Japan Corporation" by the Western industrialized countries. In the beginning of the 1980s, domestic and international conditions changed. In 1980, MITI published a report called Trade and Industry Policies for the 1980s, which predicted technical developments for reliable energy sources and less dependence on oil. It also predicted the development of highly sophisticated technology, using new materials and systems (Minami, 1991).

With the globalization of the economy and criticism from the West regarding government protectionist policies, the government turned to market liberalization and decreased direct and visible financial subsidies to chosen industrial sectors after the middle of the 1980s. Instead of being directly involved in industries, MITI now attempts to support R & D activity for basic research and plays the role of catalyst in cooperation among regional governments, industries, and universities.

In the 1990s, the government seeks to attain the high standard of living demanded by the people through productivity growth and the improvement of adequate social infrastructure. For productivity growth, a highly skilled work force and technological innovations are required.

Higher educational standards could make it possible to produce value-added products and improve the development of the service sector. Technological innovation will continue to improve productivity levels and R & D activities are the core area for it. The provision of social infrastructure will contribute not only to raising living standards but also to increasing economic growth from the supply side (Economic Planning Agency 1993).

Trade friction and the globalization of Japanese firms have forced the country to rethink management methods with an international perspective since the second half of the 1980s. Japanese companies needed to extend their corporate operations, including investment in plant and equipment, research and development; develop production facilities; and establish locally incorporated companies abroad. To implement these corporate operations, MITI continues to play an important role in the 1990s. Its future aspects focus on environmental protection and sustainable development.

VII. TRANSFORMATION OF THE SOUTH KOREAN ECONOMY

Late industrialization is characterized by three facets of growth—diversification, stabilization, and growth momentum. The transformation of the South Korean economy can be explained with these characters. In order to reach these goals, the government has played a role of entrepreneur which planned what, when, and how much to produce.

The initiative to enter new industrial sectors has come primarily from the public sphere. In the 1950s, the economic policy was under control due to its heavy U.S. foreign aid for Korean War reconstruction. Compared to it, every major shift in industrial diversification in the 1960s and 1970s was planned by the South Korean government (Amsden 1989).

The state masterminded the early import substitution project in cement, fertilizers, oil refinery, and synthetic fibers. In particular, the last improved the profitability of the textiles industry. The transformation from light to heavy industry was also initiated by the state. It was fully responsible for the push into heavy machinery and chemicals in the 1970s. Hence, it is safe to say that major milestones in South Korea's industrialization have been decided by the state.

In South Korea, as in Japan, a tradition to consider bureaucratic careers is vital in providing both legitimacy for state initiatives and nonmaterial incentives. The bureaucracy has managed to maintain itself as one of power-elite groups along with the military. The most privileged bureaucracy organ was the Economic Planning Board (EPB), headed by a deputy prime minister and chosen by former president Park Chung Hee to be a superagency in the economic area (Kim 1987). It coordinated economic policy through control of the budgetary process and the Economic Ministers Consultation Committee. Additionally, the managers of EPB were often promoted into leadership positions in other ministers (Choi 1987).

The government-led economic transformation resulted in strong ties between the regime and the largest conglomerate business (Chaebol). The Park regime was dependent on Chaebol to implement industrial transformation, which guaranteed the basis for its legitimacy (Evans 1995). These strong ties were enhanced through the military governments, the Chun regime, and the Roh regime. Two former army generals, Chun Doo Hwan and Roh Tae Woo, took over political power after former president Park Chung Hee was assassinated in October 1979.

VIII. ECONOMIC DEVELOPMENT AND GOVERNMENT STRATEGIES

A major change in the direction of the South Korean economic development began with the military government that took power in 1961. Its economic policy aimed at rapid industrial development based on export-oriented industrialization strategy, active inducement of foreign capital, and various institutional reforms (Sakong 1993; Kim 1994).

To carry out the outward-looking development strategy, the government devaluated its currency in May 1964 by almost 50% from 130 to 214 won per U.S. dollar, and large-scale foreign borrowing to finance investment in export industries flowed into South Korea. Furthermore, substantial imports of raw materials, components, and machinery were also necessary to perform the export drive policy. It provided the most successful exporters a range of benefits, including preferential access to loans at subsidized interest rates, tax incentives, discounts on power and freight costs, and access to important licenses for machinery and components (Bloom 1993).

These measures enabled a few major exporters to expand their export and led to a concentration of economic power into Chaebols, which accumulated profits and branched into new lines of business across industries to form groups. They became further diversified and grew faster than the rest of the economy. The 46 largest Chaebols grew at an average annual rate of 22.8% between 1973 and 1978; the nation's GDP grew at an average annual rate of 9.9% for the same period (see Table 1). Their share in GDP also increased from 9.8% to 17.1% during the same period (Sakong 1993). A major factor in the fast growth of the conglomerates in the 1970s was the government's new industrial policy based on the heavy and chemical industries (HCI). The government supported them further in order to reach its target of economic growth. HCI's preferential access to bank credit enabled big conglomerates participating in the government's HCI promotion policies to receive nearly 60% of the total bank loans from 1975 to 1977 and almost 95% of policy loans in 1978. It resulted in the neglect of the light manufacturing industries that were significant exporters as well as producers of daily necessities. At the same time, the overinvestment in targeted industries based on supply-side considerations occurred rather than realistic demand-side forecasts at the firm level.

Consequently, the government announced a set of comprehensive stabilization measures including restrictive aggregate demand management through a tighter monetary and fiscal stance in 1979. It means that the growth-first strategy in the 1960s and 1970s turned to stabilization policy in the 1980s, though the

Table 1 Average Annual Growth Rate of Chaebols, 1973–1978 (%)

	Total value added	Value added in manufacturing
Top 5	30.1	35.7
Top 10	28.0	30.0
Top 20	25.9	27.5
Top 46	22.8	24.4
1 to 5	30.1	35.7
6 to 10	22.8	16.8
11 to 20	19.9	22.4
21 to 46	12.8	16.4
1 to 46	22.8	24.4
GDP	9.9	17.2

Source: Sakong (1993).

latter was based on the short-term strategy. The policy shift caused severe problems in the nontargeted, labor-intensive sectors of the economy and the balance of payments crisis created by the second oil shock. However, it was well timed and South Korea took advantage of the boom in manufactured exports in the mid-1980s.

Moreover, selective industrial promotion laws oriented to sunrise industries such as electronics and petrochemicals were replaced by the Industrial Development Law in 1986 which mainly focused on rationalization of declining industries such as the textile industry, ferro-alloys, and fertilizers. The new law also supports technological upgrade instead of providing only credits. It enabled the government to establish a basic principle. The government was ready to be involved in industries only in cases of obvious market failure. In the second half of the 1980s trade liberalization became essential for maintaining a cooperative relationship with the United States in particular, and a liberalization in financial sector began with a limited form.

The close association of government and business in South Korea's economic development has been regarded as Korea Inc. (Cumings 1987; Wade 1990). However, although this government-business relationship contributed to the rapid industrialization, the national economy suffered from fundamental distortion of the competitive market structure, misallocation of resources, severe inflationary pressure, and imbalanced development of the industrial structure created by excessive government intervention until the first half of the 1980s (Kim 1994).

Furthermore, the domestic environment has changed rapidly since the end of the 1980s. The technology-intensive sector has continuously expanded at the same time as the manufacturing sector has become more sophisticated and diversified. Big conglomerates such as Hyundai, Samsung, Lucky Goldstar, Daewoo, etc., are becoming more integrated into the world economy through corporate alliances and foreign direct investments that enable them to evade government directives. Thus, the new directions of the economy ought to concern themselves with technology-related market failures based on the lack of human and relatively underdeveloped subcontractors.

In the beginning of the 1990s external environment also changed rapidly through new regional alignments and new order of world trade system based on the World Trade Organization (WTO). In order to overcome trade barriers, the government and businesses promote overseas direct investments on the one hand, and they are keen to increase their competitiveness against foreign firms on the domestic and international market on the other. Hence, the role of the government is focusing on supporting for research and development activity to upgrade technological standards. The present government has been also keen to upgrade industrial structure oriented from industrial widening toward industrial deepening, and to improve industrial competition environment created by well-developed infrastructure, stable labor and land supply, etc. (Ministry of Trade, Industry, and Energy 1994).

IX. SOUTH KOREA'S INDUSTRIAL CHALLENGE AND TECHNOLOGICAL STRATEGIES

South Korea's key industrial challenge is to keep ahead of the ASEAN-4 and mainland China by maintaining and expanding the existing technological gap and at the same time achieve higher levels of product sophistication in order to compete with other NICs as well as with Japan, the United States, and Europe. With a new global economic order, triple blocs, South Korean industry faces severe trade barriers in other blocs on the one hand, and new intraregional competition based on a rapid increase of intraregional trade connections in high-technology and knowledge-intensive goods and services in its own bloc on the other. Thus, South Korea needs to develop technology-intensive industries to survive in a dynamic international and regional environment.

Historically, Chaebol-dominant industrial structure has restricted the entry of small and medium-size firms that has resulted in serious technological dependence. Activities of small and medium-size firms based on their flexibility play an important role for innovation. To slow down Chaebol dominance and to emphasize small and medium-size firms, the government launched two strategies aimed at rapid and sustained technological development. First, South Korea struggles to upgrade its technological capacity through using imported technologies; that is, a part of the strategy is to form the nation's linkages with key multinational companies in various industrial areas. Secondly, South Korea is keen to strengthen the country's technological self-sufficiency by deepening its existing industrial and technological capabilities. To carry out this strategy successfully, an increase of R & D activities is necessary. The government promotes a participation of local industries in R & D activities through offering a large number of incentives such as depreciation allowances, investment tax credits, deferral of income tax payments, and duty-free import of selected capital goods (Simon and Soh 1994).

X. REGIONAL DEVELOPMENT STRATEGY BASED ON HIGH TECHNOLOGY

Considering that South Korea is a newly industrialized country, its industry has developed rapidly in the past 30 years. It has become a major power in electronics manufacturing and some areas of information technology (Castells and Hall 1994). South Korea has continuously upgraded its technological foundation, and the quality of technical and engineering work forces as well. This success story is based on providing necessary governmental support for the industrial and communications infrastructure, labor training credit, and trade policy, on the one hand, and the willingness of South Korean companies to increase their competitiveness in the world market on the other.

This technology policy focused on targeted fields contributing to national economic development. At the same time Chaebol-oriented economic policy based on heavy and chemical industries caused a severe regional imbalance in the territory. The government realized the need for regional decentralization. The symbolic value of national R & D facilities contributed to regional development as well as to upgrading national technology standards. Former President Park Chung Hee decided on building a new science town (Taedok Science Town) in central South Korea in 1973 (Park 1997).

In 1995, about 14,000 of South Korea's leading researchers and engineers were working on R & D activities. The total residential population has reached about 70,000, of whom about 40,000 were employees in R & D units, R & D support organizations, and their families. About 16,000 housing units have been constructed for them. The numbers of in-town organizations have reached 48 and 18, mostly industrial labs to be set up in the near future.

In addition, the Technobelt Concept was launched to connect research and industry through information and telecommunication technologies. According to the plan, Seoul and Taedok are to become technological diffusion centers connecting networks along four major technobelts. The west coast belt from Seoul to Kwangju is to specialize in energy and food production; the south coast belt from Kwangju to Pusan is to focus on heavy industry; the north-south belt connecting Seoul, Suwon, Taedok, and Pusan will be based on electronics, semiconductors, and textile industries; and the east-west belt linking Kwangju, Taedok, and Kangnung will concentrate on medical and social services research and production. This technobelt concept will contribute to the formation of a productive structure for the 21st century, and at the same time the role of Taedok Science Town will be strengthened due to its geographical location and innovative milieu as an R & D center.

To become an R & D Center and create synergy effects, Taedok Science Town has intensified the cooperative relationships among government supported institutes, universities, and industrial laboratories. The Technological Innovation Center (TIC) at KAIST carries out industry-oriented projects and facilitates technology developments in the industrial sector (Park 1997).

XI. CONCLUSIONS

The success of Japanese exports in the 1950s and the 1960s was mainly based on price advantages. In 1960, Japanese exports accounted for $40.8 billion and increased to $144.6 billion in 1980. In 1985, Japan had a huge trade surplus, almost $47 billion, with its partners. The Japanese trade surplus was increasing continuously until the beginning of the 1990s. It reached $103 billion in 1991 and increased to $144 billion in 1994. However, due to the depreciation of the yen during the second half of 1995, after the peak value of 79 yen per dollar in April, the total Japanese trade surplus for 1995 ended up with $132 billion.

Japanese economic policy represented an outward-looking strategy concentrating on exports and economic growth from the 1950s until the middle of the 1970s. During that time, the Japanese export sector used methods of mass production to better compete on the international market. Since 1975 the Japanese government has attempted to adapt its economic policy to changes in the international economy, and reached a stable economic growth rate in the 1980s.

The main goals of the Japanese technology policy are the promotion of development for creative technologies, the refinement of industrial structure, the securing of sufficient supplies of energy and raw materials, and the promotion of regional economic structures. Additionally, this policy demands an improvement of general living conditions in cities and in the industry. As a further goal, it promotes the transfer of science and technology to developing countries and strengthens Japan's cooperation with industrialized countries in the achievement of scientific and technological progresses.

Following a late industrialization based on state intervention, foreign loans, borrowed technologies, etc., South Korea has become one of the major economic powers in the Asia-Pacific region. Its economic development is regarded as a miracle of East Asia and a model for other developing nations. In the rapid economic growth period, the government chose strategic industrial sectors, which contributed to improving national competitivenesses on the world market. This government-led economic development strategy resulted in strong ties between government and industry, which enabled them to form Chaebols.

A Chaebol-oriented economic structure contributed to the rapid economic growth and at the same time faced severe trade barriers from EU and NAFTA due to its mass production system. Furthermore, domestic production costs have continuously increased because of well-organized labor unions and rocketing land prices. These negative factors pushed the industries to reorganize their structures. South Korea struggles on the technological upgrading of the industry and foreign direct investment in the region as well as in the advanced industrialized countries. In addition, the technological upgrading of the industry and regional development will make the South Korean economy grow further.

Overall, industrial policy and regional development in Japan seem to be cooperative and efficient to implement because of its matured economic level, while the regional development in Korea is regarded as a showcase for the technological upgrading in specific areas.

REFERENCES

Akamatsu, K. (1961). A theory of unbalanced growth in the world economy. *Weltwirtschaftliches Archiv*, *86*(2), 196–215.

An, J.K. (1991). *Philosophy and Technology*. Seoul: Juk San.

Bloom, M.D.H. (1993). Globalization and the Korean electronics industry. *Pacific Review* *6*(2), 119–126.

Castells, M. and Hall, P. (1994). *Technopoles of the World: The Making of 21st Century Industrial Complexes*. London: Routledge.

Cumings, B. (1987). The origins and development of the northeast Asian political economy: industrial sectors, product cycles, and political consequences. In F. Deyo (ed.), *The Political Economy of the New Asian Industrialism*. New York: Cornell University Press.

Cumings, B. (1989). Ursprunge und Entwicklung der politischen Ökonomie in Nordostasien: Industriesektoren, Producktzyklen und politische Konsequenzen. In U. Menzel (ed.), *Im Schatten des Siegers: Japan*, Band 4. Frankfurt am Main: Suhrkamp.

Economic Planning Agency. (1993). *White Paper on Japanese Economy*. Tokyo: EPA.

Evans, P. (1995). *Embedded Autonomy, State and Industrial Transformation*. Princeton: Princeton University Press.

International Monetary Fund. (1997). *International Financial Statistics, August*. Washington: IMF.

Ippei, Y. (1992). Gearing economic policy to international harmony. In G.D. Hook and M.A. Weiner (eds.), *The Internationalization of Japan*. London: Routledge.

Kang, T.W. (1989). *Is Korea the Next Japan*? New York: Free Press.

Katsuzo, S. and Conquest, C.R. (1992). The internationalization of Japanese capital. In G.D. Hook and M.A. Weiner (eds.), *The Internationalization of Japan*. London: Routledge.

Kim, K.-S. (1994). Industrial policy and trade regimes. In L.-J. Cho and Y.H. Kim (eds.), *Korea's Political Economy*. San Francisco: Westview Press.

Kim, Y.-H. (1994). An introduction to the Korean model of political economy. In L.-J. Cho and Y.H. Kim (eds.), *op. cit*.

Klenner, W. (1989). Grundzüge der wirtschaftlichen Entwicklung und der Wirtschaftspolitik seit dem Zweiten Weltkrieg. In U. Menzel (ed.), *Im Schatten des Siegers: Japan*, Band. 3. Frankfurt am Main: Suhrkamp.

Komiya, R. (1984). *Industrial Policy of Japan*. Tokyo: Academic Press.

Korhonen, P. (1994). *Japan and the Pacific Free Trade Area*. London: Routledge.

Kübler, H. (1986). *Japanische Telekommunikationsindustrie*. Munich: München Universitäts Verlag.

Minami, R. (1991). *The Economic Development of Japan*. London: Macmillan.

Ministry of International Trade and Industry. (1980). *A Report on Trade and Industry Policy for the 1980s*. Tokyo: MITI.

Ministry of International Trade and Industry (MITI). (1989). Die Perspektiven der MITI-Politik in der achtziger Jahren. In U. Menzel (ed.), *Im Schatten des Siegers: Japan*, Band. 3. Frankfurt am Main: Suhrkamp.

Ministry of Trade, Industry and Energy. (1994). *The White Paper*. Seoul: MOTIE.

Nojiri, T. (1986). Wirtschaftsentwicklung und Wirtschaftsethik in Japan. In C. von Barloewen and K.W. Meers (eds.), *Japan und der Westen*, Band. 2. Frankfurt am Main: Suhrkamp.

Park, S.-C. (1997). *The Technopolis Plan in Japanese Industrial Policy*. Göteborg: Vasastadens.

Sadako, O. (1992). Interdependence and internationalization. In G.D. Hook and M.A. Weiner (eds.), *The Internationalization of Japan*. London: Routledge.

Sakong, I. (1993). *Korea in the World Economy*. Washington: Institute for International Economics.

Simon, D.F. and Soh, C.-R. (1994). Korea's technological development. *Pacific Review*, *7*(1), 89–104.

Steven, R. (1991). Structural origins of Japan's direct foreign investment. In J. Morris (ed.), *Japan and the Global Economy*. London: Routledge.

Tatsuno, S. (1986). *The Technopolis Strategy. Japan, High Technology, and the Control of the Twenty-First Century*. New York: Prentice-Hall.

Uchiyama, Y. (1986). Japans Stellung in der Weltwirtschaft. In C. von Baloewen and K.W. Mees (eds.), *Japan und der Westen*, Band. 2. Frankfurt am Main: Fischer.

Vogel, E.F. (1989). Pax nipponica? In U. Menzel (ed.), *Im Schatten des Siegers*: *Japan*, Band. 2. Frankfurt am Main: Suhrkamp.

Wade, R. (1990). *Governing the Market*: *Economic Theory and the Role of Government in the East Asian Industrialization*. Princeton: Princeton University Press.

Wilkinson, E. (1991). *Japan Versus the West*. London: Penguin Books.

7

Deregulation for Whom? Reexamining the Retail Deregulation in Japan

Yoichiro Sato
University of Auckland, Auckland, New Zealand

I. INTRODUCTION

Small store owners and farmers in Japan were well protected throughout the post–World War II period. Johnson sees this protection as a payoff for the maintenance of the Liberal Democratic Party's (LDP) rule.[1] Dramatic social changes in Japan during postwar economic development lessened the LDP's reliance on these two groups. Nevertheless, they still exercise a significant influence both through individual LDP members and the bureaucracy, resisting and delaying necessary policy changes in the retail sector. Jurisdictional battles within Japan's central bureaucracy, and between central and local governments, further make a meaningful policy change difficult.

This study of the amendment and the eventual abolition of Japan's Large-Scale Retail Store Law (LSRSL) will reveal a strong influence of small retailers and the MITI's dilemma in implementing a major retail policy change. A broad consensus on retail rationalisation has been stalled by bureaucratic and intergovernmental disagreements, thereby inviting external pressure. Despite changes in the law and MITI's administrative guidance, informal sabotage by the local status quo interests watered down policy changes.

While the strict government regulation has failed to reverse the lack of successors for mom-and-pop stores, blind deregulation is not the answer. The recent deregulation has increased the total number of department stores and supermarkets, and their stronger bargaining power has resulted in a sharp drop on wholesale prices. However, the simultaneously expected drop in consumer prices has so far been limited to certain durable products, and this suggests that the drop is largely due to the prolonged recession of the 1990s, not the retail liberalization. As many observers have optimistically equated the retail liberalization of the 1990s with the realization of consumer interests, little attention has been paid to the increasing oligopolistic tendency in Japan's retail industry.

This chapter will review the history of the large-scale retail regulations in Japan. Political processes which led to policy changes at different stages will be analyzed. The amendment of the Large-Scale Retail Store Law in 1991, the changes in its implementation since 1994, and the new decentralized regulation to be effective in the year 2000 will be analyzed in relation to wholesale prices, retail prices, and the structure of the retail industry. Finally, based on the preceding analysis, the paper will seek a possible direction of the future reforms for Japan's retail regulations.

II. HISTORY OF LARGE-SCALE STORE REGULATION

Japan's large-store regulation has its origin in the prewar period. Expansion of department stores in the early 1900s caused conflicts with smaller retailers. Voluntary restrictions by the Department Store Association (DSA) after 1932 failed to calm the disputes, and small retailers mobilized anti–department store campaigns. In the wartime-disciplined economy, the Department Store Law, passed in 1937, regulated stores larger than 3000 m^2 in the six largest cities, and larger than 1500 m^2 in other areas. Opening new stores and expanding existing ones required a permit from the Ministry of Commerce and Industry, which examined population, number of small retailers, and other related variables in the area.[2] The law was abolished under the Allied occupation in 1947, but renewed conflicts between large and small retailers revived the old Department Store Law in 1956 with some modifications.[3]

The emergence of supermarkets and their unregulated growth during the 1960s irritated both small retailers and the already regulated department stores. MITI initially optimistically predicted that economic development and the resulting enlargement of the market would ease tension between supermarkets and small retailers, and hoped that supermarkets would be the leading force in the retail reform. However, increasing political pressure from small retailers forced MITI to issue several administrative guidance to regulate supermarkets. The DSA took the lead in discussion in the Small Commission on Retail Problems of the Distribution Division of the MITI Industrial Structure Council.[4]

Taking into consideration the interests of the DSA, the division recommended extension of the regulation to supermarkets. The division also suggested that the existing permission system be replaced by a mandatory advance reporting system. However, facing an organized protest by small retailers, the Socialist and Communist parties, and members of the Commerce and Industry Committee of the LDP's Policy Affairs Research Council (PARC), the bill was redrafted to enable MITI to screen the reporting and decide not to accept it, thereby reinstituting a de facto permit system. MITI was to consult the Large-Scale Retail Store Advisory Council (LSRS-AC) made up of people of "learned experience," including scholars and journalists, and issue recommendations or orders when necessary.

The Large-Scale Retail Store Law was passed in 1973 (see Figure 1).[5] However, the LSRS-AC remained inactive, and MITI, through an administrative guidance, forced mediation in local conferences on Commercial Activity Adjustment (CCAA), which consisted of local merchants, consumers, and scholars. The CCAA was to mediate conflicting interests through unanimous decisions. To avoid disagreements in the CCAA, it was common for large retailers to hold informal pre-CCAA meetings with local small retailers before mandatory reporting of a planned opening of the store (LSRSL, section 5) or reporting construction of the building (LSRSL, section 3).[6]

The CCAA aggregates diverse opinions in the area of planned store opening and presents a collective recommendation to the directors of the chambers of Commerce and Industry (CCI) and the Commerce and Industry Meetings (CIM), and the CCI and CIM in return report to MITI. However, informal pre-CCAA meetings had no clear rule of member selection and operation. The informal meetings became the de facto arena for interest adjustments.[7]

Opening of new supermarkets continued during the 1970s, and some stores scaled down their sizes to evade the MITI regulation (see Appendix). Many local governments passed their own ordinances to regulate these middle-size stores. MITI intended to integrate the LSRSL and other retail regulations into one law and regulate the opening of middle-sized stores based on voluntary reporting.[8] However, the plan backfired in the LDP-PARC Commerce and Industry Committee. In 1978, a new category, Class II Large-Scale Retail Store, was added to the law in order to regulate stores between 500 and 1500 m^2. Prefectural governors were given authority to screen the reporting from these middle-size stores and express their objections in consultation with prefectural Large-Scale Retail Store Advisory Council (LSRS-AC). This enhanced the authority of local governments.[9]

III. SMALL RETAILERS AND MITI

The 1979 law already indicated MITI's general direction toward retail rationalization. Ito Keiichi of the MITI Industrial Policy Bureau pointed out the variation of consumer needs, selective attitudes of consumers, extended shopping distance

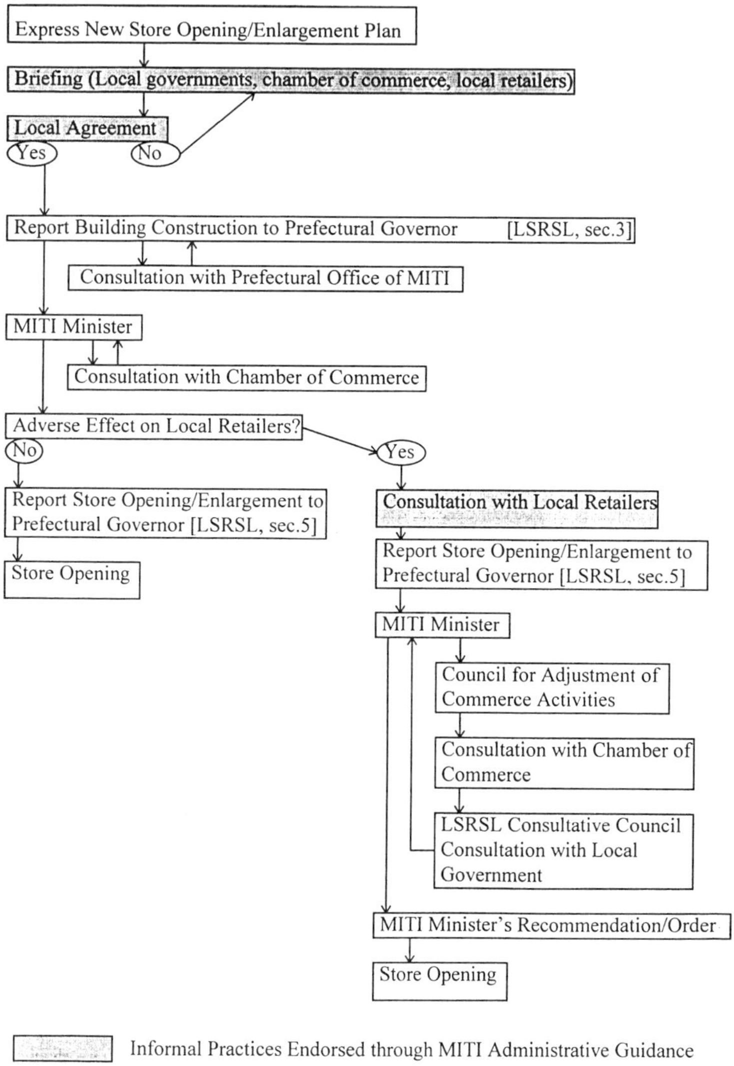

Figure 1 Large-scale retail store law. (Translated and reproduced from Nihon Keizai Shimbunsha, ed., *Daitenho ga kieru hi*, Tokyo, 1990, p. 72.)

due to motorization, and increased spare time. He stated, "In retailing, large and small enterprises will be able to co-exist, and small enterprises may enjoy prosperity depending on their innovation."[10]

However, MITI soon faced fierce resistance from small retailers. Increased local authority in the amended LSRSL intensified the conflicts between large and small retailers, and MITI requested voluntary restriction on opening of new large stores in 1981. The Discussion Group on Large-Scale Store Problems was established as a private advisory body of the chief of the MITI Industrial Policy Bureau and the director of the Medium and Small Enterprise Agency. Along the lines of the Group's recommendation, MITI in 1982 placed a one-per-year quota on the opening of new stores for each of the 10 department store enterprises, and set upper limits on the total floor size increase for each of the 13 supermarket enterprises.[11]

Small retailers were, furthermore, seeking a revival of the "permit system," which existed under the old Department Store Law. The National Shopping Districts Promotion Meeting (*Zenkoku Shotengai Shinkokai*), the National Shopping Districts Union (*Zenkoku Shotengai Rengokai*), and five other small retailers' organizations in 1981 formed the National Retailer Promotion Meeting for Amending the LSRSL and other purposes.[12]

In 1982, MITI started drafting the Vision of Retailing in the 1980s in a collective meeting of the Industrial Structure Council's Retail Division and the Medium and Small Enterprise Policy Council (MSEPC)'s Small Commission on Retailing. Whereas the 1981 discussion consisted of the Industrial Policy Bureau and the MSEA, the MSEPC was an advisory body of the Prime Minister, indicating an increased political intervention in the area of normally routinized administrative regulations. Sekio Sugioka interprets this as evidence of declined influence of the MSEA within MITI.[13] Despite the gradual consolidation of pro-reform forces within MITI, it was not the time to attempt any amendment to the LSRSL. Had the LDP got its hands into the process, a more restrictive bill would have passed with the support of all opposition parties.[14] The best MITI could do was to issue administrative guidance to appease the pressure from small retailers and the LDP without hurting the existing large stores.

Diversifying consumer tastes demanded rationalization of retailing.[15] Small retailers gradually switched their objective to compensation measures. MITI offered "special loans for computerisation," promoted grouping of small stores for information sharing on market trends, and helped "redevelopment" of shopping districts. In 1984, MITI helped small retailers plan four new shopping districts, and the number jumped to 14 in 1985. Due to rising foreign pressure to increase imports, these shopping districts were also subsidized in the name of staging "import fairs," and individual stores received loans for setting up "import corners."[16] Projects for revitalization of shopping districts were able to finance up to 65% of the cost with a low 2.7% interest rate, and under certain conditions, 80% with no interest.[17]

Not all small retailers were satisfied with these MITI payoffs. Some groups did not trust MITI at all and continued resisting relaxation of the LSRSL by relying on the increased local authority and the informal delay tactics. In many cases, an agreement with existing local shopping districts was a de facto requirement for large retailers to file a report on planned construction. According to MITI, 12 prefectures and 105 other local governments (cities, towns, and villages) had such de facto requirements. While an agreement was to be sought in informal pre-CCAA meetings, the length of the discussion there was unspecified. In some cases, more than 10 years was spent from the announcement of a plan until the actual opening due to prolonged discussions. Twenty-three prefectures and 991 other local governments had extended restrictions, regulating stores smaller than 500 m^2.[18]

The strict but informal nature of regulations tempted some large retailers into corruption. In 1981, small-store owners in Kitakami city filed a lawsuit with the Tokyo regional court for a cancelation of MITI's recommendation, complaining about the biased representation in the CCAA. Among the 18 members, three had a clear conflict of interests, and 15 were chosen from supporters of the planned construction of a shopping center.[19] While subsidies to small stores gave them much-needed breathing space, the tightened regulations against the large-store openings also allowed oligopolistic market control by the existing large retailers, especially the six dominant supermarket chains, during the 1980s.[20]

IV. POLITICS OF THE RETAIL VISION OF THE 1990s

Facing the paralysis during the 1980s, MITI concluded its Retail Vision of the 1990s in June 1989. The Vision recommended elimination of the local consent requirement and an eight-month limit on the length of CCAA meetings. MITI, local governments, Chambers of Commerce and Industry (CCI), and Commerce and Industry Meetings (CIM, or *Shokokai*) were to be authorized to close CCAA meetings after eight months without unanimous agreement. Additional restrictions by local governments were to be abolished.[21]

MITI was to issue an administrative guidance to implement these changes in the Vision. However, LDP members from districts with many small retailers demanded that MITI delay the guidance, in the wake of LDP's defeat in the June 1989 House of Councillor election due to LDP's introduction of a new consumption tax. However, the influence of the rank-and-file LDP Commerce *zoku* (politicians with interests in specific policy areas) members had declined by this time, and the leaders among the Commerce *zoku* were committed to a more market-oriented retail reform.[22] The Ministry of Home Affairs also opposed the Vision because it called for invalidation of locally imposed regulations and would "lead to encroachment of local autonomy."[23] While the MITI generally supported relaxation of the large-store regulation, abolishing the LSRSL would reduce its jurisdiction. Abolition could also mean undisciplined growth of local ordinances to regulate large stores.[24] Lacking political control over this turf battle, the Japanese government was incapable of making anything more than an incremental change.

V. FOREIGN PRESSURE MADE IN JAPAN?

Complaints by foreign exporters about Japan's complex retail system have been heard since the 1970s. However, it was only after the 1980s that the matter came up in official bilateral discussions between Japan and the United States. It is reported that an executive of one of Japan's largest supermarkets informed the U.S. government about the LSRSL, and this triggered a detailed analysis of the law by the American negotiators.[25] The LSRSL became the symbol of Japan's complex retail system, and its abolition was thought to be a part of Japan's economic liberalization and import expansion.

The U.S.-Japan Structural Impediment Initiative (SII) talks, beginning on 5 September 1989 in Tokyo, addressed the LSRSL issue.[26] On 26 September 1989, Toys R Us Inc. announced that it was going to open four to six stores in Japan in 1991 in cooperation with McDonald's Japan.[27] Toys R Us's chairman, Charles Lazarus, and President Fujita Den of McDonald's Japan, met U.S. Trade Representative Carla Hills on 4 October 1989 and received her backing.[28] In the third SII talk in February 1990, the U.S. negotiator officially demanded abolition of the LSRSL.

Expecting this U.S. demand, the LDP had postponed the SII talk, which was due in mid-January, to avoid its negative influence on the February 1990 House of Representatives election.[29] LDP's victory in this election reduced the bargaining power of small retailers. While Prime Minister Kaifu Toshiki and senior LDP members sought abolition of the law, some LDP members sympathized with small retailers. MITI and the Ministry of Home Affairs were united against abolition.[30]

While retail discussion was under way, a real-estate developer, Shuwa, and a supermarket chain, Life Store, reportedly planned a merger of four supermarket chains.[31] Shuwa's president had proudly talked about his close relationships with high U.S. officials.[32] Life Store's president was also "well connected" with LDP leaders. He publicly said "using *gaiatsu* [foreign pressure] is the fastest way for reforming the Japanese system." [33] U.S. Ambassador Michael H. Armacost had reportedly indicated the lobbying by Japanese large retailers.[34] Other U.S. diplomats also said that the U.S. demands were based on the ideas of "thoughtful" people in Japan.[35]

VI. JAPAN FEDERATION OF ECONOMIC ORGANIZATIONS

Ambiguity within the Japan Federation of Economic Organizations (JFEO) on the LSRSL also delayed retail rationalization. Retailers had only limited influence within the JFEO until Isao Nakauchi of Daiei, a supermarket chain, took the chairmanship of the Public Affairs Committee in 1989.[36]

Major corporations in the industrial sector had their own inefficient retail networks. For example, Matsushita Electronics had 27,000 affiliated stores, and Toshiba, 14,000. These companies, therefore, could not loudly advocate retail rationalization.[37]

The interest group of trading corporations, the Japan Trading Association, supported the revision of the LSRSL to ''raise a strong retail industry'' which would encounter manufacturers' dominance in retailing.[38] Japan's largest supermarket chain, Daiei's President Nakauchi Isao, criticized the industrial sector for its closed distribution practice and MITI for its interest in the preservation of its regulatory power.[39]

However, recession in the wake of the bursting-bubble economy in the 1990s forced Japanese industries to quickly rationalize. Symbolic significance of the LSRSL in U.S.-Japan disputes also made it necessary that Japan makes a meaningful concession. Thus, the JFEO shifted in favor of curtailing excessive regulations by the local governments and possible revision or abolition of the LSRSL.[40]

VII. POLITICS VERSUS ADMINISTRATION

MITI did not officially admit that the LSRSL constituted a structural impediment to American exports, because it might endanger the very existence of the law.[41] A rebuttal to foreign accusation of the LSRSL was also presented by the Japan Chamber of Commerce and Industry, in both English and Japanese, to chambers of commerce in 31 countries and foreign embassies in Japan.[42] MITI's objective was to pursue the planned retail rationalization without abolishing the LSRSL.

Facing an American demand for the abolition of the LSRSL, the LDP was divided. Prime Minister Kaifu and senior leaders sought abolition. At one point, even the LDP members elected with the support of small retailers gave up their resistance against the party leaders, shutting off the petitions by small retailers. A MITI official is reported to have called up a leader of the National Shopping Districts Promotion Meeting, leaking LDP's movement toward abolition of the LSRSL and triggering an organized protest by the Promotion Meeting, the Japan Shopping Districts Union, the Japan Specialized Store Associations League, and other groups on 19 March 1990.[43] Shocked by such an organized protest, members of the LDP-PARC Commerce and Industry Division reversed their reform-leaning stance and unanimously opposed the abolition on 28 March 1990.[44] The LDP Economic Adjustment Special Research Council also met on 29 March. The Council even opposed relaxation of the LSRSL limited to major cities.[45] The decision reflected the petition by about 150 leaders of small retail organizations at the LDP headquarters on the same day.[46] The LDP Large-City Diet Member League also decided to refuse both abolition of the law and partial relaxation.[47]

As the antiabolition force regained ground within the LDP, a compromise was reached on 2 April. A new administrative guidance was to set the upper limit to the ''adjustment period'' at 18 months. Partial relaxation (or abolition) of the law in ''specific regions'' was to be done through an amendment in two years. ''Specific regions'' was left undefined, indicating a disagreement within the LDP.[48] The U.S. side accepted this plan, while reserving the right to reraise the issue, if the plan did not produce visible results. After the SII talk, MITI demanded an increase in personnel to ''supervise the management of local Adjustment Conferences.''[49] According to Upham, this personnel increase indicated that MITI was now ready to take up the legally mandated task of evaluating store opening applications and making decisions on them: a task which MITI previously delegated to informal dispute settlements among private parties during the 1980s, partly due to the lack of financial and personnel resources.[50]

The process of the 1991 amendment reveals several interesting points. First, LDP rank-and-file members had to be more sensitive to the demands of the small retailers than their senior leaders, whereas the senior leaders had to prove their political skills by rising above parochial interests.[51] Second, small retailers' votes were less important to the LDP, when Kaifu's ''clean'' image somewhat eased the tarnished party image of the late-1980s. Finally, despite LDP leadership's clear involvement in the issue, the process which resulted in amendment, rather than abolition, of the LSRSL in 1991 indicated that MITI bureaucrats were at the ultimate helm.

VIII. AFTER THE AMENDMENT

While MITI successfully manipulated interest groups under its jurisdiction, it could not totally eliminate the influence of interest groups. A collective meeting of the Industrial Structure Council's Retail Division and the Medium and Small Enterprise Policy Council's Small Commission on Retailing concluded its report. The report emphasized the shortening of the adjustment period to one year (instead of 18 months), integration of the official AACC process and informal pre-AACC meetings into the previously inactive LSRS Advisory Council (LSRS-AC), and the relaxation on floor enlargement for import corners. Additional restrictions by local governments were to be limited in a new section under the amended LSRSL.[52]

Local chambers of commerce, in which small retailers were predominant, exercised strong influence in the informal pre-AACC meetings. The new law, consolidating the adjustment functions into the MITI-controlled LSRS-AC, would reduce the chambers' effectiveness in bargaining vis-à-vis large retailers. Therefore, the Japan Chamber of Commerce established an extralegal Commerce Problem Discussion Group (CPDG), in which the role of local chambers in "consolidating local opinions when necessary" would be preserved.[53] MITI's intent to reactivate the LSRS-AC and consolidate regulatory power into it was thus compromised when it was made mandatory for the LSRS-AC to consult the CCI and/or the CIM in case of disagreements in the LSRS-AC. Minutes of the meetings called by the CCI and/or the CIM were not disclosed to the public.[54] However, members of the LSRS-AC under the new law were appointed by MITI minister as quasi-public servants subject to confidentiality requirements and antibribery laws.[55]

The disagreement between MITI and the Ministry of Home Affairs was left unsolved. Among about 400 "overly strict" local restrictions pointed out by MITI, only 39 were abolished by May 1991.[56] Small retailers thus maintained a considerable degree of protection, despite the amendment.

IX. INCREMENTAL CHANGES AND THE CRUMBLING OPPOSITION

Within the opposition camp, a gap was widening between the "pragmatists" and the "dogmatists." The National Shopping Districts Promotion Meetings took a pragmatic position, cooperating with MITI to obtain as much budget as possible for shopping district revitalization plans. This close working relation with MITI may be due in part to the fact that the meeting's board included a retired bureaucrat from MITI.[57] On the other hand, the Japan Specialized Store Associations League focused on "political performance," such as "standing opposition meetings."[58]

The pragmatism attracted increasing support in light of the continued decline of small retailers. The tight restriction in the early 1980s ironically reduced competition among large retailers and allowed them breathing space to improve their floor efficiency. As a result, their sales per floor space increased after 1983. On the other hand, the efficiency of small retailers suffered, while some benefited from the consumer-attracting power of large stores.[59]

The structure of retail forces has also changed. According to *Nihon Keizai Shimbun* research, the proportion of retailers with a second job reached 43.7% in 1990, up by 18.5% in five years.[60]

At the same time, motorization and extended shopping distances caused conflicts between neighboring commercial zones. Commercial zones had been set for an administrative purpose. However, as shopping distances increased, regulation in one zone became meaningless when large stores opened in the neighboring commercial zones. Thus, competition among neighboring zones led to the weakening of opposition solidarity.[61]

According to a survey by the Disaster Relief Project for Medium and Small Enterprise Owners in 1990, only 17% of the respondents answered that they would not accept an opening of a large store in their commercial areas under any condition, whereas 60% said they might conditionally accept such an opening. The conditions included a regulation on operation hours, cohosting of sales campaigns and events (by large stores with local shopping districts), joining (of large stores) into local shopping districts, and payment of restructuring funds (by large stores to local shopping districts).[62]

In the 1989 supplemental budget, 26 billion yen was allocated for reactivation of small retailers, in compensation for relaxation of the regulation announced in the Retail Vision.[63] This raised the total amount of funds available to small retailers to about 45 billion yen for fiscal year 1989. One MSEA official is reported to have admitted that such a small amount of money was not for practical use but for a cosmetic purpose.[64] The MSEA worked on an additional amount in the 1990 supplemental budget in compensation for additional relaxation during the SII talk.[65]

National Union of Commerce and Industry meetings (*Zenkoku Shokokai Rengokai*) drafted ''Small Retailer Promotion Measures under the LSRSL relaxation.'' In the report, the Union. asked MITI and the MSEA for increased subsidies, long-term/no-interest loans, and preferential tax treatment for shopping district reconstruction and construction of parks and parking spaces, regrouping of stores, and job training.[66] These demands were included in a report by the Industrial Structure Council's Retail Division and the Medium and Small Enterprise Policy Council's Small Commission on Retailing.[67]

X. FURTHER DELAY IN REFORMS

Prospect of retail deregulation caused a temporary rush of applications for opening large-scale retail stores during the 1990–1991 period. However, economic recessions and saturation of the retail market slowed down store openings in 1992.[68] Despite the simplified formal application procedure, informal ''root-binding'' with local merchants continued. At the same time, department stores and supermarkets, which had already opened stores in key strategic locations, switched their focus to relaxation of the regulations on operation hours/day rather than demanding abolition of the LSRSL, which would invite further competition from other large retail chains and specialized stores.[69]

In summer 1993, the LDP lost majority in the House of Representatives, allowing a coalition of former opposition parties to place, as Prime Minister, Hosokawa Morihiro of the Japan New Party. The Hosokawa cabinet launched a series of economic deregulation programs, including revision of the LSRSL. The CCI, CIM, and other groups of small retailers insisted that there was no need for change.[70] The JFEO (*keidanren*), on the other hand, moved toward deregulation, demanding relaxation of the floor size limitation, abolition of the restrictions on business hours and days, and eventual abolition of the LSRSL.[71] During the SII talk in 1991, the United States and Japan had agreed on revision of the LSRSL within two years, including possible removal of specific cities from the application of the LSRSL. The Economic Reform Study Group, an advisory body of Prime Minister Hosokawa, was to recommend abolition of the LSRSL by 1998.[72] Nevertheless, resistance from the bureaucracy and several LDP members blocked such initiative, and the reform implemented in May 1994, for cities defined by an ordinance, was limited to raising the lower limit of the store size under regulation to 1000 m^2 (previously 500 m^2) and relaxing the regulations on business hours and days.[73] Still, the deregulation for stores between 500 and 1000 m^2 and the extended business hours/days contributed to a rush of new store opening applications and increased sales for existing stores.[74]

The Socialists left the coalition in early 1994 and eventually allied with the LDP. Although deregulation had become an irresistible political trend, the LDP was reluctant to rock the boat on the retail issue as its support was declining among its major support groups: urban salaried workers, rural farmers, and small retailers. Socialists were in a worse position as they failed to attract support among urban workers and their reliance on the shrinking population of organized farmers and small retailers increased. As Japan's economy struggled through recession, further relaxation and/or possible abolition of the LSRSL was not included in the deregulation plan in 1994 and 1995.[75] Decline in efficiency among department store establishments after the 1991 relaxation, measured through sales per square meter and sales per employee, also seemed to have contributed to the government reluctance for further deregulation (see Table 1).

Nevertheless, both internal and external pressure for the abolition intensified. As a large number of municipal regulations remained, the supermarket industry was shifting toward total abolition of the large-scale retail regulations.[76] Capping on the length of adjustment discussions in the 1991 reform did not eliminate local small retailers' resistance in the process, but prevented them from stalling it. Nevertheless, municipal regulations of stores below 500 m^2 could not be invalidated, since the LSRSL did not clearly preempt local municipalities' authority to do so.[77]

Changes in the structure of the retail industry steadily eroded the effectiveness of the regulations. The number of stores under 50 m^2 has declined. On the other hand, middle-size stores, not regulated by MITI or prefectural governor (between 50 and 500 m^2), as well as the larger stores regulated by the LSRSL,

Table 1 Department Stores in Japan

Year	#Establ	#Employees	Floor size[a]	Annual sales[b]	Sales/empl[b]	Sales/m[2b]
1984	360	170,961	6,076	7,643,754	44.1	1.27
1985	360	170,387	6,201	7,982,465	46.8	1.29
1986	365	169,989	6,310	8,416,439	49.5	1.34
1987	368	170,570	6,414	8,879,340	52.1	1.38
1988	371	175,854	6,563	9,551,819	54.3	1.46
1989	377	180,998	6,776	10,516,550	58.1	1.55
1990	378	181,613	6,942	11,456,083	63.1	1.65
1991	416	192,534	6,964	12,085,175	62.8	1.74
1992	421	194,643	7,229	11,930,277	61.2	1.65
1993	424	192,824	7,430	11,263,552	58.4	1.52
1994	428	185,790	7,571	11,024,892	59.3	1.46

[a] In thousands of square meters.
[b] In millions of yen.
Source: MITI. *Monthly Commerce Statistics*, adopted from the Distribution Economics Institute of Japan, *Statistical Abstract of Japanese Distribution*, 1996, 51.

increased in number between 1985 and 1991 (see Table 2). Smaller stores' share in the total retail sales also declined, as the number of large stores increased (see Table 3).

Efficient sales do not necessarily guarantee cheaper consumer prices. Revision of the LSRSL in the 1990s must, as MITI claims, take into account consumer interests. Larger retailers, taking advantage of the scale merit, play better bargains vis-à-vis wholesale distributors, or even get rid of the middlemen by directly purchasing from the producers. The supermarket industry was playing this role by cutting into the vertically integrated retail *keiretsu* organized by the major manufacturers.[78] Major department stores and general merchandise supermarkets have consolidated buying groups for this goal.[79] In fact, Japan's wholesale price index has declined during the 1990s, and this tendency is more true for the imported products (see Table 4).

Upham showed his optimism in Japan's retail reform in the 1990s by pointing out the increase in parallel imports since the late 1980s, among other factors.[80] However, as the large retailers choked the smaller ones, the absolute number of retail outlets has declined, and they are controlled by fewer enterprises. As a result, the Japanese consumer market has become more oligopolistic, and the benefits from the reduced wholesale prices are not shared by the consumers. The largest supermarket chains in Japan, expected in the 1970s to break the hold of the oligopolistic department store industry, have established their own oligopoly (Table 5) and now control the chains of smaller convenience stores, which skill-

Table 2 Number of Retail Outlets by Sales Space

	Number of establishments		
Floor size[a]	1985	1988	1991
under 10	85,318	83,510	72,387
10~20	308,018	280,761	246,657
20~30	287,169	267,077	239,425
30~50	376,850	367,266	360,059
50~100	263,107	271,227	282,388
100~200	88,866	96,260	109,050
200~500	36,350	48,423	56,490
500~1000	8,161	8,408	8,799
1000~1500	3,400	3,888	4,358
1500~3000	1,910	2,047	2,269
Over 3000	1,980	2,107	2,371
Unknown	167,515	188,778	206,970
Total	1,628,644	1,619,752	1,591,223

[a] In square meters.
Source: MITI. *Census of Commerce*, adopted from the Distribution Economics Institute of Japan, *Statistical Abstract of Japanese Distribution*, 1996, 19.

Table 3 Retail Sales by Sales Space

	Sales[b]			Sales %		
Floor size[a]	1985	1988	1991	1985	1988	1991
Under 10	927,803	995,322	1,028,281	0.9	0.9	0.7
10~20	4,209,588	4,228,601	4,337,198	4.1	3.7	3.1
20~30	5,681,694	5,681,385	5,806,867	5.6	4.9	4.1
30~50	11,329,360	11,706,467	12,845,380	11.1	10.2	9.1
50~100	13,804,385	15,480,074	18,081,011	13.5	13.5	12.9
100~200	8,867,116	10,064,410	12,742,469	8.7	8.8	9.1
200~500	8,926,837	11,541,579	15,246,901	8.8	10.1	10.8
500~1000	4,651,839	4,811,985	5,452,639	4.6	4.2	3.9
1000~1500	3,232,403	3,774,570	4,539,363	3.2	3.3	3.2
1500~3000	2,708,741	3,124,023	3,732,774	2.7	2.7	2.7
Over 3000	14,351,668	16,701,795	21,096,550	14.1	14.5	15.0
Unknown	23,027,629	26,729,716	35,728,670	22.6	23.3	25.4
Total	101,721,048	114,839,927	140,638,103	99.9	100.1	100.0

[a] In square meters.
[b] In millions of yen.
Source: MITI. Census of Commerce, adopted from the Distribution Economics Institute of Japan, *Statistical Abstract of Japanese Distribution*, 1996, 19.

Table 4 Indexes of Wholesale Prices and Consumer Prices

	Wholesale price			Consumer price
Year	General	Domestic products for domestic demand	Imports (yen basis)	General
1985	110.4	105.3	152.2	93.5
1986	100.3	100.3	97.7	94.1
1987	96.5	97.2	89.7	94.1
1988	95.6	96.7	85.6	94.8
1989	98.0	98.5	92.0	97.0
1990	100.0	100.0	100.0	100.0
1991	99.4	101.0	91.8	103.2
1992	97.8	100.1	86.2	104.9
1993	95.0	98.6	77.3	106.3
1994	93.1	96.9	73.0	107.1
1995	92.2	96.1	72.9	107.0
1996	92.8	95.3	79.9	107.1

The Bank of Japan; Management and Coordination Agency.
This table has been reconstructed from Management and Coordination Agency of Japan, Statistics Bureau and Statistics Center, *Indexes of Wholesale Prices, Consumer Prices, and Land Prices*.

fully evaded the tight floor size regulations under the LSRSL during the 1980s (Table 6).

Japan's consumer price index after the 1991 relaxation of the LSRSL has in fact mostly risen, despite its prolonged recession (see Table 4). A possibility that consumers are buying more expensive brands of the same product category cannot be empirically falsified, due to limited data. However, this does not seem to be the case during the current recession. Even after the additional relaxation of the LSRSL in 1994, most retail products show no price drop, with a few exceptions in furniture, household utensils, and recreational durables (Table 7).

The LSRSL's floor size–based regulations also face challenge from catalogue, television, and Internet shopping services, which have no physical stores. Proliferation of membership stores also effectively demolished the border between wholesale and retail stores, making the LSRSL obsolete.[81] The American Chamber of Commerce in Japan officially demanded abolition of the law in October 1995, and the U.S. government also demanded abolition by the year 2000.[82] The Hashimoto cabinet had set the administrative reform as its top priority, and it announced a "program for Transformation and Creation of Economic Structure" on 16 December 1996. In the program, the government promised a start of the preparation toward review of the LSRSL in 1996, but no detail of possible

Table 5 Japan's Top Retail Enterprises, 1993

	Department stores		General merchandise/ supermarket chains, co-ops	
Ranking	Company	Sales[f]	Company	Sales[f]
1	Mitsukoshi	842,372	Daiei[a]	2,015,230
2	Seibu Department Stores[b]	808,074	Ito-Yokado	1,511,553
3	Takashimaya[c]	788,462	Seiyu[b]	1,103,778
4	Daimaru	569,799	Jusco	1,005,664
5	Matsuzakaya	491,367	Nichii	789,462
6	Isetan	442,895	Uny	569,799
7	Tokyu Department Store[d]	378,841	Nagasakiya	414,563
8	Hankyu Department Stores	344,729	Izumiya	400,844
9	Kintetsu Department Stores	284,142	Coop Kobe	351,707
10	Sogo[e]	280,039	Chujitsuya[a]	321,911
11	Yokohama Takashimaya[c]	269,489	Maruetsu[a]	321,045
12	Odakyu Department Stores	235,241	Uneed Daiel[a]	298,149
13	Tobu Department Stores	188,686	Kotobukiya	281,347
14	Yokohama Sogo[e]	167,000	Tokyu Store[d]	275,691
15	Keio Department Stores	146,801	Heiwado	208,987

[a] Daiei Group.
[b] Saison Group.
[c] Takashimaya Group.
[d] Tokyu Group.
[e] Sogo Group.
[f] In millions of yen.
Source: Larke. *Japanese Retailing*, 178, 200.

revision was included. A senior MITI source was quoted for internal division within MITI.[83] As the LDP foot-dragged on the issue throughout 1996, the U.S. government repeated its demand in early 1997. MITI replied that comprehensive review of the law would be done by the end of December 1997, after which immediate actions would take place.

MITI started a joint meeting of the Industrial Structure Advisory Council and the Medium and Small Enterprise Policy Advisory Council on 21 May 1997 to have them report to the MITI minister a plan of revision. A national survey by the Prime Minister's office and a series of public hearings were planned in June.[84] Large stores were interested in abolition of the mandated number of closing days (set at 24 days per year by the 1994 revision) and the regulations on operation hours (closing at 8 PM set by the 1994 revision). However, relaxation of the regulation on new store openings did not receive much support from the

Table 6 Leading Convenience Stores Chains and Mini-Markets, 1992

Rank by sales	Store chains	Sales	#Stores	Parent company
1	Seven-Eleven	1,194,913	5,058	**Ito-Yokado (1)**
2	Lawson/Sun Chain	666,400	4,448	**Daiei (2)**
3	Family Mart	413,939	2,311	**Saison Group (3)**[a]
4	Sun-shop Yamazaki	321,950	2,427	Yamazaki Bread
5	Zennishoku Chain	265,900	1,878	Zennihon Shokuhin
6	Circle K	193,599	1,255	**Uny (4)**
7	K-Mart	142,640	1,096	Kittaka
8	Sunkusu	137,900	804	**Nagasakiya (5)**
9	Community Store	84,520	575	Kokubu
10	Monmato	74,718	442	Monmato Suto
11	Mini-Stop	74,279	440	**Jusco (6)**
12	Hot Spar	69,980	517	Kasumi
13	Seicomart	68,100	425	Nishio Maruyo
14	Coco Store	60,000	483	Izumikku
15	Spar/Hotspar	43,991	190	Tokan
16	3-8/Hi-mart	43,034	253	Hiroya
17	3-F	39,845	239	Fuji Shitio
18	Sebuon	37,770	366	Iseya
19	Spar	33,778	131	Osaka Spar
20	Family Mart	27,955	209	Chubu Family Mart

Bold indicates that the parent company is ranked within top 20 in sales for general merchandise chains.
The number in parentheses indicates GMS ranking.
[a] Saison Group also includes Seibu Department Stores, ranked No. 2 in sales among department stores.
Source: Larke. *Japanese Retailing*, 146.

large retailers due to the concern of overcompetition.[85] Some retailers also thought that total abolition of the LSRSL would lead to a rush of regulatory ordinances by municipalities in the total absence of the preempting MITI regulations.[86]

The joint meeting of the Industrial Structure Council (MITI) and the Medium and Small Enterprise Policy Council (Prime Minister's office) concluded its report in December 1997, recommending that the LSRSL be abolished. As a related measure, amendment to the City Planning Law (*Toshi keikaku ho*) was also recommended to enable local municipalities to regulate store opening from the viewpoints of traffic control, environmental protection (including garbage collection), and regional planning. These municipalities would publish zoning and size limits for land use under the new City Planning Law. Then, municipalities would evaluate individual applications for store opening in light of their

Table 7 Index of Consumer Prices, Subgroup

Item	1995	1996	1997
Food	100.0	99.9	101.7
Fresh food (fresh fish & shellfish, fresh vegetables & fresh fruits)	100.0	100.4	100.8
Food, excluding fresh food	100.0	99.8	101.8
Cooked food	100.0	100.5	102.9
Beverages	100.0	99.6	101.3
Alcoholic beverages	100.0	99.6	100.5
Furniture & household utensils	100.0	98.0	97.1
Household durables	100.0	95.8	93.3
Other furniture & household utensils	100.0	99.2	99.1
Interior furnishings	100.0	99.0	98.5
Bedding	100.0	98.0	97.8
Domestic utensils	100.0	100.0	100.6
Domestic non-durables	100.0	97.3	95.4
Clothes & footwear	100.0	101.1	103.4
Clothes	100.0	101.4	103.7
Japanese clothing	100.0	101.8	102.7
Clothing	100.0	101.4	103.9
Shirts, sweaters, underwear	100.0	101.4	104.1
Shirts & sweaters	100.0	101.3	103.8
Underwear	100.0	101.5	104.8
Footwear	100.0	100.1	102.4
Cloth & other clothing	100.0	100.2	102.1
Cloth & thread	100.0	98.9	100.3
Other clothing	100.0	100.2	102.5
Reading & recreation	100.0	98.9	100.4
Recreational durables	100.0	88.9	83.6
Other reading & recreation	100.0	99.9	102.1
Recreational goods	100.0	98.8	100.6
Books & other reading materials	100.0	100.7	102.9
Miscellaneous	100.0	100.4	102.0
Toilet articles	100.0	99.7	99.7
Personal effects	100.0	99.7	102.1
Cigarettes	100.0	100.0	101.7
Other	100.0	107.2	110.0

Based on Management and Coordination Agency of Japan, Statistics Bureau and Statistics Center, Japan in Figures, ''Indexes of Wholesale Prices, Consumer Prices and Land Prices,'' Subgroup Index for Japan.

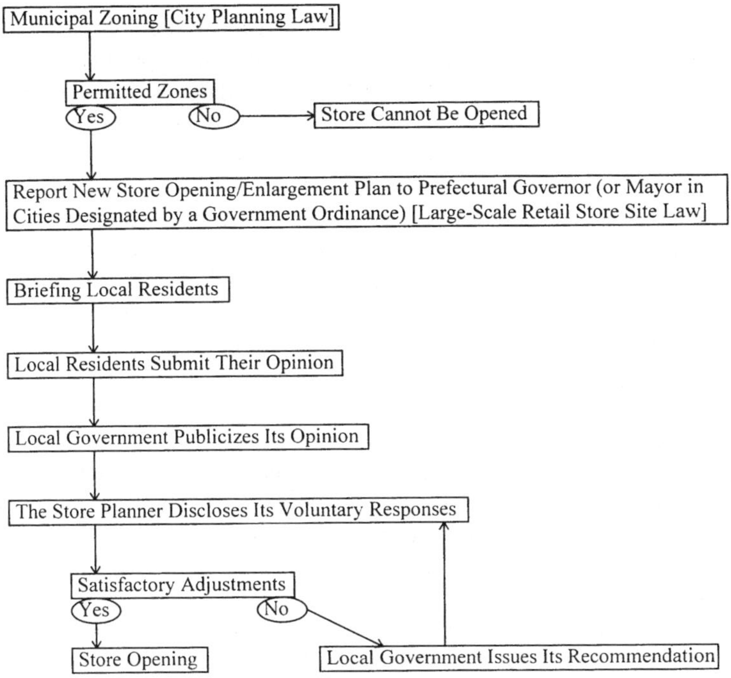

Figure 2 Large-scale retail store site law (to be implemented in 2000). (From *Nihon Keizai Shimbun*, 25 December 1997, p. 10; 24 May 1998, p. 8.)

social impact, and if necessary, issue recommendations of changes, under the Large Store Site Law (see Figure 2). Large supermarket interests, suspicious of subjective and extended regulations by municipalities in the absence of a specific definition of ''serious and irreversible'' social impact, opposed the plan. Meanwhile, small retailers also opposed the plan in the absence of a clear assurance of their participation in the municipal evaluation process.[87] However, these reform measures passed the Diet in May 1998, and the new law will be implemented in 2000. MITI is to issue guidelines to municipalities, which include uniform criteria for large retailers to consider in opening new stores.[88]

XI. CONCLUSION

The relaxation of the LSRSL involved both external and internal pressure, but MITI's control over its jurisdiction prevented abolition of the law. Relaxation of the law was more incremental than it looked due to informal sabotage at the implementation stage. Under the new law, extended local autonomy may still prevent large stores from opening. Small retailers derived their political strength through their plural access channels to the LDP, the MSEA, local governments, and the Ministry of Home Affairs. With the declining influence of the MSEA within MITI, small retailers' alliance with MITI was possible only to the extent that neither liked complete abolition of the LSRSL.

The LDP's role, backed by its political strength during the 1980s, remained that of a mediator among the status quo interests of the bureaucracy, small retailers, department stores, and supermarket chains. As small retailers declined in number, their political strength was destined to decline. Nevertheless, general decline of the LDP popularity since the late 1980s slowed down the decline of relative strength of small retailers well into the 1990s. However, the LDP in the 1990s let the MITI take a lead in deregulation, contrasting its own reregulation initiative until the early 1980s.[89]

The LSRSL failed to solve conflicts between large and small retailers. Extended shopping distance, specialization, cooperation among large and small stores, and proliferation of membership stores have made the LSRSL obsolete. However, the whole process is characterized by the absence of a consumer perspective. Incremental reforms have advanced large retailers bargaining power vis-à-vis wholesale distributors, at the cost of small retailers. However, the cost advantage gained by the large retailers has not been enjoyed by Japanese consumers. A more meaningful retail reform seems to lie in the area of antimonopoly laws.

Small retailers' resistance seems to have exhausted their ammunitions at the national level, but they have acquired a potentially strong influence via local municipalities. The structure of the retailing industry has been defined by cultural, historical, and natural conditions, and varies from one region to another.[90] The delegation of the retail regulation authority to local government levels has the potential to allow regionally unique evolution of the retail industry. However, whether MITI will set clear criteria for large stores, and whether local municipalities will refrain from setting additional criteria in evaluating store opening applications, are yet to be seen.

Keeping the above analysis in mind, I would like to conclude this chapter with some proposals. Further reform of the retail regulations should encompass all of the following goals:

1. MITI should set the minimum store size, under which store opening cannot be regulated by local municipalities.

2. Establishment of larger commercial zones for driving consumers, and smaller urban commercial zones for nondriving consumers within each ''driving'' zone by municipalities.

a. Relaxation in store size and operation hours/day regulations in the suburban driving zones.
b. Relaxation in operations hours/days, but maintain moderate store size limit in the urban nondriving zones under the local government's authority.

3. Antimonopoly monitoring and enforcement in each driving zone. The enforcement should be based not on each store's sales, but on each enterprise's sales within the zone.

All of the reform initiatives require a strong political leadership, since they will inevitably have to redraw the existing jurisdictional boundaries. Without a strong leadership, neither small retailers nor consumers would enjoy prosperity.

ACKNOWLEDGMENTS

The author expresses his special thanks to Associate Professor Robert Angel of the University of South Carolina, Associate Professor Mayumi Itoh of the University of Nevada at Las Vegas, and Masahiko Asano of the University of California at Los Angeles for their insightful comments and valuable suggestions on the earlier draft of this chapter. The author also thanks Provost Nancy Renkiewicz of the Trans-Pacific Hawaii College for the use of the college's computer facility.

ENDNOTES

1. Chalmers Johnson, Rethinking Japanese Politics: A Godfather Reports. Speech given to the Japan Society of New York, 1989, p. 15.
2. Kato Yoshitada. Kenkyu noto—Daiichiji hyakkatenho no seiritsu keii to sono tokushitsu [Research note—The legislation process and characteristics of the first Department Store Law]. *Kansai Daigaku Shogaku Ronshu*, 34:3, 1989, pp. 85–103.
3. Kato. Kenkyu noto—Dainiji hyakkatenho no tokushitsu [Research note—The special characteristics of the second Department Store Law]. *Kansai Daigaku Shogaku Ronshu*, 34:4, 1989, pp. 93–107.
4. Kato. Kenkyu noto—Daitenho kaisei to sonogo no kisei kyoka [Research Note—The amendment of the Large-scale Retail Store Law and the following tightening of regulations]. *Kansai Daigaku Shogaku Ronshu*, 35:2, 1990, pp. 122–140.
5. Kato. Kenkyu noto—Daitenho kaisei to sonogo no kisei kyoka, pp. 69–71.
6. Kato. Kenkyu noto—Daitenho kaisei to sonogo no kisei kyoka, pp. 70–73.
7. Nihon Keizai Shimbunsha, ed. *Daitenho ga Kieru hi* [The day the Large-Scale Retail Store Law is abolished]. Tokyo: Nihon Keizai Shimbunsha, 1990, p. 76.
8. Kato. Kenkyu noto—Daitenho kaisei to sonogo no kisei kyoka, pp. 123–128.
9. Kato. Kenkyu noto—Daitenho kaisei to sonogo no kisei kyoka, pp. 123–128.

10. Ito Keiichi. Atarashii ryutsutaikei mezashite [Aiming at a new retail system]. *Tsusan Janaru*, June 1979, pp. 136–140.
11. Kato. Kenkyu noto—Daitenho kaisei to sonogo no kisei kyoka, pp. 128–129.
12. Sugioka Sekio. Tasogare no Daitenho-teki chosei [The declining interest adjustment under the Large-Scale Retail Store Law]. *Ekonomisuto*, 8 February 1983, pp. 42–47.
13. Sugioka, Tasogare no Daitenho-teki chosei, p. 43.
14. Leonard J. Schoppa, *Bargaining with Japan: What American Pressure Can and Cannot Do*. New York: Columbia University Press, 1997, pp. 159–160.
15. Ogawa Shuji. Korekara no ryutsu [Retail in the future]. *Tsusan Janaru*, January 1984, pp. 70–72.
16. Charles Smith. Under threat: a shrinking army of small-timers. *Far Eastern Economic Review*, 18 December 1986, pp. 77–78.
17. Yamada Naoyoshi. Kurozu-appu tsusan seisaku—chusho kouri shogyo seisaku no tenkai [Close-up MITI Policy—the development of medium and small retail policies]. *Tsusan Janaru*, October 1988, pp. 42–46.
18. Nihon Keizai Shimbunsha, ed. *Daitenho ga Kieru hi*, pp. 10–11.
19. Matsumoto Tadashi. Meikaku ni sareta Daitenho no fubi—Iwate supa maketto sosho [The disclosed shortcoming of the Large-Scale Retail Store Law—the Iwate supermarket lawsuit]. *Hanrei Taimuzu*, 463, pp. 71–73.
20. Frank Upham. Privatizing Regulation: The Implementation of the Large-Scale Retail Store Law. In Gary D. Allinson and Yasunori Sone (eds), *Political Dynamics in Contemporary Japan*. Ithaca: Cornell University Press, pp. 264–294.
21. Nihon Keizai Shimbunsha, ed. *Daitenho ga Kieru hi*, p. 9.
22. Kusano Atsushi. *Daitenho Keizai Kisei no Kozo* [The structure of the economic regulations by the Large-Scale Retail Store Law]. Tokyo: Nihon Keizai Shimbunsha, 1992, p. 244.
23. Nihon Keizai Shimbunsha, ed. *Daitenho ga Kieru hi*, pp. 10–11.
24. Terada Takashi. *Political Economy of the Large-Scale Retail Store Law: Transforming 'Impediments' to Entering the Japanese Retail Industry*, Pacific Economics Papers No. 237. Canberra: Australia-Japan Research Centre, Australian National University, 1994, p. 22.
25. Nihon Keizai Shimbunsha, ed. *Daitenho ga Kieru hi*, pp. 7–8.
26. Nihon Keizai Shimbunsha, ed. *Daitenho ga Kieru hi*, p. 4.
27. Nancy Yoshihara. Toys R Us to Team With McDonald's in Japan, *Los Angeles Times*, 27 September 1989, p. IV-2.
28. Nihon Keizai Shimbunsha, ed. *Daitenho ga Kieru hi*, p. 30.
29. Nihon Keizai Shimbunsha, ed. *Daitenho ga Kieru hi*, p. 12.
30. Nihon Keizai Shimbunsha, ed. *Daitenho ga Kieru hi*, pp. 14–15.
31. Nigel Holloway. Chain store massacre. *Far Eastern Economic Review*, 27 July 1989, pp. 72–73.
32. Sugita Nozomu. Shuwa—Kobayashi Shacho ga Semete kita [President Kobayashi of Shuwa has come to invade]. *Bungeishunju*, October 1989, pp. 196–206.
33. Nihon Keizai Shimbunsha, ed. *Daitenho ga Kieru hi*, p. 28.
34. Shiozawa Toshiyuki. Gyosha, shohisha wo obiyakasu daitenho no honenuki [The watering down of the Large-scale Retail Store Law that threatens retailers and consumers]. *Zen'ei*, 595, 1990, pp. 161–167.

35. Clayton Jones. Attack from within: Japan retailer bucks establishment. *Christian Science Monitor*, 21 March 1990, p. 7.
36. Stefan Wagstyl. Japan's Master of Retailing. *World Press Review*, January 1989, p. 52.
37. Uncorking the bottleneck. *Economist*, 16 June 1990, p. 80.
38. *Asahi Shimbun*, 14 September 1989, p. 2.
39. Kambara Keiko. Retailer says: Government out! *Christian Science Monitor*, 16 June 1989, p. 9. Daniel Sneider. Japan's distribution system: removing a blockade to imports. *Christian Science Monitor*, 16 June 1989, p. 9.
40. Matsuzawa Takuji. A position on SII talks—the new emphasis on the consumer. *Keidanren Review*, April 1990, 122, pp. 10–12.
41. Takahashi Michinao. Unyo no ''Kaizen'' de Daitenho ha Sonzoku suru [The Large-scale Retail Store Law will continue under improved enforcement]. *Ekonomisuto*, 13 December 1988, pp. 56–59.
42. *Asahi Shimbun*, 22 July 1989, p. 3.
43. Nihon Keizai Shimbunsha, ed. *Daitenho ga Kieru hi*, p. 19.
44. *Asahi Shimbun*, 29 March 1990, p. 2.
45. *Asahi Shimbun*, 29 March 1990, evening edition, p. 1.
46. Nihon Keizai Shimbunsha, ed. *Daitenho ga Kieru hi*, pp. 20–21.
47. *Asahi Shimbun*, 30 March 1990, evening edition, p. 2.
48. *Asahi Shimbun*, 3 April 1990, p. 1.
49. *Asahi Shimbun*, 16 August 1990, p. 3.
50. Upham. Privatizing Regulations, pp. 274, 290.
51. Tatebayashi Masahiko. Kouri Ryutsu Seisaku no Keisei Katei (1)—Ogataten Kisei Seisaku no Hensen to Seiji [Making of Retail Policies (1)—Changes in the Large Store Regulations and Politics]. *Hogaku Ronso* [University of Kyoto], December 1991, pp. 61–82.
52. *Asahi Shimbun*, 22 December 1990, p. 1.
53. *Asahi Shimbun*, 9 May 1991, p. 9.
54. *Asahi Shimbun*, 22 November 1991, p. 9.
55. *Asahi Shimbun*, 24 January 1992, p. 9.
56. *Asahi Shimbun*, 11 May 1991, p. 9.
57. Kusano Atsushi. *Daitenho Keizai Kisei no Kozo*, p. 238.
58. Nihon Keizai Shimbunsha, ed. *Daitenho ga kieru hi*, pp. 22–23.
59. Nihon Keizai Shimbunsha, ed. *Daitenho ga kieru hi*, pp. 26–28.
60. Nihon Keizai Shimbunsha, ed. *Daitenho ga kieru hi*, p. 158.
61. Nihon Keizai Shimbunsha, ed. *Daitenho ga kieru hi*, pp. 51–53.
62. *Asahi Shimbun*, 13 September 1990, p. 8.
63. *Asahi Shimbun*, 6 April 1990, p. 9.
64. Smith. Under threat, p. 44.
65. *Asahi Shimbun*, 6 April 1990, p. 9.
66. *Asahi Shimbun*, 21 June 1990, p. 8.
67. Tsusho Sangyo Sho. Daitenho Kaisei Oyobi Kongo no Kouri Shogyo Taisaku no Arikata ni tsuite [The amendment of the Large-scale Retail Store Law and the retail policy in the future]. *Gekkan Chusho Kigyo*, March 1991, pp. 58–61.
68. *Asahi Shimbun*, 31 January 1992, p. 8; 9 May 1992, p. 9.

69. *Asahi Shimbun*, 1 October 1993, p. 11; 28 December 1993, p. 2.
70. *Asahi Shimbun*, 6 November 1993, p. 12.
71. *Asahi Shimbun*, 22 December 1993, p. 12.
72. *Asahi Shimbun*, 28 December 1993, p. 2.
73. *Nihon Keizai Shimbun*, 8 February 1994, p. 1; *Asahi Shimbun*, 29 January 1994, p. 11; 29 April 1994, p. 4.
74. Terada. *Political Economy of the Large-Scale Retail Store Law*, pp. 19–20.
75. *Asahi Shimbun*, 2 June 1994, p. 11; 21 June 1994, p. 3; 6 October 1995, p. 2.
76. *Nihon Keizai Shimbun*, 21 December 1995, p. 7.
77. Terada. *Political Economy of the Large-Scale Retail Store Law*, p. 19.
78. Ishida Hideto. Anticompetitive Practice in the Distribution of Goods and Services in Japan: The Problem of Distribution Keiretsu. Translated by John O. Hailey. *Journal of Japanese Studies*, 9:2, 1983, pp. 319–321.
79. Roy Larke. *Japanese Retailing*. New York: Routledge, 1994, pp. 169–175.
80. Upham. Privatizing regulations, p. 267.
81. *Nihon Keizai Shimbun*, 27 December 1995, p. 5.
82. *Asahi Shimbun*, 19 October 1995, p. 11; 23 November 1995, p. 1.
83. *Yomiuri Shimbun*, 16 December 1996, p. 9.
84. *Yomiuri Shimbun*, 22 May 1997, p. 9.
85. *Yomiuri Shimbun*, 25 May 1997, p. 2.
86. *Yomiuri Shimbun*, 22 May 1997, p. 9.
87. *Asahi Shimbun*, 25 December 1997, pp. 3, 10.
88. *Asahi Shimbun*, 24 May 1998, p. 8.
89. Tatebayashi. Kouri ryutsu seisaku no keisei katei (1), p. 69.
90. Tatebayashi. Kouri ryutsu seisaku no keisei katei (1), p. 65.

Appendix Regulations of Large-Scale Retail Store Opening

Law	Subject of regulation	Regulatory bodies	Contents of regulation	Maximum time for adjustments
1979 Large-scale retail store law	Stores over 1500 m^2	MITI (principal); Prefectural governor, Chamber of Commerce, municipal government (legally mandated consultation); local retailers (de facto participants)	Reporting of building plan, reporting of store opening and expansion plan (de facto permit system, requiring full consent of the local retailers before accepting the report)	No limit (18 months after the 1990 Administrative guidance)
	Stores over 500 m^2	Prefectural Governor (principal); prefectural MITI office, Chamber of Commerce, municipal government (legally mandated consultation); local retailers (de facto participants)	Limit on daily store operation hours (ad hoc, bargaining between local retailers and the large store), mandated store closing days (ad hoc, bargaining between local retailers and the large store)	
			One-per-year quota on new department store opening by each of the 10 major department store enterprises; enterprise-based floor increase limit on 13 supermarket chains (1982 Administrative guidance)	

Appendix Continued

Law	Subject of regulation	Regulatory bodies	Contents of regulation	Maximum time for adjustments
1991 Large-scale retail store law	Stores over 1500 (3000 in large cities designated by an ordinance) m^2	MITI (principal); prefectural governor, Chamber of Commerce, municipal government (legally mandated consultation); local retailers (de facto participants)	Reporting of building plan, reporting of store opening and expansion plan, limit on daily store operation hours (closing at 7 pm), mandated store closing days (44 days/year)	One year
	Stores over 500 but below 1500 (3000 in large cities designated by an ordinance) m^2	Prefectural governor (principal); prefectural MITI office, Chamber of Commerce, municipal government (legally mandated consultation); local retailers (de facto participants)		
1994 Administrative guidance	Stores over 3000 (6000 in larger cities designated by an ordinance) m^2	MITI (principal); prefectural governor, Chamber of Commerce, municipal government (legally mandated consultation); local retailers (de facto participants)	Reporting of building plan, reporting of store opening and expansion plan, limit on daily store operation hours (closing at 8 pm), mandated store closing days (24 days/year)	One year

	Stores over 1000 but below 3000 (6000 in large cities designated by an ordinance) m^2	Prefectural governor (principal); prefectural MITI office, Chamber of Commerce, municipal government (legally mandated consultation); local retailers (de facto participants)		
2000 Large-scale store site law	Stores over 1000 m^2	Prefectural governor, city mayor in large cities designated by an ordinance (principal); local governments, residents (consultation); MITI will issue a guideline for large stores to consider in planning a new store	Municipal land zoning (City Planning Law) Reporting of new store opening and expansion, plan evaluation from city planning perspective (such as traffic control, parking, noise, garbage problems), recommendation for altering the plan	One year

8

Democracy, Development, and the Welfare State in India

A Win-Win Policy Analysis

Noorjahan Bava
University of Delhi, New Delhi, India

I. INTRODUCTION: INDIA'S DEVELOPMENTAL GOALS

Since independence India has been preoccupied with the pursuit of the fourfold goals of democracy, planned socioeconomic development, nation building, and welfare state. These cherished values and objectives emanating from the Constitution of India have become the alpha and omega of public policies of the government for the past 50 years.

The Constitution ordains that "The State shall promote the welfare of the people by securing and protecting as effectively as it may a social order in which justice—social, economic and political—shall inform all the institutions of the national life" (Article 38). The Directive Principles of State Policy embody the objective of the State under the Republican Constitution, namely that it is to be a Welfare State and not a Police State. These directives aim at the establishment of economic and social democracy pledged for by the preamble. They emphasize that the goal of the Indian polity is not unbridled laissez-faire but a welfare state where the state has a positive duty to ensure to its citizens social, economic, and political justice with the dignity of the individual and consistent with the unity and integrity of the nation. By making them fundamental in the governance of the country, the founding fathers have enjoined upon all future governments in India the responsibility to find a middle way between individual liberty and the public good, between preserving the property and privilege of the few and bestowing benefits on the many in order to liberate the powers of all men and women equally for contribution to the common good. To achieve these grand goals of development, welfare, and democracy, the policy makers and planners of India have adopted two different sets of win-win policy packages: (1) the state-led, public sector–dominated socialist model, and (2) economic liberalization or the market-led Structural Adjustment Programme (SAP).

II. CONCEPTUAL FRAMEWORK OF STUDY

To talk of welfare/development/democracy is to talk at once of public policies in general and sectoral policies like social, economic, political, and cultural development policies in particular. A clear normative foundation and a general interpretative framework together are necessary for the assessment of social policy. None has emphasized the need for this linkage better than Max Weber[1]:

> The distinctive characteristic of a problem of social policy is indeed the fact that it cannot be resolved merely on the basis of purely technical considerations which already assume settled ends. Normative standards of value can and must be the objective of dispute in a discussion of the problem of social policy because the problem is in the domain of general cultural values.

The values of democracy, development, and welfare state are closely and positively correlated, as the following pages show. The relationship among these ideals can be hypothesized as follows:

1. Welfare state and development are closely linked as means and ends, respectively.
2. Welfare state is a short-term goal while development is a long-term achievement.
3. Welfare state enhances and strengthens democracy.
4. Democracy being a goal of development, its achievement in political, economic, and sociocultural spheres constitutes all-around development.
5. Citizen participation in all the interfaces of the decision-making process is the sine qua non of both democracy and development.

The value-loaded[2] umbrella concept of development is a multidimensional one involving normative, empirical, environmental, moral, legal, material, spiritual, individual, group, spatial, and temporal aspects essential for human development.[3] Development is measured by the extent to which the skewed distribution of factor ownership is corrected by the number of people who are lifted above the poverty line; by the education, health facilities, and housing provided to them; by the range of employment generation; by economic growth, price stability, political participation by the unorganized and disinherited majority; and by cultural progress.[4] For the purposes of this study development is operationalized as removal of poverty, unemployment, and inequality. From Third World perspective,[5] development signifies the shift from industrialization and urbanization to agriculture and rural development, from market-determined priorities to state-determined basic needs, from GNP per capita to individual/group welfare, and from centralized planning to decentralized participative planning.

Given the fact that the concept Welfare State is a confluence of many philosophical streams—conservatism, laissez-fairism, liberalism, and Fabian socialism—an undefinable abstraction,[6] there is no positive comprehensive philosophy or ideology that underlies the many policies and programs that form part of the welfare state.[7] However, it has been equated with a political system with a high degree of responsibility for the welfare of the population,[8] a kind of socioeconomic system with a dominant public sector seeking to change the conditions and circumstances under which families live but without basically changing society. The two essential characteristics of a welfare state are (1) its intense individualism which confers on the individual an absolute right to receive welfare, and (2) its collectivism that imposes a duty on the state to promote and safeguard the whole community.[9] Since the welfare state has not rejected the capitalist economy, it is a kind of capitalism softened by an injection of socialism—a mixture of semisocialism and semiliberalism. The welfare state to be worthy of name has to be at least a social security state with its assurance of a minimum standard of life (e.g., Britain before Thatcher) or at least the radically democratic and egalitarian social welfare state (e.g., Sweden) and not like "the corporate-oriented positive state" like the United States, whose primary aim is to protect the holders of property from unregulated markets and from potential redistributive demands.[10] For operational purpose the essence of a welfare state lies in government-protected minimum standards of income, nutrition, health, housing, and education and assured to every citizen as a political right, not as charity.[11]

Social development, which is an integral part of economic development, calls for human resource development. For, the human beings are the most precious assets and their all-around development leads to the generation of human capital. The basic objective of the welfare state being the concern and care of the poor and needy in particular and promotion of welfare of all citizens in general, the concept, when translated into action, can facilitate the uplifting of the poor and weaker sections of society from poverty, unemployment, and inequality, thereby paving the way for true development in society in the long run.

Economic development is concerned with how the well-being (or welfare) of people improves over time. The dominant approaches to the idea of well-being in welfare economics are fundamentally deficient. One approach based on utilitarianism focuses on "utility," and well-being is seen in terms of happiness/pleasure. The other approach sees well-being in terms of "opulence" and seeks to measure it by incomes, commodity possessions, and affluence. Under the opulence approach, economic development is seen as expansion of the availability of goods and services. The focus on the growth of GNP per capita is an especially simple version of that approach. Under the utility approach, removal of inequality, exploitation, poverty, hunger, illiteracy, and other deprivation is seen as rendered important only if, and to the extent that, there is a net utility gain through that removal. It is this obsession with utility—judging the importance of everything in the scale of utility—that is fundamentally inadequate.[12]

Under the basic-needs approach advocated by Paul Streeton,[13] "The basic needs concept is a reminder that the objective of development effort is to provide all human beings with the opportunity for a full life." The basic needs are also defined in terms of commodities, i.e., "particular goods and services required to achieve results."

There are many factors that impinge on people's welfare: consumption of goods and services, level of health, leisure, freedom rights, etc. The greater the amount consumed, the higher the level of welfare. If the process of economic development enables a person to consume more of at least one good, without requiring him to curtail the consumption of any other thing, then one can conclude that the person's welfare is improving.[14]

III. METHODOLOGY: A WIN-WIN POLICY ANALYSIS

At this juncture a brief explanation of the methodology followed by the author is in order. To achieve the goals of democracy, development, and welfare state, the policy makers and planners in India have adopted two different win-win policy packages which are popularly known as the Nehruvian (named after the first Prime Minister of India, Pandit Jawaharlal Nehru) Model from 1947 to 1991, and the Economic Liberalization Model from July 24, 1991, onward.

As evaluation of the impact of the two policy paradigms on the country's anticipated goals has been the principal objective of this study, both models have been subjected to a thoroughgoing public policy analysis in the following pages. The interdisciplinary field of public policy studies focuses attention on the nature, causes, and effects of alternative public policies addressed to specific social problems.[15] Since policy analysis by definition involves seeking to achieve or maximize given values or social goals rather than ignoring them,[16] the policy analyst has to strictly adhere to the parameters of policy studies. These include (1) an obligation on the part of the policy analyst/evaluator to be "objective" in the sense of not allowing his/her own values or biases to influence the collection, recording, presentation, and analysis of the data; (2) at least a minimum level of acquaintance with the subject matter, tools, techniques, and methods of various social sciences that impinge on public policy; and (3) skill for interdisciplinary research. Although methods of policy analysis consist of both quantitative and nonquantitative ones,[17] for the purpose of this study the interdisciplinary and multidisciplinary methodology involving a mix of philosophical, historical, legal, constitutional, political economy, political sociology, social psychology, and management approaches combined with a sprinkling of statistics has been deployed. The adoption and application of a truly integrated holistic systems approach is imperative when one embarks upon evaluation of public policies for development.[18]

A. Win-Win Policy

A win-win policy is a public policy that is capable of achieving conservative and liberal goals simultaneously; it is not a compromise policy, and above all it must be feasible in theory and practice.[19]

B. Super-Optimum Solutions (SOS)

Those win-win solutions through which all major actors or parties gain are referred to as Super-Optimum Solutions.[20] They are a special form of win-win solutions in the sense that gain exceeds the best initial expectations of each side and thus excludes a nonsubstantial gain.

C. Methodological Problem in Evaluation

The evaluation of the Nehruvian/socialist/public sector–dominated (state-led) model is based on project management methods since all the eight Five Year Plan development programs, projects, and schemes aimed at microeconomic changes in the primary, secondary, and tertiary sectors of the economy. On the other hand, structural adjustment program involved both macroeconomic changes through policy conditionalities aimed at stabilization and microeconomic reforms. Therefore the project management method is used only in respect of the latter whereas the evaluation of macroeconomic reforms is based on judgment in this paper. In fact the Bretton Woods financial institutions are themselves in a quandary as far as the selection of the appropriate methodology for evaluating the SAP is concerned.[21]

It is only after the UNICEF Report on Adjustment with a Human Face 1987 emphasized the need to protect the poor and vulnerable from the burden of the SAP that the ''Social Safety Net'' provision was included in the policies.

D. Benchmark Data

Before the evaluation of the profile of India as a welfare state begins, it will do well to recall the benchmark data about the country on the eve of independence. As far as the basic needs of life in general, and food in particular are concerned,

India was short of not only cereals but also pulses and oil seeds. In 1945–46, the per capita availability of food grains had declined steadily from 195 kg to 152 kg per year! As far as cloth was concerned, the per capita availability was 17 m in 1951. After spending Rs. 100 crores (1000 million) in producing drinking water supply in 1971, as many as 325,000 villages out of a total of 576,000 villages were without this facility. On the housing front it was estimated that in urban areas alone, which had only a little more than one crore (10 million) families, there was shortage of more than 18 lakh houses in 1951. In addition, 10 lakh houses were required for displaced persons from Pakistan.

In 1951, only 17% of the population was literate, and of every 100 children in the school age of 6 to 11, only 43 attended school. As far as health and medical facilities are concerned, the position in India was thus:

One doctor for 6300 persons againt 1000 in U.K.
One nurse for 43,000 people against 300 in U.K.
One trained midwife for 60,000 women against 618 in U.K.
One health visitor for 4 lakh against 4710 in U.K.

In short, immediately after independence India was one of the most underdeveloped countries in the world. Its per capita income was extremely low. Most people were engaged in overcrowded agriculture at a low level of productivity. There was no infrastructure for industrialization. Life expectancy was low and infant mortality high; inequalities between various sections of people; exploitation and oppression of women; scheduled castes and tribes existed.[22]

IV. WIN-WIN POLICY I: STATE-LED DEMOCRATIC SOCIALIST (NEHRUVIAN) MODEL

India adopted the strategy of development through democratic planning within the framework of a mixed economy to reach the Nehruvian vision of socialistic pattern of society. Rejecting the orthodox model of the Western capitalist economies and the radical approach of the socialist command economies, India took the middle path of "growth with equity" based on the belief that developing countries like her, where the majority still live in rural areas and where the poor are concentrated, more governmental intervention and action than the orthodox (market economy) approach advocates is required if growth with equity is to be achieved. Plan after plan reiterated India's faith in growth-with-equity approach, the chief components of which are: expansion of employment opportunities; corrections of market distortions through governmental policy and administrative action; emphasis on rural development; meeting basic needs of people; and developing small/cottage/rural industries and new international economic order which will help the poor nations of the world to receive a fairer share of the world's wealth. The Indian state assumed a lion's share of responsibility to achieve a socialistic pattern of society and its multidimensional role as planner, policy maker, catalyst, participant, regulator, manufacturer, importer, exporter, financier, and distributor under the Industrial Policy Resolution, which resulted in 1956 in the growth and dominance of the public sector undertakings (PSUs) numbering 243 units with a capital investment of Rs. 178,628 crore (1,786,280 million) as on March 31, 1991, vis-à-vis 5 PSUs worth Rs 29 crore (290 million) in 1951, and their control over the commanding heights of the Indian economy. The underlying rationale/philosophy of the expanding public sector was that the PSUs were expected to generate employment opportunities, generate surplus wealth, alleviate poverty, remove regional disparities, promote welfare, and enable India to contribute to international understanding and peace.

V. IMPACT OF THE NEHRUVIAN MODEL

In a democracy everything that the government does has to be for the welfare of the people. Planning was started with a view to improve the quality of life of the people. After four decades of planning for socioeconomic development, welfare, and nation building, India's experience is neither a runaway success nor a dismal failure.[23] Indeed India today is a major industrial and military power. It produces a wide range of different industrial goods, including sophisticated computers, military aircraft, and automobiles. It has launched its own weather satellites into space. We have one of the largest pools of scientists and engineers in the world. India is self-sufficient in food production. India has now become a nuclear power since May 1998.

A. Alleviation of Poverty

Considering the critical importance of rural development for India, our planners and policy makers had given the highest priority to it in the national agenda right from the commencement of the era of planned development. A whole lot of programs ranging from the Community Development and National Extension Services, Panchayat Raj, IAAP, IADP, to special programs for weaker sections like the Small Farmers, Marginal Farmers, and Agricultural Laborers Development Program, Command Area Development Program, Tribal Development, Hill Area Development Program, Minimum Needs Programs, Integrated Rural Development Program, Integrated Child Development Program, National Rural Employment Program, Rural Landless Employment Guarantee Program, Training Youth for Self Employment Program, Jawahar Rozgar Yojana, etc. had been implemented in order to achieve self-reliance, removal of poverty, employment generation, and all-around integrated development of rural/urban areas.

As Sukhmoy Chakravarty observes: While India had doubtless scored some success, it had left a number of people below the poverty line. The 32nd National Sample Survey showed that in 1977–78 the proportion of population in rural areas living below the poverty line was 51.2%, whereas the corresponding figure for urban areas was 38.2%. According to the 38th survey (1983–84), the figures had nosedived to 40.4% for rural and 28.1% in urban areas. This indicated the gross poverty that existed in the country, as the norm used for these purposes was based principally on caloric intake.

In terms of nutrition the average per-person availability of cereals had gone up from 334 to 429 g/day in 1986–87, though this is still not adequate to provide two square meals to the entire population. The per capita availability of oilseeds had remained static at 14 kg/year, while the availability of pulse, the main source of protein in India, had declined from 22 to 13 kg/year. Thus the economic condition of half of the farmers of India who grew coarse cereals, pulses, and oilseeds in the dry regions has not improved in the four decades since independence.

B. Employment

During the 1947–90 period the unemployment scenario of India was neither healthy nor sound. Vitiated by chronic unemployment both absolute and seasonal, the situation was quite grim. The position of unemployment within agronomy was further aggravated by wide underemployment, with 10 persons competing for every job opening. Labor being mostly landless and disorganized, wages were poor and verged on exploitation. In the industrial, mining, and infrastructural areas, the bulk of labor is unskilled, and, education being largely nonvocational, there is large-scale educated unemployment, wage differentials, deep-seated labor unrest, and militant trade unionism (undermining production and productivity in the nation).

Since an overwhelming proportion of the Indian population lives in the villages, the bulk of the unemployment is rural. The backwardness of Indian agriculture and the failure of land reforms aggravate the situation. From 1970 onward, 5 million more were added to the rural unemployed. The level of unemployment was high all over the rural sector; it was equally rapidly rising in the urban sector, and public sector employment and public works program–based palliatives failed to check this additional alarming rise.

The main factor causing the problem of unemployment had been identified as structural disequilibrium, distortions in planning, deficient employment planning, population explosion, and faulty education cover.

C. Economic Growth

While independence certainly broke the spell of stagnation in the Indian economy, the national income showed a trend growth rate of 3.6% per annum over the period of 1950–84. India's macroeconomic performance had been only "moderately good" in the terms of GDP growth rates. Allowing for the fact that for the better part of the entire plan period, population increased by more than 2% per annum, the growth in per capita income on an average basis had been somewhat less than 2% per annum. The rise in the domestic savings rate from around 10% of GDP in the early 1950s to 23% currently was quite impressive. Secondly, while India had to reckon with a fair measure of inflation from time to time, the average rate of inflation had been a "modest" one by international standards. Most often such periods were triggered by harvest failures and brought under control without resort to large-scale foreign borrowing.

There are two major reasons for this success. One is the ability to maintain a rate of growth of food production of around 31% over the period as whole. The other is the financial deepening that was experienced by the country, which allowed domestic savings to go up in monitized form. As Nicholas Kaldor and others have emphasized in the analysis of Latin American inflation, the proneness of these countries to inflation has been in large part due to their neglect of food grain agriculture. The policy of the government to tackle the problem of inflation from both demand and supply sides whenever inflation exceeded single digit coupled with political legitimacy (a poor but open democratic system is generally less tolerant of inflation than authoritarian regimes), it has in the long run helped to increase the savings rate by helping to maintain confidence in the standard of value. However, much of the saving had taken place in the housing sector and not in the public sector. Most of the public sector undertakings became white elephants.

While the trend growth rate of the industrial sector was 5% per annum during 1950–84, that of agriculture was only 2.2%, the same as the rate of population growth. Consequently, the contribution of the industrial sector to the national income had increased from 15% in 1947 to 261% in 1988, but it had not resulted in a significant increase in the percentage of total labor employed. In industry, the change had been from 10% to 15% in 40 years. Consequently, the percentage of India's labor force employed in agriculture and allied activities had changed only from 74% to 66% in the same period.

D. Health Services

India is one of the very few countries that had from the very beginning planned health services as a part of general socioeconomic development. The broad objectives of the health plans had been the strengthening of the health infrastructure and complete eradication of diseases and their integration into basic health services. The health care system was coordinated with other nation-building activities and was made a part of the community development programs and administered through a network of primary health centers, which formed the nucleus for a minimum standard of health services for the rural community.

During the First and Second Five-Year Plans, emphasis was laid on control of communicable diseases, improvement of environmental sanitation, organization of institutional facilities, training of medical and paramedical personnel, provision of maternity and child health services, health education and nutrition, and family planning. From the Second Plan onward greater emphasis on family planning had been laid by the government. During the Third Plan a shift in the approach took place from a narrow clinical to one of exclusive community education, provision of facilities near the homes of the people, and widespread effort in rural and urban communities. The Family Planning Department was established in the Ministry of Health. The Medical Termination of Pregnancy Act was placed on the Statute Book in 1972. Since 1975–76 the government has been actively implementing and expanding the Integrated Child Development Services (ICDS) which provides supplementary nutrition, immunization, health checkups, referral service, treatment of minor illness, nutrition and health education, preschool education, and other services. Out of the 5143 community development blocks in the country, the ICDS have been covered in 1551!

The experience of ICDS during the first 12 years indicated that it had the potential of bringing about a silent revolution—a profound instrument of community and human resource development. Its achievements include a decrease in malnutrition and anemia, better nutritional assessments, a significant decrease in preventable diseases, effective Anganwadi workers, fall in infant and child mortality, and positive results of community participation. The health services also include maternity and nutritional services to women. The central expenditure on the ICDS has increased over the years from 6.02 crore (60.2 million) in 1980–81 to 144 crore (1440 million) in 1987–88. There were 1054 rural projects and 497 tribal projects and 187 urban projects in the country covering 87.78 lakh children in 1988.

The fruits of development had been neutralized by the failure of the family-planning program to arrest the population growth during the period under review.

E. Weaker Sections

The Constitution of India provides for the promotion of welfare of the weaker sections through socioeconomic policies embodied in the Directive Principles of State Policy. Article 46 states: "The State shall promote with special care all the educational and economic interests of the weaker sections of the people and in particular, of the Scheduled Castes and Scheduled Tribes and shall protect them from social injustice and all forms of exploitation."

The weaker sections include not only the SCs and STs but also the physically and mentally handicapped, women, widows, orphans, socially and educationally backward classes, minorities, and so forth. Although Article 17 of the Constitution declares that untouchability is abolished and the Untouchability (offenses) Act provides penalties for preventing a person on the grounds of untouchability from entering a place of worship or taking water from a sacred tank, well, or spring and enforcing all kinds of social disabilities, the implementation of the law has been ineffective resulting in atrocities against SCs, STs, women, and others which are on the increase. Though the SCs and STs enjoy constitutionally laid down reservation of seats in Parliament and state legislatures, in public services, and for admission in colleges and universities, after the Supreme Court judgment on the Mandal Commission Report, OBC (other backward classes) have also been entitled for reservation not exceeding 27% in public employment.

The Ministry of Welfare of the Government of India administers several welfare programs for the SCs, STs, and the physically and mentally disabled. It provides financial assistance to organizations for disabled persons for the purpose of construction of building, purchase of furniture, equipment, salaries, allowances of the staff, books, contingencies, transport, journal publication, and maintenance charges; for purchases/fitting of aids of appliances and scholarship to various types of the physically handicapped—visual, hearing, orthopedic, and multiple—and the mentally handicapped for studies under its scholarship scheme.

Although women constitute roughly 50% of the population of India and the Constitution guarantees the same fundamental rights that are bestowed on men, women continue to suffer from serious social and economic disabilities. Their participation in various political, administrative, and social institutions of national life and in the process of production is negligible. Unless women are treated equally and their right to participate in the process of production, governance, and administration is vigorously enforced, and the social evils against them such as dowry, child marriage, etc. are removed, they will have to remain outside the orbit of development and its fruits. Thus participation of 50% of the women in the development process which is not there needs to be corrected.

F. Social Security

The Constitution of India provides for social security and assistance in the case of unemployment, old age, sickness, disablement, and other cases of want. It provides that the state shall within the limits of its economic capacity and development make effective provision for security; the right to work; education and assistance in the case of unemployment; old age; sickness; and disablement. The welfare state in India has been strengthened by the enactment and enforcement of the Retirement Benefit Act—Employees Provident Fund Scheme, Payment of Gratuity Act, 1972, and Family Pension—Cum Life Insurance Scheme applying to employees drawing salary up to Rs. 1000 p.m. in every factory, mine, port, oil field, plantation, shop, etc., employing 10 or more persons. The state has passed a number of labor legislations regulating the conditions of work of employees which also provide for social security. For instance, the Employees State Insurance Act 1948 covers all power-using nonseasonal factories wherein 20 or more persons are employed for a period of 12 months except in mines and railway sheds. The benefits include sickness, extended sickness, maternity, disablement, dependency, and medical benefits.

There is no dearth of social security and welfare legislation in India. But the effective and efficient enforcement of these legal measures is far from satisfactory. The chief obstacles in the way of the full blossoming of the welfare state in India are: lack of welfare society, willpower, and resources, and participation of people; corruption and inefficiency in social, political, administrative systems; the new economic policy of the government; poverty and the low position of women and workers in the unorganized sectors; the failure of the family planning program to arrest the population explosion and illiteracy.

A comparison between India's record of performance at the developmental front with those of her Asian sisters leads to the startling revelation that although India and South Korea had almost the same per capita income at about 7% that of the United States in 1950, it has gone up for South Korea to 25% in 1980 while it has remained virtually unchanged for India. Countries like Malaysia and Thailand have also shown higher performance than India with 25% and 15%, respectively. The better performance of the Asian Tigers was attributed to the economic liberalization policy implemented in those countries.

By the end of 1990 not only did India remain a very poor country, but also its income was unequally distributed as in many other countries of the world. The top 20% of the population in India had a share of more than 40% of the total consumption expenditure (income minus savings) while the share of the bottom 40% is less than 20%. The distribution of income was even more skewed than that of consumption expenditure. As a result the poorest in India, typically the landless agricultural workers, are exceedingly poor. Even by the most conservative estimate, over 35% of Indians were below the official poverty line in 1987. (The Sixth Five Year Plan defined an all-India poverty line as a per capita consumption expenditure of Rs. 65 of 1977–78 prices in rural areas corresponding to a calorie intake of 2100.) According to World Bank data for 1985, the poverty condition of India was worse than that of sub-Saharan Africa. What is even more alarming is that the percentage of population below the poverty line is higher and yet falling more slowly in India than in other, less developed Asian countries, such as Indonesia, Malaysia, and Thailand.

A significant percentage of the population is so poor that its basic needs—e.g., adequate diet, clean drinking water, health care—are not being satisfied; health indicators such as child mortality and life expectancy reflect this fact. On the literary front India's performance is one of the worst in the world. In 1947, 19% of India's population could read and write. By 1985, this had improved to only 43%, whereas during the same period China improved the literacy rate from 30% to 70%, and South Korea from 32% to 95%. India's performance is especially shocking in the light of her achievement in higher education. While the slums lacking drinking water and sanitation are increasing in metropolitan cities, thousands flee to cities every day from villages in search of better life. The stark reality and most oppressive fact of life in rural areas being the scarcity of employment opportunities, India is far from reaching the goal of a welfare state. The hypotheses of the study thus stand vindicated.

VI. WIN-WIN POLICY II: MARKET-LED LIBERALIZATION/ GLOBALIZATION PARADIGM

India witnessed a policy paradigm shift to the Structural Adjustment Program (SAP) in 1991 when the Congress under Prime Minister P.V. Narasimha Rao assumed power. The policy continued under the 13-party United Front Coalition Government as well. The SAP, which is rooted in neoliberalism, was advocated by the World Bank and IMF as the international model of development for the Third World under the influence of the new monetarists (Friedman), the new political economy, Public Choice School (Buchanan and Niksanan), and the New Right, who gave the clarion call for the rolling back of the state, reinventing the government, and establishment of the free-market economy based on liberalization. The World Bank's World Development Report, The Challenge of Development 1991, called for market-friendly development.

The components of liberalization are as follows:

1. Privatization of state and parastatal enterprises to reduce inefficiencies and government-protected monopolies
2. High interest rates and credit squeeze to reduce inflationary tendencies
3. Trade liberalization to open up the internal market and expose local industry to world market competition and boost foreign trade exchange
4. Domestic demand management leading to a lowering of state budgets and decreasing expenditure in the social sector
5. Currency adjustment to improve the balance of payments by raising import prices and making exports more competitive
6. Free-market prices to remove distortions resulting from subsidized food and fertilizers and from import taxes on luxury goods

Liberalization can be either internal or external or both. Internal liberalization signifies privatization, marketization and minimalization of the state's economic role. It calls for unfettered role for private enterprises and market forces and substantial withdrawal of the state from its regulatory, directly participative, enterpreneurial role. In contrast, external liberalization denotes globalization in terms of import liberalization; exchange rate adjustment; generally devaluation of the currency of the poorer, debtor nations; free flow of foreign direct investment (FDI) induced by liberal incentives; tax concessions; political guarantees and unfettered activities of the MNCs on the basis of their unfettered reading of market signals and profit calculus and continued curbing of labor mobility. External liberalization provides increased space freely accessible to foreign capital, goods, and services; finance and technology on favorable terms. The MNCs transcending the national barriers have become the vehicles of global economic hegemony with command over huge capital, technology, and diversified and geographically dispersed production mix; huge R & D outlay; and global markets in which Third World nations and former command economies are holding promising prospects (the emerging markets).

VII. IMPACT OF THE LIBERALIZATION MODEL

In India the implementation of the liberalization policy since July 1991 has led to decontrol, deregulation, privatization/disinvestment of the public sector enterprises; and abolition of industrial licensing for all projects except in a few strategic and environment-concerned industries. As against 17 industries that were reserved for public sector investment under IPR 1956, now only eight industries concerned with defense and strategic matters are reserved. Foreign equity participation limit has been increased from 40% to 51% under the Foreign Exchange Regulation Act; grant of automatic permission of the facility to specified list of hi-tech and high-priority industries; automatic approval of foreign collaborations in high-priority industries up to 5% of domestic sales or 8% of export sales or up to a limit of Rs. 10 million; and reduction of political and bureaucratic control and influence through measures such as:

1. Removal of the requirement of prior clearance from the government for the location of projects except in the case of large cities.
2. Allowing small-scale enterprises the option to offer up to 24% of equity in large-scale undertakings while still retaining their small-scale status.
3. Removal of the mandatory requirement that loan agreements of financial institutions with private firms formally provide for the conversion of loans into equity (convertibility clause).
4. Liberalization of the procedure for foreign exchange remittances.

A. Financial Reforms

Since the globalization policy will open up the Indian economy, changes in the EXIM policies and convertibility of the rupee have been effected. The new credit policy announced by the RBI aims at increasing the supply of money in the financial market which was subjected to liquidity crunch.

Considering the Southeast Asian currency turmoil (slide) involving devaluation of the currencies and collapse of the share markets and the resultant political crisis (e.g., Thailand), India should not rush for full convertibility of the capital account even though one of the conditions for full convertibility, i.e., inflation, has been brought down to 3.75%. India should wait till her fiscal deficit falls to 3% of GDP.

B. Removal of Import-Export Curbs

The government of India has further liberalized the import of gold. Eleven agencies have been permitted to import unlimited quantities of the precious metal for sale in the domestic market as well as for export of gold jewelry which will generate a lot of foreign exchange for the country besides preventing smuggling of gold.

C. Economic Growth

It has been argued that liberalization and globalization will open up the Indian economy, thereby facilitating faster rate of economic growth, the fruits of which will trickle down to the poor. According to the present estimate the growth rate has shot up to 6.5% thanks to the reforms vis-à-vis 3.5% before the reforms. However, economists say that India will not be able to sustain the 7% rate for long. The governor of the RBI feels that India has the potential to reach a 7% growth rate.

India has already started experiencing the inevitable negative consequence of liberalization, namely, the trade cycles. Since the economy has been hit by a sharp industrial slowdown, low business confidence, and sluggish investment, private sector magnates have urged the government to increase public expenditure to shore up demands in the economy. The recession of the economy is bound to increase the unemployment in the country as the private entrepreneurs resort to the EXIT policy.

D. Subsidy

The policy of the government toward subsidy has been denounced by both internal and external critics. While the latter (World Bank and IMF) advise the government to completely stop the subsidies so that the government can reduce its fiscal deficit, the domestic detractors have questioned its basic approach to the subsidy question which is based on a particular conceptualization of merit and nonmerit goods resulting in skewed subsidies. All merit goods are entitled at present to automatic subsidy. Under this policy the government has brought primary education and R & D under merit good entitled to subsidy and education beyond primary level under nonmerit good and therefore no subsidy. R & D is entitled for subsidy but not higher/university education. In a developing country like India, with one-third of people living below the poverty level, the ''social safety net'' and the ''human face'' of the new policy taking the form of subsidies to the Public Distribution System, to small, marginal farmers, and agricultural laborers, subsidy given to social services should continue. Recently the government hiked subsidy on a renewable energy program with a special focus on SCs and STs and poor.

E. Weaker Sections

Several ''human face'' measures have been taken up by the government. Thanks to the reservation policy, the proportion of SC and ST in central government services has gone up to 16.90% and 5.48% in 1994, respectively. Their literacy rate has also gone up to 37.41% for SC and 28.6% for the ST. A five-member National Commission for Backward Classes has been established under the 1993 Act. Preexamination coaching classes for OBCs and facilities for their economic development under National Backward Classes Finance and Development Corporation with a capital of Rs. 156.9 million to provide loans have been created.

Till the end of 1995–96, the National Scheduled Caste Finance and Development Corporation established in 1989 to provide support to economic development programs of the SC has distributed about Rs. 3000 million. The state level bodies established for the same purpose have disbursed to 87 lakh beneficiaries in 1994–95. To remove the indignity of the lowest caste and promote its liberation, a National Commission for Safai Karamcharis (Cleaning Staff) was created in 1992. A National Minority Commission has been established to take care of the interest of the minorities.

F. Corruption

The protagonists of liberalization do not hesitate to condemn public administration as the most inefficient and corrupt one. But there is growing evidence to show that corruption is built into the market economy. In their study on liberalization and corruption, Barbara Harves White and Gordon White of the Institute of Development Studies, London, question the assumption that corruption can be rolled back by eliminating the state through privatization and deregulation. The privatization of the Telecommunication Sector alone resulted in scams involving Rs. 1750 million and the resignations of a cabinet minister and a bureaucrat.

G. Privatization of the Public Sector

The Government of India's decision to grant increased financial and operational autonomy to select PSUs that have been brought under the Navratna scheme is laudable. The disinvestment and privatization of the PSU shares should be slowed down as efficiency and accountability will go up with the new policy. The decision of the government not to offload the shares of PSUs (GAIL and MTNL) in the context of the global financial crisis is a wise one. The BJP-led Coalition Government of Mr. Vajpayee is vigorously pursuing the policy of disinvestment of PSUs and privatization of the insurance to mop up adequate resources to meet the fiscal deficit of Rs. 6000 crores in the Union Budget as per the conditionalities laid down by the World Bank and IMF.

H. Unequal Treatment at International Trade

As long as the global economy is characterized by inequalities, international trade based on the principle of mutual interest of the partners cannot bring benefits to the weaker partners, i.e., developing countries like India. India's trade deficit during 1995–96 stood at $4,056.62 million as against $1,837.41 million during 1994–95. The recent decision taken by India, Malaysia, etc., at the Commonwealth Heads of Government Meeting and the Group-15 nations that a second round of trade negotiations at the WTO should be avoided and developing nations should not submit to the procedures of globalization devised by the advanced industrialized nations is correct.

I. Unemployment, Poverty, Illiteracy, and Inequality

Economic liberalization involving antilabor and antipoor exit policy, fierce foreign competition from MNCS, and emphasis on profit maximizing have resulted in the creation of greater unemployment and poverty in the country than before. Thanks to SAP, ''jobless growth'' has taken place in India as elsewhere. Not only unemployment and poverty but also inequality and corruption have increased. India's debt burden has increased. The private entrepreneurs—domestic and foreign alike—do not want to invest in infrastructural (power/road) projects, as these entail huge capital investment and long gestation periods. Privatization has led to undesirable consumerism and cultural invasion of the country. In the social sector the cost of education and medical treatment and care provided by the private sector has increased enormously to the detriment of the weak and poor.

India is destined to march into the new millennium with the largest number of illiterates in the world. Neither of the win-win policies has resolved the problem of illiteracy in the country, as they have failed to provide the most basic of human rights—education. While 30 million have no access to schooling, of the 14 million who are enrolled, only two-thirds complete the primary stage. Of the remaining, only half reach the eighth standard. The majority of the dropouts are girls.

According to the UN World Development Report 1997, India's vital development/welfare indices read as follows:

> India continues to be a Low Income Country (LIC) with a population of 929.4 million in 1995; a GNP per capita of $340; average annual growth percentage of 3.2 during 1985–95; 52.5 percent poverty-ridden people living on less than $1 a day (PPP), life expectancy at birth 62; adult illiteracy 48 percent; Central Government's current deficit/surplus as percentage of GDP minus 1.6; average annual lending rate 16.3 percent; average inflation 9.8 percent in 1985–95; Current Account Balance minus 1.8; and net present value of external debt 23 percent of the GDP.

To sum up, the debit side of the economic liberalization policy weighs more heavily than its credit side. Dissatisfaction with the new policy is growing among different sections of the people for different reasons. The small indigenous industrialists, business community, and farmers who have contributed their might to the economic/industrial development for the 50 years since India's independence are now faced with the threat of extinction—the big fish swallowing the small ones in the face of fierce competition from powerful monopolist foreign companies/MNCs. In all fairness the government has to provide a level playing field to the Indians through protection and concessions while simultaneously motivating them to modernize their enterprises with the latest technology which will help them and the country in the long run.

VIII. CONCLUSION

Under win-win policy model II, though the state activities in the Indian economy have shrunk, it does not mean that government has rolled back or that it has no function to perform. Under the impact of the new economic reforms, the Indian bureaucracy has to bring about debureaucratization, deregulation, delicensing, and decentralization of development administration. However, its performance in this regard has been far from satisfactory. India's main development goal of building a welfare state is still a distant goal. The new economic reforms have not been able to make a dent in unemployment, poverty, or inequality in the country. The gaps between rich and poor and crime and violence are increasing. Agriculture, the backbone of the Indian economy, has been neglected under the new regime of economic liberalization. The recent shortage of essential commodities and mismanagement of this sector by the Union Government points to the poor performance of the second win-win model of development, in force in the country since 1991.

ENDNOTES

1. Weber, M. (1949). *The Methodology of the Social Science*, 56–57. New York: Free Press.
2. Lin, P. (1976). Development guided by values. In R. Kothari (ed.), *State and Nation Building*, New Delhi: Allied, p. 189.
3. Bava, N. (1993). *Development and the Social Science Method: An Interdisciplinary and Global Approach*, 169. New Delhi: Uppal.
4. Adiseshiah, M.S. (1977). Planning and development. In S.K. Sharma (ed.), *Dynamics of Development*. Delhi: Concept, p. 283.
5. Islam, N. and Henault, G.M. (1979). From GNP to basic needs: a critical review of development and development administration. *International Review of Administrative Sciences*, *VI*(3), 253–678, 1979.
6. Titmuss, R.M. (1976). *Talking About Welfare: Readings in Philosophy and Social Policy*. London: Routledge and Kegan Paul, p. 145.
7. Robson, W. (1976). *Welfare State and Welfare Society: Illusion and Reality*, 12. London: George Allen and Unwin.
8. Furniss, N. and Tilton, T. (1977). *The Case of the Welfare State from Social Security to Social Equality*, 19. Bloomington: Indiana University Press.
9. Marshall, T.H. (1963). *Sociology at the Crossroads*.
10. Furniss, N. and Tilton, T. (1977). *The Case of the Welfare State from Social Security to Social Equality*, 15. Bloomington: Indiana University Press.
11. Wilensky, H.L. (1976). *The New Corporation, Centralisation, and Welfare State*, 8–9. London: Sage Publications.
12. Sen, A. (1986). The concept of well-being. In S. Gulshan and M. Shroff (eds.), *Essays on Economic Progress and Welfare: In Honour of I.G. Patel*, Bombay: Oxford, p. 175.
13. Streeton, P. (1981). *First Things First. Meeting Basic Needs in Developing Countries*, 21. New York: Oxford.
14. Mukheshwaran and Kotwal, A. (1994). *Why Poverty Persists in India*. Bombay: Oxford.
15. Nagel, S.S. (1984). *Contemporary Public Policy Analysis*. Alabama: University of Alabama Press.
16. Negal, S.S. (1980). *The Policy Studies Handbook*, 162. Lexington, MA: D.C. Heath and Co.
17. Nagel, S.S. (1984). *Contemporary Public Policy Analysis*. University of Alabama Press, p. 28.
18. Lipset, M.S. (1972). *Politics and the Social Sciences Method*, xiii–xiv. New Delhi: Wiley Eastern Pvt. Ltd.
19. Nagel, S.S. (1995). Universal values and win-win policy. *Policy Studies Journal*, *23*(2), 1–2.

20. Nagel, S.S. (1995). Universal values and win-win policy. *Policy Studies Journal*, 1–2.
21. Toye, J. (1995). *Structural Adjustment and Employment Policy: Issues and Experience*, 13–42. Geneva: ILO.
22. Bava, N. (1994). Welfare state: the Indian chapter. Paper presented at the XVI World Congress of the International Political Science Association, August 21–25, Berlin.
23. Bava, N. (1996). Welfare state and liberalisation. *Indian Journal of Public Administration*, special number on Liberalisation Policy and Social Concerns, Vol. XLII(3): 334–346.

9

Policies and Strategies of International Organizations in Combating Child Labor in India

A Win-Win Analysis*

Rupa Chanda
Indian Institute of Management, Bangalore, India

Rekha Datta
Monmouth University, West Long Branch, New Jersey

I. INTRODUCTION

Few problems confronting humanity are as baffling and complex as that of child labor. The most common cause for child labor is poverty. Poor families depend on the income of their children, who may be as young as 5 years. This is compounded by the lack of access to education.[1] How to combat child labor is a complex problem. Most countries have legislation seeking to prevent child labor. In practice, however, these are not always implemented and many developing countries continue to put their children to work. There are several challenges that developing countries encounter in the area of combating child labor. These in-

* This chapter is based on information gathered from the United Nations in India. The section on the activities and views of the various UN agencies in the area of child labor are excerpted from an ILO report titled, ''UN System in India: Position Paper on Child Labour.'' This report was prepared for the United Nations' Operational Activities for Development in India, ILO Area Office for India and Bhutan, on behalf of the UN in New Delhi, India, 1998. The authors are grateful to the UN for sharing valuable information and for suggestions and comments which helped shape this chapter. The views expressed here are solely those of the authors and not of the UN/ILO.

clude poverty, lack of access to basic and vocational education, cultural acceptance of norms such as apprenticeships and bonded labor, etc.

At what age should children be allowed to work? The minimum age at which a child should be allowed to work in a salaried position is a much debated one. In 1973, the ILO convention 138 on minimum age for employment provides: "The minimum age . . . should not be less than the age of compulsory schooling and, in any case, shall not be less than 15 years."[2]

According to one estimate, there are 120 million children between the ages of 5 and 14 working full time. Most of them are in developing countries. The number is higher when secondary activities are included.[3] India accounts for the largest number of child workers in the world. According to the 1991 census estimates, about 13 million children between the ages of 5 and 14 are engaged in child labor. This figure is considerably lower than other estimates of child labor in India, which range from 40 million to over 100 million.[4]

Child labor occurs in many countries, developed and developing alike. But it is more widespread in the developing world. In today's interdependent world, a problem like child labor transcends national boundaries. As such, it becomes critical to see how international agencies cope with the issue and the challenges they encounter from national governments in doing so. This chapter examines the role of international organizations such as that of the United Nations system in implementing programs and policies to combat child labor in India.

II. CHILD LABOR IN INDIA

Accurate data on child labor is difficult to obtain. Quite understandably, many governments downplay the extent of child labor. This is true in the case of India as well. Noted social scientist Myron Weiner explains in his 1991 study on child labor in India:

> Given the uncertainties of definition and the complexities of remuneration, it is no wonder that estimates of child labor vary so greatly in India. . . . The official National Sample Survey of 1983 reports 17.4 million child laborers, while a study by the Operations Research Group of Baroda, sponsored by the Labor Ministry, concluded that the child labor force was 44 million, including children paid in kind as well as cash.[5]

As in the international context, the total magnitude of child labor in India is very difficult to estimate. As already stated, the latest census indicates that some 13 million children between the ages of 5 and 14 are engaged in child labor.[6] Other estimates of child labor in India show the range from some 40 million to over 100 million. These higher numbers may be correlated with the number of children not attending primary schools. Over 80% of child labor in India is found in the rural sector with the remainder in the urban informal sector. About 2 million or so children are believed to be engaged in hazardous employment.

The rural child labor force is mainly engaged in agriculture and its allied activities, and in household chores. In the urban informal sector, child labor is found in small-scale cottage industries; in tea stalls, restaurants, workshops, and factories; as domestic servants; and on streets. In the nonagricultural sector, child labor is found in many activities such as:

The carpet industry in the Mirzapur-Bhadohi belt of UP
Match and fireworks industry of Sivakasi, Tamil Nadu
Diamond-cutting industry of Surat
Glass industry of Ferozabad
Pottery industry of Khurja
Brassware industry of Moradabad
Tea plantations of Assam and West Bengal
Silk-weaving industry of Varanasi
Sports goods industry in Meerut and Jullunder

Statewise, child labor is predominant in the states of Uttar Pradesh, Bihar, Madhya Pradesh, Andhra Pradesh, Orissa, Karnataka, and Tamil Nadu, and is mainly found in poor areas and among the most disadvantaged and marginalized groups in society.

There is a deep-rooted view in Indian society that child labor is caused by poverty and that elimination of child labor is not possible without first eradicating poverty. Thus, child labor is an accepted socioeconomic reality that is perpetuated by traditional attitudes and also institutionalized in practice in many parts of the country. However, as in the international context, some major causes of child labor are the exploitation of poverty made possible by unequal access to principal productive resources and assets, the lack of education, and societal attitudes.

Of late, a consensus is gradually emerging in Indian society on the importance of these factors and thus on the strategies required to eliminate child labor. Compulsory and universal primary education is increasingly being recognized as the most relevant instrument to combat child labor, along with strategies for income generation, empowerment of women, enforcement of child labor laws and minimum wage legislation, and overall convergence of social services on families with child labor.

One of the most common forms of child labor in India is *bonded* labor. Usually when a person or a family needs a loan and has no asset to stand as security, they pledge their labor or that of their children as security against a loan. In most such cases, when the debt becomes too high, it is transferred from one generation and children are "lent" as repayment of loans. Because of the high amount of the loan, the service or "labor" that was originally pledged usually increases with time and the children remain bonded sometimes for life. The service time also increases arbitrarily when the moneylenders punish their "slaves" by increasing the time they have to serve because they have either been slack or slow in their work or have disobeyed them. Bonded labor is widely used in many industries. It is especially widespread in the carpet industry; 85% of India's carpet exports come from Uttar Pradesh in northern India. Children age 6 to 9 were reportedly employed in the weaving looms in Uttar Pradesh and other parts of India.[7]

The fireworks industry in Sivakasi in the southern state of Tamil Nadu also employs large numbers of children, sometimes very young. More than a decade ago, it was estimated that 45,000 children between the ages of 3½ and 15 were employed in the match industry. Children as young as 3½ years were picked up in buses early in the morning and sent to work in match factories. Accidents are common in fireworks factories and there have been several reports of accidents and evidence of "children being roasted alive." Poverty is a major cause for the large concentration of child labor in such areas. There is also a complex mix of economic and social constraints that contribute to the perpetuation of the problem. The fireworks industry is owned by the Nader caste, which capitalizes on the fact that the region is barren and drought prone. They prevent the spread of agriculture into the area so the people are forced to depend on the fireworks industry as a means of livelihood. Thus whereas child labor is common in farmlands, where children help out on the farms, children in this region have no alternatives to working in the fireworks factories.[8]

The Indian constitution bans the use of child labor in factories and mines. For instance, Article 24 prohibits the use of children for work in factories and mines. Under Article 45, the state shall try to provide children up to the age of 14 with free and compulsory education. In addition to these and other constitutional guarantees, several laws sought to protect the underage children in factories and mines. These included the Labor Act of 1951, the Mines Act of 1952, and the Factories Act of 1954. The 1979 Committee on Child Labor appointed by the government to review the status of children concluded that despite the legislation and constitutional prohibition on using child labor under certain ages and in hazardous employment, the government had not enforced legislation banning child labor.

More recent efforts by the government to prohibit child labor have not been very effective either. For example, the Child Labor Act of 1986 does not deal with the causes of child labor but only with its consequences.[9] Also, it makes recommendations about not using children in hazardous employment without clearly defining what constitutes hazardous. This means that many employers continue to employ children in various industries for long hours in unsanitary and unhealthy conditions without violating the law.

Administrative short-sightedness and unwillingness to deal with the problem are exacerbated with the social and economic pressures by families that have to send their children to work for economic reasons.[10] Furthermore, the government has passed several laws dating back to the inception of the constitution prohibiting the use of child labor in factories but not in agriculture or the informal sector, including domestic helpers, cottage industries, and restaurants. Leading social scientists have repeatedly argued for compulsory primary education. They argue:

> No country has successfully ended child labor without first making education compulsory. As long as children need not attend school, they will enter the labor force. But Indian officials and politicians reject compulsory education, arguing that poor families need the labor and income of their children.[11]

Given the magnitude of the problem and the relative ineffectiveness of the government, many nongovernmental organizations (NGOs) and collaborative efforts by the government and nongovernmental agencies have become more prevalent in recent years.[12] Many organizations are focusing on eradicating child labor by mobilizing community participation for universal primary education.[13] Draft papers and background notes of NGOs often shed light on various aspects of the national initiatives on child labor, the existing legislation, national projects (such as the National Child Labor Projects, the Child Labor Action and Strategy Program, and the ILO's International Program on the Elimination of Child Labor). One such paper is C.J. George's ''Child Labor: The Inadequate Responses and Prevalent Myths,'' which came out in January 1996. It looks at legislation to deal with bonded child labor, the work of local activists, different approaches that have been taken to address the problem including outright abolition, and compulsory primary education. Such efforts attempt to complement the gaps still to be overcome by legislation alone. Community activism has proven to be very effective in the drive toward eradicating child labor.

III. THE UNITED NATIONS AND CHILD LABOR[14]

The United Nations and its affiliate agencies such as UNICEF and the International Labor Organization are at the forefront of the movement to eradicate child labor. When we examine the role of the UN in eradicating child labor in India, we find that it is broad and comprehensive.[15] There is a common concern for the problem in terms of protecting the child directly from exploitation, and in noting the adverse consequences of such exploitation and the factors leading to such exploitation.

The UN's comprehensive view of child labor is well reflected in some of its agencies' definitions of child labor. For instance, according to UNICEF, any child who is out of school is a child laborer or a potential child laborer. UNIFEM views child labor as any work that prevents children from enjoying their childhood. UNESCO's perspective on child labor is in terms of a group with special needs. The UN system's holistic view of child labor is also reflected in the agencies' recognition of the complex range of demand-and-supply factors that give rise to child labor. The 1996 ILO publication *Child Labor: Targeting the Intolerable* highlights numerous factors such as lack of education, societal attitudes and norms, inequities in economic and social conditions, and economic motivations as contributing to child labor. Likewise, the UNICEF report *The State of the World's Children, 1997*, presents the issue in all its complexity, discussing its various causes and solutions and exposing several myths which exist on child labor.

A. Programs and Projects Initiated by UN Agencies

There are many UN agency–supported programs specifically on child labor which are implemented by the government and by NGOs. These relate mainly to the ILO and UNICEF. Some of these programs are discussed below.

1. ILO and Programs to Eliminate Child Labor

In 1992, the ILO has introduced the International Program on the Elimination of Child Labor (IPEC). It is a major initiative and the main UN program targeted specifically at this issue. The ILO implements IPEC through various so-called action programs. IPEC aims at progressively eliminating child labor. It also emphasizes making the agencies and the public aware of the negative effects of child labor. As of 1997, 121 agreements were signed for implementing action programs under IPEC in India. Most of these programs are implemented through NGOs.

The programs that IPEC has launched are comprehensive and far-reaching. For instance, the action programs focused on the setting up of nonformal education centers, drawing local working children into these centers, and often supplementing the basic curriculum with low level vocational skills, supplementing the diet of the children, providing health care, and conducting awareness-raising campaigns for the children, their parents, the community, and employers.

Since 1993 there has been a change in focus of the programs. They shifted from providing welfare inputs to combating child labor at the local level through community support and involvement. There was more emphasis on ensuring sustainability of these initiatives. During this second phase, preventive strategies have also been included, such as enrolling children into schools before their entry into the labor force, mainstreaming children into formal schools, and providing follow-up assistance to prevent dropping out.

In addition, IPEC and Indian agencies have launched joint initiatives to combat child labor. They have established links with many new partners, including trade unions such as the Indian National Trade Union Congress (INTUC), Centre of Indian Trade Unions (CITU), the All India Trade Union Congress (AITUC), and the Bharatiya Mazdoor Sangh (BMS). They have also sensitized the national trade union leaders about the nature and magnitude of the problem of child labor under action programs. Between 1992 and 1995, at least five nationwide trade unions have taken a stand against child labor within and outside their organizations. They have made efforts to educate their workers about child labor and are influencing the central and state governments to intervene against this problem.

IPEC has also involved national employers' organizations such as the Federation of Indian Chambers of Commerce and Industry (FICCI), the Confederation of Indian Employers (CIE), and regional employers' organizations such as the Punjab, Haryana, and Delhi Chambers of Commerce and Industry (PHDCCI) in combating child labor in India.

Training inspectors is an essential step in the process of eradicating child labor. IPEC has provided support to the government through training programs for labor and factory inspectors. Under these programs, inspectors have been sensitized about the negative impact of child labor on the development of children and on the society and economy as a whole. These training programs have had a significant impact on the law enforcement machinery in the country.

To be sure, IPEC has played an important role in developing the institutional capacity of training and research institutions in combating child labor. Under its action program with the Central Board of Workers' Education (CBWE), educational modules were developed and introduced on child labor into all the CBWE's workers' training programs with a reach of 105 million workers per year. As one of its projects, the program improved the library and made it the focal point for distributing information about child labor. This strengthened the CBWE section on women and children. Many workshops on awareness raising and sensitization have also been conducted through institutes such as the National Institute of Rural Development and the National Safety Council which have been important for capacity building in the country.[16]

Another very important project that the ILO has implemented is the Child Labor Action Support Project (CLASP). This was a three-year project supporting nine specified national child labor projects. Its objectives were to enhance the central government's policy, its planning and implementation capacity, and its ability to support ongoing and future projects by state governments and NGOs.

CLASP also aimed at mobilizing communitywide support against child labor and at facilitating more efficient use of government resources. The goal was to enable a more rapid abolition of child labor in accordance with the ILO's Minimum Age Convention Number 138 of 1973.

2. UNICEF and Programs on Child Labor

UNICEF has a long history of cooperation with the government of India. Since the country's independence in 1947, it has supported programs for women and children. While UNICEF's interface with the government is through the Department of Women and Children, its various sections have regular working contacts with the Ministries/Departments of Education, Health, Rural Development, Urban Development, Welfare, and Information and Broadcasting. UNICEF's cooperation with the Ministry of Labor on the issue of child labor began in 1983.

Since then, UNICEF has been involved in a variety of activities concerning the elimination of child labor. Its main emphasis in this area has been on the prevention of child labor through primary education and other actions. UNICEF has also provided support to the setting up of the child labor section within the National Labor Institute and provided financial and technical assistance for the training of factory and labor inspectors, government officials, and NGOs, for the organization of meetings and workshops, and for studies on street children in various cities and child labor in various occupations. UNICEF field offices located in 10 states have supported state level workshops on child labor in almost all the states. In several states, UNICEF has also supported studies to compile state profiles of child labor which have been important for creating awareness about the issue and generating actions by state governments and NGOs.

UNICEF has focused on the 13 states that have the highest incidence of child labor in the country. These include Andhra Pradesh, Tamil Nadu, Uttar Pradesh, and Bihar. In Andhra Pradesh, UNICEF has supported state level studies on child labor, orientation workshops for government officials, meetings of trade unions, innovative NGO projects, and efforts for the convergence of programs. In Uttar Pradesh, UNICEF provided supplementary funds for an initiative focusing on the elimination of child labor in carpet weaving in the three main carpet-weaving districts. In Bihar, UNICEF initiated a UN interagency effort to assist the Bihar government in developing a strategy for the prevention and elimination of child labor. In Tamil Nadu, the state government and a UNICEF task force formulated a plan of action for the elimination of child labor in Sivakasi. Also, in the context of the state government's Child Labor Action Support Scheme (CLASS) in North Arcot district, aimed at eliminating child labor in the beedi-rolling industry, UNICEF provided technical input and seed capital for sensitization, education, and training; supported the district administration in developing an elimination strategy; and helped bring out a video on the project.

More recently, UNICEF has been involved in the area of child prostitution and trafficking. In 1996, it supported six regional workshops on this issue and is now working with the National Human Rights Commission to coordinate policy action and do advocacy work in this respect. In 1995, along with some other organizations, UNICEF organized a national consultation on child prostitution and will be part of a working group in this area.

UNICEF has also played an important role in the Rugmark labeling initiative. Rugmark Foundation is a joint international initiative which began in 1992. It involves UNICEF, the Indo-German Exporter Promotion Program, carpet manufacturers, and NGOs such as the South Asian Coalition on Child Servitude (SAACS). Rugmark has become a very effective mechanism to monitor, control, certify, and label carpets that are made without using child labor.[17] This was initiated in response to threats from industrialized countries of sanctions on imports of goods made with child labor. Thus, UNICEF together with Rugmark, has helped to develop an inspection system to ensure that Indian carpets are child labor free. UNICEF is a board member of the Rugmark Foundation which supervises this system and it manages the rehabilitation funds collected under this scheme.[18]

3. Other UN-Supported Programs with Bearing on Child Labor

There are UN agency programs that are not directly concerned with child labor but include the issue as a component within the overall program, or have an indirect impact in this area through some of their activities. Some of these are:

1. The *UNDP's South Asia Poverty Alleviation Program*, currently being implemented in three districts, focuses on institution building at the grass roots level, and includes child labor among several other issues. In Andhra Pradesh, under this program, UNDP is supporting the MV Foundation in various activities that have bearing on child labor. These include social mobilization, development of community infrastructure (including schools), and training of teachers and volunteers. Similar social mobilization initiatives are being considered in Madhya Pradesh, with a focus on getting children out of work and into schools through community involvement and infrastructure building.
2. The *UNDCP program for street children* focuses on children involved in drug and substance abuse. Its aim is to provide these children with access to services and information to reduce their vulnerability to drug-related risks. Although there is no direct focus on working children, since many street children are employed in ragpicking, peddling, and other activities that make them prone to drug and substance abuse, the program necessarily touches upon child labor. It addresses their working conditions on the street and tries to prevent some of the adverse consequences of such work on their health and well-being.[19]
3. *UNESCO's Learning Without Frontiers* (*LWF*) program, to be imple-

mented in six selected districts of three states in India, also has bearing on child labor. It targets the unreached and the disadvantaged who have no formal access to education, be it in the geographic, social, or economic sense. It aims to provide them with innovative and alternative learning opportunities at the basic and primary level, and in this context to strengthen community institutions and facilitate transition to formal schooling utilizing open schooling and distance education where appropriate. The campaign approach for literacy and neoliteracy programs is also supported. Since child workers are often among the marginalized and disadvantaged, the LWF program's activities have implications for child labor.[20]

4. The *UNFPA's support to the government of India's adult literacy program* includes the preparation of booklets and materials for literacy campaigns targeting the 9 to 15 age group. Many of the latter group are child laborers or have been in the past.

5. *UNIFEM's Entrepreneurship development programs for women*, such as its sericulture project in Udaipur and fisheries project in Orissa, are explicit about the positive impact on the child's well-being from an improvement in women's status in the community.

6. *WHO's projects on street children* include running informal courses on health awareness for this target group with the help of NGOs. They also aim to develop minimum standards of quality for services provided to street children.

7. *UNAIDS' activities on child trafficking* include assisting the government to obtain information regarding this problem. They also include facilitating the National AIDS Control Organization's role in strengthening State AIDS programs and in working with NGOs on social mobilization and advocacy concerning HIV/AIDS.

8. The *World Bank's sericulture project in Karnataka*, cofinanced by the Swiss Development Corporation and implemented by the state government, made a conscious effort to replace child workers in the silk industry with other means of production.

B. Joint UN System Initiatives Relevant to Child Labor

There are several joint initiatives within the UN system in India that have relevance to child labor and its elimination. Some take the form of cofinancing arrangements with allocation of responsibilities across the partner agencies. Others involve funding by one agency and implementation by another. Some others are very informal in nature and based only on exchange of information and expertise. A few of these joint initiatives are highlighted below.

1. The *Joint UN System Support for Community-Based Primary Education* is a collaborative effort including UNICEF, UNDP, ILO, UNESCO, and UNFPA. It is proposed to be implemented in selected blocks of districts in the states of Rajasthan, UP, Bihar, Madhya Pradesh, Maharashtra, Karnataka, Orissa,

and Andhra Pradesh. The aim of the program is to provide support to ongoing government efforts on universal elementary education and to make primary education more accessible and effective for primary school–age children, especially girls and children from deprived and disadvantaged communities or groups. The general objectives of this program are to enhance capacity for community participation in effective school management, improve the performance of primary school teachers, and improve the social conditions that affect attendance and performance of school-age children in selected districts through integrated social sector development programs. Of significance to child labor is that one of the criteria for selecting districts is their designation as a child labor area. Also, since this program targets the most disadvantaged and backward groups, it necessarily also covers child workers who are often from the marginalized and deprived groups in society.

2. The *UNICEF-ILO protocol* has direct bearing on child labor. It is based on the recognition that the ILO and UNICEF have complementary and mutually supportive roles to play in the progressive elimination of child labor and protection of working children. The framework for cooperation between the two agencies includes: regular consultations and coordination of policies regarding priority categories of child labor; encouraging member states to ratify and implement international standards; collaboration on research and exchange through regional and subregional workshops as well as development of methodologies for assessing and improving the condition of working children; and technical cooperation, especially in field activities of the two agencies.

3. Under the UNDP's *South Asia Poverty Alleviation Program*, UNICEF has supported initiatives with bearing on child labor in Mehboob Nagar district of Andhra Pradesh.

4. ILO and UNESCO have a *Joint Convention on the Status of Teachers* and a collaborative unit in Geneva to implement its recommendations. Enhancing the quality of teachers as a vital human resource has significant implications for school effectiveness and thus student participation and retention.

5. In the *prevention of child trafficking*, UNAIDS has provided technical inputs to the UNICEF in the latter's advocacy work and regional initiatives in this regard.

6. *In the health area*, UNDCP in conjunction with UNICEF and others (ODA, Ministry of Health) has helped carry out a survey on the behavioral and health aspects of children involved in drug abuse and HIV/AIDS.

7. *UNDCP* is cooperating with the ILO for the prevention of drugs at the workplace.

8. *UNAIDS* is working with UNICEF, UNESCO, and WHO to put HIV/AIDS-related information into the school curriculum. With funding from the various co-sponsors, UNAIDS is assisting NGOs to mainstream STD/HIV/AIDS into their activities and helping to provide targeted interventions for HIV/AIDS

to prevent risk behavior in the general population as well as defined groups such as sex workers, mobile populations, and migrants.[21]

IV. CONCLUSION

As in many other parts of the world, child labor has become a serious and widespread problem in India. It is all the more problematic because even though there is widespread concern about child labor, not everyone agrees on the solution. Especially in a poor country like India, where the majority of the population are struggling to remain above the poverty line and where a large portion of the work force is engaged in agriculture, engaging children in family farms and businesses seem the only feasible alternative to many. Instead of going to school, millions of children go to factories and farms every morning.

As already stated, making education compulsory has been suggested as a solution to ending child labor. In spite of several pleas, the government is reluctant to make compulsory education a priority. There is vested interest from many who use and employ child labor for their gains, and the government needs to be more forthright about its role if it is serious about eliminating child labor.[22]

Researchers and analysts have made several recommendations about the impact of education in eradicating child labor. Among them are suggestions that the entire primary education system be overhauled. Compulsory primary education has met with resistance in the past and the government has conveniently used it as a rationale *not* to implement it; the argument has been that poor families may need to put their children to work in order to survive economically.[23]

In the absence of government initiative, international pressures, public awareness, and nongovernmental organizations' efforts are going far in ensuring the steady consciousness about the cruel practice of using child labor to cut costs, pay low wages, and increase productivity. One such enterprise is Rugmark Foundation, which was founded in India in 1994 and has extended to Nepal. It gives license to companies to use their logo that no child labor was used in the manufacture of the carpets carrying the logo. In return, the companies have to comply with surprise inspections and other codes to ensure that child labor was not used in the manufacture of the carpets.[24] Individual success of Rugmark notwithstanding, it is a step in the direction of using public pressure and individual and group initiative to bring about changes in people's attitude toward child labor. Similar ventures are now in operation in other South Asia countries, such as Nepal and Bangladesh, and in Brazil.

The structure of the labor market will also determine whether eradicating child labor will meet with a whole lot of resistance. In markets where wages are flexible, employers will tend to hire children at lower wages. Where minimum wages are firmly determined and practiced, employers will tend to hire adults who can deliver more with the same wages. Thus, stabilizing wages may go a long way in eradicating child labor, especially in developing countries.

In the changing environment of globalization of the market, many developing countries are finding it almost imperative to engage in structural adjustment programs to compete and to qualify for various kinds of financial assistance from international lending agencies such as the World Bank and the IMF. Structural adjustment programs have also had an impact on child labor.[25] Economic liberalization has attracted more foreign investment, and the demand for labor has increased, making it easier for many industries to hire children at lower costs and meet the demands of increased production.

ACKNOWLEDGMENTS

The authors thank Mr. M. P. Joseph of the ILO office in New Delhi for his help, and Stuart S. Nagel and the Policy Studies Organization for providing the useful framework of the win-win analysis.

ENDNOTES

1. This information is from N. Burra, *Born to Work: Child Labor in India.* New Delhi: Oxford University Press, 1995; UNICEF, *The State of the World's Children 1997*, New York, 1997; and ILO, *Child Labor: Targeting the Intolerable*, Geneva, 1996.
2. *General Survey of the Reports relating to Convention 138 and Recommendation No. 146 concerning Minimum Age*, Report III (Part 4 B), Geneva: ILO, 1981, p. 73.
3. ILO, *Child Labor: Targeting the Intolerable*, Geneva, 1996.
4. Chaudhuri, *A Dynamic Profile of Child Labor in India, 1951–1991*, ILO, New Delhi, 1996. Other sources that are useful include R. Kanbargi, *Child Labor in the Indian Sub Continent: Dimensions and Implications*, New Delhi: Sage Publications, 1991.
5. Myron Weiner, *The Child and the State in India: Child Labor and Education Policy in Comparative Perspective*, Princeton, NJ: Princeton University Press, 1991, pp. 20–21.
6. Chaudhuri, *A Dynamic Profile of Child Labor in India, 1951–1991*, ILO, New Delhi, 1996.
7. Pharis Harvey and Lauren Riggin, *Trading Away the Future: Child Labor in India's Export Industries* (International Labor Rights Education and Research Fund, 1994), 53; B.N. Junyal, *Child Labor in the Carpet Industry in Mirzapur-Bhadohi* (New Delhi: ILO, 1993), 13; *Human Rights Watch, Children's Rights Project*, Sept. 1996, looks at bonded child labor in India, why it exists, domestic and international legislation on bonded child labor in various industries where it is found, Indian government programs and their failure to address the problem, and alternative solutions and recommendations to the government.

8. Christine Whitehead, The Economics of Children at Work, *New Statesman*, 12 Dec. 1986, p. 19.
9. Fernandes, ''A Critique—Towards Amendments/Restructuring of the Child Labor (Prohibition and Regulation) Act of 1986,'' draft paper, 1996.
10. For a review of the legislative history in India regarding child labor, see Myron Weiner, *The Child and the State in India: Child Labor and Educational Policy in Comparative Perspective.* Princeton, NJ: Princeton University Press, 1991.
11. Myron Weiner, Suffer the Children, *Far Eastern Economic Review*, 7 Feb. 1991, p. 26; Weiner, *The Child and the State in India*, Princeton, NJ: Princeton University Press, 1991.
12. H. Bertsch and E. Schalegger, ''Seri 2000''—concept paper for a collaborative seri-development program between the government of India and nongovernmental private sector institutions, and firms and the Swiss Agency for Development and Cooperation, 1997–2002, Beme, May 1996. This paper looks at the sericulture industry in India and makes references to the consequences of developing this industry for child labor. Also, ''Campaign Against Child Labor,'' position paper on child labor, Mumbai, 1997. This paper looks at the causative background for child labor from a socioeconomic perspective, the rural and urban features of child labor, definitional issues, and the work of CACL.
13. V. Dhagamwar, ''Eradication of Child Labor Through Social Mobilization for Primary Education,'' report on two organizations, New Delhi, 1995.
14. The programs and projects initiated by the UN system and the ILO are exerpted from the ILO Report ''UN System in India: Position Paper on Child Labour,'' New Delhi: ILO, 1998.
15. The reference here is to all the UN agencies with whom discussions were held for this paper.
16. For further details on IPEC, see M.P. Joseph, *IPEC in India, 1992–95: Looking Back*, New Delhi: ILO, 1996.
17. For more details, see Martine Kruijtbosch, *Rugmark: A Brief Resume of Concept to Reality for Visual Guarantee of Carpets Made Without Child Labor*, New Delhi: SAACS, 1995.
18. The funds are mobilized by implementing a levy of 1% to 2% on the export value of the carpets. This is used to rehabilitate children released from the carpet industry.
19. UNDCP is also supporting a project on the Rehabilitation and Prevention of Drug Abuse at the Workplace. The project is being instituted by the ILO and the Indian Ministry of Welfare. While the focus is not on child labor per se, the preventive measures have an impact on the working conditions of children and their health, and on community awareness of these problems.
20. Important components of the program are formal schooling; income generation; environmental awareness; generation of employable skills; coordination and mobilization of ministries, departments, the community, NGOs, donor agencies, the business sector, and key individuals; and local capacity building. Many of these activities have significance for the elimination of child labor.
21. There was also an interagency group consisting of UNICEF, ILO, and UNESCO working on child labor in Bihar. The goal of this joint initiative was to enable the

agencies to play complementary roles in the area of education rather than running parallel programs. However, it did not make much headway.

22. M. Weiner, Child labor in India, putting compulsory primary education on the political agenda, *Economic and Political Weekly*, Nov. 9–16, 1996.
23. K. Charnaraj, Chalking in change, *Humanscope*, July 1996. This study talks about the need for structural change in primary education to eliminate child labor and provides views on the important role played by education in this process.
24. International Labor Rights Education Fund, Rugmark label gathers support amidst carpet industry violence, *Workers' Rights News*, Aug. 1995. This article talks about steps being taken in the carpet industry to cope with trade-based pressures on carpet exports made with child labor.
25. M. Swaminathan and V.K. Ramachandran look at *Structural Adjustment Programs and Child Welfare*, Mumbai: Indira Gandhi Institute of Development Research, Aug. 1993.

10

Economic Liberalization and Federalism

The Case of India

Lawrence Sáez
University of California, Berkeley, California

Gradual political decentralization and economic liberalization policies are having a tremendous impact on India's federal system. However, the literature on comparative federalism has not explored how economic and political changes affect federal relations in India. In this paper I will first discuss India's political decentralization by way of a gradual political party realignment in the 1980s. I will then examine the dimensions of India's economic liberalization policies. I will then show how India's political reform and economic liberalization policies have impacted federal relations in India. I will argue that the political party realignment in the 1980s combined with the economic liberalization policies in the 1990s has prompted a change in federal relations from cooperative federalism to interjurisdictional competition.

The paper will show that the transformation from cooperative federalism to interjurisdictional competition will have three significant implications. First, interjurisdictional competition is bringing about striking financial disparities among states. These financial disparities may prompt greater subregional conflict. Second, the transformation in federal relations has affected the effectiveness of institutions of intergovernmental cooperation. Third, the transformation in federal relations in India has affected the ability of the Indian state to address developmental challenges.

I. TIMING AND PACE OF REFORM

The change in India's party system featured a transformation from a one-party-dominant system through the 1970s to a multiparty system of governance at the state level in the mid-1980s. The Congress Party has had episodic periods of rapid decline at the polls, particularly during the 1967 state assembly elections. These periods of sharp decline, though, have been followed by equally sudden periods of extraordinary electoral performance. The 1971 election was a period of extraordinary electoral success of the Congress Party at both the national and the regional levels. However, following its victory after the 1985 general elections, support for the Congress Party appears to have been irreversibly eroded. Since 1985, the once dominant Congress Party suffered a steadily diminished aggregate share of seats and votes in India's state legislatures (See Fig. 1).

The political party realignment in its state legislatures has had dramatic effects on India's federal system. In the 1980s there was a notable rise of regionalist political parties. These regionalist parties increased demands for a more decentralized federal system. Moreover the political party realignment has helped out the establishment of different types of party systems in India's state legislatures. At the regional level, there are still significant variations in the electoral strength

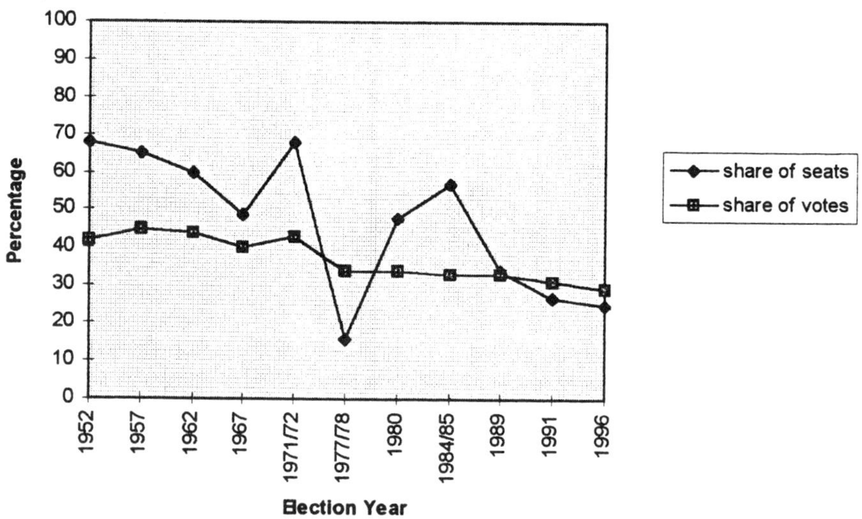

Figure 1 Congress Party's aggregate share of seats and votes in state assembly elections (1952–1996). (From Rudolph and Rudolph, 1987, 130–131; Butler et al., 1995, 133–326; Aggarwal and Chowdhry, 1996; *Frontline*, various issues (June 14, June 28, July 12, 1996); *India Today* (August 16–31, 1996).)

of the Congress Party. As James Manor has recently written, one cannot refer to the continuance of a one-party dominant system at the regional level. There has been an emergence of various types of party systems at the regional level. According to Manor, some states in India could be characterized as being one party dominant systems, some as two party systems, and others as fragmented party systems.[1] The Congress Party continues to be a prominent electoral player in states with a bipolar party system. In fragmented party systems (Assam, Bihar, Punjab, and Uttar Pradesh) the Congress begins to play a gradually insignificant role.

These parties have seized on the gradual weakness of the Congress Party to issue demands for greater decentralization. As a result of the mode of India's unique pattern of party realignment at the state level, the coordination of legislative relations and the development and implementation of economic policies has been affected. The transformation in the party system in the mid-1980s appears to be durable.

The political party realignment has been accompanied by an unrelated development, India's gradual economic liberalization in the 1990s. Some authors claim that Prime Minister Indira Gandhi began to enact some modest industrial policy reforms in 1975 and 1980 followed by additional industrial reforms and some trade liberalization policies in the mid-1980s under Prime Minister Rajiv Gandhi.[2] However, these nominal economic reforms were principally aimed at domestic industrial reform. They also featured moderate trade reforms though a slow shift from import substitution to an export-oriented strategy of growth. This strategy included the gradual rationalization of the tariff structure and the import licensing policy.[3] These modest efforts to redress India's growing current account deficit increased India's exports but also aggravated India's trade deficit (see Fig. 2).

A more substantive set of economic liberalization policies were enacted following a mounting economic crisis which reached its peak during April–July, 1991. By July of 1991, India's foreign currency assets touched a record low of $560 million, the fiscal deficit peaked at 8.4% of the gross domestic product, and the inflation rate increased to 16.7%.[4] The Congress Party government, which came to power in June 1991, introduced a new economic strategy eventually labeled as the New Economic Policy (NEP). NEP used a combination of measures aimed at economic stabilization as well as structural reform. The reforms were masterminded by Narasimha Rao's Finance Minister, Manmohan Singh, and presented before the Lok Sabha. Manmohan Singh warned that the process of macroeconomic adjustment would take at least three years to implement.[5]

The NEP included short-term stabilization measures to reduce the current account deficit in the balance of payments (BOP) and to control inflation. Long-term measures of structural reform included the elimination of import restrictions on intermediate and capital goods. Other current account liberalization measures

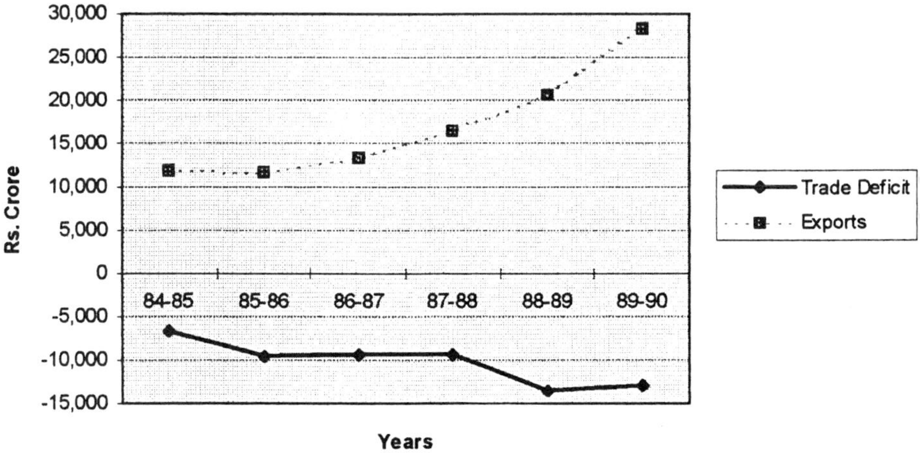

Figure 2 India's Exports and Trade Balance 1984–1990 (crore rupees). (From Centre for Monitoring of Indian Economy, *Basic Statistics Relating to the Indian Economy*, Vol. I (August 1991).)

included the gradual reduction on the average tariff protection on most goods from 300% in 1991 to 50% by 1995. These initial reforms were supplemented by financial sector reforms including adjustments in the exchange rate and on a partial convertibility of the rupee on the trade account. In addition, partial capital account reforms were introduced in the secondary capital market to facilitate portfolio investment in India's stock markets.[6]

India's conceptually sequenced economic liberalization policy has succeeded in increasing foreign direct investment inflows into India. Similarly, total portfolio equity investment, which includes foreign institutional investment, Euro-issues/GDRs, portfolio investment by nonresident Indians (NRI), and offshore funds have increased dramatically (see Fig. 3).

The dramatic increases in foreign direct and portfolio equity investments have aided in the recovery of private investment in India. For instance, gross domestic investment (as a percentage of the gross national product) has increased from 23.1% in 1991 to over 29% in 1997.[7] Moreover, according to International Finance Corporation statistics, market capitalization in India has increased from $38 billion in 1990 to $128 billion seven years later.[8]

The period of economic liberalization prior to NEP has typically been referred to as a period of ''reform with reluctance'' or ''half-hearted liberalization.''[9] Others have labeled the period of economic liberalization after the introduction of NEP as ''galloping'' liberalization. In contrast to other countries that have adopted ''shock therapy'' economic liberalization packages, India's eco-

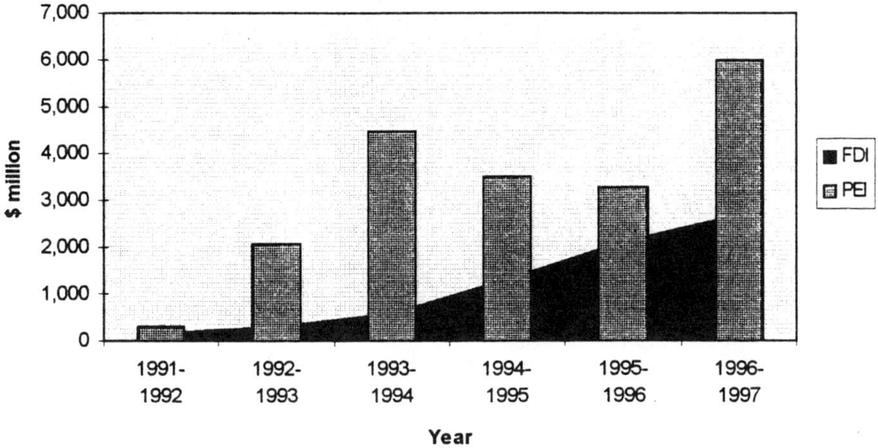

Figure 3 Foreign Direct Investment (FDI) and Portfolio Equity Investment (PEI) into India from 1991 to December 1997 (actual receipts). (From Centre for Monitoring of Indian Economy, *Annual Indicators* (December 1997), p. 8.)

nomic reforms, although crisis driven, have been comparatively gradual.[10] The gradual nature of India's economic reform process was intentional. In an interview during the initial stages of NEP, then Finance Minister Manmohan Singh forecast that the reform process had "to go on for a decade if India is to achieve her full development potential."[11]

The gradualness of the economic reforms was a matter of necessity given that the Congress Party that initiated NEP was a minority government. Prime Minister Narasimha Rao had to reach support for Manmohan Singh's economic reform package within and outside the Congress Party.[12] In contrast, although Prime Minister Rajiv Gandhi had enjoyed a clear mandate during the 1985 general elections, he later failed to capitalize on this electoral victory to lobby for internal party support for his moderate trade liberalization policies. In an analysis of Rajiv Gandhi's modest economic reforms, Atul Kohli has argued that the opposition to Rajiv Gandhi's trade liberalization policies surprisingly came from the rank and file of the Congress Party. The diffuse opposition to further economic liberalization efforts was stalled by a return to populist policies.[13] Other observers, such as Prem Shankar Jha, have noted that since the enactment of NEP, "the opposition to the reform programme within Congress seems to have virtually disappeared."[14] Moreover, the consensus-driven economic reforms have weakened the opposition to the reforms from outside of the Congress Party.

One of the advantages of India's gradual economic liberalization policies is that a consensus has been built around some key policy proposals. Instead of harming the credibility of the reforms, gradualism appears to have cemented a broad, multipartisan political consensus in favor of measured economic liberalization. The last two minority governing coalitions have coincided in their interest for increased foreign direct investment in a graduated manner, with an emphasis on investment into infrastructure development and removal of unemployment.[15] The support for increased foreign direct investment has had some unlikely advocates. Jyoti Basu, the Chief Minister of West Bengal's Communist (Marxist) Party of India controlled government, has argued in favor of economic liberalization that also protects domestic industries. Similarly, L.K. Advani, the president of the Hindu nationalist Bharatiya Janata Party (BJP), expressed that India has "to be cautious and a phased movement towards globalisation is better. I am all for liberalisation, as rapidly as possible."[16] Former Indian Prime Minister H.D. Deve Gowda argued that "the movement towards economic liberalization and foreign investment is a process that cannot and will not be stopped."[17] According to Jagdish Bhagwati, an economic adviser to former finance minister Manmohan Singh, the NEP reforms are sustainable. He argued that "the question now is not whether the reforms will be reversed but how rapidly they will be extended."[18]

At this stage there are several areas of economic policy that various political parties have been reluctant to enact legislatively at the federal level. For instance, the full convertibility of the rupee, public sector reform, the privatization of state-owned enterprises, and the opening up of certain core or strategic sectors of the economy (such as the insurance industry) to foreign investment have remained areas of disagreement. A full-fledged debate on more dramatic structural adjustment has not taken place due to the continuing shift in coalition governments at the center. Since 1989, India has had four general elections and five different minority governing coalitions. Therefore, the gradual nature of India's NEP is likely to continue as a result of coalitional entanglements in the central government because no clear support or opposition to NEP can be sustained for long.

II. INDIA'S UNIQUE BRAND OF COOPERATIVE FEDERALISM

The dual transformation of the political party realignment in the mid-1980s and the economic liberalization policies in the early 1990s has altered the structure of India's federal system. As is the case in other federations, competition and cooperation are often overlapping facets in India's federal system. India's federal system is textured by its unique historical and constitutional features. Several authors have attempted to find a theoretical middle ground between the centralizing, hierarchical features of the Indian Constitution and the demands for decentralization that eventually arose from its sociocultural diversity. Granville Austin was instrumental in addressing this continuous tension by labeling India's federal system as an example of "cooperative federalism." Austin argued that "cooperative federalism produces a strong central, or general government, yet it does not necessarily result in weak provincial governments that are largely administrative agencies for central policies."[19]

The British political scientist W.H. Morris-Jones also pointed to the unique discrepancy between India's formal constitutional structure and the demands for decentralization. He argued that "whereas the emphasis on the Constitution is on demarcation, that of practical relations is on co-operative bargaining."[20] As a result of India's socioeconomic diversity, Morris-Jones has stressed the bargaining aspects of federalism rather than its cooperative elements, as suggested by Granville Austin. Cooperative federalism, for Morris-Jones, has implications of a semblance of friendly commonality of interests, whereas bargaining implies the conflictual aspects of cooperation resulting from conflictual interests. Both Morris-Jones and Granville Austin have illustrated the practicality of cooperative federalism by showing that although the Indian Constitution imposed a stronger national government on the states, the states have been strategically essential to carry out nationally defined goals.[21]

III. RELATIONS BETWEEN THE CENTER AND THE STATES

Functionally, the relationship between the central government and the states has been occasionally coercive, particularly through the application of President's Rule. In turn, acrimony has been a defining characteristic of some other facets of federal relations in India. An area of disagreement in federal relations has been the issue of financial relations. The disparities in the distribution of resource transfers from the central government to the states have often become central in the debates about fiscal federal relations, mainly because the Constitution of India has circumscribed the tax-raising abilities of the central and state governments.

Indian states receive about 60% of their total revenue from tax receipts. The primary component of the state's total tax receipts are received from the states' sales tax. Nearly a quarter of all states' total revenues come from the sales tax. However, there is wide variation between the states' tax-raising ability. Approximately one-third of the state's total revenue constitutes the state's share of taxes collected by the central government.[22] These revenues are supplemented by direct grants and loans from the central government. In the past, in order to alleviate the state's perceived dependence on assistance from the central government, some state governments demanded more powers to impose taxes of their own. Moreover, some state governments argued that their inability to raise an adequate level of resources prompted unwanted interference from the central government into the affairs of the state governments.

Table 1 States' and Union Territories' Share of Tax Revenue (Rs. crore)

1992–93	1993–94	1994–95	1995–96	1996–97	1997–98
20,593 (27.6%)	22,294 (29.4%)	24,840 (26.9%)	29,298 (26.3%)	35,107 (26.5%)	40,253 (26.2%)

Source: CMIE, *Public Finance* (May 1998), p. 508. *Economic and Political Weekly* (May 17–24, 1997), p. 1207. (Percentage of the center's gross tax revenue in parentheses.)

India's gradual move to a market economy has not significantly altered the central government's financial relationship with the states. The Finance Commission, the national government agency that reviews tax devolution and determines resource transfers, arranges the allocation of nonplan transfers to the states. Nearly three-quarters of central government transfers to the states are approved by the Finance Commission. Despite recent efforts by the central government to reduce its fiscal deficit, the states' and union territories' percentage share of income tax revenue and Union excise duties has remained constant (see Table 1).

Table 1 shows that the states' and union territories' share of tax revenue has remained at approximately 26% of the center's gross tax revenues. The Tenth Finance Commission recommended an increase to 29% in the transfer of the center's gross proceeds of all taxes to the states. This offer was rejected by some states as being "too meager."[23]

About half of the states' nontax revenues are received as plan outlays in the form of direct grants from the central government to the states. These transfers are determined by the Planning Commission, and often serve to finance the plans of states. Since the enactment of NEP, central governmental assistance to state plans as a percentage of the center's total plan transfers has decreased slightly while assistance to union territories has remained constant (see Table 2).

Tables 1 and 2 suggest that the center's financial relationship with the states has not been substantially altered by economic liberalization. However, central government loans to finance the fiscal deficits of states have increased as a proportion of nonplan expenditures. Moreover, loans and advances to the states have increased as a proportion of the actual governmental capital receipts. However, the increase in loans and advances to the states have been offset by a decrease in capital receipts as a proportion of the central government's tax revenues (see Table 3).

Ironically, as tighter hard budget constraints have affected federal-level plan expenditures to the states, the debates about fiscal federalism have decreased. It appears that the resulting influx of foreign investment inflows in the 1990s has gradually diminished the importance of the central government as a principal

Table 2 Central Governmental Assistance to State and Union Territory Plans (Rs. crore)

1992–93	1993–94	1994–95	1995–96	1996–97	1997–98
Assistance to state plans					
15,664	19,021	20,905	18,073	21,220	25,885
(12.85)	(13.45)	(13%)	(10.1%)	(10.4%)	(11.1%)
Assistance to union territories					
1,220	956	673	688	796	837
(1.0%)	(0.7%)	(0.4%)	(0.4%)	(0.4%)	(0.4%)

Source: Ministry of Finance; Economic and Political Weekly, 32:20 (May 17–24, 1997), p. 1209. (Percentage of the center's total plan outlays in parentheses.)

source of revenues for some states. Instead, NEP has pushed some states to lobby for alternative sources of revenue, mostly in the form of additional foreign direct investment or other forms of mobile capital stock. This explains the paradoxical fact that some states, such as West Bengal's CPI (M) state government, are actively competing for foreign direct investment into their states. At the same time, the central government has recently threatened to dismiss the Rabri Devi state government in Bihar as a result of that state's continuing fiscal mismanagement.

The impact of political party realignment has been widespread across the states of India. However, the accompanying economic liberalization in the 1990s has tended to be concentrated toward a few states, mostly middle-income and high-income states (see Fig. 4).

NEP has had direct spillover effects in some states. As Figure 4 shows, three states (Maharashtra, Gujarat, and Tamil Nadu) account for nearly a quarter of the foreign direct investment proposals made in India from August 1991 to September 1996. If one also includes FDI proposals in the union territory of Delhi, three states (and Delhi) account for nearly 50% of all approved foreign direct investment approvals made in India.

Outside of foreign investment magnets, there is wide dispersal of FDI in-

Table 3 Loans and Advances to the States and the Union Territories (Rs. crore)

1992–93	1993–94	1994–95	1995–96	1996–97	1997–98
4,728	6,264	9,753	10,538	10,771	11,396
(3.9%)	(4.4%)	(6.1%)	(5.9%)	(5.3%)	(4.9%)

Source: Ministry of Finance; *Economic and Political Weekly*, 32:20 (May 17–24, 1997), p. 1208. (Percentage of the center's total nonplan expenditures in parentheses.)

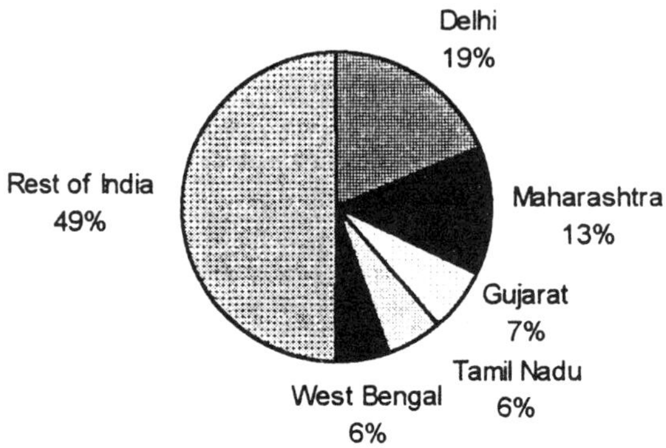

Figure 4 Comparison of FDI Proposals Approved from August 1991 to September 1996 in Selected States with All-India Totals. (From Ministry of Finance; *Economic and Political Weekly*, ''Foreign Investment Approvals and Actuals'' (May 10–16, 1997), p. 987.)

flows into other states in India. It is dispiriting to note that four of India's most populous states (Uttar Pradesh, Madhya Pradesh, Rajasthan, and Bihar) are also low-income states with comparatively minuscule FDI inflows. Since August of 1991, the combined proposed foreign direct investment to these politically powerful ''Hindi-belt'' states (Rs. crore 5058) approximates the proposed foreign direct investment to the southern state of Tamil Nadu (Rs. crore 5006). Moreover, there has only been one proposed FDI project in the politically troubled state of Jammu and Kashmir worth Rs. 8.01 crore. Assam, another state with a continuing legacy of law-and-order problems, has only received four FDI proposals worth Rs. 1.5 crore in six years.[24] Finally, the small northeastern states of Arunachal Pradesh, Meghalaya, Mizoram, and Nagaland complete the landscape of foreign investment laggards in India.

Similarly, there appears to be a high regional concentration of foreign investment in other sectors of the economy. One important sector of private investment in developing countries has been investment and remittances by expatriate communities. Since the enactment of economic liberalization measures, nonresident Indians (NRIs) have been a growing source of FDI inflows to India. From August 1991 to July 1996, the destination of nearly 50% of all investment by NRIs has gone to two states (Maharashtra and Gujarat).

Finally, another area of growing investment has been investment into export-oriented units (ESUs). ESUs serve as export promotion zones and leading states typically offer special tax incentives to foreign investors. From August 1991 to November 1996, four states (Andhra Pradesh, Orissa, Tamil Nadu, and Maharashtra) account for nearly 50% of the proposed investment into export oriented units (see Fig. 5).

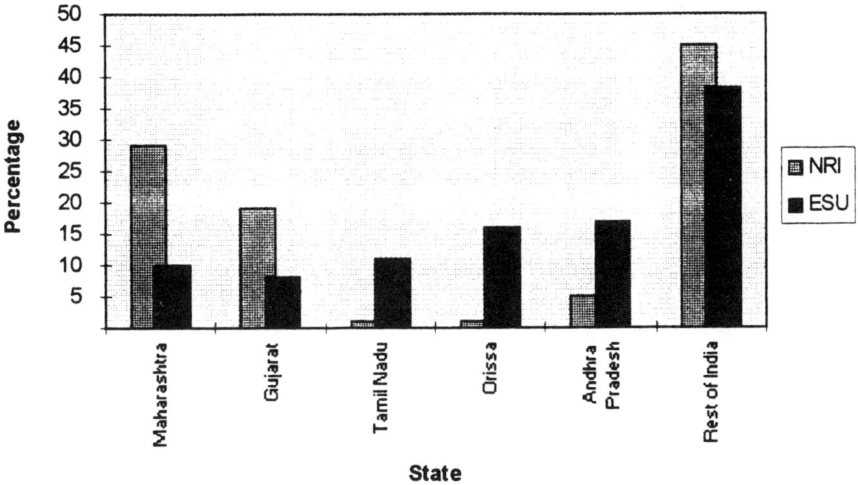

Figure 5 Percentage Comparison of Nonresident Indian (NRI) Investment Destination and Distribution of Investment into Export-Oriented State Units (ESU). (From *Indian Express* (August 14, 1996); *Times of India* (February 1, 1997), p. 15.)

Although NEP has not altered the magnitude of transfers to the states, some states have successfully supplemented their revenues elsewhere. The noteworthy concentration of FDI as well as NRI investment and investment into export-oriented state units is one of the most significant features of NEP.

A second, related feature of NEP is that political party realignment appears to have been a key factor in some states' ability to attract foreign investment. States that have developed a competitive two-party system (Andhra Pradesh, Delhi, Gujarat, Haryana, Kerala, Madhya Pradesh, Maharashtra, Orissa, and Rajasthan) have been more successful than states with unstable multiparty systems (Assam, Bihar, Punjab, and Uttar Pradesh). Thus, in addition to high income, there appears to be a correlation between political stability and ability to attract foreign investment.

IV. ECONOMIC LIBERALIZATION AND A TAXONOMY OF FEDERALISM

In light of the recent changes in India's political and economic regime types, the problems in attempting to define the application of the concept of cooperative federalism have become more perplexing. These changing circumstances force a reevaluation of federal relations in India. My analysis of the impact of economic liberalization policies on India's federal system begins with a schematic chart of federalism. This composite model combines differing approaches to the study of federalism.

In this paper federalism has been modeled along a basic distinction between the participating levels of government and the nature of their relationship.[25] Thus intergovernmental institutions (or institutions of vertical integration) represent the different tiers of government (central government and the constituent units). Interjurisdictional institutions (or institutions of horizontal integration) represent the similar tiers of government (constituent units) or governmental institutions among localities within a region.

The character and pattern of this relationship can be cooperative or competitive. Thus cooperative federalism has been defined by Jane Clark Perry, Morton Grodzins, and Daniel Elazar as the sharing of governmental functions and authority.[26] Competitive federalism has been defined by Albert Breton and John Kincaid as the rivalry and contention for resources or avoidance of a particular cost.[27] This schematic chart of federalism may be diagrammed as shown in Figure 6.

The model of federalism shown above is merely a heuristic device to - illustrate a broad transformation in the pattern of federal relations in India. The dual transformation (political party realignment and economic liberalization) has altered the traditional structure of federal relations in India. Although the diminished significance of the central government for a state's development of economic plans could encourage greater opportunities for grassroots local development and increased interjurisdictional cooperation, the impact of massive foreign investment inflows will instead push the debates about federalism in a different direction. This altered trajectory is from intergovernmental cooperation to interjurisdictional competition, which is the rivalrious and contentious relation-

		pattern of relationship	
		cooperative	competitive
participants in relationship	intergovernmental institutions	different tiers of government share functions	different tiers of governme contend for resources
	interjurisdictional institutions	similar tiers of government share functions	similar tiers of government contend for resources

Figure 6 Schematic Chart of Federalism.

ship for resources among similar tiers of government (constituent units) or among localities within a region.

V. IMPLICATIONS OF ECONOMIC LIBERALIZATION ON FEDERAL RELATIONS

Although economic liberalization has allowed some states to compete for alternative sources of revenues, the transformation of federal relations from intergovernmental cooperation toward interjurisdictional competition has several implications for federal relations in India. These implications may include social unrest, institutional design, and development.

A. Regional Inequality and Social Unrest

The concentration of foreign direct investment inflows into a few states has raised concerns about the aggravation of financial disparities among states. Some prominent critics of NEP, such as C.P. Bhambhri, have suggested that economic liberalization has ''aggravated regional imbalances and it has generated inter-state ruthless competition to attract foreign capital.''[28] In turn, some worry that these asymmetries could spark growing domestic conflict in low-income states and special-category territories that have not been destinations for foreign direct investment. Some critics of NEP, such as Amit Bhaduri and Deepak Nayyar, worry that the uneven development could result in the surfacing of religious, linguistic, and caste conflicts.[29] Similarly, Asghar Ali Engineer has also postulated that rapid economic development is often accompanied by communal violence in South Asia, largely because capitalist development ''either brings significant shifts in the socio-economic and political structure or completely transforms it.''[30]

Comparatively, magnets for foreign direct investment have higher average growths of rate in net state domestic product (NSDP) than those that have not been. For instance, Maharashtra had an average growth rate in NSDP of 11.8% for 1980–1985. Maharashtra's average NSDP growth rate has increased to 17.8% in 1990–1995. Gujarat has had an average growth rate of NSDP of 13.6% in 1980–1985 compared to 17.9% in 1990–1995. The growth rate of states that have not been magnets for foreign investment have declined in the 1990s. For instance, Bihar had an average NSDP growth rate of 11.8%. It had suffered a drop from 12.2% for the same period in 1980–1985. Assam's average NSDP growth rate has also declined from 17.8% in 1980–1985 to 11.2% in 1990–1995[31] (see Table 4).

The impact of economic liberalization on social dissent in the states needs to be evaluated in more detail. Nevertheless it is not entirely clear that economic liberalization has fostered socioeconomic dislocations in those areas that have

Table 4 Comparison of the Net State Domestic Product (NSDP) of Selected States (Rs. crore)

	Year			
State	1980–81	1985–86	1990–91	1994–95
Andhra Pradesh	7,324	13,412	31,165	50,679
Assam	2,298	5,175	9,498	14,538
Bihar	6,349	12,366	22,828	35,653
Gujarat	6,547	12,103	24,285	46,588
Himachal Pradesh	723	1,237	2,521	4,306
Jammu & Kashmir	1,050	129	2,763	3,471[a]
Karnataka	5,587	10,217	20,580	38,420
Maharashtra	15,163	26,467	57,577	111,028
Tamil Nadu	4,126	7,669	18,281	24,285[a]
Uttar Pradesh	14,012	24,669	49,496	79,024
West Bengal	9,594	17,415	31,753	49,780

[a] Latest available data for fiscal year 1993–1994.
Source: CMIE, *Profiles of States* (March 1997).

been magnets for foreign investment. Historically, Delhi and Bombay have had the largest incidence of crime compared to other metropolitan cities in India.[32] According to a study of white-collar crime patterns of India, the states of Gujarat, Rajasthan, and Karnataka accounted for 73.2% of the incidence in white collar crime for 1988 through 1992.[33]

On the other hand, there is no evidence that economic liberalization has directly served to increase crime incidence or aggravate communal conflict. The incidence of crime is not highly correlated to economic development in urban centers. The cities of Bangalore and Nagpur have the highest per capita incidence of crime. On the other hand, Hyderabad and Calcutta have the lowest per capita incidence of crime.[34] Communal conflict in India precedes the enactment of economic liberalization policies. Moreover, the occurrence of communal conflict has been dispersed and unpredictable. Communal rioting and caste-based unrest have often occurred in cities (notably Bombay) but they have also occurred in rural areas. For instance, medium-size rural cities such as Moradabad and Ayodhya have been the scene of communal riots.

B. Institutional Design

The second significant implication about this transformation will be the growing obsolescence of existing institutions of intergovernmental cooperation, such as the Planning Commission, the National Development Council, and the Zonal Councils. The Planning Commission is a national advisory body (composed of eight members appointed by the Prime Minister) which provides expertise in drawing up national development plans. The National Development Council is a body (composed of the Prime Minister, all Chief Ministers from all of the states, and members of the Planning Commission) which reviews and approves the development plans of the Planning Commission. The Zonal Councils are five regional advisory bodies which makes recommendations on an array of matters relating to its region's economic and social planning.

The Planning Commission and the National Development Council have at times assumed an important role in Nehruvian economic planning. Although extraconstitutional in nature, the bodies have not for that reason remained ineffective. They represent forms of "executive federalism" which have promoted regular and useful center-state consultation and coordination on sectoral issues. So long as the Congress Party dominated the central government and a substantial majority of the state legislatures, federal relations in India were essentially an intraparty affair. Thus, during the period of Congress Party dominance, development planning institutions, such as the National Development Council or the Planning Commission (and to a lesser extent the Zonal Councils), were tightly controlled by the Prime Minister and by influential Congress Party Chief Ministers.

In light of changes in the party system, the central government was forced to reevaluate these institutions of central planning. In 1988, an Indian government commission, the Sarkaria Commission, examined the state of federal relations in India and issued over 247 recommendations with respect to proposed changes in its administrative, legislative, and financial structure.[35] The Sarkaria Commission made modest recommendations regarding institutional design, namely the establishment of an Inter-State Council (ISC), the reconstitution of the National Development Council (NDC), and the revival of the regional Zonal Councils.

The demands from some state governments in the Sarkaria Commission represented what two theorists of comparative federalism, Amal Ray and John Kincaid, have called "second-generation strains" in India's federal system.[36] These strains originate from a redefinition of state demands on the center based on an attempt to bring about structural changes in India's federalism rather than on reinforcing constitutional restraints on the national government.

Unfortunately, with the transformation in federal relations from intergovernmental cooperation to interjurisdictional competition, changing the institutional design of intergovernmental institutions will not be able to mediate conflicts arising out of intergovernmental cooperation. Intergovernmental institutions may weaken state capability. These conflicts may represent what may be termed "third-generation strains" in India's federal system. Third-generation strains are neither an attempt to reinforce the constitutional restraints on the national government nor an attempt by state governments to bring about structural changes in India's federal system. Instead, third-generation strains on the federal system will be an attempt to define and mediate interjurisdictional competition through interjurisdictional institutions. However, at present there are no functioning interjurisdictional institutions other than ad hoc conferences of Chief Ministers and the Inter-State Water Commission. In light of the increasingly competitive patterns of federal relations in India, this absence creates a problem for horizontal integration.

In turn, this transformation explains why functional institutions of intergovernmental cooperation have not been effective. For instance, once established, in October 1990, the ISC has not lived up to its promise of serving as a significant intergovernmental forum.[37] One of the most prominent scholars of India, Francine Frankel, has suggested that the ISC is "virtually defunct."[38] Moreover, a report by the *Economic and Political Weekly* has even suggested that the meetings of the Inter-State Council were an "empty ritual."[39] Other formerly prominent governmental planning bodies such as the Planning Commission or the National Development Council have come under increasingly negative scrutiny. For instance, a report from *India Today* suggested that the Planning Commission was merely a gathering of "academic deadwood."[40] For this reason, the institutional reforms that the Sarkaria Commission proposed will be increasingly anachronistic because they will be unable to mitigate interjurisdictional competition.

C. Development

The third implication of the transformation of federal relations in India from cooperative federalism at the intergovernmental level is that the Indian state has been faced with new developmental challenges. The Sarkaria Commission surveyed a wide range of legislative, administrative, and financial views from state governments.[41] These issues have traditionally involved controversies about, among others, emergency powers, the role of the governors, and taxation authority. However, the Sarkaria Commission was not able to foresee the dramatic change brought about by NEP.

NEP has forced states to adopt major strategic and structural changes toward internal development. These developmental policy changes vary from state to state and have concentrated on foreign direct investment, investment by NRIs, and the state's industrial policy.[42] Not surprisingly, the states that have responded aggressively to implement the central government's economic reforms, particularly through the adoption of "single window clearance" to expedite clearances for industrial ventures, have been magnets for foreign investment. For instance, Andhra Pradesh and Karnataka have adopted industrial policies far more extensive than those pursued by the national government. They include special incentives for projects with investments exceeding Rs. 100 crore and sales tax deferment for new industrial units. Similarly, the state of Orissa took the initiative of privatizing its state electricity boards in 1996. Some states, like Maharashtra and West Bengal, have set up industrial promotion institutions to attract foreign investment.[43]

On the other hand, states that have adopted "green channel scheme" strategies for selected investments or states that have not responded positively to economic liberalization in the industrial sector have fared less favorably.[44] For instance, Assam has offered sales tax exemptions to small investment units and subsidizes feasibility studies. The state of Bihar offers special facilities for minority-owned (scheduled caste and scheduled tribes) enterprises.

The Indian central government continues to maintain a cooperative relationship with states on redistributive policies, notably in the field of education. States with higher FDI inflows continue to finance education with central government revenues. However, the influx of foreign direct investment has diminished some states' willingness to cooperate with the central government on developmental policies, notably in energy. High recipients of FDI are increasingly relying on extragovernmental sources of finance for developmental energy projects (see Fig. 7).

Figure 7 shows that economic liberalization has not significantly altered a state's budgetary expenditure on education. However, there is a notable reduction of budgetary expenditures on energy infrastructure by states that are high recipients of FDI. In this sense, state governments no longer cooperate with the central government but instead compete with other states for an increased share of FDI.

Similarly, India's ability to utilize revenues for development use are going

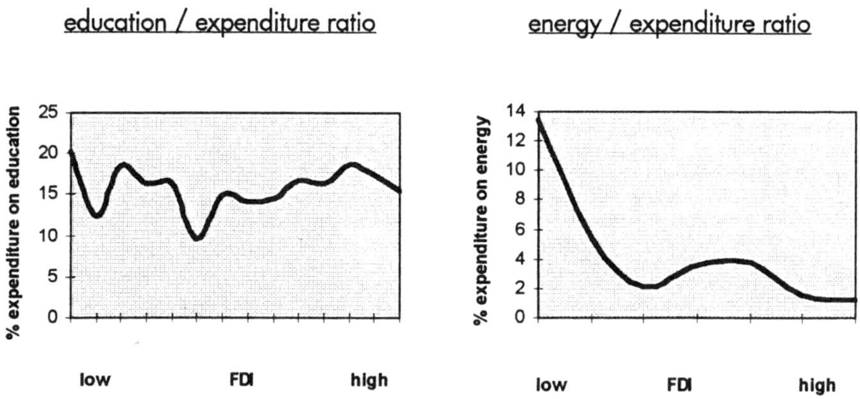

Figure 7 State's Budgetary Expenditure on Education and Energy as a Proportion of the state's Total Expenditure. (From CMIE, *Public Finance* (March 1997), p. 21.)

Table 5 Foreign Collaboration Approvals from August 1991 to December 1996 by Industry Sector

Industry	Amount (billion rupees)	Percentage of total FDI
Basic goods	312	32.70
Capital goods	93	9.79
Intermediate goods	19	2.01
Consumer nondurables	127	13.34
Consumer durables	27	2.86
Services	375	39.30
(telecommunications)	(255 billion)	(23.55)
Total FDI approvals	955	100%

Source: "Foreign Investment Approvals and Actuals," *Economic and Political Weekly*, 32:19 (May 10–16, 1997), p. 987.

to be challenging. Successive Indian governments have attempted to direct foreign direct investment toward physical infrastructure projects. Physical infrastructure projects include a wide spectrum of services such as transportation; energy generation, transmission, and distribution; and communications. Physical infrastructure is a precondition for economic growth in other sectors, principally industrial development. However, the sectoral pattern to foreign direct investment in India reveals a steady skew toward noninfrastructure areas, particularly in the consumer and service sectors. Foreign collaboration approvals have favored investment into telecommunications. This service sector accounts for nearly a quarter of total FDI approvals in India from August 1991 to December 1996 (see Table 5).

In an early analysis of the NEP and federalism, the renowned economist S. Guhan foresaw the pitfalls of unmediated competition. He expressed concern that "long-term structural adjustment will entail considerable concentration of policies and action at both levels."[45] He suggested the development of a "cooperative positive-sum approach" of policy implementation. However, owing to the ensuing transformation in federal relations, contemporary issues among state governments have remained unresolved. They include issues whose unexpected resolution is likely to benefit some states more than others. They include issues of intergovernmental cooperation regarding further foreign direct investment approvals, energy production, and the privatization of state-owned enterprises.

In practice, instead of the coordination of developmental policy through cooperative arrangements between the central government and the states, the implementation of developmental policy has served disjointed objectives. This piecemeal approach to developmental policy has failed to respond to two conflicting objectives: the capacity of the central government to meet its develop-

Table 6 Plant Load Factor of State Electricity Boards Thermal Plants in Selected States

State	1990–1991	1991–1992	1992–1993	1993–1994	1994–1995	1995–1996
Maharashtra	57.4	61.3	59.7	64.1	61.2	64.9
Gujarat	58.7	57	61.6	60.4	60.5	65.3
Tamil Nadu	63.8	55.4	65.2	69.1	68.4	76.1
Andhra Pradesh	58.3	62.1	65	68.7	70.2	77.4
Uttar Pradesh	58.3	44.4	50.5	50.1	43.9	47.3
Assam	27.7	24.7	24.3	19.9	26.7	28.6
Bihar	24	21.3	25.2	24.4	20	17.4

Source: CMIE, ''Profiles of States'' (March 1997). Data not available for Jammu and Kashmir.

mental goals, and the state government's ability to effectively implement its own industrial policy.

Finally, these dysfunctional objectives explain why the central government has not been able to coordinate its foreign investment strategy with the states. Instead, regional forces have been at the forefront of the promotion of foreign investment whereas others have not. For instance, investitures on energy as a proportion of the state's total expenditures have tended to decrease in magnets for foreign investment, whereas they have increased in laggards. However, the relative decline in public expenditures in energy production by FDI magnets has been offset by greater private sector participation in infrastructure development, particularly in energy projects. Still, state electricity boards continue to control as much as 60% of transmission and over 97% of the distribution of electricity.

Moreover, the utilization of energy has been more efficient in magnets for foreign investment. Since the enactment of economic liberalization policies, there is a growing regional divergence in plant load factor (PLF) of state electricity boards. PLF is an indicator of electrical generation efficiency (see Table 6).

Table 6 shows that high FDI states have had an increase in plant load factor (PLF) in state run electricity boards. In contrast, although laggard states in foreign investment have higher expenditures as a proportion of their state's total expenditures, they have utilized their resources less efficiently and with the greater losses in production.

VI. CONCLUSION

This paper has argued that the political party realignment in the mid-1980s combined with the impact of foreign investment inflows in the 1990s has shifted the debates about federalism from intergovernmental cooperation to interjurisdictional competition. This transformation has several implications for federal relations in India.

First, I have shown, though, that the influx of foreign direct investment has been concentrated into selected states. However, in this paper I have argued that the financial disparities between states (see Table 4) need not spark new forms of domestic unrest. Second, the attempt to alter the institutional design of intergovernmental institutions, such as those recommended by the Sarkaria Commission, will be largely outmoded. Finally, the transformation from intergovernmental cooperative federalism to interjurisdictional competitive federalism has not equipped India with the ability to properly face new developmental challenges.

Given the instability of various minority governing coalitions at the center, the continuation of India's gradual economic liberalization program is likely to remain undisturbed. However, the volatility of India's party system at the center may prevent it from addressing some of the unfavorable outcomes derived from unmediated interjurisdictional competition.

ENDNOTES

1. James Manor, ''Regional Parties in Federal Systems,'' in *Multiple Identities in a Single State*, eds. Balveer Arora and Douglas Verney (Delhi: Konark Publishers, 1995), 116–118. Out of these, only West Bengal, controlled by the Communist Party of India (Marxist), is characterized by Manor as a one-party-dominant system. The bulk of the states in India are now bipolar party systems or systems that oscillate between bipolar and three-party systems. Manor classifies Andhra Pradesh, Delhi, Gujarat, Haryana, Kerala, Madhya Pradesh, Maharashtra, Orissa, and Rajasthan as bipolar state level party systems. Manor cites the cases of Karnataka and Tamil Nadu as being examples of three-party states.
2. Christopher Candland, ''India's Economic Development: Mid-1970s to the Present,'' in *The India Handbook*, ed. Steven LaRue (Chicago: Fitzroy Dearborn Publishers, 1997), 21–23; Atul Kohli, *Democracy and Discontent*: *India's Growing Crisis of Governability* (Cambridge: Cambridge University Press, 1990), 305–338.
3. Government of India, *Report of the Committee on Trade Policies* (New Delhi: Ministry of Finance, 1985). Full text available in CMIE (September 1985).
4. M. Thiripalraju, K.G. Sahadevan, and T.P. Madhusoodanan, *Standard & Poor's Sovereign Credit Analysis*: *India* (New York: Standard & Poor, August 1996). Also see A.C. Minoche, ''The Structural Adjustment in Indian Economy: The IMF-WB Model of Growth,'' in *Structural Transformation of Indian Economy*, ed. S. Murty (Delhi: Atlantic Publishers, 1996), 29–35.
5. Lok Sabha Secretariat, *Lok Sabha Debates*, 10th Ser., vol. 5, no. 46 (New Delhi: Lok Sabha Secretariat, 1991), 51–70; *Lok Sabha Debates*, 10th Ser., vol. 7, no. 24 (New Delhi: Lok Sabha Secretariat, December 24, 1991), 271–330.

6. Thirripalraju, Sahadevan, Madhusoodanan, *Standard & Poor's Sovereign Credit Analysis: India, 76*; also see Jeffrey Orlando and Donald Gabbai, *Sovereign Risk Analysis: India* (New York: Brown Brothers Harriman and Company, 1996).
7. Asian Development Bank, *Asian Development Outlook, 1997–1998* (Hong Kong: Oxford University Press, 1997).
8. International Finance Corporation, *Emerging Stock Markets Factbook* (Washington: International Finance Corporation, 1998), 165.
9. Jagdish Bhagwati, *India in Transition: Freeing the Economy* (Delhi: Oxford University Press, 1994), 3; Kohli, *Democracy and Discontent*, 1990, 305–338.
10. N. Chandra Mohan, ''Reforms on Slow Track,'' *Business India 7* (December 1992): 50–51; Sunil Jain and Hardev Sanotra, ''Economic Reforms: Questioning the Pace,'' *India Today* 18 (November 1–15, 1993): 142–147; Rajiv Shirali, ''Will New Economic Policy Attract Foreign Investment.'' *Economic Times*, 9 August 1992, p. 5; R. Sasankan, ''Government Going Slow on Economic Reforms? *Indian Express*, 15 August, 1992, p. 1; Tapan Dasgupta, ''Dilemma Over Speed of Reforms,'' *Times of India*, 3 August, 1993, p. 11.
11. Sudeep Chakravarti and Sunil Jain, ''Reforms Will Take a Decade,'' *India Today* 18 (March 15–31, 1993): 104–105.
12. Sudeep Chakravarti, Zafar Agha, and Shahnaz Ankhesaria Aiyar, ''Bold Gamble,'' *India Today* 16 (July 16–31, 1991): 22–37; Girish Mathur, ''New Economic Policy and Need for Consensus,'' *Link* 33 (July 14, 1991): 9–11; Partha Ghosh, ''Political Aspects of Debate on Reforms,'' *Hindu* (Madras), 4 June 1992, p. 24.
13. Kohli, *Democracy and Discontent*, 306–307.
14. Prem Shankar Jha, ''Growing Consensus for Reform,'' *Hindu*, 2 September, 1992, p. 8. Also see Gautam Adhikari, ''Consensus Is the Key: Reforming India's Perestroika,'' *Times of India*, 16 July, 1991, p. 3; ''Economic Liberalisation: Toward Consensus,'' *India Today* 16 (June 15–30, 1991): 115–150.
15. Common Minimum Programme.'' ⟨http://www.allindia.com/economy/minprog.html⟩ (accessed June 1996); also see ''National Agenda for Governance.'' ⟨http://www.bjp.org/nagenta.html⟩.
16. Nilanjan Mukhopadhya and Rahul Sharma, ''I Am All for Liberalisation,'' *Economic Times* (10 August, 1993), p. 7.
17. ''Country Profile: India,'' *Emerging Markets Week* 4 (December 2, 1996): 9.
18. Jagdish Bhagwati, ''The End of Isolation,'' *Financial Times*, 24 June 1997, p. 3.
19. Granville Austin, *The Constitution: Cornerstone of a Nation* (Oxford: Clarendon Press, 1966), 187.
20. W.H. Morris-Jones, ''From Monopoly to Competition in India's Politics,'' *Asian Review* Vol. 1 (November 1967): 128.
21. W.H. Morris-Jones, *The Government and Politics in India* (London: The Eothen Press, 1964), 143. Also see Austin, *The Constitution*, 186–188.
22. Colin Bruce et al., *Economic Developments in India: Achievements and Challenges* (Washington: World Bank Publications, 1995).
23. Mahendra Ved, ''No Consensus Arrived at Yet on States' Share in Central Transfers,'' *Times of India*, 12 May 1997, p. 8.
24. ''Foreign Investment Approvals and Actuals: A Profile,'' *Economic and Political Weekly* 32 (May 10, 1997): 987.

25. This composite model of federalism draws on the work of John Kincaid, particularly in his article ''The Competitive Challenge to Cooperative Federalism'' in *Competition Among States and Local Governments*, eds. Daphne Kenyon and John Kincaid (Washington: Urban Institute Press, 1991).
26. See Jane Perry Clark, *The Rise of a New Federalism* (New York: Columbia University Press, 1938); Daniel Elazar, *The American Partnership: Intergovernmental Co-Operation in the Nineteenth-Century United States* (Chicago: University of Chicago Press, 1962); Morton Grodzins, *The American System: A New View of Government in the United States* (Chicago: Rand McNally & Company, 1966).
27. See Albert Breton, ''The Existence and Stability of Intergovernmental Cooperation,'' in Kenyon and Kincaid, *Competition Among States and Local Governments*; Breton, ''Towards a Theory of Competitive Federalism,'' *European Journal of Political Economy* Special Issue 3 (1987): 263–329; Breton, *Intergovernmental Tax and Policy Competition* (Washington: Advisory Commission on Intergovernmental Relations, 1991).
28. C.P. Bhambhri, *The Indian State: Fifty Years* (New Delhi: Shipra Publications, 1997), 221.
29. Amit Bhaduri and Deepak Nayyar, *The Intelligent Person's Guide to Liberalisation* (New Delhi: Penguin Books India Ltd., 1996), 120–122.
30. Asghar Ali Engineer, *Lifting the Veil: Communal Violence and Communal Harmony in Contemporary South Asia* (Hyderabad: Sangam Books, 1995), 17. Also see Asghar Ali Engineer, *Communalism and Communal Violence in India* (New Delhi: Ajanta Publications, 1989); S.S. Phulia, N.K. Chadha, and Surinder Nath, *Criminology* (Delhi: Friends Publication, 1992).
31. Centre for Monitoring of Indian Economy, *Profile of States* (Bombay: CMIE, March 1997): 72, 96, 120, 288.
32. Mary Tahir, *Crime in Delhi* (Delhi: National Book Organisation, 1996), 47.
33. Khrishna Mahan Mathu, *Crime, Human Rights and National Security* (Delhi: Gyan Publishing House, 1996). Also see Ashwini Sarin, ''Liberalisation Spawns White Collar Crime,'' *Indian Express*, 18 August 1995; Khrishna Andavolu, ''Alarm Bells Over Bank Frauds,'' *Times of India*, 14 March 1994; K. Madhavan, ''The White Collar Crime—The Most Devastating of Them All,'' *Frontline* (17–20 July 1993): 124–130.
34. Tahir, *Crime in Delhi*, 47.
35. Government of India, *Commission on Centre-State Relations* (Sarkaria Commission Report) (Delhi: Government of India Press, 1988).
36. Amal Ray and John Kincaid, ''Politics, Economic Development and Second Generation Strain in India's Federal System,'' *Publius* 18 (Spring 1988): 147–167.
37. Lawrence Sáez, ''Evaluating Intergovernmental Institutions: The Mixed Case of the Inter-State Council in India,'' *Administrative Change* 25, No. 1 (1997): 1–27.
38. Francine Frankel, ''Unity or Incoherence: The Problem,'' *Seminar* 459 (November 1997): 15.
39. ''Empty Ritual,'' *Economic and Political Weekly* 31 (November 9, 1996): 2960.
40. Sumit Mitra, ''Academic Deadwood,'' *India Today* (15 April 1997): 56–58.
41. Government of India, *Commission on Centre-State Relations*.

42. R. Venkatesan, *Problems in the Implementation of Economic Reforms at the State Level* (New Delhi: National Council of Applied Economic Research, 1994).
43. See Maharashtra Industrial Development Corporation, available at ⟨http://www.midcindia.com⟩ and West Bengal Industrial Development Corporation, available at ⟨http://www.wbidc.com/default.html⟩.
44. Venkatesan, *Problems in the Implementation of Economic Reforms at the State Level*, 82–93.
45. S. Guhan, ''Federalism and the New Political Economy in India,'' in *Multiple Identities in a Single State*, eds. Balveer Arora and Douglas Verney (New Delhi: Konark Publishers, 1995, p. 261).

11

Government-Business Relations and Southeast Asian Subregional Economic Growth Triangles

Gwynneth Singleton and Mark Turner
University of Canberra, Canberra, Australia

> On the one hand, politics largely determines the framework of economic activity and channels it in directions intended to serve the interests of dominant groups . . . on the other hand, the economic process itself tends to redistribute power and wealth: it transforms the power relationships among groups. This in turn leads to a transformation of the political system, thereby giving rise to a new structure of economic relationships.[1]

The rapidly growing economies of Southeast Asia of the 1990s gave predictive force to Gilpin's 1975 statement in that the economic process which drove that growth fostered two outcomes with the potential to transform the political system:

1. New institutional arrangements to facilitate regional trade in the form of subregional integrative economic zones popularly known as "economic growth triangles"
2. An expanding middle class

I. GROWTH TRIANGLES

Economic growth triangles are "transnational economic zones spread over well-defined geographically proximate areas covering three or more countries where differences in factor endowments are exploited to promote external trade and investment."[2] Also known as subregional economic zones and natural economic territories, they have proliferated in East and Southeast Asia. The original triangle involved Singapore, southern Johor in Malaysia, and Batam Island in Indonesia (SIJORI) but in 1996 the Indonesian province of West Sumatra and the Malaysian states of Negri Sembilan and Pahang were added. Other subregional economic zones have multiplied rapidly since SIJORI's establishment and now include the Southern China Growth Triangle (Taiwan, Hong Kong, Macau, and southern China); the Tumen River Area Development Program (parts of Jilin province in China, Siberia in Russia, and the Democratic People's Republic of Korea); the Northern ASEAN Growth Triangle (the northern states of Malaysia, northern Sumatra in Indonesia, and southern Thailand); and the East ASEAN Growth Triangle (Mindanao and Palawan in the Philippines, Brunei, the Malaysian territories of Sabah, Sarawak, and Labuan, and three provinces of eastern Indonesia).

Growth triangles emerged in response to pressures for regional economic cooperation and large flows of foreign investment. They are held to illustrate the increasing influence of market forces in organizing economic production according to comparative advantage.[3] They are, in short, one manifestation of the process of globalization. National borders are seen as inconvenient obstacles to the free movement of factors of production among adjacent territories in different countries. The growth triangle exploits economic complementarities in production and generates economies of scale. Government and multilateral agencies, especially the Asian Development Bank (ADB), encourage growth triangle formation, but the private sector is supposed to be the driving force, with businesses creating networks and forging relationships across national borders.

The mobility of factors of production, including capital and labor, and the liberalization of trading restrictions associated with economic growth triangles create the conditions for diminished political influence and control over business by the state.[4] However, this may be wishful thinking as growth triangles may merely represent a continuity with prevailing practice as a "statist form of regionalism in response to the challenges and opportunities of economic globalization."[5]

II. THE MIDDLE CLASS IN SOUTHEAST ASIA

Experience of the impact of economic growth on the dominant power elite can be found historically in Western Europe where economic expansion produced a business class that displaced the ruling aristocracies and transformed social and political systems.[6] A critical issue for Southeast Asian analysis is the role played by the middle class in such transformation, a topic which has absorbed social scientists throughout the developing world for many years.[7]

Most are agreed that a middle class or middle classes are increasingly evident in Southeast Asian countries, although there is a conceptual problem about who comprises the middle class.[8] Are entrepreneurs, private sector managers, airline pilots, teachers, and public servants of all grades all members? If we categorize by class position there is a major division between owners of capital and individuals who are appointed to managerial and professional positions. If classification is made by consumption patterns then the income differentials among many persons popularly identified as middle class can be considerable. Also, the different socioeconomic and cultural conditions encountered in the countries of the region mean that what constitutes a middle class in one place may not do so elsewhere. What is clear, however, is that in the Southeast Asian countries under study, economic growth has resulted in the spread of wealth to a group which has been categorized as the "middle class" even though it might more appropriately be termed the "new rich."[9]

The trade liberalization and business networking functions of growth triangles will further expand the opportunities for middle-class wealth creation. The question is whether this will translate into greater political empowerment and influence for the middle classes in terms of the Gilpin hypothesis.

This paper argues that this is unlikely to happen. The Gilpin hypothesis takes little account of the political imperatives of an incumbent governing elite determined to protect its power base. Almost four decades ago, Hoselitz[10] made the astute observation that

> It is undeniable that the dominant status group will attempt to prevent the development of a middle sector and will try to draw individuals in the emerging middle class under its influence. For an independent middle class, especially one with independent, self-determined economic sources of social strength, forms a danger to the leading political and status groups which have every interest to prevent or counteract this development.

If dominant elites or classes pursue economic growth even only for their own aggrandizement, it is inevitable that the middle class will grow. It is not inevitable, however, contrary to much Western democratic theory, that the emergent middle class will acquire the power to influence significant decisions made by the state. This study gives substantive force to the Hoselitz hypothesis by demonstrating that dominant elites in Southeast Asia strive to control the levers of power. While needing a middle class to run the growing and modernizing economy, the dominant elite formation will restrict access to the management of socioeconomic development so that they remain the principal beneficiaries and retain the power to determine significant decisions. The middle class is allowed only restricted access to such power. This pattern of domination has been achieved in the following ways:

1. Regularized and regulated corporatist cooption of business to the interests of the ruling elite, including those small and medium-size business organizations representative of the middle class.

2. Patrimonial and clientelistic relationships between the established dominant economic-political elite and business.

III. BUSINESS, GOVERNMENT, AND THE MIDDLE CLASS

A. Indonesia

Indonesia, anxious to stimulate economic development, particularly in Eastern Indonesia[11] and encouraged by the President's aspirations for the Asia Pacific Economic Council (APEC),[12] moved to deregulate and encourage private sector development.[13] President Suharto's 1990 Budget Speech stated that development of the eastern region was necessary to redress a regional imbalance in wealth due to low investment, poor infrastructure, and a lack of skilled labor.[14] Priority was assigned to Eastern Indonesia for regional funding,[15] and export-oriented policies were aimed at encouraging expansion within the region.[16]

Development policies for the region embodied an interest in decentralization to facilitate regional economic growth[17] including involvement in the emerging EAGA growth triangle. Participation in EAGA was encouraged by Indonesia's experience in the SIJORI growth triangle with Singapore and Johor in Malaysia. Following the establishment of EAGA, Eastern Indonesia experienced a higher rate of growth than Western Indonesia[18] although it is difficult to determine the contribution of EAGA-led activities to that growth. However, it has maintained the popularity of growth triangles for regional development in Indonesia and has provided additional impetus to the introduction of the growth triangle linking Sumatra in Indonesia with Malaysia and Thailand.

The emphasis on private enterprise as the engine for future growth resulted in some sections of the business community pursuing greater input into the policy process through membership of representative business associations.[19] Another effect of sustained economic growth has been the emergence of a substantial urban middle class.[20] One estimate of the Indonesian middle class for 1988 put it at 14 million persons, 8% of the population[21] while Vatikiosis[22] regards it as 10% of the population rising to as high as 15% in urban areas. However, the category is vaguely conceptualized, and the class itself appears to be fragmented. For example, Mahasin[23] identifies upper, middle, and lower fractions while Robison[24] observes several internal cleavages which affect the middle class. The most important of these distinctions are between public-sector and private-sector employees, Indonesian Indonesians and Chinese Indonesians, and Muslims and non-Muslims. The effect of such distinctions is to reduce the importance of class as a mode of group formation and basis for action.

Surveys of the middle class reveal a narrow social and political awareness and little interest in democracy despite many members of the class being exposed to Western democracies as students. Liberal reformist groups and organizations exist and draw their membership from the middle class, but in general the middle class is depoliticized. They support the regime because it has brought economic and social stability, jobs, and desirable patterns of consumption. They are therefore satisfied that it remains strong. By supporting the status quo the middle class is both defending its economic gains and distancing itself from dispossessed underclasses. Dick[25] maintains that this is manifest in "the mode of consumption" which distinguishes the middle class. Consumer items are privatized for consumption behind fences, window bars, and locked doors rather than being accessible to a wider group within the community.

By distancing itself from the lifestyle of the *kampung*, the middle class is orienting itself toward support of the state and offering no real challenge to the dominant political elite who have kept their hands firmly on the tiller—and on the till. It is a situation in which politically the middle classes have nowhere else to go as the dominant elite maintains tight control over state institutions, including the parliament, and business representation.[26] This does not, however, preclude the middle class or significant sections of it from raising questions about access to political power, but as Lev[27] observes, "The relative powerlessness of these groups by comparison with the state, seems to portend authoritarian regimes long into the future." Private wealth and independent market-oriented activity do not translate inevitably into political autonomy from the dominant elite.[28] Such views would not see growth triangles as vehicles for asserting middle class autonomy and claims for power sharing.

While big business has flourished under the New Order, it operates within an authoritarian framework of a "guided democracy" underpinned by the prescriptive tenets of the national doctrine of Pancasila, and the paternalistic reach of patronage surrounding the President and his family and their clientelistic connections.[29] Economic development at the national and local levels is guided by the overarching framework of the National Five-Year Development Plan instituted by presidential decree.[30] Business dealings are dominated by enterprises involving the presidential family, associates, and hangers-on, assisted through favorable licensing arrangements and monopolies.[31] Vertical and horizontal integration by large conglomerates owned by members of the presidential family means their tentacles extend throughout the business sector. It has been commented that "you cannot get involved in an important deal if you don't bring in at least one of the children."[32] This "surge of oligarchic corporatism"[33] given authority and legitimacy by the President reinforces patrimonial involvement as a critical factor of doing business.

Economic decentralization is unlikely to translate into substantive decentralization of political power because state regional and local administrators who operate as "state functionaries"[34] are usually retired military officers or bureaucrats with strong links to the dominant presidential and military elite.[35] These officials dominate and profit most from local business because of their inside knowledge and manipulation of government tendering and licensing opportunities.[36] This situation reinforces the lines of central authority and the system of patronage that is an intrinsic part of doing business in Indonesia, including siphoning off from government funding schemes for personal benefit.[37] That economic development of Eastern Indonesia was pursued to maintain national unity and ''extinguish the fires of separatism'' smoldering from economic inequality[38] indicates that trade liberalization to engineer economic growth has been used to shore up the power of the dominant elite. Because regional elites derive their economic well-being and political power from their association with the state, they are unlikely to pose any threat to existing institutional arrangements.

The benefits of economic liberalization which have flowed to Chinese conglomerates and other Chinese businesses have not translated into calls for greater political participation, despite their increased involvement with business associations, for several reasons. First, business representation has been neutralized politically by its cooption into corporatist structures, such as the Chamber of Commerce and Industry (Kadin).[39] Second, Chinese entrepreneurs who have benefited from trade liberalization choose to keep a low political profile for fear of refueling anti-Chinese sentiment[40] while those in provincial areas have been excluded from the political process.[41] Those who rely for their economic success on their close connections to the President and the military are unlikely to bite the hand that feeds them.[42]

Similarly, Suharto responded to discontent within the military elite by ''combining patrimonialistic inclusion with artful division,'' creating a situation where those benefiting from presidential patronage would be less willing to challenge the authority of his regime and weaken the opposing forces through his strategic use of the powers of appointment.[43]

Tanter and Young[44] have put forward the view that strains are likely to develop between the rural economic elite and independent landowners and small-business people increasingly exposed to international competition. Robison[45] also argues that this ''increasingly independent and internationalized middle class and business sector cannot forever be satisfied with careers and economic growth.'' Presumably this means they will be seeking a greater share of political power. Economic growth triangles, if they operate on free market lines as proposed, could contribute to such a trend but are not sufficient to drive it on their own. It is more probable that the retirement of President Suharto and a regime change will provide the catalyst for accelerated demands for political participation, but it may be difficult for the middle class to mobilize sufficiently or cohesively enough to break down the barriers of ''crony capitalism'' underpinned by the political power of the ruling elite.[46]

B. Singapore

Because of its limited territorial size, the central government is necessarily the facilitator and political actor in developing economic relations through subregional frameworks. The ruling power elite resides not within a presidential family, but within a political party, the Peoples Action Party (PAP), which in the 1980s shaped and managed political and state structures, spearheaded by state-owned enterprise, to induce rapid economic development.[47] The controlled utilization of foreign capital as the seedbed for economic growth marginalized local business from the political process.[48]

The spurs of trade liberalization and globalization and sluggish domestic economic growth caused in particular by the smallness of the Singapore market induced a more pragmatic and reactive approach to economic policy by the Singapore government, including loosening control on local capital[49] and encouragement of private-sector activity to maximize export and investment opportunities within the neighboring Southeast Asian region.

Singapore's involvement in economic growth triangles is symptomatic of these trends in expanding its overseas economic activities. Deputy Prime Minister Loong has stated that in the highly competitive global economic environment it makes sense for Singapore, Johor and the Riaus to pool their complementary strengths and compete against other regions for world markets.[50] For Singapore, the growth triangle facilitates the achievement of certain national objectives including restructuring the economy, becoming a high-value-added service economy and hub city, promoting the regionalization and internationalization of Singapore enterprises, providing leisure areas in close proximity to Singapore, achieving a secure water supply, and helping to promote the economic advancement of its neighbors and ASEAN out of self-interest.[51] Relative to this last point it has been suggested that the arrangements are less a triangle and more a set of bilateral agreements between Singapore as the growth pole and its two neighbors. In this interpretation the "growth triangle" is in fact a Singapore project with specific Singapore objectives.

While the growth triangle has been successful in securing private sector investment, the government continues to play a key role. Singapore's involvement in the Singapore-Johor-Riau Growth Triangle was negotiated by the Singapore government in 1989 following on a bilateral arrangement with the Johor state government and an agreement with Indonesia on liberalization of investment on Batam.[52] Private companies are encouraged to invest in the region with a range of incentives from the government's Economic Development Board, and Singaporean government-linked companies have been heavily involved in investment and joint ventures.[53] The government is directly involved in the capital and financial markets.[54]

Chalmers[55] argues that these initiatives to promote local business have resulted in the intrusion of domestic class forces into the policy-making process and less autonomy for the state. Economic development has seen the emergence of an affluent middle class[56] which has adopted a higher political profile seeking a gradual lessening of government controls.[57]

These changes have not been sufficient, however, to challenge the dominance of the PAP over the political system. The government has harnessed economic development and trade liberalization to the political purpose of retaining office,[58] assisted by effective one-party rule over a long period and the absence of a credible alternative ideology and political opposition.[59] The strong leverage of this ''controlled democracy''[60] provides a significant constraint on outside intrusion into the policy process and any challenge to the existing regime. This includes the strictures on freedom of political activism imposed by the imprisonment without trial provisions of the Internal Security Act, government censorship of the media, and, like Indonesia, the cooption of business associations seeking greater involvement in the decision-making processes into corporatist institutions.[61]

The apparent political acquiescence of Singapore's middle class might be construed as surprising, given that it is relatively the largest in Southeast Asia and therefore potentially an actor with political clout. One estimate[62] put 50% of the Singaporean population into the middle class, a result of high-sustained economic growth which has propelled Singapore's GNP per capita above countries such as Australia, Canada, and the Netherlands.[63] But it has been argued that the middle class has not called for a transformation of political life in Singapore because of the state's success in satisfying their material needs.[64] While PAP hegemony may well be regarded by many in the middle class as a suboptimal arrangement it is accepted in exchange for such benefits as material wellbeing, security, and minimal corruption.[65] The ''opportunity costs'' for replacing PAP rule would be high.

Middle-class compliance is secured less by coercion than by masterful manipulation of economic and social incentives and disincentives.[66] Also, the PAP is strategically aware and as such has demonstrated a capacity to reform political structures to maintain dominance in response to perceived societal pressures. It has accommodated the consumer aspirations of the middle class by mild liberalization. This regulatory relaxation giving greater consumer choice has also affected public housing and public health services. In this climate certain interest groups are also permitted to operate so long as they are nonthreatening to the PAP.

This combination of satisfying consumer needs, welfare security, tight regulation, and a strategic orientation to maintaining political hegemony while allowing some increased personal autonomy should keep the middle class from becoming the supporter of a democratic movement. They have benefited from the imposed meritocratic order and liberalization of the economy has produced no accompanying demand for liberalization of the political system. The establishment of the SIJORI growth triangle in 1989 has had no political effect on the middle class. Singapore already had the most liberal trade policies in Southeast Asia and an outward-looking development policy when the growth triangle was created.[67] Political problems could arise less from class forces than from perceived inequities in the distribution of growth among the triangle partners, questions of equity in investment, sensitivities over national sovereignty, and social problems resulting from rapid economic growth. The business elite in Singapore has been the big winners.

C. Malaysia

Malaysia, like its neighbors, has responded to the pressures for economic growth with trade liberalization and expansion of trading relationships, including its involvement in emerging economic growth triangles. Likewise, the potential impact of this private-sector economic growth is the development of private business interests distinct from those of the state, and changes in class structures.[68] This trend may be enhanced by linkages between Malaysian companies and business groups within the economic growth triangle sector such as Kemayan Corporation, a Malaysian company dominated by three Singaporean businessmen, undertaking several large projects in Johor, the Malaysian state closest to Singapore, and developing air links to Thailand and Singapore through its subsidiary Air Mandalay. Successful business in cases such as this depends less on the regulatory and economic policy framework developed by the government within Malaysia, and more on taking advantage of market-driven opportunities within the region.

As a result of sustained economic growth there has been a corresponding increase in the size of the Malaysian middle class. But this has not resulted in any fundamental change to the political system for several reasons: (1) the inclusion of middle class representation within the ruling coalition; (2) ethnic divisions which have prevented the development of a united and cohesive middle class; and (3) dependency on the existing political order for economic benefit because of preferential policies and patronage.[69]

While rapid economic growth has benefited Malaysian business, there has been little consequent change to the political system.[70] The reasons are very similar to those existing in Singapore—control of the institutions of government, including the bureaucracy, the armed forces, and the judiciary; and control of the business environment by UMNO, the governing party. The government's control of economic policy inexorably draws business into a close relationship with the ruling party.[71] Another significant factor has been the inclusion by UMNO of Chinese parties within its Barisan Nasional coalition government to help defuse potential points of conflict within a system that has been described as "hegemonic with accommodationist elements."[72]

The state and key business groups are interlinked because of the dependence of business on the patronage of the ruling party for access to "state-created rents."[73] The result is that "virtually all the big Malay tycoons" depend on their connections with UMNO, while the largest corporations are owned by the party.[74] For example, not only is the banking system regulated by the central bank, Bank Negara, but it also follows highly interventionist policy directives determined by it. Although some aspects of company financial operations have been liberalized, the bank can rein in those privileges if that is considered warranted for national economic policy purposes, such as limitations on loans for property development if the market for such activity should decrease. The resulting concentration of ownership within ''political oligopolies''[75] has produced a convergence of interests between business and the state which makes it difficult for business to challenge the ruling elite.[76]

This system of patronage, where the ruling party rewards its supporters with economic benefits and punishes its opponents by denying that access,[77] is a significant reason why there has been no substantive challenge to the ruling elite from the expanding middle class. Many Malay and Chinese businesspeople are dependent upon the patronage of UMNO, in the form of licences, permits, and other approvals, for their continued operation in the market.[78]

Chinese businesspeople have been forced to seek Malay partners with links to the political establishment. For example, Kamayan Corporation is controlled by Singapore-Chinese businessmen, but includes on the board a Malay with links to the banking establishment. A ''strong rapport with the state government'' makes it easy for them to do business in Johor.[79] Another major Malaysian company, Daibochi, is in a similar position, with five Chinese businessmen as major shareholders and, among its directors, Malays with links to the UMNO establishment.

The same situation occurs at the regional level where UMNO in the 1995 elections retained control of all the state assemblies, with the exception of Kelantan.[80] For example, the success of a construction company in Sabah has been attributed to the Malay owner's political links in Sabah.[81]

This dominance of UMNO at the state and national levels tends to enhance the centralization of power and political patronage within the political system. For example, in 1988, 10 of the 13 states were under UMNO Chief Ministers directly appointed by the Prime Minister.[82] It has also, as Bowie[83] explains, created ''a large and influential group of domestic bumiputra companies that are in fact the vehicles for ensuring continued UMNO political dominance.''

The risk of challenge is minimized also by what Case has called Malaysia's system of ''semi-democracy'' where the government has limited participation by opposition parties, professional associations, trade unions, and other groups, through the Societies Act. Its monopoly of media ownership, and the use of security measures also silences public criticism.[84]

The combination of government party control, patronage, and clientelistic relationships, assisted by the cooption of business in general through corporatist institutions, will ensure that participation in economic growth triangles will maintain the economic and political interests of the ruling elite.

D. Philippines

Until recently, the Philippines was ASEAN's poor performer in the race for economic growth and development. It then followed the example of its ASEAN neighbors by recording GNP per capita growth rates in excess of 5% after 1994. Elected to a six-year term in 1992, President Fidel Ramos elevated economic policy to the forefront of his agenda and embarked on an ambitious program of development guided by the vision of "Philippines 2000" which entails putting the country on a rapid track to NIC status. Liberalization of the economy has been the major policy thrust. One of the many ways in which this has been manifest has been the establishment of EAGA. This growth triangle incorporates the Philippine islands of Mindanao and Palawan in a subregional economic zone with Brunei and adjacent parts of Malaysia and Indonesia, and has been enthusiastically promoted and supported by President Ramos.[85] In this sense the Philippine experience replicates those of its neighboring growth triangle partners.

The Philippines, however, is markedly different from the other countries in this survey in its government-business relations and in the political orientation of the middle class. It has been categorized as a weak state in which the government has not gained effective control of the society. Even under the authoritarian presidency of Ferdinand Marcos there was central accommodation of provincial strongmen while a Communist insurgency grew with each succeeding year to become a significant force in almost every part of the nation. An armed Muslim secessionist movement in Mindanao further challenged the state's control of its subjects and territory.

In its postindependence history the Philippine state has rarely developed an economic vision and coherent strategy to pursue it. It has, however, through its financial institutions and policy processes, played a major role in determining financial and commercial regulations, and in so doing determined who would be successful in business. In the postindependence years the state extended its "nominal influence" into almost every sector of the economy. Paradoxically, the weakness of the state allowed and encouraged the penetration and manipulation of the state for personal gain by members of the economic elite.

McCoy[86] cites the observation of an American financial consultant in the 1950s that "business is born and flourishes in or fails not so much in the marketplace as in the halls of the legislature." The state became "swamped by the particularistic demands of powerful oligarchic forces."[87] Members of the business elite would influence legislation for the benefit of their own family operations, sometimes individually, often in blocs. Elite business families would ensure the election of one of their number to the Congress thus creating a "fused elite" where political office and substantial wealth were evident in the family.[88] If no family member held political office, then elite families would sponsor talented representatives from the middle class to look after their interests. As Simbulan[89] observed in the 1960s, no national legislator relied on official income alone. All had multiple occupations and sources of income. The state became the focus of "booty capitalism"[90] in which elites strove to secure the large material returns available from rent-seeking opportunities.

The trend toward centralization of the state under Marcos merely gave greater emphasis to the role of rents within the economy. That is, the government intervened even more in the economy to provide lucrative opportunities to selected members of the bourgeoisie.[91]

The overthrow of Marcos in a celebration of "people power" did not lead to drastic alterations in this pattern of government-business relations. Despite strong constitutional provisions outlawing the reestablishment of family dynasties in political office, the names of the new legislators often have a familiar ring. Of the 199 members of Congress elected in 1992, 164 have been identified as members of "political clans" while the most prominent legislators were classified as "business tycoons and industry leaders."[92] The percentage of entrepreneurs elected had increased from 10% in 1940 to 36% in 1992.

The middle class has played a significant role in recent political events. The people-power phenomenon in Manila which led to the overthrow of President Marcos was widely interpreted as an event dominated by the middle class. Such a predilection to middle class mobilization was not always so. When Marcos declared martial law in 1972, the middle class was largely acquiescent, even supportive, as the action seemed to offer stability in an environment of deepening crisis. Some authors have attributed this crisis in part to middle-class challenges to traditional leadership. The important lesson from these examples is that the middle class can exercise considerable influence on the political process in the Philippines by both action and inaction. Matters relating to the defense of democracy and economic crisis did lead to class action which played a part in determining the outcome of political processes.

But complicating matters are issues of class boundaries and possibilities of overdetermination in identifying particular actions as "class actions."[93] Some writers fail to delineate who or what is meant by the term middle class. Some reject the concept altogether,[94] preferring to characterize the Philippines as a two-class society. Such sentiment was registered in a recent survey where 21% of respondents in a stratified sample identified only two classes in Philippine society.[95] Hughes and Woldekidan[96] put 7% of the population in the middle class, the same figure used by Philippine market researchers,[97] although estimates of up to 30% can be found.[98] If the middle class is a political actor of increasing importance, then the population and analysts are not clear about what it is they are referring to. It does, however, appear to be "becoming increasingly a central arena of political discourse and contention."[99] It is a variegated presence with several strands of middle-class consciousness operating at any one time and, indeed, changing in content, intensity, and importance over time.[100]

There are problems, also, with attributing too much influence and power to the middle class. As has been shown above, "political clans" still crowd the national legislatures and occupy key positions in cities and provinces. Alternative avenues of political influence and action have been explored, especially in the numerous developmental and advocacy NGOs which are "primarily staffed by, managed, directed and greatly influenced by a fraction of the urban, educated middle class,"[101] yet government processes remain widely dictated by patronage.[102]

Also, there has been little democratization of wealth. The Philippines has a more unequal distribution of wealth than its ASEAN neighbors with a few hundred families dominating its economy. One of President Ramos's chief advisers described the Philippine economic system as "more Latin American than East Asian in the way it has concentrated power in a few families."[103] In such situations the elite has little incentive to change the existing political relationships among legislatures, bureaucracies, and business.

The continued development of the EAGA growth triangle may well benefit existing business elites and their multinational partners. It will not have a direct effect on the middle class as a political force, although if the triangle is successful, the class will increase its membership and relative size in Mindanao. Its power could also be boosted less by economic liberalization than by the decentralization program introduced under the Local Government Code of 1991.

This legislation represents the most radical devolution of responsibilities to subnational governments in Southeast Asia. Functions such as health, agriculture, and the environment have been devolved to local governments while there is statutory involvement of NGOs in potentially important economic planning bodies. An autonomous region in Mindanao and a new Special Zone of Peace and Development (ZOPAD), both headed by former insurgent chief Nur Misuari, complement the other decentralization measures and seem to offer opportunities for much greater local determination of affairs. However, the continued volatility of this region could still threaten economic development and lead to hasty withdrawals of foreign capital and cautious dealings by triangle partners.[104]

Despite these decentralization initiatives, the prospects for EAGA creating the conditions for a change in the relationship between state and capital in favor of the middle class remain problematic. The constraint will be the continuation, despite a greater diversity within the business community and an expanding middle class, of the incumbent clientelistic system of crony capitalism so long as business operations can only be developed or expanded by means of "privileged access to state-controlled licences, monopolies and loans."[105] What we see is the perpetuation of familiar patterns of government-business relations whereby "access to the state apparatus remains the major avenue to private accumulation and the quest for rent-seeking opportunities continues to bring a stampede of favored elites and would-be favored elites to the gates of the presidential palace."[106]

IV. CONCLUSION

The Gilpin hypothesis is correct inasmuch as political forces have determined the formation of innovative subregional economic arrangements in Southeast Asia that have contributed to the creation of wealth and its wider distribution in society. In the process, the growth of the middle class has been given a boost although the growth has been differentially experienced among participating countries and regions.

Gilpin has not been proved correct, however, in his prognosis that this will lead inevitably to a redistribution of political power among groups. Transformation of power has not occurred. There has been no erosion of the authority of established regimes. Trade liberalization has been managed by the governing elites to sustain and maintain their control of political power. Economic growth triangles as economic institutions have been the progenitors of managed "strategic trade policy"[107] rather than vehicles for radical political change.

The weakness of the Gilpin hypothesis in failing to predict these outcomes lies with an underlying precept that there is a separation of government from business and no recognition of the capacity of existing institutional actors to manage external pressures on economic development. His argument is founded on the assumption that the state withdraws as the market intrudes, yet the evidence presented in this paper indicates otherwise. In Southeast Asia the term "market" is "a nominal one because governments often intervene to shape comparative, and competitive, advantage and market forces."[108]

Southeast Asian economic growth triangles are a functional institutional response by governments and their associated business elites to manipulate and take advantage of trade liberalization and complementarities in factors of production, rather than engender a dysfunctional attack on state power by market forces. A former President of the Philippines has said that "the growth triangle concept has taken hold because it is a controlled experiment in regional cooperation . . . it offers the benefits of regional integration without great loss of economic sovereignty." Growth triangles, he states, "require no changes in national concepts of sovereignty, administration or national preferences" and, therefore, "governments can enter into them with minimum political risk."[109]

It is a natural response by the dominant economic-political group to exercise its power to forestall any challenge to its political dominance.[110] The symbiotic relationships between government and business evident in the corporatist and clientelistic arrangements of crony capitalism[111] outlined in this paper have been used as the gatekeepers against pressures for any substantive transfer of political power deriving from changes to the economic process. Economic gains from growth triangles have enhanced this resistance to political pressure by allowing the established economic-political elite to satisfy the economic needs of the middle class while at the same time maintaining and increasing its own share of the pie. The middle class is less likely to challenge the power elite so long as it is dependent on this largesse for its ''share of the spoils'' and its consumption and welfare demands are being met.

It is, in fact, a questionable assumption of modernization theory that a growing middle class is a major force in replicating Western liberal democracy in non-Western states. It has been demonstrated in Latin American development that middle classes do not have a standard universal political role.[112] They forge alliances with different classes according to their perceived interests and opportunities. Thus, they will support authoritarian rule in some circumstances, be satisfied with limited and controlled access to government through corporatist arrangements, or acquiesce when ''people-power'' revolts fail to deliver an entree into the closed shop of crony capitalism as our case studies indicate.

Economic growth triangles have not upset the existing political order. They have provided the means whereby the established economic-political elite has managed the external pressures for trade liberalization to their own advantage by doing business in the usual manner. Rather than economic growth triangles and simple middle-class expansion generating political change, it may be that the current economic crisis in Southeast Asia will be a more potent force in challenging ''the lack of accountability, generally stemming from the too-cosy relationship between government and business.''[113]

NOTE ADDED IN PROOFS

It is now two years since we first wrote this chapter and the Southeast Asian region is now emerging from the economic crisis. With the exception of Indonesia, the political order of elite domination has not been seriously challenged. The middle classes have not transformed into potent political forces agitating for change, while growth triangles can be clearly seen as epiphenomena. Thus, our central theses remain intact. Even in Indonesia where authoritarianism has been overthrown, multi-party democracy introduced, and decentralization legislation passed, crony capitalism is still evident, as is the power of the military and bureaucratic elites. Efforts to introduce greater accountability have encountered stiff elite resistance.

ENDNOTES

1. Gilpin, R. *US Power and the Multinational Corporation*. New York: Basic Books, 1975, pp 21–22.
2. Tang, M. and Thant, M. Growth triangles: conceptual and operational considerations. In M. Thant, M. Tang, and H. Kakazu (eds.), *Growth Triangles in Asia: A New Approach to Regional Economic Cooperation*. Oxford: Oxford University Press, 1994, p 2.
3. Parsonage J. Trans-state developments in South-east Asia: subregional growth zones. In G. Rodan, K. Hewison, and R. Robison (eds.), *The Political Economy of South-East Asia*. Melbourne: Oxford University Press, 1997, p 249.
4. Kumar S., and Siddique, S. *Beyond Economic Reality: New Thoughts on the Growth Triangle*. Singapore: Institute of Southeast Asian Affairs, 1994, p 48.
5. Parsonage, J. Trans-state developments in South-east Asia: subregional growth zones. In G. Rodan, K. Hewison, and R. Robinson (eds.), *The Political Economy of South-East Asia*. Melbourne: Oxford University Press, 1997, p 274.
6. Moore W. *Social Change* Englewood Cliffs: Prentice Hall, 1963. Crouch, H. *Government and Society in Malaysia*. Sydney: Allen and Unwin, 1996, p 96.
7. For example, see Johnson, J.J. *Political Change in Latin America: The Emergence of the Middle Sectors*. Stanford: Stanford University Press, 1958. Roxborough, I. *Theories of Underdevelopment*. Atlantic Highlands, NJ: Humanities Press, 1979. Johnson, D. *Middle Classes in Dependent Countries*. Beverley Hills: Sage, 1985.
8. For example, see Asian Development Bank (ADB). *Asian Development Outlook*. Manila: Asian Development Bank, 1994. Turner, M. Imagining the Middle Class in the Philippines. *Pilipinas 25*, 87–101, 1995. Cheng, T. Is the dog barking? The middle class and democratic movements in the East Asian NICs. *International Study Notes 15*(1), 1990, pp 10–17.
9. Robison, R. Indonesia: an autonomous domain of social power. *Pacific Review 5*(4), 338–349, 1992.
10. Hoselitz, B. *Sociological Aspects of Economic Growth*. Glencoe, IL: Free Press, 1960.
11. Soesastro, H. The economy: a general review. In C. Barlow and J. Hardjono (eds.), *Indonesia Assessment 1995: Development in Eastern Indonesia*. Canberra: Research School of Pacific and Asian Studies, Australian National University, and Singapore: Institute of Southeast Asian Studies, 1996, p 24.
12. Grant, B. *Indonesia*. 3rd ed. Melbourne: Melbourne University Press, 1996, p 123.
13. MacIntyre, A. Power, prosperity and patrimonialism: business and government in Indonesia. In A. MacIntyre (ed.), *Business and Government in Industrialising Asia*. Sydney: Allen and Unwin, 1994, p 244.
14. Cited in Chauvel, R. Beyond the Wallace line. In C. Barlow and J. Hardjono (eds.), *Indonesia Assessment 1995: Development in Eastern Indonesia*. Canberra: Research School of Pacific and Asian Studies, Australian National University, and Singapore: Institute of Southeast Asian Studies, 1996, pp 61–62.
15. Azis, I.J. Eastern Indonesia in the current policy environment. In C. Barlow and J. Hardjono (eds.), *Indonesia Assessment 1995: Developments in Eastern Indonesia*. Canberra: Research School of Pacific and Asian Studies, Australian National University, and Singapore: Institute of Southeast Asian Studies, 1996, p 84.

16. Azis, I.J. Eastern Indonesia in the current environment. In C. Barlow and J. Hardjono (eds.), *Indonesia Assessment 1995: Developments in Eastern Indonesia*. Canberra: Research School of Pacific and Asian Studies, Australian National University, and Singapore: Institute of Southeast Asian Studies, 1996, p 112.
17. Mboi, B. The socio-economic development of Eastern Indonesia: the role of government. In: C. Barlow, J. Hardjono (eds.), *Indonesia Assessment 1995: Developments in Eastern Indonesia*. Canberra: Research School of Pacific and Asian Studies, Australian National University, and Singapore: Institute of Southeast Asian Studies, 1996, p 125.
18. Azis, I.J. Eastern Indonesia in the current policy environment. In: C. Barlow, J. Hardjono (eds.), *Indonesia Assessment 1995: Developments in Eastern Indonesia*. Canberra: Research School of Pacific and Asian Studies, Australian National University, and Singapore: Institute of Southeast Asian Studies, 1996, p 112.
19. MacIntyre, A. Power, prosperity and patrimonialism: business and government in Indonesia. In A. MacIntyre (ed.), *Business and Government in Industrialising Asia*. Sydney: Allen and Unwin, 1994, p 255.
20. Mackie, J. and MacIntyre, A. Politics. In H. Hill (ed.), *Indonesia's New Order*. Sydney: Allen and Unwin, 1994, p 3.
21. Hughes, H. and Woldekidan, B. The emergence of the middle class in the DMCs. Paper presented for the Asian Development Bank's Sixth Workshop on the Asian Economic Outlook, Manila, 22–22 October 1993.
22. Vatikiotis, M. *Political Change in Southeast Asia: Trimming the Banyan Tree*. London: Routledge, 1996.
23. Mahasin, A. The Santri middle class: an insider's view. In R. Tanter and K. Young (eds.), *The Politics of Middle Class Indonesia*. Monash Papers on Southeast Asia, No. 19. Clayton, Australia: Centre of Southeast Asian Studies, Monash University, 1990.
24. Robison, R. Indonesia: an autonomous domain of social power. *Pacific Review* 5(4), 1992, pp 338–349.
25. Dick, H.W. Further reflections on the middle class. In R. Tanter and K. Young (eds.), *The Politics of Middle Class Indonesia*. Monash Papers on Southeast Asia No. 19. Clayton, Australia: Centre of Southeast Asian Studies, Monash University, 1990.
26. Robison, R. Transition to entrench new order oligarchies. *The Australian*, 15 July 1994, p 13.
27. Lev, D.S. Notes on the middle class and change in Indonesia. In R. Tanter and K. Young (eds.), *The Politics of Middle Class Indonesia*. Monash Papers on Southeast Asia No. 19. Clayton, Australia: Centre of Southeast Asian Studies, Monash University, 1990, pp 44–48.
28. Young, K. Middle bureaucrats, middle peasants, middle class: the extra-urban dimension. In R. Tanter and K. Young (eds.), *The Politics of Middle Class Indonesia*. Monash Papers on Southeast Asia, No. 19. Clayton, Australia: Centre of Southeast Asian Studies, Monash University, 1990, p 159.
29. MacIntyre, A. Power, prosperity and patrimonialism: business and government in Indonesia. In A. MacIntyre (ed.), *Business and Government in Industrialising Asia*. Sydney: Allen and Unwin, 1994, p 244.

30. Mboi, B. The socio-economic development of Eastern Indonesia: the role of government. In C. Barlow and J. Hardjono (eds.), *Indonesia Assessment 1995: Developments in Eastern Indonesia*. Canberra: Research School of Pacific and Asian Studies, Australian National University, and Singapore: Institute of Southeast Asian Studies, 1996, p 133.
31. Grant, B. *Indonesia*. 3rd ed. Melbourne: Melbourne University Press, 1996, p 113. Mackie, J. Property and power in Indonesia. In R. Tanter and K. Young (eds.), *The Politics of Middle Class Indonesia*. Monash Papers on Southeast Asia No. 19. Clayton, Australia: Centre of Southeast Asian Studies, Monash University, 1990, p 112.
32. Schwarz, A. All is relative. *Far Eastern Economic Review 30*, April 1992, p 54.
33. Robison, R. Transition to entrench new order oligarchies. *The Australian*, 15 July 1994, p 13.
34. Young, K. Middle bureaucrats, middle peasants, middle class: the extra-urban dimension. In R. Tanter and K. Young (eds.), *The Politics of Middle Class Indonesia*. Monash Papers on Southeast Asia No. 19. Clayton, Australia: Centre of Southeast Asian Studies, Monash University, 1990, p 150.
35. Guiness, P. Local society and culture. In H. Hill (ed.), *Indonesia's New Order*. Sydney: Allen and Unwin, 1994, pp 273–274.
36. Young, K. Middle bureaucrats, middle peasants, middle class: the extra-urban dimension. In R. Tanter and K. Young (eds.), *The Politics of Middle Class Indonesia*. Monash Papers on Southeast Asia No. 19. Clayton, Australia: Centre of Southeast Asian Studies, Monash University, 1990, p 153.
37. Tanter, R. and Young, K. Introduction. In R. Tanter and K. Young (eds.), *The Politics of Middle Class Indonesia*. Monash Papers on Southeast Asia No 19. Clayton, Australia: Centre of Southeast Asian Studies, Monash University, 1990, p 11.
38. Chauvel, R. Beyond the Wallace line. In C. Barlow and J. Hardjono (eds.), *Indonesia Assessment 1995: Development in Eastern Indonesia*. Canberra: Research School of Pacific and Asian Studies, Australian National University, and Singapore: Institute of Southeast Asian Studies, 1996, p 63.
39. MacIntyre, A. Power, prosperity and patrimonialism: business and government in Indonesia. In A. MacIntyre (ed.), *Business and Government in Industrialising Asia*. Sydney: Allen and Unwin, 1994, p 252.
40. MacIntyre, A. Power, prosperity and patrimonialism: business and government in Indonesia. In A. MacIntyre (ed.), *Business and Government in Industrialising Asia*. Sydney: Allen and Unwin, 1994, p 252.
41. Mackie, J. Property and power in Indonesia. In R. Tanter and K. Young (eds.), *The Politics of Middle Class Indonesia*. Monash Papers on Southeast Asia No. 19. Clayton, Australia: Centre of Southeast Asian Studies, Monash University, 1990, p 74.
42. Grant, B. *Indonesia*. 3rd ed. Melbourne: Melbourne University Press, 1996, p 113.
43. Case, W. Comparing regime continuity and Change: Indonesia, Thailand and Malaysia. Discussion paper No. 15, *Regime Change and Regime Maintenance in Asia and the Pacific*. Canberra: Department of Political and Social Change, Research School of Pacific and Asian Studies, Australian National University, 1995, p 12.
44. Tanter, R. and Young, K. Introduction. In R. Tanter and K. Young (eds.), *The*

Politics of Middle Class Indonesia. Monash Papers on Southeast Asia No. 19. Clayton, Australia: Centre of Southeast Asian Studies, Monash University, 1990, p 11.
45. Robison, R. Transition to entrench new order oligarchies. *The Australian*, 15 July 1994, p 13.
46. Grant, B. *Indonesia*. 3rd ed. Melbourne: Melbourne University Press, 1996, p 113.
47. Chee, C.H. The PAP and the structuring of the political system. In K.S. Sandhu and P. Wheatley (eds.), *Management of Success: the Moulding of Modern Singapore*. Singapore: Institute of Southeast Asian Studies, 1989, p 71.
48. Tremewan, C. *The Political Economy of Social Control in Singapore*. Singapore: St. Martin's Press, 1994, p 178.
49. Chalmers, I. Weakening state controls and ideological change in Singapore: the emergence of local capital as a political force. Working Paper No. 13. Perth: Asia Research Centre, Murdoch University, 1992, pp 14–15.
50. Loong, L.H. Economic co-operation through growth triangles. Press statement, 17 December 1994, p 1.
51. Smith, S.L.D. The Indonesia-Malaysia-Singapore growth triangle: a political and economic equation. *Australian Journal of International Affairs 51*(3), 373.
52. Arndt, H. Anatomy of regionalism. In R. Garnaut and P. Drysdale (eds.), *Asia Pacific Regionalism*. Sydney: Harper Educational, and Canberra: Australia-Japan Research Centre, Australian National University, 1994, p 96.
53. Parsonage, J. Trans-state developments in South-east Asia: subregional growth zones. In G. Rodan, K. Hewison and R. Robison (eds.), *The Political Economy of South-East Asia*. Melbourne: Oxford University Press, 1997, p 264.
54. Lim, L.Y.C. Singapore's success: the myth of the free market economy. *Asian Survey* XXIII (6) June. In J. Ravenhill (ed.), *The Political Economy of Southeast Asia 3*. Part One. London: Edward Elgar, 1983, p 756.
55. Chalmers, I. Weakening state controls and ideological change in Singapore: the emergence of local capital as a political force. Working Paper No. 13. Perth: Asia Research Centre, Murdoch University, 1992, pp 3, 5.
56. Rodan, G. Singapore: emerging tensions in the 'dictatorship of the middle class.' *Pacific Review 5*(4), 380.
57. Souchou, Y. Consumption and Social Aspirations of the Middle Class in Singapore. *Southeast Asian Affairs*. Singapore: Institute of Southeast Asian Studies, 1996, p 351.
58. Chalmers, I. Weakening state controls and ideological change in Singapore: the emergence of local capital as a political force. Working Paper No. 13. Perth: Asia Research Centre, Murdoch University, 1992, p 4.
59. Souchou, Y. Consumption and Social Aspirations of the Middle Class in Singapore. *Southeast Asian Affairs*. Singapore: Institute of Southeast Asian Studies, 1996, p 352.
60. Quah, J. Social discipline in Singapore: an alternative for the resolution of social problems. *Journal of Southeast Asian Studies 14*, 1983, p 127.
61. Chalmers, I. Weakening state controls and ideological change in Singapore: the emergence of local capital as a political force. Working Paper No. 13. Perth: Asia Research Centre, Murdoch University, 1992, p 5.

62. Hughes, H. and Woldekidan, B. The emergence of the middle class in the DMCs. Paper presented for the Asian Development Bank's Sixth Workshop on the Asian Economic Outlook, Manila, 21–22 October 1993.
63. World Bank. *World Development Report*. New York: Oxford University Press, 1996.
64. Souchou, Y. Consumption and Social Aspirations of the Middle Class in Singapore. *Southeast Asian Affairs*. Singapore: Institute of Southeast Asian Studies, 1996, p 353. Rodan, G. Singapore: emerging tensions in the 'dictatorship of the middle class.' *Pacific Review 5*(4), 1992, p 379.
65. Cheng, T. Is the dog barking? The middle class and democratic movements in the East Asian NICs. *International Study Notes 15*(1), 1990.
66. Cheng, T. Is the dog barking? The middle class and democratic movements in the East Asian NICs. *International Study Notes 15*(1), 1990. Quah, J. Social discipline in Singapore: an alternative for the resolution of social problems. *Journal of Southeast Asian Studies 14*, 1983.
67. East Asia Analytical Unit. *Growth Triangles of South East Asia*. Canberra: Department of Foreign Affairs and Trade, 1995.
68. Crouch, H. *Government and Society in Malaysia*. Sydney: Allen and Unwin, 1996, p 150.
69. Crouch, H. *Government and Society in Malaysia*. Sydney: Allen and Unwin, 1996, p 247.
70. Crouch, H. *Government and Society in Malaysia*. Sydney: Allen and Unwin, 1996, p 217.
71. Jesudason, J.V. Statist democracy and the limits of civil society. Paper No. 119. Singapore: Department of Sociology, National University of Singapore, 1993, p 21.
72. Zakaria, H.A. Cited in Case, W. Comparing regime continuity and change: Indonesia, Thailand and Malaysia. Discussion Paper No. 15. *Regime Change and Regime Maintenance in Asia and the Pacific* Canberra: Department of Political and Social Change, Research School of Pacific and Asian Studies, Australian National University, 1995, p 26.
73. Gomez, E.T. *Malaysia's Political Economy*: *Politics*, *Patronage and Profits*. New York: Cambridge University Press, 1997, p 4.
74. Crouch, H. *Government and Society in Malaysia*. Sydney: Allen and Unwin, 1996, p 216.
75. Gomez, E.T. *Malaysia's Political Economy*: *Politics*, *Patronage and Profits*. New York: Cambridge University Press, 1997, p 180.
76. Jesudason, J.V. Statist democracy and the limits of civil society. Paper No. 119. Singapore: Department of Sociology, National University of Singapore, 1993, p 10.
77. Jesudason, J.V. Statist democracy and the limits of civil society. Paper No. 119. Singapore: Department of Sociology, National University of Singapore, 1993, p 5.
78. Crouch, H. *Government and Society in Malaysia*. Sydney: Allen and Unwin, 1996, pp 217–218.
79. Raj, C. Thinking big. *Malaysian Business*, 16 June 1995, p 14.
80. Adid, S.A. A vote for the vision. *Malaysian Business*, 16 May 1995, p 42.
81. Raj, C. Its chase for glory. *Malaysian Business*, 1 August 1995, p 13.
82. Anwar, A. Government and governance in multi-racial Malaysia. In J.W. Langford

and K.L. Brownsey (eds.), *The Changing Shape of Government in the Asia-Pacific Region*. South Halifax, Nova Scotia: Institute of Research on Public Policy, 1988, p 106.

83. Bowie, A. The dynamics of business-government relations in industrialising Asia. In A. MacIntyre (ed.), *Business and Government in Industrialising Asia*. Sydney: Allen and Unwin, 1994, p 182.
84. Case, W. Comparing regime continuity and change: Indonesia, Thailand and Malaysia. Discussion Paper No. 15. *Regime Change and Regime Maintenance in Asia and the Pacific*. Canberra: Department of Political and Social Change, Research School of Pacific and Asian Studies, Australian National University, 1995, p 26.
85. Turner, M. Subregional economic zones, politics and development: the Philippine involvement in the east ASEAN growth area (EAGA). *Pacific Review 8*(4), 1995. Ramos, F. Cross-border 'growth triangles' promote prosperity in East Asia. *New Perspectives Quarterly*, Winter 1995, p 13.
86. McCoy, A.W. 'An anarchy of families': the historiography of the state and family in the Philippines. In A.W. McCoy (ed.), *An Anarchy of Families: State and Family in the Philippines*. Quezon City: Ateneo de Manila, 1994, p 13.
87. Hutchcroft, P. Cited in McCoy, A.W. 'An Anarchy of Families': the historiography of the state and family in the Philippines. In A.W. McCoy (ed.), *An Anarchy of Families: State and Family in the Philippines*. Quezon City: Ateneo de Manila, 1994, p 13.
88. Wurfel, D. *Filipino Politics: Development and Decay*. Quezon City: Ateneo de Manila, 1979.
89. Simbulan, D. A study of the socio-economic elite in Philippine politics and government. Unpublished PhD dissertation. Canberra: Australian National University, 1965.
90. Hutchcroft, P. Booty capitalism: business-government relations in the Philippines. In A. MacIntyre (ed.), *Business and Government in Industrialising Asia*. Sydney: Allen and Unwin, 1994.
91. De Dios, E.S. (ed.), *An Analysis of the Philippine Economic Crisis*. Quezon City: University of the Philippines Press, 1984.
92. Guitierrez, E. *The Ties That Bind: A Guide to Family Business and Other Interests in the Ninth House of Representatives*. Manila: Philippine Center for Investigative Journalism and Institute for Popular Democracy, 1994, p 4.
93. Turner, M. Imagining the middle class in the Philippines. *Pilipinas*, *25*, 1995.
94. Lynch, F. Big people and little people in the rural Philippines. In M. Hollnsteiner (ed.), *Society, Culture and the Filipino*, Vol. II. Quezon City: Institute of Philippine Culture, 1975. Carino, L. The land and the people. In R.P. de Guzman and M.A. Reforma (eds.), *Government and Politics in the Philippines*. Singapore: Oxford University Press, 1988.
95. Turner, M. Imagining the middle class in the Philippines. *Pilipinas*, *25*, 1995.
96. Hughes, H. and Woldekidan, B. The emergence of the middle class in the DMCs. Paper presented for the Asian Development Bank's Sixth Workshop on the Asian Economic Outlook, Manila, 21–22 October 1993.
97. Roberto, E.L. The validity of the socio-economic classification of the Philippine market. Asian Institute of Management Occasional Papers No. 11, 1986.

98. Hunt, C.L. *Sociology in the Philippine Setting: A Modular Approach*. Quezon City: Phoenix, 1987.
99. Pinches, M. The Philippines' new rich: capitalist transformation amidst economic gloom. In R. Robison and D. Goodman (eds.), *The New Rich in Asia: Mobile Phones, McDonalds and Middle Class Revolution*. London: Routledge, 1996, p 123.
100. Turner, M. Imagining the middle class in the Philippines. *Pilipinas*, *25*, 1995.
101. Gregorio-Medel, A. Development work is middleclass oriented as much as it is poverty oriented. In *Philippine Politics and Society*. Quezon City: Ateneo Center for Social Policy and Public Affairs, 1992.
102. Hutchison, J. Pressure on policy in the Philippines. In G. Rodan, K. Hewison, and R. Robison (eds.), *The Political Economy of South-east Asia: An Introduction*. Melbourne: Oxford University Press, 1997, p 84.
103. Almonte, J. Cited in Vatikiotis, M. *Political Change in Southeast Asia: Trimming the Banyan Tree*. London: Routledge, 1996, p 13.
104. Turner, M. Growth triangles and vicious circles: peace and development in Mindanao. *New Asia Pacific Review 3*: 2, 1997.
105. Hutchison, J. Pressure on policy in the Philippines. In G. Rodan, K. Hewison, and R. Robison (eds.), *The Political Economy of Southeast Asia: An Introduction*. Melbourne: Oxford University Press, 1997, p 77.
106. Hutchcroft, P. Booty capitalism: business-government relations in the Philippines. In A. MacIntyre (ed.), *Business and Government in Industrialising Asia*. Sydney: Allen and Unwin, 1994, p 217.
107. Drache, D. From Keynes to K-Mart: competitiveness in a corporate age. In R. Boyer and D. Drache (eds.), *States Against Markets: The Limits of Globalization*. London: Routledge, 1996, p 55.
108. Smith, S.L.D. The Indonesia-Malaysia-Singapore growth triangle: a political and economic equation. *Australian Journal of International Affairs 51*(3), 1997, p 382.
109. Ramos, F. Cross-border 'growth triangles' promote prosperity in East Asia. *New Perspectives Quarterly*, Winter, 1995, pp 12–13.
110. Reynolds, C. *The World of States: An Introduction to Explanation and Theory*. Aldershot: Edward Elgar, 1992, p 56.
111. Grant, B. *Indonesia*. 3rd ed. Melbourne: Melbourne University Press, 1996, p 113.
112. Cardoso, F.H. and Faletto, E. *Dependency and Development in Latin America*. Berkeley: University of California Press, 1979.
113. *Far Eastern Economic Review*, 8 January 1998.

12

Economic Reform and Political Legitimacy in Post-Mao China

Maria Chan Morgan
Earlham College, Richmond, Indiana

I. INTRODUCTION

Legitimacy, Samuel Huntington once observed, "is a mushy concept that political analysts do well to avoid. Yet, it is essential to understanding the problem confronting authoritarian regimes in the late twentieth century."[1] The collapse of Communist regimes in Eastern Europe has reinforced the notion that their inability to sustain the customary range of social and economic benefits for their citizens delegitimized their governments.[2] But legitimacy is not the exclusive concern of authoritarian regimes. In the late 1970s, when stagflation seemed to have strained the capacity of many social democracies in Western Europe, many pronounced that the modern capitalist states were in a crisis of legitimacy.[3] This chapter tries to address a simple controversy: Does market reform shore up or undermine the legitimacy of the Chinese government?

As Ralf Dahrendorf argues, effectiveness and legitimacy are related, but that relationship is asymmetrical.[4] Governments can be effective without being legitimate, and governments can be legitimate without being effective. However, widespread doubts in the effectiveness of governments will turn into doubts in their legitimacy. Central to the concern of this chapter is how effective market reform measures have been in making people believe that the post-Mao one-party regime is worthy of their support and obedience.

I shall first review some of the relevant literature on regime legitimacy and identify some of the gaps in the conceptualization of political legitimacy and show why prevailing theories have not been helpful for our understanding of legitimacy in a regime undergoing economic transition. Second, I want to examine how effective the newly introduced economic and political institutions have been, and what consequences they have for the government's legitimacy. I shall argue that the government's ability to build public confidence in these new institutions is essential, especially because they are so contrary to prevailing party ideology. Without people accepting the validity of these new institutions—such as property ownership, financial institutions capable of channeling public savings to productive investments, foreign direct investment which modernizes the economy, and local elections which give people greater control over local affairs—neither the regime nor the reform can be sustained. The government's willingness to introduce these new measures and its ability to institutionalize them will give their reform efforts credibility. I call these confidence-building institutions.

I shall show that market reform in China has not entailed the diminished role of the state, but I part company with those critics of the state by arguing that the force of law, however ambiguous and unevenly enforced, has lent some credibility to these new reform institutions. The result of introducing these new institutions is that the decision-making space for people has been vastly expanded. True, sometimes the action people take moves the country and economy in directions unintended by the government. Still, these new institutions are the means whereby people's scope of choices and their access to resources are increased and stabilized. The state does so by providing a legal framework, however imperfect and uncertain, to legitimize such activities. When citizens are confident enough to utilize or participate in these institutions, they have a stake in these institutions. Public acceptance and influence over these new institutions make further reform possible.

I select but a few empirical scholarly studies of the new economic and political institutions introduced under reform to indicate the extent of popular support they enjoy and the degree of credibility they gain. I choose local elections, banking and financial institutions, property ownership, and foreign direct investment because they represent some of the most politically sensitive measures that have the potential to delegitimize a regime that officially still adheres to Marxism-Leninism. I shall show how these institutions gain credibility largely because of the legal infrastructure that underpinned them, not because they deliver what they promised. Thus while economic reform in China is marked by mishaps, the new institutions are gaining acceptance and winning public confidence.

II. CONCEPTUALIZING LEGITIMACY AND EFFECTIVENESS OF GOVERNMENT

The disagreement among scholars on the effects of market reforms on political legitimacy lies in part in the confusion between normative and empirical concepts of legitimacy and in part in the difficulty of measuring the effectiveness of economic reform.

The literature on the subject of legitimacy is powerfully influenced by Max Weber's classification of the three systems of legitimacy based on tradition, charisma, and belief in the validity and rationality of the legal institutions. But Weber also identified a fourth kind of legitimacy—"the authority of substantive policies or values"—which he did not add to his classification of types of political domination.[5] Yet, substantive policies, such as macroeconomic policies that promote economic growth and stability, can be one of the most powerful justifications of obedience when people believe that the regime that asks for their support is enhancing their economic well-being.[6] But since substantive policies presumably can be produced by a government based on either tradition, charisma, or legal-rational institutions, Weber excluded them from the classification of legitimacy. This is consistent with the fact that Weber treated the three systems of domination by and large as empirical and historical rather than normative phenomena.

The normative dimension of legitimacy reasserted itself in the Marxist critique of capitalism where the state was delegitimized for serving the exclusive interest of the dominant economic class. Thus Gramsci and others have argued that people's perception or "consciousness" of their duty and obligation to a state was manipulated by the people in power. Similarly, Habermas assumes that a capitalist state cannot pursue unpopular policies producing negative outcomes such as unemployment if people had their free will.[7] By casting doubts on the legitimacy of capitalist states, Marxist and critical theorists stimulated social scientists' interest in the normative basis of legitimacy.

Not surprisingly, then, many social scientists subsequently attempt to synthesize the normative with the empirical aspects of legitimacy by suggesting that what gives legitimacy to governments should include such absolute moral imperatives as human rights and rule of law, as well as culturally determined values that have enduring validity for a particular country, such as adherence to Islamic laws for Arab countries.[8] Ralf Dahrendorf suggests that "[a] government is legitimate if what it does is right both in the sense of complying with certain fundamental principles, and in that of being in line with prevailing cultural values."[9] He goes on to suggest that the less the perceived gap between government action and basic values, the more legitimate the government. Any dissociation of government action and prevailing cultural values will meet with doubts by the people.[10] However, Dahrendorf does not link government effectiveness with economic performance.

In his examination of the tension between borderless, global financial markets and bounded, national politics, Louis Pauly argues that political legitimacy cannot be separated from the performance of the national economy.[11] He believes that the challenge to capitalist democracies today is that "two sets of priorities—a growing economy and responsible government—are today required for a critical mass of citizens to accept the authority of their state.''[12] By examining the evolving mandates of the Economic and Financial Organization of the League of Nations and the IMF, Pauly shows that concern over the legitimacy of the individual leading member states led them to prefer multilateral collaboration as a means of crisis management over policy coordination because the former requires legislative approval.

Yet, it is not just the political analysts who evaluate the legitimacy of a regime by asking whether what the government did is right and whether the government is effective in delivering what it promises. Political leaders are under increasing international pressure to legitimatize their regimes by conforming to international norms and moral standards as well as delivering tangible results for its subjects. Their inability to meet those criteria seems to have driven many Communist governments in the past to invoke ideology and nationalism to buttress their claims to power. However, Communist ideology becomes increasingly problematic for such governments to legitimatize themselves because the ideology itself was an obstacle to economic growth and development. In addition, such systems lack the mechanism to renew itself, as democratic governments do through elections. This lack of self-renewal mechanism contributes to the erosion of the legitimacy of these authoritarian regimes.[13]

The issue of legitimacy for post-Mao China is further complicated by international politics and U.S. foreign and domestic politics. There is evidence that such pressure had the effect of making the Chinese government more compliant with international conventions on as diverse a field as restrictions on missile exports, nuclear nonproliferation, and intellectual property rights.[14] American pressure on China predated the 1989 Tiananmen Square incident. In fact, ever since the Communist takeover in 1949, China has generated passionate political responses within the United States.[15] Since the Tiananmen incident in 1989, the legitimacy of the regime has been hotly disputed by both right-wing anti-Communist politicians who view China as a ''rogue regime'' or an unrepentant Red menace, and human rights activists and socialist groups who view an increasingly materialistic and nonegalitarian China as a betrayal of their postmaterialist, humanistic ideal of revolutionary egalitarianism. In the post-Mao period, the Chinese government is compelled to respond not only to domestic expectations but to foreign pressure and criticism. Market reform and China's gradual integration with the global economy are part and parcel of this process of legitimization. China's nationalistic expression which bristled at international criticism and her desired accession to the World Trade Organization to take her ''rightful'' place as a world trading power should thus be viewed in this broader context.

The next section of this paper will examine different theories regarding the relationship between market reform and political legitimacy in China. I shall address some of the substantive issues raised by these contradictory findings. Finally, I offer my interpretation of the effectiveness of reform-driven institutions. I shall show that even though some institutions fall short of delivering economic results, they expand the range of human choices, which accounts for the continued political legitimacy of China today.

III. RELATIONSHIP BETWEEN ECONOMIC PERFORMANCE AND LEGITIMACY

There are several theses regarding the relationship between market reform and regime legitimacy in China. Some argue intuitively that by raising the standard of living for many, market reform will enhance the political legitimacy of the present regime. Bartlomiej Kaminski observed for instance that ''[w]ith the declining appeal of the promise of a better future, economic performance becomes essential to state socialism's legitimacy.''[16] Others, like Stephen Haggard and Robert Kaufman, argue that economic growth contributes to long-term political stability by easing the tradeoffs between political supporters and those who are negatively affected by reforms.[17] Acute economic difficulties are shown to have contributed to the collapse of democratic regimes in Chile, Argentina, Uruguay, Brazil, Bolivia, Peru, South Korea, Thailand, Turkey, and the Philippines at various times in the 1960s and 1970s. But the most severe economic recession since the Great Depression, the 1997-1998 Asian financial crisis, did not produce similar results except in Indonesia, suggesting that factors other than economic performance have sustained the legitimacy of many regimes in Asia and Latin American countries during the crisis.[18]

Most political analysts believe that regime legitimacy cannot be based on good economic performance alone because of the cyclical nature of most economies, regime support needs be built on people's belief in the validity of system institutions. The well documented institutionalization of democracies in postwar Japan and Germany is the best example. Yet, it is doubtful that democracy could have taken hold in those countries without the anchor of economic miracles. It is the process of the translation of economic miracles to political legitimacy that is not well understood.

In *Economic Transition and Political Legitimacy in Post-Mao China*, Feng Chen argues that the incompatibility between Marxist ideology and capitalist practice forces the Chinese leaders to self-consciously legitimatize market reform measures by rationalizing them as instrumental for achieving the egalitarian goals of Marxism-Leninism.[19] Feng shows that the Chinese Communist Party is extremely sensitive to public doubts about the congruence between the government's reform-driven action and Marxist-Leninist principles. Hence, the party went to great lengths to claim the consistency of their reform policies with fundamental socialist principles. Zhao Ziyang in the early 1980s and Jiang Zemin in

1997 have both tried to win Marxist hardliners' support by justifying liberal economic reform on the ground that it would speed China along its first stage of socialist development.

But while the Chinese leaders in the short run have been able to give primacy to modernization and efficiency and justify such reform policy by borrowing heavily from liberal, capitalist economic ideas, in the long run, Marxist ideology—the fundamentals upon which the CCP depends—will be exposed as irrelevant for solving China's economic needs, and certainly cannot be offered as the best alternative to societal development.[20] Feng's point, then, is that the inherent tension between the fundamental principles of Marxism-Leninism and the instrumental principles of economic liberalism cannot sustain the regime's legitimacy.

In much the same vein, sociologist X.L. Ding identifies the challenge to regime legitimacy as the contradiction between ideological-institutional continuity and policy innovations created by economic reform.[21] While Ding and Feng Chen use different vocabularies to describe the two contradictory legitimation devices—Ding describes them as rationalism v. socialist morality, whereas Feng Chen describes them as instrumental v. fundamental justifications—their ideas are similar. However, Ding uses the concepts of counter-elite and ''institutional parasitism'' to explain a legitimacy crisis. Ding argues that political instability is created by Deng's open-door policy and economic reform because they made possible the development of ''institutional parasitism,'' which allowed the intellectuals and professionals to mount an antigovernment movement from important party-state organs such as universities, television and radio stations and news agencies.[22]

Ding explains that Deng's open-door policy gave the people, especially intellectuals, access to better information and an opportunity to compare the poor performance of China with the advances made in the West, Japan, and the other East Asian dragons.[23] Moreover, Deng's economic reform was an admission that the leadership had lost confidence in the Communist system, which they felt compelled to defend in order to stay in power.[24] Dengist reform introduced a generation of better-educated people into officialdom, many later utilized their semiautonomous organizations to voice their criticism and dissent.[25]

The problem with Ding's analysis is that even though the concepts of ''counter-elites'' and ''institutional parasitism'' are supposed to be central to his theory, it became clear that the crisis of legitimacy in 1989 was brought about by inflation and corruption quite independent of the counter-elites. In the politics of legitimation, the acquiescence of the people is left out of his analysis, because Ding made the error of equating the intellectuals with the people, portraying the 1989 democracy movement as a nationwide mass movement of opposition to the regime, when it was primarily a youth movement protesting against ineffective economic policies and government corruption.

The third school of thought believes that departure from centrally planned economies tends to weaken the Communist party's authority by redistributing power away from the center, or producing social and economic dislocations.[26] Leading this argument is Andrew Walder, who suggests that market reform altered the relationship between state and society by allowing citizens to be increasingly assertive and autonomous; it also changed the relationship within the party-state apparatus by increasing the independence of the local cadres who have access to independent wealth and income as they can patronize private entrepreneurs by virtue of their position.[27] Walder focuses on the negative effect reform has on the Communist party, but it seems possible to argue that the increased autonomy not just for local cadres, but ordinary citizens, could very well validate the very process of reform.

Against Walder's position, Yasheng Huang argues that while the center is economically less dominant as a result of market reform in relation to local governments, the center is politically still powerful because of its control of political patronage and appointment.[28] Basing his argument on principal-agent relation, Huang demonstrates the moral hazard of curbing investments in order to control inflation. He shows that central leaders have much greater incentive to control investments than local leaders because the center has to absorb a disproportionate share of the costs of inflation. With the bankruptcy of some provincial international trust and investment companies (*ITIC*s) and the enormous debts these non-banking financial institutions incurred in 1998, the center has a more powerful incentive to curb reckless investment by provinces. Thus the Chinese government has not lost its authority or capacity to enforce an austerity program to rein in inflation in the 1994-96 period, or to force bankruptcy on the ITICs, however unpopular such measures are with local officials.[29] While there are obvious problems with marketization—several boom-and-bust cycles, increasing crime and income disparity, and mounting losses for state-owned enterprises—there are few signs that the Chinese Communist party dominated regime is in imminent danger of collapse. So, what is it that holds China together in the process of market reform that the Russians failed to do?

Without attempting to address the issue of political legitimacy directly, Barry Naughton has documented how, by increasing employment and consumer goods while holding down inflation in the late 1970s, the Chinese government managed to restructure the economy with wide public support.[30] Naughton emphasizes that policy makers had no grand strategies to reform the economy between 1979 and 1983, and that the bureaucratic apparatus that dominated many state enterprises remained resistant to reform. What made progress possible at that time was the relatively flexible attitude of the top leadership plus the inability of the recalcitrant bureaucracy to move swiftly to oppose reform.[31] Marketization progressed in those days on the fringe of the centrally planned economy, legitimatized by ad hoc authority from the more flexible leaders.[32] Naughton demonstrates how, by creating "a presumption of permissiveness in the countryside," including a degree of institutional flexibility, the small changes allowed in rural policy led to rapid growth of the nonstate sector, especially in rural industrialization by the township and village enterprises (TVEs).[33] The performance of the nonstate sector was not outstanding, but its expansion changed the macroeconomic behavior of the whole economy by introducing a competitive environment to China, and helped it achieve efficiency, especially in shifting more and more economic decisions from plan to market.[34]

By 1984-85, favorable economic conditions gave policy makers the willingness to further reform and the confidence to make comprehensive plans for sustained economic growth.[35] But disagreement over different approaches at rationalizing the economy forced reformers to accept a more modest, dual-track growing-out-of-plan strategy between 1985 and 1988.[36] The characteristic of this strategy was that of the "expansion of the area subject to market regulation," and not rationalizing the control mechanisms that shaped the economy as a whole.[37] One effect of the dual-track system was a continued distortion of the price system, leading to lower rate of price increases for industrial products that were still under the plan, but higher prices for products and materials outside the plan. The result was an accelerating inflationary crisis in 1989. The government's response was the imposition of tough austerity measures which essentially derailed reform for a while and led to a crisis of confidence among urban dwellers in the regime. Yet, when recentralizing the economy failed to produce results by late 1990, the hardliners who replaced the liberal reformers after the Tiananmen incident were forced to dismantle the traditional planning apparatus and resume and accelerate economic reform.

In Naughton's account of the process of economic reform, he made it clear that "the coherence of the reform process emerged in spite of, not because of, the policies of the Chinese leaders."[38] He praised the robust, broad-based reform, but he did not think that the "quantitatively rapid economic growth" and "qualitatively significant development" were enough to confer legitimacy on the government. Despite impressive economic performance, Naughton views the government as lacking "minimum levels of accountability and legitimacy."[39]

In contrast, Susan Shirk argues that reform measures were carefully orchestrated and chosen, based on the rational calculation of political career advancement and political succession advantages. The path of reform is characterized by gradualism, administrative decentralization, and particularistic contracting (that is, fixing the level of procurement and taxation according to local abilities.) The fact that economic reform has not undermined the center is because of a mutually reinforcing support between some central leaders for particularistic reform policies, in return for political support from the provincial leaders who benefit from such particularistic policies, leading to more particularistic reform policies.[40] In short, economic reform did not undermine the center because the measures were designed to win local political support in the political succession struggle. However, for the same reason, reform is shallow rather than deep, and may not lead to an open domestic market or deep integration with the world economy.[41] Yet, contrary to what Shirk claims, studies have shown that many reform measures were dictated by economic necessity rather than political horse trading.

How, then, can we reconcile these different arguments by the leading scholars in the field? I believe that with the exception of Naughton, these scholars tend to focus on the behavior of a specific group of officials and/or vested interests in response to a narrow set of reform policies but not on the legal sinews and ligatures that were gradually put in place to remove much of the ambiguities of uncoordinated reform. The legal framework gave reform credibility by defining permissible economic and political activities, which are forever increasing. The rule of law, however frequently infringed upon, did expand ''the entire spectrum of personal choice'' for most people, as Naughton has put it.[42] Hence, I hypothesize that (1) these institutions create political space for participation in decision-making, (2) such participation in turn generates pressure for greater transparency in the economic realm, and (3) greater transparency enhances public support for the regime and its legitimacy. I shall show that public acceptance of these new institutions and measures has to do with the wider spaces for action made possible by the increasingly transparent rules. Moreover, there is significant support for these new institutions even during periods of economic downturn and political uncertainty. This may explain why, despite all the predictions of the erosion of the political authority of the party, the regime appears remarkably robust as it reclaimed the sovereignty over Hong Kong on July 1, 1997.

IV. CONFIDENCE-BUILDING INSTITUTIONS UNDER MARKET REFORM

In this section, I propose to examine the effectiveness of four new institutions associated with market reform, namely, local elections, banking and financial reform, private property ownership, and foreign direct investment. They do not represent an exhaustive list of reform measures, but they are chosen because, given their politically sensitive nature, they are most vulnerable to resistance by orthodox ideologues. I judge the effectiveness of these new institutions primarily with indirect indicators, as shown in Table 1. The indicators measure whether the opportunities provided are well exploited by individuals or organizations. Regrettably, for lack of data, some of the interpretation of public support and participation has to be by inference, but I shall try to make a reasonable case for my interpretation. I shall give a brief description of each of the reform measures and interpret their effectiveness in terms of gaining public support through expanding opportunities for participation.

Table 1 Confidence-Building Institutions Under Market Reform

Institution	Domain of autonomy	Indicators of effectiveness
Local elections	Candidate choices	Genuine competition, participation
Financial reform	Credit extension according to commerical criteria	Profits, provisions for doubtful debts, monetary stability
Property ownership	Investment opportunities	Land use rights in villages, privatization of TVEs, urban ownership of real estate
Foreign direct investment	Choice of partners; removal of control and invisible barriers	Captial inflow and its utilization; technological transfer; local employment

A. Local Elections

Local election may not seem to be related to economic reform. Yet, continued poverty in many villages and peasant discontent in the 1980s have led the government to call for more representative, and presumably more responsive, village leadership in order to obtain social stability and economic development. However, the means for doing so appear contradictory. On the one hand, for obvious reasons, the party wants to maintain control over the selection and appointment of village party secretaries. On the other hand, the government provided for competitive democratic elections at the village level with the passage of the 1987 Organic Law of the Village Committees.

Studies of elections of village committees or assemblies in the past few years point to increased and genuine competition in village elections. The central government, especially the Ministry of Civil Affairs, is an active promoter of democratic village self-rule, especially in poor areas, where concerns about political stability and economic development are greatest.[43] The government hopes that local self-rule would help assuage discontent in a period of rapid change.[44]

With economic reform and the decollectivization of rural communes, villages, unlike townships or counties, receive no budget from the upper levels, nor are they allowed to keep any portion of the tax revenues. Financial expenses have to be met locally.[45] This means that the poorer the villages, the more fees they have to levy on the already poor peasants, and the more fees they levy, the more disgruntled the peasants. Small wonder the party sees democratically elected village committee to be the logical means to legitimize fee levying, which will provide the villages with some resources to fight crime and banditry. Local elections become especially urgent since the lack of resources means that few people are willing to be appointed to be party secretaries in the poor villages.

While Seymour Martin Lipset's model of democratization would lead us to anticipate a causal relationship between increased income level and increased competition and participation, it is not the case in China. Some of the most economically advanced areas in Guangdong, China's most prosperous province, have lagged behind in implementing village elections. In other cases, the relationship is reversed. Some democratically elected village assemblies have improved village income. What seems crucial in determining the level of participation is the control and availability of resources. In poor villages, where sources of income are derived locally, for example, where land is commodified for sale instead of being collectively owned, there are more frequent elections and more participation because the stake is high. It was reported that when a village is visibly lagging behind its neighbors in getting a share of the material wealth, its inhabitants would seize the opportunity of local elections to replace their local chieftain.[46] However, where the source of village wealth is dependent primarily on private enterprises, there is lower level of participation and competition. In such cases, appointed party secretaries continue to be the key decision makers.[47]

Nonetheless, the effectiveness of village government is increasingly judged on the basis of whether it can develop collective wealth and provide jobs for its members and money for its collective coffers.[48] Where people see local election as the only means available to control their fate, they exploit that opportunity. Low level of participation is due to the availability of other means to improve one's well-being, rather than the lack of credibility of electoral institutions. In poorer areas, the state-sponsored push for democratic self-government has transformed subjects into citizens. In rich villages, control of village committees is regarded as irrelevant for citizens to pursue wealth.

Zhang Chunsheng, head of the legislative department of the National People's Congress, reported that ''about one-third of village committees are satisfying the needs and wishes of their residents. About one-third need improvement and another third are unsatisfactory.''[49] The figures seem to indicate that the credibility of local elections as a means for selecting representatives capable of developing public goods to enhance local communities is gaining ground.

B. Financial and Banking Institutions

China's financial institutions are the most spectacular failures of market reform in the 1980s. The Chinese capital market is volatile, its banking system is saddled with nonperforming assets, and the central bank has insufficient skills in risk management, limited experience in monetary management, few policy instruments, and inadequate regulatory and supervisory capacity. Many banks in China had to extend loans at administratively determined interest rates to state enterprises at the direction of the government.[50] The government resorted to the credit plan as an instrument of monetary control, giving the State Council and the People's Bank of China the power to impose strict limits on credit expansion in order to contract the economy and control inflation. But such an instrument was blunt and ineffective because state banks and state-owned enterprises managed to find numerous ways to circumvent the credit plan.

The proliferation of nonbank financial institutions such as trust and investment companies (TICs) set up by provincial governments, government agencies, and, before 1986, state banks as well, is one such means. The TICs are taking advantage of opportunities (such as availability of interbank funds) and loopholes in regulations (such as lending outside of the credit plan) to inject funds into numerous development projects. But since TICs get short-term deposits but make long-term commitments in ventures such as real estate projects and state-owned enterprises, many are insolvent. Hence the assets of many TICs are nonliquid and their operations very risky, as their business scope expands.[51] Financial sector reform is thus the sine qua non of state enterprise reform.

In November 1993, as the economy became overheated after three years of rapid expansion, the government introduced sweeping financial reforms designed to strengthen the central bank's ability to influence the economy through monetary instruments rather than administrative means. Three policy banks—Agricultural Development Bank, Export-Import Bank of China, and State Development Bank—were created to channel government-directed lending to those three areas. The reform also tried to transform four specialized banks—Bank of China, Industrial and Commercial Bank of China, Construction Bank of China, Agricultural Bank of China—into genuine commercial banks by encouraging them to acquire skills in risk and asset liability management and credit and risk evaluation, and giving them greater freedom in designing their lending program based on commercial criteria.[52]

In 1995, to deepen reform of the financial sector, the state passed the People's Bank of China Law, officially established the People's Bank of China (PBOC) as the central bank for the PRC, empowering it to supervise and regulate the financial services industry. Secondly, the Commercial Bank Law was passed, requiring the state banks to become commercial banks and prohibiting commercial banks from investing in nonbank financial institutions.[53] In addition, the Insurance Law, Securities Law, the Trust Law, and the Foreign Exchange Management Law were all passed in that year. The purpose is to strengthen the legal infrastructure of China's financial system as the basis of the financial sector reform.

Many problems persist. According to Nicholas Lardy, 25% of all the outstanding loans at the four largest specialized banks in 1997 are nonperforming.[54] Not only are the major banks unable to meet the 8% Basle capital adequacy standard, their capital adequacy rates have been falling steadily since the early 1990s.[55] But the suggestion that China will face an impending banking crisis seems exaggerated because the nonrecoverable loans are probably only 2% to 3% of the problem-loans, not 20% as some analysts suggest.[56] It is politically inconceivable that having been directed by the government to make the loans to state-owned enterprises to sustain employment in the provinces, the banks will be forced into bankruptcy by Beijing and be without support from the provincial governments benefiting from such loans. As the Asian financial crisis deepened, the Chinese government has taken bold and forceful steps to address problems in the financial system, such as the recapitalization of the state banks by setting up financial asset corporations to reduce the ratio of nonperforming loans.[57]

There are strong indications that the central bank is gaining increasing independence and management expertise, using interest rates and money supply rather than credit control as the appropriate means to influence the economy. It is widely expected that a national securities law will soon be passed to replace ad hoc State Council directives and that regulatory jurisdiction over the fast-expanding and increasingly complex securities market will be placed in the PBOC, perhaps alongside the State Council Securities Committee (SCSC).[58]

Other indicators of the effectiveness in restructuring the banking and financial sector can best seen in the increasing independence of commercial banks from local government in their lending practices and in the closure of Guangdong International Trust and Investment Company in 1998 and forcing its creditors to go through bankruptcy procedures to recover their loans. Data on the growth of assets in the hands of citizens are available. Before 1978, 96.7% of national savings came from the government and state-owned enterprises, and only 3% from private citizens. In 1996, private savings constitute 61% of the assets in financial institutions, and they do not include stocks and bonds held by individuals.[59] In fact, even during a period of high inflation (1993–95), households continued to pour deposits into the banking system. While increased personal income, the lack of alternative options of investment, and the government's decision to offer an inflation-indexed interest rates for time deposits with a maturity of three years or longer certainly all account for the increases in individual savings account deposits, the government's awareness of the danger of social disorder should there be a massive run on banks also led it to liberalize the financial market and institutionalize better supervision over the banking system.[60]

The gradual deregulation of the financial market can also be seen from the growth of foreign financial institutions in China, whose representative offices or branches had increased to over 600 by the end of 1996.[61] Even more significantly, qualified foreign financial institutions are allowed to do business in *renminbi* in Pudong, another step in easing foreign exchange controls. The decision to abolish the swap markets in December 1998 in favor of freer access to foreign exchange but better control by state banks over such activities is another example. By allowing the convertibility of renminbi on current account transactions and easing restrictions on the amount of foreign currency locals can obtain for travel abroad, policy makers are gradually moving toward full convertibility and enhance domestic and international confidence in China's economic reform.[62]

None of the above should be taken to mean that the Chinese financial market is a mature market. Internal Chinese documents indicate that policy makers recognize that the Chinese financial market lacks breadth, depth, and flexibility, that its supervisory structures require strengthening, and that institutional and private investors lack sophistication in risk management.[63] Nonetheless, the laws and regulations that are put in place have already transformed the financial market in China in a course of but 12 years.

C. Private Property Ownership

No economic institution signifies the rejection of communism as powerfully as the institution of private property. This section discusses the evolution of private property in the villages, the townships, and the cities in the form of ownership of land and real estate and the problems private ownership posed to continued official commitment to collective ownership. Since the evil of capitalism was supposed to be rooted in the control of the means of production in the hands of a few, collective ownership by the state has been the centerpiece of socialist economies. With economic reform, but with the continued commitment to Marxist ideology in China, laws dealing with private ownership are introduced piecemeal and with caution. Not surprisingly, officials have to make some ideological readjustment in defense of agricultural decollectivization, extending greater autonomy to state-owned enterprises (SOEs), and the sale of public housing.[64]

Chinese policy makers justified the introduction of the individual household contract on grounds that it was a means of restoring peasants' confidence in the collective economy.[65] Similarly, in allowing land use rights (but not land ownership rights) to be exchanged in the market, the reformers are compelled to defend their action. They legitimize it on the ground that guaranteeing peasants land use rights for 30 years will increase productivity without violating the principle of public ownership. Yet this rationalization has prevented the reformers from taking the logical step of privatizing land in the countryside.

With the introduction of individual household contracts, many production teams and brigades were disbanded, so their land got transferred back to the administrative village governments—usually at the township level or above. The confusion over ownership of land can be seen in the survey for the Asian Development Bank on land tenureship in 1996, in which a majority of rural cadres claimed that the land belonged to the administrative government, whereas most peasants believed it belonged to the village team.[66] Of the 200 households surveyed in one village, 27.5% thought that the land they cultivate belonged to the state, 22.5% thought it belonged to the government, 35% believed it belonged to the village team, and only 2% believed that the land belonged to them. In another village that had ongoing conflict with the local government over land acquisition, 100% of the villagers believe that the land belonged to the village team. In another village, 62.5% of the people believed that the land belonged to the state.[67] Most of the conflicts between peasants and village and township governments in Guizhou, Fujian, and Shandong are reported to be over land acquisition and auction.[68]

Yet, as Table 2 shows, despite public confusion over private land ownership, collective property was fast diminishing in the countryside by 1996. Peasants seemed confident enough about their ownership right over the houses they built that they would borrow money from rural credit cooperatives to build houses on land which they may not have legally owned. This accounts for the wholesale conversion of farm land to houses which changed the landscape in the countryside. It was estimated that between 1986 and 1995, about 75 million *mu* (about 5 million hectares) of cultivated land was lost to nonagricultural use.[69] The random occupation of land for private or industrial development became such a chronic problem that the State Land Administration, vested with authority to control land use, announced on April 15, 1997, that it would conduct a large-scale investigation to look into the problem of land use and abuse. [70] My prediction is that the agency will recommend zoning and the legalization of land sales.

At the township level, the ownership of township and village enterprises (TVEs) presents yet another challenge to the notion of collective property. The very evolution of TVEs in the early 1980s was due to distinctive and favorable conditions created by the command economy, which included cheap and expensive capital in the countryside (as opposed to relatively expensive labor and captial in the cities), the relaxing of a previously protected market, low tax rates, proximity to urban areas for subcontractual work, and diversity.[71]

The ownership of TVEs has long intrigued researchers. As Naughton reported, the ownership situation of TVEs varied. Around Shanghai, where the collective organizations were strong, TVEs were collectively owned and were well integrated with the urban economy through subcontracting. Around Wenzhou, where the private economy was strong, rural industries were mostly private

Table 2 Percentage of Land Belonging to Village Teams

1980	1987	1996
95.9%	65%	34%

Source: Jean Hung, *Survey for Asian Development Bank*, 1997, p. 3.

enterprises. By the late 1980s, many TVEs were privatized even though, for ideological reasons, the rural governments still registered them as if they were collectively owned.[72] In the 1990s, competition among TVEs and between TVEs and state enterprises has eroded the profitability of many TVEs. Their ability to absorb surplus rural labor began to decline as well. Hence, privatization is unlikely to resolve the problems of many TVEs, as many have already sold off their liquid assets and leased their fixed assets.[73] At issue is not privatization but improved capitalization and management of TVEs. In a survey on the causes of the failure of some TVEs, a majority of the respondents blamed it on the lack of competent leadership and lack of appropriate technology or capital rather than on government policy or lack of support from the party leaders.[74]

In response to the deteriorating economic situation of rural enterprises, the government promulgated the Township and Village Enterprise Law in October 1996 to ''support and guide the healthy development of TVEs and protect their lawful rights.''[75] The law reaffirms the special treatment of TVEs because of their role in supporting the rural economy, and extends the protection of the special concessions to TVEs (for example, in land usage, infrastructure installation, and social services provision) even if the TVEs expand their operation to the county metropolis or cities. Of special interest to us is the section of the law dealing with property rights. The law prohibits ''unlawful interference'' in the management and decisions of TVEs, but it also obligates investors and managers to ''accept the supervision of workers'' on ''matters of grave importance to the enterprise.''[76] It is clear that the government tries to balance the need to make property rights of TVEs more transparent so that these enterprises will continue to play a central role in rural development, but also to shield rural workers from the turbulence of economic reform in order to maintain regime support.

Finally, it is in the area of urban housing that the notion of private property finds its most rational expression. In 1991, the State Council pushed for housing reform in an attempt to solve the problems of shortage and deteriorating housing stocks. Reformers took the cautious approach by embracing a principle of having the state, the collective, and the individual taking responsibility for improving housing, with the aim of increasing the ratio of private to public investment in housing construction.[77] Proclaimed a State Council document: ''No longer should housing be the accumulated assets of the state for planned distribution, but houses must be turned into consumer goods for exchange in the market place.''[78]

However, the conversion of housing from state-provided social goods to marketable durable consumer goods proved tortuous. Rent subsidies and low wages have long distorted the market prices, availability, and quality of housing. Low rent and high maintenance costs of old buildings became a disincentive for home ownership.[79] Since housing workers have long been the responsibility of state-owned enterprises, under the reform proposals, they are given the task of maintaining, building, managing, assigning, and selling living spaces to workers. But without capital for developers and a home mortgage market for buyers, and with almost 75% of public sector workers living in subsidized housing in 1994, the privatization of housing remains stalled in most cities.[80] The ability to implement reform depends on the enterprises' access to state resources as well as the income of workers. Privatization of public houses thus tends to move fastest among wealthy (i.e., powerful) government organizations or profitable enterprises.[81]

Mindful of more visible income disparity, and to prevent the concentration of real estate ownership in the hands of high-income families, the State Council ordered a dual-pricing system so that the sale of public housing to high-income working families would be based on prices determined by the market, and the sale to middle- to low-income families be based on cost (which includes land acquisition, compensation for relocation, survey, planning, construction, infrastructure, management fees, and taxation).[82] But because of the remaining ambiguity about the disposal and resale of such property, the State Council further clarified the ownership issue in 1994, giving the workers who purchase their public housing at market price outright ownership and disposal rights of their property, but requiring workers who purchase their housing at cost to live in the property for at least five years before they can dispose of it.[83]

Simultaneous with encouraging the sale of public housing, the state experimented in Beijing, Chengdu, Ningbo, and Yantai with a more comprehensive housing reform system supported by a World Bank loan. The idea is to integrate the development of joint-stock real estate companies to build, sell and lease apartments with the development of a mortgage market, and the rationalization of rent and wages according to market criteria.[84] In cities such as Shanghai, a public providence fund for housing has been established since 1991, capitalized by workers' contributions. In 1996, the fund lent over 667 million yuan to work units and real estate developers to build houses and 66.2 million yuan to workers to finance their purchase of apartments.[85]

In conclusion, despite the ideological obstacles to the development of private property ownership, people's confidence in the ownership right of real estate has spurred the construction of private housing everywhere. It seems clear that the structural obstacles to the privatization of urban housing caused the slower pace of property ownership in the cities than in the countryside. But that has to do with price distortion because of heavy subsidies of workers' housing in the urban areas rather than people's lack of confidence in ownership rights. The state has played an active role in encouraging the development of a private market for housing with the introduction of a legal framework to protect property transactions as well as financial instruments to facilitate the development of real estate. This culminated in the enshrinement of private property rights in the constitutional amendment by the National People's Congress in 1999. Privatization of public housing is not yet effective because it requires income and wage reform, which the state has not mustered enough political capital to implement.

D. Foreign Investment

Few measures in economic reform are more risky to the regime's political legitimacy than opening the country to foreign direct investment (FDI). All the concessions, incentives, and investment subsidies offered to foreign capitalists seemed contradictory to the Chinese ideology of self-sufficiency and anti-imperialism.[86] In her authoritative study of foreign joint ventures in China in the period 1979-1988, Margaret Pearson shows that the government has been effective at implementing a number of specific controls (e.g., foreign exchange, repatriation of profits, maintenance of social benefits) and at negotiating favorable terms on a case-by-case basis (e.g., access to all research and development information in the transnational's home office for the duration of the joint venture). She found that the government's interest in attracting foreign investment for the purpose of economic modernization and development was balanced by the desire to protect the country from foreign domination.[87] But when such controls became detrimental to the inflow of foreign investment, the government was able and willing to make gradual and orderly adjustment without forfeiting its ultimate sovereign authority, as in the move toward the gradual convertibility of the renminbi in 1996, or the approval of what joint ventures would be established.[88]

The purpose for attracting FDI in the first place had been to import modern technology and management to enhance the economy. Toward such end, the Chinese government had offered generous concessions, such as tax holidays, accelerated depreciation allowances, and investment allowances, to attract FDI to critical industries such as chemicals, electrical engineering, motor vehicles, information-based technologies, and hotels even though politically it was risky for the government to do so. Hong Kong, Taiwan, Japan, and the United States are the major sources of FDI in China.[89] It has been estimated that China's market size, growth potential, inexpensive labor costs, and political stability are the primary reasons for foreign direct investment in China and elsewhere.

Studies have shown that before 1992, the majority of FDI from Hong Kong and Macau tended to be channeled to small-size business in labor-intensive and low-wage industries such as clothing, textiles, and electronic assembly, bringing little technology and research and development information with them.[90] Since 1992, as the government has significantly improved the foreign investment environment by promulgating laws that clarify ownership issues, deregulating many well-protected industries, and removing foreign exchange control, large multinationals with moderate and, in fewer cases, advanced technology have begun to invest in China. By the end of 1996, foreign investors began to shift into the infrastructural sector and are now allowed to own equity in roads, local railways, and power stations.[91]

The impact of FDI on local employment is a more complex issue. In many cases, foreign joint ventures were established on the base of previous SOEs, and tended to draw the best skilled manpower from existing SOEs. In such cases, FDI did not create employment but did not create unemployment either, because many SOEs are saddled with labor redundancy. In the case of Guangdong province, about 1 million people were employed in all FDI activities by the end of 1987; in Fujian province, 2.1 million workers were employed by foreign investment enterprises at the end of 1993. These employment levels suggest that FDI did not create significant employment but did not impoverish the labor market either, as critics claim.[92] For this reason, while there was occasional labor unrest related to the foreign investment enterprise's management practice of foreign invested enterprises (especially those managed by Koreans and Taiwanese), there is never widespread labor resentment against FDI.

Finally, the effectiveness of FDI should also be measured against its ability to enhance foreign exchange earnings, or at least balance their foreign exchange requirements, so that China's priority programs can be financed. The impact of FDI on China's total foreign trade has grown significantly since 1990. Its share among the national trade increased from 25% in 1992 to 37% in 1994. More significantly however is the increase in the FDI's share of the country's total exports. It has increased from 0.82% in 1984 to 16.90% in 1990.[93] The share of FDI inflows as a percentage of gross domestic capital formation has also increased, from 0.4% in 1980-82 to 4.9% in 1992.[94] However, the effects of some foreign investment enterprises on the net foreign exchange balance remained negative because of an influx of capital-goods imports necessary to support them. More worrisome is the rising level of imported nonessential consumer goods.

This section then demonstrates that while FDI was not seen as legitimate in the mid-1980s, it is now widely accepted. Moreover, in spite of the politically sensitive issue of FDI, not only has the direction of foreign investment moved to targeted industries and priority projects desired by the government, but the overall effect has been positive. The increase in FDI is faciliated by an increasingly transparent legal infrastructure put in place by the state.

V. CONCLUSION

Taken together, reform measures in the four politically sensitive areas did not achieve all their objectives, yet what I have tried to show here is that the state has given them credibility by instituting the rule of law to build participants' confidence in them. That there are now some genuinely competitive local elections that help economic growth in some areas, financial institutions capable of controlling investment and inflation, private ownership of property, greater integration with the global economy, and more effective use of foreign capital speaks for the effectiveness of economic reform. Their institutionalization has been facilitated by a legal framework which, however imperfect, has given the regime the rightful authority it seeks.

In areas not examined in this paper, such as civil service reform, legal reform, and the restructuring of state-owned enterprises, there is increasing transparency to such an extent that villagers in China have exercised what Kevin O'Brien called "rightful resistance" to defend their lawful rights and interests.[95] Without laws that provide authorized channels to lodge complaints, and without the regime's transparent policies and legitimating myths to back their claims, such defiance of officials could not have happened.

Even more revealing about increased autonomy as a result of economic reform is a national survey of Chinese local government officials conducted by the National Structural Reform Commission published in 1996[96]: 66.6% of respondents agreed that economic reform has expanded the autonomy of enterprises, especially regarding the retention of profits after tax, import and export, and product and personnel decisions; 49% of respondents believed that there is less friction between government and enterprises after economic reform whereas 24.8% said there was increased conflict. Although 83.9% of the respondents believed that the central government has a major role to play in establishing "a socialist market economy," 65% of respondents put restructuring of government organization as the most important thing in changing the administrative relationship between central government and enterprises. Last but not least, given a choice to identify the ten most serious problems with enterprise reform, almost 77.4% of respondents identified the lack of a social security system as the most serious problem, followed by obscure property rights (52.4%).[97]

The responses from people with responsibility for implementing economic reform confirm the urgency for the rule of law to be established to clarify property rights. But for a regime that has no Chinese vocabulary for "legitimacy," but only "authority" (*quanwei*), the idea of authority based on law (*hefade quanwei*) is a significant step forward.[98] Ad hoc market reform thus far seems to have the effect of moving China toward a legal-rational basis of legitimacy, even though the leaders thought ideological justification of reform measures should take primacy. The rule of law that is designed to remove some uncertainties in a specific area has the cumulative effect of expanding the domain of autonomy for more and more people and organizations. For a country that has only emerged in 1978 from a planned economy and Marxist-Leninist-Maoist orthodoxy, even these legal skeletons are significant achievements.

Critics of China's human rights record have largely ignored these improvements in the rule of law in the political economy. Whether the rule of law in the economic sphere can be divorced from the rule of law in political freedom cannot be settled by this chapter. This is not to not say that human rights are unimportant for the future legitimacy of China. Indeed, it can be argued that unless the laws are enforced with impartiality and speed, the legitimacy of the regime (and the reform associated with it) is still fragile. But just as holding down inflation and maintaining employment have won public support for reform from the very beginning, in the second stage of economic reform, the cumulative effect of building such legal infrastructure has given market reform and the officials who support it credibility. The expanded political space for both government officials at the lower levels and the citizen-participants cushioned the regime from difficulties when the economy turned sour in the mid-1980s and again in 1988–89, 1994–95, and 1998–99. While there are losers in every case, those negatively affected are not concentrated in any particular sector or region, and hence lack the power or incentive to organize their opposition to reform and to the regime itself. This chapter tries to show that the basis of legitimacy for post-Mao China is built not on economic performance, but on the institutions that require fine-tuning. The effectiveness of these new institutions is particularly apparent compared with conditions prior to reform. Fortunately for the government, the people who live in China have longer memories than critics of the regime outside of China to know and appreciate the differences.

ACKNOWLEDGMENTS

The author gratefully acknowledges the generous support from the Professional Development Fund by Earlham College to carry out research at the Universities Service Centre, Chinese University of Hong Kong for this paper. I am particularly indebted to Michael K. Ipson, Kuan Hsin Chi, and Stan Rosen for their very thoughtful and detailed comments on my earlier drafts. For helpful suggestions, I want to thank Mary Comerford, Jean Hung, and Anne Klineman.

ENDNOTES

1. Huntington, S. *The Third Wave*. Oklahoma City: University of Oklahoma Press, 1991, p 46.
2. In 1986, Stephen White took issue with the contention by such scholars as Richard Lowenthal and Marshall Goldman that Communist regimes were in serious legitimacy crisis because of a deterioration in economic performance. White ventured the idea that while lacking electoral legitimacy, these regimes made use of what he called ''mechanisms of adaption'' to process citizens' demands, expand their consultative capacities, and give them a stake in the system so as to preempt demands for far reaching changes. Needless to say, White's thesis is rendered historically obso-

lete, but his contribution is to offer a counterintuitive analysis of the relationship between economic performance and political legitimacy by asking us not to consider politics as dependent on economics. See Stephen White ''Economic Performance and Communist Legitimacy'' in *World Politics* (No. 3, 1986), pp 462–482.

3. See for instance Jurgen Habermas, ''What Does a Crisis Mean Today? Legitimation Problems in Late Capitalism'' in *Social Research*, Vol. 40 (1983), pp 643–647; and Keith Middlemas, *Politics in Industrial Society* (North Pomfret, VT: Trafalgar Square Publishing Co., 1980), Chapter 15.
4. Dahrendorf, R. Effectiveness and legitimacy: on the 'governability' of democracies. *Political Quarterly*, October-December 1980, pp. 393–410, reprinted in Roy Macridis and Bernard Brown, *Comparative Politics, Notes and Readings*, 6th ed. Homewood, IL: Dorsey Press, 1986, p 396.
5. I think Stephen White is wrong to suggest that Weber gave no direct attention to socioeconomic performance or ''social eudaemonic'' legitimation. See White, p 463. I acknowledge my source from Rodney Barker, *Political Legitimacy and the State* (Oxford, UK: Clarendon Press, 1990), p 49.
6. *Ibid.*, p 49. Barker argues that while the three types of domination are the inherent characteristics of government, involving ''the acknowledgment by those subject to and accepting authority, that the person or institutions exercising that authority are possessed of some special quality,'' it is not ''the case with the authority of substantive policies, which can be subject to constant scrutiny by the subject, whose judgment as to their inherent worth and efficient implementation is as good as that of anyone else'' (*Ibid.*, pp 50–51).
7. Barker, 1990, p 93.
8. Dahrendorf, R. (in Macridis and Brown, 1986, p 384).
9. *Ibid.*, p 384.
10. Dahrendorf, 1986, p 385.
11. Pauly, L.W. *Who Elected the Bankers? Surveillance and Control in the World Economy*. Ithaca and London: Cornell University Press, 1997, p 13.
12. *Ibid.*, p 15.
13. Huntington, *op. cit.*, p 48. Huntington, together with Jorge I. Dominquez, also offered a classification of legitimacy for modern states based on competitive election, revolution, and nationalism. The overlap between theirs and Weber's is evident, even though they emphasize a well-developed ideology rather than charisma as central to a modern revolutionary state. See Samuel P. Huntington and Jorge I. Dominquez, ''Political Development'' in *Handbook of Political Science, Macropolitical Theory* Vol. III. Reading, MA: Addison-Wesley, 1975, p 49.
14. Nathan A.J. and Ross, R.S. *The Great Wall and the Empty Fortress, China's Search for Security*. New York: W.W. Norton, 1997, pp 75, 154–155.
15. Madsen, R. *China and the American Dream, A Moral Inquiry*. Berkeley: University of California Press, 1995. Madsen argued that Americans have three ''myths'' about China. One is the liberal myth of China as troubled modernizer, another is China as Red menace as seen from the right; the third myth is China as revolutionary redeemer as seen by radical intellectuals in the 1960s. (pp 28–29).
16. Kaminski, B. *The Collapse of State Socialism*. Princeton, NJ: Princeton University Press, 1991, p 23.

17. Haggard, S. and Kaufman, R.R. *The Political Economy of Democratic Transitions*. Princeton, NJ: Princeton University Press, 1995, p 325.
18. *Ibid*., p 327. They refer to the economic recession in the 1980s and early 1990s, but the Asian financial crisis is even more severe than those.
19. Chen, F. *Economic Transition and Political Legitimacy in Post-Mao China: Ideology and Reform*. Albany: State University of New York Press, 1995.
20. Chen, F. *Ibid*., pp 198–200.
21. Ding, X.L. *The Decline of Communism in China: Legitimacy Crisis, 1977–1989*. London: Cambridge University Press, 1994.
22. *Ibid*., pp 200–201. Ding offers the concept ''institutional parasitism'' to replace the then in-vogue dichotomy between state and civil society, which Ding thinks are misleading analytical concepts for explaining the collapse of former Communist regimes. Institutional parasitism is characterized by fluid or indeterminate boundaries between the public and the private spheres, and the dependence of many nominally autonomous organizations on the Communist party for resources and appointees. Ding thinks the ''amphibious'' nature of these state institutions makes them susceptible for co-optation by the counterelites (i.e., the professionals and intellectuals) when the center is weak (see pp 77–79).
23. *Ibid*., pp 136–137.
24. *Ibid*., pp 79–80, 198–199.
25. *Ibid*., p 79.
26. Shambough, D. Losing control: the erosion of state authority in China. *Current History* (September 1993), pp 253–259.
27. Walder, A., ed. *The Waning of the Communist State: Economic origins of Political Decline in China and Hungary*. Berkeley: University of California Press, 1995 (especially Chapter 1).
28. Huang, Y. *Inflation and Investment Controls in China: The Political Economy of Central-Local Relations During the Reform Era*. London: Cambridge University Press, 1996.
29. Tao-chiu, L. Review of *The Waning of the Communist State: Economic Origins of Political Decline in China and Hungary*. edited by Andrew G. Walder. (Berkeley: University of California Press, 1995) in *China Journal* No. 37, January 1997, p 124.
30. Naughton, B. *Growing Out of Plan: Chinese Economic Reform 1978–1993*. London: Cambridge University Press, 1996, pp 94–95.
31. *Ibid*., p 135.
32. *Ibid*., pp 135–136.
33. *Ibid*., Chapter 4, especially pp 147–158.
34. *Ibid*., pp 168–169.
35. *Ibid*., pp 175–176.
36. *Ibid*., Chapter 6.
37. *Ibid*., p 243.
38. *Ibid*., p 309.
39. *Ibid*., p 310.
40. Shirk, S. *The Political Logic of Economic Reform in China*. Berkeley: University of California Press, 1993, p 150–196.

41. Shirk, S. *How China Opened Its Door: The Political Success of the PRC's Foreign Trade and Investment Reforms*. Washington: Brookings Institution, 1994, pp 6–7.
42. Naughton, *op. cit.*, p 310.
43. Oi, J. Economic development, stability and democratic village self-governance. In *China Review 1996* edited by M. Brosseau, S. Pepper, and T. Shu-ki. Hong Kong: Chinese University Press, 1996, pp 131, 134–135.
44. Melloan, G. China's Communists find beauty in local elections. *Asian Wall Street Journal*, July 22, 1997.
45. Oi, *op. cit.*, p 132.
46. Melloan, *op. cit.*
47. Oi, *op. cit.*, p 137.
48. *Ibid.*
49. Melloan, *op. cit.*
50. The best exposition of the failure of financial reform is Nicholas Lardy's *China's Unfinished Economic Revolution* (Washington: Brookings Institution, 1998). Also see *The Chinese Economy: Fighting Inflation, Deepening Reforms* (World Bank, 1996), p ix.
51. *China's Non-Bank Financial Institutions, Trust and Investment Companies*. World Bank discussion paper No. 358, 1997, pp 19–21.
52. Lardy, N. *China's Unfinished Economic Revolution*. Washington, DC: Brookings Institution Press, 1998, Chapter 3, ''The Evolving Banking System.''
53. *Ibid.*, pp 26–27.
54. *Ibid.*, p 235.
55. *Ibid.*, pp 93–96, 168.
56. Much of the controversy over the health of the Chinese banking system stems from the inability of some analysts to distinguish between nonperforming loans and unrecoverable loans. Raymond Blanchard, an analyst in Hong Kong who submitted a study of Chinese banks for the U.S. embassy in Beijing, is reported in the *Wall Street Journal* (May 12, 1997) to have argued that the collapse of one or two big banks could dash Chinese hopes for prosperity because the total financial losses could be more than 20% of China's GDP.
57. Beijing tackles bad loans. *South China Morning Post, April 27, 1999*. The first bad-debt management company, China Cinda Asset Management, will take over more than 200 billion yuan of nonperforming loans from China Construction Bank.
58. PBOC claws back powers to direct Mainland markets. *South China Morning Post*, July 10, 1997.
59. World Bank, *The Chinese Economy*, p 4.
60. World Bank, *The Chinese Economy*, 1996, p 9.
61. Macro Restructuring Research Department, State Council Research Center. An overview of reform of the financial sector. *Jingji Yanjiu Cankao*, No. 1002, Jan. 4, 1997, p 3.
62. *Ibid.*, pp 3–4.
63. *Ibid.*, p 15.
64. See Feng Chen, *op. cit.*, Chapters 4–6 on the official reformulation of concepts dealing with contract responsibility in the countryside, reforming state ownership, and extending the urban private economy.

65. Chen, op. cit., p 76. After individual household contract (IHC) was widely implemented, it was rationalized ideologically as a new type of collective economy, characterized by combining public ownership of the land with totally individualized operation of production. Yet, in order to build peasants' confidence in the IHC, because peasants did not respond to the short-term land use contract, some local authorities stipulated no time limitation at all in the land use contract. Eventually, land use can hardly be distinguished from land ownership, and the Party has to confront the thorny problem of privatization of land, which challenged the fundamental principle of the Communist party. So even though IHC was not initially intended to change property relations, it ended up having such effect. See Feng, 1995, pp 82–84.
66. Hung, J. A Survey and Recommendation on Farmland Protection and Land Tenureship in China (*Geng Di Bao Hu Yu Tu Di Cheng Bao Zhi De Kao Cha Yu Jian Yi*). Unpublished manuscript, 1997, p 3.
67. *Ibid.*
68. *Ibid.*, p 2.
69. *China Daily*, July 11, 1997.
70. *Ibid.*
71. Naughton, *op. cit.*, pp 144–161. Also see Qin Hui, "Reform and the Loss of Collective Property: A study of the Privatization of China's Township and Village Enterprises (TVEs)" (*Gaige Yu Jiti Zichan Liushi: Zhong Guo Xiang Zhen Qiye Siyou Hua Anli Yanjiu*), unpublished manuscript, 1997, who summarized the controversy about TVEs in this way: Skeptics thought TVEs were another form of state-owned enterprises set up by local governments to create employment in rural areas. Supporters on the other hand have praised TVEs as the triumph of local entrepreneurship, others hail them as exemplifying the superiority of collectivism. Postmodernists looked at them as an affirmation of the nonurban road to development, and post-Fordists look at them as a superior alternative to the assembly-line method of production (p 5).
72. Naughton, *op. cit.*, pp 156–157.
73. In an article by Huang Mingcai of the research department of Ningbo General Trade Unions, the author lamented the auctioning off of TVEs to original factory directors by local government supervisory departments without competitive bidding. See *Dangdai Sichao*, No. 2, 1997, p 31. Also see Qin Hui, *op. cit.*, p 18.
74. *Dangdai Sichao*, No. 2, 1997, Table 1.
75. Protect the continued healthy development of township and village enterprise. *Renda Gong Zuo Tongxun*, No. 3 (Feb. 1997), pp 15–17.
76. *Ibid.*, p 17.
77. *Yearbook of Chinese Real Estate Market 1996 (Zhong Guo Fangdi Chengshi Niangjian)*, p 659.
78. *Ibid.*, p 659.
79. Chinese Academy of Social Science Research Institute. Basic ideas and policy research on reform of urban housing system. *Jingji Yenjia Cankao*, No. 1010, Jan. 29, 1997, p 11.
80. *Ibid.* According to the report, Nanjing has failed to implement privatization of public housing by March of 1996, and the early implementation of housing reform in Wenzhou led to chaotic adjustment in wages and rent that caused much public resentment.

81. *Jingji Yenjia Cankao, Jan*. 29, 1997, p 6.
82. *Yearbook of Chinese Real Estate Market*, 1996, p 662.
83. *Yearbook of Chinese Real Estate Market*, 1996, p 663.
84. *Yearbook of Chinese Real Estate Market*, 1998, p 113.
85. *Ibid*., p 18.
86. Wang, Z.Q. *Foreign Investment and Economic Development in Hungary and China*. Aldershot, U.K.: Avebury, 1995, p 300.
87. Pearson, M.M. *Joint Ventures in the People's Republic of China: The Control of Foreign Direct Investment Under Socialism*. Princeton, NJ: Princeton University Press, 1991, pp 201–203, 213.
88. *Ibid*., p 202.
89. Wang, *op. cit*., p 300.
90. *Ibid*., 115. Huang, Y. *FDI in China, An Asian Perspective*. Hong Kong: Chinese University Press, 1998, p 19.
91. Wang, *op. cit*., p 115; Huang, *op. cit*., pp 71–72.
92. Wang, *op. cit*., pp 218–219.
93. Wang, Z.Q. Exports by FIEs in China 1984–94 (1995, 220).
94. Huang, 1998, Table 2.3, p 21.
95. O'Brien, K.J. Rightful resistance. *World Politics*, *49*(1), 33–35, 1996.
96. Consolidated Survey Report of Chinese Local Government Officials in *Zhongguo Zhengzhi* (*Chinese Politics*), No. 7 (July 1996), pp 41–50. The survey was conducted in 69 cities with a return rate of 95%. It was designed to tap into (1) the changing relationship between government and enterprises, (2) the perceived problems with government administration and the changing functions of central government, (3) local perception of reform benefits, and (4) knowledge of local officials about modern enterprise management system. Since some of the responses were not at all flattering, there is no reason to doubt the authenticity of the survey.
97. *Zhongguo Zhengzhi 7*, 46–47, 1996.
98. Numerous Chinese publications in the past two years have emphasized on the rule of law in economic reform. See for instance *Shi Chang Jing Ji Shi Fa Zhi Jing Ji (Market Economy Is Law-Governed Economy)* published by Tianjin, China: The Tianjin People's Press, 1995.

13

Implications of Reform in the Chinese State-Owned Enterprises

Yat Lun Chan
University of Aberdeen, Old Aberdeen, Scotland

Feng Xiao and Alex Kelvin
University of Hertfordshire, Hertford, England

I. INTRODUCTION

The aim of this chapter is to assess how successfully state-owned enterprises are reformed and reengineered. Profound transformation of state-owned enterprises (SOEs) in China is part and parcel of all-embracing economic reform which includes integration of China into the world economy, monetary policy to maintain employment and balance of payments in equilibrium, currency convertibility, exchange rate determination and management (Lau 1998), redesigning the banking sector (Zhu 1997), a better blend in private and public provision of goods and services (Briand and Kelvin 1997, 1998a; Chan and Kelvin 1998), promotion of stock exchanges and use of international capital markets (Xiao and Kelvin 1998), development of high-tech industries and establishment of venture capital mechanisms, foreign direct investment, bridging the gaps between the Chinese and international accounting systems, and improved taxation.

Prior to 1978, the allocation of resources to production units was highly centralized. Neglect of market mechanism resulted in lack of adjustment to evolving demand. The state administrative agencies were in charge of routine production activities, and enterprises lacked decision-making power. Rigid control over distribution of products resulted in considerable losses. All profits were transferred to the state. Therefore, the managers had no incentives for improvements, and declining productivity in the SOEs was widespread. Finally, there was no national welfare system outside of enterprises. The workers were guaranteed life-long employment and fixed wages irrespective of results, i.e., so-called iron rice bowls.

The initial Multiple Layer Management System was based on central government ownership. It granted production rights to ministries—metallurgy, transport, etc. Subsequently, these rights were transferred to the relevant supervisory departments which assigned these rights and management to enterprises under mandatory planning. That system had excessive levels of subordination with poorly defined property rights. These drawbacks generated high agency costs. Absence of direct relationship between remuneration and performance created ground for opportunistic behavior. Serious cumulative information asymmetries did arise. To secure employment the government subsidized SOEs and made the state banks provide them with credits on favorable terms. Under the soft budget constraint there was a bias toward overinvestment. Risks arising from the SOEs were transferred to the central government. This discouraged improvements in performance.

Therefore the Contract Responsibility System was implemented in 1983 in almost all SOEs and farms. The Open-Door Policy attracted foreign investors. Joint ventures and mergers were encouraged. The Bankruptcy Law of 1986 made provisions for closure of loss-making SOEs and reallocation of labor. The large public conglomerates narrowed down their productive activities and became more concerned with quality than quantitative output. Today most SOEs are willing to invest into subsidiaries or associated companies rather than to expand their own activities. This brings down costs and reduces the tax bill. Therefore the reform of SOEs helps to make them more efficient and contributes to the rapid development of private industries (Xie 1991). Over 15 years till the mid-1990s, the average economic growth was close to 10%. The industrial growth averaged 13.5% and rose over 20% in 1992-93. Domestic savings were within 34% to 41% range. Foreign direct investment was particularly active in the light industry (Byrd 1992). Export-driven growth was amplified through multiplier and accelerator effects, boosting economic growth.

But compared to economic success elsewhere, the SOEs, the banking and monetary sectors have been lagging behind. To prevent the long-term social impact of labor shedding, subsiding of loss-making SOEs continues. Due to a policy of "soft loans" to ailing SOEs, the "policy banks" have accumulated estimated losses from nonperforming loans equivalent to US $155 billion (Zhu et al. 1997). State bank credits covered about a quarter of the losses. The remaining three-quarters of losses used to be covered by direct government subsidies. This exacerbates deficit financing and adds to macroeconomic instability. There seem to be two confluent ways to solve the problems of SOEs, i.e., to lower their share in total industrial production, and to improve their efficiency.

II. THEORETICAL METHOD

The analytical core is based on the theories of complexity, property rights, principal-agent, and X-efficiency. These theories are interdependent and appropriate to the topic.

A. Complexity Theory

SOEs are complex adaptive systems. It is assumed that they perform best in the intermediary zone between order and chaos (Fig. 1). In Zone One of excessive restrictions organizational structures become unnecessarily stiff. Therefore the firms cannot keep up with changes which amplify uncertainty and ambiguity. Neither can they create or shape environment. Zone Three is of intense volatility where organizations tend to degenerate out of control. The intermediary Zone Two blends features of order and chaos (Medio 1992). It possesses several interesting properties such as nonequilibrium state, random behavior, and irregular hidden pattern. Since deviations from the path are limited, the pattern breeds desirable outcomes which are randomly generated (Stacey 1992). The very nature

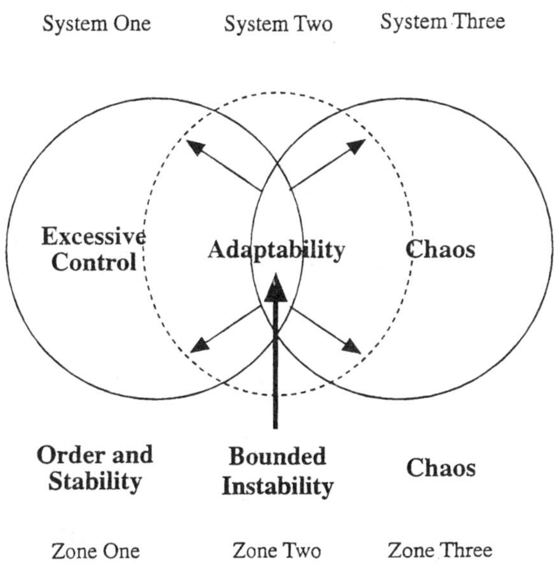

Figure 1 Complexity: three zones of activity. Expansion of Adaptable Systems Capitalizing on Bounded Instability

of instability appears essential to open up the organizations to new thinking and innovative forms of behavior. Stacey (1992) proposes a two-stage approach: (1) weaken constraints; (2) devise adaptable systems which generate desirable outcomes. The shift tends to make behavior more adaptable but at the same time more disorderly. The organizations are becoming more accommodating and more unstable. Within the zone of bounded instability, the systems are highly sensitive to small changes in environment. Managers have to develop new original mental models to confront new situations. Instability, disorder, and conflict are considered necessary to generate new perspectives (Waldorp 1992). But managers strive to reduce the unpredictability of future changes.

However, corporations face a dilemma. On the one hand, efficiency requires formal task division and streamlining of production within centralized control. On the other hand, innovative atmosphere favors informal channels of communication, dispersion of authority, and division of organization into autonomous or independent units. Decision making has to become more open and diffused involving numerous participants because no one holds enough knowledge. Expression of original and diverse proposals is encouraged. As a consequence, one has to expect and accept low consensus (Shammaki 1995). The purpose is to achieve cooperative behavior resulting in synergy. This duality requires a new perspective on control and a new distribution of authority (Wiggins 1990). The question is, How can managerial control over intended outcomes be assured under more unstable conditions?

The very nature of instability makes it hard to keep organizations in Zone Two. They tend to slide further rightward to increasing instability. Organizational structure becomes sufficiently fragmented so that differentiated learning in groups can occur. However, improved individual and group skills contribute to creation of exceptionally well-trained pools of human resources. If personal relations in companies become too tense, some members leave. Such changes can be regarded as parts of natural cycle which can be compared with the swinging pendulum of a clock. When organizations reach their limit of chaos, they would reverse the movement. Changes have to be designed and implemented in the reallocation of property rights. The outcome should be effectual and result in new ethos, new products and processes, and new organizational structures and communications patterns.

B. Property Rights Theory

Property rights entitle the owners to residual income, after costs of activities have been covered. This residual is an important incentive for efficiency and low production cost. Assignments of property rights affect motivation and behavior of economic actors. Incomplete contracts create principal-agent problems, make monitoring difficult, and result in inefficiency. The higher the value of rights relative to the costs of specifying them, the greater the attempted clarity (Furubotn et al. 1974).

The stronger the enforcement of property rights, the closer the relationship between the welfare of owners and the economic consequences of their decisions; i.e., economic considerations dominate decision making. The principals monitor the rate of return and adjust incentives for personnel. Attenuation of property rights implies limitations of the owners' rights either to change the assets or to transfer their rights. Restrictions affect the owners' expectations about their uses, value, and terms of trade (Linyu 1995).

The consumers' goodwill determines capitalization which is based on future earning capacity. Lack of transferability of public assets prevents the capitalization of future consequences of decisions (Lee 1993). While threats of bankruptcy and takeover are obviated for public enterprises, managerial discretion appears to be high. The property rights theory suggests that the public sector fails either in the provision of appropriate *incentives* or in the *monitoring* of performance. Managers would perform only at the level necessary to meet the minimum performance standards (Aharoni 1986).

C. Agency Theory

The principal-agent theory aims at increasing the overlap of interests for the stakeholders (Aharoni 1982; Jensen 1976). The normative approach applies mathematical models to explore the incentive systems and risk allocation systems. The positive approach investigates the shareholding arrangements. The main concepts of the positive approach are the agency effect, the agency cost, and the systems to reduce agency costs. The agency effect incorporates the division effect and the scale effect. The division effect means separating economic units, each possessing a different set of skills and abilities to perform various tasks. Such specialization results in higher satisfaction and more efficient production. The scale effect means that an economic unit would obtain marginal utility proportionately higher than an increase in output. The higher the scale effect, the higher the efficiency. The agency cost arises from contractual relationships between the principals and agents. This includes the expenses of drawing up and enforcing contracts and of moral hazard and transaction costs. Agency costs are major determinants of how firms are organized and how their staff is remunerated (Lee 1994). They determine motivation and explain performance. Agents are maximizing their self-interest. Such behavior is hard to discover when information asymmetry exists. However, without information asymmetry, the agents' behavior is easily observable. Most of the visible motives for opportunism would be covered by the mechanism of incentives and penalties. The unobservable behavior of the agents and the information asymmetry of the principals cause the noncooperative behavior and inefficiency, which are attributed to moral hazard and adverse selection. Moral hazard refers to the lack of effort on the part of the agents. Adverse selection refers to misinterpreting the managerial abilities (Eisenhardt 1989). The agency cost can be reduced by internal and external mechanisms. The former refers to well-defined contracts specifying responsibilities, rights, obligations and the peer pressures. The latter means that the market exerts external competitive pressures on the managers to be more efficient.

D. X-Efficiency

The X-efficiency theory suggests various degrees of rationality depending on individual interests which are not identical to those of the firm. It incorporates several concepts such as psychological elevation and effort (Tolstoy 1904), X-efficiency (Leibenstein 1978), and internalities (Arrow 1974; Wolf 1988). Tolstoy's contribution is in focusing on psychological elevation and effort as main inputs in achieving the goal in the war situation. He discovered the sources of internal inspiration, translated created motivation into effort, and converted effort into high-quality performance leading to desirable outcomes. Leibenstein used Tolstoy's concepts to formulate the new microfoundations of modern economics and developed comprehensive and systematic analytical framework. In Leibenstein's vision, performance of all factors is intrinsically unstable. People and organizations commonly work with a slack; i.e., efforts and outputs can be optimal only in exceptional circumstances. *X-inefficiency* is defined as degree to which actual output or other productivity indicators are less than their theoretically optimal levels. Effort is defined as an important variable input which determines outcomes to a large extent. Effort explains differences in performance among the individuals, the companies, and the countries.

Arrow (1974) calls the structures of rewards and penalties *internalities*. Remuneration and other quantifiable costs and benefits, which are reflected in contracts and corporate accounts, form only a subset of variables in the utility functions of economic actors. This quantifiable part can be called *tangible internalities*. However, corporate culture and individual expectations for self-actualization are largely implicit. They can be called *intangible internalities*. Wolf (1988) explicitly links internalities to the pursuit of individual goals within an organization. Such goals provide motives for individual behavior and explain team and organizational performance. The main task of the principals is to involve the employees in the pursuit of official objectives.

The assessment method is based on the following postulates. People and organizations work with a slack, and their efforts become elevated and synergetic only in exceptional circumstances. Production function is only partly specified due to the inherent complexity of the work force, incomplete contracts, and specification of input requirements in bands. Flexible nature of production functions and qualitative decision making leave important discretionary choices to the staff.

The divisional or corporate results depend on the sequence, pace, length, and portfolio of activities, and are to an extent indeterminate, because human efforts are unstable and variable. Organizational efficiency depends on patterns of information, channels of communication, and amounts of energy needed for making and implementing decisions. If improvements are possible but are considered not worth of the effort, inertia prevents changes (Leibenstein 1976:111). In times of gestation, challenges become increasingly novel and require creative solutions, learning, and development of new skills (Waeiermair 1990). Knowledge of internalities can be used to design compensation packages to increase contribution to corporate objectives. The key point is that the staff members cannot be reduced to the role of passive bystanders; they are actively shaping corporate destiny. They find equilibrium positions which accommodate their interests and balance their efforts against corporate expectations. Individual motivation and efforts depend on the inner drive, peers' expectations, organizational culture, and external contestability. Corporate performance results from individual efforts and activities.

III. SEPARATION OF OWNERSHIP AND MANAGEMENT IN THE SOES

Following introduction of the Contract Responsibility System, direct interference from the government departments was replaced by periodic assessments (Xie 1991). The purpose of removing at least some constraints was to improve adaptability and to boost creativity and innovative behavior. But ownership still remained under state control. The incentive systems attempted to relate remuneration to performance. Therefore, a certain amount of agency costs, generated by moral hazard, was reduced (Yeung 1995).

A. Separation of Ownership and Management

The Diversified Ownership Separate from Management (DOSM) stepped up instability so that individuals could brainstorm the roadblocks and come out with solutions. People became able to invest in traded shares according to their expectations and preferences. Under combined effect of contestable pressures and monitoring by the shareholders, agency costs were further reduced. The flotation of shares enhanced the division effect; i.e., each unit tends to specialize and achieve higher satisfaction. It also intensified the scale effect; i.e., marginal utilities obtained become proportionately higher than the increase in size of economic activities. Organizations are becoming more accommodating but simultaneously more unstable. Corporate performance is reflected in stock prices. Therefore, those with low performance would attract less investment. Feedback loops would contribute to improved efficiency and competitiveness. At this stage of reform Linyu (1995) and Chan (1996) propose a Transitory Unified Management System.

B. Transitory Unified Management System

In this framework, the agency relationships are structured (1) between the central government and a certain number of shareholding groups, (2) between the shareholding corporate groups and separate enterprises, (3) between individuals and enterprises, and (4) between individuals and the central government. Each public industry would set up several shareholding groups to be responsible for the supervision and operation of member firms. Shares can be issued and sold to the public in the name of member firms. Prices of traded shares will reflect objective valuation of each firm's performance. Reciprocal holding of shares can reduce mutual risk. It is assumed that ability of firms to survive in the changing environment can be enhanced.

Although China introduced new Accounting Regulations for Foreign Investment Enterprises (ARFIE) in 1992, there are still deviations from the International Accounting Standards (IAS). See Table 1. For example, the IAS require disclosure of accounting policies. In the ARFIE policies should be consistent and changes in accounting methods should be reported. Long-term investment and contingencies are not specified under ARFIE. The disparities discourage international investors from entering the market. B shares for foreign investors are traded at about 66% of A shares value in Shanghai (Xiao and Kelvin 1998).

IV. CASE STUDY—MAANSHAN IRON AND STEEL LIMITED COMPANY (MIS)

This large corporation is representative of China' iron and steel industry. It is one of the first large SOEs whose shares were floated. Its progress would be indicative for promotion of the shareholding system in medium and small SOEs. Since 1978 three reform stages were implemented: organizational and managerial restructuring, introduction of the Contract Responsiblity System, and the introduction of shareholding.

A. Organizational and Mangerial Restructuring

Three levels of organizational structure are examined: factory, workshop, and team. At the factory production plans are formulated, schedules are coordinated. Workshops set production quotas, provide technical conditions for production, improve quality of products, ensure safety regulations. Daily output schedules

Table 1 Comparison of International and Chinese Accounting Standards

Accounting issue	International accounting standards	Standards under the accounting regulations for foreign investment enterprises
Receivables	Provision for bad and doubtful debts is required	Provision is required within 3% of the year-end balance. Write-off of bad debts is permitted
Inventories	Lower of cost and net realizable value; first-in, first-out; weighted average; specific identification; and last-in, first-out methods. Provision for damaged, slow-moving, and obsolete goods	Inventories are valued at cost. First-in, first-out; last-in, first-out; weighted average; and moving average methods are used. Provision is allowed, subject to approval. Shortage, obsolescence, or damages should be accounted for in the current year's profit and loss accounts
Property, plant, and equipment	Asset valuation is at historical or updated cost. Provision for loss in fixed assets value. Income statement shows maintenance expenses	Assets should normally be valued at historical cost
Depreciation	Depreciation is calculated on the basis of historical cost, useful life, and residual value. Straight-line and accelerated methods	Estimated residual value is generally not less than 10% of original cost. Methods include straight-line and production output. Accelerated depreciation may be used subject to approval
Intangible assets: Preoperating expenses	Setup costs are charged to the income statement. Deferral is only allowed if commercial viability is reasonably assured	Preoperating expenses are amortized in equal installments over a period of not less than five years upon commencement of operation
Shareholders' equity	Share capital in foreign currency is translated at the exchange rate ruling on the date of the contribution	Share capital in foreign currency is recorded at official rate. Installments are recorded at official rate. Exchange differences are recorded in capital reserve account
Research and development expenses	Research expenditures are charged as expenses. Development costs are deferred to future operations	Deferral of research and development costs is not specified. Such costs are usually charged once incurred

Table 1 Continued

Accounting issue	International accounting standards	Standards under the accounting regulations for foreign investment enterprises
Foreign currency translation	Translation is at the date of the transaction. Monetary assets and liabilites are translated at the balance sheet date. Exchange gains or losses are charged to operating results	Translation is at the transaction date or first date of the month. Exchange gains or losses are charged to operating results. Exchange gains arising during preoperating period may be written off over five years after the commencement of operations, retained for setting off future operating losses, or carried forward until liquidation
Account for leases	Assets under a finance lease are capitalized at fair value. Finance lease rentals are split between interest and capital to approximate a constant rate of interest on the remaining balance. Operating lease rentals are charged to profit and loss account	Assets under a finance lease should be capitalized at value specified in lease agreeement. Otherwise, standards are similar to IAS. No guidance is provided on accounting for finance charges or operating lease rentals

Source: *People's Republic of China*. Deloitte Touche Tohmatsu International, publisher, 1995 edition.

are set for each team. Detailed production records and statistics are kept. Team leaders provide the work performance record for every member.

A comprehensive organizational system assures that fewer departments are involved in each operation to economize on coordination and bring down transaction costs. Managers are either specialized in departments such as research and development, sales and marketing, production, technical support, or accounting, or work in general management. Job tasks are assigned to each worker. Each working position contains several effort points. Workers choose the most preferred ones. However individuals would shift from one effort point to another depending on internal and external pressures.

B. Rewarding System

Workers need to fulfill production quotas to qualify for the basic wage. If workers produce more, they earn a bonus. Penalties are applied for low performance. The advantage is that the enterprise can control effort choices of the workers. By making workers responsible for the results of their efforts, wages approximate the value of marginal product. If total production cost is reduced below the budget target, the workshops keep a certain amount of revenue as a bonus to be distributed to the workers. Distribution among individuals depends on their efforts. Peer groups are assumed to exert pressure to affect the effort levels of individual workers. Housing policy became based on the employees' working performance and achievements. This motivates the employees to work harder and increase productivity. Housing has been substantially improved. In addition, several facilities have been developed such as nurseries, day care centers, schools, workers' rest rooms, cultural activity centers and recreation clubs.

C. Promoting Workers' Participation in Management

Prior to introducing any important policies, one month is given to let all the employees discuss them. All employees are encouraged to give their opinions which are incorporated into decision making. Before assigning tasks, the interests of each worker and employees are ascertained. The idea is to assign tasks considering individual interests. Technological innovation is promoted along with stronger efforts to provide healthy and agreeable working environment.

D. Introduction of Contract Responsibility System (CRS)

The specified responsibilities and behavior of each worker affect property rights of other individuals in the working environment. Deviations from the principals' interests would have adverse effects on the agents. Penalties reduce opportunistic behavior. Several rewarding systems are applied. The remuneration system assigns duty salaries to managers and position wages to workers. The duty salary is determined by responsibilities. Position wages are associated with various grades depending on qualifications and experience. Both systems encourage to reach the economic and technical standards.

Although the CRS has improved economic performance, the unclearly specified property rights between the state and the enterprises resulted in ambiguities. Net profits after tax were paid to the Treasury. The retained profits legally belonged to the state. But they also were treated as the corporate savings. Distribution among investment fund, welfare fund, and bonus fund was unsettled. Under soft state enforcement, bonus payments and housing construction showed signs of getting out of control. Under the CRS capital investment programs were constrained by short-term profit considerations during the contract period. Neglect of long-term profitability and return discouraged efficient resource allocation. The state tended to preserve direct control over operations.

E. Privatization by Introducing the Shareholding System

Introduction of the Shareholding System has converted the nonprofit organization into a shareholding corporation. All assets created prior to 1978 are covered by state shares. All assets created after 1978 are covered by corporate shares. Flotation and share trading enable capitalization of anticipated incomes and profits and improve economic efficiency. The A shares for local investors were listed on the Shanghai Securities Exchange. The H shares, which are designed for foreign investors into privatized SOEs, were floated on the Hong Kong Stock Exchange (Xiao and Kelvin 1998). Funds from selling the A shares are intended for expansion and modernization programs, repayment of bank loans, and working capital. Proceeds from selling the H shares to the foreign investors provide alternative funds for modernization. Besides raising money, stock exchanges create contestable pressures to reorganize management and improve international transparency and acceptability for foreign investors. The state has formally given up claims over income. The important characteristic is that the shareholders possess only the income rights; they cannot trade corporate assets.

There are two important implications. First, distribution relations have been clarified by introducing property rights over corporate assets. Second, separation of ownership and management has been achieved. A supervisory committee of three is set up to monitor activities of the board of directors and senior managers and prevent deviations from the employees' and shareholders' interests. Two members are elected by the shareholders at the general meeting, and one member is representative of the corporate employees. Each supervisor serves a three-year term and can be reelected. The supervisory committee is accountable to the shareholders and reports to their general meeting.

The board of directors is mainly responsible for decision making and monitoring activities. Their responsibilities include (1) approval of annual budgets and long-term strategic plans, (2) decisions on distribution of profits between remuneration benefits and investment funds, and (3) appointment and removal of senior managers. Operational decisions are the responsibility of senior managers. This decision-making structure should ensure that the corporation is run in line with the shareholders' interests.

F. Impacts of Reform on Corporate Performance

For the three years period 1990–92 the corporate turnover increased by 60.6%, from RMB 2284 million to RMB 3369.1 million; after-tax profit increased by over 317%, from RMB 97.7 million to RMB 407.6 million. The extrapolated annual after-tax profit, based on first five months for 1993, reached RMB 2351.7. This happened for several reasons. State control was relaxed on pricing of steel products and distribution of value added. Sales tax and tax on corporate profits were reduced. Improved incentives to managers and workers and clarified property rights also contributed to higher profits. In the first half of the 1990s the annual growth rate of corporate sales was in line with the real GNP growth and the annual steel production growth rate in China.

V. CONCLUSION

The purpose of this chapter was to evaluate impacts of reforms in Chinese SOEs and formulate suggestions. The blend of complexity theory, principal-agent theory, property rights theory, and X-efficiency theory was applied to assess the reform.

A. Evaluation Summary

First, the nature of organizational relationships was simplified. Information asymmetry and transaction costs were reduced and monitoring became easier. Responsibilities for each job were clearly defined, but motivation of managers and workers remained problematic. Second, the *contract responsibility system* reduced opportunistic behavior. The remuneration of each employee became closer related to performance. It appears that the reward system increased the employees' loyalty. Productivity and profits increased substantially. However, short-term policies resulted in neglecting the long-term interests of the principals which are served by long-term capital investment programs and industrial and business policies. Third, the *shareholding system* and the clarification of distribution rights between the state and the corporation ensured that the operational management and the distribution of profits would not be interfered with by the state. The corporation can raise funds through the stock exchanges and is more accountable for its operational and financial results.

B. Suggestions for Further Reforms

The young Chinese stock exchanges at Shanghai and Schenzhen are risky and provide low return (Xiao and Kelvin 1998). This is due to heavy regulation, poor performance of the listed companies, and narrow market. But the reform package aims at upgrading corporate efficiency. Lack of adequate legal protection appears to be the main handicap, especially for foreign investors. The regulators tend to cope with emerging problems by ad hoc short-term measures. The market has been suffering from wide fluctuations. But it appears that the economists expect an upturn in the business cycle to start soon. Then shares will become more attractive to the investors provided that most of listed companies could improve performance.

Liberalization of foreign trade is expected to result in the multiplication of joint ventures and upgraded quality of Chinese management. A blueprint to develop stock market in China was formulated in Xiao and Kelvin (1998). Suggested measures include publishing the Securities Law, tax reform, reducing import duties and export subsidies, merging the markets for A and B shares, ending listing quotas, segmenting the listed companies, and promoting the stock exchanges. The idea is to enlarge and deepen the stock market, to make it more fluid. Simultaneously it aims at reducing sensitivity to small changes in environment so that the market remains flexible but avoids overreacting to some events. This study suggests that, in addition to privatization of SOEs, further measures should be implemented.

1. Set up a national insurance scheme in China. Employees can pay monthly contributions. In this way, the retired employees would rely less on the exclusive financial support from their SOEs. The welfare burden on the SOEs will be reduced.
2. Provide training to the unemployed to improve their prospects in rapidly growing sectors.
3. Hand over services unrelated to production, e.g., hospitals, to independent organizations to remove the burden of long-term subsidies.
4. Establish a comprehensive banking system and find a solution for the loss-making SOEs.

REFERENCES

Aharoni, Y. (1982a). State-owned enterprises: an agent without a principal. In L. Jones (ed.), *Public Enterprise in Less Developed Countries*. London: Cambridge University Press.

Aharoni, Y. (1982b). Principal-agents relationships: who should control public enterprises? In L. Jones (ed.), *Public Enterprise in LDCs*. London: Cambridge University Press.

Aharoni, Y. (1986). *The Evolution and Management of State-Owned Enterprises*. Cambridge, MA: Ballinger Publishing Company.

Arrow, K. (1974). *The Limits of Organization*. New York: Norton.

Belbin, R. (1992). *Management of Teams*. Oxford: Butterworth Heinemann.

Briand, S. and Kelvin, A. (1997). Strategic alliances in global air transport. Paper for Annual Conference of the British Academy of Management, hosted by London Business School, Queen Elizabeth II Conference Centre, 8–10 Sept. 1997.

Briand, S. and Kelvin, A. (1998a). Assessment of deregulation in the European airlines. *International Journal of Transport Economics*, Feb.

Briand, S. and Kelvin, A. (1998b). Priorities and strategy for liberalisation in the European airlines. Conference paper at the 8th World Conference on Transport Research, Antwerp, July 12–17, 1998.

Byrd, W. (1992). *Chinese Industrial Firms Under Reform*. Oxford: Oxford University Press.

Chan, Y. (1996). *The Chinese Iron and Steel Industry under Reform—Case Study of Maanshan Iron and Steel Company*. Dissertation in Applied Economics, Business School, University of Hertfordshire, Hertford, England.

Davis, H. (1995). *China Business Context and Issues*. Longman Asia Limited.

Eisenhardt, K. (1989). Agency theory: an assessment and review. *Academy of Management Review*, 57–74.

Furubotn, E. et al. (1974). *The Economics of Property Rights*. Ballinger Publishing Company.

Groves, T. et al. (1994). Autonomy and incentives in Chinese state enterprises. *Quarterly Journal of Economics*, *CIX* (1), 183–209.

Jensen, M. et al. (1976). Theory of firm, managerial behaviour, agency costs and ownership structure. *Journal of Financial Economics, 3*, 305–360.

Kelvin, A. (1996). From state monopolies toward contestable and sustainable market structures: the case study of transport in Zaire. *Tijdschrift Vervoerswetenchap (Dutch Journal of Transport Science), 2*, 145–168.

Kelvin, A. (1997a). Impact model for socially low tariffs in Zairian river transport. *Annals of Public and Cooperative Economics*, *68*(1), 107–128.

Kelvin, A. (1997b). Upgrading private contribution to partnerships in view of failure in the public provision of services. Conference paper, the 24th Annual (1997) Conference Proceedings, Organisation of International Business, Academy of International Business UK. Centre of International Business, University of Leeds, 4–5 April 1997.

Kelvin, A. (1997c). Closing the gaps between decisions, implementation and performance. Case study of transport in the Democratic Republic of Congo. *Tijdschrift voor Economie en Management* (Flemish Journal of Economics and Management), *XVII*(4), 409–423.

Kelvin, A. (1997d). Identifying training strategies of task-oriented teams. Fifth International Conference on Modern Industrial Training, Jinan, Shandong province, China, 26–29 Oct. 1997.

Kelvin, A. (1998). Modelling team learning. Conference paper at the Fifteenth Annual Conference and a publication in the Proceedings of the World Association for Case Method Research and Application, Marseille, France, July 1998.

Kelvin, A. and Xiao, F. (1998). Stakeholders' preferences versus characteristics of investment programmes. Conference paper, Fourth International Conference Public and Private Sector Patnerships: Fostering Enterprise, 20–23 May 1998, Faculty of Economics, University of Ljubljana, Slovenia.

Lasagna, L. (1991). Cost of innovation in the pharmaceutical industry. *Journal of Health Economics, 10*, 107–142.

Lee, K. (1993). Property rights and agency problems in China's enterprise reform. *Cambridge Journal of Economics*, *17*(2), 183–209.

Lee, K. (1994). *Chinese Firms and the State in Transition—Property Rights and Agency Problems in the Reform Area*. East Gate.

Leibenstein, H. (1978). *General X-Efficiency Theory and Economic Development*. Oxford: Oxford University Press.

Linyu, Z. (1995). The direction of enterprise reform. *Chinese Social Sciences Quarterly, 10.*

Maanshan Iron and Steel Limited Company. (1993). *Prospectus.*

Medio, A. (1992). *Chaotic Dynamics: Theory and Applications to Economics.* Cambridge: Cambridge University Press.

Shammaki, S. (1995). *Corporate Strategy and Decision Making Process. Case Study Arab Banking Corporation International.* Dissertation. Business School, University of Hertfordshire, Hertford, England.

Stacey, R. (1992). *Managing Chaos: Dynamic Business Strategies in an Unpredictable World.* London: Kogan Page.

Tolstoy, L. (1904). *War and Peace.* London: Heinemann.

Totten, G. et al. (1992). *China's Economic Reform: Administering the Introduction of Market Mechanism.* Westview Press.

Waldorp, M. (1994). *Complexity.* London: Penguin Books.

Weiermair, K. (1990). *Studies in Economic Rationality: X-Efficiency Examined and Extolled.* Ann Arbor: University of Michigan Press.

Wiggins, S. (1990). *An Introduction to Applied Non-linear Dynamically Systems and Chaos.* New York: Springer-Verlag.

Wolf, C. (1988). *Markets of Governments.* Cambridge, MA: MIT Press.

Woodward, J. (1980). *Industrial Organisation: Theory and Practice.* London: Oxford University Press.

Xiao, F. and Kelvin, A. (1998). Strategic blueprint to develop Chinese stock market. Conference paper and a publication in the Proceedings of China International Business Symposium, 27–29 May 1998, Shanghai.

Xie, B.S. (1991). *China's Economic Policies, Theories and Reforms Since 1949.* Fudan University Press.

Yeung, T. (1995). The responsibility contract system of state-owned enterprises in China. *Prospective Accountant,* July/August, 54–55.

Zhu, S. et al. (1997). *Financial System in China.* Essay, London School of Economics, London.

14

Central-Local Conflicts in Economic Management in China

Zhong Zhu Ding
New School University, New York, New York

Central-local relations have been a long problematic issue in China's political-economic life. After Emperor Qinshihuang wiped out all other states in the mainland and established a united huge empire, the Qin Dynasty (221–207 BC), theoretical disputes and power conflicts over centralization versus decentralization became a continuing political theme in China's history. When the Communists took power and a socialist People's Republic was established in 1949, the historical dilemma in central-local relations took on some new facets. As a state-dominated socialist regime, the state monopolistically controlled most means of production and centrally planned national economic development. On the other hand, China's extremely complex social-economic conditions demanded local autonomy in order to accommodate regional differences.

The great economic structural reform since 1978 has introduced significant changes in central-local relations in terms of decentralization. While they have brought dynamic vitality to China's economy, new problems caused by these changes, such as local economic barriers, disorder in the national economy, clash in resource allocation between the central and local authorities, and the decline of state capacity in macroeconomic management, are also essentially disturbing China's development. As Jiang Zemin, the President of China, admitted in September 1995, in the process of structural reform, some provinces and regions overconsidered their local interests and therefore slackened or even resisted central government's policies. On the other hand, the central capacity in macroeconomic management weakened. The "overdecentralization" phenomenon dislocated China's economic order and damaged the national interests.[1]

It is a contradiction that the state in China exists as a corporate actor of national development on one hand, but appears as an arena of central-local conflict on the other hand. In order to achieve effective state action, a certain power of coherence and coordination, which is autonomous from localities, is necessary. However, centralized state organizations are often distressed by misleading information and commands proceeding through hierarchical channels. Therefore, many sorts of state action need decentralization to ensure efficiency. However, decentralization puts the state in a dangerous situation, decreasing its own ability to contribute to development. If decentralization makes the state unable to behave coherently in support of national goals and interests, the unique character of the state acting as a cooperative unit may be destroyed.

Although China has had since 1994 a program of ''strengthening macroeconomic control'' to strengthen the weakened state capacity in national development, research shows that at the beginning of 1998, the problems mentioned were still serious.

A critical question therefore faced Chinese reformers: Could they find an integration mechanism that combines coherence and effective coordination of the state with decentralization and active local participation in market competitions as a vital new system for development?

I. POWER DIVISIONS BETWEEN CENTRAL AND LOCAL GOVERNMENTS BEFORE 1978

As early as 1956, Mao Zedong pointed out that under the centralized system, the relationship between the centre and localities was a ''contradiction.'' The main problem was, he went further, that the local powers were too restricted. It was necessary to enlarge local power and grant localities certain independence under central plan, because, Mao justified, ''two enthusiasms,'' which referred to both central and local enthusiasms, were more beneficial than only a central control.[2] In order to stimulate local authorities' enthusiasms and creativity in social-economic constructions, and to reduce central government's heavy administrative and financial burdens, by shifting certain power of economic controls to provinces, Mao Zedong launched adjusting programs three times between 1957 and 1970, attempting to resolve the troubling dilemma in central-local relations. The results, however, were not satisfactory. When the center entrusted more power to the local authorities, the local governments would use every means to take profit incomes from enterprises in their regions as much as possible, leaving the national revenue shortage to the central government; meanwhile, the repeat constructions in regions and unreasonable competitions among provinces would get worse. Troubled by these difficulties, the center would then be forced to take back some power transferred to the localities previously. As a result, however, the local enthusiasms of economic development and potentialities were severely damaged again.

The first attempts at decentralization came in 1957–58. The adopted system gave the local governments policy and operational decision-making power. Under this system, 87% of the enterprises, which were previously controlled by the central government, were put under management of the provincial authorities. Also 75% of material distributions, which were originally monopolized by central government, were placed under local control. The local authorities were entrusted decision-making power to adjust local production plans and were also able to arrange utilization of any funds after fulfilling the submission quotation of revenue set by the state. As long as the local authorities accomplished the requirements of state planning, they could fully enjoy the enlarged decision-making power.[3]

This system enabled provincial authorities to enlarge local industries dramatically and quickly. However, the Second Five-Year Plan of development was scrapped in favour of the all-out drive of the Great Leap Forward. The Leap's unrealistic high targets, their hasty implementation and the extreme strengthening on the growth of iron and steel production encouraged the local authorities to irrationally use their power in blind extending of local iron and steel industry, causing serious economic dislocation and resource scarcities so that the national economy fell into a fatal disorder and imbalance in the first half of 1959.

As a result, to resume the national economic order, since the second half of 1959, the central government was gradually taking back most of the power which had been transferred to the localities during the period of 1957–58. Therefore, the central-local relations, by 1961, totally went back to the old situation so that the central planning controlled all the local production and allocations. Consequently, the local development declined sharply right afterward.

Two further attempts to change occurred in 1964 and 1970. In 1964 the local governments were granted greater power to allocate revenue resources and production materials. They also gained more power to decide the scale and pattern of investment. In 1970 local controls over economic development were further reinforced. The power of managing about 2000 large and medium-size industrial enterprises, construction companies, and other economic organizations was shifted from the central level to the local level. To stimulate local potentialities, the provincial power in capital allocations was institutionally ensured by the central policy. The system allowed the provincial authorities to dispose autonomously a considerable ratio of local revenue incomes for local development. The provincial governments were also granted the right to participate in decision making for the division of national revenue. Under this system, the provincial authorities had power to control 30% of the investment for capital constructions; another 30% of the investment should be arranged on the basis of agreement between the central government and the provincial governments; the remaining 40% of the investment was directly controlled by the central government.[4]

The reformed system stimulated effectively local governments' enthusiasms to enlarge their local industries and promote social-economic development. However, it also brought crises and disorder in national economy by unbalanced local industrial development and repeat constructions. The system remained in operation until a new strategy launched in 1972 by the central authorities which followed the adoption of the policy of ''readjustment, restructuring, consolidating and improving the national economy.'' By the new strategy, the central planning was reimposed in many economic areas. This new policy favored light industry as opposed to heavy industry. The related policy of narrowing the scope of capital construction created problems, particularly because the demand for machinery decreased, with the result that many engineering enterprises could not find enough work to do. Factories that found themselves in this position were forced to explore other channels, such as producing for export or manufacturing accessories and spares. In these circumstances, the national economy suffered again an inactive period.

Until 1978, all attempts at modifying the central-local relations focused mainly on the readjustment of control limits between the central and local governments, with almost no attention paid to the economic relations between the state and enterprises. Consequently, the real problems had not actually been resolved during that period.

The central-local relations therefore seemed to be caught in a vicious circle: once the centre transferred more power of economic management to the localities, the national economy would fall into disorder; the central government would then be forced to resume the rigid control by restricting local power; consequently, local development would decline and the national economy would become stagnant again.

II. EXPANSION OF ENTERPRISE AUTONOMY

Since 1980, industrial enterprises, accounting for the most of the gross output value from state industries, have been granted the right to retain part of their profits instead of turning over all of them to the state, as well as being given greater power to make their own decisions. The practice has given the management and the workers of these enterprises reason to improve production and business operations, resulting in higher income for the workers, the enterprises, and the state.

Before the reform, producers did not have the right freely to sell their products. All products, such as raw materials, facilities, and machines, were allocated to enterprises by the state according to plans. Under the new system, however, the producers were encouraged to contract with buyers beyond state plans. For example, a mine is allowed to sell its iron ore to a steelworks, and a textile mill can sell its cloth to a clothing factory. Breaking through the conventional lines of division between industries and trades, associations for various economic sections have been established to link producers with marketing agencies. The associations are composed of producers and buyers regarding particular products respectively, such as the steel association or the clothing association. These specialized associations act very dynamically to help business dealings in a market environment. The associations provide their members with updated information about market demand-supply situation for their products and organize marketing conferences to facilitate contacts or negotiations between producers, marketing agencies, and buyers.

China's bold reform had achieved significant success by 1984. This encouraged the authorities to deepen and strengthen the reform of the structure of the economy, focusing on the changes of relationship between state and enterprises, and between planning and market. At the Third Plenum of the 12th Party Central Committee, one of the most important documents on structural reform was adopted on 20 October 1984. According to the document, the goals of reform that the Chinese authorities pursued were as follows:

1. To devise a new economic system combining beneficial parts from both the state planning system and the free market system for developing a socialist commodity economy
2. To vitalize enterprises as the key to restructuring the national economy by granting them greater autonomy
3. To establish a flexible price system to suit a market demand-supply situation and to facilitate economic resource allocation
4. To separate government control from enterprises' operating process, enabling enterprises to make their economic decisions independently, corresponding to market competition
5. To create a new income distribution system to reward workers according to work performance in order to stimulate production growth.[5]

In short, the authorities sought to secure a dynamic socialist commodity economy with "Chinese characteristics."

Under the new system, enterprises have been designated by planning to bear the primary responsibility for undertaking production, construction, and service, and participating commodity circulation. The enterprises have been divided into industrial, transport, building, commercial, and service sections. In 1985, gross enterprise production in industrial section was Y344.87 billion (RMB yuan), in construction section Y41.79 billion, in transportation and postcommunication sections Y40.69 billion, in commercial section Y57.70 billion, in various services Y113.53 billion, totaling Y598.58 billion. China's gross national product (GNP) in 1985 was Y855.76 billion; the total enterprise production (Y598.58

billion) therefore formed 69.9% of GNP in 1985. Since the enterprises are of such importance, they undoubtedly need great vitality to lead the national economy.[6]

The Chinese reformers understand that this vitality can only be built in two ways: It needs to be free from unnecessary state control, and an organized internal vitality needs to exist between the managerial leadership and the workers and staff. Under the new system, an enterprise has the power to adopt flexible and diversified forms of operation; to plan its production, supply, and marketing; to keep and to budget funds; to employ and remove its own personnel; to decide on how to recruit and use its work force; to set wages and rewards; and to set the prices of its products within the limits prescribed by the state.

In the reform, each enterprise is gradually becoming an independent entitiy as both a producer and a seller of its products. The reformers believe that the producing strength and vitality would come from managerial efficiency and workers' initiative. And workers' initiative would be encouraged by benefits.

From 1985 to 1988, the Chinese government imposed three major reform measures on the urban economic structure. First, the authorities slowly reduced the central government's direct control of enterprises by perfecting a system of indirect control, under which the government controls enterprises through levying taxes instead of taking all profits. Second, the government transferred power to the publicly owned enterprises of large and medium-size operations. Such enterprises must become much more autonomous, self-managing, and responsible for their profits and losses as socialist commodity producers and managers. Third, under planning, the commodity market was developed further by allowing more products to be distributed through the market and allowing their prices to float in the market.

The new system has granted the provincial and major municipal governments much greater power in economic management since 1985. Before the reform, the provincial governments functioned only as a representative agency of central authorities to transmit and implement central planning in managing local enterprises. They had no autonomy to formulate independent planning for local industrial development. Under the new system, however, the provincial governments and major municipal governments have gradually been granted power to formulate independently their local planning of industrial development according to central guideline. Especially in the Special Economic Zones (SEZs) and Economic and Technologic Development Zones (ETDZs), the local governments have had highly autonomy to make local industrial policies.

By 1994, all the provincial and major municipal governments have been granted same power of autonomous industrial management enjoyed by the SEZs and ETDZs. The central government has now transferred the management power of most original centrally controlled enterprises to the provincial or municipal governments, except for a very few enterprises of strategic importance such as railway industry, major coastal harbours, major steel and iron corporations, and the defense industry, which are still controlled by the central government. According to a report from the State Planning Commission, by 1993, the central mandatory planning on industrial production has been limited to only 36 kinds of product, forming mere 7% of total national production.[7]

Decentralization and strength of autonomy have brought dynamism to enterprises' economic activities. From 1992 to 1994, production of state-owned enterprises maintained an annual growth of 6.8% and realized tax payment increased annually at 29%. However, the internal management continued to be a weakness of the state-owned enterprises in adapting to the competitive environment of market economy. The immaturity of modern management in state-owned enterprises has caused difficulties for their production and operation, such as an increase in material waste, decrease of product quality, and rise of production costs. Statistics show that, compared to 1993, in 1994 state-owned enterprises' material consumption increased 2.2%, production costs increased 2%, and qualified products reached only 70%. By April 1995, more than one-third of state-owned enterprises suffered economic losses.[8]

Another serious problem caused by decentralization is dramatic increase of unemployment that has contributed to social crisis. While the local authorities and enterprises have been entrusted with autonomy to pursue economic efficiency by restructuring enterprise management, including eliminating the phenomenon of human resource waste in terms of excessive employees, there is no a social security system to help unemployed people. This dilemma is also becoming an obstacle for people to transfer freely in the labor market because if they quit their jobs they may suffer extreme economic difficulty and there will be no temporary support from social assistance.

There is therefore a contradiction that although overemployment is a very common problem in China's state-owned enterprises, the reformers of central authorities cannot encourage enterprises to fire surplus employees because China has not yet established a new social security system to match the market-oriented reform. China's current welfare security system, which was established on the outdated centralized-planning economy, is in fact a ''working unit system'' rather than a ''social system.'' At the national level, there is no government-funded social security system to supply financial aid for unemployment insurance, retirement pensions, or health insurance. The current security system is completely tied to the working unit. Once a person is employed by an enterprise or government agency, he or she benefits from all kinds of welfare and security; but if a person is fired or quits, his or her welfare and security privileges will be abolished as well. Therefore, the incompatible welfare security system in the market-oriented reform has contributed a severe new social problem, causing sharp social conflicts, complaints, and even violence between unemployed workers and enterprise management and local governments.

Demonstrations of unemployed workers protested against enterprise management or local governments have become frequent events disturbing the social stability. In late 1997, laid-off workers in Hefei city, Mienyang city, and Wuhan city made violated public demonstrations against local authorities, asking for survival right. According to the *World Journal* of January 5, 1998, even in Beijing, the national capital, the dismissed workers from the 3501 Military Manufacture were preparing to take to the street for demonstration against their dismissal by the authorities. Also, the increase in the number of laid-off workers in Xinjiang Autonomous Region has become a serious troubling element causing the region's instability.[9]

III. CENTRAL-LOCAL CONFLICTS

Under the traditional centralized planning system, the central government rigidly controlled collection of taxes and allocation of revenues. When a local government increased its revenue through its own efforts, it still had to hand in any excess over the state plan to the central government. This caused indifference to profits and losses by the provinces. To stimulate local governments' enthusiasm in the market-oriented reform, in 1980 the central government initiated the fiscal decentralization reform. The 1980 reform measure was ''eating in separate kitchens,'' meaning to give local governments certain autonomy in allocating revenues. As Wang Shaoguang analyzed, ''The center hoped that decentralization would give local governments sufficient incentives to maximize budgetary revenues, thus making the fiscal 'pie' bigger, which in turn would enlarge the absolute size of the center's own slice.''[10] Under the new system, financial relations between the centre and provinces have been fundamentally changed. A fixed proportion of the province's revenue would be left at the disposal of the province; the remainder was to be handed over to the central government.

In 1985, to further decentralize, the central government announced the establishment of a new fiscal division system to divide revenue incomes between the central government and the provincial governments. This new system stipulated that (1) the national revenue was divided as central revenue, local revenue, and central-local shared revenue; (2) provincial government should set contracts with the central government to determine the expense rates of local governments based on their revenue incomes; and (3) the profits of the whole national revenues, including the central, local, and central-local shared revenues, would divided between the central and local governments based on central-local contracts.[11]

In 1988, the central government issued a new reform measure to deepen the decentralization process. The main content of this reform was to transfer the power of collecting 13 kinds of taxes from the center to local governments. The 13 taxes were: individual industrial-business income taxes, business operation taxes, individual income-adjusting taxes, individual income taxes, state-owned enterprise wage-adjusting taxes, contract taxes, farm and forest side-product taxes, slaughter taxes, living stock trade taxes, farm-market trade taxes, vehicle-boat usage taxes, real estate taxes, and bonus taxes. The revenue incomes from the 13 taxes would totally be gained by local governments; the interests or profits of these revenue incomes would totally be taken by the local governments as well.[12]

In 1989, China established officially a new system to divide revenue incomes between the central government and the provincial governments. The tax categories have been systematically differentiated to be collected by the central government and the provincial governments. Sales taxes and enterprise profit income taxes, for example, are stipulated to be collected by the central government, while the wholly owned small-business income taxes and individual income taxes are collected by the provincial governments.[13]

The new system has also specified that a proportion of enterprises' profits shall be divided between the authorities exercising control over the enterprises and the enterprises themselves. These fiscal measures have increased the power of local governments over local industry. By this division, national industrial, technologic, or infrastructural projects are still funded or cofunded by the central government, while the medium- and small-scale projects and ancillary items are funded by the local governments. According to a research by the World Bank, by 1989, the local governments had enjoyed 62.5% of China's total national revenue.[14]

Although the shift of decision-making power to local authorities from central government has brought considerable vitality in giving full scope to local creativity and potentiality, new contradictions have occurred in the changed central-local relations. Since local governments have had considerable power in local development planning, revenue allocation, and material distribution, they are able to pursue independence in economic management from the center. To maximize their own local interests and to speed up their own development pace, many local authorities in recent years have ignored national economic policies or arrangements initiated by the central government. This situation has resulted in two consequences. The first is that macroeconomic management has been disrupted in terms of repeated constructions and projects, overheated industrial growth, soaring inflation, and severe waste of social-economic resources. The second is that regional economic inequality has been drastically enlarged between coastal areas (or development zones) and inland areas (or poor remote provinces). Because of the macroeconomic management disorder, the developed provinces have taken advantage of their economic power to commit unfair market competition. The central government has been able to do very little to influence the bias; therefore, the gap between the rich and the poor has dramatically expanded in recent years.

Another problem caused by the power transfer to the local authorities is local barriers in the national market. Since the provinces have had power to design their local development strategies, they have usually tried to protect local products in market activities in their own dominions. Therefore, many provinces have issued protecting regulations or policies against products from other provinces, seriously fragmenting the national market. Consequently, from the point of view of national development, the principle of fair market competition and a united national market, which are a foundation for healthy national economy, has been challenged, and interprovincial exchanges have been disturbed at the cost of social-economic resource waste.

The reforms of the revenue system in fact reduced state revenue share and granted the localities greater power in national revenue allocation. The share rate of state revenue income in gross domestic product (GDP) was reduced to 16.6% in 1992, from 26.7% in 1979. Central revenue income, as a share of total national revenue income, was 57.6% in 1981 but declined to 45% in 1992. This situation increased dramatically the central government deficit. By 1992, the national deficit raised to Y90.5 billion, forming 3.8% of the total GDP of same year. This rate exceeded that in Western industrial countries (the average rate in these countries is usually less then 3%). In 1992, 50% of the central government's expenditures had to depend on borrowing money or issuing bonds to make payments.[15] In these circumstances, the ability of the central government in macroeconomic management decreased obviously. The traditional strong capability of the centre in mobilizing national resources to undertake strategic development projects has been severely challenged.

As local autonomy has significantly increased, the relations between the state and enterprises have hit a new problem. Past experience has verified that the extreme control of the state over enterprises would seriously damage enterprises' economic dynamics. Therefore, *fenquan rangli*, or transferring part of the central government's control over economic resources and decision-making to provincial governments and enterprises, is an important aspect of the structural reform in the post-Mao era. The central authorities were therefore attempting to grant enough autonomy to enterprises by decentralization. However, since the local authorities obtained greater autonomy in economic management and revenue allocation, they have found that taking control over enterprises is an important source for increasing local government revenue incomes, and they have been able to do so. Consequently, although the center has lifted a great deal of control over the enterprises, the enterprises are still strongly controlled by governments. The only difference is that they were controlled by the central government in the past, but now are controlled by their local governments.

Since 1994, when the Chinese People's Bank, as a decentralization measure, became a policy-oriented central bank separated from all other commercial banks, China's central government budget deficit continually increased and reached Y52.9 billion in 1996. To finance the deficits, the cental government has to borrow funds by issuing various bonds, including compulsory ones, to sell to Chinese citizens.

The transfer of power to localities and enterprises was originally designed to arouse local and enterprise initiatives. However, the overincrease of local control in resource allocations has reduced the effect of the decentralization measures. Moreover, this situation, as Dali L. Yang maintains, has "led to a far more precipitous [relative] decline in central control over resources than anticipated."[16] Consequently, as Wang Shaoguang emphasizes, the "budget revenue as a percentage of national income has dropped by a wide margin" and "the central government's share of the budget revenue has dropped by a wide margin" since 1978.[17]

The practice from 1990 to early 1998 particularly demonstrated that China's current economic decentralization has essentially weakened the capacity of central control over national investment, consumption levels, and resource allocation, resulting in the growth of inequality among regions and conflicts in resource allocations between the central and local governments. The state's capacity in coordinating and balancing national development has therefore declined.

IV. PREFERENTIAL POLICIES FOR SPECIAL ECONOMIC ZONES

The Special Economic Zone (SEZ) is a unique approach used by the Chinese reformers to undertake experiments for fundamental changes in the Chinese political economy. This approach in fact is rooted in a traditional political culture since the Communists took power in China. The basic idea is that before a policy involving fundamental change is implemented in the whole country, in order to avoid unexpected political upset or damage, the state should carry out this policy in some selected area or areas as an experiment, testing and improving the policy. When the policy has been verified by practice as feasible and the experience for implementing this policy has been gained, the new policy would be spread to the rest of the country.

In 1980, a SEZ was set up in Shenzhen, a small town at that time just linking with Hong Kong. The role of the SEZ was designed to be the basis of a bold reform experiment base to accelerate China's economic marketization and internationalization. The advantages of Shenzhen's geographic position close to Hong Kong were fully considered to facilitate attraction of foreign investment and foreign economic exchange. To support the SEZ strategy, the central government granted the SEZ government much more autonomy than other regions in economic management and preferential policies regarding foreign investment in the SEZ.

In the same year when the Shenzhen SEZ was established, other SEZs were established in Zhuhai, a city on the border with Macao, and in Xiamen and Shantou, the two closest coastal cities to Taiwan, in 1980. Later, in 1988, when Hainan Island was restructured as a province, it was announced by the central government to be the biggest SEZ in China. At this time, the special character of SEZs has been enlarged to, besides attracting foreign investment, pursuing imports from Western countries of advanced technologies and effective managerial skills that China lacks and needs.

The preferential policies for SEZs also included granting privileges of lower taxes to foreign investors. Despite a 33% tax rate on profits for foreign funded enterprises (FFEs) in other areas, FFEs in SEZs were only required to pay 15% tax on their income. Besides that, the FFEs in SEZs as well as in other provinces enjoyed a tax waiver for first two years of profits, and during the following three years, the FFEs needed to pay only 7.5% income tax. Besides those privileges, the FFEs in SEZs were exempted from paying customs duties when they imported materials, equipment, and machines for production purposes. For their exports, no taxes were applied.[18] The implementation of the preferential policy caused severe problems in terms of central government's revenue decline, conflicts between central and local governments in tax revenue allocation, and abuse of the preferential policy by foreign and joint enterprises. This situation stimulated the central authorities to adjust this preferential policy. Since July 1995, the refund rate of tax payment for foreign enterprises' exports has been reduced to between 3% and 14%. In October 1995, the central authorities decided to reduce the refund rate of tax payment further to 3%, to 9% beginning 1996.[19]

The obvious bias policy for SEZs has stirred strong criticisms from many Chinese scholars. They charged that this so-called preferential policy has in fact contributed to unequal market competition and the loss of national revenue. Wang Shaoguang and Hu Angang, for instance, argue that ''opening to outside world and absorbing foreign capital do not mean to give up the state's right to collect income taxes from domestic and foreign enterprises.'' They say that the central government's preferential policy for SEZs has caused serious loss of China's national income of tax revenue by reducing or waiving the tax payment for foreign enterprises. Wang and Hu further argue that the state's maintaining of a unified tax system and tax rate in a country is the necessary condition for a modern market economy with equal competition; therefore, China's preferential policy has in fact damaged the principle of equal market competition.[20]

As discussed previously in this research, the SEZs have more autonomy in decision making than in other areas. While foreign investment projects in other areas needed approval from the central government, the local governments in SEZs had the power to decide affairs of foreign investment and foreign trade, according the special preferential policies the center granted to the SEZs. For example, on November 26, 1981, the National People's Congress issued a special resolution to

> authorize the Guangdong and Fujian Provincial People's Congresses and their Standing Committees to formulate various specific economic regulations for their Special Economic Zones according to the principles laid down in the related laws, decrees and policies and in line with the actual conditions and special needs of the Special Economic Zones of these provinces.[21]

As a matter of fact, on August 26, 1980, the National People's Congress had issued *Regulations on Special Economic Zones in Guangdong Province* to legally grant preferential treatment for foreign investors in the SEZs. Article 4 of the Regulations stipulates:

> All items of industry, agriculture, livestock breeding, fish breeding and poultry farming, tourism, housing and construction, research and manufacture involving high technologies and techniques that have positive significance in international economic cooperation and technical exchanges, as well as other trades of common interest to investors and Chinese side, can be established with foreign investment or in joint venture with Chinese investment.[22]

The SEZs also had the power to make decisions on investment in their local social-economic construction, as long as the funds were raised by themselves, which included taxation, foreign capital, bank loans, and other resources. Enterprises in SEZs, including joint ventures, foreign-funded enterprises, private enterprises, and state-owned enterprises, enjoyed more autonomy as well. They had the right to decide their own production, operation, investment, and funding collection according to the market situation. With permission from the SEZ authorities, the enterprises can negotiate finance and technology cooperation with foreign investors or pursue funding from foreign capital.

Highly autonomous decision-making power and preferential policies for foreign economic relations enjoyed by the SEZs have stimulated remarkable economic growth in SEZs' development. By 1991, the exporting value of the four original SEZs—Shenzhen, Zhuhai, Xiamen, and Shantou—reached US $9.6 billion, forming 13.4% of China's total exporting value in the same year, doubling the 1987 value.[23] From 1979 to 1989, Shenzhen had attracted foreign investment of US $5.04 billion in contracts, $2.58 billion of which was actually employed. During this decade, Shenzhen had reached 4774 foreign investment agreements, 21.9% of total agreements for the whole of China in the same period. By 1989, Shenzhen's exporting value increased to US $2.17 billion, 153% of that value in 1987, and 4.35 times that in 1982.[24]

By 1992, Hainan, the last-established SEZ, achieved exports of US $881 million, compared to $670 million in 1991, increasing 31.6%; this was 7.63 times that value of $115.5 million in 1987. This situation indicated an average annual growth of 50.1% during this period. In the five years from 1987 to 1992, $4020 million foreign investment had been contracted in Hainan. Of that total amount, $2593 million was achieved in 1992, 4.9 times more than in 1991 and 180.3 times more than in 1987. This suggested an average annual growth of foreign investment in Hainan at 182.6% during these five years.[25]

While these special policies facilitated the SEZs to enlarge their economic ties with foreign capital and the international market, and to autonomously participate in the domestic market, the inland and non-SEZ provinces and areas strongly complained of unfair treatment by the policy bias of the central government. This situation put great pressure on the centre to enlarge the scope of decentralization to non-SEZ areas.

The bold reform policies achieved obvious success in SEZs and this situation encouraged the central government to spread the SEZ model to other areas which were considered ready for the fundamental changes. In 1984, 14 coastal cities were announced as ''opening cities'' to adopt an SEZ-style economic system, enjoying similar preferential policies to the SEZs. Since those cities had originally had good economic conditions, including relatively modernized infrastructure construction, industrial foundation, and technological facilities and personnel, they were established as ''economic and technology development zones'' (ETDZs). In 1990, the central authority announced establishment of the Pudong Development Zone, which is located in the biggest city of China, Shanghai. According to the decision, Pudong was granted even more autonomy and policy privileges than the SEZs and ETDZs had enjoyed. Thanks to the strategic position of Shanghai, the Pudong Development Zone was designed to be a ''Long Tou'' (the Head of a Dragon), meaning a leading base for the development of the Yangtze Valley area.

The reform experiment in the Pudong Development Zone (PDZ) has been successful so far. In 1994, PDZ's GDP achieved Y29.1 billion, increasing 28.6% over 1993. This growth rate doubled Shanghai's, and was 18% higher than the national average. By the end of 1994, PDZ's gross industrial production reached Y77.6 billion and realized industrial sales of Y76.0 billion, increasing 19% and 20%, respectively, against 1993. In 1994, 1035 new foreign investment enterprises were established in PDZ; their total investment was US$3.81 billion, increasing 12% and 22%, respectively, against 1993. According to statistics of 1995, there have been 2663 foreign enterprises established in PDZ, with a total investment of US$10.36 billion, forming 25% of the number in Shanghai. Among those foreign enterprises, many are branches of worldwide transnational corporations. PDZ's exports arose dramatically in 1994 as well, totaling US $1.8 billion, increasing 80% over 1993 and forming 20% of Shanghai's total exports in 1994. The practice of the new development model in PDZ has achieved a top-level performance in the country.[26]

The favorable outcomes of SEZ development model stimulated the central authorities to continuously expand this model further to the inland areas. In 1992, 10 inland cities were announced to be ''autonomous planning cities'' and six areas along the Yangtze River Valley were announced as ''development zones.'' The 10 ''autonomous planning cities'' are Nanjing and Zhenjian in Jiangsu province; Anqin, Wuhu, Tanglin, and Maanshang in Anhui province; Jiujiang in Jiangxi province; Yueyan in Hunan province; Wuhan in Hubei province; and Chongqing in Sichuan province. The six Development Zones are Shanghai-Nanjing Zone, the Hunan-Hubei-Jiangxi Zone, the Wuhan Development Zone, the Chongqing-Yichang Zone, the Panxi-Liupanshui Comprehensive Resource Development Zone, and the Wujiang Hydropower and Mineral Resource Development Zone.[27]

All these cities and zones came to enjoy all the preferential policies that the SEZs had been practicing. By 1994, almost every Chinese province was granted the same treatment of the preferential policies. From 1995 to early 1998, the central-local relations have gradually arrived a new stage of decentralization that the provinces, SEZs, ETDZs, opening cities, and development zones have gained great autonomous power in their local development.

V. NEW PROBLEMS AND NEW ADJUSTMENTS

While the spread of SEZ-style preferential policies to the whole country and the decentralization of economic allocation have vitally stimulated development strength to localities, some new problems in the transforming central-local relations have consequently appeared essentially disturbing national development as well. The first problem is irrational competition in foreign economic activities. Following the SEZ's development strategy of attracting foreign capital, competition for luring foreign investment and foreign trading among the provinces has become overheated and preferential treatment offered to foreign investors from competitive provinces has often disadvantaged the incomes of the governments. According to the author's interviews in late 1997 and January 1998 with officials of representative offices in New York from various Chinese provinces, more than 80% of foreign tradings of the provinces are negatively profited and only few foreign investments in China have contributed to the revenue increase in their provinces.

The second problem is severe loss of agricultural land because of broadly created new development zones. Encouraged by the economic success of SEZs, many provinces or regions strongly requested the central government to grant permission for them to set up their own development zones. Under this pressure, the center has in fact approved most of this kind of application during the period 1988 to 1994. However, every new development zone used agricultural lands to construct its industrial, commercial, and service buildings or bases. Considering China's giant population, agricultural production is extremely important to supply people's basic needs. Therefore, the severe loss of agricultural land has stirred strong criticism and serious concern from many scholars and officials. Since 1995, the central authorities have adopted some regulations to control the agricultural land loss. However, from 1995 to early 1998, while the pace was slowed down, the agricultural land loss continued.

The third problem is decline of the central government's capacity in macroeconomic management. As a result of decentralization by reducing central controls over production and allocation and strength of local capacity in economic management, *zhuhou jingji* (feudal princes-controlled economy) has appeared, meaning the provinces have established their own exclusive economic systems and economic barriers against others in the national market, and the central government has had difficulty in coordinating or adjusting provinces' economic activities. Influenced by *zhuhou jingji*, as Zhang Yan points out, the central revenue income has decreased since the late 1980s and capacity of central government in macroeconomic management has weakened.[28]

These problems reflect the phenomenon that state capacity in China has been significantly challenged in structural reform. The shift of central power of decision making on production and control over resource allocation to local authorities and enterprises has resulted in a dramatic decrease of central financial income. Consequently, the central government's ability in national capital investment, resource allocation, and development balance has diminished. Therefore, the state's capacity as a coordinator of the whole nation has declined. As Wang Shaohuang and Hu Angang argue, "Economy is the foundation of politics, economic power determines political capacity. The 'zhuhou jingji' will cause political decline, and the capacity of central government will be losing, the outcome will be severe."[29]

Since 1992, consequently, the disorder in the macroeconomy, such as severe inflation, unfair competition, official corruption, and a widening income gap, has occurred during the marketization process. In 1993, when the market mechanism was heavily emphasized and central control was greatly reduced, those problems became much tougher. Although the central government tried in 1994 to reduce soaring inflation, the weakened central power of control was not enough to achieve the goal. The statistics painted an even worse picture of inflation for the year. In 1994, compared to 1993, resident consumer prices increased 24.1%, retail goods prices 21.7%, retail prices for means of agricultural production 21.6%, and prices for whole sale of industrial products 19.5%.[30]

The high inflation rates were of course influenced by the structural changes owing to the pricing system reform and the fast rise of food prices due to the natural disaster the agriculture suffered, but the primary cause, as vice-premier Zhu Rongji emphasized at the World Economy Forum in January 1995, was the macroeconomic disorder that brought overheated investment of fixed capital across the whole country.[31]

This situation was a serious challenge to social-political stability. As a result, the central government announced that it would launch a series of further reform programs in 1994 to improve macroeconomic management. This series includes reforms on the financial tax system, monetary system, planning system, investment system, foreign currency and exchange system, and enterprise system.[32]

The purpose of initiating these new reform programs was to reinforce macroeconomic management to achieve a balance between general supply and general demand, and to decrease the drastic inflation crisis. The Chinese wanted to use monetary policy as an instrument to contain the inflation rate under 10%. That means the state should restrict the growth rate of money supply in a scope between 20% and 25%. Consequently, the growth rate of gross domestic production (GDP) should be reduced from 13% in 1993 to 9% in the future in order to cool down the overheated economic growth.[33]

According to a statement of Shao Zhongming, the Vice Director of the State Statistics Bureau, in an international press conference in February 28, 1995, the reform of macroeconomic management achieved breakthrough progress in 1994. In the series of reform programs initiated in the second half of 1993, including reform measures in taxation, finance, foreign exchange, foreign trade, the state paid attention to coordinate the reform process in a systematic and balanced way; the goals of the reforms were therefore achieved smoothly, and the capacity of the state in macroeconomic management has hence been strengthened. In the reform process, as the overheated economic growth was gradually controlled, the economy avoided a sharp decline under the adjustment program as that happened in the past, maintaining a continual and stable growth rate of 11.8% in 1994. In 1994, the general social supply-demand hit a basic equilibrium; the situation of international incomes and expenditures achieved a remarkable improvement and foreign trade increased dramatically, and the living standards of urban and rural residents realized further promotion.

However, Shao also admitted that there are many serious problems existed in 1994 in Chinese economic development, which have not been resolved until now. They are, for example, dramatic soaring of market prices, severe difficulties of many state-owned enterprises in production and operation, and the weakness of infrastructural constructions in agriculture. These problems are urgently needed to be resolved by state macroeconomic coordination.[34]

To resolve the macroeconomic disorder problems, it seems that the central authorities have decided to strengthen state intervention power on the basis of marketization. In the Government Work Report to the Third Section of National People's Congress opened on March 3, 1995, Premier Li Peng announced that since the severe high inflation is still troubling China's economy. The phenomenon of overheated growth still exists, and the state's macroeconomic coordinating capacity must therefore continually strengthen and improve. In national economic operations, the state must make efforts to maintain comprehensive coordination in order to promptly resolve new problems occurring in the economic development. In 1995, the central government should particularly pay attention to adjust the direction and extent of capital investments. The extent of infrastructural constructions should be seriously controlled and investments to agriculture, transportation, communication, and energy industries and their technical promotions should be particularly increased. Li also emphasized that the urban planning and urban constructions should be controlled, and the constructions of luxurious buildings should particularly restricted. Investments in the real estate industry should focus on the construction of people's residences.[35]

The new measures for reinforcing the central capability of macroeconomic control may not be a simple return to central planning, but is an effort to perfect the newly built socialist market structure with state coordinating power. The problem is, however, that state control is usually, as the free-market school claims, a negative force against market mechanisms' ability to allocate resources based on the market demand-supply situation. Therefore, to what extent state control could play a beneficial role in perfecting the market mechanism is a difficult question facing the Chinese reformers.

In fact, by the end of 1997, the consequences brought by problems in central-local relations in the structural transformation remained serious. Because of the broad financial losses of state-owned enterprises in the decentralization, the bad debts in the banks reached Y500 billion—20% of the whole assets of the banks of the nation. In the process of structural changes, unregulated operations and officials' corruptions made unclear financial losses of as high as several Y100 billion. The illegal establishment of financial agencies protected by local authorities increased the severity of the financial crisis, illegal business operations, and the instability of the monetary market.

In addition, by the first half of 1997, the number of laid-off enterprise workers reached 10 million. By the end of 1997, half of China's provinces and major cities had laid off workers, leading to demonstrations on streets. By the beginning of 1998, there were 200 million jobless laborers from rural areas, 130 million of them flowing into cities and threatening urban workers' safety and social stability.[36]

It seems that the 1998 will be a difficult year for China to maintain economic and social stability by readjust central-local relations. As Zhang Shenli argues, the current problematic central-local relations should be readjusted. To achieve proper central-local relations, the regional developments should follow the national coordination. The barriers between central and local management, barriers among provinces, and ineffective or minimally effective resource allocations must be abolished.[37]

Since the market mechanisms in China are still not mature and the related legislation for new central-local relations has not been systematically established, the simple transfer of economic power from central to local authorities, as the Chinese authorities had done in the past decade, from a ''state capacity'' point of view, is a ''nonfunctional'' power shift with unstable and irregular characteristics. To achieve efficient and rational transforming central-local relations, the Chinese may need to profoundly review and rearrange the state's functioning division between the center and the localities, and to establish systematically relevant laws and regulations to institutionalize new central-local relations in the process of economic marketization.

ENDNOTES

1. Jiang Zemin. (1995). Correctly dispose some important relationships in the socialist modernization construction. *Xinhua Wenzai* (*Xinhua Digest*), *12*, 1–5.
2. Mao Zedong. (1974). On the ten great relationships: 25 April 1956. In *Mao Tse-tung Unrehearsed: Talks and Letters: 1956–71*, 71–73. Edited and introduced by S. Schram, translated by J. Chinnery and Tieyun. Middlesex, England: Penguin Books.
3. Ren Luosun. (1980). Changes in China's economic management. *Beijing Review*, *5*, 22.
4. *Ibid*.
5. CCP Central Committee. (1984). *China's Economic Structure Reform—Decision of the CCP Central Committee*. Beijing: Foreign Language Press.
6. Guojia Tongjiju (China State Statistics Bureau). (1993). *Zhongguo Tongji Tiyao* (*China Statistics Outline*), 19–20. Beijing: China State Statistics Bureau.
7. Guojia Jiwei Zhengce Yanjiushi (Policy Study Office of China State Planning Commission). Establishing the new structure of central-local authority division in economic management. In *Woguo Zhongyang Yu Difang Jingji Guanli Quanxian Yanjiu* (Studies of Authority Division between the Central and Local Governments in Economic Management in China), edited by Guojia Jiwei Zhengce Yanjiushi, Beijing: Guojia Jiwei (the State Planning Commission), 1993, p 53.
8. *Renmin Ribao Haiwaiban* (People's Daily, overseas edition), April 20, 1995, p 2.
9. *World Journal (New York edition)*, Jan. 5, 1998, p A11.
10. Wang Shaoguang. (1994). Central-local fiscal politics in China. In Jia Hao and Lin Zhimin, eds., *Changing Central-Local Relations in China: Reform and State Capacity*, 94. Boulder, CO: Westview Press.
11. Chen Yinqi. The central-local relations in fiscal management. In *Woguo Zhongyang Yu Difang Jingji Guanli Quanxian Yanjiu* (Studies of Authority Division between the Central and Local Governments in Economic Management in China), edited by Guojia Jiwei Zhengce Yanjiushi. Beijing: Guojia Jiwei (State Planning Commission), 1993, p 69.
12. *Ibid*.
13. Guojia Jiwei Zhengce Yanjiushi (Policy Study Office of China State Planning Com-

mission). Establishing the new structure of central-local authority division in economic management. In *Woguo Zhongyang Yu Difang Jingji Guanli Quanxian Yanjiu* (Studies of Authority Division between the Central and Local Governments in Economic Management in China), edited by Guojia Jiwei Zhengce Yanjiushi. Beijing: Guojia Jiwei (State Planning Commission), 1993, pp 69, 72.

14. World Bank. *China: Revenue Mobilization and Tax Policy*. Washington: Author, 1990, p 221.
15. Guojia Tongjiju (China State Statistics Bureau). *Tongji Ziliao* (Statistical Reference), Beijing, No. 180, June 20, 1993, pp 2–5.
16. Dali L. Yang. Reform and the restructuring of central-local relations. In D.S.G. Goodman and G. Segal, eds., *China Deconstruct: Politics, Trade and Regionalism*. London: Routledge, 1994, pp 59–90, at 63.
17. Wang Shaoguang. Central-local fiscal politics in China. In Jia Hao and Lin Zhimin, eds., *Changing Central-Local Relations in China: Reform and State Capacity*. Boulder, CO: Westview Press, 1994, pp 91–109.
18. Bell, M.W., Hoe Ee Khor, and Kalpana Kochhar. *China at the Threshold of a Market Economy*, Washington: International Monetary Fund, September 1993, pp 40–41.
19. Beijing will forcefully undertake the adjustment of the preferential policy. *Central Daily News (International Edition)*, Nov. 1, 1995, p 4.
20. Wang Shaoguang and Hu Angang. *Zhongguo Guojia Nengli Baogao* (Report on China's State Capacity). Shenyang: Liaoling Renmin Chubanshe (Liaoling People's Press), 1993, pp 86–89.
21. *Selected Foreign-Related Laws and Regulations of the PRC* (Vol. 1). Hong Kong: Institute of Chinese Law and East Asia Open Institute, 1989, p 93.
22. *Selected Foreign-Related Laws and Regulations of the PRC* (Vol. 2). Hong Kong: Institute of Chinese Law and East Asia Open Institute, 1989, p 119.
23. Bell, M.W., Hoe Ee Khor, and Kalpana Kochhar. *China at the Threshold of a Market Economy*. Washington: International Monetary Fund, Sept. 1993, p 40.
24. Xiangmin Chen. The changing role of Shenzhen in China national and regional development in the 1980s. In *China in Transition*, G.T. Yu, ed. New York: University Press of America, 1993, pp 254–255.
25. *Introduction of Special Economic Zone in Hainan Province for Its 5th Anniversary Celebration*. Haicou: Hainan Zhenfa Property Co. Ltd, 1993, p 4.
26. Shi Jun. Economic efficiency in Pudong development zone. *Renmin Ribao Haiwaiban* (People's Daily Overseas Edition), Feb. 1, 1995, p 1.
27. Bell, M.W., Hoe Ee Khor, and Kalpana Kochha. *China at the Threshold of a Market Economy*. Washington: International Monetary Fund, Sept. 1993, p 44.
28. Zhang Yan. Taxes division system meets protest of the localities. *Guangjiaojin Yue Kan* (Broad View Monthly), January 1994, p 10.
29. Wang Shaoguang and Hu Angang. *Zhongguo Guojia Nengli Baogao* (Report on China's State Capacity). Shenyang: Liaoling Renmin Chubanshe (Liaoling People's Press), 1993, p 11.
30. Guojia Tongjiju (State Statistics Bureau). Statistic report on national economic and social development in 1994. *Renmin Ribao Haiwaiban* (People's Daily Overseas Edition), March 2, 1995, p 2.

31. Ban Wei. Vice Premier Zhu Rongji's speech at the world economy forum. *Renmin Ribao Haiwaiban* (People's Daily Overseas Edition), Jan. 30, 1995, p 6.
32. Guojia Jingjitizhi Gaige Weiyuanhui (State Economic Structural Reform Commission), ''Issues of Reform and Development in 1994,'' *Zhongguo Gaige* (China Reform), No. 2, 1994. p 11.
33. *Ibid.*
34. Zhang Jinshen. 1994: Chinese economy achieved five great accomplishments. *Renmin Ribao Haiwaiban* (People's Daily Overseas Edition), March 1, 1995, p 1.
35. Abstracts of Premier Li Peng's government work report. *Renmin Ribao Haiwaiban* (People's Daily Overseas Edition), March 6, 1995, p 2.
36. Chen Jinshong. Description and comments on finance and economy. *Radio Free Asia*, January 1998.
37. Zhang Shenli. Strategically adjusting the structure of state economy. *Guangming Daily*, Oct. 31, 1997, p 7.

15

Marketization After Mao

National Strategy in Postreform China, 1980–1993

Laure Paquette
Lakehead University, Thunder Bay, Ontario, Canada

I. INTRODUCTION

This article applies my own framework of strategic analysis to the People's Republic of China between 1980 and 1993. The framework allows for explanations or predictions about national strategy on the basis of certain permanent social characteristics. It was developed for the purpose of determining the overall posture of a state in conditions of high uncertainty.

The theory and method developed here make the prediction that, given China's main social values of community orientation and materialism, it should choose a direct strategy of action. For purposes of this analysis, national values are defined as the accepted standards of historical or ideological origin as well as the national heritage cherished by the population as a whole. National strategy is defined as the comprehensive direction of all the elements of national power to attain national objectives and to support and pursue the general goals provided by a nation's leaders.

The bulk of this paper is taken up by the determination of those two variables of the empirical hypothesis—national values and national strategy. Because of space limitation, the proposal for the theory of causal relationship between the two variables has been explored in detail elsewhere.[1] Once the *type* of strategy is established, however, it becomes possible to identify the actual strategy China is using and, of most interest to the policy and decision makers, to understand and make predictions about its tactics.

II. ANALYSIS

The process of analysis can be broken into four steps. The first step involves the identification of a sea change in national policies, usually a reliable indication of the last time a new strategy was introduced. Such major shifts in direction are often accompanied by major social upheavals. Russia's, for instance, is easy to identify following the disintegration of the former USSR. Step 2 involves the identification of the new tactics introduced with the new grand strategy. These tactics are the most obvious manifestations of a new strategy. By tactics I refer to the means at a state's (or any actor in the political sphere's) disposal. This stage of the analysis looks for changes in the economic, military, diplomatic, and political spheres, and they also usually provides the material for identifying the values. Values are a key factor in determining the long-term compatibility of strategies, since my own previous research shows that they underpin the entire grand strategy. The identification of values also helps narrow the range of possibilities that must be considered.

For the purposes of this analysis, national values are defined as the accepted standards of historical or ideological origin as well as the national heritage cherished by the population as a whole. This analysis is best served by a classification adapted from Talcott Parsons' typology of social values: (1) self-orientation versus collectivity orientation, and (2) materialism versus nonmaterialism.[2] The third step examines the declaratory policy or political rhetoric (official documents, speeches, debates in the legislatures, etc.) in order to identify the goals of the national strategy.

A. Identifying Stategy

National strategy is defined as the comprehensive direction of all the elements of national power to attain national objectives and to support and pursue the general goals provided by a nation's leaders. It can be identified by answering three questions:

(1) Is a particular state using strategy? The trick here is to tell a strategy apart from a plan, policy, or program. Plans, policies, and programs organize means to an end as much as a strategy does. But strategy is both an idea and an action, while plans, policies, and programs are not. A state using strategy is much likelier to use slogans or strong images. A state using plans, policies, and programs does not rely on slogans or strong images.

(2) Is the state using a national strategy? A strategy is national when it uses a broad spectrum of the means available to the state and tries to achieve objectives important to the whole rather than to parts.[3] In other words, the strategy must cut across several areas of state behavior: economic, political, cultural, military, etc.

(3) What strategy is the state using? It is not easy to pick out the exact strategy a state is using from so many possibilities. The best way to proceed is to start by reducing the number of possibilities one has to consider by identifying the type of strategy.

B. Identifying the Type of Strategy

André Beaufre's typology of strategy classifies them according to their nature: direct strategy of action, direct strategy of persuasion, indirect strategy of action, indirect strategy of persuasion. The difference between strategy of action and strategy of persuasion is straightforward: the first involves physical engagement of the state's material resources, while the second involves threats, discourse, posturing—all means and actions that require nonmaterial resources. The difference between a direct strategy and an indirect one is not quite so obvious: a direct strategy is one that changes the opponent's direction or momentum itself; an indirect strategy changes the opponent's direction using an intermediary. Once the type of strategy is identified, then those possibilities need to be considered. The next step is to identify the components of strategy, each by its own preferred source of information: (1) goal, by analysis of official statements[4]; (2) means or tactics, by direct observation; (3) style, by secondary analysis; and (4) core idea, by analysis of official statements, although this is not always possible.[5]

The fourth step identifies the strategy itself, the identification of values having provided us with the type of strategy possible. It is possible that the strategy is made explicit in the declaratory policy of a state, but if not the strategy can be identified by its characteristics. Typically, a national strategy encompasses a number of spheres. It is also true that the best strategies are not made public or even explicit in sources available to the scholar. Also, some states like Canada or South Korea in the 1990s, have no particular strategy. They simply drift, relying on incremental policy, decision making, or crisis management. This paper focuses only on two of these value dichotomies.

1. Self-Orientation Versus Community Orientation

The argument that Chinese society chooses community orientation over self-orientation is based on the content of the ''shame'' culture, the Confucian hetriage till present in the political culture, and the political ideology. This foundation is so solid and so fundamental that the value of community orientation has survived the massive social changes brought about by economic reforms.

Chinese political culture has three dimensions—the moral, the psychological, and the social. The moral dimension provides for virtue and evil, and for social and psychological inhibitions against deviation. This shame culture promotes virtue by assuring universal acceptance of a set of norms and by making behavior maximally public and discourages deviance, which is instantly confronted by unanimous reproof. The psychological dimension provides a defense mechanism of repression. The social dimension presents a duality: the Chinese masses have been taught to cultivate boundless love and self-sacrifice for the people and boundless hate for enemies of the people.

A number of scholars have remarked on the continued significance of Confucianism via the continuities of classical Chinese in contemporary culture. Many of them reinforce the primacy of the group over the individual: the cult of the Emperor and the personality cult of Mao; the rule of man instead of rule of law; the coercive power of the military; collective guilt and punishment; the wide-ranging power of the state/party on monopoly of political power; supervised and controlled grass roots community life; official ideological orthodoxy; the dominance of the state/party over individuals; the domination of society by the bureaucratic state; concentration of power in the hands of a few without institutional checks on that power; the law as a tool wielded by the ruler to control the populace; state imposition of official ideology as truth; state monopoly of communication; private individuals as subject to and property of the state; and subordination of all social groups to the state.[6]

The Chinese imperial state, founded on Confucian teachings among others, was such that no private undertaking or any aspect of public life could escape official regulation, and the same can almost be said of the Communist state. One of the cornerstones of Confucianism, moreover, is not just the subjugation of the individual to the group, but the very abhorrence of the individual, and the portrayal of the individual interest as selfishness.[7]

It is hardly necessary to discuss the content of Marxism or Communism as it has existed in China since 1949 in order to establish that community orientation is encouraged and supported over self-orientation by the Chinese ideology. What is striking about this particular national value in contemporary China is the extent to which it has held true in times of great social upheaval: the decade of the Cultural Revolution, the reforms of Deng Xiaoping, and the Tiananmen Square crisis of 1989. The Tiananmen crisis itself was couched in terms that reflect the communitarian orientation. Although to Western eyes, the students' concerns were immediate (terrible living conditions, compulsory assignments to first jobs, salaries less than those of waiters and cab drivers), the students themselves ''could not concentrate their complaints on such pragmatic, concrete personal problems *because this would expose them to the criticism of being selfish*.''[8] The government's reply in an editorial in the *People's Daily*, which was read in its entirety on state television, was to brand the students as unpatriotic and as selfishly concentrating on personal woes.[9]

2. Materialism Versus Nonmaterialism

The argument that materialism has risen above nonmaterialist concerns like ideology rests on two developments. First, the standard of living in China has been falling slowly and has reached a point below which it triggered a crisis, because the society was in danger of collapsing and taking the Communist Party system with it. In any event, a crisis over scarce resources, a strained environment, and overpopulation was imminent. Second, the previous concern over ideology was quickly downgraded. Reforms overwhelmingly emphasized business and economic development, and said nothing or little about political institutions. Characteristically, there were sudden reversals of policy, and the leaders took little trouble to reconcile their actions with previous explanations, either to the Chinese people or to other countries. These reforms were based on a need to address the material aspirations of the nation, so long denied, but they were also a significant challenge on ideological grounds. Ideology lost, and its importance was gradually and obviously decreased.

In 1979, the year he finally edged out Premier Hua Guofeng, Deng Xiaoping, the new leader of China, launched a three-year economic readjustment and a new economic strategy. This new economic strategy dominates the domestic concerns and the national political agenda to this day. By 1984, the reforms were considered both successful and popular. The 1984 meeting of the National People's Congress ushered in sweeping economic reforms, allowing for free enterprise and price reforms. For the first time since 1949, any citizen could obtain foreign exchange through the Bank of China. In March 1988, the first-ever foreign bids for leases of land use rights were held for Shanghai concessions. By 1993, the revolutionary special economic zones for foreign investment initiated in Fujian and Guandong were extended to every province in the People's Republic.[10] But there was another side to this newly minted ''socialism with Chinese characteristics.'' At the National People's Congress of 1989, the main state emphasis was on reasserting economic and political control over the country, given the 100,000 planned layoffs of coal workers, with another 300,000 by 1995, in a country where unemployment was unknown since 1949.

Military aid in terms of arms exports is a good example of how aid in general was gradually suspended to fellow Communist countries. In the 1960s, arms also constituted long-term free loans to any ideologically correct—i.e., Marxist or Maoist—state or political movement. During the Cultural Revolution, for instance, China had provided weapons to Maoist insurgents in India.[11] In the 1970s, the arms exports were really forms of aid, since they were provided without guarantee or on barter. But in the 1980s, arms were sold to any country, politically correct or otherwise, as long as they were fighting some of China's own enemies and then to anyone with the cash to pay for them. Now, China only helps those regimes which are fighting Chinese enemies, which, given reassessed threat perceptions, are increasingly few.

III. CHINESE NATIONAL STRATEGY

A. Prediction

If its national values are materialism and self-orientation, China should choose a direct strategy of action. A material state is more likely to use a strategy of action because it develops and applies material standards to the processes of cognition, evaluation, and appreciation. The state is more likely to perceive a concrete threat, to assess outcomes according to tangible realities, and to prefer action to persuasion. (In the same way, a nonmaterialist state prefers persuasion to action.) The reasons why a self-oriented state chooses a direct strategy are a little less obvious. A state which sees itself as a single unit rather than part of a group is more likely to count on its own resources to solve any problems. It will also see other states as single units, discounting the significance of alliances. In a word, it will generally apply self-oriented standards. Having established a hypothesis, it is now possible to examine the exact content of Chinese national strategy.

This particular section of the chapter is divided into three sections making the following argument: There was a national strategy under Mao Zedong which was changed under Deng; Deng's initiatives and changes constitute a strategy, having the components of style, core idea, goal and tactics; and this strategy is a direct strategy of action.

B. Previous Strategy

It is much more difficult to argue that Mao's China was governed by a single strategy than it is to do so with Deng's China, because his later, tyrannical decisions obscure in retrospect his original cohesive vision. This vision is generally known under the slogan ''fighting the people's war,'' or under the Chinese concept of *hezu liliang*, or forcing inaction by frightening the adversary.[12] The goal was ''national security, the search for power and influence, and unification.''[13] The tactics were[14]:

1. *Yuan Chiao Ching Kung*: Cooperate with the distant country against the near country.
2. *I I Chih I*: Set up one barbarian against another barbarian.
3. *Pi Shish Chi Shu*: Attack the weak and avoid the strong.

C. New Strategy

Most observers noted changes as Deng gained and finally assumed power: ''In a year since [Mao's death], the country has moved rapidly from ideological dogmatism towards eclectic pragmatism, from extreme totalitarianism towards liberalised authoritarianism, from a command economy, towards market socialism.''[15] There was also ample evidence of changes in foreign or military policy: Defence Minister's Zhang Aiping's article in the Party journal *Red Flag* showed clearly that ''China . . . is rethinking its defence strategy,'' with a new emphasis on ''strategic and nuclear war as opposed to tactical and conventional conflict,'' and ''changes in Sino-Soviet relations evident since 1982.''[16]

D. Components of Strategy

> This new national strategy could initially be seen as presuming a sequence: 1) political changes, especially the creation of a professional and highly skilled administrative bureaucracy, that in conjunction with 2) several structural economic reforms will produce 3) sustained economic growth which will, in turn, create 4) popular support and legitimacy for the regime.[17]

1. Goal

''The top priorities of the present Chinese leadership are economic development and improvement of the people's living standards, so as to sustain the legitimacy of the Chinese Communist regime.''[18] This goal was stated over and over again at meetings of the National People's Congress, the State Council, and the Party Central Committee.

2. Style

Deng's preferred style throughout this period has always been that of the power behind the throne. For instance, as early as 1986, Deng was giving hints of his retirement. He left all of his posts after putting his trusted men in place, but still pulled all the strings. This style, called his ''Soft Iron Hand,'' is obvious in his early career, when he was Zhou Enlai's lieutenant. The contrast was vivid: ''Teng tends to be assertive and even acerbic, where Chou was suave and gracious. . . . Teng is less politically secure than Chou was in his last years and accordingly cannot afford to be as relaxed on the highly charged Taiwan issue.''[19] It is also obvious in his management of the People's Liberation Army (PLA).[20] However, Deng had due regard for the PLA and was careful to retain the traditional basis of power of the military under his firm control. The chairmanship of the Central Military Commission was the post he held the longest, even after he had resigned from all the others.

A second characteristic of the Deng style is a moderate reliance on the personality cult: ''May Chairman Deng live ten thousand years.''[21] The existence of the personality cult, a well-known feature of the latter years of Mao's reign, is usually attributed to the weakness of the institutionalization of leading role positions in the party structure.[22] Just as the media reported that Mao could, according to his doctors, live to be 150 years old, so Deng's granddaughter has stated publicly that Deng could live to be 125. Deng used a highly personalized form of power. His vision and strategy were China's as long as he remained the elder statesman, and the transition away from his strategy will only be gradual. These two characteristics of his style are obvious in the way he edged Premier Hua Guofeng, leader of China between 1976 and 1980, out of power.

The story begins with Deng falling from grace for the second time in his career. As historian Antonia Fraser once said, it is sometimes difficult to remember that events so vivid in the past once lay in the future. There was an earlier Beijing Spring, in 1976, now overshadowed by the events of 1989. Then, Senior Vice Premier Deng, heir apparent to the highest office, is summarily dismissed as an ''unrepentant capitalist roader'' for having plainly displayed his sympathies for the students. By September, Mao is dead and Hua Guofeng is the leader of China. By October, the rehabilitation of Deng begins. By August 1977, Deng is again the third-ranking leader in China.

1978 is a momentous year for China and for Hua: Deng is elected Chairman and Vice Premier of the State Council again. Deng is now emerging as the driving force behind all new policies. From now on, the personalized form of power that Deng exercises is particularly obvious. The 1976 Tiananmen Square is declared ''completely revolutionary,'' a direct embarrassment to Premier Hua and a boon to Deng. In a rare example of grandstanding, Deng tells foreign journalists he chose *not* to be Premier. By 1980, Hua Yaobang and Zhao Ziyang are both promoted at Hua's expense, as Deng is pulling the strings behind the scenes. By December of that year, Hua is completely and finally edged out as Premier and Communist Party leader. The Deng lieutenants are now promoted and Zhao becomes Premier, but with Deng and Zhang Aiping as Vice Premiers of the State Council. Finally Deng, Hu, and Zhao are elected to the Party Central Committee. Given that the army is now the main centre of opposition, Deng brings it under permanent civilian control, via the new Central Military Commission enshrined in the Constitution of 1982, which he chairs himself.

3. Core Idea

Deng's core idea has become a fixture of political rhetoric in the China of the 1980s and 1990s: ''It does not matter if the cat is black or white, so long as the cat gets the mouse.''

4. Tactics

Here it is particularly clear that the national strategy is one of action, because Deng's strategy contains a large number of active interventions. The tactics used by Deng fall into three broad categories: domestic initiatives, foreign relations, and military affairs.

(a). Domestic Initiatives. Domestic initiatives can in turn be divided into three categories: how Deng attacked the gerontocracy, how Deng reformed the bureaucracy, and how Deng guided the economy.

Gerontocracy. Deng consolidated his own power by encouraging generational change in the Party. As late as 1982, the gerontocracy still survived in senior posts. In April 1985, however, Deng selected over 1000 young (meaning under the age of 60) officials as candidates of ministerial and provincial posts. The following September, the Party ousted 10 of 24 Politburo members, and 64 of 340 Central Committee members. Deng supporters dominated the new membership, with a marked reduction of the military presence on the committees. Ostensibly to combat right-left factionalism in the party, Deng required existing members to reregister, resulting in 3000 de facto expulsions. A program combating ''spiritual pollution'' was similarly successful, so much so that it was called off after only nine months. In a May 1987 address to party leaders, Zhao Ziyang tells them that they suffer from rigid thinking, ossification, and far too many elderly cadres. Finally, and this was his masterstroke, Deng resigned from most of his party posts: with the elevation of Zhu Rongji to the Vice Premiership a new generation has risen to power.

Bureaucracy. Deng was more successful in reforming the bureaucracy of China. Starting in 1982, the State Council went from 13 Vice Premiers to two, the bureaucracy from 98 government departments to 52, and the cadres staff from 49,000 to 32,000. A new state Constitution was promulgated: it reinstated the positions of State Chairman and Vice Chairman; created the symbolic position of Head of State, the State Central Military Commission, and the Ministry for State Security; returned communes to their original, strictly economic, role; and abolished life tenure in important posts. By 1984, the transformation of the Chinese state was obvious: there were regional and department boundaries, less egalitarianism in remuneration, a role for market and value in production, planning only for major projects, a program to update the laws and regulations of the last 35 years, and a campaign in favor of modernization.[23]

Economy. The Chinese economy was unquestionably the area of greatest concern and activity from 1984 on, but reconstructing it is not always an accurate business. Western economic statistics are not always available for China, and

Table 1 Selected Economic Statistics, 1985–91

Year	Event
1985	50% inflation in Beijing
1986	16% devaluation of official currency rate
1987	29% increase in exports to US $39.92 billion
	2.2% increase in imports to US $43.86 billion
	14% overall increase in trade
	9.4% increase in GNP to US $1.09 trillion
	9.1% inflation
	21% of households had decline of standard of living
	10% of households below poverty line (income = $120/Y450 p.a)
1988	27% inflation
	11% increase in GNP
	17% increase in industrial output
	2% unemployment (previously unknown)
1989	6.5% increase in exports, to US $43.27 billion
	3.9% decrease in imports, to US $38.27 billion
	4% increase in GNP
1990	20% decrease of revenue from state industry
1991	12% increase in GNP
	6.2% inflation in countryside
	11% inflation in cities

Source: Ref. 50.

official figures are not necessarily calculated on the same basis as Western economic statistics. But it is possible to form at least a partial picture of the Chinese economy (see Table 1).

These statistics are in broad agreement with the historical record of a government struggling to control an overheated economy throughout the late 1980s. As early as 1981, China received a US$717 million International Monetary Fund (IMF) loan to correct its balance-of-payment problems. The State Council announced the gradual lifting of price controls on half of all goods by 1989, the first major price reforms ever. It also ceded control over trade, imports, and exports to local jurisdictions in 1988. Beijing started combating economic crimes committed by state and Party officials. The three top economic posts in Chinese banking were shuffled, and the National People's Congress passed measures to tighten controls on the economy, controls that were only eased in the mid-1990s. Corruption is generally thought to be growing by leaps and bounds.

(b). Foreign Relations. The second leg of Deng's strategy was in the area of foreign relations. Here there were announcements about the objectives of the foreign policy of China, renewed relations with the two superpowers, renewed regional relations, and increased participation in multilateral forums.

Foreign policy objectives. Deng's first gesture was to abandon the theory of the Three Worlds, based on three now-outdated assessments: that both American and Soviet leaders were aware that total war would only bring about mutual destruction; that the world was bipolar; and that not many Second and Third World countries would participate in a united front against hegemony.[24] Instead, Deng firmly committed to an independent foreign policy based on the so-called Five Principles of Peaceful Coexistence: respect for territorial integrity and sovereignty; noninterference in domestic affairs; equality and mutual benefit; nonaggression; and peaceful coexistence.[25] In practice, these have translated into an intolerance of interference or pressure from outside; a focus on United States relations, which are improving, and with Japan, which are cordial; a lack of any attachment to an external power; and pragmatism over the pursuit of solidarity and cooperation with the Third World, on the one hand, and eventual reunification with Hong Kong and Taiwan, on the other.

Relations with the superpowers. Until the end of the cold war, China was consistently motivated by a desire to enhance its own defense capability to be able to counter the Soviet threat.[26] Initially, the USSR made several appeals for normalized relations, but Beijing was skeptical: China's entire foreign policy was devised to counter Soviet expansionism, with rapprochement to the United States, Western Europe, and Japan,[27] and Eastern Europe as a second intermediate zone.[28] Both Beijing and Washington felt a greater need to enhance mutual relations after the Soviet naval expansion into the Indian Ocean and the Asia-Pacific in the mid-1970s.[29] In the early 1980s, the Chinese were beginning to see the Soviet invasion of Afghanistan and Moscow's support for the Vietnamese invasion of Cambodia more as a threat to U.S. supremacy than as an effort to checkmate Beijing.[30] As a result, there were major changes in Beijing's threat assessment, policy goals, and evaluation of its own defense capability.[31] But

> Peking's principles in its military relations with Washington have been (1) to make all possible efforts to obtain science and technology from the United States; (2) to be sure not to allow the value of arms purchased from the United States to exceed foreign-exchange income; (3) to only buy arms which will not irritate the Soviet Union; and (4) not to rely on the United States too heavily.[32]

Despite China's best efforts, Japan, and not China, was the cornerstone of U.S. policy in Asia under Reagan.[33]

Regional relations. Regional relations generally reflected Deng's Five Principles. In South Asia, "Beijing acts on the assumption that its interest in South Asia can best be achieved by consolidating its existing ties in the region, e.g. Pakistan and inch towards long term detente with India."[34] In the 1980s, China tried to reduce regional tensions and became a fan of South Asia Arms Reduction Cooperation.[35] Relations with Vietnam have been the most troublesome in Southeast Asia. After a decade of clashes and border incidents, including a 1988 exchange of warship fire over the Spratley Islands, in 1991 China and Vietnam normalized their relations. Popular feelings against Japan remain high in China. As recently as 1985, there were student demonstrations against Japanese militarism and Japan's increasing commercial role in China. Finally, the mainland Chinese had adopted a "Big Family" strategy vis-à-vis Taiwan and Hong Kong in 1979.

Multilateral forums. China has now joined a large number of international forums, mainly economic ones. Post-Tiananmen, the Chinese were desperate to get back into a number of countries' good graces, as their vote in the United Nation on the Gulf War shows.

(c). Military Affairs. Deng has sought to modernize the PLA, to develop China's nuclear arsenal, and to increase the arms trade.

Reform of the PLA. Deng had brought the PLA under his personal control and lowered its profile and position in domestic affairs by (1) downgrading military modernization to last of the four modernizations (after industry, agriculture, and science); (2) cutting its resource allocation; and (3) changing its role in the conduct of international politics.[36] For a time, the PLA, nicknamed the "People's Liquidation Army," suffered from sabotage, public attacks, criticism, and demoralization.[37] Deng also made radical changes in the managerial, institutional, and economic spheres to foster innovation.[38] But Tiananmen overall has been good for the army: After 10 years of cuts, the Communist Party approved an increase of 15% in 1990, 12% (after inflation) in 1991, and 12% again in 1992 (see Table 2). The PLA now apparently plans to build its own aircraft carriers, and had decided to buy one from abroad.[39]

The most striking change has been the personnel reforms: China has retired 25% of troops, 70,000 to 80,000 senior PLA officers, and 2 million out of 10 million cadres.[40] Along with those retirements are renewed party controls over all changes in personnel, military policy making, promotions, and education, and an extensive ideological campaign against the PLA opposition, since mid-1979.[41] Overall, the reforms diffuse the military's channels of intervention in politics at the center and deemphasize PLA as an arm of the Party, although it remains an important domestic political actor.[42]

Table 2 Changes in Military Expenditures

Year	Change in military expenditure
1965–71	+10.0%
1971–75	−1.2%
1975–80	+1.5%
1981–90	−15.1%
1990	+15.0%
1991	+12.0%
1992	+14.0%

Source: Ref. 51.

Nuclear arsenal. The second area of significance in military affairs is China's nuclear arsenal. For the Chinese, nuclear weapons are the symbol of its self-reliance. While the outlays on conventional forces have been reduced in recent years (except in the aftermath of the Vietnam campaign in 1979), expenditure on nuclear weapons has been consistently maintained at about 5% of the overall defence expenditure. At worst, however, China can only be considered "to have limited nuclear ambitions . . . [though it] may fall into the same dilemma as the other four nuclear weapons nations: perpetually 'modernizing' their nuclear forces to overcome imagined deficiencies."[43] By 1988, it was reported to have a capability for surviving nuclear counterattack. It continued to modernize throughout 1989, but it is now the only major country not publishing information on its tests. In August 1991, China announced that it would sign the Non-Proliferation Treaty, but also improve technology and capability in its ballistic missile force.[44]

Table 3 National Strategy of the PRC

Values	Materialism, collectivism
Strategy	Pragmatism
Core idea	"It doesn't matter if it is a black cat or a white cat, so long as the cat gets the mouse"
Goals	Regime survival
Tactics	Gradual economic reform
	Retain domestic political status quo via tight control of peasants, dissidents
Style	Personalized politics

Arms trade. All of this may be being financed by the profits of the arms trade, which has mushroomed since 1985, having launched a major marketing effort in 1984.[45] It was the fifth largest arms exporter to the Third World between 1986 and 1990, up from eighth in the previous five years.[46] With ideology no longer a factor in marketing, China's status as a major power was bolstered. After Tienanmen Square, China reneged on its promise not to sell arms to the Middle East, but was as reluctant as ever to release information on its arms sales. In the 1990s, China continued to be present at all arms exhibitions in Asia and the Middle East, adding Thailand to its client list and selling as many conventional weapons as the United Kingdom. In 1992, the United States placed its Most Favored Nation status contingent on arms exports behavior.[47] In May 1992, China agreed to cooperate in the halt of the global spread of technology and equipment at a Major Arms Supplier conference, but it is not yet clear what practical measures it will be willing to take. In 1993, China sold missile components to Pakistan, resulting in a U.S. embargo on high-technology exports. Major weapons systems are now being sold in unprecedented quantities to a broad spectrum of states among Beijing's allies and others, which have fat bank books rather than correct ideology. The quality of weapons is far more consistent and China has begun to compete in providing larger-scale arms requirements of states, though the quality gap is still telling.[48] Characteristically, as its arms trade and marketing are growing quickly, China has playing a larger role than ever before in arms control.

IV. CONCLUSION

There have been three tests of Deng's strategy (see Table 3), the so-called three shocks[49]: the lessons learned in Vietnam; the introduction to Western arms technology after missions of military experts were sent overseas; and the advent of SDI in March 1983. According to Alex Gliksman, this led to a reinforcement of its nuclear posture. A fourth shock, the events of Tienanmen Square, also failed to alter the basic values of community orientation and materialism or the basic course on which Deng is set. As Milovan Djilas once said, a revolution cannot change a nation, only the form of power and the form of property.

What of the future of Deng's strategy? Inevitably it seems tied to Deng himself, given the high degree of personalization, but his strategy did not die with him. At present, the survival of the central government appears to be tied in part to the strength of its resolve and the resolve of the Ministry of State Security and the PLA to maintain social order. Even now, they are not entirely successful. We can be certain that China will continue to talk one way and walk another, jettisoning commitments or reversing course according to the dictates of pragmatism.

Is China trying to become a regional power? Deng Xioaping purged the general staff in the hopes of ensuring a reformist succession after his death. The Chairman of the Central Military Commission, Jiang Zemin, a hard-liner, is taking more and more power, so much so that experts are beginning to suggest that the succession struggle is over. China is voting in the same direction as the other permanent members of the Security Council of the United Nations. On the other hand, the military budget has grown. Since the layoff of soldiers by the hundreds of thousands, these increases must be going to procurement and technological modernization. The tendency to democratization, apparent in the postwar world, is particularly intense in Communist China, currently undergoing a social revolution of massive proportions. From a nuclear standpoint, there is not much to inspire confidence in China: it supports the principles of the Non-Proliferation Treaty, but it has targeted countries with nuclear ambitions for its nuclear marketing.

ACKNOWLEDGMENTS

I thank for their assistance at the University of National Defense of the People's Liberation Army, Senior Colonel Professor Deng Feng, Vice Director, Senior Colonel Professor Liu Chunzhi and Senior Colonel Professor Liu Siqi; at the China International Institute for Strategic Studies, Mrs. Gao Wenmei, Senior Research Fellow and Founding Member, Senior Colonel Yu Hua Dong, Executive Director, Admiral Professor Luo Renshi, Senior Research Fellow, Senior Colonel Sa Benwang, Senior Research Fellow, Mr. Zhang Wu Tang, Standing Council Member, General Mu Huimin, Secretary General, and Mr. Wang Tongle, Administrative Officer; at the Shanghai Institute for International Studies, Professor Chen Peiyao, Acting President. I also thank Christine Straehle and Piero Pucci for establishing a chronology of events in China between 1984 and 1993, and Nicole Cody for later research assistance.

ENDNOTES

1. Laure Paquette. *National Strategy and National Values*. Ph.D. dissertation, Kingston, Ont.: Queen's University, 1992.
2. Talcott Parsons' classification in R.F. Bales, Edward Shils, and Talcott Parsons, *Working Papers in the Theory of Action* (Glencoe, IL: Free Press, 1953), *passim*; Michael Sullivan, *Measuring Global Values* (New York: Greenwood, s.d.), *passim*.
3. Ray S. Cline. *World Power Trends and U.S. Foreign Policy for the 1980s*. Boulder, CO: Westview Press, 1980, 2.

4. Although he calls it aims. F.B. Ali. The principles of War. *Journal of the Royal United Services Institution for Defence Studies* 108 (May 1963), 159–165.
5. ''The entirety of traditional practices and habits of thinking which, in a society, governs the organization and the use of the military forces in the pursuit of political objectives.'' Author's translation, as quoted by Bruno Colson, ''La culture stratégique américaine,'' *Stratégique* 8 (1988), 15–82, 33. The original reads: ''l'ensemble des pratiques traditionnelles et des habitudes de pensée qui, dans une société, gouvernent l'organisation et l'emploi de la force militaire au service d'objectifs politiques.''
6. Fu Zhengyuan. Continuities of Chinese political tradition. *Studies in Comparative Communism XXIV*(3) (September 1991), 259–280, 262.
7. Cal Clark. The nature of Chinese Communism and the prospects for Teng's reforms. *Issues and Studies 21*(1) (January 1985), 12–37, 21.
8. Lucian Pye. Tiananmen and Chinese political culture: the escalation of confrontation from moralizing to revenge. *Asian Survey XXX*(4) (April 1990), 331–347, 334. Emphasis mine.
9. Hu Qili, then a recognized moderate and ally of Zhao Ziyang. Beijing edition of *People's Daily*, April 26, 1989.
10. Jonathan Pollack. Changing perceptions of East Asian security and development. *Orbis 29* (1985–86), 771–795, 782.
11. *World Armaments and Disarmament: SIPRI Yearbook 1980*. London: Taylor and Francis, 1980, 76.
12. Richard W. Fieldhouse. Chinese nuclear weapons: an overview. *World Armaments and Disarmament: SIPRI Yearbook 1986*. London: Taylor and Francis, 1986, p. 100.
13. Harold C. Hinton. *Communist China in World Politics*. Boston: Houghton Miflin, 1966, 109.
14. Edward S. Boylan. The Chinese cultural style of warfare. *Comparative Strategy 4* (September 1982), 336–353, 342.
15. A. Doak Barnett. Ten years after Mao. *Foreign Affairs* (Winter 1986), 32–47, 37. Joseph Y.S. Cheng. China's foreign policy in the 1980s from anti-hegemony to modernization diplomacy. *China Report 21*(3) (May-June 1985), 197–222.
16. *Summary of World Broadcasts*, BBC FE/7272 2.3.82. Jonathan D. Pollack. Changing perceptions of East Asian security and development. *Orbis 29* (1985–86), 771–795, 777.
17. Cal Clark. The nature of Chinese Communism and the prospects for Teng's reforms. *Issues and Studies 21*(1) (January 1985), 12–37, 32.
18. Joseph Y.S. Cheng. China's foreign policy in the 1980s from anti-hegemony to modernization. *China Report 21*(3) (May-June 1985), 197–222.
19. Harold C. Hinton. Teng Hsiao-p'ing's management of the superpowers. *Issues and Studies 23*(4) (April 1987), 11–25, 14.
20. Wei-chin Lee. Iron and nail: civil-military relations in the People's Republic of China. *Journal of Asian and African Studies XXVI*(1–2) (January 1991), 132–148.
21. An allusion to the cultist slogan ''May Chairman Mao Live Ten Thousand Years.'' Fu Zhengyuan. Continuities of Chinese political tradition. *Studies in Comparative Communism XXIV*(3) (September 1991), 259–280, 264.
22. Graeme Gill. Personality cult, political culture and Party structure. *Studies in Com-*

parative Communism: An International Interdisciplinary Journal XVII(2) (Summer 1984), 111–122, 113.

23. Chang Ya-chün. Military relations between Peking and Washington. *Issues and Studies 23*(4) (April 1987), 59–78.
24. Joseph Y.S. Cheng. China's foreign policy in the 1980s from anti-hegemony to modernization diplomacy. *China Report 21*(3) (May-June 1985), 197–222, 200.
25. *FBIS-CHI*. 19 April 1985, p. E2.
26. Robert G. Sutter. *Chinese Foreign Policy After the Cultural Revolution, 1966–1977*. Boulder, CO: Westview, 1978, 34–37.
27. Joseph Y.S. Cheng. China's foreign policy in the 1980s from anti-hegemony to modernization diplomacy. *China Report 21*(3) (May-June 1985), 197–222, 208.
28. Joseph Y.S. Cheng. China's foreign policy in the 1980s from anti-hegemony to modernization diplomacy. *China Report 21*(3) (May-June 1985), 197–222, 214.
29. Robert G. Sutter. *Chinese Foreign Policy After the Cultural Revolution, 1966–1977*. Boulder, CO: Westview, 1978, 34–37.
30. Gerald Segal. China's security debate. *Survival* (March-April 1982), 68–69.
31. Christopher E. Stowell. China's defense market comes of age: a view from the US of the US-China defense relationship. *International Defense Review* (December 1985), 1922–1923.
32. Chang Ya-Chün. Military relations between Peking and Washington. *Issues and Studies 23*(4) (April 1987), 66.
33. Harold C. Hinton. Teng Hsiao-p'ing's management of the superpowers. *Issues and Studies 23*(4) (April 1987), 11–25, 20.
34. Steven I. Levine. China and South Asia. *Strategic Analysis 12*(12) (January 1989), 1107–1126, 1107.
35. Pramod K. Mishra. China and South Asia. *China Report 21*(5) (September-October 1985), 403–413, 412.
36. Eberhard Sanschneider. The Chinese Army after Tiananmen. *Pacific Review 3*(2) (March 1990), 113–124, *passim*.
37. Eberhard Sanschneider. The Chinese Army after Tiananmen. *Pacific Review* 3(2) (March 1990), 113–124, 122.
38. *World Armaments and Disarmament: SIPRI Yearbook 1985*. London: Taylor and Francis, 1985, 261.
39. *South China Morning Post*, 3 March 1993, p. 1. *Der Spiegel*, 8 March 1993, p. 157.
40. *FBIS-CHI*, 10 April 1985, p. E3. *Asian Wall Street Journal Weekly* (Hong Kong ed.), 15 April 1985. *New York Times* 6 March 1985 and 21 April 1985. *FBIS-CHI*, 14 June 1985 p. W1.
41. John Frankenstein. Military cuts in China. *Problems of Communism 34*(4) (July 1985), 56–60, 58.
42. Deng Xiaoping. *Selected Works of Deng Xiaoping*. Beijing: Foreign Language Edition, 1983, 365–366. D. Banerjee. PLA and the 13th Chinese Communist Party Congress. *Strategic Analysis 12*(3) (June 1988), 217–231, 225–226.
43. Richard W. Fieldhouse. Chinese nuclear weapons: an overview. *World Armaments and Disarmament: SIPRI Yearbook 1986*. London: Taylor and Francis, 1986, 111.
44. Richard Fieldhouse. Chinese nuclear weapons: an overview. *World Armaments and Disarmament: SIPRI Yearbook 1986*. London: Taylor and Francis, 1986, 84.

45. Gerald Segal, Anne Gilks. China and the arms trade. *Arms Control 6*(3) (Dec 85), 256–281, 256. *World Armaments and Disarmament: SIPRI Yearbook 1985*. London: Taylor and Francis, 1985, 356.
46. *World Armaments and Disarmament: SIPRI Yearbook 1980*. London: Taylor and Francis, 1980, 65.
47. *World Disarmament and World Armaments: SIPRI Yearbook 1991*. London: Taylor and Francis, 1991, 279.
48. Gerald Segal, Anne Gilks. China and the arms trade. *Arms Control 6*(3) (December 1985), 256–281, 260.
49. Alex Gliksman. Emerging technology and China's changing security requirements. *Washington Quarterly 10*(3) (Summer 1987), 133–144, 133.
50. *World Armaments and Disarmament: SIPRI Yearbook 1985–1992*. London: Taylor and Francis, 1985–1992.
51. Based on constant 1978 U.S. dollars. Source: *World Armaments and Disarmament: SIPRI Yearbook 1980*. London: Taylor and Francis, 1980, 152–153.

16

Hong Kong

The World's Freest Economy and Its Liberal Policy

G. Mac Nie
Fort Valley State University, Fort Valley, Georgia

Enbao Wang
University of Hawaii at Hilo, Hilo, Hawaii

I. INTRODUCTION

Hong Kong became a colony of the United Kingdom after the Opium War between the United Kingdom and China from 1839 to 1842. In 1984 the governments of the United Kingdom and China signed an agreement on Hong Kong. According to the agreement, the United Kingdom would return Hong Kong to China in 1997. Also in the agreement, China pledged that Hong Kong would be, under the principle of "one country, two systems," a Special Administrative Region (SAR) of China with a high degree of autonomy. China also agreed that Hong Kong's capitalism and way of life would remain unchanged for 50 years after the transfer of sovereignty. Based on the agreement, Hong Kong was returned to China on July 1, 1997.[1]

What was the economic relationship between the United Kingdom and Hong Kong from 1842 to 1997? Because the original purpose of British occupation of Hong Kong was to trade with China, since 1841, when Hong Kong became a British possession, Hong Kong has served as a nontariff free port. During the Victorian era in the 19th century, the British government carried out colonial reforms as well as other liberal economic policies and started to grant some of its colonies self-government.[2] However, London did not relinquish its oversight of Hong Kong's financial budget of income and expenditure until 1958, when Hong Kong was granted financial autonomy.

Hong Kong's real economic development began in the 1950s. In 1958, Britain granted financial autonomy to Hong Kong. Fortunately, 19th-century values of economic liberalism in Britain continued to influence official thinking and practice in Hong Kong. The Hong Kong government leaders, including the decision makers of both the former colonial government and the current SAR, realized that private individuals and companies held the responsibility for the creation of wealth. Government intervention would frustrate the private operation that is coordinated by the market mechanism and damage the growth rate of the economy. Consequently, the Hong Kong government continued to carry out a policy of economic liberalization that is called ''positive nonintervention.'' Interestingly, the United Kingdom and other postindustrial economies have diverged somewhat from laissez-faire principles since the beginning of the 20th century. Increasing governmental intervention in the economy of these countries diluted the principle of the classical economic policy.[3] On the contrary, Hong Kong did not follow the policy direction of its colonial home ruler and grew as a sincere disciple of the free-market principle when it was still a developing economy.[4]

After the experiment of a free market economic policy for over forty years, Hong Kong has become a vigorous industrial power without recourse to outside economic assistance, despite formidable obstacles arising from political and economic circumstances beyond local control. This paper identifies Hong Kong as a model of economic development and offers theoretical discussions of economic policies put into effect in Hong Kong.

The rest of the paper is organized as follows. Section 2 explains the reasons that Hong Kong has been practicing the classical economic policy and summarizes the major points of the policy. Section 3 introduces the economic performance of Hong Kong and shows that Hong Kong's sheer free market system brings prosperity to this economy. Section 4 provides a theoretical explanation that supports Hong Kong's positive non-intervention policy used in the development of the Hong Kong economy. Finally, Section 5 presents concluding remarks.

II. HONG KONG: THE WORLD'S FREEST ECONOMY AND ITS POLICY

Hong Kong has been ranked the world's freest economy by the Heritage Foundation and the *Wall Street Journal* for four consecutive years.[5] Milton Friedman, Nobel Laureate, also praises Hong Kong as the freest market economy on Earth.[6] Hong Kong is also considered by some economists and policy makers as a model of economic freedom to deal with the plight of depressed cities in the advanced postindustrial economy.[7] The title of the world's freest economy offered by the

Heritage Foundation and the *Wall Street Journal* is based on an index that empirically measures the level of economic freedom in countries around the world.[8] The two main reasons for Hong Kong's liberal policy have been the natural and geographic conditions that Hong Kong has and the nonparty government administered by career civil servants.

First, Hong Kong has a land area of just over 1000 km^2, only 12% of which is arable. It has hardly any local mineral resources and no indigenous sources of fuel except timber. Seventy percent of its water supply is piped across the border from China. As a result, Hong Kong has to import 80% of the food for its residents and all the raw materials and fuels for its industrial activities. If foreign countries ceased to export to Hong Kong, the residents of Hong Kong would quickly be reduced to poverty and starvation. In addition to the necessary condition for trade, a wide, deep, and sheltered harbor provides Hong Kong with excellent and sufficient conditions for international trade. These natural conditions determine that export-oriented and free-trade policies are Hong Kong's *raison d'être* and lifeline. To attract foreign investment, respond quickly to world prices, and maintain competitive advantages in international markets, it is wise for an entirely externally dependent economy like Hong Kong to carry out a series of outward and liberal policies that will be discussed later in this section.

The second reason is that there had been no political parties in Hong Kong and the Hong Kong government was administered by career civil servants before 1991. Before Hong Kong was returned to China on July 1, 1997, the British government via a governor appointed by the Queen ruled it. By 1991, when the British had ruled Hong Kong for 150 years, there were no free elections and no political parties in Hong Kong. The government was run by career civil servants without any elected political officials or legislators to control their activities. In fact, Hong Kong's political system, under British rule, gave the government of Hong Kong a free hand to pursue its nonintervention policy. In 1991, the colonial government started introducing democracy and elections into the Legislative Council (Legco) and then political parties emerged. However, the executive-led system and the nonintervention economic policy remained unchanged even after the United Kingdom returned Hong Kong to China in 1997.[9]

What are the major elements contained in Hong Kong's positive nonintervention economic policy? Based on Hong Kong's practice, the policy can be simply summarized as *free trade, low taxes, small government, prudential budgetary management (or fiscal restraint), no control over monetary policy, minimum regulation, and providing good infrastructure*.[10]

A. Free Trade

Owing to historical reasons and natural conditions, Hong Kong policy makers consistently pursue a policy of openness and rely more heavily on the international division of labor and foreign trade than do most other economies. In stark contrast to Japan and the other East Asian newly industrial economies (NIEs), Hong Kong has refrained from protecting and subsidizing its industries and imposed the lowest restriction on exports and imports in the world. There are neither import tariffs nor export subsidies. Duties are levied on some commodities such as liquors and tobacco, but irrespective of whether they are imported or manufactured locally.

B. Low Taxes

Since Britain granted financial autonomy to Hong Kong in 1958, the Hong Kong government has continuously adopted the low-tax policy that was pioneered by William E. Gladstone, British Prime Minister and a leading political advocate of the classical economic policy of laissez-faire throughout the second half of the 19th century. The rationale behind this policy is that ''Cheap government would leave more money in the pockets of the people. Their ability to spend would mean greater demand for goods and higher investment by producers. The result would be a thriving economy and, in turn, a contented population.''[11] Except for three small oil-rich countries and the Bahamas, Hong Kong has the world's lowest tax rates.[12] The corporate profit tax has been 16.5% since 1994.[13] Individuals pay a maximum standard rate of 15% on salaries. In the 1995/96 budget, an estimated 62% of the labor force was out of the tax net, and only 2% of income earners were required to pay tax at the 15% standard rate. For instance, a married couple with a combined household income of HK$204,000 (US$26,342) would only just pay HK$80 (US$10.33) in direct taxes.[14] There is no tax on interest earnings, dividends, or capital gains. Hong Kong's low-tax policy guarantees the minimum restrictions and costs imposed on the private sector.

C. Small Government

To make sure that the colony of Hong Kong would not be a financial burden, one of the Britain's key policies toward Hong Kong was that the governmental expenditure of the colony had to rely on its own resources. Therefore, beginning in the 1840s, the size of the Hong Kong colonial government was deliberately reduced as small as possible.[15] Since the small government policy is consistent with the nonintervention principle, after Hong Kong received financial autonomy from Britain, the policy continued to be carried on. Table 1 shows the size of Hong Kong's public expenditures relative to the GDP from the fiscal years 1961/62 to 1996/97. During this period, the public sector averaged less than one-fifth of the gross domestic product.

Table 2 shows the size of the public sectors of selected countries in 1980 and 1993. Hong Kong's public sector is among the smallest. Usually, the ratio

Table 1 Size of the Public Sector in Hong Kong

Financial year	Size of the public sector (%)	Financial year	Size of the public sector (%)
1961/1962	13.8	1979/1980	14.0
1962/1963	13.7	1980/1981	15.6
1963/1964	13.3	1981/1982	17.2
1964/1965	12.9	1982/1983	18.5
1965/1966	13.2	1983/1984	18.1
1966/1967	13.1	1984/1985	15.5
1967/1968	12.0	1985/1986	16.0
1968/1969	11.7	1986/1987	15.3
1969/1970	10.9	1987/1988	13.9
1970/1971	10.9	1988/1989	14.2
1971/1972	11.1	1989/1990	15.6
1972/1973	12.1	1990/1991	16.3
1973/1974	12.3	1991/1992	16.2
1974/1975	14.3	1992/1993	15.8
1975/1976	13.4	1993/1994	17.3
1976/1977	11.7	1994/1995[a]	16.8
1977/1978	12.6	1995/1996[b]	17.6
1978/1979	14.2	1996/1997[c]	17.6

[a] Revised estimate.
[b] Budget estimate.
[c] Forecast value.
Source: Tang (1995).

of government spending to GDP is lower when an economy is less developed. Yet, Hong Kong is now ranked among high-income developed economies, but its government expenditure measured by percent of GDP is still lower than the government expenditure of most developing economies. Among the high-income economies, Hong Kong's public sector is the smallest. Compared to many developed capitalist countries in Europe whose government expenditures have reached more than one half of their GDP, Hong Kong, as a highly developed economy, continuously pursues a classical nonintervention and laissez-faire policy. The government refrains itself from spending its revenue on activities that might interfere with the private sector except for providing essential support services such as housing, education, railroads, airports, and, to a lesser extent, health care.

D. Prudential Budgetary Management

The prudential budgetary management is another aspect of the Hong Kong government's nonintervention policy, because the "living-within-our-means" rule

Table 2 Government Expenditures of Selected Countries

Selected economies	Government expenditure (% of GNP) 1980	1993	Selected economies	Government expenditure (% of GNP) 1980	1993
Low-income economies			22 Chile	29.1	22.6
1 Rwanda	14.3	31.9	23 Greece	34.4	43.1
2 Kenya	26.1	28.9	24 Korea, Rep.	17.6	17.1
3 India	13.2	16.9	25 Portugal	34.1	42.3
4 Nicaragua	32.3	39.5	High-income economies		
5 Ghana	10.9	21.0	26 New Zealand	39.0	36.6
6 Pakistan	17.7	24.0	27 Spain	27.0	35.1
7 Zimbabwe	35.3	36.2	28 Israel	72.4	44.2
8 Sri Lanka	41.6	26.9	29 Australia	23.1	28.2
9 Egypt	53.7	46.6	30 Hong Kong[a]	15.6	17.3
Middle-income economies			31 United Kingdom	38.2	43.4
10 Indonesia	23.1	18.9	32 Italy	41.0	53.4
11 Cameroon	15.5	18.3	33 Singapore	20.8	19.7
12 Philippines	13.4	18.1	34 Canada	21.8	25.8
13 Ecuador	15.0	15.4	35 Netherlands	52.7	53.9
14 Peru	20.4	14.0	36 Belgium	51.3	50.9
15 Tunisia	32.5	33.2	37 France	39.3	45.5
16 Thailand	19.0	16.3	38 Austria	37.7	39.7
17 Panama	33.4	32.1	39 Germany	. . .	33.6
18 Turkey	26.3	25.9	40 Sweden	39.5	53.9
19 Venezuela	18.7	19.2	41 United States[b]	21.7	23.8
20 Brazil	20.9	25.6	42 Denmark	40.4	45.5
21 South Africa	23.1	32.6	43 Japan	18.4	. . .

[a] The Hong Kong data come from Table 1.
[b] Federal government only.
Source: World Bank (1995) pp. 180–181.

restricts the Hong Kong government in economic affairs including its using a deficit fiscal policy. The Hong Kong government has constantly followed that rule and balanced its budget. According to Xunzi, an ancient Chinese philosopher, to be prudent in public spending, to improve the well-being of the people, and to maintain good reserves are the ways to make a country prosperous.[16] This Chinese doctrine is consistent with the Western classical view of a balanced budget. According to classical economic thought, prudential budgetary management is the best long-term public finance policy. A more straightforward reason for Hong Kong to avoid budget deficits and debt finance reflects the belief that deficit financing leads inevitably to an increase in the domestic money supply. Because Hong Kong is an externally dependent economy, an increase in the domestic money supply would push up domestic costs and prices, causing a decline in exports and output. Although the adjustment process would bring internal costs and prices back into line with world prices, in the short run, resources would be reallocated and economic efficiency will be reduced.[17] Table 3 illustrates government fiscal balances of advanced economies from 1989 to 1998. It clearly demonstrates that except Hong Kong and Asia's other NIEs, almost all advanced economies run at deficit financing. By comparing Table 3 with Table 4, which shows economic growth in advanced economies from 1989 to 1998, one can easily find that during the same time period, Hong Kong and other Asian NIEs have achieved much higher GDP growth rates than other advanced economies. From the comparison, one can easily conclude that the prudential budgetary management of Hong Kong and other Asian NIEs is closely correlated with their higher economic growth. Since the balanced budget is exogenously determined in Hong Kong, the high rates of GDP growth can be considered to be endogenously affected by the policy.

E. No Control Over Monetary Policy

From 1974 to 1983 the exchange rate of the Hong Kong dollar was operated under the flexible exchange rate system. However, since September 1982, fear of the Chinese takeover and uncertainty about the future of Hong Kong have led to a portfolio shift for many investors and a significant outflow of capital. On October 17, 1983, the Hong Kong government took a drastic step to peg the Hong Kong dollar to the U.S. dollar at US$1 = HK$7.8. Since then the Hong Kong government's ability to use monetary and interest rate policy has been strictly circumscribed. Although the usefulness of maintaining the currency peg continues under debate, there has been no doubt about the government's determination to keep the economy stable. After Hong Kong returned to China in 1997, the Hong Kong SAR government continued to maintain the link. During the Asian monetary crisis beginning late 1997, relying on a plenty of foreign reserves, the Hong Kong dollar was the only currency in that region that maintained its pegged exchange rate against the U.S. dollar.[18]

F. Minimum Regulation of the Private Sector

In Hong Kong, economic affairs are conducted in an environment of virtually unfettered free enterprise. Government policy has long dictated an essentially hands-off approach toward the private sector. There are no restrictions on the movement of capital and little protection or subsidies for particular industries. Unlike Singapore and South Korea, the Hong Kong government has refrained

Table 3 General and Central Government Fiscal Balances in Advanced Economies

	1989	1990	1991	1992	1993	1994	1995	1996	1997	1998
General government fiscal balance										
Advanced economies	−1.1	−2.0	−2.7	−3.7	−4.2	−3.4	−3.2	−2.7	−2.0	−1.8
Major industrial countries	−1.2	−2.1	−2.7	−3.8	−4.3	−3.5	−3.4	−3.0	−2.3	−2.1
United States	−1.7	−2.7	−3.3	−4.4	−3.6	−2.3	−2.0	−1.4	−1.5	−1.3
Japan	2.5	2.9	2.9	1.5	−1.6	−2.3	−3.7	−4.6	−2.9	−2.7
Germany	0.1	−2.0	−3.3	−2.8	−3.5	−2.4	−3.5	−3.8	−3.3	−2.9
France	−1.1	−1.4	−2.0	−4.0	−5.8	−5.8	−5.0	−4.1	−3.3	−3.4
Italy	−9.9	−11.0	−10.2	−9.5	−9.6	−9.0	−7.1	−6.8	−3.3	−4.1
United Kingdom	0.9	−1.2	−2.5	−6.3	−7.8	−6.8	−5.6	−4.4	−3.1	−2.1
Canada	−2.9	−4.1	−6.6	−7.4	−7.3	−5.3	−4.1	−1.8	−0.3	0.3
Other advanced economies	−0.8	−1.7	−2.6	−3.5	−4.0	−2.8	−2.3	−1.6	−0.9	−0.6
Spain	−0.28	−3.9	−5.0	−4.1	−7.5	−6.2	−6.6	−4.4	−3.2	−3.0
Netherlands	−4.7	−5.1	−2.9	−3.9	−3.2	−3.4	−4.0	−2.3	−2.2	−1.8
Belgium	−6.4	−5.6	−6.6	−7.2	−7.4	−5.1	−4.1	−3.4	−2.9	−2.6
Sweden	5.4	4.2	−1.1	−7.8	−12.3	−10.3	−7.9	−2.5	−0.8	0.3
Austria	−2.8	−2.2	−2.7	−1.9	−4.2	−4.8	−5.3	−3.9	−2.5	−2.8
Denmark	−0.5	−1.5	−2.1	−2.9	−3.9	−3.4	−1.9	−1.6	−0.1	—
Finland	6.3	5.3	−1.5	−5.9	−8.0	−6.2	−5.2	−2.6	−1.9	−0.7
Greece	−14.4	−16.1	−11.5	−12.3	−14.2	−12.1	−9.2	−7.6	−5.1	−3.5
Portugal	−2.3	−5.5	−6.6	−3.5	−6.8	−5.7	−4.9	−4.0	−2.9	−2.5
Ireland	−1.8	−2.3	−2.2	−2.4	−2.2	−2.0	−2.4	−1.0	−1.6	−1.6
Luxembourg	4.6	5.0	−0.4	−0.8	0.5	0.9	0.4	−0.1	−0.1	−0.1
Switzerland	0.8	—	−2.1	−3.5	−3.7	−2.8	−1.8	−2.2	−2.9	−2.5
Norway	3.6	4.2	2.1	−1.7	−1.4	0.4	3.3	6.3	6.3	7.3
Israel	−5.8	−4.5	−4.4	−3.1	−2.3	−1.2	−3.1	−4.2	−3.2	−2.5
Iceland	−4.6	−3.3	−2.9	−2.8	−4.5	−4.7	−3.1	−1.7	−1.0	−0.7
Korea	0.2	−0.6	−1.6	−2.6	−1.0	3.3	3.0	1.0	1.0	1.0
Australia	1.5	0.5	−2.2	−4.4	−4.5	−3.4	−2.1	−1.5	−0.9	−0.1
Taiwan Province of China	3.6	0.8	0.5	0.3	0.6	0.2	0.4	0.2	0.2	0.2
Hong Kong	2.1	0.7	3.2	2.5	2.3	1.3	−0.3	0.3	1.8	1.5
Singapore	9.9	11.4	10.3	11.3	14.3	14.2	12.7	8.6	8.9	7.8
New Zealand	−1.8	−2.3	−2.3	−4.6	−0.7	2.2	3.7	3.2	2.7	3.2

	Average 1979–88	1989	1990	1991	1992	1993	1994	1995	1996	1997	1998
Advanced economies	2.9	3.7	2.7	1.2	1.9	1.2	3.1	2.5	2.5	2.9	2.9
Major industrial countries	2.8	3.6	2.5	0.8	1.8	1.0	2.8	2.0	2.2	2.6	2.6
United States	2.7	3.4	1.3	−1.0	2.7	2.3	3.5	2.0	2.4	3.0	2.2
Japan	3.8	4.8	5.1	4.0	1.1	0.1	0.6	1.4	3.6	2.2	2.9
Germany	1.8	3.6	5.7	5.0	2.2	−1.1	2.9	1.9	1.4	2.3	3.0
France	2.2	4.3	2.5	0.8	1.2	−1.3	2.8	2.2	1.3	2.4	3.0
Italy	2.7	2.9	2.2	1.1	0.6	−1.2	2.1	3.0	0.7	1.0	2.4
United Kingdom	2.5	2.2	0.4	−2.0	−0.5	2.1	3.8	2.5	2.1	3.3	2.8
Canada	3.2	2.4	−0.2	−1.8	0.8	2.2	4.1	2.3	1.5	3.5	3.4
Other advanced economies	3.5	4.5	3.9	2.9	2.4	2.0	4.5	4.2	3.7	3.8	4.1
Spain	2.3	4.7	3.7	2.3	0.7	−1.2	2.1	2.8	2.2	2.8	3.4
Netherlands	1.6	4.7	4.1	2.3	2.0	0.8	3.4	2.1	2.7	3.0	2.9
Belgium	1.5	3.4	3.7	1.6	1.7	−1.3	2.3	1.9	1.4	2.3	2.2
Sweden	2.2	2.4	1.4	−1.1	−1.4	−2.2	3.3	3.6	1.1	2.0	2.5
Austria	2.1	3.8	4.3	2.8	2.0	0.4	3.0	1.8	1.1	1.7	2.8
Denmark	2.1	0.6	1.6	1.2	0.2	1.5	4.2	2.7	2.4	2.7	2.5
Finland	3.8	5.7	—	−7.1	−3.6	−1.2	4.5	4.5	3.2	4.4	3.4
Greece	1.8	3.8	—	3.1	0.4	−1.0	1.5	2.0	2.6	3.0	3.1
Portugal	2.8	5.7	4.0	2.2	1.7	−1.2	0.7	2.3	3.2	3.3	3.5
Ireland	3.1	6.1	8.0	2.1	4.0	3.1	6.5	10.3	7.0	6.3	5.6
Luxembourg	4.2	9.9	3.4	5.4	5.8	8.5	4.1	3.5	3.7	3.7	3.5
Switzerland	2.2	3.9	2.3	—	−0.3	−0.8	1.0	0.1	−0.7	0.7	2.3
Norway	3.2	0.9	1.9	3.1	3.3	2.8	5.0	3.3	4.8	4.2	3.2
Israel	3.6	1.2	6.1	6.3	6.6	3.5	6.8	7.1	4.4	4.8	4.8
Iceland	4.0	0.2	1.2	1.3	−3.4	0.9	3.5	2.1	5.5	3.0	2.4
Korea	7.8	6.4	9.5	9.1	5.1	5.8	8.6	8.9	7.1	5.6	6.3
Australia	3.3	4.4	1.4	−1.1	2.3	3.4	5.2	3.2	4.0	3.2	3.7
Taiwan Province of China	8.1	8.2	5.4	7.6	6.8	6.3	6.5	6.0	5.6	6.0	6.3
Hong Kong	8.2	2.6	3.4	5.1	6.3	6.1	5.3	4.8	4.5	5.0	5.0
Singapore	7.3	9.6	9.0	7.3	6.2	10.4	10.1	8.8	7.0	6.6	6.1
New Zealand	1.9	0.8	−0.2	−1.7	0.9	5.0	5.9	3.4	2.7	3.7	3.0

Source: International Monetary Fund (1997), p. 132.

from promoting specific industries. The role of the government in Hong Kong's industrial development has been more facilitating than guiding, and more indirect than direct. Although the Hong Kong government welcomes foreign investment, it offers no specific incentives to attract it, and there are no rules to exclude it from particular sectors. Laws and statutes in Hong Kong carry clear commitment to private property. The legal system allows private transactions to be relatively free of administrative encumbrance, and offers protection against fraud by the legal enforcement of contracts. The formation of companies is easy and straightforward. Business license fees are modest and are waived for small, one-person businesses. The industrial relations system in Hong Kong is also decentralized. The government plays a minimal role in influencing the relationship between workers and employers. It has never attempted to set a minimum wage or interfere in private managerial prerogatives.

G. Good Infrastructure

The Hong Kong government attaches great importance to economic infrastructure including education, transportation, communication, energy provision, and financial services. Infrastructure is an important means to facilitate free trade and enlarge the extent of both internal and external markets and to accumulate human and physical capital. Because the supply of most of infrastructure is not sufficiently profitable for the private sector, but its social benefits are great, the Hong Kong government makes supplying it one of its most important duties. In 1994, Hong Kong had the busiest container port in the world. The mainly underground Mass Transit Railway made Hong Kong one of the most heavily used carriers in the world. Telecommunications are excellent: more than 5% of the population use cellular phones, and per-capita pagers are the highest in the world. Energy consumption per head has one of the highest rates in Asia.

III. HONG KONG'S ECONOMIC ACHIEVEMENTS

Hong Kong provides an example of what a high economic growth rate it can achieve. In 1965, Hong Kong had a per-capita GDP of $2279. As a result of practice in economic freedom, its per-capita wealth rose nearly 10-fold, to $21,650 in 1994.[19] Compared with many countries, such as Canada, Australia, and the United States, that enjoy rich resources and huge land areas, Hong Kong is a territory with limited space and resources. However, the people of Hong Kong have made unimaginable achievements in this tiny area that include:

Per-capita wealth in Hong Kong increased 10-fold in 30 years (1965-94).[20]
Hong Kong's per-capita GDP exceeded the United Kingdom's in 1994.

Hong Kong was the world's eighth-largest exporter of goods and services in both 1995 and 1996. Table 5 shows that the projected world export share for Hong Kong in 1997 and 1998 will exceed Canada's and therefore move Hong Kong to seventh position.
The port of Hong Kong handled 13.3 million containers in 1996. It has been the world's largest container port for five consecutive years. It handles more containers than the whole of Britain.
Hong Kong is the fourth-largest international financial center after New York, London, and Tokyo. Eighty-five of the world's top 100 banks have operations in Hong Kong. The external assets of Hong Kong's banking sector rank fourth in the world, and foreign exchange turnover places Hong Kong fifth in the world.
Hong Kong has the sixth-largest stock market in the world and the second-largest in Asia next to Tokyo.
Hong Kong had $65.9 billion in foreign exchange reserves by the end of 1996, and ranked seventh in the world.
Hong Kong's per-capita foreign currency reserve ranks second in the world after Singapore's.
Hong Kong ranks sixth in the world in household spending power.
In 1993, Hong Kong became the first major city in the world to have a completely digital telecommunications network. It has the second-highest rate of mobile-phone use in the world.
Hong Kong is Asia's most popular travel destination.
Hong Kong has two of the world's top 10 billionaires.[21]

It is a clear message showing that ecomonic freedom brings prosperity to Hong Kong.

The next section offers theoretical discussions to show why Hong Kong can achieve such a great success.

IV. CLASSICAL THEORY OF ECONOMIC GROWTH

From our discussion of Hong Kong's economic policy in Section II it can be concluded that except for providing necessary infrastructure, the government function in economic affairs has been restrained at a minimum level, while private enterprise, free trade, and competition are being pursued. The policy is guided by classical economic thought. Two aspects of the classical theory justify private enterprise and free trade with minimum government intervention that lead to the efficient operation of the economy and significant growth and development. First, the competitive free market system results in the efficient allocation of resources. Second, the Smith theorem of *the division of labor that depends on the extent*

Table 5 World Export Market Shares for Selected Economies (*Percent of world goods and services*)

						Projections	
	1970–79	1980–89	1990–94	1995	1996	1997	1998
United States	12.4	12.2	13.1	12.6	12.8	13.2	13.2
Japan	6.3	7.9	8.1	7.9	7.2	6.8	6.7
Germany	10.3	9.7	10.3	9.8	9.4	8.8	8.7
France	7.0	6.6	6.4	5.9	5.7	5.4	5.4
Italy	4.4	4.4	4.9	4.8	5.0	4.8	4.7
United Kingdom	6.0	5.6	5.3	5.0	5.1	5.2	5.1
Canada	4.0	3.7	3.4	3.4	3.4	3.5	3.5
Hong Kong	1.0	1.6	3.0	3.4	3.4	3.6	3.8
Korea	0.7	1.5	1.9	2.4	2.4	2.5	2.6
Singapore	0.7	1.3	1.9	2.4	2.4	2.5	2.5
Taiwan Province of China	0.7	1.5	1.9	2.0	2.0	2.2	2.2
China	0.7	1.1	1.7	2.4	2.4	2.6	2.7
Indonesia	0.6	0.8	0.8	0.9	0.9	1.0	1.0
Malaysia	0.5	0.7	1.0	1.3	1.3	1.4	1.5
Thailand	0.3	0.4	0.9	1.1	1.1	1.1	1.2
Argentina	0.5	0.4	0.3	0.4	0.4	0.4	0.4
Brazil	0.9	1.0	0.8	0.8	0.8	0.8	0.9
Mexico	0.6	1.0	1.0	1.1	1.2	1.3	1.4
Czech Republic	0.5	0.4	0.3	0.5	0.4	0.5	0.5
Poland	0.9	0.5	0.4	0.5	0.5	0.6	0.6
Russia	2.5	1.5	1.5	1.5	1.5	1.6	1.5

Source: International Monetary Fund (1997), p. 72.

of the market states that free trade and other liberal policies are important because they contribute to broadening the extent of the market and therefore deepen the division of labor that, in turn, spurs economic growth. Due to the collapse of the Soviet System and the failure of numerous state-run enterprises in many countries, market-oriented reforms have become the widely adopted remedies. This fact manifests that the first part of the classical theory, the free-market mechanism that leads to the efficient allocation of resources, has been widely accepted. However, the second part of the theory has been largely ignored in modern literature on economic growth and development. Therefore, we will focus our discussion around the second aspect of the classical theory, the classical theory of the division of labor and economic growth.

A. Division of Labor

In *The Wealth of Nations*, Adam Smith (1937) first discusses the division of labor. He points out that the division of labor increases productivity and, therefore, increases the production of wealth. In a well-known example of production of pins, he gives a vivid description, as follows.

Without the division of labor, a workman could make one pin a day, and certainly could not make 20. If the pin-making work can be divided into a number of branches and each of those branches can be an individual business, then the whole business of making a pin can be divided into about 18 distinct processes. Smith had seen a small manufactory of this kind where 10 men were employed, and where some of them performed two or three distinct operations. With the necessary machinery, they could make 48,000 pins a day. Consequently, the average productivity of each worker is at least 4000 times greater than the average productivity without the division of labor!

Smith gives three reasons for the productive powers resulting from the division of labor. First, each worker develops increased skill and dexterity in performing one simple task over and over. This phenomenon is also called *learning-by-doing* if we use a contemporary phrase. As a result, with the division of labor, the cost of training a skilled worker can be reduced. This means return to skilled labor (labor with human capital added) can be increased. Second, time is saved by not shifting from one kind of work to another. We can take this phenomenon as a managerial progress resulting from the division of labor. Third, machinery can be invented to increase productivity once tasks have been simplified and routinized through the division of labor. When a man makes a complete pair of shoes by himself, there could be no single machine to do his work, for it is too complicated. But when shoemaking was broken down into a series of simple operations, tools and machines could be invented to replace hand labor relatively easily. This feature reduces the costs of using machines and developing new technologies, and therefore increases returns to both physical and human capital.

We can conclude that the division of labor significantly reduces the cost of production, stimulates both physical and human capital accumulation, and accelerates technological progress. It is a theory of increasing returns discovered by Adam Smith 200 years ago. We should say that the division of labor is the fundamental driving force that leads to economic growth and ''the fundamental principle of economic organization.''[22]

B. Classical Theory of Trade-Driven Growth

Speaking of the trade theory, one may immediately associate it with the Ricardian model and the Heckscher-Ohlin model. Both models are based on the principle of comparative advantage or making use of divergent conditions of technology or resources between countries. The theoretical conclusions drawn from both models are very important but not universal. There are alternative types of modern trade that are based on non-comparative-advantage trade. One is called ''slicing up the value chain.''[23] A second is intraindustrial trade (IIT), or two-way trade in similar products among countries with similar resource endowments and technology conditions. Data show that the IIT grows fastest of all trade.[24] Both comparative-advantage trade and non-comparative-advantage trade rest on the international division of labor. From this point of view, we can conclude that the division of labor is the root cause of trade of any type (international, interregional, interindustrial, or intraindustrial).

Adam Smith's very significant contribution to the theory of trade-driven growth is his profound theorem of *the division of labor that depends on the extent of the market*. According to this theorem, opening trade and reducing government intervention are important because they result in a broader extent of the market that, in turn, drives economic growth via a more specialized division of labor.

Allyn Young (1928) points out that a doctrine of increasing returns is equivalent to Smith's theorem of the division of labor that depends on the extent of market. He evaluates the theorem as ''one of the most illuminating and fruitful generalizations which can be found anywhere in the whole literature of economics.'' And Stigler (1951), Negishi (1989), West (1990), and many others have supported this evaluation. Only by widening the market and creating more demand for the product can the full benefits gained from the division of labor be realized.

Now let's use the classical theory of economic growth to explain how Hong Kong has been quickly developed. Because Hong Kong is a nontariff free port, the prices of imports are low. Since most of consumption and capital goods in Hong Kong are imported from overseas markets, low prices of these imports plus low tax rates lead to low costs of labor and capital that are used to produce cheap products for export and domestic uses. With the competitive advantage from selling cheap products, Hong Kong's business firms win a large share of both international and domestic markets. The broadened extent of the market allows Hong Kong's firms to step on more specialized division of labor and facilitate technology progress. Consequently, a high rate of economic growth results.

Again, let's take a look at Hong Kong's historical role in the international division of labor and trade style. Because of the Communist revolution in China after World War II, local businessmen and industrialists fled from Shanghai, the largest city of China, to Hong Kong. The Hong Kong economy then reoriented from *entrepôt* trade to manufacturing for export. As companies have shifted their manufacturing facilities from Hong Kong into China to take advantage of lower operating costs since early 1980s, the main trend in the Hong Kong economy has been the switch from domestic exports to re-exports. From 1989 to 1994, re-exports rose by 174%.[25] A more recent trend has been a shift in China trade patterns away from re-exporting through Hong Kong to simple transshipment through the territory. It appears to be the result of China's greater maturity in product processing and auxiliary services as well as its port facilities. The growth of transshipments reinforces Hong Kong's role as a major control center for trade servicing and financing in East Asia. Over the past decade, Hong Kong's exports of services, including transportation, travel, trade-related services, and financial services, have grown rapidly. The changing role of Hong Kong in the international division of labor implies that the more and more productive division of labor in Hong Kong fits in with a broader and broader extent of the market. The market is opened up through Hong Kong's long-term export-oriented and liberal economic policy. Today, the extent of market accessed by Hong Kong is so large that as a small economy with a tiny area, Hong Kong became the eighth-largest world exporter of goods and services in 1996. The data provided by the International Monetary Fund projected that Hong Kong would maintain its momentum as a rising power after returning to China and would replace Canada as the seventh-largest world exporter in 1997 (see Table 5).

V. CONCLUSIONS

Hong Kong is widely recognized as the world's freest economy and is one of the best examples of economic development. Since 1958, when Hong Kong was granted financial autonomy by London, the Hong Kong government has followed the classical laissez-faire doctrine and a positive nonintervention policy. This policy can be summarized as free trade, low taxes, small government, prudential budgetary management (or fiscal restraint), no control over monetary policy, minimum regulation, and good infrastructure.

Through 40 years' practice of economic freedom, Hong Kong has moved from a poor economy to an advanced, high-income economy. From 1965 to 1994,

Hong Kong's per-capita wealth increased almost 10-fold. By 1994, Hong Kong's per-capita GDP has surpassed that of the United Kingdom, its colonial ruler.

The Hong Kong economic policy is guided by classical economic thought. The classical theory of the free-market system discussed in this paper includes two aspects: the free-market mechanism that leads to the efficient allocation of resources, and expanding the extent of the market that spurs economic growth via a more specialized division of labor. Since the free-market mechanism is well known and widely accepted by contemporary economists and policy makers, this paper lays emphasis on the classical theory of trade-driven growth. Hong Kong's economic development can be well explained by the classical theory of economic growth.

ACKNOWLEDGMENTS

The authors want to thank John P. Formby for his generous support in many aspects, and Carol A. Cassel and Charles G. Leathers for their helpful comments. The authors are responsible for any omissions or errors.

ENDNOTES

1. For more detailed discussions about the Sino-British agreement and the Chinese policy toward Hong Kong, please see endnote 9 in Section II and Wang (1995).
2. The laissez-faire doctrine was first proposed by Adam Smith. In his book *The Wealth of Nations*, Smith urges British to abandon the mercantilist colonial system and replace it with a free-trading system. Smith concludes that, after the colonies were granted their economic independence, there would continue to be a mutually profitable and harmonious trade between the less developed former colonies and their previous imperial master (see Semmel, 1993). However, it was Prime Minister William Ewart Gladstone who is the leading figure to carry out a series of the 19th-century liberal policies including free trade, low taxes, and colonial reforms in Britain from 1860s to 1890s. For more details, see Rabushka (1979), Knaplund (1927), and Bebbington (1993).
3. In the first decades of the 20th century, Britain's relative economic power declined because of the rise of other European countries, the United States, and Japan. The liberal policies of the Victorian era, including free trade, low taxes, small government, and the gold standard, were greatly challenged by the United Kingdom's rivals. During the interwar years, Britain's rivals invented, for commercial competition, new weapons such as dumping, currency manipulation, and quotas, and also used the old weapons such as tariff barriers. In 1931, the United Kingdom was forced to relinquish the gold standard and the principle of free trade, which had been in

place for almost a century, in favor of a policy of protection. Also, domestically, since the 1930s Keynesian economics as new policy replaced classic liberalism in Britain. Under the pressure of socialist theories and labor unions, the welfare state seemed to be ideal while the 19th-century laissez-faire that was the cornerstone of the British economic prosperity became a problem. Since then, in Great Britain and other industrial countries, increasing governmental intervention in the economy diluted the principle of the classical economic policy. For more detailed discussions about increasing governmental intervention in industrialized economies, see Endacott (1964, p. 286) and Lo (1992, pp. 8–17).

4. In Section II, we offer two reasons to explain why Hong Kong carries on a classical liberal economic policy. Also see Hopkins (1971) and Luk (1995).
5. See Johnson et al. (1998).
6. See Holloway (1995).
7. See Butler (1981).
8. The index consists of 10 elements: trade policy, taxes, government consumption of economic output, monetary policy, capital flows and foreign investment policy, banking regulation, wage and price controls, protection of property rights, business regulation, and the strength of the black market. Each element is scored separately, with the average of all elements for a country constituting a rating of that country's level of economic freedom. See Holmes et al. (1997) for more detailed explanations of how to measure a country's economic freedom with the index.
9. According to the Sino-British Joint Declaration of 1984, Hong Kong was to become a Special Administrative Region (SAR) of China and as such would enjoy a high degree of autonomy. In 1990, the Chinese National People's Congress, China's legislature, stipulated the Basic Law of the Hong Kong SAR that incorporates all Chinese policies toward Hong Kong. According to the Basic Law, Hong Kong's private ownership and free market, the core of the Hong Kong economy, remain unchanged. Hong Kong will continue to have an independent financial system and the Chinese central government will not levy taxes on Hong Kong. Hong Kong will continue to have an independent monetary system and the Hong Kong dollar, as the legal tender of the SAR, will continue to circulate and to be freely convertible. And Hong Kong will remain a free port. In addition to the economic system, Hong Kong's current executive-led political system will be preserved. Under the Basic Law, the chief executive of the SAR is elected by the Hong Kong people and appointed by Chinese central government. Tung Chee-hwa, the first appointed Chief Executive of the SAR, is a no-party businessman. Like the British governor, the chief executive will have dominant power within the Executive Council (Exco) and will be authorized to appoint and dismiss members of the Exco. The legal and judicial system will also remain basically unchanged except for those aspects related to sovereignty. For more detailed issues about the Basic Law and SAR, see Wang (1995).
10. See Chen (1984), Tang (1995), Miners (1995), and Mesquita et al. (1996).
11. See Bebbington (1993), p. 92.
12. The three small oil-rich countries are Bahrain, United Arab Emirates, and Kuwait. In all the three countries, the government owns almost all oil resources and manages oil production. Consequently government revenues in these countries largely rely

on the selling of oil and oil products. In the Bahamas, import duties are a main source of government revenue. (See Johnson et al., 1998).

13. The corporate profits tax rate was lowered from 17.5% to 16.5% in April 1994.
14. Economist Intelligence Unit, "Country Profile: Hong Kong and Macau," 2nd quarter, 1997. p. 18.
15. See Endacott (1964), pp. 286–287.
16. See Tang (1995), p. 182.
17. See Rabushka (1979), p. 8.
18. Another example is China's currency, which maintained a fixed rate against the U.S. dollar during the 1997 Asian Crisis. However, the Chinese currency is still unconvertible in the world market.
19. Based on 1994 per-capita GDP, using purchasing power parity; from *The World Bank World Atlas 1996* (Washington: World Bank, 1996). Also see Holmes et al. (1997), p. 18.
20. Ditto.
21. Most of the data listed here come from Mesquita et al. (1996).
22. See Stigler (1951), p. 193.
23. See Krugman (1995).
24. Lindert (1991), pp. 95–97.
25. Economist Intelligence Unit, "Country Profile: Hong Kong and Macau," 1995–96.

REFERENCES

Bebbington, D.W. (1993). *William Ewart Gladstone*. Grand Rapids, MI: William B. Eerdmans.

Butler, S. (1981). *Enterprise Zones*. New York: University Books.

Chen, E.K.Y. (1984). The economic setting. In D.G. Lethbridge (ed.), *The Business Environment in Hong Kong*, 2nd ed., 1–51. Hong Kong: Oxford University Press.

Economic Intelligence Unit. *Country Profile: Hong Kong, Macau*. London: United Kingdom, 1995–1996.

Economic Intelligence Unit. *Country Profile: Hong Kong, Macau*. London: United Kingdom, 2nd quarter, 1997.

Endacott, G.E. (1964). *A History of Hong Kong*, 2nd ed. Hong Kong: Oxford University Press.

Hopkins, K. (1971). *Hong Kong: The Industrial Colony: A Political, Social, and Economic Survey*. Hong Kong: Oxford University Press.

Holmes, K.R., Johnson, B.T., and Kirkpatrick, M. (1997). *1997 Index of Economic Freedom*. Washington: Heritage Foundation and *The Wall Street Journal*.

Holloway, N. (1995). Paradise lost. *Far Eastern Economic Review, 158*(55), Feb. 23.

Johnson, B.T., Holmes, K.R., and Kirkpatrick, M. (1998). *1998 Index of Economic Freedom.* Washington, DC: Heritage Foundation and *The Wall Street Journal.*

Knaplund, P. (1927). *Gladstone and Britain's Imperial Policy*. New York: Macmillan.

Krugman, P.R. (1995). Growing world trade: causes and consequences. *Brookings Paper on Economic Activity*, *1*, 327–362.

Landreth, H. (1976). *History of Economic Theory*. Boston: Houghton Mifflin.
Lindert, P.H. (1991). *International Economics*, 9th ed. Homewood, IL: R.D. Irwin.
Lo, C.P. (1992). *Hong Kong*. London: Belhaven Press.
Luk, Y.F. (1995). *Hong Kong's Economic and Financial Future*. Washington: Center for Strategic and International Studies.
Mesquita, B.B., Newman, D., and Rabushka, A. (1996). *Red Flag over Hong Kong*. Chatham, NJ: Chatham House.
Miners, N. (1995). *The Government and Politics of Hong Kong*, 5th ed. Hong Kong: Oxford University Press.
Negishi, T. (1989). *History of Economic Theory*. Amsterdam: North-Holland.
Rabushka, A. (1979). *Hong Kong: A Study In Economic Freedom*. Chicago: Graduate School of Business, University of Chicago.
Richardson, G.B. (1975). Adam Smith on competition and increasing returns. In A.S. Skinner and T. Wilson (eds.), *Essays on Adam Smith*, 350–360. Oxford: Clarendon Press.
Semmel, B. (1993). *The Liberal Ideal and the Demons of Empire*. Baltimore: Johns Hopkins University Press.
Skinner, A.S. (1987). Smith, Adam. In J. Eatwell, M. Milgate, and P. Newman (eds.), *The New Palgrave—A Dictionary of Economics*, Vol. 4, 369–375. London: Macmillan.
Smith, A. (1937). *An Inquiry into the Nature and Causes of the Wealth of Nations*. New York: Modern Library, 1937.
Stigler, G.J. (1951). The division of labor is limited by the extent of the market. *Journal of Political Economy*, *59*, 185–193.
Tang, S.-H. (1995). A critical review of the 1995–1996 budget. In Y.L. Cheung and S.M.H. Sze (eds.), *The Other Hong Kong Report—1995*, 157–182. Hong Kong: Chinese University Press.
Wang, E. (1995). *Hong Kong, 1997: The Politics of Transition*. Boulder, CO: Lynne Rienner Publishers.
West, E.G. (1990). *Adam Smith and Modern Economics*. London: Edward Elgar.
Young, A.A. (1928). Increasing returns and economic progress. *Economic Journal*, *38*, 527–542.

17

State Revenue Administration Problems in a Transition Economy

State Revenue Service of the Republic of Latvia*

Maiga Dzervite
Latvian State Revenue Service, Riga, Latvia

I. INTRODUCTION

A country's Tax Administration issues are the backbone of any fiscal system and the core for its success. This is particularly true and important for countries in transition, because of these countries' severe needs to finance their reforms and to keep a tight monetary policy that would be supported by a broadly balanced general government budget and complemented by a tax-based revenue policy.

While there are many differences among the countries in transition at the fiscal, legal, and cultural levels, there is also a wide range of similarities. The author is trying to address some of the similar problems, assessing the operation of the tax administrations of countries in transition based on the situation in three Baltic countries[1] and in Latvia particularly.

Since the regaining of their independence in 1991, the three Baltic countries have been engaged in comprehensive structural, institutional, and social changes in order to switch their societies to democracies and their economies to the market ones, to transform their economies from centrally planned to a market-based system. After becoming independent it was necessary to establish several new gov-

* The views expressed are those of the author and do not necessarily represent those of the Latvian State Revenue Service.

ernmental institutions or totally change the operational policy of old ones. Among these were the tax and customs administrations. At first these two bodies, as in many countries, and not only in the countries in transition, were separate and had a status of a legal person. Collection of internal taxes in Latvia was the task of the State Finance Inspection Board, while foreign trade taxes were collected by the Customs Department.

At that time these two main state fiscal policy implementation bodies functioned without close coordination among themselves—there was no cooperation on methodological issues related to some parallelly administrated taxes and duties, as well as to the execution of control functions. Both administrations also were developing their own information technology systems, which were not compatible.

By the end of 1993 the Government of Latvia, the only one of the three Baltic countries, had decided to reorganize the tax and customs services into an integrated revenue administration in order to collect revenue more effectively at minimum cost. In accordance with the law passed by Saeima (Latvian Parliament) on November 25, 1993, the two agencies were merged into the State Revenue Service (SRS) on April 1, 1994. In the new institution a new department, Financial Investigation, was established.

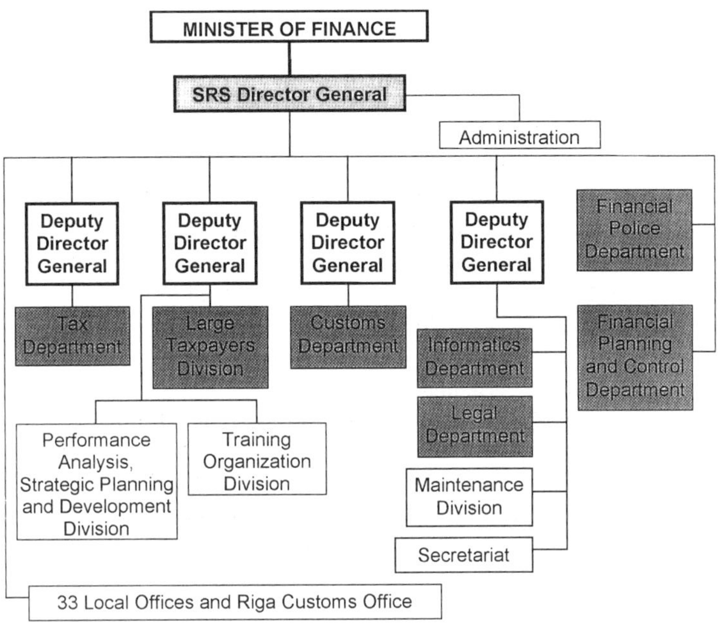

Figure 1 Flow chart of structure of the State Revenue Service, 1998.

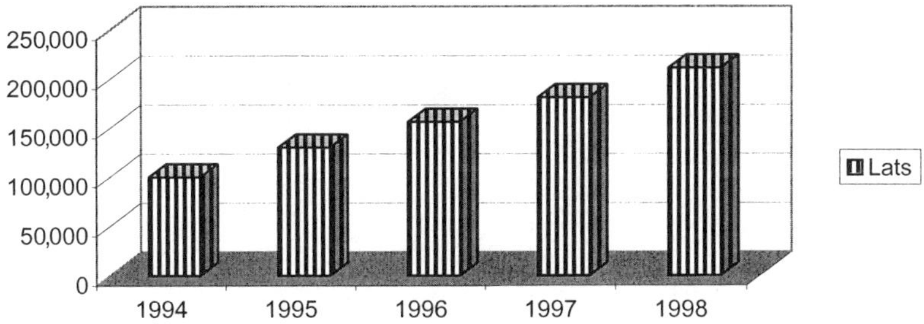

Figure 2 State basic budget tax revenues administrated by SRS per SRS employee 1994–98 (thousand Lats).

The SRS with slightly more than 4000 employees ensures tax administration and implementation of tax and customs policy throughout all of Latvia with almost 100,000 corporate taxpayers and more than 1.1 million individual taxpayers. The SRS consists of the headquarters, 33 local offices, and Riga the customs office (Fig. 1). The current average annual input, which each SRS employee[2] contributes to the state and local government budget revenues is approximately US $300,000 (Fig. 2). At the same time to secure current state and local budget revenues the SRS spends less than 3% of collected budget revenues (Fig. 3). After establishment of an integrated institution, the efficiency of administration and collection of taxes into state and local government budgets has significantly improved (Fig. 4).

After the merger of the two institutions, tax administration operations did not substantially change, only became more efficient. On the contrary, customs

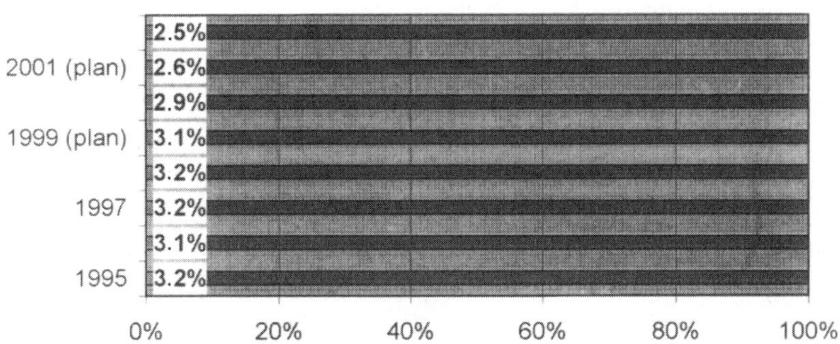

Figure 3 SRS expenditure for the collection of one Lat into central budget (percentage) 1995–2002.

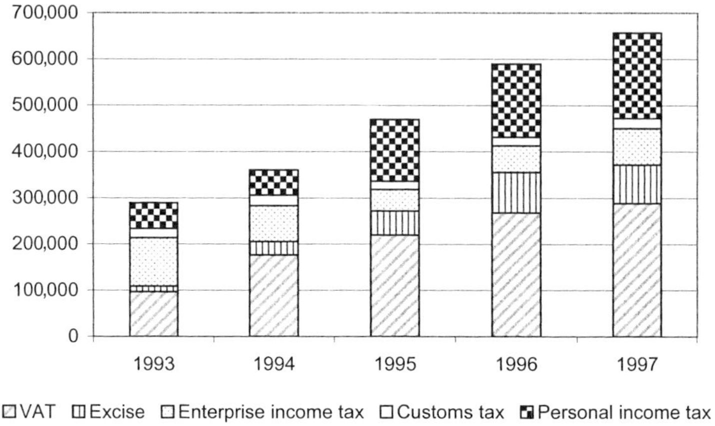

Figure 4 Tax revenues (administered by SRS 1993–97 (thousand Lats).

operations in Latvia, as in the other two Baltic countries, until 1993 were oriented toward enforcement of restrictions on imports and exports, not to revenue collections. During the past three years, when the customs administration merged with the tax administration, there has been significant progress in adapting customs' procedures and working methods to a market economy and to trade liberalization, as well as in preparations and adjustments of these methods toward joining the European Union. In this short span of time, Latvian customs has introduced a number of international instruments and standards, including the harmonized system for the tariff classification of goods and the principles of the GATT code for the valuation of taxable goods, continuous development of the IT system, and introduction of an ''online'' system for exchange of information between 43 border-crossing points and the SRS headquarters.

II. ASSESSING THE PROBLEMS

Rapid changes in the political and economical environment in Latvia, the increasing speed of the implementation of economic reforms, and the process of accession to the European Union have made it necessary to define and try to find solutions in the area of tax and customs administration. Here are some of the problem areas:

1. Modernization of the SRS to ensure a smooth transition to operational regime corresponding to the demands of E.U. directives in the fiscal area.

2. The enormous program of economic reforms and restructuring implemented by our country since regaining independence in 1991, as well as the

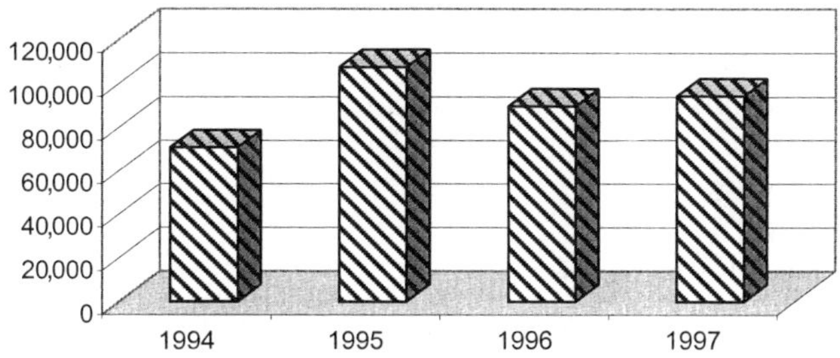

Figure 5 State basic budget tax debts 1994–97 (thousand Lats).

balanced budget announced by the government caused the need for the SRS to ensure maximally possible and stable revenue to the state budget.

3. The large number of tax arrears (Fig. 5) accumulated in the years 1992–1994 called for the necessity to expend the existing and to establish new structures within the SRS, as well as to improve and develop methods and tools to enforce the debt collection.

4. The taxpaying process is very much hands-on within the SRS.

5. The tax payment process is heavily paper-oriented with the same information keyed into databases at various points in the process—by the taxpayer himself, by the receiving banks, by the State Treasury Department, and by the local SRS office. There is no electronic exchange mechanism in place yet.

6. The customs staff, as it was basically formed in 1991–92 and with no really independent customs administration before 1991, needs basic education and comprehensive special training (more than 38% of customs officers have only a high school education, and only in 1997 did the first 50 students graduate from the Riga Technical University Institute of International Economic Relations and Customs).

7. Permanently changing the legal environment and contradictory interpretations of the legislation have caused the need for ''chain'' training system, including on-the-job training, for the tax staff as well as customs staff.

8. Necessity to create a good tax system (including tax administration issues), which would be not only one where rules are simple, transparent, and perfect from the legal point of view, but also one that can reach the targets set by the government with minimum costs and maximum benefit.

III. SOLUTION OF THE PROBLEMS

Main directions in the reforms, which have been made in the SRS recently (in 1995–96) or are on the way now:

1. Needs for changes in the law on the SRS
2. Restructuring of the SRS
3. Introduction of contracting elements and a new remuneration system for employees
4. Changes in the work planning:
   Business plans
   Targets for local office work
   Two years' general SRS operational program, State Revenue and Customs Policy Implementation, which is the background for the budget financing request
   Implementation of the elements of strategic planning with the forecasts of revenues administrated by the SRS
5. Comprehensive on-the-job training and introduction of the "chain" training system

A. Needs for Changes in the Law on the SRS

Since establishment of the Latvian State Revenue Service, it operates under the special law "On State Revenue Service." The law was created in a short time and that is why it was composed of different articles that looked like separate unconnected parts, like "a patchwork." Moreover, there was no flexibility, which was definitely needed in a rapidly changing legal and administrative environment of the country in transition.

The main reason why the amendments to the Law on SRS were enacted by the end of August 1996 was the necessity to make the law more uniform and also flexible to make the required structural changes in the SRS. The need to encourage the staff to work more efficiently and to increase their sense of responsibility about the common achievements of the SRS was another reason. This is why a specific amendment was made to change the status of the SRS staff from civil servants to employees whose hiring is based on individual contracts and collective agreements. Totally there were almost 100 amendments finally approved by Saeima on January 16, 1997.

A general summary of the amendments to the Law on the State Revenue Service, made in August 1996 and approved by Saeima in January 1997:

Law on Civil Service does not apply to SRS officials
Law on SRS allows for a more flexible organizational structure
Employees are employed on contract system—easier to hire-and-fire
Contracts and wage scales are more flexible

The law defines the State Revenue Service as "a state administration institution operating under the supervision of the Ministry of Finance and ensuring registration of taxpayers, collection of taxes, duties and other state compulsory payments on the territory of the Republic of Latvia and on customs borders, as well as implementing state customs policy and settling customs matters.''

The main tasks of the State Revenue Service are defined as follows:

1. To ensure collection of state taxes, duties, and other compulsory payments administered by the State Revenue Service on the territory of Latvia and on customs borders.

2. To implement the state customs policy and ensure protection of customs borders.

3. Within the framework of authority set out by the law to exercise control over the execution of the anticorruption law as well as over the observance of additional restrictions on state officials set out by other laws.

4. To prevent and detect offenses in the field of payment of state taxes, duties, and other compulsory payments set out by the state.

5. To ensure training of employees from institutions subordinated to the State Revenue Service in tax legislation act application matters.

6. In accordance with the order established by laws and regulations of the Cabinet of Ministers to register and account taxpayers and control conformity of registration documents to the requirements of the law and the actual situation.

7. From January 1998 a new task has been added—administration of the social tax.

8. The new structure of the law became more logical and consequent (Table 1), and overlapping with other laws was reduced as much as possible.

B. Restructuring of the SRS

Undoubtedly, a good organizational structure of tax and customs administrations helps to a high extent to solve many problems. That is why the Latvian State Revenue Service was and still is in the process of restructuring. Therefore the SRS tries to adjust its organizational structure to changing economical environment.

The actual restructuring started in 1995, when local-level offices had been restructured by functions (Fig. 6) and were no longer tax-oriented. At the same time that the local offices were reorganized by size of enterprises (businesses), by the end of 1995 the Large Taxpayers Division (LTD) was established to deal with the large taxpayers' cases. However, the headquarters' structure remained as it was. The drawbacks of the existing law did not allow the SRS global structural changes.

The amendments simplified the procedure for creation of new structures not only within headquarters but also at the local level. This is particularly important now, when discussion in the government is almost over for the creation of three levels of state administration: local, regional, and central levels.

Table 1 Structure of the Law on State Revenue Service with Incorporation of Amendments Approved by Saeima (Latvian Parliament) on January 16, 1997[a]

Chapter 1. State Revenue Service's tasks, structure, and principles of operation
- Article 1. State Revenue Service
- Article 2. Main tasks of State Revenue Service
- Article 3. Structure and officials of State Revenue Service
- Article 4. Director General of State Revenue Service
- Article 5. Director of territorial institution of State Revenue Service
- Article 6. Execution of requirements of State Revenue Service officials

Chapter 2. Tasks of State Revenue Service and rights of officials in tax (tees) administration matters
- Article 8. Tasks of State Revenue Service in tax (tees) administration
- Article 10. Rights of officials in tax administration

Chapter 3. Tasks of State Revenue Service and rights of officials when implementing customs policy
- Article 11. Tasks of the State Revenue Service during implementing of customs policy
- Article 13. Rights of customs officials

Chapter 4. Tasks of the State Revenue Service's finance police and rights of officials when detecting violations of law in the sphere of state revenues
- Article 14. Tasks of the State Revenue Service's finance police in the detection of violations in the sphere of state revenue
- Article 16. Rights of the officials of the State Revenue Service's finance police in the process of disclosing violations in the sphere of state revenues
- Article 16.1. The right of the officials of the State Revenue Service's finance police to apply physical force and special means
- Article 16.2. Rights of the officials of the State Revenue Service's finance police to use a firearm

Chapter 5. Status of the State Revenue Service's officials and employees, their responsibility and the appeal procedure, material provision of the State Revenue Service
- Article 19. Status of the State Revenue Service's officials and employees
- Article 19.1. Dismissal of State Revenue Service's officials
- Article 20. Legal protection and social guarantees of State Revenue Service's officials (employees)
- Article 21. Responsibility of the officials (employees)
- Article 22. Procedure of the appeal against the decisions and instructions of State Revenue Service's officials
- Article 23. The procedure of compensation for damages incurred due to an unlawful act of a State Revenue Service's official
- Article 24. Material provision of the State Revenue Service
- Article 25. Identity cards and distinctive marks of the State Revenue Service's officials
- Article 26. Symbols and stamps of the State Revenue Service

Table 1 Continued

Transition regulations. The main tasks of the State Revenue Service under the Chapter 1, Article 2, are defined as follows:

1. To ensure collection of state taxes, duties, and other compulsory payments administered by the State Revenue Service on the territory of Latvia and on customs borders
2. Implement the state customs policy and ensure protection of customs borders
3. Within the framework of authority set out by the Law to exercise control over the execution of anti-corruption law as well as over the observance of additional restrictions on state officials set out by other laws
4. Prevent and detect offenses in the field of payment of state taxes, duties, and other compulsory payments set out by the state
5. To ensure training of employees from institutions subordinated to the State Revenue Service in tax legislation act application matters
6. In accordance with the order established by laws and regulations of the Cabinet of Ministers to register and account taxpayers and control conformity of registration documents to the requirements of the Law and actual situation
7. From January 1998 a new task will be added—administration of the social tax

[a] After amendments several articles (NR. 7, 9, 12, 15, 17, 18) were deleted and some (NR. 16.1, 16.2, and 19.1) were added.

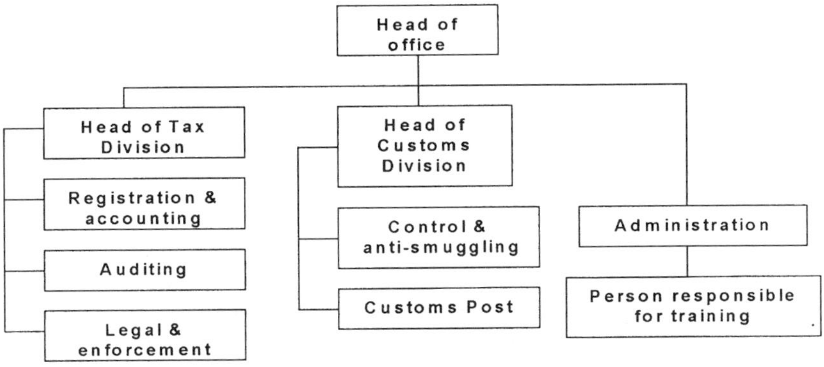

Figure 6 Structure of typical local tax office in Latvia.

An important objective in this process was the increase of level of efficiency and effectiveness of all SRS offices. The amendments allowed the merger of functions that the tax and customs administrations have in common, like strategic and development planning, IT systems, legal service including collection and enforcement actions, international affairs, etc. (Fig. 1). However, even if the ideas are right and would be accepted by all parties involved in these changes, the process of reorganization (as always whenever the human interests are involved) will take time and, hence, is still not finished.

Unfortunately, for countries in transition there often is not much time available to check all possible problems and to solve them in the real ''pilot office.'' Changes in the economic and political environment often call for rapid measures, with, sometimes, only a few weeks for preparation. Time in these countries is compressed and requires prompt actions. Therefore, it is of utmost importance at least to evaluate ''a priori'' all pros and cons and prepare a maximally detailed master plan before actions are taken. Such a plan was prepared with regard to the creation of the Large Taxpayers Division, which now administrats taxes of slightly more than 200 large taxpayers.

The LTD handles every aspect concerning the taxes of a large taxpayer: levying (sending out assessment and processing returns), collection, enforcement, and audit. Clusters of logically related corporations and shareholders, subsidiaries, and branches are treated as if they were one fiscal entity. For each taxpayer or entity a file is kept which contains all the information (tax returns, audit reports, letters, payment orders, etc.) necessary for an integrated approach. This and other information is stored on a computer connected with the local network. The information beginning 1994 is immediately available on each taxpayer (entity) and is continuously updated. The important achievement of the LTD is the speed with which individual cases are handled. Maximum handling times are set for tax assessments, taxpayers' appeals, and requests. On the contrary, a short processing time would quickly give taxpayers a certainty on their tax position, with a reassuring feeling that their cases are being given due care and attention. Since all the fiscal affairs and information of the taxpayer are located in one unit, the workload (levying, collection, and audit) can be handled quickly and efficiently.

C. Contracting Elements and New Remuneration System for Employees

In accordance with the amendments to the law on SRS, the Law on Civil Servants does not apply to the SRS officials anymore, as they are now under the Labor Code. This permits the managers to be more flexible promoting the staff members on their career. This also allows the application of simpler procedures to hire and fire the SRS personnel, substantially reducing the amount of money and time spent to organize open contests whenever a staff position becomes available.

The new remuneration system, passed by the government by the end of 1996, introduced not only higher monthly salaries, but also a system of benefits:

Additional payments for long service in the SRS (30% after 5 years of service; 40% for 5–10 years, and 50% for more than 10 years)
Additional payments for higher responsibilities
Implementation of the system of bonuses
Introduction of performance contracts (monthly salary could be up to eight times higher than the regular one) for senior managers and for specific staff positions.

Signing of the performance contracts depended on the results of defense of the business plans, which were incorporated into the contracts as targets and objectives of these contracts.

The first step toward implementation of the contracting system was a contract between the Minister of Finance and the Director General. Signing the performance contracts between the Director General and the directors of local SRS offices was the next step, and finally the performance or regular contracts between the directors and their staff members were signed. Now there are also collective agreements in place.

D. Changes in Work Planning

Work planning elements were introduced in the work of SRS in order to make tax administration cost-effective (in terms of cost-benefit ratios) and flexible, due to the rapid changes in world economic conditions and in the countries in transition economies. Up to 1996 there was no detailed and uniform long-term development concept or program for implementation in the SRS. In 1996 the first attempt was made to start strategic planning in the SRS.

The working group for the "brainstorming" that would create something totally new and unprecedented was put together for the first time in the SRS. In a short time—less than three weeks—under the supervision of the author, an exhaustive program was ready for presentation to the government and was successfully defended there. At the same time it became clear that business planning, as a management tool, should be expanded.

The program for 1997 "State Revenue and Customs Policy Implementation" (Fig. 7) consisted of two subprograms representing equally important branches of the SRS work—state tax administration and state customs policy implementation. As the SRS has two additional functions that are not directly connected with its principal tasks, they also are reflected in the program as subprograms: "Economic and Financial Audits at the Request of Law Enforcement Bodies" and "Inspection of Legitimacy of Public Officials' Income." Uniform measures which ensure the mutual functioning and development of all of these

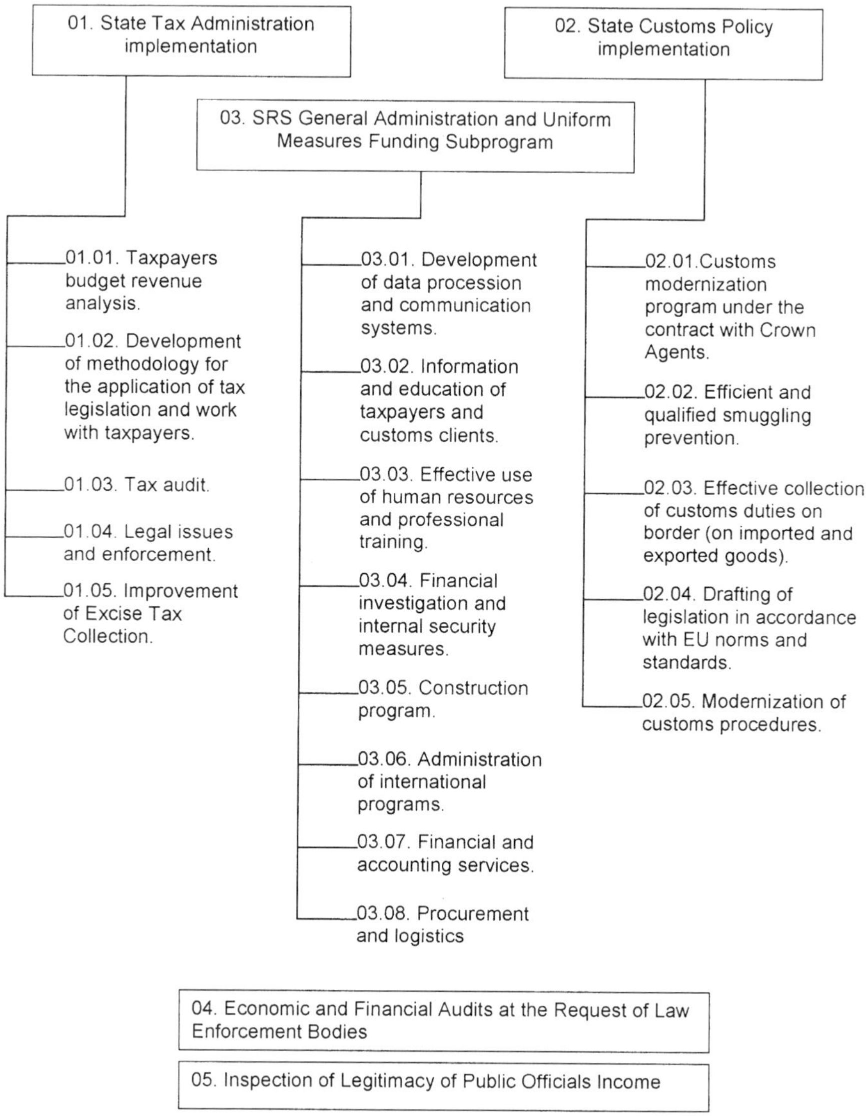

Figure 7 Structure of state revenue and customs policy implementation program for 1997.

subprograms were developed in the "SRS General Administration and Uniform Measures Funding Subprogram."

Each subprogram consisted of several projects (on the whole there were 18 projects) with a detailed discussion of existing problems, possible solutions to these problems, and defining additional resources necessary to achieve the purpose of the respective project. Following a short introduction by the Ministry of Finance, all programs, subprograms, and projects had a uniform layout including targets, problems, tasks and priorities, expected results, legal background, explanations and clarifications, saving measures, and economic background.

The next step toward creation of a comprehensive, well-prepared strategic program was the new SRS program—for 1998 and 1999—with the same title—"State Revenue and Customs Policy Implementation" (Figs. 8–10). The structure of this program differs substantially from the first one. While there are also five subprograms and the first (the basic) is "State Tax Administration and Customs Policy Implementation," priority in this program has been given to the

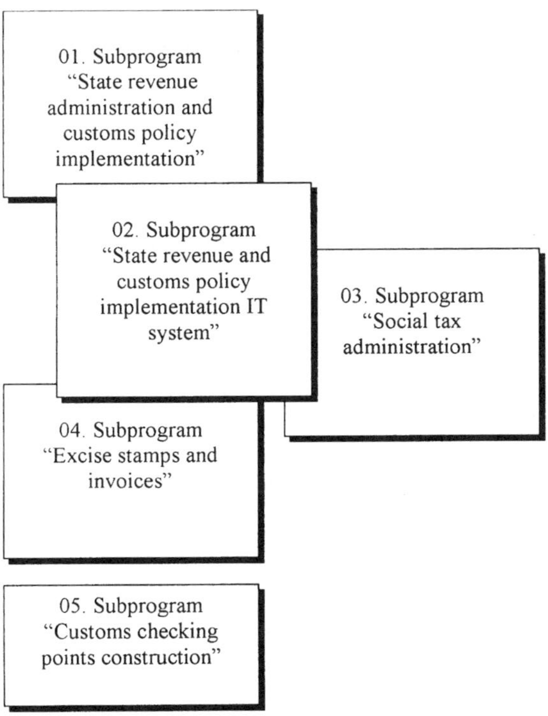

Figure 8 State revenue and customs policy implementation programs for 1998–99.

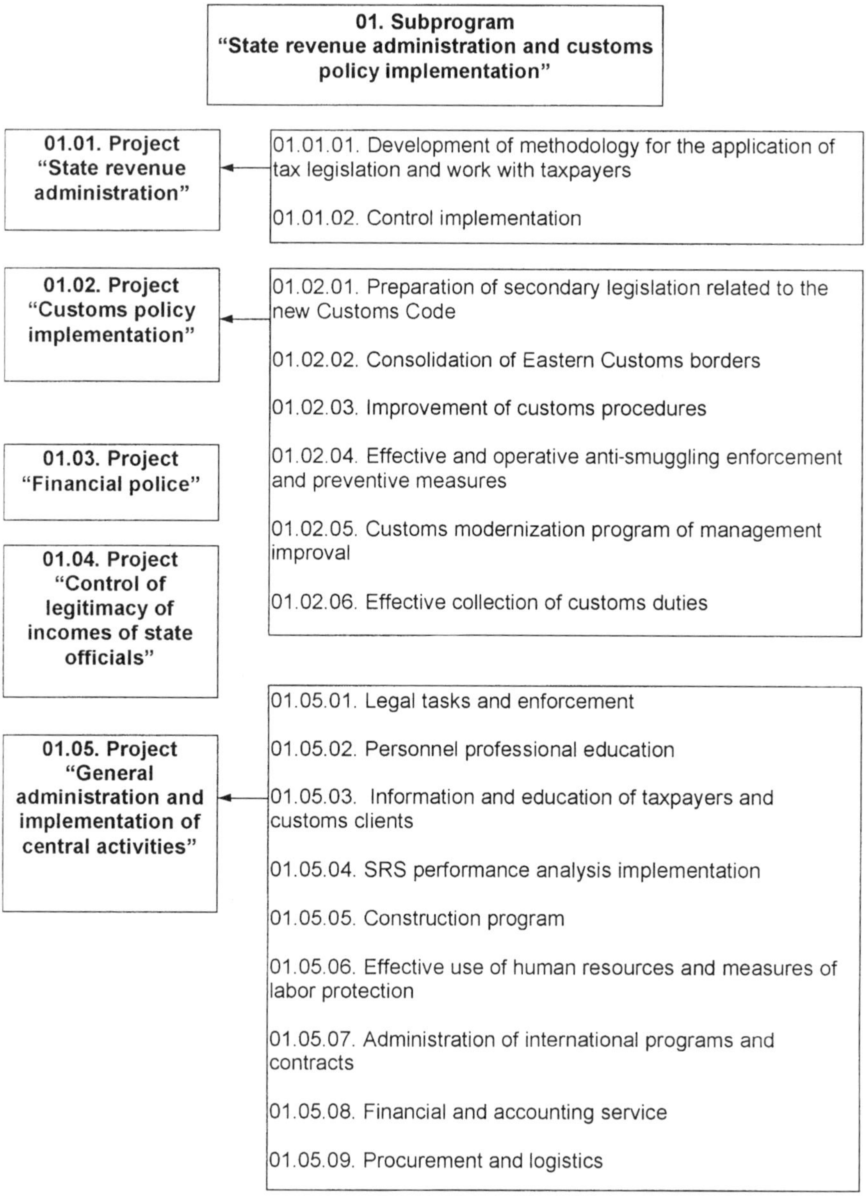

Figure 9 Projects and activities for the new SRS program for 1998–99.

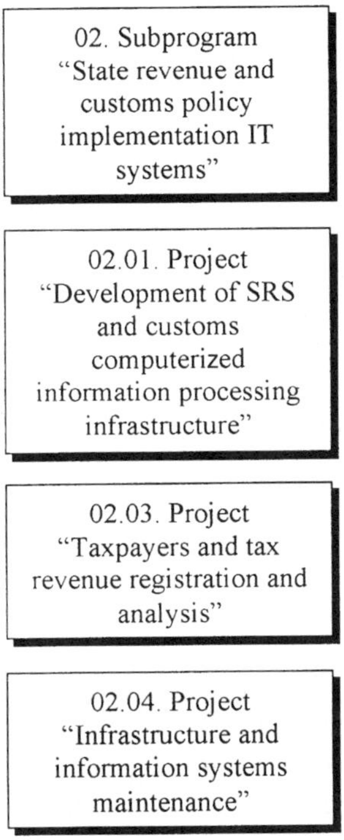

Figure 10 More projects and activities for the new SRS program for 1998–99.

IT system (subprogram "State Revenue and Customs Policy Implementation's Informatization System") and the new Taxpayers Register as a core of the whole system.

It is clear that one of the important prerequisites for the successful functioning of the SRS is the ability to register big blocks of information, to process them quickly, and to ensure access for all persons involved in tax administration. World experience shows that successful coping with such tasks is impossible without the use of modern information-processing technologies. Therefore, the SRS throughout all of its short period of existence has paid great attention to computerization. Currently there are operating about 1000 PCs in the SRS (on average one of four employees), the majority of which are logged into local networks; logging of computers to the SRS global information system is on its way now. A detailed master plan was created by the help of the technical assistance from the E.U. Phare program, and further developments in this area are planned by SRS specialists.

The SRS faced a new enormous task in 1997—to take over from the Ministry of Welfare and from January 1998 to start to administer the social tax. Thus one of the subprograms was related this issue.

The last two subprograms—''Excise Stamps and Invoices'' and ''Building of Customs Control Posts''—were separated basically for the financing reasons as budget funding was necessary and possible to allocate separately from the other three subprograms.

Hence, the whole program was divided into five subprograms with 11 projects and 17 measures. Understanding that the number of tasks performed by the SRS could not be atomized—it will always be necessary to work with each taxpayer and customs client separately in auditing, tax enforcement, customs control, financial investigation, etc.—and that the collection of substantially more taxes without increasing the number of staff would therefore be inconsistent, the SRS proposed that at the present stage of development, taking into consideration the economic and financial state of the country, it would be necessary to choose a combination of extensive and intensive development model.

The extensive development would ensure the improvement of the SRS work results in the near future, but intensive in the long run. The extensive development would ask to increase the amount of additional financial resources. The intensive development would need considerable financial injections within the next two or three years, but, judging by the experience of other countries (e.g., the Czech Republic, Hungary, New Zealand, and others), this would allow a gradual reduction in the funds necessary for the operation of the SRS, increasing and ensuring stable total state revenues.

Therefore on the whole the SRS program for the 1998 outlined:

1. Effective use of the existing resources (work organization and selection of staff; placing and training; ethics; financial encouragement of staff; economic usage of financial and technical means) and increase of the work intensity
2. Upgrading and simplification of tax administration and customs procedures
3. Development of the new IT system with uniform communication system
4. Increased education of taxpayers
5. Implementation of state investment program, first of all at the customs border-crossing points

The first experience with the creation of the SRS strategic program reaffirmed the conviction of the SRS management that it was necessary to move further toward a well-organized business planning system within the SRS. In November 1996, a decision was taken by the director general of the SRS to introduce the business planning for the local SRS offices up to headquarters' offices. The time schedule was:

A handout and clarification (explanation) of how to create a business plan were prepared.

One-day seminar "How to create a business plan" was arranged for the directors of the local SRS offices and for the senior officials of the SRS headquarters.

Revenue forecast by taxes for 1997 for each local office was prepared by the newly established Performance Analysis, Strategic Planing, and Development Division at the Headquarters.

After 1 month all local offices presented, at the special commission headed by the Director General of the SRS, their business plans and target figures for the revenue collection and defended them one by one.

After successful defense and agreement with the commission, the contracts with the directors of local SRS offices were signed.

Analyses and control of results achieved were conducted by the local offices each month.

Results achieved by each regional SRS office in the first half of the year were presented.

At the moment all regional SRS offices are preparing, defending, and implementing their new business plans for 1998. The SRS is in the process of developing business plans of headquarters of the SRS for years 1998–99. That would allow to prepare in a timely manner the overall SRS work program for 1999, design of which will be started in April 1998.

At the end of 1997 the long-term Strategic Plan for the SRS was created. The strategic plan of the SRS consists of the definition of the SRS mission, short description of operting environment, SRS performance results, and future vision. The main body of the strategic plan includes the following strategic goals for 1998–2002:

Improve the efficiency of performance

Achieve simpler internal regulation on tax collection ways and procedures

Propose the necessary amendments in the legislation of the Republic of Latvia

Modernize SRS information system

Taxpayers education

Customs modernization

Strengthening of the eastern customs border

E. Comprehensive On-the-Job Training

Comprehensive on-the-job training and introduction of the "chain" training system within the line of overall personnel management policy are the basic prerequisites for increased efficiency and intensity of the SRS staff work performance. Figure 11 shows a level of education of the SRS staff.

To handle the fiscal situation of the taxpayers, tax personnel now need to have a sound knowledge of more than one type of tax. Taxpayers, especially corporate entities, are confronted with different kinds of taxes, so tax staff must be adequately equipped with expert knowledge and skills empowering them to make the right decisions independently.

A strategic plan of training of the SRS staff has been developed in the SRS. The activities of different SRS structural divisions and the relations among them as well as interaction among different stages of the training system should be observed in order to implement the strategic plan for training.

There are five main stages of implementation of a unified training system (Figs. 12–15).

1. Analyzing the Problem

The first stage comprises the necessity to clear up whether the certain problem in the State Revenue Service can be solved by training and to determine the main directions for training.

2. Determining Training Needs

It is important to evaluate the education and professional qualification of each employee. After summing up this information it becomes possible to determine the priorities of training needs. In order to achieve good results in determination of training needs it is necessary:

To evaluate and improve the job descriptions
Develop work-place descriptions
Analyze the actual adequacy of personnel, to compare the difference be-

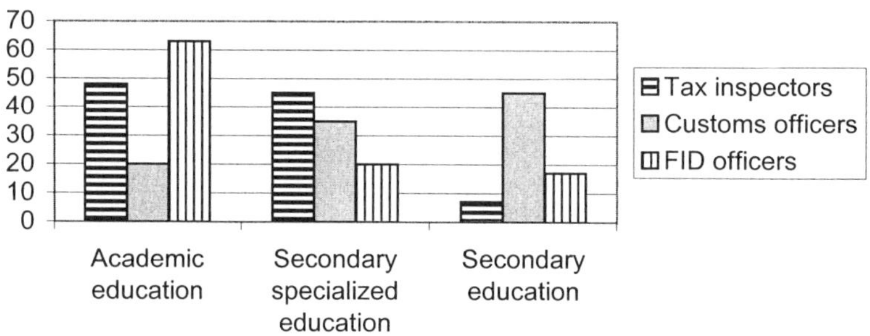

Figure 11 Level of education of the SRS staff in 1997 (percentage).

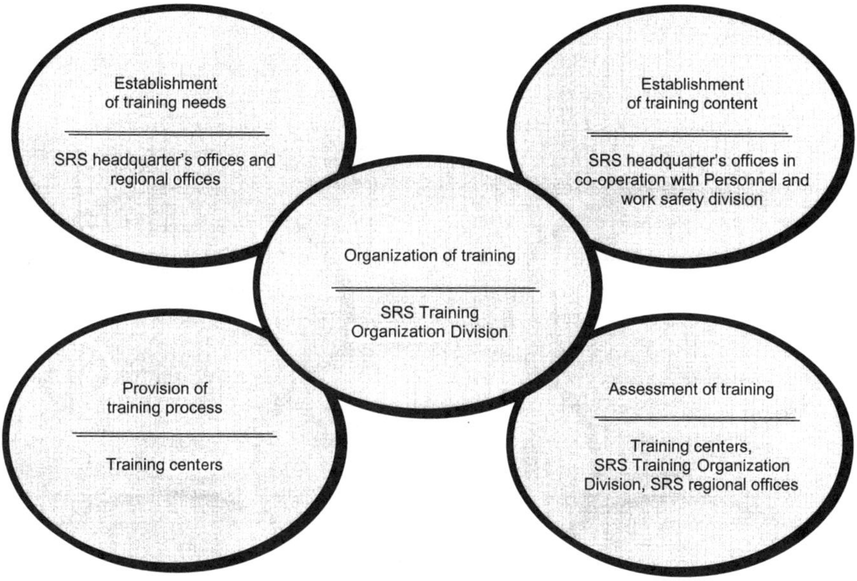

Figure 12 Phases of the strategic training plan.

tween the actual and required level of competence, basing on the job descriptions and workplace descriptions

Determine training needs and define the training goals

Calculate the limits for financial, personnel, time, and technical resources

Sum up the proposals for raising professional education and qualification of SRS staff in the regional SRS offices, taking financial limits into account

Evaluate the proposals on raising professional education and qualification requirements to create annual and perspective plans

Develop and coordinate annual and perspective plans for raising professional education and qualification of SRS officers, based on the proposals submitted and the financial resources allocated for training needs

3. Determining Training Contents

To determine training contents and amount and level of complexity, it is necessary to make preliminary inquiries, taking into account the experience and education of the officers to be trained as well as abilities to use the existing knowledge in practical work. To have a qualitative determination of training contents it is necessary:

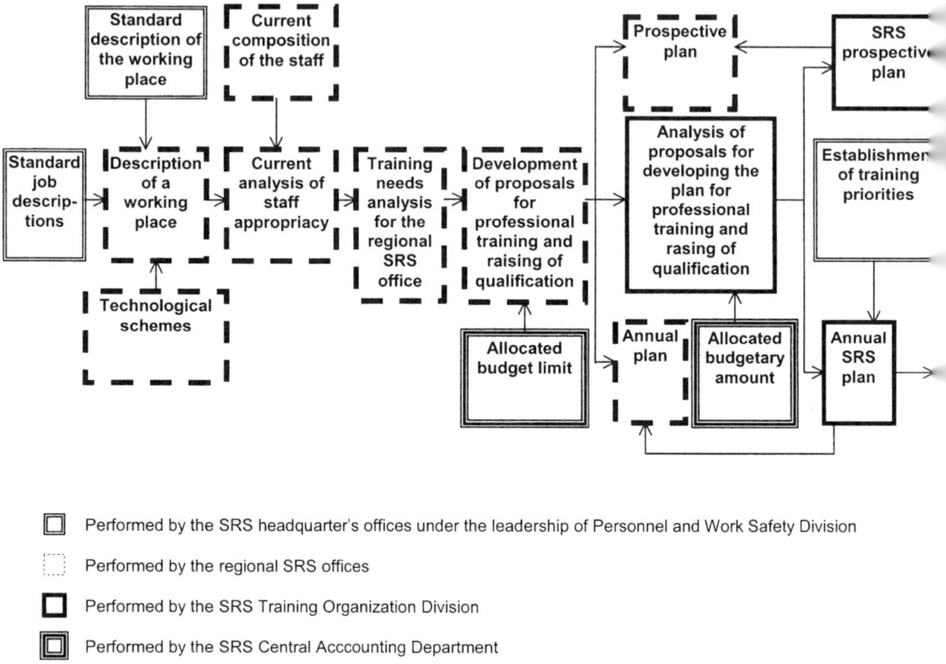

Figure 13 Development and coordination of plans for professional training for SRS staff.

To present the results of analysis of training needs to the management of the SRS

Sum up the training priorities determined by each department of the SRS according to the requirements set by the tax and customs legislation

Prepare training plans and programs based on the training needs and priorities determined

Submit the training plans and programs to management of the SRS for approval

4. Training Organization

Training must take place in due time and in relation to organizational changes or changes in procedures and work processes. This includes:

Presenting of the programs for training courses to SRS central administration and management of regional authorities

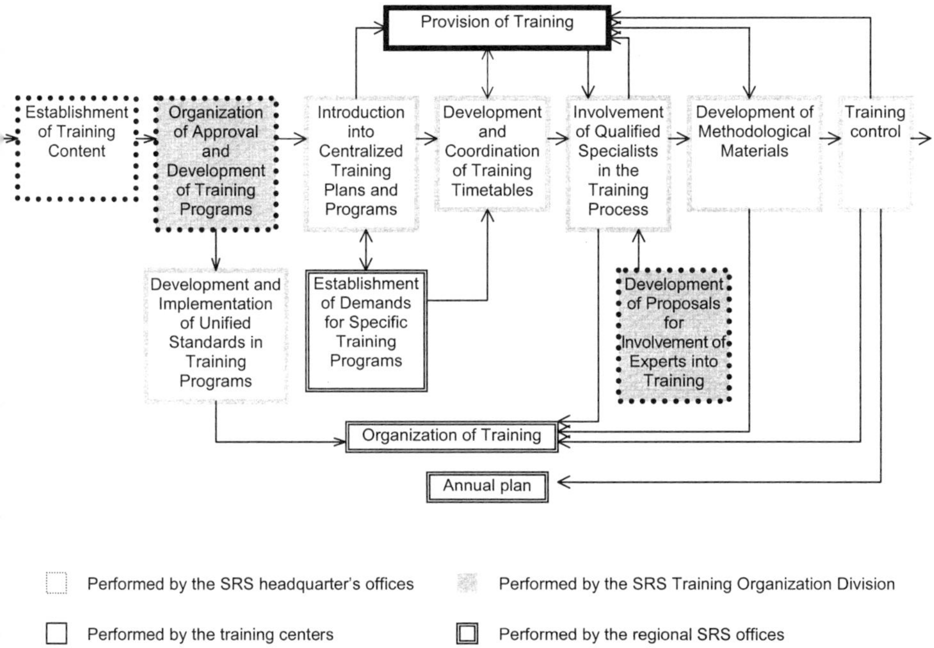

Figure 14 Organization of training.

Receiving and summing up of requirements for the number of officers involved in each training program, taking into account the limits of state budget allocated for organization of centralized training courses
Working out of training schedules
Summing up of information about planned training activities at the regional authorities within the limits of allocated budget means
Controlling of the quality of training activities organized by the regional authorities and the efficiency of the allocated budget means
Working out and implementing unified demands for organization of certain training programs at the regional authorities
Working out handouts and methodological materials
Identifying of qualified specialists and involving of them in trainers work
Organizing of train-the-trainers activities
Working out proposals for implementation of a financially motivated system in order to bring highly qualified customs specialists into trainers work

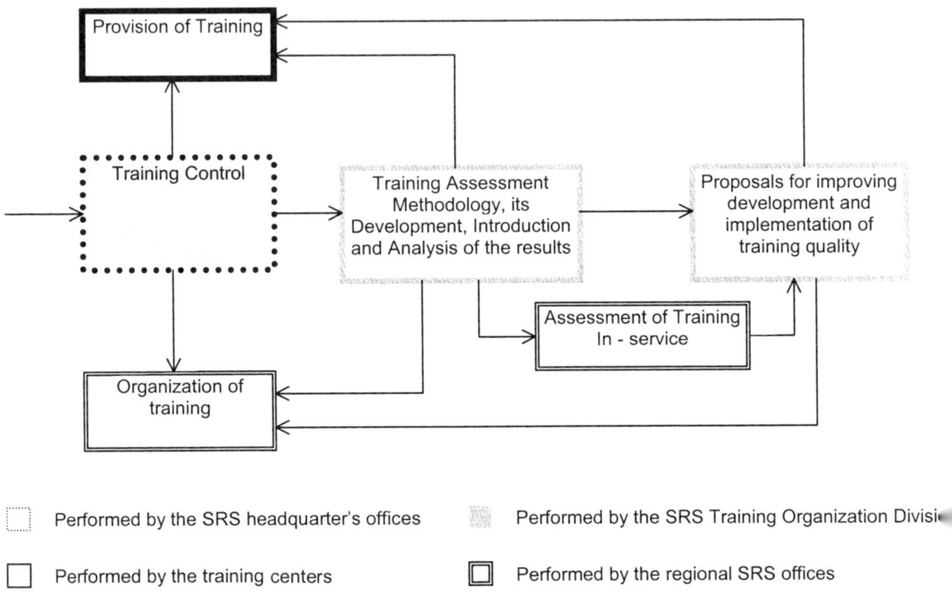

Figure 15 Assessment of training.

5. Evaluation of Training

This is an important stage in the training process. Evaluation of quality and effectiveness of a training course asks for developing of the unified methods for training evaluation according to evaluation standards and levels, implementation of the system of training evaluation, and analysis of the results of training evaluation and developing of proposals for raising of training quality.

Apart from the stages of a unified training system the strategic plan of the training organization aims:

- To set up regional training centers (for example, in Latgale and Kurzeme districts for differentiated training of customs officers)
- Plan and organize acquiring of professional education at the Latvian universities and institutes
- Draft a perspective plan for raising professional education and qualification of SRS staff in order to develop a long-term training strategy
- Acquire experience of foreign countries in successful training organization
- Set up training board

IV. CONCLUSION

The Latvian State Revenue Service, like other tax and customs administrations in countries in transition, is searching for the optimal, most effective operational and organizational structure. The Latvian SRS is steadily moving from a fragmented system to an integrated approach. Although there was no thorough and extensive planning, it was comprehensive and intensive, so the actual reorganization of the SRS was carried out over a short period of time and in a smooth manner. The experience of the Latvian SRS in solving the problems raised by the transition process from a centrally planned to a market-based system could be used as an example for other countries in transition.

As a result of described reforms and developments within the SRS, tax revenues administrated by the SRS (Fig. 16) increased by 81.8 million Lats, or 17.8%, in 1997 in comparison with 1996.

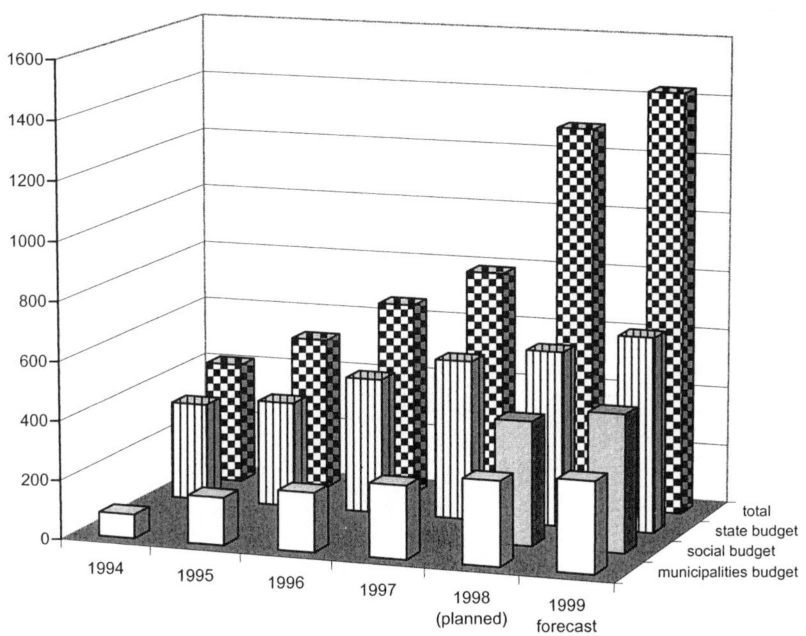

Figure 16 Tax revenues administered by SRS 1994–99 (million Lats)

ACKNOWLEDGMENTS

I would like to thank all the advisers of the IMF and especially Mr. Chris Murray, who contributed to the issues of planning, and Mr. Jan Jansen, head of the Training Division in the Swedish National Board of Customs, for his valuable ideas about the organization of training process.

ENDNOTES

1. Estonia, Latvia, and Lithuania are three Baltic countries which in 1991 regained their independence and reestablished their own states.
2. Including SRS management, tax inspectors, customs officers, and technical, support, and service staff.

18

From Corporatism to Etatism

German Policy Networks Before and After Unification

Thomas König
University of Uonstanz, Uonstanz, Germany

I. CORPORATIST STRUCTURE

The breakdown of the East German economy, increasing unemployment, and low foreign investment rates forced the German Government to take action against what has been called the ''German disease'' (*Newsweek* 1996:18; *The Economist* 1996:19). Following the ''concerted action'' of the 1970s, the Labor Minister invited prominent employer and employee organizations to collaborate on the reform of German labor law (*BMA* 1996:1). Despite the institutional and political challenges posed by German unification, the macrostability of the labor network among interest groups and public actors promised the success of the traditional German consensus instrument for interest mediation, the Alliance for Labor among governmental, employer, and employee peak organizations. From a societal perspective such arrangements among only a few peak organizations are advantageous if they reduce the decision-making costs to an amount which exceeds the losses incurred by non-participants (Buchanan and Tullock 1965: 76).

The prospect of success for the German Alliance of Labor can be studied by either social choice or network analysis. According to social choice theory, we must take into consideration the voting rights and preferences of government, employer, and employee peak organizations with regard to wages, working-time regulations, dismissal conditions, etc. (Cartellieri 1994:3). In this respect, we can easily predict the outcome of the Alliance for Labor: While we expect arrangements to be made on wages and working-time regulations among employers and employees at the firm level, employer and employee peak organizations have no voting rights on labor law at the federal level. The German government can take into account the employers and employee preferences at the federal level, but the governmental potential for policy change is restricted by different party majorities in the Bundestag and Bundesrat (König 1997; König and Bräuninger 1997).

From a network perspective, reducing decision making costs presupposes the political leadership of government as well as interest groups having monopolies of representation in the employer and employee sector, since peak organizations have to represent their functional sector effectively (Schmitter 1996:5). This precondition of monopolizing labor peak organizations has often been studied indirectly by macrostructural indicators, in particular by scales of corporatism correlating the degree of unionization with economic welfare (Schmidt: 1982: 246; Lehmbruch 1984:61, 75; Cawson 1986:42; Czada 1987:24, 25). However, these studies often assume that corporatist structures correspond with economic growth (Keman 1996:10). Hence, they focus on the macrostructural development of Western societies rather than on the study of the relationship between labor organizations determining the prospect of success for the Alliance for Labor. Measures of corporatism give little insight either into the internal relationships among interest groups or into their access relationships to government. Macrostructural indicators disregard the microfoundation of corporatism that requires the analysis of interorganizational relationships between all relevant labor organizations. In view of a microfoundation we must identify the participants in labor decision making and study their relationship pattern.

Organizations such as interest groups, parties or ministries participate in the process of legislative decision making in Western societies (Laumann and Knoke 1987:381). The relationship between those organizations can be described by network analysis where we distinguish between private and public actors. The latter have formal voting rights in legislative decision making, whereas private actors dispose information in order to get access to public actors (Pappi et al. 1995:339). Due to the traditional conflict between capital and labor, we find a large number of organizations that are unable to access all public actors in the labor policy domain. Inversely, we also expect some labor organizations to have privileged access to public actors. Consequently, we analyze the information transfer relations of more than 100 labor organizations trying to influence legislative decision making in the labor policy domain before and after unification. These interorganizational relationships specify the boundaries for (labor) policy making during the 1980s and '90s. As our focus, we are looking for certain access patterns as a precondition for the Alliance for Labor.

From an interorganizational perspective, organizations can perform different roles in the information transfer to public decision makers (Benson 1982:140).

Since many organizations do not have direct access to public decision makers in large policy domains, they may contact a broker who can give them indirect access to public decision makers. In this sense, a broker performs a prominent role, and has a monopoly if he controls the indirect access to all public decision makers in cases of no direct access. Accordingly, dummy or irrelevant policy domain actors are organizations which have no direct and no indirect access to any public decision maker. However, in systems characterized by sectoral segregation among employers, employees, professionals, etc., we seldom find either an unconsidered sector or a monopolist controlling all functional sectors. Instead, we identify organizations that have prominent broker roles within their functional sector because they channel the access to public decision makers. If an organization is a prominent broker for its functional sector, we call it a peak organization. Besides employer and employee organizations, a public actor can also be considered as a peak organization if it controls the access relationships between other public actors.

In order to examine the prospect of success for the Alliance for Labor we classify the German system of interest mediation by the distribution of broker roles among more than 100 labor organizations. Ideally, we can distinguish between types of interest mediation according to the role distribution among public and non-public organizations: Ideal types of interest mediation reveal the dominance of public decision makers when they distinguish between clientelist and etatist patterns of inter-organizational relationships in policy networks (König 1995:280). The pluralist pattern of interest mediation refers to the market allegory of competing (labor) non-public-interest groups with direct access to public decision makers, while the corporatist pattern is characterized by a few prominent interest groups controlling the access relationships of the employer, employee, and governmental sector. A corporatist pattern is considered to be the ideal precondition for the Alliance for Labor, since it reveals representation monopolies of a few peak organizations channeling the access of the governmental, employer, and employee sectors.

Our empirical results show that all functional sectors—represented by employees, employers, professionals, social security organizations and other public interest groups such as churches, welfare, or minority groups—have had direct access to public decision makers before and after unification. Despite some changes in the group homogeneity of several functional sectors, the contact density of all 100 labor organizations has also remained approximately the same. Looking at the roles of organizations, however, there was a corporatist structure among government, a peak organization of the unions and of the employers before unification. Today, the increased demand for coordination between the different party majorities in the Bundestag (first chamber) and in the Bundesrat (second chamber) have transformed the corporatist into an etatist structure. Public administration actors dominate present German labor policy making, while the peak organizations of the nonpublic employer and employee sector became relevant during the 1990s. In sum, the precondition for the Alliance for Labor existed during the 1980s, but due to the actual situation of different party majorities in both chambers, no peak organizations in the labor policy domain are in the position of being able to channel the indirect access of their functional sector.

The remainder of this paper is divided into four sections. First, we present our concept of corporate actors in the labor policy domain before and after unification. Our emphasis relies on an institutional perspective of access relationships directed toward public decision makers with formal voting power. Second, we describe the situation in the German labor policy domain before and after unification. Two surveys on labor organizational elites—the first in 1988 and the second in 1994—define our empirical basis. Third, we analyze the direct and indirect relationships of more than 100 organizations using a typology that distinguishes broker roles by their channels to public decision makers. Finally, we compare the preconditions for the Alliance for Labor by specific broker roles.

II. LABOR POLICY DOMAIN BEFORE AND AFTER UNIFICATION

Peak organizations are to be understood as prominent organizations having privileged access to public policy making. They represent interests in specific functional sectors, such as those of employers or employees, and take the floor for these sectors in public affairs. Government itself is often interested in maintaining a strong collaboration with peak organizations as the sectoral prominence of the latter may guarantee a smooth implementation of public policies. In this sense, Offe (1985) identified private peak organizations holding semipublic positions in Germany, which means that the participation of these interest groups in public policy making is not only accepted but encouraged by the German government.

The members of peak organizations are, for their own part, often organizations representing the aggregate interests of smaller groups. The formal structure of the German parent union, the Deutscher Gewerkschaftsbund (DGB), provides a good example of the formal role of a peak organization. Its members are not individual employees but specific unions acting autonomously, in particular in bargaining on wages. In the field of labor policy, the DGB represents German unions, which is also recognized by public decision makers as the legitimate representative of the employee sector. Beyond the DGB we find other unions, but they are not able to compete with the DGB monopoly on employee representation in the field of labor policy. German employer interests are organized in two parent associations, the associations of employers (BDA) and of industry (BDI). The BDI mainly concentrates on the industrial sector and entrepreneurs, whereas the BDA represents the employer sector in the field of labor policy. Although other organizations deal with employer interests in the labor domain, the division of labor between BDA and BDI promises the role of a peak organization channeling employer access to public decision makers.

Under these conditions—formal peak organizations in the employer and employee sectors as well as a parliamentary system strengthening the role of governmental actors in the public sector—we find macrostructural settings favoring the success of the Alliance for Labor between governmental, employer and employee peak organizations. Despite these formal settings, the prospect of success for the Alliance for Labor depends on the interorganizational characteristic of a corporatist structure that promises lower decision-making costs in labor policy making by maintaining a small set of efficient peak organizations. Concerning the efficiency of peak organizations for the Alliance for Labor, the governmental side should perform a monopolistic role among the organizations of the public sector, whereas a credible commitment to the smooth implementation of labor policy requires monopolies in the employer and employee sector (Lehmbruch 1984:61). Since formal settings cannot provide sufficient information about the preconditions for the Alliance for Labor, we assess the role of peak organizations empirically.

To analyze interorganizational structures, we introduce our concept of a neoinstitutional policy domain analysis which builds on the framework of the Organizational State concept developed by Laumann and Knoke (1987). According to the Organizational State, national public policy making is primarily segmented into policy domains—an assumption which comes close to the concept of *mesocorporatism* in sectoral policy networks (Cawson 1985). Second, in contrast to former elite studies on contacts among individual personalities, corporate actors such as parties, ministries, or interest groups dominate public policy making in Western societies. Third, the relationships between corporate actors can be determined by specific policy domain networks which we study using the tools of social network analysis (Kenis and Schneider 1991:30).

We add to this concept our perspective on the relevance of institutional settings by specifying the targets and the direction of policy domain relationships. Accordingly, our analysis of prominent roles in labor policy making does not take into account all relationships among policy domain actors. Since public decision makers take the final vote on labor policies, we focus on the relationships between and toward public decision makers. Public decision makers compete in labor decision making, and interest groups try to influence those outcomes. Hence, when we study public policy making in general and labor policy making in particular, we can identify the set of formal decision makers by the procedural settings of (labor) legislation. Interest groups do not belong to this set, but they usually (try to) get access to public decision makers.

Most corporatist studies of the 1980s emphasized the access of interest groups to ministries or public offices (Schmitter 1989; Streeck 1994). Parliament was often disregarded because during the 1980s the same parties held majorities in both German chambers. Rather than complying with this assumption we offer an empirical answer to the congruence of governmental and parliamentary actors by taking into consideration all public decision makers having voting power on labor policies. Apart from the Ministries of Labor, Justice, Finance, Internal Affairs, and Economic Policy, the parliamentary groups of the CDU/CSU, FDP, SPD, and GRÜNE in the 1980s, and CDU/CSU, FDP, SPD, B90/GRÜNE, and PDS in the 1990s, may offer access to labor policy making. Moreover, German legislation provides bicameral settings for public policy making including either the consent of a second chamber majority or the option to file an objection with the second chamber majority. The members of the second chamber therefore complete the set of public decision makers consisting of ten *Länder* (without Berlin) before, and 16 *Länder* after unification. In sum, 19 public organizations before, and 25 public decision makers after unification are the access targets of all labor policy domain actors. Only the answer of one public actor of the 1980s is missing.

Voting power is the formal criterion for the selection of relevant policy domain actors. Another criterion is based on the relevance of organizations in labor policy making. To identify relevant domain organizations without voting power we applied the criterion of being invited to hearings on labor policies. We identified 21 and 28 (three missing) other political organizations like parties or party-affiliated organizations which participated in two or more hearings on labor policies between 1983–87, and 1990–94, respectively. Eighty-one interest groups (four missing) before, and 49 (nine missing) after unification also met this criterion, which can be categorized according to the following sectors: unions (17 of 18 before; 8 of 9 after), employers (21 of 23 before; 8 of 11 after), professionals (12 before; 9 of 10 after), social security organizations (13 before; 12 after), other public interest groups (18 of 19 before; 12 of 16 after). The response rate is 96% before and 89% after unification, and more so-called ''other political actors'' participated in labor policy making before unification, while the sectoral rate of participation changed differently. Since only a single East German organization joined the set of relevant labor organizations after unification, our first hypothesis on minor modifications of the nonpublic system is confirmed.

The 121 actors before and 100 organizations after unification are our samples of relevant labor policy domain participants. Having identified the set of relevant domain actors, we must still assess the relationships between those organizations in order to determine the prospect of success for the Alliance for Labor. We compare the access of the 121 and 100 organizations to public decision makers, and focus on privileged access of organizations in the public, employer, and employee sectors with regard to the corporatist type of interest mediation. Privileged access to public decision makers outlines only one side of a corporatist structure. Another perspective on corporatism deals with the implementation of policies. In this case, the targets of access may change, since parliamentary groups may have no voting power in the implementation phase. We leave out this second side of corporatism and concentrate on the following question: How have peak organizations dominated the access to public decision makers before and after unification?

III. ACCESS RELATIONSHIPS IN POLICY DOMAIN NETWORKS

A major empirical research problem concerns the measurement of interorganizational relationships and their aggregation to patterns of interest mediation. In contrast to cross-domain (Laumann and Knoke 1987; König 1996) and cross-national comparisons (Pappi et al. 1995; Knoke et al. 1996), we are interested in a longitudinal social network analysis. The longitudinal perspective also allows us to examine assumptions about the stability of network contacts which is normally used to generalize the cross-sectional findings. In most policy network studies, interorganizational relationships are conceptualized as being rather stable, allowing material and immaterial resources to be channeled within a social system (Knoke et al. 1996). We will assess the assumption on the stability of policy domain network relationships by comparing the access relationships of labor policy domain actors to public decision makers before and after unification. Moreover, we look for a specific structural pattern in the labor policy domain, namely for the corporatist structure among governmental, employer, and employee peak organizations with regard to the Alliance for Labor.

For the measurement of access relationships we can question interviewees on their access either directly or indirectly. The direct question is whether the interviewee is offering or looking for access to other organizations. A shortcoming of this is that access has a rather unspecified meaning. The other option is to measure access indirectly but specifically. We measure the inter-organizational linkages indirectly by a confirmed information network because the hearings on labor policies already indicate a demand by public decision makers for valuable labor information (König 1993:355). The special features of our information network are the confirmation of the relationship by both interviewees and the direction of the information transfer which specifies the actors' relationship. We look at the information transfer from both the supply side and the demand side of labor information. We first asked the representatives of the organizations whether they send valuable labor information to other organizations, and if so, to list all organizations to which they offer this information. Then, all interviewees were asked whether they receive valuable labor information from other organizations, and to list all organizations from which they receive this information.

Their responses define two policy domain networks, the first of sending and the second of receiving information. Although we asked about information transfer in both cases, the transposed sending network is not the same as the receiving network and vice versa. The sending network contains the names of organizations to which the interviewee supplies information, and the receiving network lists organizations whose information the interviewee actually uses. Both networks can be analyzed separately, but we can also combine them in a confirmed information network that still indicates the direction of the information flow. The advantage of combining both networks is that we get rid of the so-called social dynamic effect which stresses responses coming from less prominent organizations in social network analysis. Less prominent organizations often mention their provision of information to prominent organizations, regardless of whether the latter in fact make use of the offer. Without confirmation, the responses of less relevant organizations would establish an (artificial) relationship between both organizations.

In the confirmed information network, a relationship is only accepted if both the sender and the receiver of valuable labor information confirm the direction of the information transfer. However, we still have to decide whether to use the sender's or the receiver's perspective. Despite its confirmation, the network is not necessarily symmetrical because the relationship between a receiver and a particular sender may still differ from their relationship in the other direction. Since we are looking for the dependence of public decision makers on outside information, we use the confirmed receiver perspective. Accordingly, the flow of information indicates the access of actors to public decision makers. An organization has access to a public decision maker if the latter demands information and the former supplies it. Reciprocal access exists only if both confirm their mutual demand and their mutual supply. In the confirmed receiver matrix, the receivers are the rows and the senders the columns, and since we are interested in the access to public decision makers, we only look at the public decision makers as confirmed demanders of information and all organizations as confirmed suppliers of information. More precisely, the dependence of public decision makers on other actors is confirmed in the rectangular receiver matrix of the size 19×121 before, and 25×100 after unification, which we call the access matrix. We assess this access matrix in order to compare the patterns of labor interest mediation before and after unification.

Recent cross-national studies on access patterns discovered a corporatist pattern of German interest mediation (König 1992; Pappi and König 1995; Knoke et al. 1996). Most qualitative studies also found a corporatist structure in former West Germany (Katzenstein 1987:35; Hancock 1988:136). The corporatist structure of Germany is especially significant in relation to the pluralist type of American interest mediation (Lijphart and Crepaz 1991:240; Pappi et al. 1995:298). These findings are based on cross-sectional studies assuming the stability of actor relationships. We now examine whether the relationships among policy domain actors are principally stable, but we must also take into account the changes of the macro-structural settings over time. We expect minor modifications in the non-public system because the former German Democratic Republic (GDR) did not allow for a system of nonpublic organized interest mediation (Lepsius 1991: 71). With regard to the changes of the public system, we must distinguish between two political events which may have influenced the labor policy domain since 1989. First, the enlargement of the second chamber with the accession of the five new *Länder* in 1989, and second, the situation of different party majorities in both German chambers that may have influenced the organizational relationships since April 1991. Our comparison of the patterns of labor interest mediation will show the differences between the labor policy domain before and after unification. We therefore have to aggregate the interorganizational relationships of all policy domain actors.

For the aggregation of interorganizational relationships, social network analysis offers two concepts, blockmodel and affiliation analysis. Blockmodel analysis focuses on the structural equivalence of actors, classifying pairs of actors according to their relational similarity to all other actors. Affiliation analysis is based on the connectedness of actors, emphasizing the existence of linkages among actors. According to structural equivalence, a pair of actors can have similar positions because they have the same ties to other actors without being connected themselves (Knoke et al. 1996:201). In contrast to the position-oriented criterion of structural equivalence, our concern is the specific roles of actors in their functional sector. Therefore, we apply a simple connectedness measure to aggregate actor relationships to structural patterns.

To study structural patterns in both policy domains we analyze specific diadic relationships among policy domain actors when we focus on broker roles. Direct access means that an actor has the possibility to present his own political opinion to a public decision maker. There is still a difference between access and influence, but the possibility to present his opinion is likely to increase the influence on a public decision maker because the latter will take into account the weights of arguments for and against labor policies (Pappi and König 1995:732). Hence, it may be useful to use indirect access to public decision makers if no direct access exists and if the broker shares the opinion because he belongs to the same functional sector.

Although we concentrate on access relationships in the labor policy domain, the high number of domain participants and of access targets gives rise to the suspicion that no policy domain actor has the ability to contact all public decision makers directly. Another reason is that both special features, the confirmation and the direction of information transfer, increase the reliability of our access data, but they also reduce the density of the access relationships among policy domain actors. In the confirmed receiver matrix, only a few actors will have direct access to all public decision makers, but network analysis may help detect another type of access, the indirect relationship to public decision makers. Indirect relationships between two actors depend on a broker, and the number of necessary brokers indicates their path distance. A path distance of length two means that two actors have no direct access themselves, but have direct access to the same other organizations which may connect them indirectly. We assess those indirect relationships because brokership may provide insights into the hierarchical structure of the interest mediation system.

We expect to find brokers who can connect public decision makers with actors having no direct ties to them. We look for peak organizations performing specific broker roles by controlling the indirect access to public decision makers. In this sense, a corporatist structure presupposes that a small set of actors channels the access relationships of their functional sectors. Accordingly, peak organizations perform broker roles connecting the members of their functional sector with public decision makers. This definition assumes that all domain actors seek access to public decision makers—a plausible assumption for interest groups. Moreover, we must still examine whether these organizations have no direct access to public decision makers; otherwise the role of a broker is irrelevant.

IV. ACCESS TO PUBLIC DECISION MAKERS

A. Direct Access

We examine the direct and indirect relationships of labor policy domain actors before and after unification on the basis of their mutual participation in information transfer. Rather than trying to determine their access relationships directly, we derive their access contacts from the rectangular confirmed receiver information matrix which enabled good predictions regarding event outcomes in different national labor policy domains (Knoke et al. 1996:152). The density of the overall 121×121 and 100×100 confirmed information network before and after unification is 0.7 (1007/14,250) and 0.8 (795/10,000), respectively. On the one hand, we expected the slight increase in the latter network density because a smaller set of actors increases the contact probability in a policy domain network. On the other hand, the densities are quite similar, confirming our hypothesis on high macro-stability of the labor domain network.

These densities refer to all details of information transfer, but we are interested in the rectangular access matrix to public decision makers. Table 1 lists the confirmed access contacts to public decision makers in the first column. The density of the rectangular access matrix to public decision makers is 0.09 (212/2280) before, and 0.13 (353/2574) after unification. Since the densities of the rectangular access matrix are significantly higher than those of the overall information networks, labor policy domain actors primarily focus on access to public

Table 1 Number of Sectoral Relationships to Public Actors Before and After Unification

		Public actors (n = 19) (n = 26)	Political actors (n = 21) (n = 25)	Unions (n = 17) (n = 8)	Employers (n = 21) (n = 8)	Professionals (n = 12) (n = 9)	PIGs (n = 18) (n = 12)	Social security (n = 13) (n = 12)	Sum (n = 121) (n = 100)
Before	Direct access density	45	52	19	30	19	26	21	212
		.13	.13	.06	.08	.08	.08	.09	0.09
After	Direct access density	137	79	25	9	14	32	37	333
		.21	.12	.12	.04	.06	.10	.12	0.13
Before	Indirect access density	164	175	159	136	77	117	156	984
		.48	.44	.49	.34	.34	.34	.63	.43
After	Indirect access density	188	233	80	41	43	115	140	840
		.29	.36	.38	.20	.18	.37	.45	.33
Before	Diadic relation	377	436	250	291	167	223	403	2147
After	Diadic relation	448	533	149	80	78	207	284	1779
Before	Concentration	2.30	2.49	1.57	2.14	2.17	1.91	2.58	2.18
After	Concentration	2.38	2.29	1.86	1.95	1.81	1.80	2.03	2.12

decision makers. Although the access relationships increased after unification, only 13% of all possible contacts to public decision makers are realized directly.

On closer inspection, the findings in the functional sectors differ extremely, and the different number of actors cannot sufficiently explain the density changes. Despite the higher number of public decision makers after unification, these actors raised their contact density from 13% before, to 21% after unification. We presume that the reason for the higher density of public actors is the situation of different party majorities, which since April 1991 has increased the demand for coordination among public decision makers. Before unification congruent party majorities discharged the party governmental actors to communicate with opposition actors. Today, opposition actors not only have better access to most governmental actors, the contacts among the higher number of members of the second chamber have also increased significantly. North-Rhine Westfalia, the majority leader of the opposition in the second chamber, now has a prominent position among public decision makers.

Whereas contact density slightly changed among the other political actors from 13% to 12%, the smaller set of unions doubled their direct access to public decision makers after unification. The results among employers show that the smaller number is not the reason for the unions' increase from 6% to 12% as the smaller set of employers lost half of their access relationships to public decision makers. Today, employers realize only 4% of all possible direct contacts compared to 8% before unification. The professionals also lost some direct contacts to public decision makers, while the access density of the social security organizations remained constant.

To sum up, the direct linkages show that some actors have better access to public decision makers than others. Moreover, public decision makers themselves have different positions in the access networks. However, these results cannot give a satisfactory answer to the question whether there is a corporatist structure of interest mediation in the labor policy domain defined on a representation monopoly in the governmental, employer and employee sector. These monopolies only exist if the sectoral access to public decision makers is channeled by the corresponding peak organizations. According to the direct linkages, most actors have no access to public decision makers. To contact public decision makers these actors must engage a broker. In the final section, we assess the structural pattern in both policy domains with regard to the roles of brokers.

B. Indirect Access

For the analysis of interest mediation patterns it is more useful to distinguish between specific broker roles than to follow the chain of brokership with regard to an increasing path distance. Therefore, we do not take into account the brokers of brokers etc., but we study the specific role of brokers more closely. In order to specify distinct broker roles, we distinguish between general indirect, and specific indirect access. Columns 3 and 4 of Table 1 list indirect relationships with path distance of length 2 indicating the general opportunity to contact a public decision maker indirectly. Before unification, 984 indirect contacts existed to public decision makers giving a density of 0.43. Since there are more direct linkages after unification the density of indirect ties is at 0.33, lower than before unification.

The indirect densities of the functional sectors to public decision makers before unification can be described as follows: the public sector with 0.48, the other political actors with 0.44, and the employees with 0.49 realized almost half of all possible indirect access to public decision makers; employers, professionals and public interest groups had about a third of indirect contacts, whereas the social security organizations had a density of 0.63. Except for public interest groups, which slightly increased their indirect density, the indirect access of almost all sectors decreased by about 10 to 20 percentage points after unification. Despite this decrease almost all labor policy domain actors are able to contact public decision makers by engaging a broker. However, there is a difference between the choice of one or several brokers. In the latter case, interest mediation is less hierarchically structured.

With regard to the hierarchical structure of interest mediation, the degree of brokership concentration can be measured by the relation between path distances of length 2 and the number of specific diadic relationships. Path distances of length 2 measure the general opportunity to contact a public decision maker indirectly, whereas the diadic relationships show how often an actor has an indirect access opportunity via specific brokers. Since an actor may engage the same broker to provide access to different public decision makers, the number of diadic relationships cannot be lower than the number of path distances with length 2. Columns 5 and 6 of Table 1 list the number of diadic relationships before and after unification, and the concentration of brokership is listed in columns 7 and 8 of Table 1, measured by the relation of diadic relationships and path distances of length 2. A low value means a high concentration of brokerships, whereas a high value expresses the opportunity to select different brokers for indirect access to public decision makers. Accordingly, the overall concentration increased from 2.18 to 2.12 after unification. The degree of concentration did not change within the public and employee sectors, while it increased within all other sectors. The increase in overall concentration is another indicator promising good conditions for the Alliance for Labor, since fewer organizations perform broker roles after unification. However, we must still find out whether a small set of peak organizations dominates the employer, employee, and public sectors.

For the analysis of the access network patterns, we study the different roles of brokers with regard to the types of sender, broker and receiver of information (Fernandez and Gould 1994). According to Figure 1, we call the broker a representative of his functional sector if he is also member of the sender sector. Being

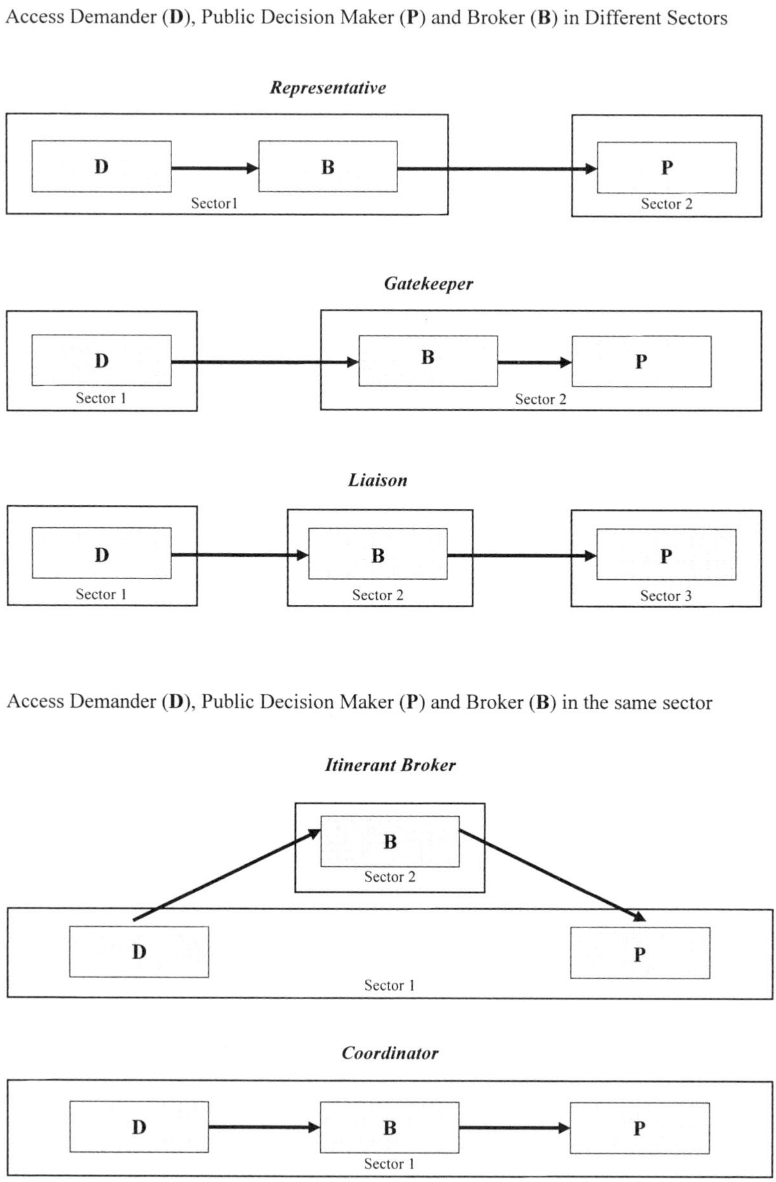

Figure 1 Roles of brokers between and within sectors.

Demand for Access							
	Public Actors	Other Politicals	Unions	Employers	Professionals	PIGS	Social Security
Public Actors	Coordinator	Gatekeeper	Gatekeeper 1				
Other Politicals		Representative	Gatekeeper 2				
Unions			Representative				
Employers	Itinerant			Representative		Liaison	
Professionals	Broker	Liaison			Representative		
PIGS				Liaison		Representative	
Social Security							Representative

Figure 2 Roles of broker by different functional sectors.

an exclusive representative is precisely the role of a peak organization. A gatekeeper is a broker who is himself a member of the public sector. A liaison is the brokership between three different functional sectors: the demander of access contacts a broker of another functional sector who is not a public decision maker. A broker acts as a coordinator if he links two other public decision makers, whereas an itinerant broker connects two public decision makers without belonging to the public sector himself.

In Figure 2 we have listed the different broker roles grouped along the type of organizations in the labor policy domain. Access brokers are listed in the rows, access seekers in the columns. Another property, the specific access to public decision makers, is indicated by the cell of public decision makers themselves who may perform the sole role of coordinator. Other brokers channeling the access to public decision makers are representatives of their functional sector, and an ideal corporatist structure consists of a dominant coordinator, and prominent representatives of the employer and employee sectors channeling the access of their members to public decision makers exclusively. By contrast, the gatekeeper roles indicate the dominance of public decision makers in other functional sectors. In this sense, we can distinguish between roles of gatekeeper 1 and gatekeeper 2: the former are public decision makers and the latter are other political actors. If gatekeeper I dominates the access relationships in the labor domain, we call the network pattern an etatist structure, whereas the dominance of gatekeeper 2 corresponds to a party-oriented structure. Another structure is the pluralist type which indicates the competition among representatives of all functional sectors (König 1995:280).

Table 2 corresponds to Figure 2 listing the number of broker roles and the name of the broker organization channeling most of the broker roles within a sector. Comparing the network before and after unification shows that the FDP—a member of the coalition government preparing the ground for the Kohl Government in 1982 (König and Liebert 1996:82)—dominated the public sector before unification by performing the coordinator role in 38 of all 71 cases. After unification North-Rhine Westfalia has 102 of 295 coordinator roles in the public sector, indicating the increased relevance of opposition actors in a situation with different party majorities. However, since the SPD dominance is replaced by the Ministry of Labor (BMA) in the sector of other political actors, the situation of different party majorities does not favor all opposition actors. First and foremost, different party majorities stress the position of administrative actors like North-Rhine Westfalia in the public sector and like the BMA in the sector of other political actors. This conclusion is also confirmed by the changes within the sector of other political actors because the labor committee members of the FDP lost their representative role in the Ministry of Women and Youth (BMJF). In sum, party actors of the governmental coalition and sometimes of the opposition were the central brokers in the public sector before unification, whereas administrative actors dominate the labor policy domain network after unification.

In the sector of the employees, the DGB can partially defend its representative role although it is less important after unification. Whereas the DGB had an absolute monopoly with all 114 representative roles before unification, the SPD is the central broker channeling 37 of 99 indirect access relationships to public decision makers. Besides the SPD, the gatekeeper 2 and liaison roles are more important than the DGB representative, indicating the unions' loss of autonomy within their functional sector. The DGB losses are also shown by the fact that the organization acts neither as an itinerant broker nor as a liaison in the public sector. In the employer sector, the role of representatives changed dramatically. Before unification, the BDI and BDA had three quarters of all brokerships within the employer sector, but after unification the employer must contact a BMA office (13) or the SPD opposition (15) to get indirect access to public decision makers. Since both employer organizations also lost their itinerant broker and liaison roles in the public sector, the public decision makers are less dependent on the employee and employer organizations after unification.

The other sectors have been dominated by labor committee members of the FDP performing a gatekeeper role before unification, whereas the SPD opposition or a BMA office have dominant positions for these organizations after unification. The social security organizations still perform a remarkable role in the labor policy domain because they have privileged direct and indirect access to public decision makers. In sum, the results of the nonpublic sectors show that

Table 2 Actor Specific Number of Broker Roles and Prominent Brokers to Public Actors Before and After Unification

		Access demand						
	Broker	Public Actors	Other Politicals	Unions	Employers	Professionals	PIGSe	Social Security
Before	Public actors	**71** (FDP 38)	**89** (SPD 30)	**43** (SPD 30)	**71** (SPD,FDP 23)	**42** (SPD 20)	**66** (SPD 36)	**65** (FDP 35)
After		**295** (NRW 102)	**235** (BMA 53)	**99** (SPD 37)	**28** (SPD 15)	**49** (SPD 24)	**107** (SPD 51)	**119** (SPD 42)
Before	Other politicals	**129** (BMA II 50)	**94** (FDP-AS 36)	**51** (FDP-AS 24)	**98** (FDP-AS 44)	**66** (FDP-AS 47)	**67** (FDP-AS 17)	**104** (FDP-AS 43)
After		**72** (BMFJ 34)	**122** (BMFJ 40)	**21** (BMA I 4)	**43** (BMA IV 13)	**17** (BMFJ 8)	**76** (BMFJ 57)	**127** (BMA III 63)
Before	Unions	**37** (DGB 35)	**49** (DGB 48)	**114** (DGB 114)	—(—)	—(—)	—(—)	**94** (DGB 94)
After		**10** (IGBSE 5)	**69** (IGBSE 24)	**14** (DGB 7)	—(—)	**1** (CGB 1)	**4** (DGB 3)	**4** (DGB 4)
Before	Employer	**107** (BDI 73)	**121** (BDI 62)	**24** (BDI 17)	**91** (BDI 44)	**13** (BDA 7)	**8** (BDI 8)	**12** (BDA 8)
After		**1** (DILL 1)	**14** (BDA 14)	—(—)	—(—)	—(—)	—(—)	—(—)
Before	Professionals	**7** (KBV 7)	**22** (BÄK 14)	**10** (BÄK 6)	**10** (BÄK 8)	**20** (BÄK 10)	**6** (DKG 6)	**41** (KBV 20)
After		**2** (MB, DLJu 1)	**1** (DKG 1)	**1** (DKG 1)	—(—)	**2** (KBV, AGBL 1)	—(—)	**2** (KBV 2)
Before	PIGS	**17** (KDB 10)	**12** (BAGFW 4)	**3** (DBJR 2)	**4** (KDB 2)	**7** (BAGFW 5)	**61** (BAGFW 22)	**12** (DS 4)
After		**18** (KDB 9)	**47** (KDB 20)	—(—)	—(—)	—(—)	**17** (KDB 11)	**9** (DV 9)
Before	Social security	**9** (AOK 5)	**49** (AOK 18)	**5** (VdAK 3)	**17** (AOK-BV 5)	**19** (BK, AOK 5)	**15** (AOK 9)	**75** (BK 20)
After		**50** (AOK 12)	**45** (BA 29)	**14** (BA 12)	**9** (BA 7)	**9** (AOK-BV 4)	**3** (AOK 2)	**23** (BA 10)

Organizations: *AGBL* = AG bäuerliche Landwirtschaft; *AOK* = Bundesverband AOK; *BA* = Bundesanstalt Arbeit; *BAGFW* = Bundesarbeitsgemeinschaft freien Wohlfahrtspflege; *BÄK* = Bundesärztekammer; *BDA* = Bundesvereinigung Dt. Arbeitgeberverbände; *BDI* = Bundesverband Dt. Industrie; *BK* = Bundesknappschaft; *BMA*, *BMA I, II, III, IV* = BM Arbeit und Sozialordnung sowie Abteilungen 1, 2, 3, und 4; *BMFJ* = BM Frauen u. Jugend, *CGB* = Christlicher Gewerkschaftsbund, *DBJR* = Dt. Bundesjugendring, *DGB* = Dt. Gewerkschaftsbund, *DILL* = Verband Arbeitsdirektoren Stahl Dillinger; *DKG* = Dt. Krankenhausgesellschaft; *DLJu* = Bund dt. Landjugend; *DS* = Dt. Städtetag; *DV* = Dt. Verein öffentliche-private Fürsorge; *FDP-AS* = FDP-Mitglieder Ausschuβ Arbeit u. Sozialordnung, *FDP* = FDP-Bundestagsfraktion, *IGBSE* = Industriegewerkschaft Bau, Steine, Erden, *KBV* = Kassenärztliche Bundesvereinigung; *KDB* = Kommissariat dt. Bischöfe; *NRW* = Landesvertretung Nordrhein-Westfalen; *MB* = Marburger Bund; *SPD* = SPD-Bundestags-fraktion; *VdAK* = Verband dt. Angestelltenkrankenkassen.

the decreasing indirect contacts led to a reduction of interest group monopolies after unification. Although macrostructural indicators such as the boundaries of the labor policy domain network, its overall densities, and the general concentration of brokership indicate the network stability before and after unification, there is a remarkable change on the microlevel concerning the modification of the roles of organizations in all functional sectors. In the public sector North-Rhine Westfalia has the coordinator role, while the employee and employer peak organizations lost their role in both sectors.

V. CONCLUSION

Due to the losses of employer and employee organizations, the preconditions for the Alliance for Labor are lacking after unification. In the non-public sectors there is no peak organization able to control its functional sector. Whereas the dominance of the DGB and the BDA/BDI outlined a corporatist structure before unification, the actual members of the employer and employee sector have not only more direct access to public decision makers, but their indirect access is also channeled by gatekeepers. The weaker position of the DGB and the BDA is also compounded by their losses in other sectors. However, the losses of the former employer and employee peak organizations occurred for different reasons. The DGB gave up its representative role due to the increasing direct links of other unions to public decision makers, while the other employer organizations do not profit from the reduction of the BDA monopoly. Two reasons may explain the disaster of the employers after unification. First, an internal power shift among the coalition government diminished the FDP's influence, the key governmental actor for employers before unification. Second, governmental actors abstain from demanding for employer information by referring to the situation of different party majorities.

The answer is provided by the changes of the overall structural pattern of interest mediation. The almost unchanged concentration of brokership already shows that the corporatist interest mediation pattern has not become a pluralist type as in American labor policy (Pappi and König 1995:740). Administrative public actors dominate in situations of different party majorities because the government majority of the first chamber has to coordinate action with the *Länder* governments of the second chamber. Due to different party majorities we find an etatist structure with predominant administrative actors rather than pluralist competition among all domain actors. In postunification Germany we no longer find those preconditions that were responsible for the success of corporatist arrangements, i.e. peak organizations in the public, employer, and employee sectors. Instead, the situation today shows a tendency toward bureaucratic labor policy making.

REFERENCES

Benson, K.R. (1982). A framework for policy analysis. S. In D. Rogers et al. (eds.), *Interorganizational Coordination: Theory, Research, and Implementation*, Ames, IA: Iowa State University Press, 137–176.

Buchanan, J.M. and Tullock G. (1965). *The Calculus of Consent. Logical Foundations of Constitutional Democracy*. Ann Arbor, MI: University of Michigan Press.

BMA/Bundesministerium für Arbeit und Sozialordnung. (1996). Programm für mehr Wachstum und Beschäftigung—Maßnahmen im sozialpolitischen Bereich, Bonn.

Cartellieri, U. (1994). Arbeitslosigkeit in der Bundesrepublik Deutschland—Ansatzpunkte zur Behebung des Arbeitsmarktproblems, Aus Politik und Zeitgeschichte B 12–13: 3–8.

Cawson, A. (ed.). (1985).*Organized Interests and the State. Studies in Meso-Corporatism*. Beverly Hills, CA: Sage.

Cawson, A. (1986). *Corporatism and Political Theory*. Oxford: Basil Blackwell.

Czada, R. (1987). The impact of interest politics on flexible adjustment policies. In H. Keman and P. Whiteley (eds.), *Coping With the Economic Crisis. Alternative Responses to Economic Recession in Advanced Industrial Societies*, 20–53. London: Sage.

The Economist. (1996). Germany—Is the model broken?, 4–10 May, 19–21.

Fernandez, R.M. and R.V. Gould. (1994). A dilemma of state power: brokerage and influence in the national health policy domain. *American Journal of Sociology 99*, 1455–1491.

Hancock, D.M. (1988). *West Germany. The Politics of Democratic Corporatism*. Chatham, NJ: Chatham House Publishers.

Katzenstein, P.J. (1987). *Policy and Politics in West Germany. The Growth of a Semisovereign State*. Philadelphia: Temple University Press.

Keman, H. (1996). The Logic of Accomodation: Consensual Politics and Corporatist Intermediation Vis-à-Vis Internationalization of Politics and Economics. Paper presented at the 8th SASE Conference (Geneva).

Kenis, P. and Schneider, V. (1991). Policy networks and policy analysis: scrutinizing a new analytical toolbox. In B. Marin and R. Mayntz (eds.), *Policy Networks: Empirical Evidence and Theoretical Considerations*. Frankfurt/M: Campus.

Knoke, D., Pappi, F.U., Broadbend, J., and Tsujinaka, Y. (1996). *Comparing Policy Networks. Labor Politics in the U.S., Germany, and Japan*. Cambridge: Cambridge University Press.

König, T. (1992). Kollektive Entscheidungsfindung im Politikfeld Arbeit: Ein modellorientierter Politikfeldansatz. *Politische Vierteljahresschrift 42*, 597–621.

König, T. (1993). Die Bedeutung von Politik-Netzen in einem Modell politischer Entscheidungen und privater Einflußnahme. *Journal für Sozialforschung 4*, 343–367.

König, T. (1995). Die Koordination in politischen Verhandlungssystemen. *Kölner Zeitschrift für Soziologie und Sozialpsychologie 47*, 268–294.

König, T. (1996). Freiwilligkeit und Zwang in internationalen Verhandlungen: Eine Modellierung von Kooperation und Konflikt an den Beispielen der Europäischen Union und der Antarktiskonferenz, Mannheim (Habilitationsschrift).

König, T. (1997). Politikverflechtungsfalle oder Parteienblockade? Das Potential für politischen Wandel im deutschen Zweikammersystem, *Zeitschrift für Staatswissenschaft und Staatspraxis 2*, 135–159.

König, T. and Bräuninger, T. (1997). Wie wichtig sind die C-Länder? Die Politik der Bundesregierung in der Zustimmungs- und Einspruchsgesetzgebung. *Zeitschrift für Parlamentsfragen*, in print.

König, T. and Liebert, U. (1996). Germany: party influence or chancellor rule? In J. Blondel and M. Cotta (eds.), *Party and Government*, 78–90. London: Macmillan.

Laumann, E.O. and Knoke, D. (1987). *The Organizational State*. Madison, WI: University of Wisconsin Press.

Lehmbruch, G. (1984). Concertation and the structure of corporatist networks. In J. Goldthorpe (ed.), *Order and Conflict in Contemporary Networks*, 60–80. Oxford: Clarendon.

Lepsius, R.M. (1991). Ein unbekanntes Land. Plädoyer für soziologische Neugierde. In B. Giessen and C. Leggewie (eds.), *Experiment Vereinigung. Ein szialer Großversuch*, 71–76. Berlin: Rotbuch-Verlag.

Lijphart, A. and Crepaz, M. (1991). Corporatism and consensus democracy in eighteen countries. Conceptual and empirical linkages. *British Journal of Political Science 21*, 235–256.

Newsweek. (1996). The German disease. Sick at heart? March 18, 18–23.

Offe, C. (1985). *Disorganized Capitalism: Contemporary Transformation of Work and Politics*. Cambridge: Polity Press.

Pappi, F.U., König, T. (1995). Les organisations centrales dans les reseaux du domaine politique: une comparaison Allemagne–Etas-Unis dans le champ de la politique du travail. *Revue Francaise de Sociologie 36*, 725–742.

Pappi, F.U., König, T., and Knoke, D. (1995). *Entscheidungsprozesse in der Arbeits-und Sozialpolitik. Der Zugang der Interessengruppen zum Regierungssystem über Politikfeldnetze. Ein deutsch-amerikanischer Vergleich*. Frankfurt: Campus.

Schmidt, M.G. (1982). Does corporatism matter? Economic crisis, politics and rates of unemployment in capitalist democracies in the 1970s. In G. Lehmbruch and P.C. Schmitter (eds.), *Patterns of Corporatist Policy Making*. London: Sage.

Schmitter, P.C. (1989). Corporatism is Dead! Long Live Corporatism. *Government and Opposition 24*, 54–73.

Schmitter, P.C. (1996). Corporatist Intermediation Meets the Global Economy: Is There Going to Be a Predictable Winner or Loser? Paper presented at the 8th SASE Conference (Geneva). Instituto Juan March.

Streeck, W. (1994). Pay restraint without incomes policy: institutionalized monetarism and industrial unionism in germany. In R. Dore, R. Boyer, and Z. Mars. (eds.), *The Return to Incomes Policy*. London: Pinter.

19

Political Economy of Income Distribution in Britain

Demography, Market, and Party Politics, 1979–1987

Rosa Mulé
University of Warwick, Coventry, United Kingdom

I. INTRODUCTION

The aim of this paper is to identify the probable causes of the pattern of income distribution in the United Kingdom over the 1980s. In June 1994 the Institute for Fiscal Studies reported that "the proportion of the UK population with income below half the national average has more than doubled in the past 30 years"; most of the increases occurred in the 1980s. The report showed that the income share of the top decile of the population rose from 22% to 25% during the three decades (*Financial Times*, 2 June 1994:10). In February 1995, the *Rowntree Inquiry into Income and Wealth* found that the trend toward increasing inequality accelerated rapidly between 1977 and 1990, reaching a higher level than recorded since World War II. Not only has the gap between rich and poor increased dramatically over the past 20 years, but the incomes of the bottom 10% were no higher in the early 1990s than in the late 1960s (Goodman and Webb 1994). These findings call into question the widespread view in the 1950s and 1960s that reductions in income differences are natural byproducts of economic development or of liberal democracy (Downs 1957; Kuznets 1955). The British experience clearly indicates that political economists are confronted with a new intellectual challenge. This paper seeks to address this challenge by drawing upon theoretical and empirical work on the political economy of income inequality in Britain, and by suggesting that party politics played a significant role in the widening gap between rich and poor. The political science literature dealing with the redistributive impact of parties has rested upon partisan theory or demand driven vote-maximizing models (Denters 1993; Hibbs and Dennis 1988; Tufte 1978). Some of the core propositions of these two schools of thought are radically antithetic, portraying a schizophrenic image of party behavior. On the one hand, the ideology of the party in power is the best predictor for the allocation of costs and benefits. On the other hand, electoral imperatives dictate variations in redistributive policies which in turn affect socially undifferentiated voters.

Despite their differences these views share fundamental assumptions, including a conception of a political party as unitary actor and the idea of preference homogeneity among party leaders.[1] In addition, most scholars believe that redistributive policies aim at improving the relative position of one social class, itself regarded as internally fairly homogeneous. Accordingly the population is subdivided into distinct classes, defined as lower-, middle-, and upper-income groups.

Advances in the theory of political parties suggest that so simple a model may be unsuited to analyzing the redistributive impact of parties in a significantly fragmented and heterogeneous society. Theoretical work on political parties has long argued that parties are not monolithic entities and are instead more fruitfully conceived of as organizations (Duverger 1951; Lawson 1994; Michels 1959). Within these organizations party actors strive for relative dominance and engage in coalition building and dissolution (Kitschelt 1994; Panebianco 1988); the making and breaking of internal coalitions, each with its own agenda, are perceived as the driving force of party life. The upshot is that special forms of bargaining and negotiations continuously evolve during the formulation of redistributive policies. In devising these policies leaders may primarily be concerned with gaining and retaining power in their own party as well as maximizing votes or pursuing ideologies. Innumerable examples show that battles over party platforms are often acrimonious because the outcome stands as symbolic evidence of who controls the party, rather than as a guideline for the making of public policy (Ware 1987: 125–126). Consequently when analyzing party politics and policies we should focus on what Cyert and March (1992:41–44) define as *organizational slack*, the use of discretionary power between organizational actors.

These considerations provide excellent reasons to alter the traditional manner in which we have studied the phenomenon of the redistributive impact of ruling parties. It seems reasonable to assume that shifting internal alignments may generate a dynamic process whereby new dominant factions attempt to translate the gains at the party level also into redistributive gains for their actual or potential supporters. The main question involved in assessing redistributive policies is therefore how internal conflict and cooperation affect those policies. To answer this question it is necessary to move beyond the unitary actor model and to relax the related assumption of preference homogeneity.

This paper examines the politics of income redistribution in Britain between 1979 and 1987 by applying recent theoretical developments in the party politics literature. The paper is divided into two parts. The first part looks at nongovernmental effects on income inequality, setting the growth of income inequality in the United Kingdom in an international contest, the second part concentrates on the driving forces behind the redistributive strategies of the Conservative governments, evaluating the impact of demographic and market forces in changing patterns of income distribution. Having assessed the contribution of government cash transfers to inequality movements,[2] and having established that transfer policies exert significant redistributive effects, we briefly explore the peculiarities of the electoral arena over the 1980s and focus on intraparty dynamics. The analysis highlights three key political factors that could have affected income inequality outcomes: the changing nature of strategic games within the Conservative Party, the introduction of sequential elections in 1975, and the minority status of right-wingers.

II. TRENDS IN INCOME INEQUALITY

It is important to investigate how measured inequality fared under the Conservative government. From Table 1 we see that over the 1970s and 1980s there was a wide diversity of experiences across countries, with rising inequality in more than half of the sample.[3] Yet one of the sharpest increases occurred in the United Kingdom where the Gini coefficient rose 2.7 percentage points. Considering the

Table 1 Income Inequality in Nine Countries for Posttax-Posttransfer Adjusted Income (Gini index %)

Country	Late 1970s early 1980s	Mid-1980s	Absolute change	Relative change
Israel	33.7	33.0	−0.7	−2.1
United States	33.0	35.5	+2.5	+7.5
Canada	32.4	31.1	−1.3	−4.0
France	30.8	30.4	−0.4	−1.3
Australia	30.2	30.9	+0.7	+2.3
United Kingdom	27.6	30.3	+2.7	+9.7
Norway	24.9	24.3	−0.6	−2.4
West Germany	23.0	26.4	+3.4	+14.8
Sweden	19.9	22.9	+3.0	+15.0

Source: Computed by the author from LIS data sets for Canada 1975, 1981; Israel, 1979, 1986; United States 1979, 1986; France 1979, 1984; Australia 1981/82–1989/90; United Kingdom 1979, 1986; Norway 1979, 1986; West Germany 1978, 1984; Sweden 1981, 1987.

Table 2 Income Inequality in the United Kingdom 1969–1986 (Adjusted Household Posttax-Posttransfer Income)

Year	CV	Gini	Theil
1969	67.9	29.8	15.9
1974	67.3	28.7	14.8
1979	53.8	27.6	12.7
1986	64.7	30.3	16.5
	Percentage change		
1969–79	−21	−7	−20
1979–86	+20	+10	+30

Source: Computed by the author from LIS.

fact that income distributions change very slowly this increase must be considered substantial. In Sweden, the Gini coefficient climbed 3 percentage points, in West Germany 3.4 points, and in the United States the index by 2.5 percentage points. But the upward trend was not universal. In some countries the Gini coefficient dropped, suggesting that while international forces were at work, national factors were also significant. Inequality continued to fall in Norway, Israel, Canada, and France, with the decline in Gini ranging from −1.3% in France to −4.0% in Canada.

A closer look at the pattern of income inequality in Britain reveals that the trend is divided into two periods marked by a downward shift between 1969 and 1979 and an ascending tendency between 1979 and 1986 (Table 2). The striking feature of Table 2 is that in the first period the three inequality indices dropped while under the Conservative governments there was a clear reversal of the trend.[4] Between 1979 and 1986 all indices rose, with the growth ranging from 10% to 80%. This unanimity of the three indices is important because it reduces the possibility that results are dependent on the particular index used.

It would, however, be unrealistic to assert that government policies were exclusively responsible for the widening gap between rich and poor. It is well known that other factors, such as demographic movements and market forces, often affect income differentials. For this reason in the next section I decompose the structure of income inequality to identify non-government determinants of inequality growth. I first examine demographic and market effects and then go on to evaluate the distributional impact of government transfers.

A. Demographic Effects: Age and Household

The demographic variables most commonly analyzed in the literature on income inequality are the age profile of the population and the household size and composition. As Cowell (1995:130) put it, a drop in inequality could be an optical illusion if we have not allowed for demographic changes, or how income varies between and within different age groups. Alterations to the age structure, including lower birth rates or the growing number of elderly, may affect the distribution of income among individuals. Elderly people are overrepresented in lower-income groups and therefore the aging of the population may widen income differentials. By the same token, rising inequality could be the outcome of changing household size and composition. In the postwar period the number of large families steadily declined while the number of single households and lone parents gradually increased. Smaller households may have a negative distributional effect because they prevent income pooling.

To assess the impact of demographic movements on the size distribution of income I decompose distributional comparisons for age groups and household types into between- and within-group comparisons. Disentangling the within-group and between-group inequality components is essential in order to isolate the redistributive role of the Conservative government: the higher the contribution of the between-groups components, i.e., the stronger the association of the grouping factor with aggregate inequality, the more negligible the distributional consequences of transfer policies.

Mookerjee and Shorrocks (1982) report that over the 1970s the growing number of elderly people contributed to rising inequality in Britain to the point where subtracting the "age effect" from aggregate inequality meant a reversal of the trend. Recent findings, however, suggest that the age effect was much less significant in the 1980s (Jenkins, 1995). Table 3 sets out the results of the age decomposition between 1969 and 1986.[5] The pattern highlights again a sharp contrast between the 1970s and the 1980s. It is evident that the age effect was roughly stable during the 1970s, while there was a downward trend from 1979 to 1986, when the Theil index dropped from 1.5% to 0.6%.[6] Because aggregate

Table 3 Contribution of Changes in Within and Between Age Group Component in Total Inequality, United Kingdom 1969–1986 (Adjusted Posttax-Posttransfer Household Income; Theil inequality index %)

Year	Total inequality	Within-group inequality	Age effect (between-group inequality)
1969	15.9	14.3	1.5
1979	12.8	11.4	1.4
1986	16.5	15.9	0.6

Source: Computed by the author from LIS. By the time I started this section the 1974 U.K. LIS data set was unfortunately not available.

Table 4 Contribution of Changes in Within and Between Households Types to Total Inequality, United Kingdom 1969–1986 (Adjusted Posttax-Posttransfer Household Income; Theil Inequality Index %)

Year	Total inequality	Within-household inequality	Between-household inequality
1969	15.9	13.7	3.1
1979	12.8	9.9	2.9
1986	16.5	14.2	2.3

Source: Computed by the author from LIS.

inequality in the same period grew by 16.5% we can safely conclude that the ageing of the population had a low distributional impact. A closer look at Table 3 reveals that what dominated was the contribution from changes in inequality within age group. These results corroborate existing research showing that demographic movements have not significantly contributed to the changing shape of income distribution in Britain (Jenkins 1995).

The second demographic variable considered in this paper is the household size and composition. Different household types may affect the distribution of income when their concentration varies.[7] In Britain, as in many other industrialized countries, there has been a secular decline in average household size. Reasons include greater mobility, a trend toward younger people living independently of their parents, and higher divorce rates (Kiernan 1989). The impact of these changes is likely to reduce equality all the more because they prevent income pooling. Table 4 shows that between 1969 and 1986 inequality between household types was fairly stable, implying that the growing proportion of smaller households had marginal effects on total inequality while within-household inequality had a strong distributional impact. These results unambiguously demonstrate that demographic movements in Britain over a period of about fifteen years had low distributional consequences.

B. Market Effects

The marginality of demographic variables in changing patterns of income inequality strongly suggests that other forces were at work. A further step in the examination of the structure of income inequality is to assess the role of market income (i.e., original, pretransfer income). Wage differentials, for instance, have received great attention from analysts of income distribution in Britain (Gardiner

1993; Gosling et al. 1996). Several studies have detected a clear link between income inequality and wage dispersion. Figure 1 represents the proportion of the population in four income classes, defined in relation to median income, for the period 1969–1986.[8] The picture that emerges is striking. The proportion of the population with less than 50% of median income more than doubled between 1969 and 1986. What is more, while the proportion of poor workers grew by 3.7 percentage points between 1969 and 1979, its growth accelerated under the Thatcher governments, climbing 8.6 points. At the same time, the richest income category, with more than twice median income, almost tripled, again with the highest increase of 11.4 points occurring from 1979 to 1986. On the other hand,

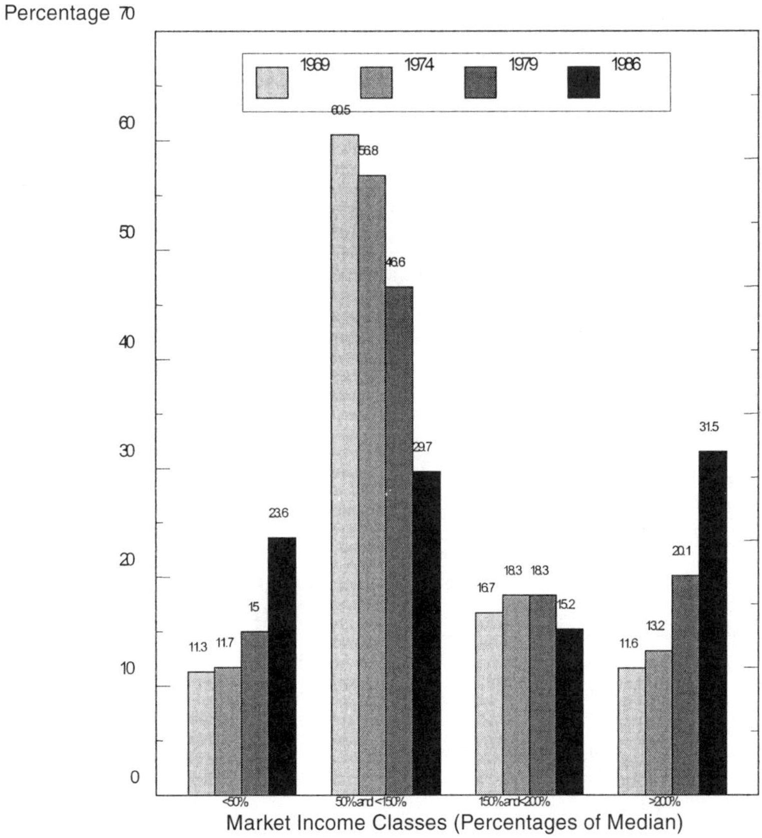

Figure 1 Proportion of the population in different market income classes. Head of household aged 20 to 64. United Kingdom, 1968 to 1986.

upper-middle-income groups were much less affected, since their number dropped slightly from 16.7% to 15.2%.

A noteworthy feature of Figure 1 is that over the 1980s the distribution of market income was more spread away from the middle: the falling percentage of workers with middle range incomes was associated with growth in the lower and upper tails of the distribution. As in other countries, income polarization in the market sphere mainly reflected structural and technological changes (OECD, 1993). There was an expansion of the secondary labor market, with an increase in temporary and part-time workers employed in low skilled jobs.

C. Distributional Consequences of Government Transfers

The distributional role of market forces can better be understood by examining variations in the Gini coefficient induced by government intervention. Table 5 presents the results for selected income definitions. From the table we see that while market income inequality (before government intervention) rose consistently throughout the period, between 1969 and 1979 inequality in posttransfer income (i.e., after government intervention) declined roughly by 5% but grew again in the 1980s by 10.8%. This indicates a less effective role played by cash income in reducing inequality and suggests that policy changes contributed to the ascending movement. Hence, the Conservative government did not offset the disequalizing impact of market forces; on the contrary, it sustained market income inequality with the retrenchment of redistributive policies.

One reason was that many Conservative supporters viewed the welfare state as a main cause of economic decline. Welfare benefits allegedly imposed a burden

Table 5 Gini Coefficient (%) for Selected Income Definitions, United Kingdom 1969–1986

Year	Market income (1)	Posttransfer Income (2)	Reduction from transfers (1) − (2)
1969	43.9	33.2	10.7
1979	46.9	31.5	15.4
1986	53.6	34.9	18.9
	Percentage change		
1969–1979	+6.8	−5.1	
1979–1986	+14.5	+10.8	
1969–1986	+22.3	+5.1	

Source: Computed by the author from LIS.
Income is adjusted with the OECD equivalence scale.

on the taxpayer, stifled incentives to work and to save, and undermined individual self-reliance.

While the provision of social services was not substantially altered, the real break with the past came about in social security policies (Hill 1990). The Thatcher government was distinctive because "none of its predecessors had dared to cut social security spending" (*The Economist*, 22 December 1979:13). Under the Social Security Acts of 1980, 1982, 1986, and 1988 the Conservative government established new rules that made take-up benefit more limited and difficult.

In other areas the *lack* of change was just as important. Despite the sharp rise in unemployment in the early 1980s, no variations were made to the level and duration of unemployment benefits. The cumulative effect of these measures was that between 1978–79 and 1983–84 the number of social security claimants increased by 138.4% but spending on income-related benefits increased by only 110.6% in real terms (Atkinson et al. 1986:30). This shows a real decline in the benefit per claimant produced by the abolition of the earnings-related supplement and the taxation of benefits.

Other redistributive measures limited the availability of benefits to women in general, and married females participating in the labor market in particular (Hill 1990:5). Since 1979 successive Conservative governments relied on a rhetoric of the family and a reassertion of Victorian values to justify cuts in welfare spending (McDowell 1989:179). Harsh measures included cutbacks in the real level of child benefit and the taxation of supplementary benefits which affected the standards of living of lone-mothers.[9] The redistributive impact of these measures is easily gauged by looking at Figure 2 which shows the trends in the Gini values for pretransfer, posttransfer and posttax incomes between 1969 and 1986. It is evident that the distributional impact of the transfer system is far stronger than that of the tax system. The distributional pattern traced in Figure 2 shows that inequality declined steadily in posttransfer and posttax income until 1979, while it increased in pretransfer (original) income since 1974, thus corroborating the results in section three on the important role of market income differentials in the acceleration of income inequality.

It is worth pointing out that under the Labour government of 1974–79 the Gini values for posttransfer (and posttax) income continued to decline, suggesting that the social security system had equalizing effects. This decline in posttransfer Gini was consistent with the pattern traced since the 1960s. By contrast, Figure 2 clearly indicates that the advent of the Conservative government in 1979 marked a departure from previous experience, with considerable increases in the Gini values for all three income concepts.

The Conservative government exacerbated income inequality by attacking the "culture of dependency" in general, and unemployed people in particular. For Nigel Lawson, the Chancellor of the Exchequer, the social security system encouraged "idleness and irresponsibility" (quoted in Gilmour 1992:125). Para-

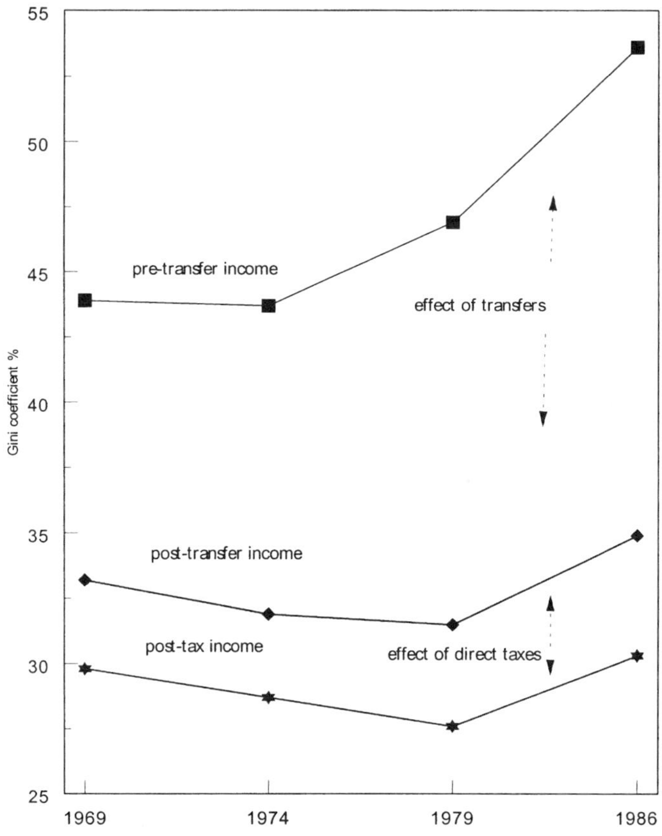

Figure 2 Inequality in pretransfer, posttransfer, and posttax income, United Kingdom, 1969 to 1986.

doxically, however, there was scant evidence to support the belief that transfer benefits generated disincentives to work. In 1977 only 50% of those eligible were claiming FIS (Family Income Supplement) while 24% of Supplementary Benefits remained unclaimed; in 1979 only 60% of those eligible were claiming the 1% benefit (*Social Security Statistics, Great Britain* 1981:253). In 1986 official estimates reported that the Supplementary Benefit unclaimed was running at 25%, which meant that Ł410 million a year went unclaimed (*Guardian*, 5 November 1986). But if the take-up rate was relatively low, then other reasons presumably lay behind the Conservative attack on scroungers. We must therefore look beyond the government's rhetoric to understand the driving forces behind income redistribution.

III. THE ROLE OF PARTY POLITICS

A. Electoral Competition

A widely held view regarding changes in redistributive policies points to electoral competition as a main cause of policy changes. In the British case two factors are particularly noteworthy, the geography of voting and the weakness of party competition. Over the 1980s the geographical distribution of votes coincided with differences in the principal bases of poverty. The majority of Conservative voters lived in the affluent South, whereas Labour supporters were chiefly concentrated in the poor counties of the North. Between 1979 and 1983 the number of beneficiaries in the North increased from 15.7% to 20% while in the Southeast it grew from 9.4% to 9.7% (Walker and Walker 1987:47-48). These figures reveal that higher unemployment, low-paying jobs, and poverty were of different magnitude and significance in the two regions.

Furthermore, in the South the poor were most likely to be elderly; poverty in the North, by contrast, was more likely to be associated to redundancy and joblessness (Green 1996). Perhaps this spatial concentration explains why social security policies penalized the unemployed and protected the pensioners, at least in the short run. Although pensions were curtailed in the medium long term, they were increased in the short term. Pensions grew in real terms by 7% between 1978-79 and 1983-84 (Sked and Cook 1993:346).

Since the losers of the economic and social transformations of the 1970s were spatially concentrated, the Conservative government deployed what Krieger (1986:86) dubbed "arithmetical particularism." Such electoral strategy relied on making sectional appeals by affecting the economic position of targeted groups. Thus, redistributive costs and benefits may have been apportioned between risk categories in order to manufacture the electoral majority. One consequence of this electoral strategy was to exacerbate income polarization between North and South. Although the North-South divide predates the 1980s, Walker (1987:13). claims that the Conservative government "helped to widen and deepen these divisions, sometimes to a catastrophic extent."

Another point to note is that cutbacks in cash transfers were facilitated by the peculiarities of party competition. It is important to appreciate that interparty competition steadily abated over the 1980s. Divisions within the Labour Party over proposals of internal constitutional change absorbed the energies of the Labourites. In the late 1970s and early 1980s Labour's strategy shifted further to the left opening a political vacuum in the centre of the ideological space, soon filled by the formation of the Social Democratic Party in 1981 (Whiteley 1983: 2–6).

Entrance in the electoral arena of a new political rival impinged on intraparty politics. It mitigated opposition within the Conservative ranks against the antiegalitarian stance of right-wingers because several Tory moderates were exposed to the Alliance's advance in their constituencies (Riddell 1983:46–47). Modifications in the electoral arena thus changed the options available to Conservative groupings, strengthening the internal position of right-wingers. What is more, the landslide victory in 1983 showed that Opposition parties were not a likely alternative.

B. Reshaping the Party Identity

Lack of credible competitors meant that the government had only been prepared to compromise in social security policies when pressure had been exerted from within its own supporters (Ogus et al. 1988:11). Against this background it is surprising that most statements about Thatcher's redistributive policies have paid little or no attention to intraparty politics. Yet the years between 1979 and 1982 were marked by the internal struggle for real control of the party, a time in which contradictions and dilemmas were particularly acute (Jessop et al. 1988:19). In this struggle rival groupings attempted to defend or mold their own identity at the same time as they shaped the party image. One group opted for defending the old party identity by praising the virtue of traditional policies, while the other preferred to "modernize" it by embarking on a new course. In general, when a political party acquires a new image this testifies to the end of an era and to the success of those new faces holding positions of responsibility in the internal hierarchy. Seen in this perspective, strategic repositioning among party elites may shed some light on the driving forces behind changes in redistributive policies.

Several observers have noted that the main goal of the Thatcherites was to recraft the party identity. Although the ideological battle over redistributive policies was cast in economic terms, "ultimately the economic arguments were means to a still more ambitious end—Keith Joseph's insistence that the party must move away once and for all from its previous position" (Deakin 1987:86). Gamble (1995a: 100) aptly remarked that the "appeal to monetarism was much more than a set of techniques for controlling the money supply." Bulpitt (1986: 33) argued that the "dictates of party management . . . ensured that a link would be made with the statecraft of monetarism." These authors agree that the Conservative appeal to monetarism was not entirely guided by economic reasons; rather, party politics reasons were at work. By the mid-1980s right-wingers had finally achieved their principal goal when the term *Thatcherism*, whatever its meaning, became part and parcel of the Conservative identity (Jessop et al. 1988:6).

C. From Implicit to Explicit Games

Understanding the interplay between internal strife and party identity, and their joint redistributive impact, involves tracing the roots of strategic games within the party. I analyze power relations between party actors by adopting a two-stage strategy (Dowding 1991:53-54). In the first stage, I trace the development of the choice situation: How did party coalitions find themselves in this situation? Were there modifications in the incentive structure that could have affected the bargaining position of these elites? The second stage focuses on bargaining processes over the content of transfer policies.

Borrowing from Schelling (1980:21), we may interpret the evolution of bargaining between the Conservative elites as a shift from tacit to explicit games. Tacit games are those where players watch and interpret each other's behavior, partners cannot or will not negotiate explicitly; by contrast, in explicit games the conflict of interest is publicized and overt. Tacit and explicit games are not thoroughly distinct concepts, since various gradations of the two games may exist.

Analysts of the Conservative Party have recognized the pervasiveness of tacit games. As one observer noted, "Conservatives . . . engage in ideological conflicts using sophisticated codewords and themes which resonate with the cognoscenti but cannot easily be picked up by outsiders" (Dunleavy 1993:124-125). Tacit games enhance loyalty and unity because they promote close cooperation and coordination.

From the mid-1960s, however, there has been a significant increase in the incidence and publicity of intraparty conflict. There had been more dissenting MP votes under Edward Heath from 1970 to 1974 than in the previous 25 years, between 1945 and 1970 (Norton 1978:115). But the differences with pre-1970s discord there were qualitative as well as quantitative. Conservative MPs traditionally expressed their disagreements by joining ad hoc alliances from issue to issue. This pattern of internal alignments gradually changed over the 1970s, with a substantial number of MPs dissenting on the same issues (Norton 1978:244). More stable and vociferous alliances signaled that the structure of strategic games was shifting from tacit to explicit.

Various hypotheses have been advanced to explain the new form of internal revolt. Some authors claim that the party was facing a generational turnover and that young Conservative MPs had developed a less deferential attitude toward party policy (Budge et al. 1988:55). The main problem with this interpretation is that a generational turnover is an insufficient condition for tilting the internal balance of power. It is not self-evident that it should always trigger variations in bargaining strength between party elites. Others maintain that the real issue was the authoritarian and confrontational personalities of Heath and Thatcher which fueled internal bickering (Norton 1978:217–255). In my view explanations in terms of personalities are unwarranted because they sidestep the crucial question regarding the dynamics of power within the party organization.

A more convincing interpretation holds that changes in the leadership selection rules since 1965 altered the distribution of power and fomented internal strife (Evans and Taylor 1996). Prior to 1965 the Conservative leader "emerged" out of informal discussions in the ranks of the party notables. This procedure endowed the leader with considerable power; all authority and policy emanated from the top. The rules introduced in 1965 did not alter significantly the relationship between the leader and the party because once elected there was no provision for his/her formal removal. But in 1974 two electoral debacles led to internal backlash against the concentration of power in the hands of the then leader, Edward Heath. As a result in 1975 two major modifications in the selection rules were introduced. First, the 15% votes requirement on the first ballot was replaced by a requirement of 15% of all eligible voters, in addition to an absolute majority. Second, and more important, provision was made for regular election at the beginning of each new parliament and in each subsequent session.

Consequently, the formal security of tenure of the party leader was brought to an end. It may be argued that Conservative leaders never enjoyed security of tenure, and that the regulations merely formalized the realities of existing relationships. Several Conservative leaders had been informally ousted by the members of parliament. Alec Douglas-Home, Harold MacMillan, Anthony Eden, Winston Churchill, and Neville Chamberlain all resigned because of loss of confidence among their close allies (Bogdanor 1994:86-96).

Evidence suggests that the new rules did mark a departure from previous experience. Bogdanor (1994:96) concedes that "neither Mrs. Thatcher, nor perhaps John Major, would have been selected under the old methods." With the new methods the election of Thatcher was the result of strategic voting. Thatcher was elected because she was the only serious candidate willing to challenge Heath and *not* because there was a widespread commitment to her views (King 1985: 97; Shepherd 1991:176–177). Research findings report that in 1975 the estimated share of Thatcherite MPs as a proportion of the Conservative parliamentary party was between 10% and 25% (Crewe and Searing 1988:371). Hence Thatcher was the leader of a minority group and was elected primarily because Heath had been unable to ensure reelection under the new rules.

D. Sequential Elections

The most significant modification brought about by the new rules was the increased dependence of the leader on the support of the parliamentary party. From 1975 the Conservative leader had first to secure reelection as leader and therefore satisfy the wishes of the faithful MPs. The fact that the leader was directly dependent on the favors of the Conservative MPs raised his/her sensitivity to the views of backbenchers, "the probability of removal may be low; but the risks to the individual [leader] are high" (King 1991:29).

The Conservative leader was now facing the problem raised by "sequential elections." Sequential elections obtain because to gain or retain office leaders must win the favors of different types of constituencies, including MPs, party activists, and voters (Aranson et al. 1970). Such conditions create a dilemma to party leaders if, for example, the wishes of party activists differ from those of the wider electorate. Comparative research on the leadership selection found that the ''process of selection may constrain the style and behaviour of those selected, either because of the resources required, or because of the need to ensure reselection where that is necessary'' (Marsh 1993:229).

Changes in the leadership selection rules in the Conservative Party signified that the potential threats of candidates standing against the incumbent could prove damaging for the party's image and thus give some leverage to dissident MPs.[10] In this way the introduction of sequential elections in 1975 impinged on the options available to the bargaining partners. We have seen that the election of Margaret Thatcher to the leadership was the outcome of strategic voting, which meant that Thatcher was ''sincerely'' supported by only a minority of MPs, the so-called dries.

The dries were a small group of Conservative MPs identified with 19th-century liberalism, the main watchwords being initiative, duty, independence; they were overtly inegalitarian and believed that wide differences in income were both natural and desirable. In the words of Joseph and Sumption (1977:1), the cornerstone of the new strategy was ''to challenge one of the central prejudices of modern British politics, the belief that it is a proper function of the State to influence the distribution of wealth for its own sake.'' This strategy was reflected in the abolition of the Royal Commission on the Distribution of Income and Wealth in 1979, signaling the changed priority toward distributional issues.

The majority of Conservative MPs, the so-called wets, were less sympathetic to such views. They claimed that the Tory tradition, going back to Disraeli, stressed the primacy of community over individuality (Gilmour 1992:142–177). They also believed that some degree of state intervention for the relief of poverty was necessary, and that less privileged groups should be protected.

Deep disagreement over redistributive issues between wets and dries,[11] and especially the minority status of the dries, accounted for their ideological spurt, so unusual among Conservative leaders. ''Margaret Thatcher was a Conservative rarity in her readiness to identify Conservatism in unambiguous ideological terms'' (Whiteley et al. 1994:127). Minority groupings are sometimes more ideological than majority ones because purposive incentives develop to compensate for other incentives (e.g., status and money) controlled by the larger group.

A further consideration is that the ideological crusade of the dries helped cement their internal divisions. Many figures, such as Rhodes Boyson, Lord Beloff, Paul Johnson, Alfred Sherman, and Alan Walters, had changed their political allegiances at least once before and thus might be expected to do so again. These people had been recruited from varying sources; some had been Liberals, others

Labour supporters. ''Since their beliefs were shaped more by their antipathies than by a common positive vision, the need for a constant unifying enemy was particularly urgent for them'' (Denham and Garnett 1994:271).

These considerations suggest that the endorsement of an overtly antiegalitarian stance by the dries is explicable also in terms of intraparty dynamics. Changes in the leadership selection and reselection rules represented a turning point in the history of intraparty politics by shifting the nature of strategic games from tacit to explicit. In turn, this modification fostered two relatively stable coalitions, the dries and the wets. Because the dries shaped their own identity against the identity of left-wingers, the process entailed the abandonment of the old redistributive principles supported by moderate Conservative groups, and a departure from the traditional party identity. In this manner intraparty dynamics contributed to alterations in income redistribution. Conservative right-wingers were molding their identity by devising redistributive policies in stark contrast to those preferred by left-wingers.

Besides triggering the dries' ideological spurt, the minority status of Thatcherites had another major consequence. It meant that on coming to office the Prime Minister had little choice but to appoint as Cabinet ministers Heath's most able and effective supporters, including William Whitelaw, Jim Prior, Ian Gilmour, Peter Carrington, and Quintin Hogg. Thatcher also brought in people like Peter Walker, the symbol of Heathite interventionism, and Christopher Soames, a typical traditional Tory. Although the significant aspect was that the Cabinet was a moderate faction, four key posts were given to Thatcher's closest supporters. Geoffrey Howe was appointed Chancellor of the Exchequer, John Biffen, Chief Secretary of the Treasury, Keith Joseph, Secretary of State for Industry, and John Nott, Secretary of State for Trade.

On coming to office the divisions between the wets and the dries grew steadily worse. Prior's reaction to the 1979 budget eloquently expressed this dissension: ''It was really an enormous shock to me that the budget which Geoffrey [Howe] produced the month after the election of 1979 was so extreme'' (Prior 1986:119). As the economy slumped and unemployment soared, the attack on social security benefits provoked an outright revolt within both the Cabinet and Conservative MPs. In 1981 the unemployment rate stood at 13% and most Cabinet members were expecting less stringent monetary rules.

The Blackpool Conference held in 1981 displayed the two faces of a divided cabinet. Michael Heseltine, Secretary of State for the Environment, criticized the right-wing emphasis on independence and self-help because ''self help [had] a limited meaning in an inner city community where 40 percent of the young kids may be without work'' (*Times*, 16 October 1981:2). Internal disputes over the relationship between the Conservative party and sections of the British population were sparked by different opinions regarding the identity of the party organization. Hardliners wished to mold it as the party of free-market principles, initiative, and duty; the wets believed that the government should not relinquish its responsibility for the relief of poverty. Arguably, the most significant aspect of the Blackpool Conference was the surfacing of the dilemma of sequential elections. Had the Conservative leader satisfied the wishes of moderate Cabinet ministers and those of the wider electorate, she would have annoyed the party's rank and file.

Thatcher skillfully deployed different sources of power to placate internal tensions (Thatcher 1993:138–139). Thatcher's demagogic appeal to activists is perhaps one reason why party membership rose under her leadership, after years of relentless decline. Her attention to the rank and file raised activists' perception of their importance for the party organization. Survey findings suggest that since the early 1980s Conservative members have been feeling more influential in the decision-making process of the party organization. (Whiteley et al. 1994). By distributing purposive incentives through attacks on scroungers and on the welfare state, the Conservative leader was able to promote and reinvigorate the loyalty of party members and to use this fidelity as an ammunition against internal rivals.

Thatcher's appeal to the party rank and file and the successful campaign for membership recruitment warned the wets that Conservative activists wanted a radical change from previous redistributive policies. Her popularity among Conservative members and their readiness to identify with Thatcherite policies helped to assuage the wets' internal opposition.

The second strategy Thatcher deployed to ease the strains between wets and dries was to relax public expenditure. Growth in government outlays in the early 1980s was mostly the effect of automatic stabilizers, but it was also the outcome of internal opposition. "The relenting on cuts took some of the edge off the cabinet anger. It is regarded as signalling the start of the 'wet appeasement' " (*The Economist*, 24 October 1981:29). For Shepherd (1991:178), Thatcher always tempered her radicalism with an overriding desire that the Conservatives should hold office with her as their leader. Sequential elections persuaded the Conservative leader to restrain her policy ambitions. Faced with the pragmatics of power, Thatcher appealed to the party rank and file and appeased the wets; in this way she was able to forge an internal alliance and to retain the leadership although she was supported by a minority coalition of MPs.

E. Breaking the Internal Alliance on Social Security Policies

The differences in social policy exposed the deep divisions in the Conservative ranks so much that internal turmoil over Thatcherite social policy was regularly reported by the press. The *Times* described how "the Government suffered one of its biggest backlash revolts of the present parliament . . . when 13 Conservative

MPs voted to restore the 5% that was cut from unemployment benefits in 1980'' (18 March 1982:1). For the *Financial Times* this revolt was ''the most determined piece of internal dissent Mrs. Thatcher has suffered'' (14 July 1982). It was clear that any further pressure would risk splitting the party asunder.

Internal wrangling reached a climax in the summer of 1981 during the discussions preparing the budget. The Treasury requested spending cuts for 1982–83, below the totals derived from the March white paper. Thatcher recounts in her memoirs how this proposal sparked ''one of the bitterest arguments on the economy, or any subject, that I can ever recall taking place at Cabinet during my premiership'' (Thatcher 1993:148).

Fierce reactions to the 1981 budget acted as a springboard for a Cabinet reshuffle. According to Francis Pym (1984:8), ''Margaret Thatcher saw this crisis as a personal challenge to her resolve and became doubly determined not to give an inch on the economic strategy.'' Between 1981 and 1982 the Prime Minister dropped three well-known wets: Ian Gilmour, Lord Privy Seal; Christopher Soames, Leader of the Lords; and Mark Carlisle at Education, and brought in three men on whom she could rely: Norman Tebbit, who was appointed Minister of Employment; Nigel Lawson, Minister of Energy; and Norman Fowler, who became Minister of Health and Social Security.

Figure 3 illustrates the dynamics which induced the cabinet reshuffle and ended the search for a compromise in social security policies. The top part of the figure shows the agreement (A_1) on social security spending and taxation as the equilibrium solution of bargaining games between the wets and the dries. Point A_1 was attractive to the dries because by appeasing the wets it deferred the threat of a leadership reselection and while retaining party unity.

The lower half of Figure 3 depicts a typical situation in bargaining theory where weakness may be strength (see Schelling 1980). As unemployment mounted, the wets moved to position W_1, which challenged the redistributive policies of the dries. At this critical point two institutional features insulated Margaret Thatcher from losing control of policy making. The constitutional role of prime ministers in appointing and reshuffling their cabinets was ''undoubtedly one of the most important ways in which a prime minister [could] exercise power over the whole conduct of government'' (Thatcher 1993:25). Another salient aspect was the strong institutionalization of the Conservative party which typically concentrates power in the hands of the dominant coalition and hinders the formation of stable organized factions (Panebianco 1988:130–141). Prime-ministerial prerogatives and strong institutionalization meant that the wets had to grudgingly accept Thatcher's policy-making authority.

The Cabinet reshuffle and the electoral landslide of 1983 crushed the wets as a coherent force within the party. Thatcherite ideas became so dominant that social policy ceased to be a divisive issue among MPs during the second Conservative term (Garry 1994). In this new scenario the Fowler report of 1986, described at the time as the most radical since Beveridge (Evans 1996), could easily

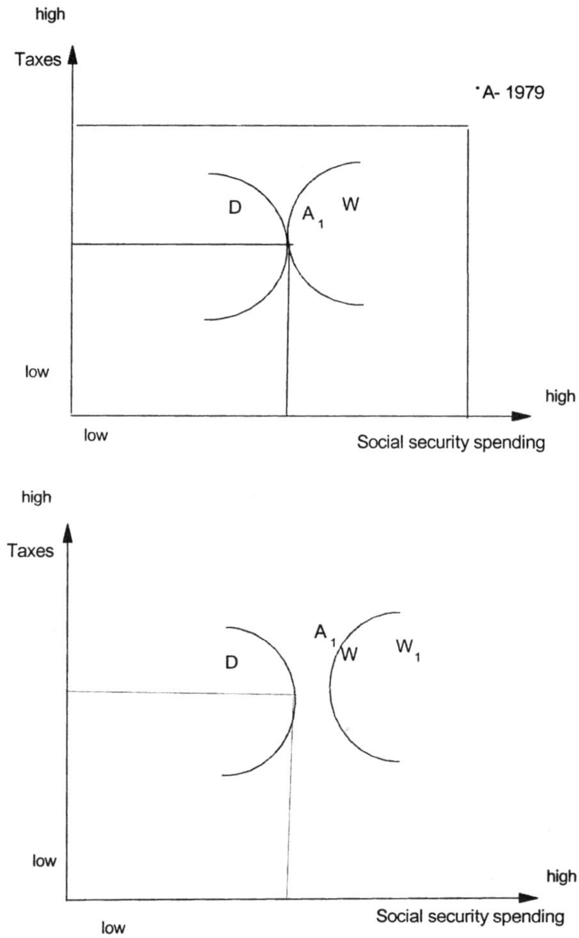

Figure 3 Making and breaking alliances on redistributive policies, Conservative Cabinet, 1979 to 1982.

mark a retreat from any serious commitment of insuring individuals against risk (Lister 1991).

IV. CONCLUSIONS

Over the 1980s income inequality in the United Kingdom grew faster than elsewhere, suggesting that national factors played a crucial role. By decomposing the structure of inequality it was possible to highlight the low distributional impact of demographic variables, such as the growing number of elderly and the smaller size of households. On the other hand, income polarization in the market sphere had strong disequalizing effects.

This wider dispersion of market differentials was not offset by government intervention. On the contrary, the Conservative government exacerbated income inequality by attacking the culture of dependency. Conservative rhetoric, however, concealed an asymmetry in the distribution of costs and benefits among beneficiaries. Until 1986 cash benefits protected the elderly living in the affluent South while cutbacks in the level and scope of unemployment benefits exposed the people out of work to the risk of poverty. This is not to say that pensioners gained from Thatcher's redistributive policies. Indeed, the indexation of pensions to prices rather than earnings meant that the relative position of pensioners to people in worked deteriorated. What I am pointing out here is that the *relativities* between pensioners and unemployed changed in favor of the elderly. The Thatcher government capitalized on the geographical distribution of poverty in Britain and was able to forge new coalitions of voters between people in work and pensioners. Manipulations of entitlement rules were encouraged by the weakness of interparty competition and the lack of a credible alternative to the Conservative government.

But explanations of Thatcher's redistributive policies have focused too exclusively on electoral concerns. The argument developed throughout this paper suggests that shifting internal alignments were important in exacerbating income inequality. Manipulations of eligibility and entitlement rules over the 1980s also reflected strategic repositioning between wets and dries. We have seen that the consolidation of the internal coalition led by Thatcher was intimately connected to redistributive questions. Three elements lay behind the antiegalitarian crusade of the dries. First, the dries shaped their own identity against the identity of left-wingers, which meant the abandonment of the redistributive principles traditionally supported by the moderate Conservatives. Second, they were a minority group within the party and therefore they distributed purposive incentives to their followers to compensate for other types of incentives usually distributed by the majority coalition, such as status and money. Third, the ideological spurt helped cement their internal divisions.

Nevertheless, intraparty dynamics can only be understood within the limits and opportunities offered by the institutional context. We have seen that during the first Thatcher term sequential elections posed a potential threat to the leader which altered the direction of transfer policies advocated by the dries. This threat perception in the context of a dynamic process of bargaining accounted for the concessions of the dries both in public expenditure growth and in the level and scope of unemployment benefits.

There were at least two other institutional factors which helped to understand the Conservative onslaught against the culture of dependency during the second Thatcher term. The strong institutionalization of the Conservative party was reflected in the concentration of decision-making authority in the hands of the leader. This factor accelerated the demise of the wets from the center of the political scene. The other institutional feature was the ample margin of freedom conferred by Westminster systems on prime ministers that provided Thatcher with the requisite autonomy to depart from postwar consensus on social security legislation.

Hence a combination of institutional environment, intraparty politics, and vote mobilization strengthened the antiegalitarian stance of the dries. In this manner the dries could reapportion redistributive costs and benefits at the expense of low-income families, who were identified either with the Opposition or with the Tory wets. Overall, these results indicate that the widening gap between rich and poor in Britain was not accidental and that party politics contributed to the accelerating pace of income inequality over the 1980s.

More generally, this paper shows that reconstructing the history of intra-elite negotiations and conflicts in the light of their policy impact, an area not yet adequately researched, can offer an altogether richer and more suggestive account of the redistributive impact of ruling parties. Focusing on internal governance exposed an important dimension thus far concealed by the unitary model. It revealed that party elites were connected to disjointed groups rather than to social classes regarded as units. In such circumstances party groupings designed redistributive policies to tighten or loosen their ties with specific sections of the population in order to enhance their internal position. This view addresses often neglected questions regarding the role of intraparty politics in the protection, exclusion, discrimination, and suppression of social identities.

ENDNOTES

1. For a detailed discussion of these arguments see Mulé (1997).
2. I am looking at transfer policies rather than tax policies because cash transfers are considered to be the main mechanism for income redistribution (Ringen 1987).
3. Until recently comparisons of income distributions within countries and between countries have been hampered by the lack of comparable income data (Smeeding et al. 1989). This drawback in comparative distributional analyses has been partially offset by the release of the Luxembourg Income Study (LIS) microdata sets. The salient feature of the LIS data is that a large number of income and demographic variables have been drawn from national, usually government sponsored, surveys and have been made comparable across the datasets. More confidence can be attributed to the fact that distributional outcomes are not merely the result of changing concepts and definitions imposed on the data.
4. I have chosen these three indices because they are sensitive to different income

groups: the coefficient of variation is top-sensitive, that is, it magnifies inequality changes for upper income groups; the Gini coefficient is modal-middle-sensitive, and the Theil index is sensitive to low-income groups.

5. The population is partitioned into seven age groups: <25, 25–34, 35–44, 45–54, 55–64, 65–74, 75+.
6. I use the Theil index for analytical convenience because it is easily decomposable into subgroups of the population (see Cowell 1995).
7. The population is partitioned into six household types: one adult, two adults, three adults, one adult with children, two adults with children, three adults with children.
8. I subdivide the working population into four income classes, one low-income category, a very broad middle category, an upper-middle, and a very high income category. This categorization is to provide cutoff values of unequal size, so that alterations in the share of market income at the top and at the bottom of the distribution is more easily detected.
9. Although this paper is chielfy concerned with cash transfers it should be mentioned that the tax system was made more regressive. There was a shift away from direct to indirect taxation by replacing the previous split rates of Value Added Tax (VAT), 8% and 12.5%, with a single rate of 15%. The Conservative government initially cut the top marginal tax rate on earned income from 83% to 60%, and later reduced it to 40%. It also cut the basic rate of income tax from 33% to 30%, later reduced to 25%. Raising the VAT at 15% added about 4% to the Retail Price Index, at a time when inflation was resurgent and oil prices were rising. Higher indirect taxation was needed partly to finance reductions in income tax at both the top marginal tax rate and the basic rate.
10. The leadership contest between Major and Redwood of July 1995 highlighted the devastating effects on party unity of the visibility of the leadership battle. Major's victory was tarnished by the fact that "218 votes meant that 109 Tory MPs did not cast their votes for Major" (*The Economist*, 8 July 1995).
11. The distinction between "wets" and "dries" is a rather simplified account of Conservative groupings. For a more nuanced description of Conservative thought and tradition see Aughey and Norton (1981).

REFERENCES

Aranson, P. and Ordeshook, P. (1972). Spatial strategies for sequential elections. In R. Niemu and H.F. Weisberg. (eds.), *Probability Models of Collective Decision-Making*, 298–331. Columbus, OH: Charles E. Merrill.

Atkinson, A.B. (1986). *Social Insurance and Income Maintenance*. STICERD Welfare State Programme, discussion paper WSP/11. London: London School of Economics.

Atkinson, A.B. (1996). Seeking to explain the distribution of income. In J. Hills. (ed.), *New Inequalitites*, 19–48. Cambridge: Cambridge University Press.

Bogdanor, V. (1994). The selection of the party leader. In A. Seldon and S. Ball (eds.),

Conservative Century. The Conservative Party Since 1900, 86–96. Oxford: Oxford University Press.

Budge, I., McKay, D., Rhodes, R., Robertson, D., Saunders, D., Slater, M., and Wilson, G. (1988). *The Changing British Political System: Into the 1990s*. London: Longman.

Bulpitt, J. (1986). The discipline of the new democracy: Mrs Thatcher's domestic statecraft. *Political Studies XXXIV*, 19–39.

Cowell, F. (1995). *The Measurement of Inequality*. Hemel Hempstead: Harvester Wheatsheaf.

Crewe, I. and Searing, D.D. (1988). Ideological change in the British Conservative Party. *American Political Science Review 82*(2), 361–384.

Cyert, R. and March J. (1992). *Behavioral Theory of the Firm*, 2nd ed. Oxford: Blackwell Business.

Deakin, N. (1987). *The Politics of Welfare*. London: Methuen.

Denham, A. and Garnett, M. (1994). ''Conflicts of Loyalty'': Cohesion and Division in Conservatism, 1975–1990. In P. Dunleavy, and J. Stanley. (eds.), *Contemporary Political Studies*, 270–277. London: Political Studies Association of the United Kingdom.

Denters, B. (1993). The politics of redistribution in local government. *European Journal of Political Research 23*, 323–342.

Dowding, K. (1991). *Rational Choice and Political Power*. Aldershot: Edward Elgar.

Gamble, A. (1995). *The Free Economy and the Strong State*, 2nd ed. London: Macmillan.

Downs, A. (1957). *An Economic Theory of Democracy*. New York, Harper & Row.

Dunleavy, P. (1993). The political parties. In P. Dunleavy, A. Gamble, I. Holliday, and G. Peele (eds.), *Developments in British Politics*, 123–153. London: Macmillan.

Evans, M. (1996). Fairer or Fowler? The effects of the 1986 Social Security Act on family incomes. in J. Hills (ed.), *New Inequalities*, 236–264. Cambridge: Cambridge University Press.

Evans, B. and Taylor, A. (1996). *From Salisbury to Major: Continuity and Change in Conservative Politics*. Manchester: Manchester University Press.

Gardiner, K. (1993). *A Survey of Income Inequality over the Last Twenty Years. How Does the UK Compare*? STICERD Welfare State Programme, discussion paper WSP/100. London: London School of Economics.

Garry, J. (1994). *The Internal Politics of the British Conservative Party and Margaret Thatcher's Position as Leader*. Unpublished MA thesis, University of Galaway.

Gilmour, I. (1992). *Dancing with Dogma*. London, Simon & Schuster.

Goodman, A. and Webb, S. (1994). *For Richer, for Poorer: The Changing Distribution of Income in the United Kingdom, 1961–91*, Commentary No. 42. London: Institute for Fiscal Studies.

Gosling, A., Machin, S., and Meghir, C. (1996). What has happened to the wages of men since 1996? In J. Hills (ed.), *New Inequalities*. Cambridge: Cambridge University Press.

Green, A. (1996). Aspects of the changing geography of poverty and wealth. In J. Hills (ed.), *New Inequalities*, 265–291. Cambridge: Cambridge University Press.

Hibbs, D. and Dennis, C. (1988). Income distribution in the United States. *American Political Science Review 82*, 467–488.

Hill, M. (1990). *Social Security Policy in Britain*. Hants, U.K.: Edward Elgar.

Jenkins, S.P. (1995). Accounting for inequality trends: decomposition analyses for the U.K. 1971–1986. *Economica 51*, 6–12.

Jessop, B., Bonnett; K., Bromley, S., and Ling, T. (1988). *Thatcherism. A Tale of Two Nations*. Oxford: Polity Press.

Joseph, K. and Sumption, J. (1979). *Equality*. London: John Murray.

Kiernan, K.E. (1989). The family: formation and fission. In H. Joshi (ed.), *The Changing Population of Britain*, 27–41. Oxford: Basil Blackwell.

King, A. (ed.). (1985). *The British Prime Minister*. London: Macmillan.

Krieger, J. (1986). *Reagan, Thatcher and the Politics of Decline*. Cambridge: Polity.

Kitschelt, H. (1989). The internal politics of parties: the law of curvilinear disparity revisited. *Political Studies 37*, 400–421.

Lawson, K. (ed.). *How Political Parties Work*. Westport, CT: Praeger.

Lister, R. (1991). Social Security in the 1980s. *Social Policy and Administration 25*, 21–33.

Marsh, M. (1993). Introduction: selecting the party leader. *European Journal of Political Research 24*, 229–231.

Michels, R. (1959). *Political Parties: A Sociological Study of the Oligarchical Tendencies of Modern Democracy*. New York: Dover.

Mitchell, D. (1991). *Income Transfers in Ten Welfare States*. London: Avebury.

Mookherjee, D. and Shorrok, A. (1982). A decomposition analysis of the trend in UK income inequality. *Economic Journal 92*, 886–902.

Mulé, R. (1997). Explaining the party policy link. In *Party Politics 3*, 493–512.

Norton, P. (1978) *Conservative Dissents*. London: Temple Smith.

Ogus, A.I., Barendt, E.M., and Buck, T.G. (eds.). (1988). *The Law of Social Security*. London: Butterworth.

Panebianco, A. (1988). *Political Parties: Organization and Power*. Cambridge: Cambridge University Press.

Pym, F. (1984). *The Politics of Consent*. London: Hamilton Hamish.

Prior, J. (1986). *A Balance of Power*. London: Hamish Hamilton.

Riddell, P. (1983). *The Thatcher Government*. Oxford: Robertson.

Ringen, S. (1987). *The Politics of Possibility*. Oxford: Clarendon Press.

Schelling, T. (1980). *The Strategy of Conflict*, 2nd ed. Cambridge, MA: Harvard University Press.

Shepherd, R. (1991). *The Power Brokers*. London: Hutchinson.

Sked, A. and Cook, C. (1993). *Post-war Britain*. London: Penguin Books.

Thatcher, M. (1993). *The Downing Street Years*. London: HarperCollins.

Tufte, E. (1978). *Political Control of the Economy*. Princeton, NJ: Princeton University Press.

Walker, A. and Walker, C. (eds.). (1987). *The Growing Divide. A Social Audit 1979–1987*, 129–138. London: Child Poverty Action Group.

Ware, A. (ed.). (1987). *Political Parties: Electoral Change and Structural Responses*. Oxford: Blackwell.

Whiteley, P., Seyd, P., and Richardson, J. (1994). *True Blues: The Politics of Conservative Party Membership*. Oxford: Clarendon Press.

20

National Industrial Policy in the Context of Supranational and Subnational Policy Expansion

Niels Christian Sidenius
University of Århus, Århus, Denmark

> In contrast, European integration combines elements of continued state authority with the creation of decentralized subnational power and the development of supranational decision-making bodies.
>
> —Marks and McAdam (1:119)

I. THE PROBLEM

The Danish political debate about membership of the European Community and about further integration into the European Union has, among other things, focused upon the domestic impacts of membership. Impact may refer to economic consequences of membership, an issue of long standing in the Danish debate due to the importance of agriculture in Denmark and the weight of the CAP in the EU, or it may refer to more political consequences of membership. At one end of the debate about policy making and policy we find the issue of loss of democratic control because many decisions are actually made by bureaucrats and interest associations outside the spotlight of democratic institutions (2); at the other end of the debate we find the issue of loss of sovereignty due to the integration through creeping transfer of decision-making power to the EU institutions, e.g., by way of majority decision making.

The impact of European Union membership can be analyzed at the level of the political system, at specific policy areas or with regard to policy-making institutions. This chapter has a double aim. On the one hand it analyses a single policy sector, *in casu* national industrial policy; on the other hand national industrial policy is analysed from the perspective of multilevel governance (cf., e.g., 3, 4) by relating it to industrial policy at the EU level as well as to industrial policy at the regional level.

National industrial policy is seen as a dependent variable, and questions in this perspective are: Has Danish industrial policy at the national level changed since the late 1980s, and to what extent can this change be accounted for, first, by EU policies and, second, by the regions' efforts at increasing their role in the domestic as well as the European industrial policy? Has there, in other words, been a withdrawal of centralized state policy and due to which supranational and subnational pressures? But national industrial policy is also seen as an independent variable, as a potential promoter of industrial policies at the regional or municipal level. The question is, then, what role the state has played in the expansion of industrial policy at these levels.

The first hypothesis of the paper is that both the effects of EU politics and policies and of regional industrial policy on national industrial policy have been relatively limited and that changes of national industrial policy to a large extent have to be attributed to other factors. The second hypothesis is that the expansion of regional industrial policy to a very limited degree has been caused by national state initiatives.

These hypotheses do not deny the impact of EU as an agenda setter and policy maker, neither in general nor within specific sectors, *in casu* industrial policy. The Internal Market directives and their implementation (5) are a case in point, just as the Internal Market has had a number of more general welfare expansion effects, though not to the extent envisaged by the Cecchini report (5: 24ff.). And although the removal of NTBs has had a positive bearing on individual companies, a majority of companies in the EU state that they have not been effected by this initiative (6:26). Rather, the hypotheses problematize the huge and unconditional impact that is often attributed to EU initiatives in the political debate.

II. DESIGN

Analytically the relations between Denmark, and any other member state, and the EU with respect to industrial policy can be divided into four elements. The first regards the national attitude towards EU industrial policy and it relates to questions as the definition of industrial policy, its aims and the specific areas to which industrial policy is applied. The second element concerns the scope and means of industrial policy: what regulatory measures and how much money are used on industrial policy, and what share of the cake goes to Denmark. Third, the impact of EU industrial policy is at stake, whether it relates to policies that have to be carried out one way or another or it relates to inducements to carry out specific industrial policies. Finally, the relations between Denmark and the EU also include the Danish participation in EU industrial policy-making, whether it aims at blocking or promoting specific policies. The chapter deals with aspects of all four elements but mainly with the third one on impact.

National industrial policy during the last decade is defined as the industrial policy agenda and discourse, including strategic planning and analysis, which has been initiated by the Ministry of Business.[1] Omitted, therefore, are initiatives by other ministries and decisions actually passed by the Folketing. The analysis is mainly conducted on the basis of a number of planning documents and policy statements of the Ministry of Industry, and its results are therefore only of a preliminary nature.

The analysis of the evolution of regional industrial policy, as potentially initiated by the state, concerns the discussion between the government, on the one hand, and the counties and municipalities on the other hand regarding the room of manoeuvre of subnational government with respect to local and regional industrial policy. This analysis is based on national industrial policy documents and decisions, general statements from the associations of the regions and the municipalities.

A third way of measuring the EU impact on Danish industrial policy might have been to analyze the political activity of interest associations. The integration of interest associations has for years been an institution in Danish policy making, penetrating formulation and implementation of policies (7), and this might change due to increased competencies of the EU. This has already been demonstrated, however, not to be the case, neither in general, nor with respect to business associations (8,9). There is no simple shift in domestic interest intermediation (10:10), and Danish interest associations actually increase their Brussels-related political activity as well as their domestic political activity. In this context we therefore dare to suspect that it also holds for their political activity vis-à-vis industrial policy and the Ministry of Business.

The first section of the paper maps the diverse causes of change of industrial policy, internal as well as external, in this way putting the impact of the EU into perspective. The following section presents Danish industrial policy at the national level in order to specify changes caused or induced by the EU. The second section analyzes the causes and impacts of regional industrial policy expansion.

III. CAUSES OF POLICY CHANGE

It seems to be a fact that the changing policies and procedures of the EU have had an impact upon the member states with respect to policy, regulatory tradition, and interest representation. By the expansion of EU competencies each member state face a changing political environment which permanently challenges and diminishes their scope of control of this environment (cf. 11). The EU redefines "existing political arrangements . . . in altering traditional domestic policy networks, in creating incipient Europe-wide networks based on intricate multilevel bargaining, in triggering institutional change . . . and in reshaping the opportunity structures of both member states and firms" (12:343).

In their edited volume *The European Union and National Industrial Policy*, Hussein Kassim and Anand Menon state that in spite of many claims of power migration from the member states to Brussels "the precise impact of EU action on the member states has been curiously under-researched" (13:1). This may partly be explained by the fact that EU impact on the member states only very seldom manifests itself in a clear-cut way immune from the interference of other change causes. This of course makes impact analysis a complicated matter.

From a public policy viewpoint as well as from an international-politics perspective, effects of Europeanization and internationalization, respectively, are to be sorted out from other factors. Kassim and Menon assert that EU action may have a bearing upon national policy substance and on national policy making, that this impact can take place in different ways, but also that policy change—nationally as well as at European level—may result from the "complex interaction of different factors" at different levels (13:5). Through analyses of diverse policy areas it is concluded that the impact of EU action has been both direct and indirect, but also that it has been very differentiated and often limited (14). Menon and Hayward suggest that the differentiated performance of EU action can be explained by several factors, such as the decision-making mode within the Union, variations among the member states regarding policy preferences and institutional arrangements, and differentiations among industrial sectors impacted upon. And—to elaborate on the complexity already mentioned—alternative pressures on national policy and policy making are at work, factors emanating both from within the state (e.g., financial pressures) and from outside its borders, primarily shifting global economic interaction and interdependence (14).

From the point of view of internationalization Keohane and Milner assert that not only pressures from the international economy but also exogenous political pressure has an impact upon domestic politics, acting simultaneously with economic internationalization (15:255ff.). Internationalization may put into question even well-established domestic institutions, e.g., the "embedded liberalism" compromise combining state intervention in the economy with openness. But domestic institutions also shape the ways in which internationalization impacts policy, for instance by giving access and voice to specific organized groups. This takes place by "blocking price signals," i.e., by setting up impediments between the world economy and domestic policies, by "freezing coalitions and policies," i.e., by sticking to path dependent and political structure maintaining strategies,

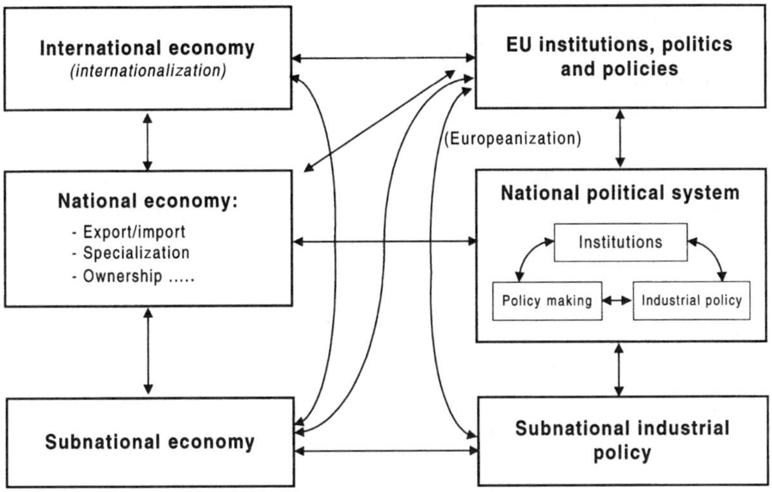

Figure 1 Causes of national industrial policy change.

and by ''channeling responses to change'' into changes at the international level (15:249ff.).

When combining the two perspectives—public policy and international relations—the focus on the changes of institutions, politics, and policies at the national level amounts to a complex web of interwoven causes, and this complexity is further augmented by adding changes at the subnational level. Figure 1 tries to depict that complexity.

Figure 1 makes it clear that the impact of the EU on Danish industrial policy is supported by and mediated through a range of factors which makes an unambiguous description difficult, not to speak of a reliable measuring of the weight of the diverse factors of change (cf. 10:3; 5:20). A further, mediating and complicating factor is the domestic political discourse in general or at specific areas, which—though reflecting perceptions of the international and national economy and the EU development—cannot be reduced to effects of these phenomena. Reflections and experiences of past policies form part of this picture, too.

IV. EU AND DANISH INDUSTRIAL POLICY—MUCH ADO ABOUT NOTHING?

Although Danish industrial policy has historically included a number of diversified measures aiming primarily at promoting exports, lowering the cost of capital investment, and speeding up technological change, it has never been a showcase of public policy as in some other countries, e.g., France, Italy, and Sweden. Expenditure has not reached the same level of GDP as in most other West European countries, and state-owned enterprises has not taken the fancy of many politicians as regards the production of goods. And Denmark has for years opted for a liberalized international trade, a policy mirroring the export-import dependency and the traditional role of agriculture in the national economy. This picture still holds as a valid description of industrial policy in Denmark (cf. 16, 17, 18:343ff.).

Around the early 1980s new initiatives with respect to the promotion of R&D and of specific technologies (information technology, primarily) were introduced (cf. 19), somewhat questioning the use of the concept of a liberal policy. This embryonic new policy did not change in 1982 following the takeover by a Center-Right government led by the Conservative People's Party; on the contrary, the period 1986 to 1989 witnessed the hitherto most serious attempt at introducing a structural policy element in the national industrial policy and some efforts at weakening the decade long corporatist structures of policy making (17,20,21).

At this time, the EC industrial policy was mainly about the rules of competition including state subsidies (articles 92 and 93) with rather little impact on national industrial policy. The passing of the Single European Act and in particular the Internal Market Program changed this, at least potentially, but the 1986 program on industrial policy says next to nothing about EC industrial policies, including R&D programs, not even about the prospects of a European industrial policy and the Danish policy with respect to it (20).

A. Industrial Policy 1989 to 1993

The launch of the Internal Market Program into the Danish industry policy strategy takes place in the 1989 Review of Business Policy. The internal market is said to challenge Danish business with respect to the breakdown of structural barriers, and the importance of industrial locomotives and of more R&D is emphasized. Danish participation in the EC technological programmes has to be increased as has the participation in major public projects in the other member states (22).

The elaboration of "Strategy 92" states that the evolution of the internal market represents "some of the until now greatest challenges" to Danish business (23:193), although the current problems of balance in the Danish economy will be neither solved nor reduced by the internal market itself. The competitiveness of major companies will not be impacted upon, reserving the drastic repercussions to the small firms, especially those focusing at the domestic market (23: 212). Public policy in accordance with this description is mainly a better general policy (e.g., financial policy, public rules, and procedures), targeted initiatives increasing participation and influence in Brussels and improving terms of standardization, and, finally, a thorough information to companies which will then have to act on that basis (23:23ff.).

At this point of time Danish industrial policy was focusing at the competitive sector, promoting its conditions of further internationalization (22:1ff.). This helps to explain why, after all, the EC and its Internal Market Programme has such relatively little bearing on the strategy of Danish industrial policy. Companies have to adapt to their new environment, and so has policy; but the EC cannot be seen as a major cause of change of industrial policy strategy. Denmark obviously has to adapt to and implement EC directives, etc., and we will return to that later. And of course this aspect of policy making can be found in the political debate, as is evidenced by the negotiations about the 1990 state budget (24:Nov. 23, 1989).

Following the negotiations of the 1990 state budget, the Minister of Industry resigned. There were several reasons for his unexpected withdrawal, but the resignation was associated with the budget cut of the expenditure on industrial policy which symbolized the end of the short life of a more structured industrial policy.

The next Review of Business Policy was presented to the Folketing in 1991 (25). It has a more liberal color than the previous one and a more explicit attitude to EC industrial policy, speaking about the division of labour between the national and the EC policies. It also mirrors the important foreign trade between Denmark and the other Nordic countries.

The Review deals with three of the four aspects of EC industrial policy mentioned previously. Globalization is seen as something different from the evolving internal market, exerting new pressure on EC business policy and making a coordination of industrial and trade policies necessary. EC industrial policy has to promote free competition more than contributing to structural adaptation; therefore it has to expand the internal market and develop general outline provisions for business. The division of labour between the member states and the EC has to rest on the principle of subsidiarity, and "business policy in Denmark is not rendered superfluous" as it has to set up productive general provisions for business and to promote the expansion of resource areas (25:9). EC has to reduce direct subsidies and be more reluctant on sectoral policies, and taxation of business has only to be introduced if it is consistent with EC aims regarding regional development, SMEs, and R&D. Danish participation in EC matters has to be increased with respect to international standardization, terms of direct subsidies, and R&D.

The fourth element of EC industrial policy, which is almost absent in the Review, relates to the impact of EC on Danish policy. The only direct mentioning of this aspect is the change of the Law of Competition in 1989 (25:11), which can be characterized as modernization without making it consistent with the dominant EC paradigm, though. We will return to this later.

The 1991 Review of Business Policy is important in understanding the nature of the reflection of EC industrial policies into the national business policy strategy, but it does not introduce a more dominant position of the EC in the national business policy discourse. The change of government in early 1993 into a coalition led by the Social Democratic Party created the new Ministry of Business Coordination (cf. note 1), which furthered the focus on a comprehensive national business policy. This took place on the background of the Maastricht Treaty of February 1992 which for the first time introduced industrial policy in the treaties (article 130). This innovation is said to have been difficult due to the opposing attitudes of member states (Germany, U.K., Netherlands, and Denmark vs. France, Belgium, and Italy) with respect to the scope, means, and procedure of a common industrial policy. The inclusion of article 130 was a victory of the latter group of countries' (whereas the substance of the article clearly favored the former group of countries') ''liberal-competitive'' paradigm of EC industrial policy which was further strengthened by the decision on unanimity in industrial policy matters put forward by Germany (26:148ff.).

B. Industrial Policy Since 1993

The 1993 Review of Business reinforces two trends of the previous Review, of 1991. First, globalization is seen as the important environment parameter as it strengthens the competition among the countries and regions of Europe (27:37); second, business policy ought to direct itself toward all spheres of business and, with inspiration from Michael Porter, it has to rely predominantly on the making of general outline provisions (27:19ff., 38ff.). In this context, business policy gains greater importance, and the repercussions of an inappropriate national policy become more severe (27:37). ''The important question of business policy is which initiatives to introduce, which tasks to perform at the national level and at the EC level, i.e., how to implement the principle of subsidiarity,'' and the answer to this question is that EC industrial policy should only deal with those tasks that can profitably be taken care of at the community level, including research programs and structural schemes, whereas all other tasks have to be conducted by national authorities (27:117).

From a Danish perspective, EC business policy ought to further the competitiveness of European companies through free and open markets but also—and this is a new point—in a sustainable way, ''considering the environment and supporting a high level of employment'' (27:88). Still, the Danish government wants to expand the internal market and to make it more effective, as it wants to influence the R&D programs, making them more precompetitive and more useful to Danish business. The attitude toward the structural policies is critical, because the programs are too small and run the risk of being turned into sectoral programs (27:91ff.).

The Review lists the business policy initiatives of 1992 and 1993, and only two of them qualify as being directly related to the EC. The first is a new agreement on the financing of shipbuilding—which is a very prominent issue in national business policy—the second is related to regional business development, i.e., the cofinancing of EC supported regional programs. To this should be added adaptations of the regulation of customs, duties, and the VAT induced by the internal market (27:415ff.). All in all not much considered the momentum of the EC at the time and the public debate in Denmark about the Maastricht Treaty.

It is implicit in the above analysis that Danish business policy is very much in line with article 130 of the Maastricht Treaty with its intention of not being an instrument to the introduction of competition distorting measures. And in the following years most political energy is devoted to the formulation of a national business policy strategy on the basis of globalization, technological innovation (information technology in particular), and the restoration of the welfare society. This focus on the national policy strategy emphasizes the establishment of general outline provisions and a rationalization of policy measures, and it makes EU business policy a secondary issue. The attitude toward EU business policy aims, scope, and means and increased Danish participation in EU policy making have already been described and it does not really change in the period 1994 to 1996.

The 1994 Review of Business allows a more quantitative description of the impact of EU business policy on Danish business policy; 140 policy measures are one way or the other related to enterprises, and of these 45 measures include EU (28:318ff.). These measures are partly in accordance with EU regulations or they are obligatory to all member states, and they are related to the primary sectors, to regional development schemes or public R&D programs directed at business (28:319, 338ff.). Business promotion, excluding agriculture and the fishing industry, amounted in 1991 to DKR 4094 billion (accounts) and in 1994 to DKR 8230 billion (budget). The amount of EU cofinancing increased, too, but its share of total expenditure decreased from 7.8% to 6.3% (cf. 28:328). If we finally look at the national regulatory initiatives in 1993 and 1994, just a few are related to EU regulation, e.g., initiatives with respect to home banking, product safety, tele competition, customs code, research in information technology, and national cofinancing of EU regional development programs (28:349ff.).

The 1995 Review of Business further develops the strategy put forward in 1993, emphasis continues to be on the national creation of general business outline provisions aiming at a welfare society restoration; but now the welfare and consumer services are also seen as important policy issues in other EU member states and as being promoted by the EU Commission (29:313).

The Danish government is satisfied with the general paradigm of EU business policy, because it is to a certain degree ''business policy without money,'' e.g., with respect to the Commission strategy on a dialogue between public and private agencies and companies. General outline provision and increasing policy coordination aiming at a more fair competition, modernization of public agencies, increasing industrial cooperation, and the promotion of immaterial investments is seen as a productive industrial policy strategy (29:195ff.), implicitly in overall accordance with the Danish strategy. It is therefore also stated with content that the EU Regional Fund implies the "possibility of limiting the direct company related elements," favoring general outline provisions (29:419), as is the new tendency of combining Commission initiatives with private and national project financing (29:215).

Among the main Danish issues regarding EU business policy (e.g., a more effective internal market, more standardization, a more knowledge-based business and R&D policy regarding generic technologies) we find the issue of more control with illegal state subsidies (29:193ff.). Together with other countries Denmark has been in favor of more transparency on the Commission's administration of the rules of state subsidies, and their classification into general and specific outline provisions—and provisions regarding, e.g., transport, coal and steel, and shipbuilding—is seen as a step forward, though a more hidebound administration continues to be on the agenda (29:210ff.). National participation in task forces and programs ought to be increased as it might improve the compliance with the original aims of large EU programs and increase their business directedness (29: 219ff.).

EU information in Denmark vis-à-vis business is characterized as confused, leaving companies without a satisfactory overview; therefore the Ministry will rationalize and increase its own efforts and improve coordination with other public and private supply of EU business information. This also holds for the information about EU R&D programs, especially with respect to SMEs (29:401ff.).

Among the 1994–95 business initiatives relatively few qualify as directly EU related, e.g., a broader use of EU structural funding in the 5b areas, companies' environmental steering, and registration of trademarks (29:431ff.). Such initiatives cannot be seen as a violation against the demanded separation between EU tasks and national competencies which bases the former on particular circumstances and causes (29:194).

The 1996 Review of Business presents the business strategy in accordance with the previous years, and Denmark is still one of the liberal hard-liners with respect to business policy. Core areas are public regulation, access to knowledge, access to investment capital, public-private cooperation, and conditions of international competition, including the Danish effort in the EU, e.g., with respect to the protection of patents and the transparancy concerning support of shipbuilding (18:43ff.). The description of the resource areas reveals some other impact from the EU business policy, e.g., the novel food directive (18:171ff.), and specialized analyses point to further EU relatedness, e.g., liberalization of establishment rules, unit trusts, tele infrastructure, and the control of the food industry (18:

265ff.). To this could be added the Law of Competition which needs to be tightened and to a certain extent harmonized with the dominant EU paradigm on competition (30:122). In 1997, the Danish government was prepared—against the policy stance of dominant business associations—to leave the traditional paradigm of allowing mergers, etc., until possible negative effects on competition had been demonstrated (31). This innovation in the direction of adaptation to EU rules of competition is probably one of the more important, though indirect, impacts on business policy from EU membership and the internal market.

C. Implementation of EU Directives

This analysis can fruitfully be supplemented by a quantitative analysis of those statutory requirements which implement EU directives. It is supposed to provide a fairly accurate estimate of the impact of the EU on this aspect of Danish policy making. Though to some extent of a technical nature, since 1986 the Market Committee of the Danish Folketing has been entitled to receive a list of directive proposals of the coming EC Presidency, and since the mid-1990s the information of the Folketing about directives also includes estimates of their impact in Denmark, particularly with respect to environment, health, labour market and consumer protection (32). Figures are presented in Table 1 which demonstrates that existing legislation with EU reference makes up only a small proportion of total existing legislation. This is striking when we look at all policy areas—2.7% for acts and 5.1% for government orders—but although the proportion is higher with respect to the Ministry of Business—12.6% for acts and 5.1% for government orders—it cannot be characterized as encompassing or dramatic. Together with

Table 1 Danish Legislation with EU Reference, 1991–1996

		Acts	Acts in toto	Govt. orders	Govt. orders in toto
Ministry of business					
Existing legislation ultimo 1996		17	135	45	882
Repealed legislation ultimo 1996		23		13	
Legislation enacted 1991–1995		34		51	
All ministries					
Existing legislation ultimo 1996	(mean)	51 (2.4)	1888	327 (15.6)	6363
Repealed legislation ultimo 1996	(mean)	68 (3.2)		140 (6.7)	
Legislation enacted 1991–1995	(mean)	101 (4.8)		377 (18.0)	

Source: (33:1995ff.).

the Ministry of Food and the Ministry of Environmental Protection and Energy, the Ministry of Business makes up one of the most EU influenced ministries.

The integration of EU policy into national policies and policy making is of recent date, however, which is also demonstrated by Table 1. Within the Ministry of Business 34 out of 40 laws, and 51 out of 58 government orders have been enacted throughout the period 1991-95, which amounts to 85% and 88%, respectively; and within this period, the number of enacted acts and orders has increased year by year (33:49ff.). For the ministries in toto the figures are 85% and 81%, respectively. The increased weight of EU policies is also proven by the fact that they, in 1995, constitute 15% of all new legislation within the Ministry of Business (33:29,37).

D. Conclusion About Industrial Policy

EU institutions, politics, and policies do have an impact upon Danish industrial policy. National policy making has become Europeanized in the sense that EU policy is taken into consideration in the national discourse, and attitudes with respect to EU industrial policy definition, aims, and areas have been formulated. Europeanization also manifests itself in the increasing Danish participation in EU policy making, in casu in the working groups and committees of the Council and the Commission. We have also seen that national legislation with an EU reference increases from the early 1990s, implying a growing impact on legislation in detail. The direct bearing of EU institutions, politics, and policies on Danish industrial policy is therefore confirmed (Table 1). And since the late 1980s the national industrial policy administration has gained a much more international perspective, evidenced by the numerous international comparisons included in the reviews of business.

When we turn to the question of the more direct impact on the substance of the national industrial policy discourse and strategy the conclusion becomes more ambiguous. National industrial policy strategy of today cannot be understood without including its relations with EU industrial policy, but one effect of this has also been to emphasize subsidiarity and an effort to more precisely define the content, role, and necessity of national industrial policy, leaving EU industrial policy the marginal areas—except for R&D and regional funding. The state of the national economy, the task of the welfare state restoration, and increasing employment seem to be more important than the impact of EU policy in understanding the changes of national industrial policy. Ironically, this becomes more pronounced in the period since the passing of the Maastricht Treaty than before, because government and organizational change gives an impetus to an encompassing redefition of national industrial policy, making changes of national politics a cause in itself of industrial policy change. In Figure 1, our attention as to policy change causes is therefore moved from EU institutions to the national (and international) economy as well as to the national political system.

There are probably a number of causes to this state of affairs. One is that Denmark and other countries have been able to avoid an EU industrial policy of a more interventionist or structural nature, and have succeeded in including industrial policy of a more liberal-competitive nature in the Maastricht Treaty (article 130). This is matched by a relative congruency between Danish and EU industrial policies in recent years, both focusing on general outline provisions, the challenge of globalization, and the importance of the service sector and employment growth. The major issue at which Denmark is at odds with EU industrial policy concerns the weight and lack of transparency of state subsidies. Denmark is at the bottom when member states' use of this support is compared,[2] and it has tried to have it cut in other member states, but without much success. Because of the general good match between Danish and EU industrial policy, Denmark has not been forced to change much of its own policy.

A second cause might be that the expected economic effects of the Internal Market Program—which might have caused national political initiatives—have not yet been produced. On some parameters the real effect approximates the one expected, e.g., with respect to decreasing home-bias and rising foreign direct investments, but on others the results have been less impressive, e.g., macroeconomic growth, price-leveling, and labor mobility (30:154ff.).

V. REGIONAL INDUSTRIAL POLICY—A DYNAMIC OF ITS OWN

Would one expect a country with 5 million inhabitants living on about 44,000 km^2 to have an abundance of local and regional business policies, including political activity in Brussels? If one takes as point of departure the hypothesis that regional distinctiveness causes ''friction between regional and national governments and, hence, of subnational mobilization'' (34:44ff.), the answer should be no. The Danish society is with respect to most parameters very homogenous in a regional perspective, e.g., concerning ethnicity, religion, language, and standard of living (cf. 29:126). Among the EU member states Denmark uses the smallest proportion at regional purposes (18:354), and in an EU-wide comparison Denmark is treated as just one region (18:390). If, alternatively, one focuses on the tradition of local and regional government, on decentralization of government and, on the weight of the municipalities in public expenditure (cf., e.g., 35, 36), one might also expect local and regional business policies, as is actually the case (e.g., 37–41).

A. Regional Industrial Policy Prior to 1989

The main national scheme for regional development was set up by the state in 1958 following local pressure to do something about the ''islands'' of Jutland with a very high level of unemployment. The period from 1958 to 1980 saw the expansion of this state initiated regional development, including the support of the setting up of a number of local and regional business councils and offices. The 1980s was a period of growth of local and regional business policies outside the original development areas, too. EU-financed programs were introduced with the backup of state cofinancing. The 1990s have been a period of coordination, EU programs have gained importance, and local and regional business strategies and programs have flourished in most municipalities and counties (42:22).

This expansion of local and regional business policy has not been guided by much formal regulation but by the non-formalized code of municipal authority, *Kommunalfuldmagten* (43:20ff.). Direct subsidization has been prohibited, in particular regarding individual companies, and has usually been avoided. The measures developed have been of a general nature, setting up general outline provisions for the growth and employment of local business, concerning, e.g., technological change, export promotion, intraregional cooperation, and participation in EU programs. Throughout the 1980s, the fight against unemployment increased the attention and responsibility of municipalities and counties with respect to their labor market policy as well as business policy potentials, and policy imitation took the expansion a bit further. The state of affairs of local and regional business policy in the mid- and late 1980s is described in *Indenrigsministeriet* (44).

This report about the municipalities and business policy was produced by the Ministry of the Interior, which was (and is) in charge of the general supervision of the municipalities and counties, and it mirrored the general reluctance of the national political parties[3] and the central administration of giving the municipalities a broader access to business promoting measures. The committee that made the report agreed that municipalities still should not be allowed to subsidize individual enterprises, but the representatives of the municipalities were in favor of creating a limited possibility of participating with investment capital in development companies and activities; this proposal was not, however, supported by the representatives of the ministries (44:101ff.).

B. Regional Industrial Policy 1989 to 1993

The 1989 Review of Business Policy (22) did not include regional business policies, and the 1990 general Act on Business Promotion was very brief on this matter, although an intraministerial working group was set up to analyze how the regional policy aspects might be taken care of by the new Business Development Council (45).

The 1991 Review of Business Policy (25) confirmed the traditional role of counties and municipalities in providing a good local and regional administration and service. The government, however, considered three ways in which subnational governments' tasks could be made more precise: with regard to the cofinancing of EU regional funding, by setting up regional business development programs; together with the state; and by enlarging the scope of participation in systems export (25:16). This new opening for the business policy aspirations of municipalities and counties was not an act of goodwill by the Center-Right government. The Review was given to the Folketing on April 24, 1991, but a week earlier, on April 18, 1991, the Socialist People's Party had asked the Prime Minister about the government's future plans concerning the guiding principles for business policy by local and regional authorities. A resolution was passed, almost in unanimity, including the later three elements of the Business Policy Review''provided they are conducted without distorting the competitiveness of private business'' (46: 1990/91:4848–4893).

This compliance to some of the policy ambitions of subnational governments was caused by their continuous efforts, especially by the National Association of Local Authorities, to inform and persuade the Folketing about their just cause. It was carried out through analyses, publications, and meetings with MPs (e.g., 37, 47–49) and, we suppose, through internal pressure in the two dominant parties at subnational level, the Social Democratic Party and the Liberal Party. The counties and municipalities were able to evoke a reaction because many local authorities had initiated or supported a local business policy irrespective of their party political composition, and, on top of that, the traditional cores of local business initiatives, the municipalities to which the regional development measures were applied, were very often led by the Liberal Party (cf. 50:45–52;40: 124–126;41:126–130;38:48–49).

The efforts of the associations of the subnational governments might not have had the eventual impact upon the outline provisions of local business policy, at least not at this time, without a political entrepreneur and a balance between the political parties in the Folketing, which was unfavorable to the government. The Socialist People's Party several times tried to enlarge the room for subnational business policy action; the question to the Prime Minister, April 18, 1991, and the majority opposition in the Folketing—also including the Social Democratic Party and the Social Liberal Party—put pressure on the government to act.

In May 1992, two bills were passed improving the room of maneuver of the counties and municipalities. The first one was introduced on Oct. 30, 1991, by the Minister of Industry in accordance with the resolution of April 18, 1991 (51); the second bill was introduced on Oct. 31, 1991, by the Social Liberal Party aiming at promoting subnational authorities' cooperation with joint-stock companies concerning investment capital and management (52). The first bill was passed with some amendments, which were not supported by the government, though in the end it was passed with the votes of the government too. The other bill, however, was passed without the consent of the government. With the change of government in January 1993, the two former major governing parties, the Conservative People's Party and the Liberal Party, in opposition returned to their previous negative attitude against the broadened scope of subnational governments' business policy.

C. Regional Industrial Policy Since 1993

The governments since January 1993, led by the Social Democratic Party, have gradually reformulated the combination of national and subnational business policy. To further increase the cooperation between public agencies and private enterprises, Act No. 383, 1992 (51), has been changed so that subnational governments in specific cases are allowed to support individual companies (53); counties and municipalities have obtained the right, for other public authorities, to carry out tasks which they already perform (54); and Act No. 384 has been made permanent (55).

The major substance of the policy reformulation is found in general policy statements, however. The main change is that the government and the central administration abandons the previously negative attitude towards the business policy innovation of subnational governments, which at best was regarded as separate policy measures, in favor of an attitude that sees it as an integrated part of the overall business policy in Denmark. A second major change is that subnational business policy is welcome when integrated with other policy measures. This new policy stance is mirrored in the annual Review of Business (29: 19), but it is most clearly elaborated in a joint committee of ministries and subnational governments (56) and in a comprehensive Regional Policy Review 1995 (42).

In contrast to the previous report on subnational business policy (44), the new report on the coordination of regional business promotion was submitted in unanimity. Its point of departure was the desirability of municipalities and counties making up joint business policy action plans (56:38), which were found in too few cases (56:35), and which would become more necessary due to the expected rise of local business promotion following the Act No. 383 (56:6). More cooperation, coordination, and division of labor among counties, municipalities, technological information centers, and other actors in regional business promotion was demanded to improve efficiency vis-à-vis companies and to utilize public resources more carefully. This plan also included the role of the state and its interplay with other actors in local business promotion which was to be conducted in consideration of state business policy (56:6ff.).

Coordination should be within a fixed framework but set up on a voluntary basis and not according to some centralized plan, and a number of alternative models for cooperation was outlined (56:8, 38). The main message of the report seems to be, though, that regional business promotion ''ought to build on the same strategy and the same principles which form the basis of state business policy,'' i.e., transfer of technology; public-private cooperation; increase of competencies concerning management, quality, and innovation; and information about national as well as international business promoting action with a bearing on local business (56:54). The report states that regional business promotion should not be turned into a competition between public funds but rather, through openness and transparency, establish a level playing field, e.g., with respect to the conditions of development contracts. This would parallel state business policy and the Danish policy stance in Brussels; accordingly, public cofinancing of development projects in one or more companies was, in the main, left to state agencies, including support of SMEs and other long-term economic inducements (56: 55ff.).

Recommendations of the report include a general congruency with state business policy, aiming at business *in toto* and larger coherent business areas, i.e., crossing the boundaries of municipalities and counties; openness and transparency in combination with a help-to-self-help principle; a supply of services governed by regional demand, implying the integration of business in planning and implementation; coordination with other policy areas; and direct cofinancing by the state only. Finally, the Business Development Council is asked to set up ''regional business policy coordination''as a new policy initiative (56:62ff.).

The strategy of the Regional Policy Review 1995 is said to build a bridge—not to the next century, but between national and regional business policy. The main challenge is coordination and connection in regional business policy promoted by a new invention to further develop regional business development programs: business centers integrating more participants and more policy areas. More generally, the report advocates a more simplified, goal-oriented, and coordinated subnational business policy; increased efforts with respect to public-private cooperation; more new ideas and activity by the municipalities and counties regarding new initiatives in national business policy; more coherence between EU-financed programs and the needs and initiatives within the regions with respect to outline provisions; and a more uniform and more efficient administration of EU structural funds in Denmark with the aim of increasing connexions between policies at the national and subnational levels (42:7ff.).

National business development is considerably dependent on regional outline provisions which have more specific effects than national outline provisions. Many national policies also demand a subnational implementation which opens for a dialogue on the development of national business policy, e.g., with respect to the regional follow up on the analyses of resource areas. There are therefore several reasons why the subnational authorities should expand their active role in regional business policy (42:24, 43ff.). On the other hand, the state has regional business policy tasks, too. By participating in establishing regional business development programs it promotes regional policy coordination; acts directly in regional business policy through the labour market system and the technological information centers; and has an impact on the general outline provisions of all companies through national business policy. The proposal of regional business centers intends to improve the total effect of all policy actors' regional efforts (42:164ff.).

The subnational governments no doubt appreciated the broadened scope of their possible business policy, which they had advocated for years. But this new policy freedom ran the risk of being turned into an illusion by another element of the new government business strategy—i.e., that of integrating subnational policies into national business policy and of ''undermining''municipality and county constituencies by defining business policy on the basis of areas of effect.

When the Regional Policy Report 1995 was to be read by the Folketing in early 1996, the National Association of Local Authorities (NALA) interfered through a pamphlet with the subtitle *Documentation to the Folketing* (57). The National Association carefully promoted evidence of much and very diverse cooperation across municipality boundaries initiated prior to as well as after the invention of regional business development programs. By this documentation the NALA wanted to state that regional business policy was not unfair competition on public money, and that it was less and less restricted to the formal political-administrative units, the municipalities, and counties. The NALA also wanted to avoid any introduction of ''bureaucracy or centralism into the business policy'' (57:16)—a reference to the concept of business centers which were only to be put into effect following certain guidelines. e.g., on the basis of local and regional initiative, and with consultative status only (57:15ff.). Finally, utilizing the general change of national business policy to the advantage of outline provisions, the NALA points to the fact—already accepted by the government—that any efficient national business policy mirrors regional differences (57:32ff.).

The 1996 Review of Business reiterates the proposal of business centres, and this potential controversy between the government and the subnational authorities is not really settled yet. The general business strategy of the government of larger cooperation between levels of authority and policy areas—to which the subnational authorities agree, in particular when coordination takes place regionally—is put forward concerning regional business and labor market policy. The rationale of the state's business policy in the regions is changed from a responsibility of ''equality of results'' to ''equality of preconditions'' transferring responsibility of the regional development to the regions (58:19). This increased regional responsibility might, in combination with the coordination of regional business and labour market policy, strengthen the regional corporatist pattern of policy making.

D. Conclusion About Regional Industrial Policy

Subnational industrial policy has changed during the 1990s. The room of maneuver of subnational governments has been extended and the number and resources of policy measures have increased. In this change is included efforts to coordinate business policy with other policy areas, more cooperation across the boundaries of municipalities and counties, and more cooperation across levels of authority, i.e., between national and subnational business policy.

The increased business policy competencies of subnational governments are caused by subnational efforts, but aided by the political balance in the Folketing. Subnational governments have gained more indirect importance to local business through the decentralization of the public sector during the last decades, but the expansion of a more direct business policy has mirrored the demand of local politicians and business (43:18). The reformulation of national business policy—which makes the impact of national business policy measures more dependent on decentralized implementation—includes, however, efforts of the state to integrate subnational business policy into the national policy and its emphasis on outline provisions, technological development, and the restoration of the welfare state. This does not necessarily implicate a changed substance of subnational governments' business policy, but the embrace by the state does at least indicate that changing policies and roles of public authorities often occur in ambiguous ways.

VI. CONCLUSIONS

Referring to Figure 1, the primary impact on Danish industrial policy is seen as deriving from the composition of the national economy and its challenges, but also changes within the national political system as such are perceived as important in understanding industrial policy changes. As the national economy is heavily impacted upon by the international economy (59), this factor also has an important, though more mediated, bearing on the national industrial policy. To some degree EU policy, directly or through the EU strategy in international institutions, also has effects on the agenda and making of national business policy. In comparison with the other factors EU is evaluated as having the smallest impact, although it is increasing. Effects of subnational governments on national business policy are found to be very limited. Although the changes of national business policy and of the framework of subnational business policy occur simultaneously, the latter has not caused the former. In general the analysis confirms the first hypothesis.

The second hypothesis is also confirmed, because subnational governments have been the main promoter—in some periods the only one—of local and regional industrial policy. For years the state policy was very restrictive regarding new measures in this area, but changes occurred in the 1990s, especially after the change of government in January 1993. This bottom-up process has recently come up against a top-down initiative by the Ministry of Business trying to integrate subnational business policy into the national strategy. This effort also mirrors, however, the need of the state of a nationwide as well as a local and regional implementation of national business policy.

The development of industrial policy at the EU level, as embryonic as it may be, and the increased business policy competencies of subnational governments constitute business policy as multilevel governance. National industrial policy is increasingly difficult to understand without reference to EU and subnational industrial policy, just as EU industrial policy has to take national policies into consideration and subnational industrial policy has to cooperate with national level policy. But multilevel governance does neither in general imply nor in our case find evidence of an unambiguously weakened national level policy.

Relatively speaking, the weight of national-level business policy has diminished but it has not been withdrawn. It has to depend partially on EU policy as it also has to integrate an expanding subnational business policy into a broader national policy. But the major decisions as to strategy, aims, and measures—including major policy changes which have occurred recently in Denmark—have been made at the national level mirroring other factors than EU and subnational policy.

ENDNOTES

1. As we shall see, a turn in national industrial policy was taken by the new Ministry of Business Policy Coordination in 1993. This ministry was set up following the change of government in early 1993, in 1994 it was merged with the Ministry of Industry into the Ministry of Industry and Business Policy Coordination and later that year renamed into the Ministry of Business (though excluding agriculture and the fisheries).
2. Support of shipbuilding is the major exception to this.
3. The more general exception to this was the Socialist People's Party which several times had put forward ideas and proposals regarding the economic room of maneuver of the municipalities. The Social Democratic Party had at times supported this policy, but only in opposition.

REFERENCES

1. Marks, G. and McAdam, D. (1996). Social movements and the changing structure of political opportunity in the European Union. In: G. Marks et al. (eds.), *Governance in the European Union*, 96–120. London: Sage.
2. Bundgaard-Pedersen, T. (1995). Demokratiproblemer i danske EU-beslutnings-processer. In: M. Madsen et al. (eds.), *Demokratiets mangfoldighed:Tendenser i dansk politik*, 404–442. Copenhagen: Forlaget Politiske Studier.
3. Jachtenfuchs, M. and Kohler-Koch, B. (1996). Hrsg. Europäische Integration. Opladen: Leske + Budrich.
4. König, T., Rieger, E., and Schmitt, H. (1996). Hrsg. Das europäische Mehrebenensystem. Frankfurt am Main: Campus.
5. Økonomiministeriet. (1997). Danmark i det økonomiske samarbejde i EU '97. København.
6. Europa-Kommissionen. (1997). *Det indre marked og fremtidens Europa*. Luxembourg: De Europæiske Fællesskaber.
7. Christiansen, P.M. and Sidenius, N.C. (1995). Korporatisme på retur? *Politica 27*(4), 436–449.
8. Sidenius, N.C. (1996). Organized Interests, Governance and the European Union: The Case of Denmark. Paper presented in "The Transformation of Governance in the European Union" workshop at the ECPR Joint Sessions of Workshops, Oslo, March 29–April 3.
9. Sidenius, N.C. (1998). A collective action problem? Danish interest associations and euro groups. In: J. Greenwood and M. Aspinwall (eds.), *Collective Action in the European Union: Interests and the New Politics of Associability*, 81–107. London: Routledge.
10. Rhodes, M., Heywood, P., and Wright, V. (1997). Towards a new Europe? In: M. Rhodes, P. Heywood, and V. Wright (eds.), *Developments in West European Politics*, 1–15. London: Macmillan.
11. Mény, Y. Muller, P., and Quermonne, J.-L. (1996). Introduction. In: Y. Mény, P. Muller, and J.-L. Quermonne (eds.), *Adjusting to Europe. The Impact of the European Union on National Institutions and Policies*, 1–22. London: Routledge.
12. Wright, V. (1995). Conclusion: the state and major enterprises in Western Europe: enduring complexities. In: J. Hayward (ed.), *Industrial Enterprise and European Integration. From National to International Champions in Western Europe*, 334–359. Oxford: Oxford University Press.
13. Kassim, H. and Menon, A. (1996). The European Union and state autonomy. In: H. Kassim and A. Menon (eds.), *The European Union and National Industrial Policy*, 1–10. London: Routledge.
14. Menon, A. and Hayward, J. (1996). States industrial policies and the European Union. In H. Kassim and A. Menon (eds.), *The European Union and National Industrial Policy*, 267–290. London: Routledge.
15. Milner H.V. and Keohane, R.O. (1996). Internationalization and domestic politics: a conclusion. In R.O. Keohane and H.V. Milner (eds.), *Internationalization and Domestic Politics*, 243–258. Cambridge: Cambridge University Press.

16. Sidenius, N.C. (1983). Danish industrial policy: persistent liberalism. *Journal of Public Policy* 3(1), 49–62.
17. Sidenius, N.C. (1989). *Dansk industripolitik. Nye løsninger på gamle problemer?* Århus: Hovedland.
18. Erhvervsministeriet. (1996). *Erhvervsredegørelse.*
19. Christiansen, P.M. (1988). *Teknologipolitik mellem stat og marked. Dansk teknologipolitik 1970–1987.* Århus: Politica.
20. Industriministeriet. (1986). *Industripolitisk redegørelse 1986 og Regeringens erhvervspolitiske program for byerhvervene.*
21. Arbejdsministeriet et al. (1986). *Debatoplæg om vækst og omstilling. Krav til strukturpolitikken.*
22. Industriministeriet. (1989). *Strategi 92. Erhvervspolitisk redegørelse.*
23. Industriministeriet. (1989). *Dansk erhvervsliv på vej til det indre marked.*
24. *Avisårbogen* (annual).
25. Industriministeriet. (1991). *Erhvervspolitisk redegørelse 1991.*
26. Christoffersen, P.S. (1992). *Traktaten om Den Europæiske Union. Baggrund, forhandling, resultat.* København: Jurist-og Økonomforbundets Forlag.
27. Ministeriet for Erhvervspolitisk Samordning. (1993). *Erhvervspolitisk redegørelse 1993.*
28. Industri-og Samordningsministeriet. (1994). *Erhvervsredegørelse 1994.*
29. Erhvervsministeriet. (1995). *Erhvervsredegørelse 1995.*
30. Finansministeriet. (1996). *Finansredegørelse 96.*
31. Act No. 384. (1997). *Konkurrencelov*, June 10, 1997.
32. Sidenius, N.C. (1997). Problems searching a solution: the role of the Folketing in Danish European Community politics. In G.-E. Isaksson (ed.), *Inblickar i nordisk parlamentarism*, 193–220. Åbo: Åbo Akademi.
33. Retsinformationsrådet. (1995f). *Retsinformation. Årsberetning.*
34. Marks, G., Nielsen, F., Ray, L. and Salk, J. (1996). Competencies, cracks and conflicts: regional mobilization in the European Union. In G. Marks, F.W. Scharpf, P.C. Schmitter, and W. Streeck (eds.), *Governance in the European Union*, 40–63. London: Sage.
35. Bogason, P. (1987). In E.C. Page and M.J. Goldsmith (eds.), *Central and Local Government Relations. A Comparative Analysis of West European Unitary States*, 46–67. London: Sage.
36. Kjellberg, F. (1988). Local governments and the welfare state: reorganization in Scandinavia. In B. Dente and F. Kjellberg (eds.), *The Dynamics of Institutional Change. Local Government Reorganization in Western Democracies*, 39–69. London: Sage.
37. Kommunernes Landsforening. (1987). *Undersøgelse af lokale erhvervsrådgivningsinitiativer.* København.
38. Kommunernes Landsforening. (1992). *Kommunernes erhvervspolitik—kompetence, samvirke og ansvar.* København.
39. Jørgensen, H. and Lind, J. (1988). Decentrale politikker for jobskabelse og erhvervsudvikling i Norden, 13–49. *Helsingfors; Nordrefo.*
40. Gertsen, K. (1990). *Kommunal erhvervspolitik.* Ms. thesis, Department of Political Science, University of Aarhus.

41. Juhl, C. (1992). *Amtskommunal erhvervspolitik—økonomi, politics og policy.* Ms. thesis, Department of Political Science, University of Aarhus.
42. Erhvervsministeriet. (1995). *Regionalpolitisk redegørelse 1995.*
43. Jensen, T.P., Maskell, P., Arnberg, S., Hansen, M.B., and Ranis, T. (1997). *Erhvervslokalisering og vækst.* København: AKF Forlaget.
44. Indenrigsministeriet. (1998). *Kommunerne og erhvervspolitikken*, betænkning nr. 1153.
45. Act No. 394. (1990). *Lov om erhvervsfremme*, June 13, 1990.
46. *Folketingets Forhandlinger* (annual).
47. Kommunernes Landsforening. (1988). *Kommunale udviklingscirkler. Erfaringer, resultater og forløb—en sammenfatning.* København.
48. Kommunernes Landsforening. (1991). *Kommunernes bidrag til 90'ernes erhvervspolitik.* Debatmøde mellem kommunerne og Folketingets erhvervsudvalg og kommunaludvalg, March 14, 1991. København.
49. Den Kommunale Højskole i Danmark and Kommunernes Landsforening. (1991). *Lokal erhvervs-og arbejdsmarkedspolitik.* København.
50. Hansen, P.E. (1981). *Erhvervs-og udviklingsrådene—organisatoriske elementer i den regionale og lokale erhvervsudvikling.* Institut for Statskundskab, AU (mimeo).
51. Act No. 383. (1992). *Lov om kommuners og amtskommuners deltagelse i erhvervsudviklingsaktiviteter*, May 25, 1992.
52. Act No. 384. (1992). *Lov om kommuners og amtskommuners samarbejde med aktieselskaber mv.*, May 25, 1992.
53. Act No. 1089. (1993). *Lov om ændring af lov om kommuners og amtskommuners deltagelse i erhvervsudviklingsaktiviteter og om ophævelse af lov om kommunal og amtskommunal støtte til forskerparker*, December 22, 1993.
54. Act No. 378. (1995). *Lov om kommuners og amtskommuners udførelse af opgaver* for andre offentlige myndigheder, June 14, 1995.
55. Act No. 289. (1996). *Lov om ændring af lov om kommuners og amtskommuners samarbejde med aktieselskaber mv.*, April 24, 1996.
56. Industri-og Samordningsministeriet. (1994). *Koordinering af regional erhvervsfremme.* Betænkning nr. 1262.
57. Kommunernes Landsforening. (1996). *Kommunernes erhvervspolitik—erfaringer og udfordringer. Dokumentation til Folketinget.* København.
58. Erhvervsfremmestyrelsen. (1997). *Samspil mellem regional erhvervs-og arbejdsmarkedspolitik.*
59. Tsoukalis, L. and Rhodes, M. (1997). Economic integration and the nation-state. In M. Rhodes, P. Heywood, and V. Wright (eds.), *Developments in West European Politics*, 19–36. London: Macmillan.

21

Divergent Paths of Product Market Regulation in France and Germany, 1970–1990

J. Gunnar Trumbull
European University Institute, Florence, Italy

I. INTRODUCTION

Beginning in the 1970s, Germany and France experienced a rapid growth in political activity focused on consumption. In Germany the number of consumer-related laws grew from a total of 25 in 1971, to 338 in 1978.[1] In France the number of laws and ministerial decrees relating to consumption increased from a total of 37 in 1971, to 94 in 1978.[2] Government funding to consumer organizations increased fourfold in both France and Germany during this period. This display of government solicitude was mirrored in both countries by apparently genuine consumer concern over product quality and price. One indication was the growing popularity at the time of consumer magazines offering the results of comparative product tests. In France, the combined distribution of the journals *Que Choisir*? and 50 *Millions de Consommateurs* grew from 90,000 in 1971, to over 700,000 in 1975. In Germany, circulation of the journal Test grew from 120,000 to 510,000 over the same period.

This paper compares government efforts to improve consumer protection in France and Germany between 1970 and 1990, focusing specifically on policies oriented towards product price and product quality. It finds that projects to protect consumer interests in Germany have proceeded in a manner that has been relatively friendly to producers. In France, by contrast, consumer protection has come at a much higher cost to producer interests and autonomy. This policy divergence is puzzling given the strong political influence of business associations in both countries. One goal of the paper is to explain how apparently similar policy objectives resulted in different policy outcomes.

The answer to this question may be important for three reasons. First, product markets are highly structured by government regulations and institutions. In *The Great Transformation*, Karl Polanyi has argued that the notion of free markets for labor, capital, and raw materials rested on the fiction that these inputs to production were commodities.[3] This paper suggests that a similar analysis holds true for product markets. Attempts to create free product markets in the postwar period evoked a regulatory countermovement intended to protect consumers against the adverse consequences of treating consumer products as simple commodities. Indeed, product market regulation today rivals labor and capital market regulation in its scope and intensity.

Second, economic theory and empirical analysis strongly suggest that such product market regulations can have an impact on a country's economic performance. Koekijk et al., for example, have found that product market regulations may play a far greater role in a country's economic performance do national labor market regulations.[4] Moreover, national difference in product market regulation have increasingly been impugned as nontariff barriers to free trade, both within the European Union and among other global trading partners. A better understanding of the origin and impact of these regulations should advance our understanding of national economic performance.

Finally, the paper attempts to demonstrate that the structure of national product markets can best be understood through an explicitly political analysis. Jacques Ghestin, a longtime participant in French consumer policy formation, has stressed the fundamentally political nature of consumer regulations.

> It is a matter of knowing to what extent we should encourage the production and distribution of products in large quantity, permitting a certain number of defects for which the consumer will suffer the consequences, and to what extent we should place a heavier weight of responsibility on producers and distributors in order to pressure them to produce less, but also to produce better. Such a choice, whose economic and social consequences can be considerable, is essentially political.[5]

The second, related goal of this paper is to elaborate a general methodological approach for studying nascent policy areas. Conventional policy analysis in comparative politics has tended to focus on three sorts of societal constraints: institutions, ideas (or culture), and interests.[6] These approaches have deep roots in Marxist, sociological, and liberal analysis, respectively. While this constraint-based approach to social explanation has proved fruitful in traditional policy areas—for example, labor relations, in which actors understand intuitively what institutions, ideas, and interests pertain—it offers less leverage in entirely new areas of policy.

The problem is that nascent policy efforts are generally not bound by constraints from institutions, ideas, and interests. Indeed, they commonly face uncertainties along each of these dimensions. What institutional framework will be relevant to an entirely new area of policy? What ideas or cultural interpretations should apply? What are the interests of the important social actors? In most nascent policy efforts, these questions are open to multiple interpretations. What for traditional policy debates appear as constraints, become, in new policy areas, a broad menu of possibilities.[7] The critical question for new kinds of policies, therefore, is *how* actors select from the menu of ideational, interest, and institutional options.

The case of consumption regulation suggests that two kinds of questions can assist researchers to understand how this selection is made. The first is a question about the *legitimacy* of the policy. On what grounds should the government act to address the perceived problem? The second is a question about *capacity* to implement a policy. What solution to the perceived problem might actually work? A focus on *legitimacy* and *capacity* has the advantage of posing explicitly political questions. While these questions are general in nature, they nevertheless reflect the genuine uncertainty, contingency, and compromise that underpin the creation of novel policies. They are the questions to which institutions, ideas, and interests form the answers.

II. PRODUCT PRICE

The first oil embargo in 1973 caused the French and German governments to rethink the way in which consumer prices were set. The French government responded by increasing the level of administrative regulation of product prices. The German government, by contrast, left price setting largely in the hand of producers. And whereas both governments also attempted to initiate programs to better inform consumers about price, only France was able to mobilize political and social actors to pursue this goal forcefully. The result has been a high level of administrative intervention in price formation in France, and relatively great producer autonomy in Germany.

A. France: Price Fixing

France has a long history of government price regulation. Authority for government intervention in price setting is grounded in ordinances 45-1483 and 45-1484 of June 1945, which were themselves restatements of the Code of Prices (*Code des prix*) established under the occupying government in October 1940.[8] These ordinances were unusual in that they placed absolute authority over prices in the hands of the administration, as well as full authority to deploy police or military forces to apply any price restrictions. In principle, at least, the government could even have enforced prices far below production costs. Although the scope of administrative prerogative in France is uncommon, the use of price controls is by no means unusual. Sweden has applied extensive price restrictions over much of the postwar period, and even the United States experimented with a price freeze under the Nixon Administration in 1974.

Price regulation in France began in earnest with the first burst of inflation in 1957, and ended in 1986. During this time, two major shifts were made in the nature of price regulation, resulting in three distinct approaches to price control. In the first period, from 1957 to September 1974, price regulation imposed a minimal burden on producers. While the price of products already on the market could only be increased subject to direct approval from the Ministry of Economy and Finance's Office on Competition and Price (*Direction de la concurrence et des prix*), new products, by contrast, could be priced at the discretion of the producer and required no justification based on the actual costs of production. Producers of new products had simply to register their intended price list with the government at least two weeks before actually putting their goods up for sale. This permissive stance towards new products, designed to promote innovation, also had the effect of encouraging companies to drop traditional products and reintroduce them under new names and with slight modifications in order to be able freely to increase their prices.

Under pressure of high inflation, new legislation in 1974 sought to fill this innovation loophole by requiring that all new products be registered with the Office on Competition and Price, including a justification for the proposed price. The Office then had one month to object to the proposed price. If the company heard nothing within one month of submission, it was free to proceed with is proposed pricing. The problem was that the 1970s saw an extraordinary growth in product kind and number, and it quickly became clear that the administrative burden of this new approach was overwhelming to both companies and the government. The government simply could not evaluate enough proposals to have an overall impact on inflation.

A final change was made in December 1976.[9] According to the new scheme, producers could sign a moderation agreement (*engagement de modération*) consenting to price ceilings that had been previously negotiated between trade associations and the government. These ceilings were set based on sectoral growth rates determined by the Office on Competition and Price from production information provided by companies in the sector. In more concentrated sectors, companies were commonly able to negotiate price ceilings individually with the government.[10] These agreements were not legally binding, in the sense that companies were free to sell products above the negotiated ceiling, but in this case they needed to apply for permission for their proposed price with the Office on Competition and Price, as they had done before the 1976 reform. As an increasing number of sectors agreed to moderation agreements, the total volume of price regulations issued by the administration declined, from 137,000 in 1978, to 91,500 in 1979, to 61,300 in 1980.[11]

The French embrace of price control signaled a clear superposition of popular interest over the interests of the business community. The CNPF had long called for the abolition of administered prices. They also opposed the negotiated ceilings introduced by the Barre government in 1976, which they felt gave government control of prices the spurious legitimacy of contractual consent. French unions, represented by their consumer association OR-GE-CO, also felt that free competition rather than price restraints was the appropriate response to rising prices: "We insist at least that the conditions of free competition be saved, because they are, in the current state of things, the only guarantee of the consumer."[12] In their view, French companies were simply not price competitive. In a trade union survey conducted in 1969 they had found that of 8000 companies operating in France, only 500 had competitive prices. The rest were, in their words, "deplorably organized."[13] In 1976 they approved of the Barre plan to created negotiated ceilings, which at least permitted limited competition below the negotiated level. But they also stressed the need to attack the structural causes of inflation, which they felt meant establishing true competition in distribution and price formation.[14]

Given that labor and management both opposed administered prices, why did successive governments, first on the right, then on the left, support the policy? The reasons have to do with *legitimacy*. The legitimacy of price controls derived, in part, from popular support for their use. A series of public surveys on inflation conducted in the 1970s showed that support for price controls increased with the growth in inflation. In 1970, 27% of the population supported price controls as a means of protecting the value of the franc. Support rose to 35% in 1974, 47 percent in 1976, and a peak of 76% in 1982.

Legitimacy was also grounded, however, in a French intellectual tradition of just prices ("*prix juste*"), and the economic entitlement that this implied. Price increases in 1911, for example, led to consumer boycotts that resulted in three deaths, 136 injuries, and 396 arrests.[15] History showed that price increases in France were likely to be attributed to a lack of government action rather than to shifting conditions of supply and demand.

B. Germany: Price Maintenance

Unlike France, Germany has traditionally granted producers extraordinary powers to determine the retail price of their goods. The core of this tradition was resale price maintenance (RPM, or Preisbindung), a practice permitted until 1973 that allowed producers to stipulate in their distribution contracts the final sales price of branded goods. Because RPM effectively eliminated price competition among retailers, it helped producers to establish and maintain a stable level of profitability, both for themselves and for their distributors. While in principal such vertical collusion fell under the scrutiny of the Cartel Office (*Bundeskartellamt*, or BKA), with whom companies were required to register RPM contracts, the practice was in fact rarely restricted.[16] With the threat of price increases from the first oil shock, the Bundestag amended Germany's competition law (*Gesetz gegen Wettbewerbsbeschränkungen*, or GWB) to prohibit RPM. This move was particularly championed by the Ministry of Youth, Family, and Health in the expectation that retail competition would help to hold down prices for consumer products.[17]

A similar effort had been made in France twenty years before, in 1953, when RPM was proscribed in conjunction with the Pinay stabilization plan to hold down consumer and industry costs. But producers quickly found that they could effectively control resale prices, even without RPM, through selective distribution practices. In France, the *Fontanet* circular of March 1960 responded to this problem by advocating that companies be prohibited from taking punitive actions, such as refusing distribution (*refus de vente*), against retailers wishing to offer discounts on their products. Enforcing vertical contractual freedom of this kind has remained a mainstay of French competition policy.[18]

In Germany, by contrast, the government has retained a variety of legal provisions that continue to assist companies in influencing the sales price of their goods in the absence of RPM. First, the 1973 GWB amendment did not explicitly prohibit the use of recommended prices (*unverbindliche Preisempfehlungen*) as unions and consumer groups had called for. Two kinds of recommended prices are commonly used in Germany: those printed onto product packaging (*Verbraucherpreisempfehlungen*), and those presented in the form of a list for exclusive use by the retailer (*Händlerpreisempfehlungen*). While prices printed on packaging could arguably help consumers to compare product prices for the same product among several retailers, unions and consumer organizations argued that prices presented in the form of price lists that are never seen by consumers do not offer this benefit, and instead abet price collusion.[19]

This assessment is reinforced by producer reactions to the banning of RPM. Between 1973 and 1975, retailers report that while the overall use of recommended prices remained nearly the same, the use of retailer price lists grew from 22% to 37% of their total stock, while the use of recommended prices targeted at the consumer fell from 30% to 14%. The shift was most dramatic for small shops (those with annual sales below 250,000 DM) for whom the use of retailer price lists nearly doubled, from 22% to 42% of their inventory, while consumer price recommendations fell by half, from 45% to 22% of inventory.[20] Unable to stipulate sales prices in their contracts, manufacturers appear to have moved to less direct means of enforcing price levels. Indeed the BKA, which tracks the use of recommended prices, has essentially recognized that retail list recommendations are tantamount to RPM.[21] But legal provisions for restriction of effective RPM (GWB §18 and §26 II) have been interpreted by the BKA largely to the advantage of branded goods producers: ''Protection of brands and distribution, not protection of the consumer, is . . . still the predominant criterion for interpreting GWB regulation.''[22]

Second, a group of laws restricting sales practice have diminished retailers' ability to exert downward price pressure on producers. Typical of these is the Discount Law (*Rabattgesetz*), enacted first in 1933, which prohibits discounts or in-kind gifts of value greater than 5% of the cost of the product. The law does not prohibit sales on, for example, overstocked or seasonal goods—these are regulated by another restrictive law, the *Zugabeverordnung*—but it does require that retailers sell goods for no less than 95% of their labeled value. Practices not permissible for German retailers under the *Rabattgesetz* include volume or loyalty discounts, sales inducements, coupons, or inflated price labeling.[23] The original goal of the law appears to have been to discourage the cooperative movement and repress immigrant shopkeepers who were willing to compete on narrow profit margins.[24] More recently the law has been upheld as a protection for consumers who might otherwise face price discrimination because they were less able or willing to haggle with sales staff for better prices.[25]

The effect of the *Rabattgesetz* on retail pricing is twofold. First, the *Rabattgesetz* makes it easy for distributors to monitor the actual retail sales prices retailers are using. Second, producers cannot use volume or loyalty discounts to reward their good customers—tactics that have helped retailers in other countries to consolidate their customer base, giving them greater power in negotiating contracts with producers.

Like French price controls, Germany's policy of price maintenance, deployed through recommended prices and retail restrictions, was grounded in reasons of *legitimacy*. One source of legitimacy was the confluence of economic interests. Industry, not surprisingly, strongly favored recommended prices. But consumers, too, found them useful. A 1973 survey found that 87% of men and 82% of women favored recommended prices printed on packaging. Those who favored it felt that it helped them to compare product prices and that it protected them against overreaching by retailers.[26] Moreover, the peak association of German retailers (*Hauptgemeinschaft des deutschen Einzelhandels*, or HDE) has argued that list recommendations, which are not made public to consumers, assist retailers in calculating what prices they should charge.[27] The *Bundestag*, in a move to appease all parties, permitted recommended prices of both kinds.

Why, however, has the BKA acquiesced to what amount to collusive practices? A second source of legitimacy for these pricing policies derives from the postwar tradition of German political economy, *ordoliberalism*, that crystallized in the Freiburg School and formed the basis of Ludwig Erhard's postoccupation economic initiatives of 1957. The ordoliberal principle of competition espoused by the BKA embraces Schumpeterian rather than liberal market assumptions.[28] From this perspective, market regulations should be deployed foremost to optimize economic transactions by balancing the position of market actors through increased transparency.[29] Consistent with this view, the central concern of the BKA in respect both to recommended prices and to the *Rabattgesetz* has been price transparency. Hence their concern with recommended prices has primarily been that manufacturers would label product packaging with artificially elevated recommendations (*Mondpreisen*), thereby permitting retailers to offer apparently attractive reductions from the manufacturer's price.[30]

Similarly, the fundamental ordoliberal argument in favor of the *Rabattgesetz* is that without it, retailers would increase products' labeled prices so that they could offer consumers greater nominal discounts without affecting their profitability. Even the peak consumer association, the AgV, which might normally be expected to oppose the restrictive Rabattgesetz, argued that its elimination would result in an 20% to 30% increase in nominal prices. In the words of the AgV head Helmut Lenders, ''that would be totally impenetrable for the consumer.''[31] Ordoliberal arguments for regulated market transparency drive much of the debate surrounding consumer protection in Germany.

C. Price Politics

France and Germany both imposed regulations in the 1970s to ensure that all consumer products were displayed with their prices in order to facilitate comparative shopping. In Germany, the 1973 Price Information Act (*Preisangabenverordnung*) accompanied the prohibition on RPM, since retailers were then in principle allowed to offer the same goods for different prices. In France, product labeling was required by decree in 1971 and reinforced through supporting regulation in 1976. In both countries clear price information was seen to be a key in holding down retail prices. But whereas in France this new emphasis on comparative price shopping enjoyed enthusiastic endorsement from both government and consumer organizations, similar efforts by consumer organizations and the government in Germany were quickly abandoned.

1. Price Activism in France

In France, the move in 1976 to a system of free price competition below negotiated price ceilings opened the way for greater price competition between companies operating below those ceilings. To emphasize this, the government of Raymond Barre undertook a number of projects to ensure that consumers had access to adequate information about product prices. In November 1977, for example, Barre announced a four month series of state-sponsored radio shows that would provide a forum for callers to report on their strategies for finding inexpensive products. The goal was to help consumers shop more wisely in order to put a check on abusive increases in prices. In the words of the newly appointed Secretary of Consumption: "Every idea helps us to better defend your budget."[32] The theme was repeated in 1979 when the Economics Minister, Michel Monory, called on consumers to compare prices before buying in order to help hold down inflation.[33]

Consumer groups in France were enthusiastic supporters of price labeling and comparative price shopping, and they frequently mobilized their participants to visit stores in order to evaluate the extent to which the pricing regulations were being heeded. A study conducted in Paris in June 1976 found that 28% of retailers and 30 percent of service providers failed to display the price of their goods or services. The worst offenders included furniture stores (52%), florists (56%), and pharmacies (74%).[34] The scale of these price surveys (*relevés de prix*) could be enormous. During the week beginning on 20 November 1979, for example, 110 local affiliates of the Federal Consumers Union (*Union fédérale des consommateurs*, or UFC) surveyed 27,735 stores in 160 cities in France. Mobilized under the slogan "not seen not bought" (*Pas vu pas pris*), they found that 38 percent of the stores visited had not displayed prices on their products.[35]

Unsatisfied with the level of consumer awareness of product price, the Ministry of Consumption under the new Socialist government in 1983 initiated a pilot project in the Region Nord–Pas-de-Calais to offer consumers objective comparative information on product prices. Cooperating with the Regional Council on Consumption (*Conseil regional de la consommation*, or CRC) in Lille, they established 100 computer terminals accessible to the public on which product price information was made available to consumers. These local centers for price information (*Centres locaux de l'information prix*, or CLIP), which accounted for 60% of the Ministry of Consumption's yearly budget, were relatively well received. A survey conducted in 1986 by the CRC of Lille found that 85 percent of the population of the region knew of the program, compared with only 30% in 1984. Of those, 40 percent stated that they used the information for purchases (33.6% of the total population). Furthermore, 22% of the users reported shifting to products that were less expensive, and 18% reported shifting to retailers that were reported to be less expensive.[36] A survey of retailers found that 64% favored the program, 54% felt the price information was useful for their business, and 13% reported using CLIP information to set their own sales prices. Over half of the retailers felt that CLIP had an impact on their consumers, although only 34% reported that consumers used this information directly in their product choice.[37] Five new CLIP regions were included in France's five-year plan of 1984, with each of these sites offered a grant of 5 million francs from the federal government to be matched by an equal contribution from the regional governments.[38]

2. German Consumer Education

Germany in 1973 saw the beginnings of a similar collaboration between the government and consumer groups to raise public awareness about price, but unlike France this effort quickly faltered. In the summer of 1973 Germany's Social-Democratic Party (SPD) launched a program for consumer education (''*Verbraucheraufklärung*'') with the goal of better informing citizens about prices and price formation. As a part of this program Germany's peak consumer association (*Arbeitgemeinschaft der Verbraucher*, or AgV) sponsored two busses to travel to 60 cities in Germany under the slogan ''Together for Reasonable Prices.'' They handed out brochures, showed films, and offered computerized tests that measured consumers' knowledge of prices.

More controversial was the project ''*Aktion gelber Punkt*'' (yellow dot protest) which was initiated by the publicity department of the SPD and pursued most enthusiastically by the SPD's Young Socialists faction.[39] The yellow dot referred to yellow stickers that were attached, as a call to boycott, to the display windows of stores that had particularly high prices. The program had been modeled on the ''*Rote-Punkt-Aktionen*'' of the late 1960, in which leftist community organizations used red labels to protest price increases in local transportation. Memory of these *Rote-Punkt-Aktionen*, which had called out the first consumer boycotts in post-war Germany, lent a radical tone to the SPD's new project.[40]

This attempt to create a politics of price in Germany was supported by labor but strongly opposed by business. Retailers felt particularly threatened by the SPD action, and in what was called the ''greatest ever sign of retail solidarity'' launched a counter-campaign against the government's program. Their posters read, ''Retailers also oppose rising prices. We favor stability!''[41] The association of branded products called the *Aktion Gelber Punkt* ''Consumer politics in the mode of class conflict'' (''*Verbraucherpolitik in Klassenkampfmanier*''). The peak employers association (*Bundesvereinigung der Deutschen Arbeitgeberverbände*, or BDA) launched a campaign against the SPD program under the slogan ''*Gelber Punkt–roter Markt–toter Markt*'' (''Yellow dot–red mark–dead market''), in which they claimed that the goal of the SPD was to dismantle the free market altogether: ''The goal of the yellow dot is apparently to eliminate the market economy.''[42]

By the fall of 1973 the SPD had already begun drawing away from price as a political issue. In October SPD leader Holger Börner assured the DIHT that the *Aktion Gelber Punkt* was not an attack on the market system. He explain that the party had switched from focusing on wage formation as the cause of inflation because they felt that companies had increased prices more than was required by wage increases.[43] At the same time Martin Grüner, the Parliamentary State Secretary for the Economics Ministry, confirmed that price controls were not compatible with Germany's market economy. He did, however, affirm the usefulness of protests that have the goal of informing consumers about price increases and alternative product choices.[44]

Why did price politics flourish in France but miscarry in Germany? The explanation lies in part in the different capacities of consumer organizations in the two countries. Whereas French consumer groups enjoyed a broad and activist local membership, the key German consumer groups had, and continue to have, only a token number of individual members. French groups, therefore, were able to mobilize an enormous membership to undertake the daunting task of price surveys. German consumer groups, because they could not hope to mobilize consumers on this scale, quickly found that the politics of price lay outside of their organizational capacities.[45]

For the governments, the difference appears to stem most strikingly from different conceptions of legitimate government interference in price formation. In France, governments on both the right and left were authentically interested in informing consumers about price so that they could play a role in holding down inflation. Since price had always been an arena of government action in France, providing comparative price information was seen merely as an extension of this responsibility. In Germany, by contrast, the goal of the SPD in launching their Consumer Education campaign appears to have been to convince the general public that prices were being set by business and not by the government. Rather than trying to control price increases, in other words, the SPD was trying to exonerate itself from blame for growing inflation. An internal document of the SPD made this argument clearly: "The state does not create prices. Industry decides about at least 80 percent of price creation. In addition we must consider the multiple anti-competitive practices, that have been common up until now. Both of these facts should make it clear, who really sets prices."[46] Prices in Germany, in other words, were set in the production sphere, through the process of wage negotiation and concerted action, not through any policy under control of the government.

III. PRODUCT QUALITY

A second set of regulations and institutions arose in the 1970s around the quality of consumer products in France and Germany. Governments in both countries were concerned that producers seemed to be designing obsolescence into their products at a time when real disposable incomes were shrinking. Faced with higher prices and lower incomes, consumers were urged to keep products for longer and to emphasize repair over replacement.[47] Unions too worried that lower levels of product quality would lower producer demand for skilled labor, thereby reducing wages for the entire work force.

Attempts to improve product quality proceeded in two stages in both France and Germany. In the first stage, the governments worked with producers and consumers to design informative product labels that would assist buyers in evaluating the relative quality of products on the market. So long as these labels were objective and voluntary, producers were staunch advocates of the process. Following the early success of technical labeling, however, both France and Germany experimented with more comprehensive labeling projects that sought to provide consumers with composite scales to reflect different aspects of product quality. These qualitative projects both faced strong opposition, and both eventually foundered.

The second attempt to improve product quality in both countries was a move to incorporate consumer interests into the design phase of production. Germany did so by introducing consumer representatives into its system of technical standards formation. France, by contrast, attempted to promote collective accords between consumer and producer interest groups in which acceptable standards of quality and design were negotiated. In the end, Germany's system succeeded because it drew on the capabilities embodied in Germany's production institutions. France's approach, by contrast, attempted to create an entirely new forum for setting quality, but one in which producers were extremely hesitant to participate.

A. Quality Labels

1. French Product Labels

In France, informative labeling for consumer products was launched as a collaborative effort by the National council of French employers (*Conseil national du patronat français*, or CNPF) and the National Consumption Institute (*Institut national de la consommation*, or INC). In September 1970 they founded the French association for product labeling (*Association française pour l'étiquetage d'information*, or AFEI), a nonprofit organization in the public interest with the goal of designing and distributing model product labels. The content of the labels was to be strictly factual, and negotiated among consumer and industry representatives. Different kinds of labels were negotiated for different product lines, and their use was strictly voluntary. The first label appeared in 1972. AFEI had issued 300 labels by 1974, 1000 by 1978, and 1300 by 1980.[48]

Following on the success of AFEI, and amid growing concern over product quality, an effort was made to extend the range of informative labeling beyond objective product dimensions to include composite indicators that would approximate qualitative characteristics of interest to the consumers, such as durability and usefulness. The model for this initiative was the Swedish VDN-Skala, established in 1951, that provided relative product quality information on five-point scales. By 1971 the VDN-Skala had been successfully applied to 110 different kinds of products.[49] Following this lead, the Ministry of Industry and Research under Michel d'Ornano created in November 1975 a ''*Service de la qualité*'' under the Direction des Mines.[50] This *Service de la qualité* would work with AFEI to create new qualitative product labels. The proposal was endorsed by the President, the Ministry of Commerce, and the INC. The association of companies that produce electrical goods (CEDEF-GIFAM), which was likely to be heavily influenced by the new label format, gave a restrained approval: ''We accept this project rather favorably but we remain concerned by the modality of the dialogue with the consumers.''[51]

In 1976 the project was taken on by the newly appointed Secretary of Consumption, Christiane Scrivener, as a flagship for her campaign to promote consumer interests. After protracted closed-door discussions with industry, she helped to write and pass a law on consumer information on 10 January 1978 that provided for so-called Quality Certificates (*certificats de qualification*). The content of the Quality Certificates was to be negotiated between industry, consumers, and the administration. The first range of products to be labeled under the new scheme, for example, was shoes. Each kind of shoe would be described on three separate scales measuring comfort, durability, and a third composite category called *finition*. In addition to offering measures of quality, the project also provided for enforcing a minimum level of guaranteed quality, to be set by the Ministry of Industry.[52] Product testing to establish product quality levels was to be carried out by the National Testing Laboratory (*Laboratoire national d'essais*, or LNE), an organization that, with 350 employees and a 44-million-franc budget, was probably not prepared for the task.[53]

Because many products were expected to fall short of the requisite level of quality specified by the Ministry of Industry, it was projected that 280 product brands would disappear from the market because of the Quality Certificates.[54] The ambitious goal, to have all products relabeled in this way by the end of 1981, was checked, however, by the election of Mitterand's Socialist government, which quickly eliminated the project. Rather than pursue qualitative labeling further, the new government had a different idea for promoting quality: they would attempt to engage consumer not just at the point of purchase, but in the product design process as well.

2. German Product Labeling

Product labeling followed a similarly disappointing trajectory in Germany. Informative product labels were initiated in 1964 by the German Institute for Product Safety and Labeling (RAL *Deutsches Institut für Gütesicherung und Kennzeichnung*, formerly the *Reichsausschuß für Lieferbedingungen*). Founded in 1925 with the goal of certifying raw materials for production, RAL was discontinued in 1942, when wartime production conditions caused quality levels to sink below the acceptable threshold set by RAL. The organization was resurrected in 1952 under the influence of Ludwig Erhard's Economics Ministry as a committee of the German Standards Committee (*Deutsches Normenausschuß*, DNA), the precursor to the German Standards Institute (*Deutsches Institut für Normung*, or DIN). The main goal of the new RAL was to create product quality symbols for both industrial and consumer products that assured conformity with a minimal level of safety and quality. RAL recognized 68 such symbols in 1960, 103 in 1978, and 145 in 1995.[55] Over half of these quality symbols applied to building materials, with the rest going to consumer products and, to a lesser extent, to agricultural products.[56] Although RAL focused its efforts primarily on quality symbols, it also issued standard specifications for product colors (*RAL-Farben*), and certificates of provenance (*Herkunftsgewährzeichen*, such as for Lübecker Marzipan).[57]

RAL began issuing informative product labels under the name RAL-*Testate* in 1964. Like the proposed French quality certificates, these informative labels included scales for the properties of the product that consumer and producer representatives agreed would be helpful to the consumer. The value of the product being sold was marked on a scale that indicated its position relative to the full range of products on the market. Companies interested in including an RAL-*Testate* on their product packaging had to submit the product to a testing center for evaluation. Like the RAL quality symbols, products that did not meet DNA minimum standards were not allowed to incorporate the DNA-*Testate* on their packaging.

By 30 April 1974, RAL had created *Testate* for 122 product kinds, including household electronics (vacuum cleaners were big users), cooking wares, metal goods, plastic and leather goods, textiles, and cleansers. Heat storage units all are sold with RAL-*Testate* because the electric companies only allow products with this marking to be sold. One in four RAL-*Testate* tests were requested by mail order companies, who sought a means to convey more information to consumers who did not have direct access to their products. A survey by the *Institut für Warenlehre des Haushalts und Verbraucherforschung* of the University of Gießen reported that one in six housewives living in the country were familiar with the RAL-*Testate*.[58]

Despite this early success, the RAL-*Testate* enjoyed a short life. On 26 August 1973, RAL separated from the DNA. The impetus came not from RAL or DNA administration, since they had worked well together and continued to collaborate after the separation, but from pressure by Germany's peak association for the household equipment industry (*Hauptgemeinschaft der Deutschen Hausgeräteindustrie*, or HDHI). As a member of DNA, the HDHI was concerned that the rising prominence of consumer politics would soon draw political scrutiny to RAL activities. If RAL remained in DNA, they argued, then the entire process of standard setting in consumer goods could become politicized, with consumer groups and the government requesting input into the standard setting process. While most members of DNA made industrial products that would be unaffected by consumer politics, they acceded to the wishes of the HDHI and banished RAL.[59]

Under its new charter as an independent organization, the RAL in 1973 invited diverse participation in order to secure its neutrality and legitimacy. Consumer organizations, trade unions, peak production associations, and chambers of commerce now participated in RAL-*Testate* design. Consumer and producer groups met in a newly created RAL Committee on RAL-*Testate* (*Ausschuß RAL-Testate im RAL*) to set priorities for products to be considered and product values to be included on labels. As the HDHI had feared, this new negotiating table became a forum for imposing minimum quality and safety limits for the purposes of the RAL-*Testate*.[60] The effect was to create a negotiating arena outside of DIN for product standard setting, and the business response to this move was hostile. Even the Consumer Council (*Verbraucherrat*, or VR) of DIN opposed the new RAL-*Testate* format. When RAL applied in 1974 for a contract from the Economics Ministry to help finance the cost of the new RAL-Testate system, it was turned down. By 1975 RAL abandoned the RAL-*Testate* program altogether, returning to its original focus on quality symbols.

3. Germany's Product Information System

Unlike France, Germany did not abandon all effort to create an information labeling system that could address the specific needs of the consumer. When the Economics Ministry turned down RAL's request for support for the RAL-Testate system, it also approached the BDI and other associations for proposals of an alternative product information system. After two years of discussions, the AgV, Economics ministry, and Stiftung Warentest worked with RAL to pass a 1977 law setting guidelines for the provision of product information in Germany (*Richtlinien für Produkt-Information in der Bundesrepublik Deutschland*).[61]

In order to implement this new set of guidelines, a working group of prominent social and economic associations[62] came together in 1977 to create an alternative set of informative labels that would provide end consumers with standard, objective measures of the most important qualities of a product. This new *Produkt-Informationssystem* (PI) was distinct from the RAL-*Testate* in that it focused on measurable qualities of products rather than attempting to create a composite or qualitative scale. To ensure that the information provided was both accurate and useful to consumers, the PI comprised two standing committees, each with representation from industry, consumer groups, and retailing. The Community Board for Product Information (*Gemeinschaftsausschuß für Produkt-Information*, or GA-PI) was responsible for setting the operating guidelines of the PI system. A second Technical Committee for Product Information (*Fachausschuß für Produkt-Information*, or FA-PI) was responsible for the content and form of the PI, as well as the enforcement of guidelines set down by the GA-PI.[63] Both committees were kept small so that they could work effectively.

In January 1979 RAL and DIN collaborated to created a private company, the German Society for Product Information (*Deutsche Gesellschaft für Produktinformation GmbH*, or DGPI) that took over management and promotion of the PI system in Germany. This new management ensured that neither the government nor consumers would interfere in PI labeling.[64] In 1980 DGPI signed a contract with the Economics Ministry to assist in providing Product Information, and to transpose European level environmental quality requirements into German product information labels.[65] By 1984, 20 PI labels had been produced, and an additional 16 were in production. Although DGPI was later amalgamated into DIN, the PI system continues to be used in Germany, particularly for white wares, electronics, gas, oil and coal equipment, heating pumps, and solar panels.[66]

The German and French experiences with product label reform in the 1970s followed similar paths. Both began with strictly informational labeling and attempted to move from there to labeling product quality based on results of product testing. In both cases these efforts were thwarted. But the similarity of their experience also reveals important differences in national *capacities* to provide product information. In Germany, consumer product labeling grew out of the RAL, an organization originally created to provide a service to producers by ensuring the quality of raw materials. In France, consumer product labeling began as an equal collaboration of producers and consumers in a new organization, AFEI. Similarly, RAL's attempt to negotiate quality thresholds for RAL-Testate was rebuffed primarily by industry, which was able to have the program eliminated and the more business-friendly PI system erected in its place.

In France, by contrast, qualitative product labeling failed not simply due to industry opposition, which does not appear to have been decisive, but from lack of political resolve and institutional capacity in the government administration. France's traditional administrative capacities proved incapable of assessing the huge volume of products that industry could produce, and political change served to undermine the labeling project. Product labeling in Germany, in other words, proceeded by the grace of industry, whereas in France it responded more closely to capacities and political interests of the government.

B. Consumer Participation

Beyond simply informing consumer about product quality, politicians in France and Germany were also pushing for greater consumer participation in the design process. In Germany, where standard setting was highly centralized in the DIN, consumers groups were able to participate in product standard setting through the creation of a consumer advisory council within the DIN. This kind of participation was possible in part due to the high level of technical competence among German consumer representatives, which allowed them to engage usefully in technical committee meetings for products of particular relevance to consumers. In France, by contrast, consumer organizations were encouraged by the government to negotiate directly with the sectoral business groups, and later with companies individually. This approach was necessary in part due to the weaker position of the French standard setting organization, AFNOR. It was also better suited to the capacities of consumer organizations in France, as their wide grassroots support gave them a claim to negotiate with industry associations on behalf of all consumers. Hence a combination of distinctive national organizational capacities guided Germany and France towards different solutions to consumer participation in product design.

1. Germany's Verbraucherrat

On 8 October 1974, the DNA decided in agreement with the Economics Ministry to accept public funds to create a Consumer council (*Verbraucherrat*, or VR) within DIN to represent consumer interests. While industry, lead by the BDI, opposed this so-called ''partnership in-house solution''[67] to the problem of consumer access to standard setting, the decision was part of a larger negotiation between DNA and the government. Beginning at the end of 1973, the government had approached the DNA for an agreement to provide significant federal funding in exchange for taking on duties that the government felt were central to the standardization process. One of these, as affirmed in the governments first consumer report of 1971, was to incorporate consumer interests into the standard setting process.[68] As a result of these negotiations, on 1 September 1975 DNA signed an agreement with the government making it the exclusive standard setting organization in Germany, and changing its name to the current German Institute for Standards (*Deutsches Institut für Normung*, or DIN). According to the terms of this agreement, set out in DIN 820 which governs the operations of the organization itself, consumers would sit on an equal footing with producers on the VR.[69]

The new VR had three goals: to oversee the standards process, to help select cases of interest to consumers for standardization, and to organize consumer representation on relevant DIN technical committees. The five members of the VR were selected, each for three years, by the president of the DIN in consultation with the AgV and the Economics Minister. The work of the VR has been very successful. Government support grew from 328,000 DM in 1975 to 451,000 DM in 1980, while the number of consumer representatives participating in DIN technical committees grew from 370 in 1976 to over 600 in 1980.[70] In 1982, 1,884 of 21,400 standards issued by DIN were found to be relevant to consumers according to VR criteria.[71] By 1989, about 2,400 of DIN's 25,700 standards were found by the VR to be relevant to consumers.[72] Hence consumer-relevant technical standards have consistently accounted for about 9% of all technical standards issued by DIN. Germany's "partnership in-house solution" has proved itself an effective tool for promoting the consumer interest in product design.

2. Consumer Accords in France

The third Barre government, inaugurated in 1978, pursued a different strategy for involving consumers in the process of product design. Rather than trying to integrate consumer representatives into industry associations, the new economics minister René Monory called instead for consumer associations to function as a counter force to industry: "Le contre pouvoir consommateur doit être développé."[73] To this end he called for the quadrupling of state funding to consumer associations, from 1 MF in 1978 to 4 MF in 1979.[74] He also eliminated the position of Secretary of Consumption, which under the previous government had focused its quality efforts on administrative intervention in production. While Monory liked to call himself the "Minister of Consumption," the actual administration of consumer affairs was taken up instead by a newly created *mission consommation*, lead by Danièle Achach, of the newly renamed *Direction de la concurrence et de la consommation* (formerly the *Direction de la concurrence et des prix*) in the Economics Ministry[75] This shift emphasized Monory's view that consumption should be treated on an equal footing with production. Product specifications should, on this view, be set through a process of negotiations between representatives of producers and their consumer counterparts.

The idea of negotiating directly with consumer groups had long been favored by much of French industry as an alternative to direct government intervention. In 1975 the CNPF appointed Paul Simonet head of a new commission on industry, commerce, and consumption (CICC) with the goal of presenting a united front to consumer organizations. The CNPF was, in the words of Simonet, "very open to all forms of concertation, especially in the domain of information. . . ."[76] The Consumption Committee of the Seventh French Plan in 1976 advocated just such a dialogue between consumers and producers, although members of the business college noted a "certain climate of hostility" among the consumer representatives.[77] The director of customer relations at Air France, Jean-Georges Marais, echoed in 1977 that such a concertation was indispensable.[78] And a survey conducted by the École supérieure de commerce of Lyons in 1976 found that 24% of French companies had already engaged in dialogues with consumer associations.[79]

The innovation of the 1978 Monory program on these earlier efforts was to encourage collaboration on all aspects of the production process, something that the CNPF had long opposed. Monory charged the formerly neutral National

Consumption Institute (INC) to support consumer associations in cultivating a "consumer counterforce to counterbalance the technical advantage of producers and the effects of advertising."[80] The CNPF's CCIC held regular meetings with consumer associations from November 1979 to March 1981.[81] In the context of these meetings, consumer representatives met with representatives of industry sectors to negotiate standards of quality and use that were felt to best suit consumer needs in that field. While such partnerships were voluntary, companies that accepted negotiated standards could advertise this as a selling point. By 1989, 49 voluntary accords had been signed between consumer associations and professional associations. Of these, 36% treated house construction, 20% used car sales, 18% small retailing, 8 percent furniture, and 6% dry cleaning.[82]

One such voluntary agreement was signed between consumer associations and UDAC, the largest retail store association. According to the agreement, retailers following a set of negotiated guidelines would be allowed to post in their store-front a sticker of a blue, white, and red fleur-de-lis that read: "Engagement du commerce, j'adhère".[83] The guidelines included marking rebates as a percentage of the proper price, indicating prices 'tout compris' including services and other charges, posting clearly information about service after sale, and a guarantee to replace goods that do not function properly or are damaged in delivery. Like many such accords, the program was well received but not very widely used. A 1981 survey of 663 stores in Marseilles found that only 27 stores (4% had placed the *fleur tricolore* in their window.[84]

3. The Corporatist Solution

The victory of Mitterand's Socialist party in 1981 put a new emphasis on such collective agreements, but their goal was to make agreements negotiated between consumer and professional groups legally binding. The Socialists signaled the importance of this initiative by creating a Ministry of Consumption, to which it appointed Christine Lalumière as minister.[85] The project was explicitly modeled on the 1936 labor law, which had granted labor unions the right to negotiate contract terms at the sectoral level. Because a corporatist strategy of this kind would have ramifications for many other areas of consumer regulation, Lalumière created a committee to rewrite the full body of consumer law in France, headed by the lawyer and consumer advocate Jean Calais-Auloy. Significantly, no representatives of industry were included on the committee.[86]

This corporatist agenda was strongly supported by consumer associations, who by 1981 had become so frustrated with the imbalance in their discussions with industry that they decided to boycott further talks until the government intervened in the negotiation process. They felt that only binding sectoral agreements would give them sufficient influence.[87] Jacques Ghestin, a lawyer and spokesman for consumer groups, argued that the government should assign authority over product quality, including the terms of consumer contracts, to professional associations. "In reality," he argued, "I don't see why professional organizations that are able to speak legitimately for their members about work conditions could not do the same in relation to sales conditions."[88]

But this move toward a corporatist solution to consumer demands was opposed both by the business community and by the Ministry of Justice. The business community argued that the analogy with labor contracts was a false one. They felt, first, that consumers were not dependent on producers in the way that employees are on their employers, since consumers face few obstacles to shopping around.[89] Second, the Paris Chamber of Commerce and Industry argued that the variety of interests in the professional community, which encompassed production, wholesale, retail, and services, would put them at a disadvantage at the negotiating table with consumers.[90] Jean Levy, who succeeded Paul Simonet in 1982 as head of the CICC, felt that binding collective conventions could only hurt production. In response to a proposal that retailers post the price-per-kilo and price-per-liter for foods, for example, he argued that this would hurt the quality of products in the market by focusing consumer attention on price. "There would be an invasion of mediocre and low-quality products."[91]

The Ministry of Justice also opposed a corporatist approach to consumer regulation. While they felt that agreements between consumer groups and professional associations should be encouraged, they emphasized that these must remain voluntary. Consumer groups, they argued, were not adequately similar to trade unions. Whereas workers had a "unity of life, unity of training, class consciousness, and direct impact on their work environment," consumers remained necessarily dispersed and disunited.[92] Furthermore, corporatist devolution of control would undermine administrative authorities such as the Commission on Abusive Clauses, which regulated retail contracts. In place of devolution they advocated non-legal means of enforcement, arguing that consumer-friendly brands such as FNAC and Leclerc had done very well in the marketplace.

In 1983, under mounting fiscal pressure, the government underwent a radical change of orientation towards business that caused it to dismiss the Calais-Auloy committee to rewrite the consumer law. It opted instead for a middle road, creating a forum in which consumer and professional groups could meet in the presence of the government administration. On 12 July 1983 it transformed the National Consumption Committee (*Comité national de la Consummation*, or CNC), which had been created in 1960 as a forum for consumer associations to express their interests to the government, into the National Consumption Council (*Conseil national de la consummation*, also CNC), a body in which professional associations would participate on an equal footing with consumer groups. The body's new goal was "to permit the confrontation and the concertation among the representatives of professionals, the public services, and the public powers."

Composed of a consumer and a producer college, the body meets four times per year.[93]

4. Quality Contracts

In December 1982 the newly created Minister of Consumption under the Socialist government, perceiving the probable failure of binding consumer accords, initiated a program to improve product quality by encouraging individual companies and consumer groups to enter into ''contracts for the improvement of quality'' (*contrat pour l'amélioration de la qualité*). Unlike consumer accords, these quality contracts were negotiated for a short time and on an individual basis, and were considered binding on participating companies. Products or services that had been approved in a set of contract negotiations with officially recognized consumer groups could be indicated with mark ''Approved'' (''*marque 'approuvé'* '').[94]

These quality contracts had a mixed reception among consumer groups. The Socialist and Communist consumer groups strongly favored quality agreements, and some companies even negotiated them through their own labor unions. The Communist consumer group INDECOSA-CGT even complained that the government was not applying sufficient pressure on the large nationalized companies to sign quality agreements with consumer associations.[95] The independent consumer group UFC, on the other hand, remained critical of the ''approuvé'' program because they felt that it produced few results for consumers and had supplanted the more effective ''quality certificates'' program attempted by the previous government.

By 1985, 59 companies had signed quality contracts with consumer associations for a duration of one or two years.[96] Of these, 33 companies signed contracts to improve the quality of services, and 26 companies signed quality contracts on a total of 305 different products. By 1986, 134 quality contracts had been signed.[97] But a survey in 1986 also showed that only 16% of the population recognized the ''approuvé'' certification.[98] In hindsight, this system of quality contracts appears to have been largely ineffectual.[99]

In sum, while France and Germany both attempted to introduce consumer interests into the product design phase of production, the solutions they chose were very different, as were the levels of success they achieved. Their divergent approaches were driven primarily by the *capacities* of the producer and consumer groups involved. In Germany, product standards were widely promulgated and accepted by producers, and consumer groups embodied a high degree of technical competence. In France, by contrast, consumer groups had a broad legitimacy but little specific technical expertise, and AFNOR standards were not used by a sufficient number of producers to be an attractive target for asserting consumer interests. The German strategy appears to have been both simpler and more effective than the elaborate collaborative efforts attempted in France.

IV. CONCLUSION

Faced with similar pressures to promote consumer interests against those of producers, France and Germany appear to have chosen very different strategies. In Germany, product market regulation has rested heavily on the institutions of production. Manufacturers were given a strong role in price formation, in the expectation that centralized wage bargaining would help wages to keep pace with prices. Efforts to improve product quality rested on Germany's standard setting body, DIN. In France, by contrast, the arena for consumer policy lay outside of the production sphere. Prices were set largely within the government administration, and product quality was promoted through negotiations between consumer and producer groups.[100]

The reason for this difference has to do less with the political power of industry, which is considerable in both countries, and more with the different *capacities* and *legitimacy* that the two countries brought to the problem. First, France and Germany enjoyed different business, government, and consumer *capacities*. In Germany, the production sphere enjoyed a high associational capability, and consumer groups cultivated a strong technically competency. Hence consumer policy could most easily be addressed through existing producer institutions. In France, by contrast, the state had evolved strong regulatory capacities, and consumer organizations, though not technically sophisticated, were grounded in a broad grass-roots membership. Consumer demands in France could therefore be best addressed through a joint effort of administrative and consumer group activism.

Second, the two countries also found different grounds for establishing the *legitimacy* of their new consumer policies. In France, an historical emphasis on the idea of a 'prix juste' justified, indeed called for, government intervention to fight inflation. Similarly, French concern for product quality was modeled on labor market conflict, legitimating a set of negotiations between consumers and producers. In Germany, by contrast, the ordoliberal tradition emphasized the basic importance of market transparency to competition, trusting informed consumer choices to press for lower prices and higher quality.

The political logic behind this divergence in French and German policies appears to extend to other consumer policy areas. Germany, for example, has no legal recall duty for manufacturers either for technical products or for food, whereas France in 1983 granted its ministries the right to have any consumer product removed from the market and barred from manufacture or import if it is thought to pose a danger.[101] Similarly, product liability law in Germany is premised on proof of negligence in production, design, or advertising, whereas French product liability has been applied in a strict way that does not consider whether the producer was or was not at fault. Through an understanding of the political formation of consumer policies, we may be able to generalize about the ways in which countries have regulated a wide range of product market dimensions. And while it is beyond the scope of this paper to evaluate the impact of the French and German strategies, it does seems likely that different kinds of product market regulations may encourage different kinds of competition and innovation.

ENDNOTES

1. Willi Laschet, ''Verbraucher sind auch Kunden,'' in Hartwig Piepenbrock, Conrad Schroeder editors, *Verbraucherpolitik kontrovers* (Koln: Deutscher Instituts-Verlag, 1987), p 60.
2. ''La protection et l'information des consommateurs: des progrès décisifs,'' *Les Notes Bleues* (Paris: Service de l'information du ministre de l'économie et des finances, 1978), pp 14–20.
3. Karl Polanyi, *The Great Transformation* (New York: Rinehart & Co., 1944), pp 130–162.
4. Kees Koekijk, Zhen Kun Wang, and L. Alan Winters, ''Market Opening, Regulation, and Growth in Europe,'' *Economic Policy 23* (October 1996), pp 443–467.
5. ''Il s'agit de savoir dans quelle mesure il convient soit d'encourager la fabrication et la distribution de produits en grandes quantités, quitte à admettre certains défauts dont l'acheteur subira les conséquences, soit de fair peser sur les producteurs et distributeurs une responsabilité plus lourde afin de les inciter à produire moins, mais à produire mieux. Un tel choix, dont les conséquences économiques et sociales peuvent être considérables, est essentiellement politique.'' Josée Doyère, ''Les acheteurs sont mal protégés contre les défauts de fabrication,'' *Le Monde*, 28 May 1975.
6. Peter Hall, ''The Role of Interests, Institutions and Ideas in the Comparative Political Economy of the Industrialized Nations,'' in Mark Irving Lichbach and Alan S. Zuckerman editors, *Comparative Politics: Rationality, Culture, and Structure* (New York: Cambridge University Press, 1997).
7. Ann Swidler has argued that culture operates in this way, acting as a constraint during times of continuity, but as a toolbox during times of change. Institutions, ideas, and interests may have a similarly dual character. Hence, in policy debates experiencing continuity, institutions bind, interests maximize, and ideas constrain. In entirely new policy areas, by contrast, culture and ideas become a toolbox, interests are revealed as plural, and institutions provide alternative possible regulatory fora from which actors can and must select. Ann Swidler, ''Culture in Action: Symbols and Strategies,'' *American Sociological Review 51* (April 1986), pp 273–286.

8. Hervé Dumez and Alain Jeunemaître, *Diriger l'économie: L'Etat et les prix en France, 1936–1986* (Paris: Harmattan, 1989).
9. Reinhard Angelmar and Bernard Yon, ''New Product Price Controls in France'' in *Journal of Consumer Policy 2*(1) (1978), pp 43–49.
10. How this information should be used in setting price levels was evidently problematic, and higher officials in the Office on Competition and Price reportedly watched Germany price levels closely. (Jeunmaitre, pp 53–54.)
11. ''L'activité de la Direction Générale de la concurrence et de la consommation en 1980,'' *Revue de la concurrence et de la consommation 15* (1981), p 4.
12. ''Nous insistons pour que soient au moins sauvegardees les conditions d'une libre concurrence qui reste, dans l'etat acutel des choses, la seule garantie du consommateur.'' Jacques Dubois, ''Reparlons des prix. . . ,'' *Information Consommateur* 1 (1971), p 3.
13. ''Editorial,'' *Information Consommateur 69*(2) (1969), p 2.
14. Jacques Dubois, ''Le plan Barre et le consommation,'' *Information Consommation OR-GE-CO 18* (Sept.–Oct. 1976), p 1.
15. Luc Bihl, *Une histoire du mouvement consommateur* (Paris: Editions Aubier Montaigne, 1984), pp 214–216.
16. Norbert Reich, ''Neue Tendenzen des kartellrechtlichen Verbraucherschutzes in der BRD,'' *Zeitschrift für Verbraucherpolitik 1*(3) (1977), p 236.
17. Katherina Focke (Bundesminister für Jugend, Familie und Gesundheit), ''Verbraucherpolitik in der Marktwirtschaft,'' *Bulletin des Presse-und Informationsamtes der Bundesregierung 65* (30 May 1973), p 643.
18. F.D. Boggis, ''The European Economic Community,'' *Resale Price Maintenance*, edited by B.S. Yamey (London: Weidenfeld and Nicolson, 1966).
19. *Verbraucherbeirat Jahresbericht*, 1977.
20. Erich Batzer, Erich Greipl, Eugen Singer, *Handhabung und Wirkung der unverbindlichen Preisempfehlung* (Berlin: Duncker & Humblot, 1976), p 121.
21. *Kartellamt Jahresbericht*, 1975.
22. ''Schutz der Marke und des Vertriebsweges, nicht Schutz der Verbraucher ist, wie in vielen Vorschriften des UWG immer noch 'vorverstandenes' Auslegungskriterium für diese Vorschriften des GWB''; Norbert Reich, ''Der Schutz des Verbrauchers vor überhöhten Preisen und einseitigen Preiserhöhungen—das GWB als Verbrauchergesetz,'' in *Verbraucher und Recht*, Norbert Reich, Klaus Tonner, and Hartmut Wegener editors (Göttingen: Verlag Otto Schwartz & Co., 1976), pp 73–74.
23. Georg Klauer and Helmut Seydel, *Zugabeverordnung und Rabattgesetz Kommentar* (München: Verlag Franz Vahlen, 1993), pp 100–103.
24. Reuters New Service, Western Europe, March 2, 1994.
25. Olaf Sosnitza, *Wettbewerbsbeschraenkungen durch die Rechtsprechung: Erscheinungsformen und Ursachen auf dem Gebiet des Lauterkeitsrecht* (Baden-Baden: Nomos Verlagsgesellschaft, 1995), p 144.
26. ''Einstellung der Verbraucher zur Preisempfehlung,'' *Wirtschaft und Wettbewerb* (May 1973), p 325.
27. Norbert Reich, ''Neue Tendenzen des kartellrechtlichen Verbraucherschutzes in der BRD,'' *Zeitschrift für Verbraucherpolitik* 1/3 (1977), pp 237–241. The HDE

also opposed recommended prices printed on packaging on the grounds that they were damaging to retailers because they restricted their freedom.

28. Manfred E. Streit, ''Economic order, private law and public policy: the Freiburg School of Law and Economics in perspective,'' *Journal of Institutional and Theoretical Economics 148* (1992), pp 687–689.
29. François Souty, *La Politique de la concurrence en Allemagne Fédérale* (Paris: Presses Universitaire de France, 1996), pp 110–115.
30. ''Verbraucherpolitik nicht nur als 'Feuerwehr,' '' *Süddeutsche Zeitung*, 13 March 1973.
31. ''Das wird für den Verbraucher völlig undurchsichtig.'' Wulf Petzoldt, '' 'Mondpreise' mit schwindelerregenden Rabatten,'' *Vorwärts* 13, 22 March 1984.
32. Rosemonde Pujol, ''Campagne d'information: ''Acheter mieux—déposer moins,'' *Figaro*, 15 Nov 1977.
33. Luc Bihl, ''Le contre-pouvoir des consommateurs,'' *Le Monde*, 5 Dec 1979.
34. ''La publicité des prix a l'égard des consommateurs,'' *Note Documentaire*, Direction générale de la concurrence et des prix, 4 June 1976.
35. ''Une enquête de l'Union Fédérale des consommateurs,'' *Le Monde*, 12 Dec 1979.
36. ''CLIP de Lille,'' *Consommateurs Actualités* 523 (17 Oct 1986), p 16.
37. ''CLIP: Impact sur les commerçants,'' *Consommateurs Actualités* 538 (13 Feb 1987), p 25.
38. ''Le prix de l'information,'' *Consommateurs Actualités* 517 (5 Sept 1986), p 4.
39. Herbert Kremp, ''Zielpunkt Unternehmer,'' *Die Welt*, 11 Oct 1973.
40. ''Autofahrer gegen ölkonzerne—Boykott letzte Waffe der Konsumenten,'' *Frankfurter Rundschau*, 24 July 1982.
41. ''Auch der Einzelhandel ist gegen steigende Preise Wir sind fur Stabilität!'' Wolfgang H. Glöckner, ''Aktion 'Gelber Punkt'—Ins Rote verfälscht,'' *Vorwärts*, 18 Oct 1973.
42. ''Der Gelbe Punkt jedoch will offenbar weg von dieser Marktwirtschaft, will sie umstrukturiern, aushohlen, verplanen!'' ''SPD beschwichtigt Unternehmer,'' *Süddeutsche Zeitung*, 13 Oct 1973.
43. *Ibid.*
44. ''Auch Verbraucher können Stabilitätsbeitrag leisten,'' *Süddeutsche Zeitung*, 9 Oct 1973.
45. Hartwig Piepenbrock, ''Die Legitimation der Verbraucherverbände zur Wahrnehmung von Verbraucherinteressen,'' in Hartwig Piepenbrock, Conrad Schroeder editors, *Verbraucherpolitik kontrovers* (Koln: Deutscher Instituts-Verlag, 1987), p 101.
46. ''Der Stadt macht im wessentlichen die Preise nicht. Die Unternehmer entscheiden uber mindestens 80 prozent der Preisentwicklung. Zusätzlich hat man dabei die Vielzahl von wettbewerbsfeindlichen Praktiken zu bedenken, die bisher blich sind. Beides sollte endg, ltig klarmachen, wer die Preise wirklich macht.'' ''SPD bereitet eine Kampagne gegen Unternehmer vor,'' *Die Welt*, 7 September 1973.
47. Josée Doyère, ''Les acheteurs sont mal protégés contre les défauts de fabrication,'' *Le Monde*, 28 May 1975.
48. AFEI was eliminated in 1984. Pierre Frybourg, (president of AFEI) ''L'Etiquetage d'Information,'' *Revue de la concurrence et de la consommation 12* (1980), pp 14–

16; ''L'Etiquetage informatif vous aide dans vos achats,'' *Information Consommation Or-Ge-Co* 27 (Mar-April 1978), pp 3–4; Jacques Dubois ''L'affichage des prix . . . ne doit etre qu'un premier pas,'' *Information Consommateur 72* (1) (1972), pp 3–4.

49. Adrian Weser, *Warenkennzeichnung—ein Mittel der Verbraucherinformation* (Verlag Göttingen: Otto Schwartz & Co, 1976), pp 126–133.
50. *Le Monde*, 22 Nov 1975.
51. ''Nous accueilons plutôt favorablement ce projet mais nous demeurons préoccupés par les modalités du dialogue avec les consommateurs.'' Rosemonde Pujol, ''Protection du consommateur: d'Ornano intervient,'' *Le Figaro*, 20 Nov 1975.
52. Jean Calais-Auloy, *Droit de la Consommation* (Paris: Editions Dalloz-Sirey, 1992).
53. Gisèle Prevost, ''Qualification de produits industriels,'' *Les Echos*, 27 Sept 1979.
54. Elisabeth Rochard, ''Pour informer les consommateurs: un 'certificat de qualification',*'' Le Matin*, 27 Jun 1979.
55. RAL Deutsches Institut für Gütesicherung und Kennzeichnung, *70 Jahre RAL-Gütezeichen: Eine moderne Idee feiert Geburtstag* (Sankt Augustin: RAL, 1995), p 22.
56. Adrian Weser, *Warenkennzeichnung—ein Mittel der Verbraucherinformation* (Verlag Göttingen: Otto Schwartz & Co, 1976).
57. Bornecke, Jürgen. *Handbuch der Verbraucherinstitutionen*. Bonn: Verlag Information für die Wirtschaft, 1982.
58. Adrian Weser, *Warenkennzeichnung—ein Mittel der Verbraucherinformation* (Verlag Göttingen: Otto Schwartz & Co, 1976), pp 124–125.
59. Annemarie Bopp-Schmehl, Uwe Heibült, and Ulrich Kypke. *Technische Normung und Verbraucherinteressen im gesellschaftlichen Wandel*. Frankfurt am Main: Haag & Herchen Verlag, 1984.
60. ''Grundsätze für Gütezeichen,'' *Bundesanzeiger*, 23 March 1974.
61. Willi Laschet, ''Verbraucher sind auch Kunden,'' in Hartwig Pipenbrock, Conrad Schroeder editors, *Verbraucherpolitik kontrovers* (Koln: Deutscher Instituts-Verlag, 1987).
62. The group included the Economics Ministry (BMWi), RAL, the peak consumer association (AgV), the Stiftung Warentest, the peak industry association (BDI), trade associations, DIN, and the federal association for materials testing (Bundesanstalt für Materialprüfung, or BAM).
63. Members included five producer representatives, three from BDI, two from retailing industries, five from AgV, one from DIN, and one from BAM. Jürgen Bornecke, *Handbuch der Verbraucherinstitutionen* (Bonn: Verlag Information für die Wirtschaft, 1982), p 326.
64. Annemarie Bopp-Schmehl, Uwe Heibült, and Ulrich Kypke, *Technische Normung und Verbraucherinteressen im gesellschaftlichen Wandel* (Frankfurt am Main: Haag & Herchen Verlag, 1984), p 86.
65. Reinhard Hector, ''Verbraucherpolitische Aspekte aus Sicht der Gebrauchsgüterindustrie,'' in Jürgen Bornecke editor, *Verbraucherpolitik in der Sozialen Marktwirtschaft* (Köln: Verein für wirtschafliche und soziale Fragen, 1984), p 28.
66. Hans-W. Micklitz, ''Three Instances of Negotiation Procedures in the Federal Republic of Germany,'' *Journal of Consumer Policy* 7 (1984), p 213.

67. ''Partnerschaftliche lm-Hause-Lösung''; Christian Joerges, Josef Falke, Hans-Wolfgang Micklitz, and Gert Brüggemeier, *Die Sicherheit von Konsumgütern und die Entwicklung der Europäischen Gemeinschaft* (Baden-Baden: Nomos, 1989), p 186.
68. *Verbraucherbericht*. Bundestagsdrucksache VI/2724, 1971.
69. In 1962 the DNA established a committee for product usefulness (*Ausschuß Gebrauchstauglichkeit*, or AGt) on which consumer representatives held four seats, but their influence was little, and the committee was eliminated after the formation of the VR.
70. Bopp-Schmehl et al., p 214.
71. Annemarie Bopp-Schmehl, Uwe Heibült, and Ulrich Kypke, *Technische Normung und Verbraucherinteressen im gesellschaftlichen Wandel* (Frankfurt am Main: Haag & Herchen Verlag, 1984), p 216.
72. Christian Joerges, Josef Falke, Hans-Wolfgang Micklitz, and Gert Brüggemeier, *Die Sicherheit von Konsumgütern und die Entwicklung der Europäischen Gemeinschaft* (Baden-Baden: Nomos, 1989), p 187; Jérôme Darigny, *Normalisation-certification-essais: leur devenir, leurs enjeux industriels dans l'Europe du marché unique* (Paris: University of Paris I (Sorbonne) thesis, November 1989), p 16.
73. René Monory, *Inauguration des Locaux de L'institut national de la consommation* (Paris: Ministre de l'economie, Service de l'information, March 1979), p 3.
74. ''René Monory: davantage de moyens pour informer les consommateurs,'' *Démocratie Moderne*, 22 Nov 1979.
75. Jean Marchand, ''Une 'mission consommation' au ministère de l'Economie,'' *La Croix*, 17 Jun 1978.
76. ''Nous sommes tres ouverts a toute forme de concertation, plus particulierement dans le domaine de l'information. . .''; ''Opinions sur la fonction consommation et la libre entreprise,'' *Humanisme et Entreprise 102* (April 1977), p 16.
77. Commisariat General du Plan, *Rapport du comité Consommation: Préparation du 7e plan* (Paris: Documentation Française, 1976), p 16; Jacques Dubois, ''Les consommateurs dans le 7ème plan,'' *Information Consommation OR-GE-CO* 15 (March-April 1976), pp 1–2.
78. ''Je voudrais affirmer qu'une concertation est indispensable.'' Jean-Georges Marais, ''Le consommateur, cet inconnu?'' *Humanisme et Entreprise 102* (April 1977), p 69.
79. ''Le Consumerisme,'' *Libre Service Actualités* 632 (30 June 1977), p 134.
80. ''Pouvoir consommateur [pour] contrebalancer la technicité des producteurs et l'action de la publicité''; Gisèle Prevost, ''Consommation: 'l'agressivité' de l'INC préoccupe de plus en plus le CNPF,'' *Les Echos*, 28 May 1979.
81. Jean Marchand, ''M. Monory veut des consommateurs puissants,'' *La Croix*, 28 Sept 1979.
82. ''Accords négociés entre associations de consommateurs et professionels,'' *INC Hebdo* 624 (3 Feb 1989), p 14.
83. ''La charte 92,'' *50 Millions de Consommateurs* 122 (Feb 1981).
84. *Consommateurs Actualité* 282 (3 April 1981).
85. Created by decree 81-704 of 16 July 1981.
86. Chambre de commerce et d'industrie de Paris, ''La Politique de la Consomma-

tion,'' rapport présenté au nom de la Commission du Commerce Intérieur par Messieurs Lefeubvre et Blat (adopted 14 Jan and 11 March 1982).

87. Didier Ferrier, *La Protection des Consommateurs* (Paris: Dalloz, 1996), p 80.
88. ''En realité on ne voit pas pourquoi les organizations patronales qui peuvent engager valablement leurs adherents quant aux conditions de travail, ne pouraient pas le faire quant a leurs conditions de vente.'' In ''Négociation collective: le point de vue des juristes,'' *Que Savoir 43–44* (June–July 1982), p 53.
89. Josée, Doyère, ''Des 'conventions collectives' de la consommation rendront obligatoires les engagements des professionnels,'' *Le Monde*, 5 Dec 1981.
90. Chambre de commerce et d'industrie de Paris, ''La Creation du Conseil National de la Consommation,''rapport présenté au nom de la commission du Commerce Intérieur par M. Gaucher (adopted 19 May 1983), p 10.
91. ''Ce serait l'envahissement par des produits médiocres et de mauvaise qualité''; Elisabeth Rochard, ''Le CNPF ne veut pas de conventions collectives de la consommation,'' *Le Matin*, 19 Feb 1982.
92. Ministère de la Justice, ''Observations sur l'eventualité de conventions collectives entre les organizations de consommateurs et les professionnels,'' (Paris, 14 March 1980), p 2.
93. Chambre de commerce et d'industrie de Paris. ''La Creation du Conseil National de la Consommation.'' Rapport présenté au nom de la Commission du Commerce Intérieur par M. Gaucher (adopted 19 May 1983), pp 4–5. The producer college had been moved from the board of directors of the INC, where they had been before, facilitating the more confrontational role of the INC.
94. Jean Calais-Auloy, *Droit de la Consommation*(Paris: Editions Dalloz-Sirey, 1992), pp 49–50.
95. ''Contrats de qualité,'' *Consommateurs Actualités* 498 (28 Feb 1986), p 17.
96. ''Contrats d'amélioration de la qualité,'' *Consommateurs Actualités 501* (21 March 1986), pp 17–19.
97. ''Contrats de qualité, quatre ans apres. . . ,'' *Consommateurs Actualités* 530 (5 Dec 1986), p 17.
98. ''Qualité: les consommateurs veulent un label unique européen,'' *Consommateurs Actualités 604* (9 Sept 1988), p 20.
99. Jean Calais-Auloy, *Droit de la Consommation*. (Paris: Editions Dalloz-Sirey, 1992), pp 49–50.
100. Accordingly, whereas the German consumer debate transpired primarily in a technical setting, informed by research projects sponsored by the government, while the French debate occurred in the public eye, with every interest group publishing its own consumer journal to convey their opinion.
101. Josef Falke, ''Post Market Control of Technical Consumer Goods in the Federal Republic of Germany,''in *Post Market Control of Consumer Goods* edited by Hans-W. Michlitz (Baden-Baden: Nomos Verlagsgesellschaft, 1990), p 342; ''La nouvelle Commission de la sécurité des consommateurs,''*Consommateurs Actualités 570* (20 Nov 1987), p 11.

22
Mexican Crisis in the Internationalization of Finance

Jong Gook Back
Gyeongsang National University, Chinju, Korea

I. FINANCIAL CRISIS IN MEXICO IN 1994

The Mexican financial crisis, which occurred in December 1994 and proceeded until the first quarter of 1995, was the fine example to show a close relationship between domestic prosperity and financial internationalization in a Third World country.[1] Mexico has tried to open her financial system in the belief that it would contribute to further her prosperity (Back 1994; Grinspun and Cameron 1996). However, the crisis came as a surprise. It destroyed Mexico's prosperity as well as her sovereignty. The Mexican economic system actually collapsed in 1994. Only the international financial package of $53.8 billion led by the United States could calm the crisis. The Mexican financial system became under the supervision of the U.S. Treasury. Therefore, many observers began to scrutinize the effects of globalized financial system. Did Mexico afford the effects of her internationalization? If international financial markets have their own motivations and logic in relation to the Mexican conditions, how can one of newly industrializing countries (NICs) such as Mexico follow up it?[2]

There are various explanations over the causes and effects of the 1994 financial crisis in Mexico. Cameron and Aggarwal summarized some explanations: liberalist, mercantilist, and structuralist (Cameron and Aggarwal 1996). Neoliberals, according to Cameron and Aggarwal, try to maintain their conviction of open world economy as the maximum benefits for the NICs. They argued that the crisis was triggered not by foreign capitals but by the erroneous policies of the Mexican investors and their government. They also opposed the American bailout because it would make a wrong signal and create moral hazard in Mexico as well as the international financial community.

The argument of the mercantilists is similar in its causes but different in its prescriptions from that of neoliberals: the crisis is the sample of vulnerability of small nation-states on foreign savings. The efforts of bailout led by the United States show nothing less than the power of the larger players for their national interests. In the Mexican case, the United States intervened directly because the North American Free Trade Agreement (NAFTA) links the interests of the United States to those of Mexico. Excessive interdependence leads to conflict. The state has to have capacity to control it.

Structuralist arguments put an emphasis upon the unequal structure of national and international communities. The internationalization of a community has to pay the social costs of adjustment and conditionality. The crisis was one of the costs. The deepening of social inequality of Mexico led to political instability. The international financial community quickly responded. As the theorists of dependency and postimperialism argue, as a result, transnational class alliance is shaping policies. Structural reforms of egalitarian society and foreign debt reduction were needed to solve the problems.

There is a new trend of convergence among theories. For example, neoliberal institutionalists generally accept the role of the state and the effects of economic structure as mercantilists and structuralists do. These explanations have a theoretical juncture, too. For example, this study will break down the juncture into some functional dimensions: political, technocratic, and institutional. After scrutinizing the dimensions, this paper will pay more attention to the role of domestic ruling coalition. As Rogowski shows the case in international trade (Rogowski, 1989), the structure of the Mexican ruling coalition matters in Mexico's responses to the effects of financial internationalization. Especially, the cohesion of the Mexican ruling coalition works as a major factor to integrate other factors and enhance their explanatory power.[3] The Mexican ruling coalition has changed from the so-called revolutionary family to a neoliberal one after several crises since the 1970s. Rapid liberalization of new ruling coalition was neither to keep its old members nor to secure its new members—the Mexican capitalists. In the successive crises, as a result, major parts of the ruling coalition tended to defect rather than cooperate. The 1994 Mexican crisis is a part of the Mexican crises in her developmental process. And these crises become more internationalized and integrated. Therefore, this paper will discuss these agenda as followings: (1) the rise of the Mexican neoliberal developmental strategy since the 1980s as a solution of the Mexican dilemma; (2) the relationship between the changing structure and development strategy of the Mexican ruling coalition and the rapid internationalization of the Mexican finance; (3) the causes and process of the crisis; and (4) a review of behaviors of foreign investors as an independent variable.

II. OLD CRISES AND NEW BORROWINGS

Since the Mexican Revolution of 1910 the Mexican regime had enjoyed a considerable political stability and stable economic growth. It is really the feat of Mexico, which was hardly found in the Third World countries. Because the Mexican ruling coalition was formed as a compromise of revolutionary forces and was institutionalized in the Partido Revolucionario Institutional (PRI), the Mexican regime was solid as a rock. Some historical accidents such as the increasing oil revenue had also contributed to economic boom and consolidated the regime.

However, the Mexican regime had gradually and evidently deteriorated since the 1960s. The warning sign of debt crisis as well as political crises enlarged the notion of the Mexican crisis among domestic and foreign observers. For example, the default of Mexico for foreign loans led some Western banks to bankruptcy or on the verge of bankruptcy. Because of bad effects of the Mexican default upon international financial system, Western countries became more interested in the Mexican affairs. Especially, the United States has had a deep concern with the Mexican affairs in their geographical proximity and increasing economic interaction.

Even before 1994, therefore, the Mexican crisis was a major theme in the Mexican study. A large number of the Mexican studies are indulged in studying the causes and effects of the Mexican crisis.[4] In one of the classical studies, Raymond Vernon configured the Mexican crisis as Mexico's populist dilemma within its ruling coalition (Vernon 1965). The struggle between *politicos* and *tecnicos* was on the horns of a dilemma that the measures for political efficiency would destabilize the political regime. If not, the regime would be unstable too, because of its inefficiency. Either way would lead to the instability of the regime. Vernon argues that it comes from the populist structure of the Mexican regime.

The Mexican crisis may not be a kind of the "collapse of a capitalist system," as Petras and Vieux argue (Petras and Vieux 1992). As Back summarizes, during the 1980s, Mexico showed a relatively stable structure of industry and trade, with slightly lower economic growth rate and higher rate of inflation, compared with those of other Latin American countries (Back 1992; 76). Just before the 1994, Mexico enjoyed the same "reasonable growth" (Mishkin 1996). Only the signs of immediate crisis were found in the figures of foreign debt services and high rate of fiscal deficit. These figures are interrelated in fact. The high debt services cause a high fiscal deficit. Therefore, the problem was mainly financial in both crises. Mexico's heavy borrowing from foreign savings and inability to serve the debts cause the crises. Thus, the Mexican crises were largely political rather than economic.

The reasons why Mexico has had to borrow so heavily are her need of capital for development but low domestic saving. In fact, Latin American countries have suffered their low domestic saving vis-à-vis their East Asian counterparts. Sebastian Edwards finds that the difference of per capital income growth explains the difference of saving rate more than structural differences (Edwards 1996). Low per capita income growth and higher political instability cause lower domestic saving. As well as the demand side of foreign capital, the development of its supply side has influenced. The development of Euromarket makes private finance than foreign direct investment and public loan available as a major source of foreign saving. In addition, technological development of international finance contributes to the heavy borrowing of Mexico since the 1970s. The agenda has changed from ''the supply of capital to support the development of Third World countries'' to ''the ability of developing countries to manage their monetary and exchange rate policies to avoid the undesirable effects on aggregate demand and inflation in the globalization of the international financial system'' (Gurría 1995).

The internationalization of finance could work as a pushing factor of the Mexican borrowing. However, Frieden's findings do not necessarily make sure that the inflows of foreign capital cause economic development in Mexico as well as other Latin American countries.[5] Demetriades and Hussein argue that financial development is not a leading sector in the process of economic development (Demetriades and Hussein 1996). There are bidirectionality and even some evidence of reverse causation between the variables. Therefore, even though the development of international financial system could work as a pushing factor, the domestic factors such as the expansionary development strategy and the lack of capital explain the heavy borrowing of Mexico much more.

There emerges a dialectic process of foreign finance between crisis and development in some Third World countries such as Mexico. In order to consolidate the legitimacy of the state, the state has to show good performances of economic development. It needs big capital for huge investment, however, which the state usually does not have. Foreign savings could afford it, searching for better return. Third World countries welcome them. However, because of its inefficiency, the efforts of the state to increasing debt easily lead to debt crisis. Debt crisis results in weakening the legitimacy of the state. Even though it is not a predetermined course, it is found common in the Third World countries.

III. EFFORTS FOR LIBERALIZATION IN MEXICO

Liberalization as a part of new development strategy must be a beginning of new crises. If Mexico had kept her economic system closed as North Korea did or managed as South Korea did, she would not worry about financial crises (at least, not sudden crises) or enjoy indebted economic growth. It is well known that Mexico changed its development strategy from import-substitution Industrialization to export-led industrialization since the 1970s.[6] Mexico already passed the easy stage of import-substitution industrialization in the 1950s. From this period the Mexican production of basic consumer goods was enough to meet the domestic demand. Domestic markets were saturated. Now, Mexico needed the production of intermediary goods or capital goods for the production of final goods. The vast amount of capital and high level of technology for upgrading the stage, however, were rare resources in Mexico.

The PRI coalition regarded the change of development strategy as the transition to neoliberal economic reforms. There were several reasons why Mexicans believed neoliberal economic reforms were solutions. First, neoliberal mood swept the United States and Latin America as a solution for the long stagnation in this region. The Reagan Administration and IMF encouraged Mexico to adopt neoliberal economic reforms as the American and Chilean examples showed. IMF quibbled in interpreting even the success of Korean case as the success of neoliberal strategy.[7] As well as external forces, the pressures from the Mexican capitalists such as capital flight leave little room to the Mexican government to choose anything else. Second, the PRI coalition could not go along with its populist dilemma any more. They felt that the revolutionary legitimacy became not enough to maintain the coalition. If the revolutionary legitimacy does not work any more, then they must rely on the economic performance to get popular support. The major members of the ruling coalition were ready to pay political costs to survive.

The selection of Carlos Salinas de Gortari in 1988 was the sign of the ruling coalition to give up its revolutionary legitimacy: the negation of the so-called presidential pendulum in which the Mexican presidency had swayed between right and left in turn. When rightist Miguel de la Madrid gave a *dedazo* to more rightist Salinas, the leftist section of the ruling coalition led by Cúautemoc Cárdenas and Profirio Muñoz Ledo defected the PRI. The PRI had relied upon a conviction that neoliberal economic reforms could increase efficiency and contribute to rapid economic growth. This conviction was intensified under the Salinas administration. ''By midterm in the sexenio of Carlos Salinas de Gortari (1988–1994), the dispute between neoliberals and national-populists appeared to have been resolved in Mexico. Neoliberals were firmly in control of economic policy making'' (Grinspun and Cameron 1996:162). As well as domestic liberalization, Salinas devoted to open the Mexican economy such as ''integración silenciosa'' through NAFTA (Middlebrook 1991). Gurría summarizes the economic reforms since De la Madrid and strengthened by Salinas (Gurrí 1995:196-202).

Stabilization and structural change policies were major parts of neoliberal economic reforms. The first job to stabilize the Mexican economy was the reduction of public expenditure. To reduce the vast fiscal deficit of the Mexican government, populist welfare spending and the size of government had to be reduced. The privatization of public enterprise could also contribute to stable economy in both ways. The selling of public firms in deficit owned by the government would give extra money to the government and reduce government's fiscal burden to subsidize the public firms. These policies had to be accompanied with the measures to balance the public account and get the prices right. The Salinas government tried to adjust public revenues through tax reform and corrected the prices by liberalizing tariffs of goods and services provided by the public sector.

Neoliberal economic reforms for structural change were more ambitious. The most dramatic measure of liberalizing the Mexican economy was to promulgate NAFTA. As a form of expanded maquiladora industry, NAFTA aimed to liberalize trade and investment and to integrate the North American markets. Even though there were some asymmetric arrangements among the NAFTA countries, Mexico made up her mind to liberalize economy in an unprecedented speed. The Salinas government also pushed economic deregulation.

Financial policies were major parts of Mexico's neoliberal economic reforms. As Gurría argues, there were some characteristics of capital inflows (Gurría 1995:205–210). First, portfolio foreign investment in Mexico rapidly expanded from US$4.5 billion in 1990 to US$54.6 billion in 1993. Salinas' heavy reliance on portfolio foreign investment was eminent while the share of portfolio investment of total capital inflows was 80% before 1994 and 50% even in 1994 (Cameron and Aggarwal 1996;976). This rapid expansion of portfolio investment was encouraged by combined factors:

1. The Mexican government encouraged portfolio foreign investment
2. There was a higher relative yield of Mexico's assets compared to those offered by markets of industrialized countries[8]
3. Mexico's financial solvency, measured by several indicators that reflect a more solid position
4. The lower risk perceived by foreign investors with regard to Mexico's domestic economic situation
5. The lower risk of suffering losses in the real value of assets, caused by a contingent devaluation due to a preestablished sliding of the exchange rate
6. The modifications to the legislation to provide more protection to foreign investors, for example, the approval of amendments of Rule 144-A on October 22, 1992.

In fact, those measures were a collection of securing foreign investment in Mexico. Mexico also encouraged capital repatriation. As Back argues, capital flight as a capitalist strike against the populist dilemma was the major factor to push the Mexican ruling coalition toward a neoliberal development strategy (Back 1992). The triumphant neoliberal faction of the ruling coalition tried to provide all possible guarantees for capital repatriation. For example, the Mexican government guaranteed positive real interest rates and a single flat rate of 1% only on repatriated capitals. This so-called stamp tax was introduced in August 1989 and guaranteed an anonymous tax (Gurría 1995:213).

Measures to control inflation were essential because stabilizing prices was the very condition of high capital inflows and massive capital inflows would create inflationary pressures. Salinas installed a specified ban of the Peso's fluctuation in order to sterilize inflationary pressures. His government also limited banks' foreign currency liabilities: 10% foreign currency borrowing equivalent to 10% of the bank's total liabilities as well as 15% liquidity coefficient for dollar liabilities invested in low-risk or risk-free assets. In hindsight, these measures were not enough to keep the value of the Peso stable. They did not function well in the 1994 crisis. It is evident that there was a contradiction between inducing and restricting measures for foreign capital inflows. If they began with political motives, however, can they stop at an appropriate crossroads?

The strangest thing was Salinas' exchange rate policy. Gurría argues that this policy was ''more responsive'' through the reform of November 1991 (Gurría 1995). The core of this policy was to dismantle dual control system of exchange rate since 1982 and widening the fluctuation bank: ceiling of 20 centavos per dollar to 40 centavos with fixed floor in the daily level. The Mexican officials believed that this system was enough to respond the fluctuation of exchange rate and that ''some problems posed by capital flows can be solved more easily'' (Gurría 1995:218). This band system of exchange rate was far from the liberalization of free exchange rate. It is very interesting to find that the Mexican officials would rather worry themselves about the excessive capital inflows! The liberalization of the economy did not accompany with the liberalization of the exchange rate. Mexico chose free capital inflows but not free exchange rate. The ability of Mexico to protect the value of the peso was out of question then.

Free capital inflows without free exchange rate seems to be contradictory to neoliberal reforms. However, it is not so contradictory if it means the desperate efforts of Mexico to induce foreign capitals. Neoliberal technocrats of Mexico believed that the fixed rate of exchange would guarantee the value of the peso and capital gains in Mexico. In order to stabilize the exchange rate Mexico would sacrifice the domestic reserve of foreign currency in the short term. But, in the long run, Mexico could enjoy enough foreign capital for economic growth. Because they believed that Mexico was attractive enough for foreign investors, on the other hand, they had to quell the rush of foreign capital inflows. ''The greater flexibility of the exchange rate also helps to discourage capital inflows of a very short-term nature'' (Gurría 1995:218).

IV. DIMENSIONS OF THE CRISIS

The 1994 financial crisis appeared as a sudden attack on Mexico and her neoliberal technocrats. The macroeconomic situation of Mexico in 1994 took good shape. Many observers believed that structural adjustment and stabilization policies were recovering the Mexican economy. International organizations such as IMF and OECD announced their favor upon the Mexican efforts of liberalization and their results. Foreign investors regarded Mexico as one of very promising emerging markets for the opportunity of business. In fact, the Consumer Price Index of Mexico was down from 26.7% of 1990 to 9.8% of 1993 in comparison to the end of the previous year. The Gross Domestic Product of Mexico was also relatively stable—it was 4.4% in 1990 and 0.4% in 1993. Interest rate per year was also stable decreasing from 37.36% in 1990 to 15.34% in 1994. The growth rate of total investment was positive except in 1993. There were some bad signs such as excessive national consumption and still increasing foreign debts. However, any scholars could not expect the 1994 crisis as much as the collapse of the Berlin Wall.

There are many explanations to explain the dimensions of the crisis, as Cameron and Aggarwal provide (1996). This paper already argues that there is a convergence among theories. Rather than striving to find theoretical differences, therefore, it is useful to find a concrete historical development. Sometimes, a chronological description enables us to escape from the fallacy of confusing causes and effects.

The history of the crisis showed that the Mexican government had tried to maintain Mexico attractive for foreign investors. In fact, every government in the world has to protect its currency from the attacks of domestic and international currency investors. The Mexican case is nothing particular. Since January 1994, however, the sequence of political shocks might lead the decline of Mexico's credibility that culminated in the devaluation in December.

The reserves of foreign currency by the central bank are a good indicator of the credibility crisis. On January 1994, the Bank of Mexico held nearly $25 billion in reserves despite the burst of the Chiapas rebellion. Its reserves grew to $30 billion in February. However, after the March 23 assassination of Luis Donaldo Colosio, the central bank had to intervene in the market. Its reserves declined to $17.5 billion by the end of April. There was a happy interim from May to November with no attack on the peso and little central bank intervention. A new round of attacks on the peso again occurred in mid-November and followed the most devastating attack on December 21. The central bank had to spend $4.5 billion in a single day to defend the peso. It proved to be futile.

The political dimension of the crisis could explain some causes. It is evident that the instability of the peso just followed the occurrence of political instability. When Salinas proudly presented the beginning of NAFTA on January 1, 1994, *los indios* in the jungle of Chiapas responded with their rebellion. It was dramatic enough for foreign investors to understand the vulnerability of neoliberal ruling coalition in Mexico. Unfortunately, on March 30 even the presidential candidate of PRI Luis Donaldo Colosio was shot to death in Tijuana, the place that represents Mexico's liberalization. Worse than that, the PRI indulged in infighting within the party and conducted a troublesome investigation over the assassin of its Secretary General, Jos Francisco Ruiz Massieu, on mid-November. Political instability might contribute to credit instability.

However, political dimension should not be overemphasized. Political instability such as those of 1994 was nothing new in Mexico since the mid-1960s. Assassinations and disappearances have increased in Mexican politics. If political instability matters, the results of the 1988 election did much more. In the presidential election, Salinas won 50.46% of the popular vote. However, the *New York Times* reported that wide range of cheating and brutality presented and people perceived it well (June 28, 1988). In addition, there were some differences between the Colosio assassination and the Massieu assassination according to policy alternatives. Therefore, the examination on the technocratic dimension of the crisis is also useful.

The technocratic dimension of the crisis is meaningful by its explanatory differences. Cameron and Aggarwal find the meaningful differences among Mexico's technocratic management in March and November 1994 (Cameron and Aggarwal 1996:978). In March 1994, when the assassination of Colosio might call the attacks on the peso, officials from Hacienda (the finance ministry) such as José Angel Gurría, the head of NAFINSA, headed off a speculative attack with various effective measures. Gurría negotiated a $6 billion swap with the United States Treasury. They shut down the Mexican stock market (or Bolsa de Valores) for a day. In order to win back the confidence of foreign investors, they called foreign investors around the world. Salinas also played an important role to invite business and labor leaders to re-sign the corporatist *pacto económico*.

In contrast, in November 1994, several technocratic measures were inappropriate and too late. On November 20, 1994, Pedro Aspe, the Secretary of Hacienda, opposed devaluing the peso and Salinas and Zedillo agreed, in spite of declining reserves. Even the new Secretary of Hacienda in the Zedillo government, Jaime Serra Puche, announced optimistic "economic criteria for 1995" which business leaders found insufficient. The most ridiculous meeting was on December 12, 1994, when Serra invited business elite to discuss the devaluation of the peso. "The meeting gave the bankers the opportunity to buy dollars before Serra's announcement of the devaluation, and billions of dollars fled the country in a matter of hours. 'It's the first time in history that a devaluation was consulted on,' commented former finance official Jesús Silva Herzog" (Cameron and Aggarwal 1996:979).

Political and technocratic dimensions are very useful to understand the integrated causes of the 1994 Mexican crisis. The review of its political and technocratic dimensions clearly tells us how neoliberal policies have failed to keep the promise of stable and shared economic growth for Mexico (Green 1996; Grinspun and Cameron 1996). The case study confirms that the factors influencing the Mexican economy were so diverse and the neoliberal premise of market was so naive. The meeting of December 12 is particularly important to understand the sequence of the crisis. Serra might intend to ask the help of his friends to protect the peso; that is the economic base of their ruling coalition in the meeting. His friends, however, quickly defected from their coalition.

As many observers argue, it is also necessary to review the behaviors of foreign investors as an independent variable. It is because that foreign investors assumed lion's share of Mexico's finance even though the defection of Mexico's capitalists would contribute to the crisis, As Cameron and Aggarwal argue, the crisis demonstrated how the construction and maintenance of increasingly complex domestic and international coalitions could play important role to manage the crisis (Cameron and Aggarwal 1996:978). Let's pay more attention to the behaviors of international finance as an independent actor does.

Since 1994 the Mexican crisis has been known as a model of how the internationalization of finance can have a devastating effect in a developing country. However, this simple argument might justify the autarky. However, too simple cry for a new autarky including chauvinism must be as much harmful as a liberal conviction of internationalization as panacea to heal every disease. Usually the effects of internationalization have been exaggerated. In fact, it is too soon to believe that globalization denationalizes countries and leads all countries to pursue the same policies (Garrett 1995). Until now, at least, leading multinational corporations as major initiators of globalization are not converging and markets are not replacing political leadership among countries (Pauly and Reich 1997). But it is also true that globalization of goods and assets is undermining the effectiveness of state-based collective action and, thus, changes the logic of collective action (Cerny 1995).

Mishkin provides a useful explanation based on an institutional dimension of the Crisis: a consolidated theory of 'asymmetric information' (Mishkin 1996). According to Mishkin, asymmetric information could lead to adverse selection and moral hazard in financial market because of scarce resources and principal-agency problem. The sequence of the Mexican crisis began with a lending boom, which was created by an unrestricted solicitation of foreign capital and the privatization of banks in the early 1990s. The lack of credible institutions intensified the vicious spiral of uncertainty in Mexico. The political shocks in 1994 also contributed to the vicious spiral. Mishkin concludes that "the financial crisis leads to such a substantial worsening of adverse selection and moral hazard problems in financial markets that there is a collapse in lending and hence in economic activity" (Mishkin 1996:52). Figure 1 shows the structure of Mishkin's argument.

Although Mishkin's explanation is helpful to understand the behaviors of foreign investors in the 1994 financial crisis, his argument misses some logical knots. First of all, the effect of international finance is meaningless if the portion of foreign capital inflows were small in total capital inflows in Mexico. Because of Mexico's new neoliberal development strategy, portfolio foreign investment

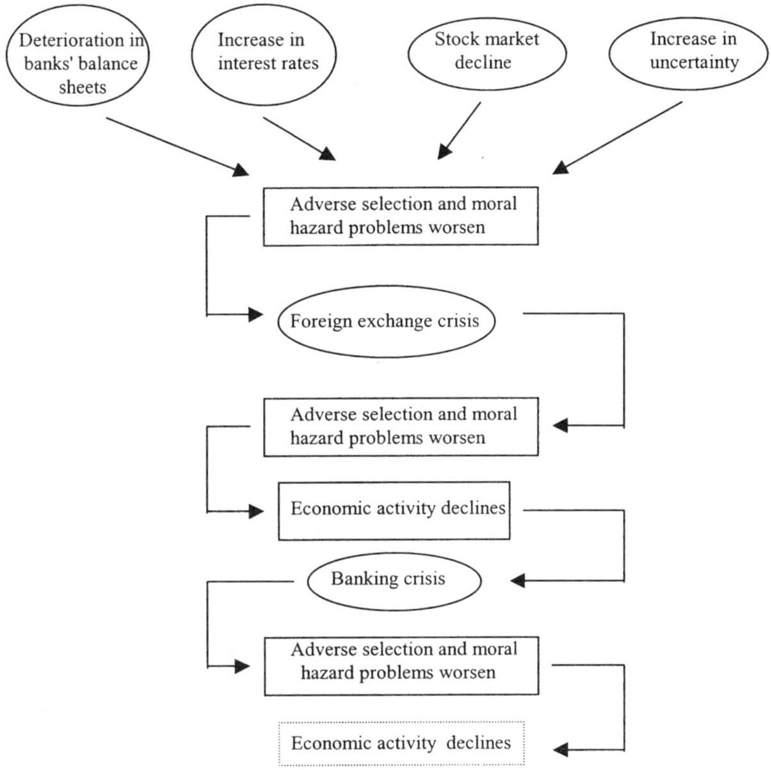

Figure 1 A hypothetical sequence of structural factors in the Mexican financial crisis of 1994. (From Mishkin 1996:45.)

in Mexico was rapidly expanding from \$4.5 billion in 1990 up to \$54.6 billion in 1993, which assumed 50% of total capital inflows in Mexico even in 1994. The 1994 crisis began with the outflows of foreign portfolio investment of \$10 billion on the fourth quarter of 1994. The central bank reserves of about \$18 billion could not cope with the magnitude and speed of the outflows.

The tighter integration of Mexico with the United States in 1994 was ambivalent in explaining the crisis. Financial integration of Mexico with the United States contributed not only to initiate the crisis but also to control it rapidly. The role of North American investors is decisive in capital inflows in Latin America. Mexico becomes a major beneficiary (Culpeper 1995). The prospect of regional integration through NAFTA intensifies the position of Mexico in international financial market, as neoliberals in Mexico expected. However, there is a backlash. Mexico became more easily influenced by any American policies. From February 1994 the U.S. Federal Reserve began to raise the interbank federal funds rate to calm incipient inflationary pressures in America. This U.S. policy succeeded in keeping inflation in America but put upward pressure on Mexican interest rates (Mishkin 1996:47). An increase of interest payments tends to lower households' and firms' cash flow and cause deterioration in their balance sheets. Deterioration of private sector balance put a negative effect on domestic saving and loan security in turn.

The United States already has the power to shape international financial regime. Not only in Latin America but also in the world, the United States enjoys a decisive role in international capital flows. The American share of foreign direct investment, portfolio investment, bonds, and bank claims in the international financial community are dominant, even though there are also considerable shares of Japan and Europe. For instance, according to Frieden, if there were 1% interest in United States, there would be \$3 billion or \$4 billion in new interest charges in the bid debtors in the NICs (Frieden 1987:143). This effect would easily create debt crises in some financially unstable countries.

The integration of Mexico with the United States explains the reason why the United States tried to bail out Mexico so quickly. This rescue package for Mexico includes \$20 billion U.S. Treasury's Exchange Stabilization Fund of 10-year maturity, \$6 billion U.S. Federal Reserve's short-term bridge financing, \$10 billion Bank of International Settlement credit, and \$17.8 billion IMF credit. The last one was odd because it assumed 688% of the Mexican quota. The United States enforced it in spite of the abstain of six European members (Cameron and Aggarwal 1996:979–981). The total amount of the package is \$53.8 billion. This size of the Mexican bailout package is too big to compare with the Marshall Plan of \$15 billion in the mid- 1940s. The security and economic concern of the United States on Mexico can only explain such a quick, enormous and impressive rescue activity.

Of course, there were very strict conditionality measures: (1) oil revenue as collateral; (2) buy back the pesos; (3) require approval in advance of every withdrawal of funds by the U.S. Treasury; (4) set up a fund backed by the World Bank as a form of socialized risk. It means that Mexico becomes under tight financial control of the United States. Even though President Zedillo insists on the sovereignty of Mexico as the first national goal in his National Development Plan 1995–2000, one pillar of sovereignty/financial ability already collapsed.

V. DEVELOPMENT STRATEGY RECONSIDERED

The 1994 Financial Crisis in Mexico is political as well as economic as summarized in Figure 2. Misunderstanding of the nature of the crisis might cause bad prescriptions. For example, Ramírez already warned that neoliberal deflationary prescriptions of IMF would create a vicious cycle of low growth rate and debt

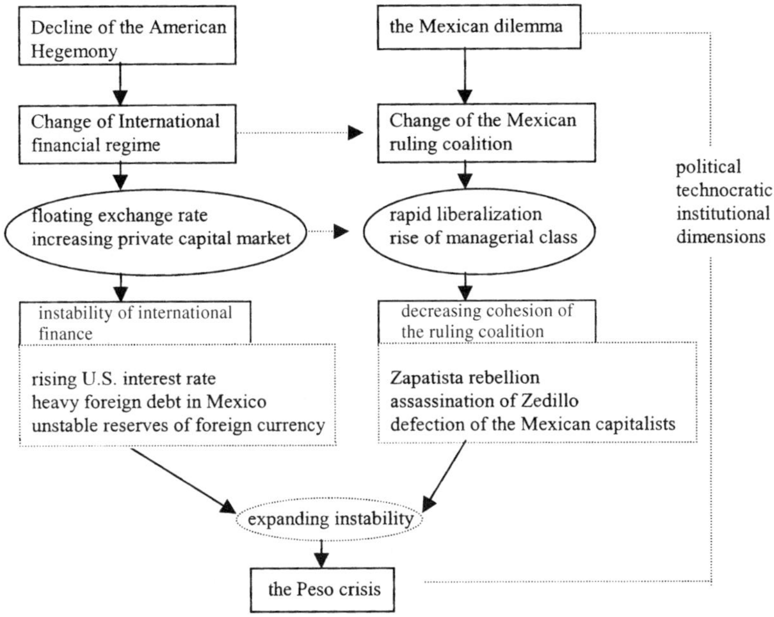

Figure 2 Sequence of structural factors in the Mexican financial crisis of 1994.

crises in Mexico (Ramírez 1996). Cutoffs of governmental spendings and a rise in taxes could not guarantee economic recovery in Mexico.

The effects of internationalization upon Mexico have proved to be enormous. In every stage and dimension, external factors influenced the decisions of the Mexican government and capitalists. However, the degree of ruling coalition's cohesion determinated the degree of influence. The Mexican ruling coalition accepted neoliberal strategies as new alternatives. Neoliberal strategies, in return, caused the change of the ruling coalition. Populist parties departed the coalition. Capitalists, however, were reluctant to pay costs for the new coalition. Therefore, the new development strategy could not work as its theory did. It is time for Mexicans to find their own development strategy, which the majority of Mexicans can agree.

ENDNOTES

1. ''Internationalization'' and ''globalization'' will be interchangeable in this paper. The proponents of ''globalization'' tend to emphasize its particularities than the term of

''internationalization'' (Marshall 1996). However, I found little meaningful difference in the usage of the terms (Back 1995).

2. Even in the United States, financial markets work independently from the conditions of American economy. As in the 1987 crash, the sudden bust in the stock and bond markets in April 1994 occurred when the American economy looked healthy. Michael Metz, one of investment strategists for Oppenheimer & Co., concurs: ''Financial markets have a world of their own and motivations of their own'' (*Time*, April 11, 1994).
3. In my doctoral research about the automobile policies in Mexico and South Korea, I emphasized the explanatory power of the ''cohesion of the ruling coalition'' (Back 1990). Frieden also put an emphasis on it as ''What determines economic policy? the character of socioeconomic interest groups and their patterns of cohesion and conflict'' (Frieden 1991:7).
4. Héctor Guillén Romo, *Orígenes de la Crisis en México 1940/1982* (México, D.F.: Ediciones Era, 1984); Forrest D. Colburn, ''Mexico's Financial Crisis,'' *Latin American Research Review 19* (1984): 220–224; David Brooks, ''Mexico: Whose Crisis, Whose Future?,'' *Report on the Americas 21* (Sept/Dec 1987): 13–39; Jorge G. Castañeda, ''Mexico at the Brink,'' *Foreign Affairs 64* (Winter 1985/86): 287–303; Brian Latell, *Mexico at the Crossroads: The Many Crises of the Political System* (Stanford: Hoover Institution, 1986); José Ayala and Clemente Ruiz Durán, ''Development and Crisis in Mexico: A Structuralist Approach,'' in *Latin American Political Economy: Financial Crisis and Political Change*, edited by Jonathan Hartlyn and Samuel A. Morley (Boulder: Westview Press, 1986), 243–264; Roger S. Leeds and Gale Thompson, *The 1982 Mexican Debt Negotiations: Response to a Financial Crisis* (Washington: Foreign Policy Institute, Johns Hopkins University, 1987); Peter H. Smith, ''Crisis and Democracy in Latin America,'' *World Politics 43* (July 1991): 608–634; James Petras and Steve Vieux, ''Latin America's Free Markets,'' *Monthly Review 44* (May 1992): 9–20; Judith Teichman, ''The Mexican State and the Political Implications of Economic Restructuring,'' *Latin American Perspectives 19* (Spring 1992): 88–104.
5. Frieden finds that the Mexican borrowing has shown some particularities in the Latin American patterns of borrowing: (1) borrowings were associated with increased imports; (2) investment grew substantially; (3) public spending strongly correlated with borrowing; (4) capital inflows were associated with real appreciation (Frieden 1991: 82). Particularities in borrowing patterns might show the different responses of each country to international finance.
6. For instance, Miguel D. Ramírez, ''Mexico's Development Experience, 1950–85: Lessons and Future Prospects,'' *Journal of Inter-American Studies and World Affairs 28* (Summer 1986): 39–66; David R. Mares, ''Explaining Choice of Development Strategies: Suggestions from Mexico, 1970–1982,'' *International Organization 39* (Autumn 1985): 667–697; L. Antonio Aspra, ''Import Substitution in Mexico: Past and Present,'' *World Development 5* (1977): 111–123; Ren Villarreal, ''The Policy of Import-Substituting Industrialization, 1929–1975,'' in *Authoritarianism in Mexico*, edited by Jos Luis Reyna and Richard S. Weinert (Philadelphia: ISHI, 1977), 67–107; Jong Gook Back, ''Two Roads Toward Export-Led Industrialization: A Comparative Analysis of Government Policies and Corporate Strategies in South Korea and Mexico,'' *Social Science and Policy Research 12* (1990): 105–135.

7. *Forbes*, as much as the IMF, recommended that one way to start solving the international debt crisis would be for Mexico to send a study group to South Korea (*Forbes*, May 7, 1984, p. 23).
8. According to Roy Culpeper's investigation, annualized investible total returns (percent returns measured in US$) during the period of 1988–1992 was 115.1 in Argentina, 90.6 in Venezuela, 60.5 in Brazil, and 55.2 in Mexico, 15.6 in the United States, and −2.2 in EAFE (Europe, Australia, and Far East's developing countries) (Culpeper 1995:17).

REFERENCES

Back, J.G. (1990). *Politics of Late Industrialization: The Origins and Processes of Automobile Industry Policies in Mexico and South Korea*. Ph.D. dissertation, UCLA.

Back, J.G. (1990). Two roads toward export-led industrialization: a comparative analysis of government policies and corporate strategies in South Korea and Mexico. *Social Science and Public Policy 12*, 105–135.

Back, J.G. (1994). Mexico as a neoliberal forerunner (in Korean). *Quarterly Sasang (Fall)*, 49–78.

Back, J.G. (1992). The change of political regime and econonomic crises in Mexico (in Korean). *Korean Journal of International Relations 32*, 61–84.

Blanco Mendoza, H. (1994). *Las Negociaciones Comerciales de México con el Mundo*. México, D.F.: Fondo de Cultura Econ mica.

Calvo, G.A., and Mendoza, E.G. (1996). Mexico balance-of-payment crisis—a chronicle of a death foretold. *Journal of International Economics 41*, 235–264.

Cameron, M.A., and Aggarwal, V.K. (1996). Mexican meltdown: states, markets, and post-NAFTA financial turmoil. *Third World Quarterly 17*, 975–987.

Culpeper, R. (1995). Resurgence of private flows to Latin America: the role of North American investors. In *Coping with Capital Surges* edited by Ricardo French-Davis and Stephany Griffith-Jones. Boulder: Lynne Rienner Publishers, 1–40.

Demetriades, P.O., and Hussein, K.A. (1996). "Does financial development cause economic growth? Time-series evidence from 16 countries. *Journal of Development Economics 51*, 387–411.

Economist Intelligence Unit. *Country Report: Mexico*. 1st Quarter 1994, United Kingdom.

Edwards, S. (1996). Why are Latin America's savings rates so low? An international comparative analysis. *Journal of Developing Economics 51*, 5–44.

Frieden, J.A. (1987). *Banking on the World: The Politics of American International Finance*. New York: Harper & Row.

Frieden, J.A. (1991). *Debt, Development & Democracy: Modern Political Economy and Latin America, 1965–1985*. Princeton: Princeton University Press.

Fuentes, C. et al (1996). *México 2000: Los Compromisos con la Nación*. México: Plaza & Janís.

Girón, A., Ortiz, E., and Correa, E. (1995). *Inegración Financiera y TLC: Retos y Perspectivas*. México, D.F.: Siglo Veintituno Editores.

Green, D. (1996). Latin America: neoliberal failure and the search for alternatives. *Third World Quarterly 17*, 109–122.

Gurría, J.A. (1995). Capital flows: the Mexican case. In R. Ffrench-Davis and S. Griffith-Jones (eds.), *Coping with Capital Surges: The Return of Finance to Latin America*, 189–224. Boulder: Lynne Rienner Publishers.

Haggard, S. and Maxfield, S. (1996). The political economy of financial internationalization in the developing world. *International Organization 50*, 35–68.

Kang, C.S.E. (1997). U.S. politics and greater regulation of inward foreign direct investment. *International Organization 51*, 301–333.

Marshall, D.D. (1996). National development and the globalization discourse: confronting ''imperative'' and ''convergence'' notions. *Third World Quarterly 17*, 875–901.

Middlebrook, K.J. (1991). The ties that bind: ''silent integration'' and conflict regulation in U.S.-Mexican relations. *Latin American Research Review 26*, 262–287.

Mishkin, F.S. (1996). Understanding financial crises: a developing country perspective. *Annual World Bank Conference on Development Economics*, 29–77.

Morales, I. (1997). The Mexican crisis and the weakness of the NAFTA consensus. *Annals of the American Academy of Political and Social Science 550*, 130–172.

Oks, D. and van Wijnbergen, S. (1995). Mexico after the debt crisis: is growth sustainable? *Journal of Development Economics 47*, 155–178.

Pastor, M. and Wise, C. (1994). The origins and sustainability of Mexico's free trade policy. *International Organization 48*, 459–489.

Purcell, S.K. (1997). The changing nature of US-Mexican relations. *Journal of Interamerican Studies and World Affairs 39*, 137–152.

Ramírez, M.D. (1996). The latest IMF-sponsored stabilization program: does it represent a long-term solution for Mexico's economy? *Journal of International Studies and World Affairs 38*, 129–156.

Roett, R. (ed.). (1996). *The Mexican Peso Crisis: International Perspectives*. Boulder: Lynne Rienner Publishers.

Rogowski, R. (1989). *Commerce and Coalitions: How Trade Affects Domestic Political Alignments*. Princeton: Princeton University Press.

Vásquez, I. (1997). The IMF through a Mexican lens. *Orbis 41*, 259–276.

Vernon, R. (1965). *The Dilemma of Mexico's Development*. Cambridge: Harvard University Press.

23

Elections and Democratization in Mexico

Tax Policy in the "Opposition" Congress[1]

Kenneth C. Shadlen
Brown University, Providence, Rhode Island

I. INTRODUCTION

This chapter examines the effects of increased partisan competition on economic policy making in contemporary Mexico. National midterm elections of July 1997 produced important changes in that country's political landscape, as the ruling Institutional Revolutionary Party (PRI), which has dominated virtually all realms of Mexican politics since the late 1920s, lost its majority in one house of the Mexican Congress.

Many observers, in Mexico and the United States, quickly reported the 1997 elections as a watershed event—as the definitive moment in the country's transition from authoritarianism to democracy. In contrast, this chapter presents a nuanced interpretation of the effects of the elections and the state of democratization in contemporary Mexico. I suggest that we regard these most recent events as additional steps in a drawn-out, incremental transition. Much is new in Mexican politics, but the essence of a drawn-out, incremental transition to democracy is that many features of the old regime endure. To be sure, the 1997 elections deepened the process of democratization, increasing both the President's accountability to the Congress and the opportunities for opposition political parties to extract concessions and further their legislative agendas. Yet I caution against overstating the impact of the 1997 election results, especially regarding the direction of economic policy and the power of the Presidency and PRI.

The first part of the chapter situates the 1997 elections in the context of the longer process of political change and democratization in Mexico. I argue that Mexico is best understood as a case of a negotiated democratic transition, but one that is fundamentally complicated by the civilian nature of the regime and the prominent role of electoral politics before and during the transition. The second part offers a careful examination of the immediate impact of the elections on contemporary Mexican policy making. It does so by focusing on a conflict between the new, opposition Congress and the President over tax policy in the making of the 1998 national budget.

II. MEXICAN TRANSITION IN COMPARATIVE PERSPECTIVE

Mexico should be regarded as a special instance of a negotiated transition from authoritarian rule to democracy.[2] Many Latin American countries that currently have democratic governments were under the rule of authoritarian regimes in the 1960s to 1980s. In most countries, transitions from authoritarianism to democracy featured some form of negotiation between outgoing military officials and leaders of civilian-controlled movements and political parties. An important hallmark of such transitions was that the generals, as they prepared to return to the barracks, would typically enter into formal or informal agreements regarding some of the basic contours of postauthoritarian rule. The distinguishing characteristic in Mexico, however, is that we are witnessing a transition from a *civilian*-authoritarian regime. That is, the authoritarian incumbents are not military officials, but civilian politicians with distinct patterns of political recruitment and career mobility.

The civilian nature of Mexico's authoritarian regime complicates the dynamics of transition by making incumbents more wary about relinquishing formal political power.[3] This is so for a pair of reasons. First, quite simply, civilian authoritarians have nowhere to go. Military leaders, upon leaving office, have jobs and pensions to fall back on. Civilian leaders lack these institutional bases of support.[4] Put another way, since military authoritarians have dual incumbencies, they can leave one office (government) while retaining the other (military); civilian authoritarians, in contrast, have only one incumbency, and consequently they are more reluctant to relinquish governmental power. The second reason why civilian authoritarians are generally more reluctant to leave power is that they lack the means to protect themselves once out of government. In Latin America, most outgoing military leaders negotiated or imposed limits on future civilian leaders' ability to hold them accountable for human rights abuses.[5] The bottom line for military ex-authoritarians is that if new civilian leaders in a democratic government abrogate, or threaten to abrogate, the agreements negotiated during the transition, military leaders have the resources to fight back and protect themselves, both individually and institutionally.[6] Put quite simply, even out of formal political power, ex-authoritarian military leaders still possess guns, tanks, and other coercive instruments. Civilian ex-authoritarians, in contrast, are presumably subject to prosecution, like other citizens.

One might ask just what sort of prosecution Mexico's authoritarians fear. Though physical violence has been an important instrument of social control in the Mexican regime, Mexicans have for the most part not been subject to the sorts of human rights abuses as were citizens in the military-authoritarian regimes.[7] But the PRI has abused its authority in other ways over the course of seven decades of rule, giving political incumbents ample reasons to fear civilian prosecution. One area is of corruption (a common quip in Mexico is that "a poor politician is a poor politician"). Corruption played a key role in sustaining the civilian-authoritarian regime, greasing the gears of the political machine—it allowed leaders to reward loyal behavior, and it served as an effective tool to keep potential dissidents in line. Investigations of and prosecution for extensive corruption committed by the PRI throughout its long tenure, then, become analogous to the issue of human rights.[8] Because the PRI cannot negotiate or impose a corruption amnesty, key figures in the party dread the prospect of losing power.

Civilian authoritarians' fear of life in a Mexico not dominated by the PRI has produced an incremental and extraordinarily drawn-out transition. Whereas military leaders throughout Latin America negotiated the terms of their *exit* from formal political power, Mexico's civilian leaders have been attempting to negotiate their *preservation*. This is not simply a desire to negotiate a future political system that preserves a role for them. Rather, fear of being a minority force in a post-PRI democratic regime motivates them to retain dominance.

This comparative optic sheds light on the PRI's political strategies of the past two decades. As the global wave of democratization has swept through Latin America, Mexico's incumbent rulers have attempted to engineer a transition from a PRI-dominated authoritarian regime to a PRI-dominated "democracy." Take, for example, the realm of electoral reforms, where the strategy is most evident. The PRI has insistently worked to control the pace and depth of modifications to the state-controlled electoral system. Historically, the civilian authoritarian regime sustained itself through regular elections. The elections, of course, were hardly fair: the PRI had unlimited and unrivaled access to state resources, opposition parties faced substantial obstacles to both formation and mobilization, and the government could use fraud to assure the results it wanted.[9] Yet because elections played a central role in the Mexican political system, electoral rules have been a focal point of political conflict in recent years.

Two reinforcing dynamics have driven the initiative for electoral reform. First, reform has been engineered from above, by the PRI. This has been a response to citizens' demand for more voice and representation, most typically in the wake of political or economic crises. Thus, since the 1960s, PRI and state officials have introduced piecemeal electoral reforms that have made it easier for opposition parties to register and that have increased opposition representation in Congress.[10] Second, reform comes from below, spearheaded by opposition political parties. Once the opposition gains some power, it then has the resources to push for more reforms. Of course, since the opposition's power remained limited, reforms were not possible without PRI participation. Thus, the process of reform remained both incremental and controlled, from above, by the PRI.

The prominence of electoral institutions and the recurrence of electoral reforms were double-edged for the PRI. On the one hand, elections gave the civilian-authoritarian regime a formal, democratic veneer, it channeled dissent through electoral institutions, and it prompted the PRI to develop a mechanism for nonviolent political succession. On the other hand, the PRI could, conceivably, one day, lose an election. That is, the same institutions that lent stability to the regime could be used against it: democratization need not be preceded by revolution. Furthermore, even though electoral reforms were incremental, the reform process always risked snowballing out of the PRI's control: electoral reform might give the opposition increased power, which would lead to more reforms, which, in turn, would produce greater opposition power, and so on. This risk has made the retention of control over the transition even more of an imperative for the PRI.

The combination of benefits and risks derived from the prominence of electoral institutions drove PRI strategy through the first half of the 1990s, as government leaders cautiously acceded to the opposition's demands for electoral reform while striving to avoid losing control of the process. However, a series of events in recent years caused the process of electoral reform to snowball out of the PRI's control.

III. CRISIS, REFORM, AND THE 1997 ELECTIONS

The December 1994 devaluation of the peso and ensuing economic crisis of 1995-96 precipitated a massive outburst of popular opposition.[11] Inflation, diminished expectations, and a general decline in living standards, along with a deepening of corruption scandals involving high government officials (including the family of former President Carlos Salinas de Gortari), provided the fodder for electoral setbacks in many state and local elections through 1995 and 1996. In the two years after the devaluation, the PRI lost state and local elections in three states (Baja California North, Guanajuato, and Jalisco) to the center-right National Action Party, PAN,[12] and it lost important municipal elections in the State of Mexico to the center-left Party of the Democratic Revolution, PRD (e.g., ''Ciudad Neza,'' a large city on the eastern outskirts of Mexico City).

The crisis also increased pressures on the administration of President Ernesto Zedillo to enter into negotiations for additional electoral reforms. The PRI retained the upper hand, but this time was negotiating from the weakest position yet, and consequently was forced to cede more ground to the opposition. Among other things, the electoral reform of November 1996, finalized after more than a year of negotiations, included limited campaign finance reform, improved opposition access to the media, and popular election for the Mayor of Mexico City. Most importantly, the reform bolstered the autonomy of the Federal Electoral Institute (IFE) to enforce the new laws and oversee a clean electoral process. One observer, citing the new IFE's importance and autonomy, has referred to it as ''essentially a fourth branch of power.''[13] Incremental electoral reforms, eroding government legitimacy, and deep economic crisis, then, provided the setting for the critical mid-term elections of July 1997. In addition to the mayor of Mexico City and governors in a number of states, the elections would produce a new 500-seat Chamber of Deputies.

In arguably the cleanest elections in Mexican history, both in terms of the playing field and the actual counting of the votes, the PRI suffered a major setback.[14] Though the PRI retained a plurality in the 500-seat Chamber of Deputies, its 239 seats fell short of a majority.[15] PRD leader Cuauhtémoc Cárdenas won the race for Mayor of Mexico City, and his party obtained a strong majority in the capital's local assembly. Outside of Mexico City, the PAN obtained its fifth and sixth governorships, winning the states of Nuevo León and Querétaro.

Thus, it appeared that the incremental process of electoral reform had indeed snowballed. Reform, plus ongoing civic mobilization in response to the economic crisis, government management of the crisis, and corruption, came together to produce the PRI's most significant defeat ever. The following section considers the effect of the 1997 elections on policy making by presenting a case study of the new legislature's attempt to impose its fiscal priorities over those of the executive in the making of the 1998 national budget.

IV. FISCAL POLITICS IN THE "OPPOSITION" CONGRESS

Historically, the Congress has not merited the attention of analysts of Mexican politics, as it was dominated by large majorities of PRI deputies who remained subservient to the President. Rarely did legislation emanate from within the congress: those initiatives presented by opposition parties tended to be frozen in committee, and PRI representatives, entirely subordinate to the President, infrequently proposed initiatives of their own. Virtually all legislation that passed out of congress was introduced by the President, and the President's initiatives tended to be approved unaltered.[16] In short, Congress served to rubber-stamp the President's initiatives. A quick review of recent legislation suggests that the President's domination over Congress had continued into the 1990s. Arguably the most significant changes in economic policy, such as the revision to Article 27 that officially terminated Mexico's land reform, the new law on foreign investment, and the North American Free Trade Agreement (NAFTA), were simply presented to the PRI-dominated legislature and passed quickly and overwhelmingly.

Historically, budgetary politics also conformed to this pattern of presidential dominance and legislative passivity. Although Mexico's constitution affords Congress the authority to ''review and approve'' federal budgets, the budgetary process was typically a last-minute and uncontested affair: days before the deadline for Congress to pass a budget, the President would submit a budget to his loyal Congress, which would pass it with minimal scrutiny, analysis, or discussion.[17]

The opposition's victories in the 1997 elections were quickly billed as an event that would mark the end of PRI domination and *presidencialismo*. In particular, the 1998 federal budget, which needed to be passed by the end of the legislative session in December 1997, would quickly move to center stage and become the most important piece of economic policy to be contested, democratically, in Mexican history. The new political landscape produced by the July 1997 elections promised to transform budgetary politics from a sleepy and uncontested affair into an arena of intense conflict—a crucible for the new world of executive-legislative relations in democratic Mexico. As Porfirio Muñoz Ledo, leader of the PRD's congressional delegation in Congress (and former party president) proclaimed, ''We are entering a new era in which the executive is not going to impose laws on us.''[18]

In an unprecedented act of boldness and initiative, Congress presented its own budget; and the opposition's fiscal goals differed in important regards from what the President was proposing. The key point of conflict was the value-added tax (IVA). In March 1995, as part of an economic stabilization package that followed the peso devaluation, the Zedillo administration raised IVA from 10% to 15%. Two and one-half years later, with the economy appearing to have rebounded from the depth of the crisis, both the PAN and the PRD insisted on lowering IVA. Both sides assailed the regressive nature of the value-added tax, and both argued that it unfairly placed the burden of economic adjustment on the poor.

Despite the appearance of opposition consensus and the general popularity of lowering the tax, the President was adamant that IVA should be kept at 15%. The Zedillo administration presented various arguments against lowering the sales tax. Most directly, the government argued that improved economic growth and consumption in 1997 demonstrated that a fiscal stimulus was not necessary.

At the same time as he presented the budget to Congress in November, for example, Treasury Secretary Guillermo Ortíz announced projected GDP figures for the final quarter of the year that would make growth in 1997 the largest since before the debt crisis of 1982.[19] Furthermore, the Zedillo Administration calculated that a reduction in IVA would undermine Mexico's fiscal balance and spark inflation, which, in turn, would jeopardize the country's ability to attract foreign capital. Quite simply, the President's team asserted that Mexico's dependence on short-term capital inflows made fiscal balance imperative.[20] This concern was voiced by the President, cabinet officials, and leaders of the PRI in Congress, all of whom admonished the opposition for their cavalier approach toward taxation. As one PRI leader charged, ''Don't blame the PRI and the government if the financial markets strike us in the worst of ways.''[21] Finally, the Zedillo Administration opposed lowering IVA for fears that doing so would further increase Mexico's dependence on oil exports. Approximately 40% of the government's revenues come from oil revenues, and a reduction in another important source such as IVA would increase Mexico's vulnerability to changes in global oil markets.[22]

The opposition rejected virtually all of these arguments and forced President Zedillo and Treasury Secretary Ortíz to embark on an extensive public relations campaign to defend their proposed budget. Ortíz himself was compelled to appear on multiple occasions in front of Congressional hearings. For example, he presented the budget on November 11, and then returned to the Chamber of Deputies for three days of hearings the following week. These hearings produced extensive, and often heated, debate, in which the opposition publicly assailed the President's budget and put the Secretary on the defensive. In fact, after his first appearance, Secretary Ortíz was ushered out of the chamber by PAN and PRD cat-calls that the President's budget would not pass.[23]

Though the PRD and PAN differed on some of the details of their own proposals, as we will see in more detail below, in October and November of 1997 they both insisted on lowering IVA, and they dismissed virtually each point made by the Zedillo Administration. They argued that Mexico's purported economic recovery was not reaching most of the population—that the aggregate growth figures presented by the government masked growing inequality and social deficits. Not surprisingly, such criticism was voiced regularly by the center-left PRD, throughout the 1997 electoral campaign and during the legislative session. Yet it was not just the PRD, but also the center-right, conservative PAN, which emphasized concerns with social justice and inequality in criticizing the President's budget. According to the PAN's coordinator for economic affairs in the Congress, ''We intend to make deep corrections in this budget. We intend to confront the enormous deterioration in Mexicans' quality of life, and the vast breach between the haves and the have-nots.''[24] The opposition also refuted the administration's claims that lowering IVA would necessarily increase the budget deficit and indicted the government of hyperbolic fear-mongering with the constant warnings that a reduction in IVA would necessarily wreak havoc on Mexico's standing in international capital markets.[25] From the PRD's perspective, the revenues lost by reducing IVA could be offset with increases in personal income and capital gains taxes. From the PAN's perspective, reduced tax revenues could be offset with reductions in government spending and streamlining of the state bureaucracy.

Thus, as of late November, the two sides appeared headed for a deadlock. The administration was forceful in presenting and tenacious in defending its conservative budget and assured the renegade Congress that no budget would be signed into law that included a tax cut, while the opposition remained intransigent in its insistence upon lowering IVA. After days of hearings with Secretary Ortíz, for example, the PAN's Sada Zambrano asserted, "We cannot approve the economic package on the terms with which it was presented."[26] Likewise, the PRD's Muñoz Ledo continued to insist that the July 1997 elections gave Congress a mandate to continued to defer to the elections as a mandate for altering the government's taxing and spending priorities: "There is a mandate. There is a social majority, an electoral majority, and a parliamentary majority that wants a reduction of IVA."[27] A collision appeared to be in the making between two determined forces. The emboldened, ambitious, and evidently united opposition Congress was taking on the historically indomitable Mexican Presidency. The people were challenging the crown.

V. THE PRESIDENT VS. THE CONGRESS

President Zedillo prevailed. In December 1997, the PAN joined the PRI in Congress to pass a slightly modified version of the President's budget, retaining IVA at 15%. The President won with a three-pronged strategy of (1) relying upon the unwavering support of the still-subordinate Senate to convince the opposition of the futility of seeking to reduce the tax; (2) weakening the opposition parties' resolve by frightening them with the potential consequences of passing a budget that lowered IVA; and (3) dividing the opposition by exploiting the distinct political and economic projects upon which the façade of unity was balanced. Each dimension of this strategy sheds light on interesting and important complexities of Mexico's democratization process.

First, the President made it clear that the Senate would not lower the value-added tax. Historically, of course, PRI dominance was not limited to the Chamber of Deputies. The Senate was equally subservient; it too acted as a mere rubber stamp of the President's initiatives. Importantly, the 1997 elections did not eliminate the PRI's dominance within the upper house. Of the Senate's 128 seats, only 32 were disputed in the 1997 elections, distributed by proportional representation in a single national constituency.[28] Thus, the 1997 electoral setback did not remove the PRI's firm control over the upper house, as it retained a majority of 59%. Notwithstanding proclamations of independence on the part of some PRI Senators in the so-called Galileo Group, President Zedillo was assured of support: no reduction in IVA would pass through the Senate so long as the President opposed it. All of this underscores an obvious, but easily overlooked, point about democratization in Mexico: if Mexico is becoming more democratic, and if the Mexican Congress is becoming more important, than *all* of Congress is important—both houses. Any expectation of dramatic change that does not take into account the power and constitution of the Senate is misleading.

The second strategy deployed by the President was to frighten the opposition with the potential costs of intransigence. This conflict had little precedent in Mexican politics. It was not at all clear what would happen were no budget to be passed by the December deadline. The absence of continuing resolutions, in particular, and the unclear constitutional provisions to deal with such a legislative stalemate, in general, created a great deal of uncertainty regarding the effects of failing to pass a budget.[29] President Zedillo's adamant opposition to lowering IVA converted this uncertainty into an asset. Metaphorically, the situation can be aptly described as a game of "chicken," in which the worst outcome for both actors would be produced by a mutual failure to cooperate.[30] For both sides, no budget was even worse than the other's budget; the paralysis and uncertainty produced by deadlock and the inability to pass a budget would have more damaging effects on Mexico's economic recovery than would the budgets proposed by either the President or the opposition. Both sides feared the economic and political consequences of deadlock and stalemate, and both sides sought to avoid such an eventuality by pressuring the other into conceding. In this "game," however, the President used his first-mover advantage, and the firm support of the Senate, to weaken the opposition's resolve. Though the two sides were equally intransigent, the Zedillo administration made it appear that blame for deadlock and crisis should be attributed to the "irresponsible" challenge to presidential authority on the part of opposition deputies. Deadlock would weaken Mexico's position in international capital markets, which in turn would produce a profound economic crisis, the President argued; and culpability would lie with *them* (the opposition) and not *us* (the government and PRI) if the failure to pass a budget with IVA at 15% produced financial instability.

This strategy was not unprecedented for the PRI. A key element of the PRI's 1994 electoral campaign, which followed the outbreak of fighting in Chiapas, was that opposition gains would produce a situation of ungovernability and crisis. Once again, in 1997 the PRI equated the opposition's increased parliamentary power to risky, impulsive legislative behavior that could have potentially disastrous consequences for the Mexican economy. Though in reality the President and the PRI were no less adamant than the opposition and therefore no less responsible for the impending legislative deadlock, the strategy was clearly to make it appear that ungovernability and crisis would be the opposition's fault. And with the backing of loyal supporters in both houses of Congress and the bully pulpit of the Presidency, Zedillo had the ability to frame the debate in this way.

The third dimension of the government's strategy was to exploit the differences between the PRD and the PAN, and thus divide the opposition. In retrospect, this was not such a difficult task, for the PRD and PAN, notwithstanding a facade of unity, entered into the budget and IVA debates with distinct economic and political projects. As a result, the PAN was easily induced into defecting from the opposition coalition.

For the PRD, the budget debate was about much more than taxing and spending. Since the PRD was formed in 1989, it has been Mexico's most consistent critic of the neoliberal economic model; and while the party's economic message has become more mainstream in recent years, it remains highly critical of many aspects of the neoliberal model (e.g., NAFTA). With regard to the budget, lowering IVA was a way to expand mass purchasing power, and thus constituted one component of a larger neo-Keynesian economic strategy that would place greater emphasis on the domestic market.[31] Thus, the conflict over IVA was really just the first step in altering a model of economic development that the party's leadership regards as exclusionary and regressive, and the PRD sought to interpret the PRI's 1997 electoral defeat as a referendum on neoliberalism. In the words of the PRD's Muñoz Ledo, "On July 6 the people of Mexico won. What did we win? We won the possibility to change profoundly unjust economic policies."[32]

For the PAN, on the other hand, the budget debate was never about neoliberal policy, which the party generally supports. The party's leadership never regarded the budget conflict as a conflict over neoliberalism and fiscal conservatism. As early as October the *panista* leadership made it clear that the PAN would not necessarily act in concert with the PRD on economic policy issues,[33] and in December, when criticized by the PRD for abandoning the opposition coalition, the PAN responded that its leadership never regarded the July 1997 elections as providing a mandate to challenge neoliberalism.[34] From the *panista* perspective, lowering IVA could not, and should not, be part of a larger strategy to reverse the deep economic reforms of the 1980s and 1990s. Thus, the PAN was easily swayed by the President's insistent suggestions that lowering IVA would undermine the entire process of economic reform.[35]

To be sure, PAN leaders relished the opportunity to gain votes on a generally popular issue, and the party had good reason to try to distance itself from a model of development that public opinion data showed to be in increasing disrepute after the 1994 peso devaluation. And though PAN leaders supported the general thrust of the neoliberal economic model, they assailed the elitist and regressive characteristics of how it had been implemented under Presidents

Salinas and Zedillo. Lowering IVA, then, in response to popular discontent, made sense in this regard. Yet the PAN's insistence on lowering IVA ought to be interpreted as a challenge to fiscal priorities within the neoliberal parameters.

Within the neoliberal parameters, the PAN sought to use the IVA issue to extract political and economic concessions. Most of all, the conflict presented the PAN with an opportunity to portray the Zedillo Administration, and the PRI more generally, as captured by an inflexible, technocratic elite that failed to appreciate the human costs of economic austerity and the post-1994 economic crisis. For a party that advocated an economic platform that was quite similar to the President's, but that went to great lengths to highlight the supposed distinctiveness of its envisioned ''social market economy,'' this was an invaluable political opportunity. Thus, the PAN took advantage of its new legislative powers to drive home this distinction by being sure to go on record in support of lowering the tax. For example, the congressional committee responsible for the budget, chaired by the PAN, went so far as to separate IVA from the rest of the budget to allow for a purely symbolic vote on the tax that would isolate the President. On two occasions, the PAN and PRD approved reductions in the IVA in the Chamber of Deputies, apart from other budgetary matters, knowingly sending the bill to certain defeat in the Senate. On the eve of the first of these votes, the leader of the PAN's parliamentary delegation declared, ''We do not, by any stretch of the imagination, believe that the Senate will approve [a reduction in the tax], but at least we are making it clear to the public that we fought for it.''[36]

The budget debate also offered the PAN the chance to advance its agenda with regard to federalism. In particular, the PAN was using IVA as a lever to extract more transfers from the national government to states and municipalities, the areas of government where the PAN has made the most significant gains in the 1980s and 1990s. Indeed, by initiating the legislative session with a hardline approach and bringing the President to the bargaining table, the PAN was able to extract more concessions than has typically been the case for opposition parties in the Mexican legislature.

VI. EVALUATION

The conflict over the 1998 budget can be interpreted in various ways. In some ways, the episode appears to fit the classic adage, ''the more things change, the more things stay the same.'' Historic 1997 election results notwithstanding, the President and PRI got their way. The 1997 budget conflict, then, ought to qualify enthusiasm over the ''opposition'' Congress: not all of Congress has opposition majority, and divisions between PRD and PAN mean that on many issues, opposition majority will not be equivalent to opposition control. On this second point, it is important to underscore that even within the Chamber of Deputies, the PRI remains the largest party: it is only the minority party to the extent that the opposition can stay united.

Notwithstanding the sobering implications of such continuities, the budget conflict can also be interpreted in another way that highlights some subtle, yet important, changes in executive-legislature relations. The President's budget underwent unprecedented public scrutiny. As indicated, the Treasury Secretary was subjected to days of intense questioning by a legislative body that shared little of its predecessors' passivity and docility. In addition, the budget brought about a degree of executive-legislature negotiations that is rare for economic policy issues in Mexico. Though the President's political strategy was served by presenting the 15% IVA as a *fait accompli*, the PAN's strategy was also served by positioning itself as the power broker in Congress and thus engaging the President in extensive negotiations over other aspects of the budget. Once the PAN indicated its willingness to come to the President's side in early December, intense negotiations ensued between this party and the executive. The PAN's gains should not be overstated, but the budget that passed did contain some modifications of the President's original budget. These include, for example, an improved mechanism for transfers from the national government to states and municipalities, increased transparency in public spending, cutbacks in the state bureaucracy, and reductions in the President's unchecked, discretionary budget. These changes, subtle as they are, do represent important indicators of an increased accountability of the President to the popularly elected Congress. Thus, Mexico does appear to be fulfilling Klesner's expectation that the new political landscape and the ensuing balance of power between branches of government would force the President and his cabinet to develop bargaining skills and strategies that are part of democratic rule.[37]

Other effects of the 1997 elections also point in the direction of incremental changes that, though less dramatic than what many expected, remain quite important. The areas where the recent electoral results are the most significant are those issues that are both within the jurisdiction of the lower house, and those upon which the PAN and PRD are in agreement. Though few issues satisfy both criteria, two are worth noting. First, exposing the PRI's corrupt practices is one of the few items where the PAN and PRD find themselves in agreement, and the opposition can use congressional committees to open official hearings, something that PRI-controlled committees had blocked in the past. Having lost its majority in Congress, PRI deputies lose the ability to close corruption investigations.[38] Thus, the Congress reopened hearings on misuse of funds related to a government-run food distribution agency (Conasupo).[39] Second, and most critically, the opposition's majority gives Congress the tools to prevent the PRI from rolling back political reforms. The ability of the snowball to keep growing, to return to a metaphor used earlier in this chapter, remains limited, as any electoral reforms continue to require PRI support (in the Senate). Yet the opposition majority should serve as a bulwark to withstand any PRI efforts to undermine IFE's autonomy, for example, and to reverse the 1996 electoral reforms. In July 1998, for example, opposition representatives offered a quick and hostile reaction to the PRI's proposal to reduce the Chamber of Deputies from 500 to 300 seats by eliminating the 200 seats allocated by proportional representation.[40]

VII. CONCLUSION

A transition from authoritarianism to democracy does not necessarily bring a marked break with the past. The nature of negotiated transitions is that a good deal of the underlying political and social orders remains in place under the new democratic regime.[41] This tendency is particularly true in the case of Mexico, where the transition has been so protracted, incremental, and drawn out.

This chapter's focus on the opposition Congress' attempt to lower the national value-added tax over the objection of the President brings to light this uneasy combination of continuity in the midst of change. Many observers expected the opposition Congress to defeat the PRI and slay the beast of *presidencialismo*, once and for all. Yet analysis of the first major confrontation between the President and the opposition Congress demonstrated the salience of some important continuities: the PRI's control over the Senate, the bargaining superiority of the President, and, most importantly, programmatic divisions between the two leading opposition parties. In sum, then, while the 1997 elections represent an important moment in Mexico's incremental transition from a civilian-authoritarian regime to a democracy, the difference between political and economic life before and after July 1997 is not black and white.

ENDNOTES

1. Portions of this chapter appeared in ''Continuity Amid Change: Democratization, Party Strategies and Economic Policymaking in Mexico,'' *Government and Opposition*, Vol. 34, No. 3 (Summer 1999).
2. On transitions from authoritarianism to democracy, see G. O'Donnell and P. Schmitter, *Transitions from Authoritarian Rule: Tentative Conclusions About Uncertain Democracies*, Baltimore, Johns Hopkins University Press, 1986; A. Przeworski, *Democracy and the Market: Political and Economic Reforms in Eastern Europe and Latin America*, New York, Cambridge University Press, 1991. For an early group of case studies of the Latin American countries, see the essays in *Transitions from Authoritarian Rule: Latin America*, G. O'Donnell, P. Schmitter, and I. Whitehead (eds.), Baltimore, Johns Hopkins University Press, 1986.
3. The perspective emphasizing the complexities and difficulties of transition from ci-

vilian-authoritarianism should be contrasted with that presented in the early work on this topic by Guillermo O'Donnell. O'Donnell suggested that democratization might be more problematic in military-authoritarian regimes, principally because of the destruction of civilian institutions, the militarization of society, and the bundle of difficult, postmilitary rule issues that come to the fore in the wake of their departure. See ''Introduction to the Latin American Cases,'' in *Transitions from Authoritarian Rule: Latin America*, pp. 10–11.

4. This characteristic is accentuated in the Mexican case, where circulation among political elites and economic elites tended to be minimal. See P. Smith, *Labyrinths of Power: Political Recruitment in Twentieth-Century Mexico*,Princeton, Princeton University Press, 1979.
5. The terms of these agreements usually remain cloudy. Brazil and Peru appear to be examples of negotiated immunities. In Chile the amnesty seems to have been imposed.
6. Witness, for example, the recurrent mobilizations of the Chilean military in the 1990s, when civilian governments threatened to reopen investigations into human rights abuses.
7. For an excellent analysis that places state violence in the context of the broader array of the Mexican state's instruments of social control, see J. Adler Hellman, ''Social Control in Mexico,'' *Comparative Politics 12*(2), 1980.
8. This point was emphasized by Adolfo Aguilar Zinzer at a talk at the University of California, Berkeley, in October 1996. See also, J. Bailey and A. Valenzuela, ''The Shape of the Future,''*Journal of Democracy, 8*(4) 1997, pp. 52–53.
9. See, among others, Pablo González Casanova, *Democracy in Mexico*, New York, Oxford University Press, 1970; J. Molinar Horcasitas, *El Tiempo de la Legitimidad*, México, D.F., Cal y Arena, 1991.
10. For more on reformism and adaptation, see S. Morris, *Political Reformism in Mexico: An Overview of Contemporary Mexican Politics*, Boulder, Lynne Rienner Publishers, chapters 3, 4, and 8.
11. The economic crisis, of course, was preceded by the outbreak of conflict between the government and the *zapatistas* in the southern state of Chiapas. Though the Chiapas conflict has remained localized, many of the issues promoted by the rebels resonated throughout Mexican society, further eroding the legitimacy of the PRI government.
12. In two of these states, Baja California and Guanajuato, the incumbent governors were from the PAN, suggesting that voters were not rejecting incumbents in general, but specifically punishing the PRI.
13. C. Lawson, ''Mexico's New Politics: The Elections of 1997,'' *Journal of Democracy, 8* (4) 1997, p. 15.
14. A good comparison can be made with the national elections of August 1994, where the vote count was generally accepted as fair, but where the playing field remained quite uneven. See W. Cornelius, ''Un balance norteamericano del proceso electoral mexicano de 1994,'' *Nexos* (Mexico City), *202*,1994, pp. 13–17. For concise overviews of the 1997 electoral results, see C. Lawson, ''The Elections of 1997,'' and J. Klesner, Democratic Transition? The 1997 Mexican Elections,'' *PS: Political Science & Politics, 30* (4), 1997.

15. Following the electoral formula included in the 1996 reforms, 300 seats were chosen by plurality votes in single-member districts (SMD), and 200 seats were allocated according to proportional representation (PR). The final vote count gave PRI 165 SMD seats and 74 PR seats, for a total of 239. The PRD won 70 SMD seats and 55 PR seats, for a total of 125. The PAN won 64 SMD seats and 57 PR seats, for a total of 121. Of the remaining 15 seats, the Mexican Green Party (PVEM) won 8, and the Workers' Part (PT) won 7.
16. González Casanova, *Democracy in Mexico*. See also S.K. Purcell, *The Mexican Profit-Sharing Decision: Politics in an Authoritarian Regime*, Berkeley, University of California Press, 1975, pp. 32–33.
17. Bailey and Valenzuela, pp. 51–52.
18. *New York Times*, 10 November 1997. The budget, though the most important area, was not the only instance of executive-legislature conflict. For example, one of the first things that the opposition's self-named Group of 4 (G4, for the four parties that controlled 261 of 500 seats) did was to deny President Zedillo permission to leave the country.
19. GDP growth in 1997 of 7.1% was the highest since 1981.
20. For example, in a speech delivered at the Mexican stock market, the President asserted that ''under current international financial conditions, the margins for prudent and responsible maneuvering are very narrow and at times practically nonexistent.'' ''Zedillo reiterates call for conservative fiscal policy,'' Associated Press, 17 November 1997. Taken from Mex2000 e-mail distribution list.
21. *Excelsior* (Mexico City), 19 November 1997.
22. *SourceMex*, Volume 8, Number 40, 5 November 1997.
23. They shouted, ''It will not pass, it will not pass.''
24. Rogelio Sada Zambrano, quoted in the *New York Times*, 10 November 1997.
25. *Excelsior*, 19 November 1997.
26. *Excelsior*, 19 November 1997.
27. Tim Duffy, ''Chamber Session Highlighted by IVA Debate,'' *The News* (Mexico City), 26 November 1997.
28. These special seats, which were to replace the 32 senators elected for six-year terms in 1991, are for only three years. The 2000 elections will produce an entirely new, 64-seat Senate, in which all members will be elected according to a national PR formula, and which will be renovated in its entirety every six years.
29. Bailey and Valenzuela, p. 52.
30. This can be contrasted with the ''prisoners' dilemma,'' in which each actor's worst outcome comes from making unilateral concessions.
31. Consistent with this approach, another element of the PRD's budget proposal was wage increases for public employees.
32. *Reforma* (Mexico City), 12 November 1997.
33. *Reforma*, 22 October 1997.
34. According to Francisco Paoli Bolio, leader of the PAN's congressional delegation, ''At no moment did the PAN either conceive or accept the election of July 6 as a vote to change economic policy. That is false. . . !'' *La Jornada* (Mexico City), 15 December 1997.
35. In fact, the more the PRD made the budget issue into something larger about neolib-

eral policy, and the more the Zedillo Administration argued that lowering IVA would destroy Mexico's fiscal balance, the PAN became increasingly ripe for defection from the opposition coalition.

36. Francisco Paoli Bolio, Bloomberg Business Wire, 2 December 1997. Taken from Mex2000 e-mail distribution list.
37. See Klesner, ''Democratic Transition?,'' p. 709.
38. Klesner, ''Democratic Transition?,'' p. 704.
39. In a similar light, the Congress embarked on an investigation into the 1968 massacre at Tlatelolco, where hundreds of protesters were gunned down by a special unit of the Mexican police. The Congress even subpoenaed the testimony of ex-President Luís Echeverría (1970–1976), who was Secretary of the Interior at the time.
40. *SourceMex*, July 29, 1998.
41. See, for example, F. Hagopian, ''Democracy by Undemocratic Means: Elites, Political Pacts, and Regime Transition in Brazil,'' *Comparative Political Studies 23* (2), 1990; B. Loveman, ''*Mision Cumplida*?, Civil-Military Relations and the Chilean Political Transition,'' *Journal of Interamerican Studies and World Affairs, 33* (3), 1991.

24

Implementing Argentine State Reform

Union Cooperation or Conflict?

Dora Orlansky
University of Buenos Aires, Buenos Aires, Argentina

I. TO SHRINK THE STATE IS TO ENLARGE THE MARKET

The widespread crisis of the model of an interventionist state and the emergence of a globalized neoliberal economy have led to a reshaping of state, society, and economy relations. The fall of statism goes back to the 1970's and the reversal of the tendency of the treble affluence which spanned four decades and consisted of the simultaneous growth of the GNP, income of families, and public expenditure. The expansion of state intervention had been until then a widespread process; even in the most conservative regimes of capitalist countries the state had turned into the economy regulator, a large-scale industrial producer, as well as an arbiter and conciliator between the concurrent social interests (Cameron 1978; Lindebeck 1985). Different interpretations of political economy based on the theories of fiscal crisis (O'Connor), of state overload (Buchanan and Tullock), and the ungovernability (Offe) submitted, from different angles, the system's impossibility to respond to the rising economic and social demands considered legitimate by the different sectors of society (Orlansky 1991).

According to the *public choice* approach the "political market" is a stimulus in itself. "One peso, one vote," the paraphrase of the liberal dictum "One citizen, one vote," is the key to the expansion of the public resources. In other words, the growth of the public sector[1] is the rational counterpart of the electoral wishes or—in a wider sense—of the social demands aggregation. From another angle, Buchanan stresses the particular interests of politicians and bureaucrats struggling for political and administrative power as the determinant factor to the growth of the public sector.

An alternative point of view is the neomarxist explanation (O'Connor) which holds that what unleashes the expansion of the public sector are requirements essential to the capitalist system. The main reasoning lies in the need of state assistance to capital by providing infrastructure, aid to industries, responsibility in education, health, and, generally, the welfare of the poorer sectors. The "fiscal crisis" of the 1970's, according to O'Connor, was due to capitalist pressures on the state. However, O'Connor's theory sounds today less plausible. The market, based on profitability, has taken charge of several public services whereas the state in the mean time has eliminated welfare programs and shrunk social expenditure (Self 1994).

II. TURNING POINT: FROM STATISM TO STATE REDUCTION

One of the novelties of the democratization process in Latin America is the drastic reformulation of development strategies. The reduction of the state has become a central component of public policies in the region. Argentina seems to be one of the pioneers in the attempt to legislate in this area. Nevertheless, the implementation of policies looking specifically toward the retrenchment of the state has been a very late strategy compared with some other countries in western Europe (United Kingdom, Spain, France) and Latin America (Chile, Mexico, Bolivia); in some of them the process had been initiated as early as the late 1970's, just as the reverse of the "treble affluence" was detected. In the case of Argentina, chronic inflation and external loans were perhaps the blurring factors that prevented an accurate diagnosis.

A consensus about the idea that the public sector should be largely transformed had emerged in Argentina only by the ending of the 1980s. Although the economic base had been eroded by permanent massive budgets deficits, Argentina was unable for many decades to accept any economic discipline. But hyperinflation and instability during the last months of the Alfonsin (Radical Party) Administration—and the critical transition period from the day on which Menem (Peronist Party) was elected—facilitated a political agreement between the two major parties.[2]

To produce the most important changes in the historical role of the state in economics, two laws were enacted without any obstruction: in August 1989, the State Reform Act (23696), and on September 1, the Economic Emergency Act (23697). A "new administrative order"[3] consisting basically in unusual constraints over the public sector was defined from the begining of the Menem Administration. To accomplish these goals, other normative tools were issued by the executive branch: the increasing use of executive orders and mega-executive orders, the so-called *decretos de necesidad y urgencia* known in Argentina as *el decretazo* (Ferreira Rubio and Goretti[4]). Under the newly enacted legislation public programs that ''in any way prevent the market economy from working'' would be eliminated (Mega-Executive Order 2476 of 11/26/1990).

Besides the relentless privatization process of state-owned enterprises, many other impressive changes have been implemented in almost every area of the federal government; this wide and diverse spectrum ranges from regulatory activity to provision of goods and services.

The cutback of the public sector can be considered a political turning point in Argentina: not only has the Menem Administration undertaken a task that had been too difficult for previous governments, but public opinion including business and labor has largely supported it. The government reaction and the favorable public response has been unprecedented.

III. LABOR REORGANIZATION IN THE PUBLIC SECTOR

The National System for the Administrative Profession, known as SINAPA (Executive Order 993/1991), replaced the previous public administration labor law that had been issued by the military regime of 1973 (Decree 1428). Once more by enacting an executive order, the Menem Administration overstepped parliamentary proceedings and avoided congressional scrutiny.

Therefore, from 1991 a new legal framework was in force for personnel of the federal government and the municipal government of the City of Buenos Aires. Labor conditions were redefined: salaries, promotions, positions, levels, categories, etc. As a matter of fact, the conversion from the previous hierarchical listing of 24 categories to the new one of six implied the redefinition of levels, categories, and salaries for all personnel. The results of equivalences were not satisfactory for the greater part of employees. Conflicts began when thousands of complaints were filed on the grounds of violation of constitutional rights because their salaries were lower than in the past. However, the discretionary application of the recategorization policy had the union leaders consent; the influential Menemist civil servants union (UPCN) was informally consulted and its members benefited from the process of reclassification.

Another important source of patronage discretion has been the design and the results of the so-called ''competition for the executive positions'' in public bureacracy. Extensively advertised ''open selection'' concealed the fact that qualification consisted of a ranking where the highest position was filled by three names presented as candidates, among which the political authority made a decision. There has been practically no remotion; a *parti pri* favoring those who had been appointed by same authorities prior to selection. Both ''replacements'' of categories into the new labor framework and ''competitions'' for executive positions have concealed subtle maneuvers of political manipulation; these legal devices improve the former ones like voluntary resignation, compulsive retirement, conditioned dismissal, etc.—implemented between 1989 and 1991 during the first stage of the Menem Administration.

The role of unions has been included ambiguously in the National System for the Administrative Profession (SINAPA). Only the pro-government union of federal civil servants has been allowed to send a delegate ''to see but not to vote'' (an ''inspector'') when decisions about recruitment or promotion are made. Nevertheless, the powerful Menemist union is currently able to accomplish an informal particularistic influence. Conversely, the other major public employees union (ATE) that does not agree with the ''pro-Menem syndicalism'' has been excluded. For the ordinary civil servant the loss of public employment tenure rights has no precedent: under the renewed ''merit system,'' two successive annual evaluations that are not approved cause dismissal without compensation.

Another striking feature of labor policy consists of a strong salaries polarization. Salary dispersion has been magnified even though an increase of around 20% of the whole salary mass was forecast from the new administrative system implementation. Moreover, salary freezing is applied at any cost, except at the highest levels where salaries are permanent and substantially raised.

Since the System for the Administrative Profession (SINAPA) was passed, the insistence to make salary increases depending on a fuzzy concept of productivity imposed budget restraints that did not allow better compensation. The idea of allocating a minimum stake of resources to finance the ''system of positions with executive functions,'' better known as ''critical positions,'' was accepted from the beginning. The purpose is to give better salaries only to those who have greater responsibilities. That is to say, the ''extremely selective increases'' concept prevailed.

The passing of SINAPA means that a general reorganization with a great salary dispersion was carried out under a new listing of categories. In 1993 the ''critical positions with executive functions'' had a salary level of around 4900 Argentine pesos (or U.S. dollars), 20 times the salary of the lowest category (level F = 280 Argentine pesos) and more than twice the salary of the equivalent position in the previous category listing (category 24 = 2400 Argentine pesos). The budgetary incidence of ''critical positions'' does not burden substantially up to now. Appointments as a *fait accompli* began at the end of 1991 when the Treasury went through a critical situation and the possibility of delaying payment of salaries was analyzed.

The selection committee for ''executive-function positions'' includes government authorities and experts. Two other members having the status of inspectors (without formal power to make decisions) are (1) a representative of the

Women's National Council, a federal agency of women's rights), and, as mentioned above, (2) a delegate of the Menemist Federal Union of the Civil Servants (UPCN). Article 38 of the National System of the Administrative Profession (SINAPA) provides for another way of privatization of state reform. Textually it says that ''for the purposes of identifying candidates that shall be timely proposed, the Selection Committee shall ask for the cooperation of firms that are specialized in personnel search and selection.'' Thus, for the first 10 critical positions of the economic area, and then for others, the government hired international consultants. This project was financed by a grant of the United Nations Development Program (UNDP). However, there is no guarantee that holders of critical executive positions will maintain their positions or remain in their executive functions because of the permanent mutations of federal government. A change of minister currently implies not only a replacement of the political appointees but a new administrative reorganization (a ''new order''); consecuently, the ''administrative reform'' of the latest minister is neglected.

IV. THREE DIMENSIONS OF STATE REFORM

State reform—defined as the effects on the state apparatus of the reshaping of state, society, and economy relationship—resulted basically in the following: privatization of the state-owned enterprises; decentralization of social functions; and, what is perhaps not so obvious, the politicization of the national administration (Orlansky 1994).[5]

A. Privatization of the State Business Sector

Under the rallying cry of ''all power to the market,'' the state companies were privatized at a fantastic pace, unprecedented as compared to the experiences in the United Kingdom during the Thatcher administration or Chile ruled by Pinochet. (The case of New Zealand would be more like the Argentine experience [Peters 1994; Self 1994].) As a result of the privatizations, the state company sector went from 347,240 employees in 1989 to 66,731 toward the end of 1993; almost 40% of that difference is due to voluntary resignations and layoffs (114,538) and this probably has increased unemployment and subemployment. In 1995 the total amount of employees in state-owned enterprises was 27,500. Indeed, privatization was the only instrument which led to the ''genuine'' shrinking of the national state in terms of public employment.

As pointed out by Gerchunoff and Canovas (1995), the implementation of privatization policies was in itself basically a political message, the need to show unequivocally through hard facts the reversal of a state tendency historically associated with Peronism. Moreover, the rhetoric chosen by decrees and laws was clear upon setting down the rules for the game. An orthodox market model was imposed by and ''emergency decree'' in 1990 (1757/90) establishing, verbatim, that those agencies and regulations that ''hinder the smooth functioning of the market shall be eliminated.''

B. Decentralization of Social Functions

The basic social functions (health, education) and some welfare programs spanning the whole country were transferred away from the central administration toward provincial and local administrations. This transference completed the neoconservative process started by the military regime 1976–1983. During the current stage approximately 340,000 public employees were transferred from the national administrative level to the provinces and municipalities, thus creating new administrative structures.

In fact, the national administration got rid of personnel whose volume has been historically rising (teachers, hospital personnel, social assistance programs, etc.). It simply ceased being responsible for the administration and delivery of social services—high schools, hospitals,[6] local welfare programs—without even designing a specific reform policy, and this change of payroll led to the creation of new public administration positions at local and provincial levels. In other words, the greater number of public employees working for provincial administrations and municipalities is—certainly—a direct consequence of the decentralization policy. The national administration disregarded functions and personnel without previously establishing any reform criterion. As the unemployment rate has been rising and practically unchecked (1989, 8.4%; 1995, 18.6%; 1997, 17.2%), the national administration imposes upon the provincial governments the task of reducing the volume and the salaries of public employees, as well as restricting the working conditions. The central government expects that the political cost of this adjustment will be borne by the provinces (particularly if their governments do not belong to the same political party).[7]

Thus, through privatization and decentralization, the national government alleges that it reduced its personnel as compared to 1989: approximately 320,000 posts from the previously state-run companies and 284,000 posts from state social functions; actually, the latter were a mere administrative level transfer.

C. Politicization of the National Administration

State reform has intensified the political profile of the national administration. Political recomposition is a direct result of the restructuring that begun in 1989. Once the state companies were privatized and the social role decentralized under the advocacy of fiscal federalism, the volume of national administration personnel ''shrinks''; at the same time, the quantitative incidence of personnel in political posts is greater, *not only* in relative terms. In absolute terms there has been an increase in the volume of posts in the most political government sectors: the Presidency, the Ministry of the Interior, and the Ministry of Economy (Orlansky 1994).

The state overdimensioning in political areas suggests that the national administration has been ''politicized''; in other words, it has become politically hypertrophied. Empirically, this process is noticeable in the expansive creation of top governmental structures (secretariats, undersecretaries) and in the clientelistic and corporative control (by the Menemist UPCN public employees union organization) of the labor scene, that is, in the recruiting, repositioning, and promotion of the civil service.

Affirming that the state is being ''politicized'' might sound tautological, but what is unusual is the degree of its extension to the political state sphere of the official party, conflicts among sectors, and its general and particular interests. As a consequence of this dynamic the state has been fragmented and there are interbureaucratic nets of undue concentration of personal power (i.e., the case of Minister of Economy Cavallo (1991–1996): his meddling with organisms beyond his jurisdiction). As already submitted in other studies—for example, Greece (Sotiropoulos 1994)—the extent of the infiltration of the party factionalism within bureaucratic structures has reduced the limited autonomy of the administrative system. However, it is true that the role of the civil service is becoming more and more politicized, irrespective of the degree of party involvement of its members (Peters 1994).

V. UNION ACTION: CONFRONTATION DYNAMICS

During the first democratic government (Alfonsin, 1983–1989) after the military regime, a new stage of reorganization and restructuring of the basis for union power commenced. The rules and regulations established by the military regime were derogated and the unions started their institutional consolidation: the regulations in force before the dictatorship were put back in practice, union elections were called for late in 1984, the CGT union central organization was normalized, and the Union Association law was passed (23551/87) (Palomino 1988).

However, between 1983 and 1989, in spite of the consolidation of its political role, the relation of the unions with the Alfonsin government was difficult and permanently conflictive. The economic policy was questioned, as well as the negotiation of the foreign debt. This and the continuous demands of salary increases resulted in 12 general strikes during that administration. The year 1988 exhibited the highest rate of labor conflicts of the decade (N = 949), an increasing conflictive trend begun to rise as from 1986. (''Conflict'' is defined here as a strike or other force measure, and does not include those economic demands that have not been channeled through active protest measures [Fraga 1991].) Most force measures were taken by unions of the public sector; the fall of public employees' salaries and the demand for better working conditions were some of the precipitating factors. The two institutions which represent the public employees of the national administration (ATE, State Workers Association; and UPCN, National Civil Personnel Union) were responsible for 72% of the conflicts which took place in 1988, under Alfonsin (Radical Party) administration.

In July 1989 when Menem (Peronist Party) was sworn in, hyperinflation and the fiscal deficit seemed to be irreversible:

> In that context, and close to the point of ungovernability, as soon as the Menem administration took office the State Reform Act and the Economic Emergency State Act were passed. According to an unprecedented political pact submitted by the executive the Radical Party, the main opposition party, gave the official party its vote in Congress. With these legislative instruments a ''new administrative order'' was inaugurated, which basically consists of the redefinition of the interactive relations of the public and private sectors and the setting of unusual restrictions to the public sector . . . (Orlansky 1991).

One of the central points of this strategy was the State Reform Act 23696 passed on August 8, 1989. Its aim was to transfer public companies to the private sector; it included a list of more than 20 enterprises and agencies subject to privatization. The government asked for the collaboration of unions to avoid demands and tensions, and accept the labor flexibility acts.

Some union sectors agreed but others did not accept the new proposals submitted by the government, and showed it. Even though in 1989 there was a slight drop in the number of conflicts of state unions, the teachers' union was at the top of the list. Also in 1990 the teachers and state workers had the most force measures. The conflict arising from the adjustment policy was inevitable: in fact, between January and November 1991, despite a drop in the total of conflicts (N = 587), 66% of them were of state unions.

Nevertheless, the year 1991 marked the end of an era of unions as a power factor (CEUNM 1994). On one hand the union opposition to privatizations could not pressure or redefine the process which did not change course. On the other hand, new laws modifying crucial labor issues such as work accidents, strike control, etc., were treated at Congress in 1991. ''Menemism'' precipitated the break of the identification of the union movement with Peronism, which was historically the key to union power in Argentina. The result is that 1992 was the year with the fewest labor conflicts since 1982 (N = 281), and this level held throughout 1993 and 1994.

According to an official report:

> It must be admitted that it is a fact that in Argentina, in spite of an excessively ideological and confusing debate, the proposals for deregulation and privatization had popular consensus, as an effect of the calamitous results of the state management. As from 1988 several projects were begun which faced stern opposition, but after the change of government (Alfonsin to Menem in 1989) state reform acts were passed, thus giving the new government the instrument to carry state reform out (Chumbita 1992).

VI. FROM CONFRONTATION TO NEGOTIATION

While the state reform policies were implemented, the relation between government and unions went through two different stages. The first, of opposition to the state company privatization policy: between 1989 and 1990 there was the number record of state union conflicts with the current administration (N = 751 in 1989; N = 864 in 1990). The second stage, readaptation with the will to negotiate: in 1991 the number of conflicts dropped (N = 587), decreasing even more in 1992 (N = 279). The teachers' unions continued to be the most stubborn unions (N = 57 in 1992 ; N = 89 in 1993; N = 58 in 1994).

But the decrease in the number of labor conflicts was due to the ''weakening'' of the union power. Its most significant indicators are the reduction in the number of union representatives at Congress (1983, 35; 1989, 23; 1991, 18; 1995, 10); the decentralization of the collective bargaining—by conditioning salary raises to each company's productivity; and the actual fracture—although not acknowledged by the government[8]—of the structure of a single central organization.[9]

The different behaviors in each sector suggest however, a possible ''pragmatic'' readaptation when faced with the deep transformations, particularly in the privatized state companies. A good example of this is the railway workers, who had the highest number of conflicts in 1985 (11% of the total) and the lowest (3%) in 1993.

Certainly, unions have lost political power. But the economic power of some unions grew at the same time: they now control—or they will do so in the near future—an important part of the shares of privatized companies (shared ownership programs); they have the direct management of ex-state companies; they participate in the (privatized) retirement insurance and pension businesses; they are involved in retraining programs with public funds or provided by international agencies, etc. Furthermore, in different ways, half the ''welfare state'' is run by the unions through their social security services: health care, tourism, social assistance, housing programs, etc. (*La Nacion* 01/02/94).

The privatization and deregulation policies turned a large part of the previously adamant unions into negotiating unions with a considerable influence in the administration of new business opportunities as a result of state retrenchment. The unions, formerly worried about the worker's interests representation and opposed to decisions adopted (privatization, deregulation, limitation to the right to strike, etc.), turned into ''business unions.''

VII. COST-BENEFIT OF THE RECONVERSION: FOUR HYPOTHESES

According to the former Labor Minister (Caro Figueroa) ''unions had an important role in the period of confrontation,'' precisely when the *Justicialista* (Peronist) Party was the opposition. But when Peronism took office ''it turned to support the consolidation of a trade-off model between government and the unions.''[10] According to the Labor Minister's interpretation the government left unchanged the single representation model—although attenuated in practice—of centralized negotiation, and of union control over the social security services. In exchange, ''unions proved to be cooperative and sometimes more than that, they were who managed economic crisis and labor reconversion'' (*La Nacion* 01/02/94).

But the unionist behavior of the public sector unions, including the unions of the privatized companies,[11] is not even: it varies from conversion toward organizations concentrated on business activities, on the one hand, all the way to the opposite, the fighting profile representing the interests of its rank and file, on the other.

The unions and their leaders are concerned with the new business opportunities related to privatized companies—for example, the management of the shares corresponding to the Shared Ownership Program (i.e., telephone workers' union: Telephone Workers Federation of the Argentine Republic; FOETRA)[12] and the participation in the new pension and retirement insurance funds management, one of the privatized social functions, jointly with international finance entities (e.g., electric energy workers' union: ''Luz y Fuerza'' Worker's Federation; FATLyF). These union organizations, whose strategy is oriented basically toward the consolidation of its economic structure, share the leadership of the General Confederation of Labor (CGT), the ''one and only'' central organization officially acknowledged.[13] The negotiations between the CGT and the government deal with the work accident act project which would allow the unions to participate in the work risk insurance business (ART, Work Risk Insurance Management). Even more, the same political actors (CGT and the Menem Administration) agreed in avoiding the deregulation of social security services, one of the main sources of union economic power in the past (today they must receive state grants), are threatened by deregulation that would eventually imply that the worker could engage health care services directly, eliminating the practice of contributing compulsorily to the union.

The CGT also includes the UPCN (National Civil Personnel Union). Their organization—as opposed to ATE (State Worker's Association)—has a particular corporative influence on public employment regarding recruiting, repositioning, and promotion, in accordance with SINAPA resolutions. Moreover, its leaders have got appointments in the management level of governmental agencies.

Quite opposite is the situation of the state workers' union, ATE (State Workers' Association), which leads the fighting unions grouped in the Argentine Worker's Congress (CTA), that represents especially the health care workers, teachers, civil service employees, particularly in the provincial and local levels, etc.[14] It proved its organizing capacity leading during 1994 both a nationwide manifestation and a general strike.

In brief, the unions belonging to the state sector at the beginning of the current administration could be classified through a gradient spanning form confrontation to negotiation according to the following set of *hypotheses*:

1. As from the setting in motion of the various mechanisms of the state reform, the state unions have redefined *differentially* their interaction profile with the government.
2. The different union profiles range from the highest level of *negotiation* to the highest level of *confrontation*.
3. State and former state unions have redefined their union action profile according to the higher or lower degree of negotiation (or conflict), associated to the existence (or not) of *benefits/incentives* for the employees, the organization, and/or the union leaders.

In fact, if the unions are classified in three large categories according to the three dimensions of the state reform, the impact of the reform policies is different according to the following order:(1)*ex-state-owned enterprises* (telephone companies, steel, oil, railways, electricpower, etc.); (2)*central administration* under a new civil service system (UPCN, with hegemonic influence); and (3)*decentralized public health care and education services* (ATE, teacher's unions).

First, the greatest reform impact corresponds to the privatized (or leased) sector with a sharp cutback in personnel. In the second place, it is the ''politicization'' effect in the national administration, with a heavy clientelistic circulation.[15] Finally, in last place, health care and education services, and other social programs since they were ''merely transferred'' to the provincial or municipal jurisdictions.

But, precisely, as established in the third hypothesis (''benefits/incentives''), the reform policies implied (or not) the selective distribution of resources to employees and/or the organization and/or its leaders. In the privatized companies the benefits consisted of large payments as compensation for those who retired[16]; the inclusion of employees in shared ownership programs (FOETRA); the incorporation of union leaders into the companies' boards (State Oil Company); the direct union ownership of former state companies (Fiscal Coal Fields, YCF, by FATLYF). At the national administration level: the inclusion (coalition) of unions (UPCN) in the decision-making personnel policies, a prior general salary increase, besides the UPCN leaders appointments in federal administration agencies. Instead, there were no similar incentives in the processes of personnel transference in the fields of education, health care, and social welfare to provincial and local administrations.

The three hypotheses together explain (1) the change from confrontation to negotiation in the state and former state sectors, (2) the relative differences between unions, and (3) the determining factors of the diversity. As a logic consequence, the *fourth hypothesis* concludes that the highest intensity of the union conflict upon putting into practice is associated with the lack of incentives for the personnel, the organization and/or the leaders. As a matter of fact, most economic demands and political demonstrations—even with unusual violence as in the cases of the provinces of Jujuy, Santiago del Estero, Cordoba, San Juan—correspond to unions of local and provincial administrations, including education, health care, and social programs, threatened with an impending structural adjustment and subject to the discretionary federal administration fiscal policy.

VIII. FINAL REMARKS

This paper has tried to explain the different reactions of state unions faced with the process of state reform. Four hypotheses have been submitted which relate the dimensions of the reform (privatization, decentralization, politicization of the federal administration apparatus) and the type of union reaction according to the existence and distribution of benefits (political, economic, financial, administrative, etc.) among various beneficiaries (employees, organizations, union leadership).

The proposed outline allows two explanations to the different responses of the public sector unions: on the one hand, the diachronic transformation of the unions of privatized companies, which went from confrontation to conformity; and on the other hand, the persistence of conflicts in local and provincial administrations, threatened with a (still pending) policy of structural adjustment.

The state reform in Argentina was a later process compared with other Latin American countries (Chile, Mexico, Bolivia) and, at the same time, it was put into effect as a shock treatment. The sudden disappearance of the state as an arbiter, regulator, and direct agent in the production and the provision of various goods and services is expressed in the fall of the national administration (central and state companies) purchasing power; in 1989 those acquisitions were over $20 billion and in 1994 it dropped to a fifth of that.

Furthermore, the economic policy has corroded the gravitation capacity of all type of sectorial corporations and institutions, even in the private sector. The union organizations and the enterprise groups whose functions were to struggle for a participation in the national income diluted the collective actions based in their aggregated demands. The administrative capacity of each union, each company or each enterprise group per se was the widespread answer to the revolutionary transformations produced by privatization and deregulation in the economic sphere.

The submitted hypotheses—even if they refer to a recent process—proved to be sustainable, although it is too early to draw conclusions. However, 1995 emerged as a turning point for the economic policies outcomes: the unemployment rate has exploded at a persistent level reaching the 18%. Thus, a new profile of new labor conflicts has irrupted into the sociopolitical stage.

ENDNOTES

1. Following Lane (1993) three functions delimit the public sector: the public resources allocation, public redistribution, and public regulation.
2. State reform has been incited by Menem Administration (1989–1995), the second elected President. Alfonsin (1983–1989) was the first President coming to office after seven years of military rule. Therefore, state reform in Argentina is definitely related to democratization.
3. The expression ''new administrative order'' alludes to the primitive new international order, coined by U.S. former President Bush, and paraphrased as the ''new international disorder.''
4. Through executive orders the President passes acts taking for himself congressional law-making power, without its consent. This exercise of discretional power fits well into the concept of ''imperial presidency.''
5. The State Reform policies were included mainly in the mentioned *two acts* of 1989 (23696, ''State Reform,'' and 23697, ''Economic Emergency'') and *four executive orders*: in 1990, 435 ''State Rearrangement''; 1457 named ''To Accelerate the State Reform'' and 2476 ''State Rationalizing: Main Regulations Regarding the Situation of Personnel''; in 1991, 992, ''Administrative Profession National System (SI-NAPA).''
6. With regard to public hospitals, the contracting-out system was added to decentralization toward subnational governments. In this way maintenance and support tasks in charge of private contractors have been capturing most of the budget while doctors', nurses', and administrative personnel salaries were frozen. A survey carried out at a first-rate hospital (Hospital Posadas, Province of Buenos Aires) shows that salaries out of 68% of 1989 budget were reduced to 48% one year later, while the

opposite happened with increasing costs of private contractors, given the same services.

7. ''The Secretary for Social Development (Eduardo Amadeo) stated that several provinces will benefit from the measures the national government will announce to face unemployment. Coincidentally, except Misiones, in the other four districts, Salta, Chaco, Jujuy, and Formosa, the governor elections are still pending, which piece of information the official failed to include in the announcement'' (*La Nacion* 07/24/95). This is an example of the politizased use given to the job policies.
8. In 1997, the government recognizes (for tactical reasons) the existence of another workers' central organization.
9. The existence in practice of four peak labor organizations went against the principle of the single union legal capacity which hinders the formation of more than one worker's general confederation. Unionism is divided in one extremely pro-Menem CGT, which still has power granted by the government; in the antagonistic extreme, the CTA (Labor Association of Argentina); and the MTA (Labor Movement of Argentina) which is a group of unions, basically of the private sector, which split in 1994 from the CGT, less condescending with the official economic policy.
10. The association between incentives and union behavior results from the general analytical framework of Grindle and Thomas (1991). According to these authors the reactions for or against the reform policies arise during its planning or when it is put into practice; and the government's capacity to carry out successfully the original plan depends on the resources available to overcome the opposition caused by the reform policy.
11. The unions of the formerly state-owned companies and privatized organisms maintained their organizational continuity. Naturally the number of affiliated members dropped due to the reduction of personnel (the electricity companies, for example, lost 50%, railway 60%, steelworks 70%, and oil 80%). It is also presumed—no information is available—that there is a negative tendency in the will to affiliate to unions.
12. The participation of personnel in shared ownership varied according to the sector: 20% in steelworks; 14% in postal workers; 10% in electricity, telephones, water works, etc.; and only 5% in natural gas. The system applied in Argentina consists in that the shares of the privatized companies are transferred to the employees as a whole for a period of nearly 10 years, managed by the union leadership (*Prensa Economica* 197-1993).
13. The current legislation on union associations which through its legal capacity figure creates a monopoly of a single central union organization, goes back to the Peronism of 1946, inspired on the Fascist ''Carta del Lavoro.'' This regulation does not reflect the union reality and does not comply with the 1987 ILO convention accepted by Argentina, which points out that the imposition of a single union organization by means of legislation constitutes an interference of the government on the exercise of the freedom to associate.
14. ATE also included personnel from the former military-industrial complex, a great part of which were liquidated due to the lack of buyers, as opposed to the privatized utilites companies. As from 1989, and despite having also union representation of the central administration personnel—the civil service—it was excluded of all par-

ticipation by the new labor legislation (SINAPA, Administrative Profession National System) under the monopoly since then of the Menemist UPCN.

15. For a description of ''political inflation''—in other words, the mechanisms of clientelistic circulation, expansion of the structures and of the top levels of the national administration, etc.—see Orlansky (1994).
16. ''Early retirement'' has been linked with latter unemployment, specially for women and middle-aged ex-workers of ex-state companies.

REFERENCES

CEUNM (Centro de Estudios para la Nueva Mayoria): *Informative Bulletins* #39, 1990; #53, 1991; #54 and #64, 1992; #68 and #75, 1993; #77, 1994. Buenos Aires.

Cameron, D.R. (1978). The expansion of the public economy: a comparative analysis. *American Political Science Review 72*, 1243–1261.

Chumbita, H. (1992). Participación de los trabajadores en la propiedad de empresas. Experiencias y modelos. El programa de Propiedad Participada. Paper presented in the seminar *Nuevos Escenarios de las Relaciones Gremiales*. INAP. Buenos Aires.

Fraga, R. (1991). La Cuestion Sindical. Buenos Aires: Centro de Estudios para la Nueva Mayoria.

Gerchunoff, P. and Cánovas, G. (1995). Privatizaciones en un contexto de emergencia económica. *Desarrollo Económico 136*(34), 483–512.

Grindle, M. and Thomas, J. (1991). *Public Choices and Policy Change. The Political Economy of Reform in Developing Countries*. Baltimore: John Hopkins University Press.

Lane, J.E. (1993). *The Public Sector. Concepts. Models and Approaches*. London: SAGE Publications.

Lindbeck, A. (1985). Redistribution policy and the expansion of the public sector. *Journal of Public economics 28*, 309–328.

Orlansky, D. (1991). El nuevo orden administrativo. Reforma del estado y empleo público en la Argentina 1989-1991. In *Reestructuración y Regulación Institucional del Mercado de Trabajo en América Latina*. Serie de Investigación 98. Geneva: Instituto Internacional de Estudios Laborales.

Orlansky, D. and Orciani, M. (1994). La reconversión sindical después de la reforma del estado. Paper presented at the *2do Congreso Nacional de Estudios del Trabajo*. Buenos Aires, Aug. 25–27, 1994.

Orlansky, D. (1994). Democratization, state reform and political inflation. Paper presented at the *XVI IPSA Berlin World Congress*.

Palomino, H. (1988). Hacia una nueva relación entre sindicatos y estado en Argentina. Paper presented at the *XVII Congreso Latinoamericano de Sociología*. Uruguay. CISEA.

Peters, B.G. (1994). Alternative models of governance: the changing state and the public service. Paper presented at the *XVI Berlin IPSA World. Congress*.

Self, P. (1994). *Government by the Market? The Politics of Public Choice*. London: Macmillan.

Sotiropoulos, D.A. (1994). Bureaucracy and civil society in contemporary Greece. Paper presented at the *XVI IPSA Berlin World Congress*.

25

Neighbors, Informal Job Brokers, and the Employment Problem of the Urban Poor

Can Dispersal Strategies Improve Access to Informal Job Networks?

David A. Reingold
Indiana University, Bloomington, Indiana

I. INTRODUCTION

In *When Work Disappears*, the renowned sociologist Williams Julius Wilson argues that one of the defining characteristics of contemporary U.S. inner-city neighborhoods—as compared to 50 years ago—is their higher levels of joblessness. Poor urban communities that once exhibited relatively stable patterns of formal private sector employment now struggle to keep a third of their adult population working. This change is traced to a myriad of causes including transformations in the nation's production process, shifts in the distribution of industrial job opportunities, the suburbanization of business, shifts in labor supply, high commuting costs, persistent housing segregation, the outmigration of non-poor inner-city residents, intended and unintended consequences of federal programs, historic discrimination, selective employer hiring practices, and processes that take place in communities lacking consistent contact with the formal labor market. Included among these processes is the potential for residents of poor urban neighborhoods to be at a disadvantage in the labor market since they infrequently interact with individuals who have access to information about job openings. As a result, some urban residents may become embedded in communities where few residents work and many collect welfare and/or make money through the drug trade, and individuals who want to work may find that they do not know people with stable work histories who can help them find a job.

Aside from explaining why poverty concentration may have a self-perpetuating effect on joblessness, this hypothesis is also related to the use of housing mobility programs, such as mixed-income housing programs, scattered-site public housing development, and Section 8 rental subsidies—including the U.S. Department of Housing Urban Development's Moving to Opportunities Demonstration. These initiatives assist low-income, mostly nonwhite families to leave high-poverty neighborhoods and move to higher-income areas.[1] An important assumption of these programs is that relocation can address some of the negative consequences associated with life in areas of high poverty concentration, such as limited access to employment information, excessive commuting costs, inadequate public services, fear of crime, and low residential satisfaction.

The potential mismatch between low-skilled urban job seekers and informal job brokers has been investigated in an emerging academic literature (for a review of this research see Briggs 1997; Jencks and Mayer 1990). Research in this area has found support for the hypothesis that concentrated poverty increases the likelihood of joblessness, particularly among teenagers (O'Regan 1991; O'Regan and Quigley 1991, 1993) and women (Fernandez and Harris 1991; Rosenbaum and Popkin 1991); however, none of these studies have been able to investigate prime-age working men or test the actual mechanisms that connect poverty concentration with joblessness (Tienda 1991; Briggs 1997).

To address these issues, I examined the employment outcomes of displaced workers who lost their jobs after a Chicago based inner-city printing plant closed. I interviewed these workers and documented their postdisplacement employment outcomes, including the receipt and transmission of informal employment information. The rate of job finding through neighbors is then analyzed by the characteristics of the respondent's neighborhood. As a result, it is possible to test—albeit indirectly—whether concentrated poverty affects employment outcomes by limiting informal job information provided by neighbors.

Before presenting the findings, however, it is important to review some of the relevant issues and concepts raised in the research literature. This will help provide a context for the following analysis, while elucidating some of the more important issues that revolve around the study of urban poverty, job finding, and neighborhood interaction.

II. BACKGROUND

The basic formulation that poverty concentration increases joblessness by disconnecting residents from informal job networks is relatively straight forward. It acknowledges the well-documented fact that a plurality of workers find jobs through personal contacts (for a review of these survey findings see O'Regan [1991]). It also recognizes that individuals who are embedded in social networks comprised of people who know of job openings and can make successful referrals will likely experience more social mobility and lower rates of unemployment (Granovetter 1974/1995; Holzer 1987; Montgomery 1994). Finally, it assumes that neighbors are an important source of informal employment information, and inner city residents lack access to informal job brokers.

Support for this last assumption is based largely on the presumption that recent social, political, and economic transformations affecting poor urban communities have resulted in the social isolation of inner city residents, increasing the social distance between inner-city residents and mainstream institutions and organizations, and furthering their dependence on neighbors and other community residents for basic resources and social support (see, for example, Stack 1974; Venkatesh 1997). The result is a pattern of hyperhomophily whereby the ties of the urban poor possess limited human capital and an inability to reach distant social circles (Fernandez and Harris 1991).

These limited patterns of social contact are thought to influence informal job brokering in several ways. As noted previously, the flow of informal employment information may be reduced since individuals who want to work may find that they do not know people with stable work histories who can help them find a job. This creates a paradox where the relative importance of neighbors as informal job brokers may increase in areas of concentrated poverty as the social distance between inner city residents and other parts of the city grows. Moreover, as abhorrent behavior becomes a fixture of inner-city life, residents may choose to distance themselves from one another, so as to avoid any contagion effects.[2] The perception that exposure to fellow community residents can diminish one's life chances would likely have a stifling effect on general perceptions of trust and, therefore, informal job brokering among neighbors.

Unfortunately, little is known about the role neighbors actually play in linking inner-city job seekers with job vacancies. The best measure of neighbors as job brokers comes from a stratified random sample of minority households and/or those in low-income census tracts in Los Angeles. Johnson and his colleagues (1996) found that of the 295 employed adult female respondents who found their job through a personal contact, 47.1% were directly assisted by job information obtained from a neighbor. As for ethnic and racial differences, only 32.7% of white respondents found their current job through a neighbor compared to 59.8% of Hispanics and 38.4% of blacks. It is unknown whether there are gender differences, since the analysis is restricted to female respondents, and it is unclear whether these racial and ethnic differences are the result of variation in neighborhood poverty levels. It also remains unclear whether the adaptive strategies used by some inner city residents to navigate an uncertain and sometimes dangerous neighborhood environment dampen the transmission of job information among neighbors. Nevertheless, these findings suggest that inner city residents, particularly Hispanics, actually transmit significant amounts of successful informal job information.[3]

Construing these results as proof that inner-city residents are *not* disconnected from locally based informal job networks deserves further comment. The problem with this interpretation is that we do not know if the employment information obtained through a neighbor occurred in the community where the interview took place. For example, a respondent could have been living in a rural Mexican town when a neighbor told her of a job opening located in Los Angeles. As we might expect, this hypothetical respondent might have reacted to the news of an employment opportunity by changing her residential location. Unfortunately, it remains unclear whether respondents who were assisted by neighbors in finding a job were helped by individuals within their current community or a community where they resided at the time of the interview. Failing to account for this type of scenario in cross-sectional survey research could lead to very misleading conclusions about the relationship between informal referrals, neighborhood poverty, and joblessness.

The need to avoid this type of mistake has heavily influenced the nature of research on this subject. For example, use of census employment data at the metropolitan level to measure the relationship between concentrated poverty and joblessness encounters the problem of simultaneity whereby the causal direction between concentrated poverty and joblessness is unclear. That is, concentrated poverty may increase joblessness by cutting residents off from informal job networks, but an increase in unemployment could also lead to an increase in the concentration of poverty "if the new poor respond to their income loss by moving to higher poverty areas" (O'Regan 1993). One way to avoid this problem is to study the employment of youths, whose residential choice is seen as influenced by their parents' employment prospects rather than their own (see, for example, O'Regan 1991; O'Regan and Quigley 1991, 1993). Even though much of this research tends to support the notion that inner city joblessness is, in part, the product of poverty concentration which limits access to informal employment brokers—particularly through familial networks—it remains unclear whether these results can be generalized to adults.

To be more specific, patterns of association and interaction among youths (as well as the elderly) may be more limited to familial contacts and persons in close physical proximity to their place of residence. As individuals enter adulthood they accumulate personal contacts. Over time these personal ties have a chance to become geographically dispersed. For working-age adults, therefore, the flow of information may be more likely to transcend the physical and social boundaries of residential communities. As a result, we might expect youth employment outcomes to be more dependent than working-age adult employment outcomes on access to informal job information through neighborhood-based ties.

There is some support for this assertion in the network literature (for a review of the literature on neighborhoods and social networks see Wellman and Leighton [1979]). For example, Oliver (1988) studied the structure and characteristics of social support networks among adult black residents from three Los Angeles communities—one of which is a poor central-city area. He found that in this area of poverty concentration roughly half of the ties reported by respondents were extralocal, i.e., outside of the respondent's neighborhood.[4] While it is unclear whether these social support networks actually tap access to job opportunities, they do suggest that the social support networks of inner city adult residents are not bounded exclusively by physical borders of neighborhoods.

Other studies from the social network literature on neighbor networks have found that respondents living in high-income areas of Nashville, Tennessee, know more neighbors than residents living in lower-income areas (Campbell and Lee 1992). However, the increased volume of social contacts who are neighbors in affluent areas is frequently accompanied by greater superficial familiarity with neighbors, and more frequent neighbor contact appears to occur in poorer areas (Guest and Lee 1983; Fischer et al. 1977). If we assume that a preponderance of jobs are found through acquaintances or weak ties (Granovetter 1995/1974), then these findings suggest that residents of poorer neighborhoods will be at a disadvantage since they tend to know fewer neighbors, and the neighbors they do know tend to be friends, close friends, or family.

Another way that researcher's have overcome the difficulties of measuring the effect of neighborhood poverty on joblessness is to use the experiences of participants in social mobility programs, specifically Section 8 recipients. The most widely cited example is Rosenbaum and Popkin's (1991) research on inner-city public housing residents in Chicago who experienced a change in residential location to the suburbs or non-poor areas of the city as a result of a court order (*Gautreaux* v. *Chicago Housing Authority*) which required the local housing authority to allocate rent vouchers to residents who had been unlawfully assigned a public housing unit based on their race. Through a mailed questionnaire distributed in 1988, these researchers randomly sampled 342 voucher recipients, all of whom were minority female heads of households. The participants who moved to a nonminority area of the city were used in their analysis as a no-change control group and were compared with movers who now live in the suburbs. Comparisons between within-city movers and suburban movers is rationalized on the basis that participants had limited discretion in their residential choice. The difference between pre- and postemployment outcomes for both suburban and within-city movers can be interpreted as the degree to which poverty concentration affects joblessness.

Rosenbaum and Popkin's results indicate that 30.2% of within-city movers were unemployed before moving but found employment after moving. Of those participants employed after moving, suburban movers were 16% more likely to be employed after moving than were within-city movers. Therefore, these results indicate that adult black mothers from inner-city neighborhoods who undergo an exogenous change in residential location do experience higher employment levels.[5]

Unfortunately, these researchers did not report how respondents found their new job. While the observed increase in work activity may be the result of greater access to informal employment information, it may also be the result of a Hawthorne effect and/or a renewed sense of self-efficacy and opportunity prompted by the receipt of a housing subsidy (for a review of shortcomings in the evaluation of housing mobility programs see Briggs [1977]). In other words, it remains unclear from existing evaluations of housing mobility programs *how* neighborhoods and poverty concentration affect levels of joblessness.

One way around these difficulties is to use data collected from recently displaced workers. This setting provides the conditions of a ''natural experiment'' whereby a population is exposed to a treatment; i.e., the exogenous shock of a job loss, and the postdisplacement experiences of workers, most notably their ability to find employment through neighbors that supply informal employment information, can be linked to the socioeconomic status of their communities. This setting creates the necessary conditions to test whether neighborhood poverty actually varies the flow of informal job information among neighbors without having to worry about the problem of simultaneity or related issues associated with the use of cross-sectional data.

The primary shortcoming of this strategy is generalizing the informal job brokering experiences of dislocated workers who tend to live in nonpoor communities and have stable work histories to residents of poor urban communities who frequently lack contact with the formal labor market. While this issue is important, this external validity problem can be minimized by studying the experiences of dislocated workers from an inner-city business.

To this end, this chapter analyzes the postdisplacement experiences of workers who lost their job after an inner-city plant closing and examines whether transmission of informal job information and finding a job through a neighbor are associated with particular types of neighborhoods. This will be followed by a test of whether effective informal job brokers are less likely to live in poorer communities. Both empirical exercises will help gauge the degree to which neighborhood poverty affects residents' access to informal information about employment opportunities and may help explain why many inner city residents suffer from weak labor force attachment. But before presenting the findings, it is necessary to discuss the data and describe the variables and measures used in the analysis.

III. DATA SOURCES AND RESEARCH PROCEDURES

The data used in this analysis are the result of 95 interviews conducted with dislocated workers who lost their jobs after a plant closing in 1993. In all, roughly 650 workers were affected. In-depth face-to-face and telephone interviews were conducted with every living worker who had not retired, transferred to another plant within the same company, or received disability insurance because of health problems. Workers who reported any job search activity or were already working at a new job, including enrollment in an educational program, were included in the study. Also included were any respondents who had been dismissed by the plant but were later hired by a different division of the same company. A 47% response rate was obtained.[6] Of the 95 workers interviewed, 38 were conducted face-to-face and 57 over the phone.

The Reservoir Press,[7] located on Chicago's near south side, was the original division of a multinational printing enterprise, manufacturing everything from local telephone books to mail order catalogs and the *New Testament*. During its illustrious 150+ year history, the plant and many of its workers saw their employer become one of the world's largest printing companies as industrial printing was transformed from the old letterpress method to state-of-the-art off-set and gravure printing. During the same period, many of these same workers saw the neighborhood around the company grow into one of the city's most concentrated areas of black poverty.

Situated in the shadow of a large convention center and 1000 units of high-rise public housing, the area surrounding the Reservoir Press is similar to many poor urban communities around the nation. Once the home of such wealthy families as Armour, Pullman, and Field, it is now one of the city's poorest and least populated areas. In 1989, almost 94% of the area's residents were black, more than 60% lived below the federal poverty line, and the great majority of the area's residents lived in Chicago Housing Authority complexes.

The company's official explanation for closing the plant was the cancelation of a contract which accounted for approximately 60% of the facility's production. The company also noted the factory's unusual vertical design which created inefficiencies in the production process (compared to newer, horizontally designed facilities). Moreover, higher labor costs in Chicago compared to other ''greenfield'' production sites in neighboring states further legitimized the decision to close the plant and reassign the remaining contracts to other production facilities.[8]

The decision to study the postdisplacement job search and informal job brokering activities of workers from the Reservoir Press is the result of several factors. First, access to the names, addresses, and phone numbers of all affected employees made it considerably easier to conduct a systematic study (for a detailed account of this research project see Reingold [1998]). Second, the exogenous shock of a job loss, simulating the conditions of a natural experiment, avoids the problem of simultaneity. Third, these data allow for an analysis of the relationship between the transmission of informal employment information and neighborhood characteristics, whereas with traditional cross-sectional survey methods, it would be very difficult, if not impossible, to assign community-level indicators to individual cases at different residential locations and points in time, depending on when and where this employment information was exchanged. Fourth, the immediacy of a plant closing and the response of those affected workers to search for employment creates an excellent environment for conducting research on informal labor market activities. Not only does it help overcome some retrospective memory problems, but it also allows for more detailed and nuanced questions concerning the exchange of informal labor market information.

Since this research is designed as an exploratory case study and not a random sample of the general population, concerns over its external validity are minimized. It is important to note, however, that the Reservoir Press has a number of desirable properties which make the experiences of its workers similar to those of the larger universe of dislocated workers and other laborers in traditional rust-belt industrial urban centers. First, the firm is located in a dynamic and diverse labor economy which is not dependent on any one firm or industry. Second, none of the workers belonged to a formal labor organization. Third, the printing business is not traditionally thought of as belonging to a trade-sensitive industry. All of these characteristics make the circumstances of the affected Reservoir employees similar to those of the general population of displaced workers, as well as to other employees in the manufacturing sector of similar urban centers.

It is important to note that the typical Reservoir employee is much closer to the stereotypical image of a traditional blue-collar worker than a member of the urban underclass. This places limits on the degree to which the experiences of these workers can be generalized to inner-city residents. However, if the post-displacement outcomes of Reservoir workers are affected by the socioeconomic composition of their neighborhood, and the ability of neighbors to informally broker employment opportunities, then a stronger case could be made to support the hypothesis that concentrated poverty increases joblessness.

The dependent variable in the analysis is whether respondents found their current job through word of mouth and whether their personal contact was a neighbor. These measures are supplemented with several indicators of the respondents' ability and/or willingness to transmit job information. Respondents were also asked if they helped others in their job search, as well as the total number of individuals assisted, and the number of people who were eventually hired as a result of the respondent's help. The independent variables in the analysis include several individual-level characteristics, such as sex, age, education, and race. In addition, community-level indicators were extracted from the 1990 decennial census. Each respondent was then assigned the characteristics of the community in which s/he lived at the time of his/her job search.[9] The community-level measures in the analysis include the percentage of black residents, the percentage of residents below the federal poverty line, and the percentage of residents who are unemployed.

The basic strategy used to analyze the data is to look at differences in neighborhood-level characteristics between those respondents who found their most current job through the help of a neighbor and those who did not. Similarly, differences in neighborhood characteristics and the ability and willingness to exchange informal job information is also analyzed. Both empirical exercises will further our understanding of whether neighborhood poverty increases unemployment by disconnecting residents from word-of-mouth employment information.

IV. FINDINGS AND DISCUSSION

Table 1 presents the average characteristics of respondents. As these figures illustrate, the typical employee of the Reservoir Press, regardless of race, was a middle-aged married man with a high school education and almost 29 years of work experience with this one employer. A little more than one-third of the respondents lived in Chicago, and 57.9% lived in surrounding suburbs. Almost 82% of the black respondents were city residents and lived in communities that were almost exclusively black. In 1990, the average poverty rate for these communities was 20.8% and had an average unemployment rate of 16.7%. In contrast, the majority of white respondents were suburban dwellers and lived in communities where two-thirds of the population was also white. These communities had an average poverty and unemployment rate that was half that of the communities where black respondents lived. Given Chicago's notorious reputation as one of the nations most segregated cities, it is not surprising to find that these respondents also lived in highly segregated communities that have significant differences in their rates of poverty and unemployment.

At the Reservoir plant, most respondents were skilled blue-collar workers who either operated the printing presses and binding equipment or repaired the plant's machinery. Several of these workers were also involved in pre-press operations, such as cylinder making and color coordination. A number of the semiskilled workers were fork-lift operators or machine operator helpers. Unskilled workers were mostly material handlers. They were responsible for moving, stacking, and taking away the finished product as it came off binding and printing machines. The average hourly wage across all occupations was $18.10.

As the figures indicate, whites earned, on average, $4.65 per hour more than blacks. This is a result of a segregated work force at the Reservoir plant where blacks were more likely to occupy lower-paid unskilled and semiskilled positions and whites filled the higher-paid skilled and supervisory occupations.

Table 1 Average Characteristics of Respondents

	All	White	Black
Average age	51.2	51.7	50.1
Percentage female	9.5	3.3**	21.9
Percentage married	73.7	82.0**	59.4
Average years of education	12.9	13.0	12.7
Residential location			
City	34.7	11.5**	81.3
Suburb	57.9	78.7**	15.6
Other	7.4	9.8	3.1
Community characteristics			
Percentage poor	9.3	3.3**	20.8
Percentage unemployed	8.7	4.5**	16.7
Percentage black	33.6	6.9**	85.1
Average years at Reservoir	28.7	30.1*	26.9
Last Reservoir occupation[a]			
Unskilled	8.4	0**	25.0
Semiskilled	32.6	23.0**	50.0
Skilled	38.9	52.5**	12.5
Clerical/sales/service	6.3	6.6	6.3
Supervisory	13.7	18.0*	6.3
Average Reservoir hourly wage[b]	18.10	19.87**	15.22
Percent currently employed	83.2	83.6	84.4
Current occupation[a]			
Unskilled	27.5	24.5	34.6
Semiskilled	13.8	3.8**	34.6
Skilled	26.3	34.0**	7.7
Clerical/sales/service	18.8	22.6	11.5
Supervisory	13.8	15.1	11.5
Percent currently self-employed	14.8	18.9	7.4
Average current hourly wage[b]	10.49	11.23*	9.06
N	95	61	32

Sources: Compiled by author from interviews conducted with dislocated workers from the Reservoir Press and U.S. Census (1989).

[a] Due to rounding error, percentages do not add up to 100%.

[b] Nonhourly employees were excluded from these calculations. The measure of average current hourly wage and percentage self-employed only include employed respondents.

Two-tailed t-tests: * = $p < .10$; ** = $p < .05$; asterisks show contrast between white and black respondents.

However, most respondents, regardless of race, were able to find employment after the plant closed, but postdisplacement wages were 40% below predisplacement levels.[10] The general pattern which accounts for some of these wage losses is that large numbers of skilled and semiskilled Reservoir employees are currently employed in much lower-paying unskilled positions.

Table 2 presents the most important method for finding respondents' current job.[11] Roughly half of all employed respondents found their jobs through word of mouth. This rate of finding jobs through friends and relatives is slightly higher than prior research on dislocated workers (see literature cited in O'Regan [1993]). Perhaps the questionnaire's attention to the use of multiple job search methods may account for some of this difference. Advertisements were the next most important method for finding a job, followed by walkins and other sources; these include finding jobs through organizations such as churches, schools, and neighborhood associations. As for racial differences, blacks were slightly less likely to have found their job through personal contacts or advertisements but were more likely to use public employment agencies and other organizations. It is also important to note that a significant number of respondents found jobs without actively searching. In all, 28.8% of currently employed respondents reported no job search activity (not shown in tables). This is relatively consistent with other social survey research on the percentage of nonsearchers (Granovetter 1995/1974:142–44).

The relationship between the respondent and the personal contact responsible for helping him/her find a job was evenly divided among relatives, good friends, friends, and acquaintances (see Table 3a). While blacks were slightly

Table 2 Most Important Method for Finding Current Job

	All[a]	White	Black[a]
Personal contact	51.4	54.2	43.5
Advertisement	26.4	33.3**	13.0
Unsolicited application	11.1	10.4*	13.0
Other source	5.6	2.1	13.0
Public employment agency[b]	4.2	0*	13.0
No method most important	1.4	0	4.3
N	72	48	23

Source: Compiled by author from interviews conducted with dislocated workers from the Reservoir Press.

[a] Due to rounding error, percentages do not add up to 100%.

[b] No respondents found their current job through a private employment agency.

Two-tailed t-tests: * = $p < .10$; ** = $p < .05$; asterisks show contrast between white and black respondents.

Table 3a Relationship to Personal Contact Who Was Most Important in Helping Respondent Find His/Her Current Job

	All	White	Black
Relative	23.8	20.7	25.0
Good friend	26.2	27.6	25.0
Friend	19.0	27.6**	0
Acquaintance	31.0	24.1	50.0
N	42	29	12

Source: Compiled by author from interviews conducted with dislocated workers from the Reservoir Press.
Two-tailed t-tests: * = $p < .10$; ** = $p < .05$; asterisks show contrast between white and black respondents.

more dependent on relatives for informal job brokering, the noticeable racial difference is in the importance of acquaintances and friends. Among black respondents who found their jobs through word of mouth, 50% of the personal contacts were acquaintances, compared to 24.1% for whites. Similarly, no black respondents who found their job through word of mouth relied on the help of a friend, whereas 27.6% of the personal contacts who assisted white respondents find jobs were friends.

Perhaps these findings reflect group differences in the definition of what distinguishes good friends from friends and acquaintances. One way to investigate this possibility is to compare the length of time a respondent knew his/her personal contact and look at differences across race and the type of relationship. For the most part, no substantial differences exist. Blacks who found their job through an acquaintance knew their personal contact for an average of 6.5 years, compared to 4.5 years for whites (not shown in tables). Similar differences exist for relatives and friends. While the small sample size limits any definitive conclusions, it appears that blacks from the Reservoir Press were much more reliant on weak ties for access to the labor market than whites, who were more dependent on friends.

Table 3b presents the average characteristics of personal contacts who most directly helped respondents find their current job. In general, most respondents knew their personal contact for extended periods of time. Almost all personal contacts and respondents were from the same racial group, but a significant number of white respondents who found their current job through word of mouth benefited from information that came from an individual who belonged to a different ethnic group. About a third of the respondents who used informal methods to obtain their current job were assisted by former coworkers from the Reservoir

Table 3b Selected Characteristics of Personal Contact Who Most Directly Helped Respondent Find His/Her Current Job

	All	White	Black
Average years known personal contact	19.9	20.7	17.8
Same race	94.9	96.2	91.7
Same ethnicity	78.8	66.7**	100
Lives in same neighborhood	32.5	33.3	33.3
Worked at the Reservoir Press	31.7	42.9**	8.3
Supervisor at Reservoir Press	9.8	10.7	8.3
Works at firm of current job	70.0	71.0	58.3
Works in printing industry	28.2	38.5**	8.3
N	42	29	12

Source: Compiled by author from interviews conducted with dislocated workers from the Reservoir Press.
Two-tailed t-tests: * = $p < .10$; ** = $p < .05$; asterisks show contrast between white and black respondents.

Press. Some of these contacts had been laid off around the same time as the respondent, while others had left many years earlier and, when they heard of the plant closing, contacted former coworkers (or were contacted by them) about possible employment opportunities. All of these latter contacts had remained in the area, working for other printing companies, and most were in supervisory positions that enabled them to directly influence hiring decisions. Since many of these contacts were white, they tended to assist ex-coworkers who also were white. As a result, 42.9% of the personal contacts used by whites had worked for the Reservoir Press whereas only 8.3% of personal contacts used by blacks had worked for the company.

It is worth noting, at this time, that respondents who had several work experiences before their first Reservoir job were no more likely to find work through word of mouth than those who had worked their entire careers for this one employer. Contacts from former jobs (aside from those at the Reservoir plant) played no role in helping any respondents find work. Therefore, in these data it does not appear that "staying too long in one's job . . . forecloses future mobility by truncating the pool of personal contacts one might otherwise have built up" (Granovetter 1995/1974:85).

As for the importance of neighbors in the job brokering process, 32.5% of respondents who found their current job through word of mouth were directly helped by someone who also lived in the respondent's community. This is true for both black and white respondents. These figures are fairly consistent with the Johnson et al.'s findings discussed above which found that 32.7% of whites and

28.4% of black women who found their current job through word-of-mouth were assisted by neighbors (1996).

To investigate the possibility that finding a job through a neighbor is associated with a community's poverty level and unemployment rate, Table 4 presents the average community-level characteristics for respondents who found their jobs through a neighbor compared to those who found their jobs through other methods and those who are not working. These figures indicate that respondents who found their jobs through neighbors do not live in communities that are dramatically different from those who found their job through some other method or those who were not working.[12] Overall, respondents who found their current job through a neighbor lived in communities with a poverty rate of 10.2%, an unemployment rate of 8.3%, and a black population of 31.1%. In contrast, respondents who found their current job through other methods lived in communities with a

Table 4 Average Characteristics of Respondents' Community Area by Method of Finding Current Job

	Community area poverty level (%)	Community area unemployment rate (%)	Percentage of blacks in community area	N
All				
Found current job through neighbor	10.2	8.3	31.1	12
Found current job through other methods	9.4	8.9	34.2	66
Not working	8.3	8.4	33.1	16
Whites				
Found current job through neighbor	4.1	4.7	12.0	8
Found current job through other methods	2.9*	4.2*	5.6	42
Not working	4.5	5.9	8.1	10
Blacks				
Found current job through neighbor	22.2	15.5	69.2	4
Found current job through other methods	21.5	17.6	87.6	23
Not working	16.6	13.6	86.0	5

Source: Compiled by author from interviews conducted with dislocated workers from the Reservoir Press and U.S. Census (1989).
Two-tailed t-tests: * = $p < .10$; ** = $p < .05$.

poverty rate of 9.4%, an unemployment rate of 8.9%, and a black population of 34.2%. Finally, respondents who were not working lived in communities with a poverty rate of 8.3%, an unemployment rate of 8.4%, and a black population of 33.1%.

To confirm the hypothesis that neighborhood poverty increases unemployment by limiting access to informal employment information, we would expect to find lower rates of poverty and unemployment in those communities where respondents who found their job through a neighbor reside. Clearly, these minimal differences do not support the notion that neighborhood poverty decreased the likelihood of finding a job through a community member.

The results do not change much when the analysis is done separately for blacks and whites. However, it does appear that blacks who found their current jobs through neighbors lived in more racially integrated communities than did those who found their job through some other method or those who were not working. Specifically, blacks who found their jobs through a neighbor lived in communities in which 69.2% of their community were black whereas those who found their job through other methods or were not working lived in communities where 87.6% and 86.0% of their communities were black, respectively. While the small number of cases in these categories prevents these differences from being statistically significant, they do suggest that more racially integrated housing patterns provide blacks with greater access to informal employment information through neighbors. However, support for this possibility is weakened, since almost all of the neighbors who helped black respondents find jobs were also black.

To further investigate the possibility that neighborhood level poverty may increase unemployment by limiting access to informal employment information, an analysis of respondents' job brokering activity is presented in Tables 5 and 6. In general, roughly half of all respondents, regardless of race, had informally helped an ex-coworker in his/her job search since the plant had closed. Respondents assisted an average of six different people, while more than two thirds of all respondents helped someone get a job.[13] Black respondents were considerably more likely than white respondents to have brokered a successful match between a job seeker and job vacancy.

Again, for these results to be consistent with the hypothesis that neighborhood poverty increases unemployment by limiting access to informal employment information, we would expect to find "good" job brokers living in communities with less poverty and unemployment and "bad" job brokers residing in communities with higher rates of poverty and unemployment. The results suggest that if any differences exist, they are in the opposite direction. That is, respondents who helped others find a job lived in communities with higher poverty and unemployment rates compared to respondents who did not offer similar assistance.

Table 5 Respondents' Job Brokering Activity (number of cases in parenthesis)

	All	White	Black
Percentage who helped others in job search	49.4 (85)	52.6 (57)	48.1 (27)
Average number of people helped in job search	6.5 (42)	6.2 (30)	7.2 (12)
Percentage who helped others find a job	67.6 (37)	57.7** (26)	90.9 (11)

Source: Compiled by author from interviews conducted with dislocated workers from the Reservoir Press.

Two-tailed t-tests: * = $p < .10$; ** = $p < .05$; asterisks show contrast between white and black respondents.

Table 6 Average Characteristics of Respondents' Community Area by Job Brokering Activity

	Community area poverty level (%)	Community area unemployment rate (%)	Percentage of blacks in community area	N
All				
Helped others in job search	9.4	8.5	29.9	43
Didn't help others in job search	9.3	8.9	36.6	41
Helped others find job	9.8*	9.4	36.4	25
Didn't help others find job	4.1	4.9	10.1	12
White				
Helped others in job search	3.0	4.3	4.4	30
Didn't help others in job search	3.9	4.8	10.6	26
Helped others find job	3.7	4.9	3.5	15
Didn't help others find job	2.4	3.8	2.0	11
Black				
Helped others in job search	24.1	18.2	88.7	13
Didn't help others in job search	19.9	17.0	87.3	15
Helped others find job	19.0	16.2	85.9	10
Didn't help others find job	23.0	17.0	99.0	1

Source: Compiled by author from interviews conducted with dislocated workers from the Reservoir Press and U.S. Census (1989).

Two-tailed t-tests: * = $p < .10$; ** = $p < .05$.

For example, black respondents who helped others in their job search lived in communities where 24.1% of the population were poor and 18.2% were unemployed, whereas black respondents who did not help others in their job search lived in communities where 19.9% of the population were poor and 17.0% were unemployed. Similarly, black respondents who helped others find a job lived in communities where 19% of the population were poor and 16.2% were unemployed, whereas black respondents who did not help others find a job lived in communities with a poverty rate of 23% and an unemployment rate of 17%. While successful black job brokers tended to live in slightly less racially segregated communities (85.9% black compared to 99% black), the difference is not statistically significant.

Overall, these results suggest that for dislocated workers from the Reservoir Press finding a job through a neighbor is *not* closely associated with neighborhood poverty or unemployment. How can we reconcile these results with the research discussed at the beginning of this chapter which shows that at the aggregate-level youth unemployment increases with poverty concentration? The most obvious answer is that access to the labor market through social networks operates differently depending on age. As noted previously, it is possible that as individuals enter adulthood, their social networks become less and less defined by geography. Teenagers begin with networks that are almost exclusively bound by the community in which they reside. As they and other members from their childhood network become older, establishing their own households in different locales, network composition becomes less bounded by a particular residential community. Therefore, it is possible that youth unemployment is negatively affected by neighborhood poverty at the same time that working-age adult unemployment is either marginally affected or has no impact.[14]

This raises an interesting question of whether growing up in communities with high levels of concentrated poverty reduces employment opportunities later in life by truncating the number of contacts in one's social network that could provide access to labor market opportunities in the future. It is not difficult to imagine an individual who has grown up in an urban ghetto and is shut out of word-of-mouth employment opportunities later in life, since his/her childhood network is largely composed of similar individuals who are also weakly attached to the labor market. Unfortunately, the design of the current study and its lack of lifelong longitudinal data on residential location does not permit an investigation of this hypothesis.

It is also possible that concentrated poverty does limit adult labor market access by isolating individuals from word-of-mouth employment information but only after a community's level of poverty concentration reaches a particular threshold. If only a few respondents from the Reservoir Press lived in communities that surpassed this hypothetical level of concentrated poverty needed to observe the constriction of informal job brokering, then the lack of a significant relationship between neighborhood poverty and access to informal job information may simply be an artifact of the data and not a shortcoming of the theory. While some research has found nonlinear effects on the structure and composition of social networks (Fernandez and Harris 1992), as well as on school dropout rates and teenage childbearing (Crane 1991), it is unclear whether such effects exist for receipt and/or transmission of informal employment information.

V. CONCLUSION

The role of social networks as a mediating mechanism for the rise of ghetto joblessness has received considerable attention by social scientists and policy makers. To move this discussion forward, this paper uses data from interviews with dislocated workers who lost their job as a result of an inner city plant closing to systematically analyze the relationship between neighborhood poverty and finding jobs through community ties. The postdisplacement experiences of the Reservoir Press employees suggests that communities with a higher proportion of employed adults do not necessarily provide greater access or flow of informal job information. Accordingly, the exchange of successful job information may *not* be substantially lower in highly concentrated poverty communities.

The implications of these findings suggest that explanations of increased inner-city joblessness, other than the hypothesized mismatch between job seekers and informal job brokers, need to be given more consideration. These include employer discrimination (Kirschenman and Neckerman 1991; Kasinitz 1992; Wilson 1996; Turner 1997), residential segregation (Massey and Denton 1993), and the deindustrialization of the urban employment base from goods-producing manufacturing sectors to the knowledge intensive service sectors (Wilson 1987; Kasarda, 1989, 1995).

These findings also suggest that the benefits associated with housing policies designed to move mostly black inner city residents to mostly white suburban communities, such as the Section 8 program and scattered site public housing, are likely not the result of increased access to informal job networks. As noted above, other plausible explanations include a Hawthorne effect and/or a renewed sense of self-efficacy and opportunity prompted by an exogenous change in residential location. Unfortunately, the preceding analysis is unable to test either of these other possible explanations.

Before concluding, it is important to mention the limitations of the data used in this paper. First, the case study design limits the use of these findings to draw inferences about urban labor markets in general. While there are many similarities between the respondents in this study and the larger universe of dislocated workers, as well as workers in traditional rust belt cities, it is unclear whether these results can be generalized to residents of the inner city. Second, the small number of respondents compared to large-scale cross-sectional social science surveys is a source of concern. Although this data may not suffer from some of the reliability problems that frequently plague larger data collection efforts, it is unknown whether the experiences of these workers are unique. Lastly, the low response rate may further skew the results; however, the emotional nature of plant closings and job loss makes the task of achieving a high response rate difficult.

Given these shortcomings, future research should improve on the present effort by systematically investigating whether inner-city joblessness has in fact increased as a result of poverty concentration through lack of access to informal employment information. Clearly, more needs to be learned of the structural constraints which limit economic opportunity in modern urban centers. The role of social networks as a mediating mechanism in fostering high unemployment and other social ills is too often investigated as a residual explanation. That is, more research is needed that *directly* tests the significance of social networks in determining economic and social outcomes. Such efforts will be invaluable to social scientists and policy makers as they struggle to understand the causes of contemporary urban poverty.

ENDNOTES

1. The extent to which participants in these programs actually experience a dramatic change in the status of their neighborhoods is subject to interpretation. In Chicago, for example, a recent study conducted by researchers at the University of Illinois at Chicago found that families using Section 8 vouchers to find private apartments are clustered in communities with black populations over 90% and where there are also large concentrations of poverty (McRoberts 1997).
2. Ethnographic studies of ghetto communities conducted in Baltimore show that many residents are faced with the difficult task of raising children in a dangerous and unpredictable environment (Furstenberg 1993). To ''protect'' themselves and their children, parents develop an ''individualistic strategy of family management'' whereby parents try to segregate their children from the surrounding community, insulating them from the potentially harmful environment. This may result in attempts by parents to teach their ''children to resist the local culture, encouraging them to feel different from (and better than) their neighbors. Other parents, less confident in their ability to internalize their values, maintain a tighter rein of control. . . . These parents are extremely wary of entrusting their children to the care of others, especially others in the immediate neighborhood'' (Furstenberg 1993:238–239). The tendency of some inner-city residents and families to insulate themselves from an uncertain environment may mean that they are less likely to interact with neighbors. Moreover, these adaptive risk management strategies may tend to increase the level of distrust among neighbors and eliminate any willingness to trans-

mit job information to other community members. This may be particularly true among the more established and economically successful residents who may also be more likely to know of employment opportunities.

3. The increased use of informal job search methods among Hispanics is likely the result of language barriers, limiting the use of formal job search methods.
4. Modest differences were found in the spatial distribution of social ties by levels of neighborhood poverty concentration. Residents of an economically heterogeneous inner city area, as well as residents from a working- and middle-class black suburb, reported social support networks where extralocal ties accounted for 62% and 59%, respectively. While these figures illustrate that residing in areas of poverty concentration is likely to increase dependence on neighbors for social support, the magnitude of these differences is relatively small.
5. A related stream of research has studied the impact of mixed-income housing on the life chances of low-income tenants (for a review of the most recent findings on these housing programs see Schwartz and Tajbakhsh [1997]). Preliminary results suggest that mixed-income housing programs do not increase low-income tenants' employment rates or access to informal employment information.
6. It is important to note that other dislocated worker surveys have been able to achieve much higher response rates (see, for example, Ashton and Iadicola [1989]). Most of these data collection efforts have been conducted on unionized workers. This is in part because unions are often interested in sponsoring such research. Documenting the negative consequences of job loss can be used to increase leverage in future negotiations. It can also be used in legal conflicts between affected workers and their previous employer. In general, labor organizations provide legitimacy to dislocated worker surveys, and may even directly encourage (and even compensate) members who participate. The downside of studying unionized workers is that they constitute only a small fraction of the American work force, and are not terribly representative of workers in general.
7. The actual name of the company has been changed to ensure the anonymity of the respondents.
8. Even though the decision to close the plant did not come until 1993, the number of employees at this facility had been declining for the past 25 years. At its height in the early-1970s, this facility employed more than 7000 people. As old contracts expired, new contracts were diverted to other newly constructed or acquired plants that were perceived as more efficient. It is interesting to note that the timing of this decline began soon after the civil disturbances of the late 1960s—some of which occurred in the same neighborhood as the Reservoir Press.
9. For respondents who live in Chicago, the community-level unit of analysis is the community area, whereas noncity respondents were assigned the characteristics of their suburbs or townships. All of these localities usually incorporate several census tracts. While these units do not perfectly capture the ecological boundaries of actual communities, they do provide a reasonable portrait of the area in which respondents reside.
10. These losses are consistent with other research on dislocated workers (see, for example, Hamermesh [1989]; Jacobson et al. [1993a,b]). This research has shown that some of the difference in pre- and postdisplacement wage levels can be explained

by firm-specific skills, efficiency wages, and implicit contracts. The firm-specific hypothesis states that many displaced workers are thought to possess skills that are especially suited for their old positions and these skills in their new position do not translate into equivalent productivity gains. These firm-specific skills, it is argued, prevent dislocated workers from finding employment at similar rates of compensation since their skills have no external demand. As for the efficiency wage hypothesis, dislocated workers frequently received wage premiums in their previous position either because of the threat of unionization or because such premiums raised worker productivity on their old job. These efficiency wage arguments assume that workers' productivity depends in part on their wages. Higher than market-clearing wages not only increase unemployment for others, but increase the costs of being fired and help deter shirking. Lastly, dislocated workers may experience large earning losses due to their involvement in implicit contracts while employed in their predisplaced jobs. This concept implies a nonbinding commitment in which the employer offers benefits such as above market wages, long-term employment, and above-average working conditions in exchange for the employee's understanding that he/she will forgo shirking and/or quit for better opportunities.

11. In order to avoid underestimating the importance of finding jobs through word of mouth, respondents were asked to name and rank all of the job search methods used in obtaining their current job. Since only a few respondents reported using multiple job search methods, these figures are based on the method the respondent considered most important in finding his/her current job. It is also important to note that several respondents were working multiple jobs. In these cases, the most important job (either in terms of hours or wages) is included in this analysis.
12. Only two respondents changed residential location at the time of the interview. Each found his/her new job while still living at his/her old address, and as a consequence, were assigned the community characteristics of this residential location.
13. The measure of helping others find a job likely contains some measurement error since some respondents were not aware of whether their job search assistance produced a job offer and whether that offer was accepted.
14. An analysis of respondents' average age by job finding method does provide some support for this hypothesis (not shown in tables). On average, respondent's who found their job through a neighbor were 48 years old, compared to respondents who found their job through some other method were 54 years old. This difference is statistically significant at the $p < .10$ level.

REFERENCES

Ashton, P.J., and Iadicola, P. (1989). The differential impact of a plant closing on the reemployment and income patterns of displaced blue- and white-collar employees. *Sociological Focus* *22*(2), 119–142.

Briggs, X. (1997). Moving up versus moving out: neighborhood effects in housing programs. *Housing Policy Debate* *8*(1), 195–234.

Campbell, K.E., and Lee, B.A. (1992). Sources of personal neighbor networks: social integration, need, or time? *Social Forces 70*(4), 1077–1100.

Fischer, C.S., et al. (1977). *Networks and Places: Social Relations in an Urban Setting*. New York: Free Press.

Furstenberg, F.F. Jr. (1993). How families manage risk and opportunity in dangerous neighborhoods. In *Sociology and the Public Agenda* edited by W.J. Wilson. Newburry Park: Sage Publications.

Granovetter, M. (1995/1974). *Getting a Job: A Study of Contacts and Careers*, 2nd ed. Chicago: University of Chicago Press.

Guest, A.M., and Barrett, L.A. (1983). The social organization of local areas. *Urban Affairs Quarterly 19*.

Hamermesh, D.S. (1989). What do we know about worker displacement in the U.S.? *Industrial Relations 28*(1), 51–59.

Holzer, H.J. (1987). Informal job search and black youth unemployment. *American Economic Review 77*, 446–452.

Jacobson, L.S., LaLonde, R.J., and Sullivan, D.G. (1993a). *The Costs of Worker Dislocation*. Kalamazoo, MI: W.E. UpJohn Institute.

Jacobson, L.S., LaLonde, R.J., and Sullivan, D.G. (1993b). Earnings losses of displaced workers. *American Economic Review 83*(4), 685–709.

Jencks, C. and Mayer, S. (1990). The social consequences of growing up in a poor neighborhood. In *Inner City Poverty in the United States*, edited by National Research Council. Washington, DC: National Academy Press.

Johnson, J.H., Bienenstock, E.J., and Farrell, W.C. (1996). Bridging social networks and female labor force participation in a multi-ethnic metropolis. Unpublished manuscript, Department of Sociology, University of California, Los Angeles.

Kasarda, J.D. (1989). The urban industrial transition and the underclass. *Annals of the American Academy of Political and Social Science 501*, 26–47.

Kasarda, J.D. (1995). Industrial restructuring and the changing location of jobs. In *State of the Union: America in the 1990s*, Vol. 1, edited by R. Farley. New York: Russel Sage Foundation.

Kirschenman, J. and Neckerman, K.M. (1991). The meaning of race for employers. In *The Urban Underclass*, edited by C. Jencks and P.E. Peterson. Washington, DC: Urban Institute.

Massey, D.S., and Denton, N.A. (1993). *American Apartheid: Segregation and the Making of the Underclass*. Cambridge, MA:Harvard University Press.

McRoberts, F. (1997). Ruling halts steering of poor to suburbs. *Chicago Tribune*, Aug. 29.

Montgomery, J.D. (1994). Weak ties, employment, and inequality: an equilibrium analysis. *American Journal of Sociology 99*(5), 1212–1236.

Oliver, M.L. (1988). The urban black community as network: toward a social network perspective. *Sociological Quarterly 29*(4), 623–645.

O'Regan, K.M., and Quigley, J.M. (1991). Labor market access and labor market outcomes for urban youth. *Journal of Regional Science and Urban Economics 21*, 277–293.

O'Regan, K.M., and Quigley, J.M. (1993). Family networks and youth access to jobs. *Journal of Urban Economics 34*(2), 230–248.

O'Regan, K.M. (1993). The effect of social networks and concentrated poverty on black and Hispanic youth unemployment. *Annals of Regional Science 27*, 327–342.

Reingold, D.A. (1999). The private sector as a sociological laboratory. *American Sociologist 30*(1), 75–88.

Rosenbaum, J.E., and Popkin, S.J. (1991). Employment and earnings of blacks who move to middles-class suburbs. In *The Urban Underclass*, edited by C. Jencks and P.E. Peterson. Washington, DC: Urban Institute.

Stack, C.B. (1974). *All Out Kin: Strategies for Survival in Black Communities*. New York: Harper and Row.

Tienda, M. (1991). Poor people and poor places: deciphering neighborhood effects on poverty outcomes. In *Macro-Micro Linkages in Sociology*, edited by J. Huber. Newbury Park, CA: Sage.

Topa, G. (1995). Social interactions, local spillovers and unemployment. Unpublished manuscript, Department of Economics, University of Chicago.

Turner, S.C. (1997). Barriers to a better break: employer discrimination and spacial mismatch in metropolitan Detriot. *Journal of Urban Affairs 19*(2), 123–141.

Venkatesh, S.A. (1997). A three-tier model: how helping occurs in urban poor communities. *Social Service Review*. December: 574–606.

Wellman, B. and Leighton, B. (1979). Networks, neighbors, and communities: approaches to the study of the community question. *Urban Affairs Quarterly 14*(3), 363–390.

Wilson, W.J. (1987). *The Truly Disadvantaged: The Inner City, the Underclass, and Public Policy*. Chicago: University of Chicago.

Wilson, W.J. (1996). *When Work Disappears: The World of the Urban Poor*. New York: Alfred A. Knopf.

26

U.S. Public Policy Toward a Dynamic Increasing-Returns Industry

Henry E. Kilpatrick, Jr.
George Mason University, Fairfax, Virginia

> But in the increasing returns case, laissez-faire gives no guarantee that the "fittest" technology (in the long run case) will the one that survives.
> —W. Brian Arthur (1994:27)

I. INTRODUCTION

Besides enumerating and explaining a number of ways that dynamic increasing returns might be achieved, this paper discusses the application of competition policy, regulatory policy, intellectual property rights, and industrial policy to those segments of the computer industry thought to exhibit this behavior. The assumption behind the analysis and discussion contained herein is that some reasonable policy goals are as follows: to increase production (but not above efficient levels) while minimizing costs, and to mitigate the potential lock-in effects associated with dynamic returns. Equity goals, such as income distribution, may be just as important if not more so as a matter of policy, but they are much more complicated to consider particularly when the knowledge base in this new theoretical arena is so minuscule. This analysis will serve more to open the subject up for discussion rather than to provide systematic evidence as to the appropriate policies. There is not enough known yet as to whether the theory has general applicability to a large segment of American industry, although casual observation strongly suggests that it does have great importance in some critical technologies, including semiconductors and software.

Increasing returns was at least foreshadowed, if not adequately theorized, by Adam Smith (1776, reprinted 1910), who noted that the division of labor is limited by the extent of the market. Smith advanced his economic ideas as Western society changed from an agricultural epoch to the inaugural of the industrial era. As this age in turn changed into a more advanced industrial age marked by large-scale industry rather than small local pin factories, Marshall and others developed the notion of economies of scale as well as the concepts of internal and external returns to scale. As this era now changes into a technological age, the notion of dynamic increasing returns is being developed to describe the characteristics of what are probably the most productive industries of this period in terms of economic output.[1] In Internet jargon, one might say that this theory is under ''heavy construction,'' and all of its implications are not yet fully known. However, it is important to understand the policy as well as the theoretical implications of dynamic returns.

II. BACKGROUND

Smith argued that competition would work to society's advantage in advancing public policy in the dawning industrial age of his time when policies promoting cartels and mercantilism were no longer useful. Later, when large-scale industry and monopoly became a concern, trust busting and monopoly regulation were used to advance public policy (at least in the United States). In fact, the static increasing returns to scale literature teaches that competition is not compatible with increasing returns, i.e., the ''core'' is empty.[2] However, when many of those industries believed to be characterized by dynamic returns (for example, advanced electronics and electronics products such as semiconductors, computers, communications equipment and software)[3] are examined, one observes what appears to be unrelenting competition, even in those cases where government aid in one form or another is provided to all the competitors. In fact, product cycles may be so short that patents are useless.[4] This is not compatible with economists' old and somewhat outdated understanding of increasing returns industries represented by huge power plants, railroads, telephone lines, and pipelines. The theory of monopolistic competition, which trade theorists such as Paul Krugman (1991), as well as endogenous growth theorists (Gene M. Grossman and Elhanan Helpman, 1991) use in order to get around the technical modeling problems of static increasing returns, does not appear to be compatible with real-world observations of increasing returns industries. Furthermore, W. Brian Arthur (1990a) argues that there are cases in which agglomeration economies in the regional location of industries grant increasing returns but do not imply monopoly, and that his results should be transferable to other circumstances.[5]

The theory of dynamic returns conjectures a disequilibrium hypothesis rather than making use of the neoclassical Newtonian equilibrium. Thus it is extraordinarily hard to model and test empirically. To a large extent, this theory is based upon the physics of thermodynamics. In fact, these new concepts of economic growth and behavior may have as much to do with a movement to a thermodynamic rather than a Newtonian metaphor in science and social science philosophies as they do with observations of the changes in the economy.

III. THEORY AND SOURCES OF DYNAMIC RETURNS

Nicolas Kaldor equated ''dynamic economies of scale'' to ''learning by doing'' (Kaldor 1972, in Buchanan 1993:85–105; see also Arrow 1962). Indeed, this is part of the story, but not the entire story. Arthur (1988) posits a self-reinforcing, dynamical economic system in which dynamic increasing returns (but no longer simply returns *to scale*) lead to the following possibilities: (1) multiple equilibria, or a technological solution is picked that is not necessarily the best choice; (2) dynamic inefficiency if the winning technology is inferior to the losing technology; (3) lock-in, or inability to exit the dominant technology, even if there is a more efficient one available; and (4) path dependence,[6] or a prevailing solution which is determined as much by historical events as purely rational action.

A. Mathematics of Increasing Returns

Mathematically, the engineering and economic concept of *returns to scale* is simply the change in output due to a change in an index of inputs. The economics of increasing returns to scale implies a production function in which a proportional change in the units of input results in a greater than proportional increase in output. Formally, a production function for an industry may be defined as follows:

$$Q = f(L, K, H)$$

and is homogeneous of degree h at time period 1 where Q = output, K = capital input, L = labor input, and H = human capital.

If inputs are increased in proportion at time period 2 such that:

$$\mathrm{o}^{h}Q = f(\mathrm{c}L, \mathrm{c}K, \mathrm{c}H)$$

then there are increasing returns to scale if $h > 1$, decreasing returns to scale if $h < 1$, and constant returns to scale if $h = 1$. Or, to state it simply, if inputs are doubled, outputs will double under constant returns, more than double under increasing returns, and less than double under decreasing returns. Note that varying returns are also possible. Varying returns, as the designation implies, posit a nonconstant ''h.''

It should be noted that the relative simplicity of the mathematical production function belies the empirical difficulties in its estimation. In addition to the inherent accounting and measurement problems, available data are restricted to actual rather than potential production. Aside from the major inputs of capital and labor, it may be difficult to properly identify as well as quantify the additional inputs necessary for production. Human capital is particularly difficult to quantify (Mankiw et al. 1992).[7] Furthermore, the mix may change over time, and business cycles and other macroeconomic phenomena will also affect output. Finally, the level of abstraction inherent in the model, and the apparent mathematical restrictions, as found in previous attempts at empirical estimation, are problematic.

These are merely some problems with the production function. The dynamic increasing returns concept is realistically a dynamics problem, with a time variable present, while the traditional mathematical characterization of the production function and the most common measurement tools are essentially static. Furthermore, when cost, output, and pricing are all put into play, it is discovered that the concept of increasing returns is not compatible with any notion of pure competition, but tools for dealing with oligopoly are too underdeveloped to cope with the problem very well.

B. Pricing and Dynamic Returns

While beyond the scope of this paper, the pricing decisions of industries characterized by dynamic increasing returns are quite important. Economic theory argues that sunk costs are bygones; only decisions at the margin matter. However, there is the issue of discerning and measuring the proper costs to consider in a marginal analysis. The marginal cost of the new technology includes all fixed costs involved in setup, while the marginal cost of the old technology may include only what it costs to operate it. Therefore, the time period over which costs are measured is crucial. Also, particularly if the technology product is an intermediate good rather than a consumer good, the savings in costs from adopting the new technology must be measured. This suggests cost-benefit analysis.

No competitive equilibrium price exists in an increasing returns world of either the static or dynamic variety characterized by more than one producer.[8] This phenomenon was characterized earlier as ''empty core'' theory. Again, this theory posits a circumstance (generally, but not necessarily, characterized by oligopoly or monopolistic competition) which exists because no stable coalitions can be formed; i.e., there is too much competition for the market. This suggests that government intervention in the production of the good or service, or even actual production by the government, may not result in a price that is more inefficient than that resulting from the interplay of market forces, since the market will not enforce efficient pricing. Multiple equilibria can be explained by the theory of the empty core. Note that a natural monopoly has a filled core, due to the ability of producer and consumer to form stable coalitions, even though the coalitions do not offer a competitive situation (thus, this structure is ''second best''). In general, it is oligopolies that exhibit the phenomenon.

C. Sources of Increasing Returns

What are the factors that generate increasing returns? As referenced previously, the classical and early neoclassical economists noted that the division of labor is the historical foundation of increasing returns. Most of this century's literature, written while its authors witnessed the growth of industry into large-scale production, has been devoted to economies to scale. Scale economies are available due to high fixed costs and low marginal costs per unit of production, thus allowing for the average cost to drop over a wide range of output. Only more recently has the literature returned to the tradition of examining the division of labor, particularly with regard to human capital. Theodore Schultz (1993:8), citing Allyn Young's approach (which, as he says, is based upon Adam Smith's), lists a number of generalized generators of increasing returns beginning with the division of labor.[9] James Buchanan and Yong Yoon (1996) also take the approach of examining the division of labor, but theirs is in a more classical tradition.

Economies of scale in production were viewed by most neoclassical economists as the primary, if not the sole, means of generating increasing returns of any variety. In fact, the economics literature sometimes appears muddled in this regard, with increasing returns to scale and economies of scale used interchangeably.

Economies of scale are important, but may no longer be the most important means of generating dynamic increasing returns in a modern economy characterized by high-technology industries. The literature, as well as observations and analysis of the production system, indicates that the following potential generators of nonconvexity can be specified:

1. Production economies which, as mentioned, consist of economies of scale from large-scale production of a single product. In addition, economies of scope from large-scale multiproduct production should be included as a production economy.
2. Network externalities, or coordination effects where the addition of a member to a network results not only in that member receiving a gain in utility, but all members currently in the network benefit from the addition of the new member up to a level at which it is no longer beneficial for those not currently in the network to join (for example, the Internet).[10]

3. Learning effects, which improve products or lower costs over time.[11]
4. Adaptive expectations, whereby the presumed dominance of a particular product or service creates a self-fulfilling demand for that product or service (also described by Arthur as informational increasing returns).
5. Production standards, which are specified dimensions of production, quality, and/or function which are imposed upon producers of a particular technology (or good or service) by government, trade associations, or other bodies for the purpose of standardization.
6. The existence of gateway technologies, which allow the interchangeable use of two or more products or product designs.
7. Historical path dependence, or the summation of chance occurrences over time.
8. Agglomeration economies, or economies derived from shared spatially referenced inputs (economies of clustering, which include improvements in communication among suppliers, and among those who work for competing interests).
9. Transfer economies, which are transactions economies derived from location networks. These are similar to agglomeration economies, but the emphasis is on trade among the networked parties.
10. Technological feedback (or autocatalytic) economies which allow advanced production quality and standards due to the enhanced quality of inputs; that is, makers of inputs to a process supply higher and higher quality inputs, which makes the outputs of higher and higher quality, which creates greater demand for the outputs. This process continuously feeds back into the system.
11. Organizational improvements within firms, industries, or economies. This catch-all category includes improvements in internal management structure, better communications between customers and firms, improvements in institutional factors such as property law and enforcement, leadership for regional strategy development and other things that enhance the production process over time.[12]

This list is not necessarily exhaustive. Furthermore, one would expect multicollinearity among these listed variables. In addition, further analysis is needed of cause and effect, particularly with regard to historical path dependence, which some contend to be a property of nonconvex systems, rather than a cause of the phenomenon (see Arthur 1989). Moreover, Levy (1992) notes that even in principle, it is difficult to distinguish between returns to scale and technological progress at the level of an industry or economy. Hence, one would expect even more difficulty in empirically separating the various contributors to dynamic increasing returns.

Table 1 Contributions and Sources of Dynamic Scale Economies

Contributions to increasing returns	Internal to the firm[a]	External to firm,[b] internal to industry	External to firm, external to to industry
Production economies (scale and scope)	×		
Network externalities	×	×	
Learning effects (R&D, training and education)	×	×	×
Adaptive expectations (informational increasing returns)		×	×
Production standards		×	
Gateway technologies	×	×	
Historical path dependence		×	×
Agglomeration		×	×
Transfer economies	×	×	
Technological feedback (autocatalytic economies)		×	
Organizational	×	×	

[a] ''Internal to the firm'' is defined as those increasing returns that are generated internally.
[b] ''External to the firm'' is defined as those increasing returns that are generated externally, but influence a number of firms that are able to capture them. Note that property rights cannot always be properly assigned to these returns to scale, with resultant market failure. Also, the concept of industry presented here does not include input suppliers.

Table 1 indicates whether these factors are internal to the firm; that is, generated internally, external to the firm but internal to the industry, external to both the firm and the industry, or any possible combination of these. For example, economies of scale and scope are always generated internally. On the other hand, production standards are imposed upon (or self-imposed upon) entire industries from outside the individual firm. Autocatalytic factors come into play from outside the firm and industry, if one assumes the industry in question is selling final goods to consumers, rather than inputs to the process.[13]

The processes, which link these causal variables to the inputs in production function(s), are not well known and are a part of current research efforts into the theory of dynamic returns. What is known is that these variables will act to augment the inputs of human capital, labor, and physical capital in various ways.

D. Dynamic Returns: Both Positive and Negative Effects

The primary benefits of dynamic returns are quite obvious—more goods and services at lower and lower production costs over time. One might wonder if there is anything at all problematic with this. There is an obstacle to economic nirvana that concerns policy analysts, as one might expect, or at least there is in theory. This is the phenomenon known as ''lock-in.''That is, as mentioned earlier, a particular inferior technology may become ''locked in'' to the production process while more dynamically efficient technologies are available.[14]

The existence of dynamic returns lowers per unit costs of a good or service. This makes it more attractive to produce and consume (in fact, dynamic increasing returns may be viewed as a positive externality). While this would normally appear to have great benefit to society (once it can come to grips with the inherent pricing problems), there may also be adverse side effects in the long run. Society may lock in to an inferior and more expensive technology and fail to develop a newer technology.

How might this happen, especially if the newer technology could also be produced under dynamic increasing returns? Production under older technology is likely to be at a point which is further down the firm or industry's long run average cost curve than the newer technology would be at its inception, and existing producers of the old are unwilling to convert to the new.[15] It may be possible that production using old technology has settled into a competitive equilibrium, whereas the newer technology can only be produced under non-equilibrium conditions (inefficient oligopoly where no coalitions are formed to bring about a movement toward equilibrium). Finally, existing institutional arrangements within organizations may hamper the ability to adopt the new technology.[16] Bresnahan and Trajtenberg (1992) similarly argue that institutions display more inertia than leading technologies, and as a ''general-purpose technology'' era comes to a close, an economy may get stuck with the ''wrong'' institutions.[17]

There are two paths that are likely to be followed. First, the owners of the new technology, hypothesizing that it will eventually supplant the old, could adopt a pricing strategy that makes it competitive with, and possibly positioned to replace, the old technology. However, this implies losses until a level of production is reached to allow profits to be made. This pricing strategy depends entirely upon the ''deep pockets'' of the potential producer as well as risk and present value analyses. Hence, it can be seen that there is a potential for market failure, whereby the free market does not adopt the production decision that is most efficient in the long run, even though the short run decision appears efficient. As Arthur et al. (1987) outline: ''For non-ergodic systems—like competing technologies with sufficient increasing returns to adoption—these properties of the macro-structure that emerge—*non-predictability*, potential *non-superiority* and structural *rigidity*—appear to be common and to some degree inevitable.''[18]

Arthur (1989a:717) argues that the positive feedback effects leading to potential lock-in are derived from four sources: large fixed costs, learning effects, coordination effects, and adaptation expectations. He further maintains that all but the expectations effects are associated with high-technology products. Hence modern high-technology economies and sectors are presumed to be more likely to show self-reinforcing mechanisms than traditional ones such as agriculture and basic manufacturing.

It is still an open question as to whether the size of the firms that dominate the industry plays any role in dynamic returns. Certainly large firms would be more able to take advantage of traditional economies of scale and scope by being able to bear large fixed costs. Zoltan Acs and David Audretsch (1990, Appendix D) cite a Small Business Administration study which uses the Small Business Innovation Data Base. In 1982, in the category of semiconductors and related devices (SIC 3674), small firms had 29 innovations and large firms had 91. However, this is a rather dated study and may be skewed by merger activity if large firms bought up small ones during the period. Furthermore, the entire database shows that small business had 2104 innovations and large firms had 2834 during the period.

IV. POLICY ANALYSIS OF DYNAMIC RETURNS INDUSTRIES

A. Competition Policy

There are three policy options with respect to a perceived lack of competition in the marketplace (or the exertion of market power by a monopoly or oligopoly):

1. Break up market power through the use of government's legal powers of antitrust or antimonopoly policy and enforce more competition.
2. Take a "hand-off" approach and leave the market alone, waiting for the dynamics of the market to eventually create competition.
3. Use government regulation to set prices, conditions of service, standards, and other market variables of interest to consumers. This has traditionally been done in the United States through the use of the regulatory agency.

All three of these options have philosophical supporters and detractors. There are also those who generally consider themselves to be pragmatic and allow the particular circumstances to decide which option is preferable.

Competition policy in the United States has historically been marked by the public's fear of monopoly power of large corporations and a confidence in competition. Consequently, legal antitrust action has been used over much of the past century to break up large firms with significant market power and to prevent or alter the terms of merger agreements if the newly created firm increased concentration substantially. Where there were natural monopolies and oligopolies such that this was not feasible, regulatory commissions were established to regulate these firms that operated in critical industries.

The first antitrust law in the US was the Sherman Act of 1890. The Clayton Act of 1914 and the Federal Trade Commission Act of 1914 followed it. In addition, as will be discussed below, there are a whole host of laws that regulate privately owned monopolies and oligopolies. These include the Interstate Commerce Act of 1887, the Federal Power Act of 1921, The Federal Communications Act of 1934 and the Natural Gas Act of 1938. Most, if not all, states now regulate intrastate public utility monopolies.

The goal of US antitrust and regulatory intervention has been to enforce (or to attempt to replicate) laissez-faire notions of economic competition against what is perceived to be excesses of big business. U.S. antitrust laws can be viewed as a means to restore ''balance'' in the marketplace by creating additional competition or preventing mergers that limit competition. The enforcement of these laws has varied over the political cycle, as has the enforcement of administrative regulations.

At present, U.S. antitrust laws, when they are strictly enforced at all, are generally enforced only against some few horizontal mergers.[19] Vertical mergers are not seen to be a significant problem, except in the case of regulated companies where vertical integration may possibly be used to evade regulation.[20] In fact, many U.S. economists believe vertical integration is efficient.[21]

This historical antitrust paradigm began to break down in the 1980s, with the advent of global competition from well-crafted consumer durables and high tech goods that poured into U.S. markets. The *Merger Guidelines*, first issued in 1984 and revised in 1992, set forth the government's position as to how mergers and acquisitions would be viewed from the standpoint of antitrust enforcement. The fact of the matter is that there have been few large mergers challenged in recent years, although there are often some agreements concerning divestiture made with the Department of Justice prior to the mergers being approved. Furthermore, there are no current challenges to those firms that have simply grown large, even if they meet the Department of Justice thresholds for possessing significant market power.

Large plant size does not appear to be necessary to capture dynamic returns, particularly since simple economies of scale are no longer as important as they once were. There are over 1200 semiconductor manufacturing plants in the world. Semiconductor plants are not completely fungible, but the existence of this large a number would appear to indicate that plant size is not as important as it is in other industries, although it is certainly important for certain types of chips. Also, computer technology often moves so fast that there may be little to be gained by horizontal merger. For example, as Don Kash and Robert Rycroft (1996:8) point out, none of the dominant manufacturers of the 5.25-in. floppy disk are competitors today in the market for 3.5-in. disks.

However, there are large firms, such as Microsoft, that some investigators believe to be anticompetitive, possessing significant market power and being willing to use it. In fact, a case has been made that Microsoft's Windows software, the dominant computer operating system, was until recently an inferior technology. Due to apparent strategic errors of Apple Computer as well as path dependent processes, the major computer manufacturers (most of which are essentially commodity producers at present, having adopted an open system by assembling computers from others' parts rather than crafting their own) continue to use the Windows software. However, certain aspects of the Windows technology are now believed to be virtually the same as the vaunted Apple technology was a decade ago.

While evidence is scant, it would appear that a more stringent antitrust policy toward large software manufacturers could be applied with favorable results, presuming the possible losses to society from monopolization and lock-in of inferior technology.[22] This is not without its drawbacks, including the fact that in the fast-moving world of high technology, a giant may be displaced through competition before the Department of Justice or Federal Trade Commission could act, given Constitutional guarantees of due process. However, one should consider that these companies are granted potential monopoly rights through government-enforced intellectual property rights. While Bill Gates may complain that the government is meddling in his business, he is not rushing to disavow his copyrights.

However, the situation changes somewhat in other potential dynamic returns industries such as the semiconductor industry, where dynamic forward pricing behavior is common.[23] At least with regard to DRAMs, which are more or less ''commodity chips'' (as opposed to the technologically more advanced logic chips), the Japanese industry caught up with and surpassed the U.S. industry. It did so by protecting its home markets and exploiting economies in its ability to sell to the open U.S. market as well as its own and European markets.[24] This implies increasing returns due to production economies as well as causes of a more dynamic nature. Antitrust action in this industry may not be useful. Furthermore, the industry leaders change quite rapidly. ''Moore's law,'' which is Gordon Moore's observation that the semiconductor chip's capacity doubles every 18 months due to technological advances, has meant an 18-month product cycle in the industry. Hence, antitrust policy must still be applied on a case-by-case basis. There do not appear to be any general rules insofar as the application of antitrust to dynamic returns industries.

B. Regulatory Policy

Current regulatory policy (or regulatory policy toward monopolies and oligopolies, so as not to confuse it with environmental, health, and safety policy) is still directed toward industries believed to be natural monopolies, but the old system is breaking down. No industries subject to traditional regulation currently exist where changing technology and markets have not forced changes in the regulatory structure to allow more competition. This competition does not always extend to the retail customer, where congestion and other costs might quickly outweigh the benefits of deregulation in many instances (i.e., one gas distribution and one electric distribution system are all one neighborhood can usually stand).

Very high fixed costs and very low marginal costs mark traditional regulated industries. The same is true of semiconductors to some degree. Software is characterized by high R&D costs and very low costs of production. However, the marketing of software is costly. Furthermore, competition among semiconductors and software does not create congestion costs as would happen in certain traditionally regulated industries, and eminent domain is not necessary for the necessary property rights to deliver the product to the customer.

A good case can be made that regulated industries have become locked-in to inferior technologies during certain periods of their history. It has been argued that regulatory agencies have been partially responsible. Some also make the argument that regulatory policy has been used to shield the industries from competition and made the situation worse. However, there is the countervailing argument that monopoly power leads to greater inefficiencies and society is stuck with a second-best solution. The latter argument has generally prevailed, although, as mentioned, more competition is becoming a reality in the traditionally regulated industries.

Nothing in the current small body of literature on dynamic returns appears to have implications for regulatory policy as practiced in the United States. However, there has been little focus on traditional regulated industries in this literature, even though most of the industries cited (high-technology industries) strongly affect the telecommunications business. Whether the current approach of increased deregulation of traditional monopolies and large-scale oligopolies will prove to be the last word in regulatory policy remains to be seen.

C. Intellectual Property Rights

Intellectual property rights include patents and copyrights. These rights, as noted by Scherer and Ross (1990:620), were first granted in 15th-century Italy. In the United States, they flow from Article I, Section 8 of the U.S. Constitution, which states that Congress shall have the power "to promote the Progress of Science and useful Arts, by securing for limited Times to Authors and Inventors the exclusive Right to their respective Writings and Discoveries."

It is well known that intellectual property rights grant monopolies, some of which have great value and others that do not. There are two major policy aspects to intellectual property rights, international and domestic, and a large number of issues within each. Interestingly, the United States awards patents to the first to invest, while most countries award them to the first to file (Ostry and Nelson 1995:89). There is great concern over international protection of intellectual property rights and harmonization of laws as well as treaties to allow international enforcement. Ostry and Nelson (1995:91) advocate a regime in which both foreign and domestic firms are treated similarly within a given country, regardless of whether international harmonization of intellectual property rights takes place. They also argue that a more open process is needed in the United States and that the objective of harmonization should be more concerned with reducing transaction costs rather than strengthening these rights.

It again appears that there is no cohesive policy applicable to all dynamic returns industries insofar as either international or U.S. policy is concerned. Patents generally offer little protection in the dynamic world of the semiconductor manufacturer, who, as noted, has to have new products on the market continuously. This would also appear to carry over into computer manufacturing, where the life cycle is very short. However, copyright protection for the software industry is a different matter altogether. It is extremely simple and, more important, very cheap to copy software and sell it in world markets.

D. Industrial Policy

Industrial policy is a set of ideas, the formalization of which is elusive. One reason for this difficulty is that the term ‘‘industrial policy’’ has become a loaded word that means different things to different people. Chalmers Johnson (1986:201) argues that industrial policy is first of all an attitude and only then a matter of technique. Others have written books describing their particular perceptions of industrial policy. One simple definition is that an industrial policy is whatever government's policy toward industry is. This is too simple a definition from which to draw useful policy conclusions. Reich (1987:114) suggests that a nation's industrial policy is the sum total of its microeconomic policies. This definition not only seems overly broad and virtually useless, but it also belies the controversy on the subject. Few if any people would dispute the fact that government has microeconomic policies and certainly most citizens would agree that government should have microeconomic policies. The industrial policy controversy is over the nature and extent of government's involvement in the private economy through its use of microeconomic policies. There are those who purport to oppose industrial policy, but who are advocates of various interventionist microeconomic policies. (For example, some economists believe in an interventionist antitrust policy. However, they oppose industrial policy when they believe it amounts to ‘‘targeting’’ certain businesses for growth, believing the market does a better job of this than government. Also, there are those who believe in interventionist domestic policies, but believe the United States should practice free trade.) Hence, industrial policy must be defined more narrowly.

Graham (1992:3) argues that a comprehensive industrial policy is a set of sector-specific economic policies that together are aimed strategically toward certain national goals. This is a good shorthand definition of industrial policy. A succinct, but detailed definition of industrial policy is provided by the Organisation for Economic Cooperation and Development (OECD, 1992:11):

> A certain convergence has now been reached around a set of principles that broadly favour policy measures which do not interfere with the market process directly and instead attempt to improve its mechanisms. Such policies tend to be of a horizontal nature; they are market-correcting or market-enhancing, aimed directly at specific and known market flaws, or at promoting industry generally, and in particular the (labour and infrastructural) inputs available to industry.

The major justification for an industrial policy is the externality argument, of which the purest aspect is the ''public good'' (Stiglitz 1986:87–89). The ''owners'' of semiconductor research cannot exclude others from its use once the research is disseminated. The marginal cost of producing an additional unit is essentially zero, particularly since research is normally a fixed-cost item. Another way of looking at it is that this research is said to give off positive externalities. That is, those other than the researcher or the funding entity may enjoy the benefits of the research. Since all the benefits cannot be captured by the researcher or those who fund the research, market allocation of the research funding decisions will result in the market providing less of the service (social science research) than is socially optimal. However, by the same token, since market signals do not work as well here as they normally would in the production of other goods and services, society is left with the difficult decision of deciding how much publicly funded semiconductor research is optimal. This is accomplished through the political markets.

The definitions given do not make it entirely clear that industrial policy is generally used as an arm of foreign policy; i.e., it involves international trade. As Gruber (1996:723–724) notes, international specialization based upon factor endowments (or the Heckscher-Ohlin assumptions of international trade, which flow from the Ricardian notions of comparative advantage) is not characteristic of the semiconductor industry. It is also not likely to be characteristic of any dynamic increasing returns industry. Gruber attributes this to learning economies. However, the entire list of contributing factors to dynamic increasing returns may be cited.

It is in the sphere of industrial policy that most attention has been paid to industries that are taken for granted to be characterized by dynamic returns—the high-technology industries. Government has provided much help here, particularly when it can be brought under the rubric of defense policy. Government played a key role in the development of the semiconductor and computer industries as well as the Internet. Tyson (1992:88) claims that up to 100% of the semiconductor industry's output was purchased by the U.S. military in the early years. Harrison (1994:24) notes that as recently as the mid-1980s, Santa Clara

County (the location of Silicon Valley) remained one of the top three recipients of defense contracts in the United States. An "iron triangle" existed among the Defense Department, the industry, and Stanford University in the early years while the industry developed (Harrison, 1994:117–122).[25] This industry has clearly benefited from a steady relationship with the government.

In addition, the DRAM producers have benefited from trade policy designed to keep the Japanese from "dumping" product into the U.S. markets.[26] Furthermore, the government helped establish Sematech in response to the Japanese Very Large Scale Integration (VLSI) program, which "reverse-engineered" U.S.-produced semiconductor manufacturing equipment and improved it for the benefit of a number of large Japanese producers who were part of the program. U.S. government response brought the U.S. industry from the brink of disaster and made it competitive again, although Korea is now becoming the world leader in DRAM chips.

The United States will practice industrial policy of sorts whether economists like it or not as long as the country maintains tis constitutional democracy. It is important to ascertain where such a policy might do some good and seek to improve it, as well as to attempt to mitigate damages form where it will inflict damage.

E. Path Dependence and Market Failure

Path dependence, simply put, is the idea that where you go depends upon where you start and the path you follow. It is the notion that small occurrences, even if they are purposive events, at critical points in time play a large measure in determining future outcomes. These occurrences can be both purposive and random or a mixture of both.[27] An example often given is the location of the semiconductor industry in Silicon Valley. One finds no logical explanation for its location, other than that certain people who were instrumental in the industry's founding wanted to live there. Path dependence is a violation of the neoclassical economic model, which views all events as occurring due to activity of rational actors. Hence, path dependence is a market failure in terms of traditional analysis.

Robertson and Langlois (1994:364) claim that institutional lock-in is a technological lock-in of the type posited by Arthur and David. They argue that this is different from the evolutionary lock-in that results from path dependence and routines rather than from increasing returns. This lock-in is said to be caused by transactions costs (more or less frictional costs which are lost to the system) and bounded rationality (which is the concept that rationality is bounded by limits of knowledge). The difference seems to represent some notion of a difference between a traditional Newtonian physics-based neoclassical economics, and an institutions-based evolutionary economics. However, the concept is not well presented by its authors. In fact, North (1990b:34–35) believes one may extend the concept of technological change to institutional change, and by implication, the lock-in effects are related. North argues that, whereas in a neoclassical economic system based upon Newtonian optimization, static competition and decreasing returns (or at best constant returns), institutions hold no interest, institutions do matter in an increasing returns world.

While Arthur is referenced above as stating path dependence and lock-in are possible outcomes of increasing returns, he does not get into the issue of lock-in as a result of path dependence. While path dependence may not be responsible for traditional static increasing returns, it may contribute to dynamic increasing returns in a positive feedback mechanism over time.

F. Policy Regarding Lock-In

Robin Cowan (1990) argues that even with complete central control, when the technologies are improving and the central authority cannot precisely predict the paths of development, it is possible to lock-in to an inferior technology. Cowan's analysis points toward the potential for "moderate" government intervention in certain cases, particularly when there is no incentive for an adopter to experiment with what appears to be an inferior technology, since the market will undersupply experimentation.

Liebowitz and Margolis (1997, 1994, 1991, 1990) make the case that lock-in does not likely occur in a competitive market. However, theirs is a static, neoclassical case that ignores the potential for dynamic inefficiencies. While the evidence of lock-in is sparse and disputed due to the nature of the phenomenon, and the fact that controversial, counterfactual methods are necessary to show its existence, the theory is intuitively appealing. Paul David's (1985) article on the subject of the QWERTY keyboard and Arthur's (1994, 1990b) exposition of Betamax technology are logically convincing even if hotly disputed by Liebowitz and Margolis.

V. CONCLUSION

The theory of dynamic increasing returns has both positive and negative implications for economic growth and productivity. Policy goals should obviously focus upon promoting the positive and minimizing the negative, but discerning the difference is rather difficult at this point and one would not wish to be locked in to inferior policy. Scholars are in the very early stages of attempting to figure out all the implications of dynamic returns. There is currently a lack of empirical work to support what has been done on a theoretical level, which itself is still at a level Richard Nelson (1994:31) would call "appreciative theorizing." The theory needs to be formally modeled and tested empirically, using the methods of regression and frontier analysis. Hence, policy analysis remains incomplete, but investigators must begin to think about such things.

ENDNOTES

1. Some would characterize this as dynamic increasing returns to scale. However, ''scale'' is a word of better use when applied to the old-style, heavy-industry, increasing-returns industries.
2. Multiple equilibria can be explained by the ''theory of the empty core,'' which posits a circumstance (generally, but not necessarily, characterized by oligopoly) which exists because no stable coalitions can be formed; i.e., there is too much competition for the market (see Telser, 1994). This is merely a fancy phrase and theory for some of the aspects of imperfect competition. Note that a natural monopoly has a filled core, due to the ability of producers and consumers to form stable coalitions, even though the coalitions do not offer a competitive situation (thus, this structure is ''second best''). Economists since Marshall have identified the empty core problem. Most production function modeling gets around the problem by assuming constant returns to scale, although the assumption of external economies of scale is another way of modeling this while preserving the competitive equilibrium model.
3. Most of these products, other than consumer electronics, and, in particular, the semiconductor industry, are ''general-purpose technologies'' or building blocks for the production of other goods and services.
4. Although copyrights are useful in the creation of software due to the ease in which it can be copied.
5. It is more succinctly stated in Arthur's article that increasing returns, if bounded, do not guarantee monopoly outcomes. Of course, while perhaps some of the literature may imply that increasing returns leads to monopoly, this is incorrect. Increasing returns instead leads to unstable equilibria, which may lead to monopoly. Monopoly is a stable equilibrium.
6. Douglass North (1990b:112) ties path dependence directly to increasing returns as follows: ''Path dependence comes from increasing returns mechanisms that reinforce the direction once on a given path. Alterations in the path come from unanticipated consequences of choices, external effects, and sometimes forces exogenous to the analytical framework.''
7. Proxy variables are generally used in modeling, as this article demonstrates.
8. As Paul R. Krugman notes, economies of scale at the plant level inevitably imply imperfect competition (1994:7).
9. Schultz's list, which includes advances in technology and ideas and knowledge as economic entities, is far too general to be functional.
10. See Schelling (1978) for limits to network advantages.
11. R&D, education, and learning by doing create these learning effects. Also see Jin (1994) for a discussion of learning capability.
12. To the best of the author's knowledge, factors 8–11 have not previously appeared as contributors to dynamic returns.

13. In the author's semiconductor example, the industry may be responsible for generating increasing returns downstream.
14. Note that Liebowitz and Margolis (1994, 1990) argue that there are no impediments to efficiency in the form of lock-in that is known as "historical lock-in." At least, they argue, this is not a problem in two cases (typewriter keys and recorders) where good arguments have been made (David 1985; Arthur 1994) that inefficient historical lock-in did exist.
15. Initial production using new technology may involve "forward pricing," that is, pricing under long-run expectations rather than short-run conditions.
16. These existing institutional arrangements can also be viewed in terms of "process technology." An example of this may be found in a comparison between the General Motors (GM) J-system management, which was adopted in the 1920s, and Toyota's newer "Toyota production system." Toyota's system involves a combination of the just-in-time system with heavy reliance on the keiretsu form of organization with its suppliers. Toyota's newer system allowed it to dominate automobile production in the 1980s, by producing greater quality at a lower price (see Keller 1993). Since this system enhances efficiency, may be transferable without affecting the transferee's ability to use it, and may be nonexcludable, it has the attributes of a public good and may be thought of as a technology. However, since the arrangements may partially depend on culture, values, and the particular actors involved, they may also be described as institutional. Separating the institutional from the technology may prove to be complicated.
17. General-purpose technologies are technological building blocks upon which a significant portion of society's productive capacity may rest. Semiconductors are general purpose technologies.
18. Ergodic theory is the theory of long term statistical behavior of dynamic systems.
19. Although the recent enforcement action against Microsoft, Inc., for allegedly attempting to dominate the Internet browser industry through tying arrangements may signal an end to weak enforcement.
20. For current antitrust policy on vertical mergers, see the U.S. Department of Justice and Federal Trade Commission *Horizontal Merger Guidelines* issued April 2, 1992.
21. Shepherd (1979) presents opposing viewpoints on the subject by Robert H. Bork as well as Walter Adams and Joel B. Dirlam. Mainstream neoclassical opinion has been tilting towards Bork's position in recent years, whereas institutional economic opinion has argued that economies of scale and scope of whatever size are efficient as long as government regulates to prevent antisocial corporate behavior.
22. The Justice Department concurs with this assessment judging by its recent action against Microsoft.
23. Dynamic forward pricing is pricing at the projected level of future sales volumes and making use of corresponding costs, rather than pricing to cover current costs by current sales.
24. See Tyson (1992:85–154) and Flamm (1996) for a discussion of U.S.-Japan trade in semiconductors.
25. *Iron triangle* is borrowed from the political science field. As explained by Lowi and Ginsburg (1994:276–277), an iron triangle, as defined originally, is a pattern of stable relationships between an executive branch agency, a congressional committee

or subcommittee, and one or more organized interest groups. The alliance reinforces their agenda against drastic change or abolition.

26. Arguments as to whether this is good policy or bad may also be found in Tyson (1992) and Flamm (1996). The issue is too complicated for a full discussion in this thesis.
27. It is not necessarily easy or even possible in every case to separate the random behavior from the purposive.

REFERENCES

Acs, Z.J. and Audretsch, D.B. (1990). *Innovation and Small Firms*. Cambridge, MA: MIT Press.

Anderson, P.W., Arrow, K.J. and Pines, D. (1988). *The Economy as an Evolving Complex System*. Redwood City, CA: Addison Wesley.

Arthur, W.B. (1994). *Increasing Returns and Path Dependence in the Economy*. Ann Arbor: University of Michigan Press.

Arthur, W.B. (1990a). ''Silicon Valley'' locational clusters: when do increasing returns imply monopoly? *Mathematical Social Sciences 19*, 235–251.

Arthur, W.B. (1990b) Positive feedbacks in the economy. *Scientific American 262*, 92–99.

Arthur, W.B. (1989a). The economy and complexity. In D.L. Stein (ed.), *Lectures in the Sciences of Complexity*, 713–736. Redwood City, CA: Addison-Wesley.

Arthur, W.B. (1989b). Competing technologies, increasing returns, and lock-in by historical events. *Economic Journal 99*, 116–131.

Arthur, W.B. (1988). Self-reinforcing mechanisms in economics. In *The Economy as an Evolving Complex System: SFI Studies in the Sciences of Complexity*. Redwood City, CA: Addison-Wesley.

Arthur, W.B., Ermoliev, M., and Kaniovski M. (1987). Path-dependent processes and the emergence of macro-structure. *European Journal of Operations Research 30*, 294–303.

Arrow, K.J. (1962). The economic implications of learning by doing. *Review of Economic Studies 29*, 155–173.

Bresnahan, T.F. and Trajtenberg, M. (1992). General purpose technologies: engines of growth? *NBER Working Paper #4148*.

Buchanan, J.M. and Yoon, Y.J. (1996). Generalized increasing returns, Euler's theorem and competitive equilibrium. Paper presented at Public Choice Seminar, Center for the Study of Public Choice, George Mason University, Fairfax, VA, Oct. 16.

Bingham, R.D. (1998). *Industrial Policy American Style: From Hamilton to HDTV*. Armonk, NY: M. E. Sharpe.

Buchanan, J.M. and Yoon, Y.J. eds. (1994). The *Return to Increasing Returns*. Ann Arbor, MI: University of Michigan Press.

Cowan, R. (1991). Tortoises and hares: choice among technologies of unknown merit. *Economic Journal 101*, 801–814.

David, PA. (1992). Heroes, herds and hysteresis in technological history: Thomas Edison and 'The Battle of the Systems' reconsidered. *Industrial and Corporate Change 1*(1), 129–179.

David, P.A. and Bunn, J.A. (1988). The economics of Gateway Technologies and network evolution. *Information Economics and Policy*, 3(1988): 165–202.

David, P.A. (1985). Clio and the economics of QWERTY. *American Economic Review 75*(2), 332–337.

Flamm, K. (1996). *Mismanaged Trade: Strategic Policy and the Semiconductor Industry*. Washington, DC: Brookings Institution Press.

Lowi, T.J. and Ginsburg, B. (1994). *American Government: Freedom and Power*. New York: W. W. Norton.

Graham, O.L. Jr. (1992). *Losing Time: The Industrial Policy Debate*. Cambridge, MA: Harvard University Press.

Grossman, G.M. and Helpman, E. (1991). *Innovation and Growth in the Global Economy*. Cambridge, MA: MIT Press.

Gruber, H. (1996). Trade policy and learning by doing: the case of semiconductors. *Research Policy 25*(5) 723–739.

Johnson, C. (1986). The institutional foundations of Japanese industrial policy. In C.E. Barfield and W.A. Schamba, ed., *The Politics of Industrial Policy*. Washington, DC: American Enterprise Institute.

Kash, D.E. and Rycroft, R.W. (1996). Unpublished manuscript.

Krugman, P.R. (1990). *Rethinking International Trade*. Cambridge, MA: The MIT Press.

Liebowitz, S.J. and Margolis, S.E. (1997). Are network externalities a new source of market failure [online]? Available at. *http://wwwpub.utdallas.edu/~liebowit/netwextn.html*

Liebowitz, S.J. and Margolis, S.E. (1994). Network externality: an uncommon tragedy. *Journal of Economic Perspectives 8*(2), 133–150.

Liebowitz, S.J. and Margolis, S.E. (1991). Market processes and the selection of standards. Unpublished paper.

Liebowitz, S.J. and Margolis, S.E. (1990). The fable of the keys. *Journal of Law and Economics 33*, 1–26.

Mankiw, N.G., Romer, D., and Weil, D.N. (1992). A Contribution to the Empirics of Economic Growth. *The Quarterly Journal of Economics 107*(May), 408–437.

Marshall, A. (1994). Correlation of the tendencies to increasing and to diminishing returns. In J.M. Buchanan and Y.J. Yoon, ed., *The Return to Increasing Returns*. Ann Arbor, MI: University of Michigan Press.

Marshall, A. (1920). *Principles of Economics*. London: Macmillan.

Nelson, R.R. (1994). Economic growth via the coevolution of technology and institutions. In L. Leydesdorff and P. Van den Besselaar, eds., *Evolutionary Economics and Chaos Theory*, New York: St. Martin's Press, 22–32.

Nelson, R.R. and Winter, S.G. (1982). *An Evolutionary Theory of Economic Change*. Cambridge, MA: Belknap Press.

North, D.C. (1990a). A transactions theory of politics. *Journal of Theoretical Politics 2*(4), 355–367.

North, D.C. (1990b). *Institutions, Institutional Change and Economic Performance*. New York: Cambridge University Press.

OECD. (1992). *Industrial Policy in OECD Countries: Annual Review 1992*. Paris: OECD Publications.

Ostry, S. and Nelson, R.R. (1995). *Techno-Nationalism and Techno-Globalism*. Washington, DC: Brookings Institution.

Reich, R.B. (1987). An industrial policy of the right. In P. Peretz (ed.), *The Politics of American Economic Policy Making*. Armonk NY: M.E. Sharpe.

Schelling, T.C. (1978). *Micromotives and Macrobehavior*. New York: W.W. Norton.

Scherer, F.M. and Ross, D. (1990). *Industrial Market Structure and Economic Performance*. Boston: Houghton Mifflin.

Schultz, T.W. (1993). *Origins of Increasing Returns*. Cambridge, MA: Blackwell Publishers.

Shepherd, W.G. (ed.). (1979). *Public Policies Toward Business*. Homewood, IL: Richard D. Irwin, Inc.

Smith, A. (1994). Of the division of labor. Reprinted in J.M. Buchanan and Y.J. Yoon, eds., *The Return to Increasing Returns*. Ann Arbor, MI: University of Michigan Press.

Smith, A. (1910). *The Wealth of Nations*. Reprinted by Everyman's Library, New York: Alfred A. Knopf.

Stiglitz, J.E. (1988). *Economics of the Public Sector*. New York: W.W. Norton.

Telser, L.G. (1984). The usefulness of core theory in economics. *Journal of Economic Perspectives 8*(2), 151–164.

Tyson, L.D. (1992). *Who's Bashing Whom*? Washington, DC: Institute for International Economics, 85–154.

U.S. Department of Justice and Federal Trade Commission Horizontal Merger Guidelines issued April 2, 1992.

Index